ON THE BORDER
WITH MACKENZIE

OTHER TITLES IN THE FRED H. AND ELLA MAE MOORE TEXAS HISTORY REPRINT SERIES

ON THE BORDER WITH MACKENZIE

or Winning West Texas from the Comanches

★★★

BY

ROBERT G. CARTER

FOREWORD BY CHARLES M. ROBINSON III

Texas State Historical Association
Austin

To the memory of General Ranald S. Mackenzie, that gallant
Colonel of the Fourth U. S. Cavalry, whose star set in the
overshadowing darkness of a clouded night, and to those heroic
officers and soldiers of that command—my brave and devoted
comrades of the Plains—who, by their untiring energy and zeal,
their unrecorded sufferings, hardships, and many sacrifices, did
so much to make civilization possible on the borders of far
Western Texas—this imperfect story of their services,
is most sincerely and affectionately dedicated.

Copyright © 2007 by the Texas State Historical Association. Printed in the United States of America.

Library of Congress Cataloging-in-Publication Data

Carter, Robert Goldthwaite, 1845-1936.

[On the border with Mackenzie]

On the border with Mackenzie, or, Winning west Texas from the Comanches / by Robert G. Carter ;
foreword by Charles M. Robinson III.

p. cm. -- (Fred H. and Ella Mae Moore Texas history reprint series)

Originally published: Washington, D.C. : Eynon Printing Co., [c1935].

ISBN 978-0-87611-228-1 (hardcover : alk. paper) ISBN 978-0-87611-246-5 (paper)

1. Texas--History--1846-1950. 2. Mexican-American Border Region--History--19th century. 3.
Frontier and pioneer life--Texas. 4. Frontier and pioneer life--Southwest, New. 5. Indians of North
America--Wars--1866-1895. 6. Comanche Indians--Wars. 7. United States. Army. Cavalry, 4th--
History--19th century. 8. Mackenzie, Ranald Slidell, 1840-1889. 9. Soldiers--Texas--x Biography. I.
Texas State Historical Association. II. Title. III. Title: On the border with Mackenzie. IV. Title:
Winning west Texas from the Comanches.

F391.C337 2007

976.4'05--dc22

2007001242

5   4   3   2   1   11   12   13   14   15

Published by the Texas State Historical Association.

Number 23 in the Fred H. and Ella Mae Moore Texas History Reprint Series.

∞The paper used in this book meets the minimum requirements of the American National Standard for
Permanence of Paper for Printed Library Materials, z39.84—1984.

Index adapted from the 1961 edition published by the Antiquarian Press, Ltd., N.Y.

CONTENTS

★★★

Contents

Foreword

★★★

Not long ago, I suggested that Robert G. Carter's *On the Border with Mackenzie* is "part memoir, part embellishment, and part fabrication."[1] While that comment still holds, it requires qualification. It generally is agreed that any tall tale, legend, myth, or story is based on a truth, and this certainly must be the case with Carter. Although it could be said that he was given to exaggeration and hyperbole, and he never let events interfere with a good story, it also must be said that *On the Border with Mackenzie* is grounded in true conditions of the Texas frontier and the frontier military of the 1870s. It also presents a true picture of his commanding officer, Col. Ranald S. Mackenzie, the brilliant, half-mad commander of the Fourth Cavalry. Historians, of course, will insist on pure fact. Philosophers, however, accept that truth transcends fact and is an entity of itself.

I made the comment about Carter's work in an introduction to an edited volume of the diaries of his contemporary, soldier-scientist-memorialist John Gregory Bourke, and one should always be cautious in drawing comparisons between individuals. Yet, because of time, place and circumstances, one must compare the two. Certainly, there were parallels. They were born within eight months of each other. Both were boy soldiers in the Union army, who used that experience to gain entry to West Point, where they knew each other and graduated within a year of each other. Both were posted to the frontier, and wrote of their experiences in the Indian Wars. Here, however, they diverge.[2]

---

[1] Charles M. Robinson III (ed.), *The Diaries of John Gregory Bourke, Volume One, November 20, 1872–July 28, 1876* (Denton: University of North Texas Press, 2003), 3.

[2] Francis B. Heitman, *Historical Register and Dictionary of the United States Army from its Organization, September 29, 1789, to March 2, 1903* (2 vols.; Washington: Government Printing Office, 1903), I, 232, 288; Dan L. Thrapp, *Encyclopedia of Frontier Biography* (3 vols.; 1988; reprint; Lincoln: University of Nebraska Press 1991), I, 144–145; 236. In his diary, Bourke recalled that at West Point, "Bob was as

Bourke's writings were based on his monumental, and reasonably accessible diaries, and can be verified by file after file of official documents. In his own lifetime, he achieved the respect of the historical and scientific community. In fact, when one considers his most famous work, *On the Border with Crook,* appeared more than four decades before *On the Border with Mackenzie,* it is hard to imagine that Carter did not see himself as doing for Mackenzie what Bourke did for Maj. Gen. George Crook. This is especially evident in the nearly identical titles. If Bourke's overall work is more factual than Carter's, it also must be admitted that Bourke had his own blind spots; he sometimes chose and carefully edited his facts to gloss over Crook's numerous flaws, and to give credence to his own views.[3] Realizing this, historians have been able to work around these lapses, and *On the Border With Crook* is recognized as an Indian War memoir *sans pareil.*

In considering Carter, however, the lines are less clearly defined, the work more ambiguous. His publications are scantier than Bourke's, and his papers not so readily available. He did not handle masses of official correspondence as Bourke did for Crook. Nor did Mackenzie rely on Carter for favorable publicity as Crook relied on Bourke. Thus, Carter's limited writing must be checked against a variety of other sources, and when checked, sometimes appears wanting. The real value of *On the Border with Mackenzie* is its comprehensiveness for time and place. In his foreword to the 1961 reprint, Jeff C. Dykes wrote, "Scholars were quick to recognize that ON THE BORDER WITH MACKENZIE contains the most complete account of the Indian wars of the Texas frontier in the [Eighteen] Seventies available to date," which may be presumed to be the date of initial publication in 1935.[4] While there is no question it has been superseded by William H. Leckie's *The Military Conquest of the Southern Plains* among others, it remains the most complete account written by an actual participant. And though there

strong as a bull and as brave as a lion." John Gregory Bourke, Diary (124 vols.; United States Military Academy Library, West Point, N.Y.), XXXVI, 752.

[3] Although *On the Border with Crook* was published after Crook's death, Bourke strove to honor his memory and never publicly mentioned the quarrel that had disrupted their friendship during the last four years of Crook's life. See Joseph Porter, *Paper Medicine Man: John Gregory Bourke and His American West* (Norman: University of Oklahoma Press, 1986), and Charles M. Robinson III, *General Crook and the Western Frontier* (Norman: University of Oklahoma Press, 2001).

[4] J. C. Dykes, foreword to Robert G. Carter, *On the Border With Mackenzie or Winning West Texas from the Comanches* (1935; reprint; New York: Antiquarian Press, Ltd., 1961), xi.

may be flaws in detail, along with good, healthy doses of exaggeration and even fabrication, the basic story rings true. One almost is reminded of another crusty, vain, boastful, yet basically honest old soldier, Bernal Díaz del Castillo, whose memoir of the conquest of Mexico also is the most complete account written by an actual participant. Like Carter, Díaz exaggerated, and became imaginative. But just as Díaz's work is essential to anyone writing about the conquest, so Carter's is essential to anyone writing about the Fourth Cavalry on the Texas Plains.

Robert Goldthwaite Carter was born in Bridgton, Maine, on October 29, 1845, the youngest of four brothers. In 1857 the family moved to Massachusetts, where his father became heavily involved in politics and state affairs. The oldest brother, Eugene Carter, graduated from West Point in 1861, and was commissioned a second lieutenant in the Eighth Infantry. Brothers John and Walter joined the Massachusetts Volunteer Infantry as ordinary soldiers, and on August 5, 1862, sixteen-year-old-Robert followed them, enlisting as a private in Company H of the Twenty-second Massachusetts Infantry. His service record contains nothing outstanding. He remained a private until his discharge on October 4, 1864, one of the tens of thousands of undistinguished Union soldiers who endured the dangers and terrible hardships of the war.[5] At least, that is how he saw himself. In fact, the four Carter brothers were intelligent, observant, literate, and articulate. Writing to each other and to their parents, they generated a massive number of letters, which Robert later transcribed and published as *Four Brothers in Blue: A Story of the Great Civil War from Bull Run to Appomattox*. This work, which started as a series in the *Maine Bugle* in 1896, was completed as an essentially self-published book with a total printing of two hundred copies in 1913. In our own time, *Civil War* magazine has named it one of the one hundred classic books of the war.[6]

Carter entered West Point in 1865, and graduated thirty-eighth in his class in 1870, after which he was posted to the Fourth Cavalry as a second lieutenant. Married on September 4, Carter and his new wife departed for

[5] Heitman, *Historical Register*, I, 287–288; Thrapp, *Encyclopedia of Frontier Biography*, I, 236; Carter, *On the Border With Mackenzie*, xxiii–xxv.

[6] The 1913 edition of *Four Brothers in Blue* was reprinted by the University of Texas Press in 1978, and the University of Oklahoma Press in 1999. The two university editions have introductory material by Frank Vandiver and John M. Carroll, from which this information is taken.

his first duty assignment, Fort Concho, Texas. There was a delay of six weeks in New Orleans because the city was under quarantine for yellow fever, after which the couple took the steamer from Brashear City (now Morgan City) to Indianola, Texas, then traveled overland to Fort Concho via San Antonio. The life of an army wife was primitive at best, and initially he suggested his wife remain behind, first in New Orleans and then in San Antonio, until he could see to suitable quarters. She rejected the idea, and accompanied him the entire trip. The last 230 miles from San Antonio to Fort Concho took fifteen days, in the company of a remount detachment driving fresh horses to the post. They arrived on November 20, 1870.[7]

Mackenzie took command of the post on February 25, 1871. Unlike Bourke, who introduced General Crook at length, Carter said very little at the outset, developing the colonel's character as the narrative progressed.[8]

One month after Mackenzie's arrival, the command was posted to Fort Richardson, from which Carter was to see most of his action. His two daughters were born there. The year was busy for the Fourth Cavalry. In May, a band of Indians massacred seven teamsters. Mackenzie tracked the raiding party back to Fort Sill, where Gen. W. T. Sherman already had arrested three of the chiefs, Satanta, Satank, and Big Tree, for their part in the affair. Satank jumped a guard and was killed, but Mackenzie returned to Texas with Satanta and Big Tree, who ultimately received life sentences (they later were released on parole). Then, in late summer, Mackenzie took a scouting expedition in what he erroneously assumed was pursuit of the Kiowa chief Kicking Bird.

The expedition did not achieve its goal (Kicking Bird actually was trying to bring the various Kiowa factions into line to conform with government edicts), but it saw action. In one fight, on October 10, Carter's leg was crushed when his horse stumbled and fell on him. Almost twenty years later, he was breveted to first lieutenant for "specially gallant conduct in action" during the fight, and in 1900 received the Medal of Honor for "most distinguished gallantry in action against Indians . . . in holding the left of the line with a few men during the charge of a large body of Indians after the right of the line had retreated[,] and by delivering a very rapid

---

[7] Heitman, *Historical Register*, I, 288; Carter, *On the Border with Mackenzie*, chapters 1 and 2.

[8] Carter, *On the Border with Mackenzie*, 57–58; John Gregory Bourke, *On the Border with Crook* (1891; reprint; Alexandria, Va.: Time-Life Books, 1980), 108–113.

fire[,] succeeded in checking the Indians until the other troops came to the rescue." Carter did not seek immediate medical attention, and the leg continued to trouble him.[9]

Carter also participated in Mackenzie's attack against the Kickapoos and Mescaleros at Remolino, Mexico, on May 18, 1873. For that action, he later was breveted to captain for gallantry. Although he was promoted to first lieutenant on February 21, 1875, he was forced to retire the following year because his leg had become worse, and he was listed as "permanently disabled." The leg later was reset and healed properly, but his various applications for reinstatement were denied. He taught school and headed the Washington bureau of the Public Service Publishing Company of New York. He wrote various pamphlets, several of which later were incorporated into *On the Border with Mackenzie*, as well as *The Old Sergeant's Story*, a compilation of letters between himself and Sgt. John Charlton, who served under him in the Fourth.[10]

Besides their daughters, the Carters had a son, Robert D. Carter, who entered the army and retired as a lieutenant colonel. After fifty-three years of marriage, Mary Carter died on November 24, 1923. In a letter of condolence, Gen. Charles King, himself a distinguished author of army life on the frontier, called her "that wonderful little Army heroine," and told Carter, "The history of your own career in the Civil War and in the old 4th Cavalry is almost without a parallel but, to my knowledge and belief, hers stands unrivaled."[11] On January 22, 1926, their son died. Carter himself lived another ten years, dying in Washington on January 4, 1936, as far as is known, the last survivor of the Fourth Cavalry who had served under Mackenzie in Texas. He, his wife, son, and daughter-in-law are buried in Arlington National Cemetery.

On the Border with Mackenzie began with articles that were published in *Outing* and *Youth's Companion* magazines as early as 1886, some fifty years before the book itself was released. One of the *Youth's Companion* articles, "The Massacre of Salt Creek Prairie and the Cowboys' Verdict," an account of the 1871 massacre and subsequent trial of Satanta and Big Tree, was

[9] Heitman, *Historical Register*, I, 288; Thrapp, *Encyclopedia of Frontier Biography*, I, 236.
[10] Ibid.
[11] King to Carter, Dec. 24, 1923, reprinted in Carter, *On the Border with Mackenzie*, 45.

reprinted as a pamphlet in 1919. Others reprinted that year were "Tragedies of Cañon Blanco: A Story of the Texas Panhandle," and "The Mackenzie Raid into Mexico." They were followed in 1920 by "On the Trail of Deserters: A Phenomenal Capture by Captain Robert Goldthwaite Carter," and "Pursuit of Kicking Bird: A Campaign in Texas 'Bad Lands.'" Each of these pamphlets was issued in a printing of one hundred copies for private distribution. They later were incorporated as chapters of *On the Border with Mackenzie*, although they also were included on their own in the 1961 reprint of the book. Additionally, "The Cowboys' Verdict" was reprinted in *Five Years a Cavalryman; or, Sketches of Regular Army Life on the Texas Frontier, Twenty Odd Years Ago*, by H. H. McConnell, a veteran of the Sixth Cavalry at Fort Richardson. This book was published in Jacksboro, Texas, in 1889. Between Carter and McConnell, "The Cowboys' Verdict" has become the standard account, although, unfortunately, it is one of those instances in which Carter allowed himself to exaggerate.

So what, specifically, did he exaggerate? For one thing, the jury itself. "Every cow boy juror had been industriously whittling the bench with his hunting knife and squirting tobacco juice at a crack. . . . They all hitched the 'shootin irons' or 'wee-pons,' which were strapped to their hips, to the front, rolled their shirt sleeve a little higher."[12]

Wee-pons? One almost hears Jeff York as Mike Fink in the Walt Disney film, *Davy Crockett and the River Pirates*. By stretching a point, Juror Peter Lynn might have been called a "cowboy," insofar as he was a cattle rancher. On the other hand, Jurors Daniel Brown, Evert Johnson Jr., and Stanley Cooper were local merchants. The foreman, Thomas W. Williams, was the brother of James D. Williams, who would serve as governor of Indiana from 1877 until his death in 1880. Most, if not all, the jurors were leading citizens of the community.[13] Fortunately, the account of the trial in *On the Border with Mackenzie* is the condensed version, and does not have all the flamboyant and somewhat dubious detail of the original.

Although the short biographical sketch above mentions Carter's participation in the so-called Kicking Bird pursuit in 1871, and the Remolino fight of 1873, missing is any reference to Mackenzie's fight at Palo Duro

---

[12] Carter, *On the Border with Mackenzie*, 101.

[13] Charles M. Robinson III, *The Indian Trial: The Complete Story of the Warren Wagon Train Massacre and the Fall of the Kiowa Nation* (Spokane: The Arthur H. Clark Co., 1997), 104.

Canyon, Texas, on September 28, 1874, one of the pivotal actions of the Red River War of 1874–1875. *On the Border with Mackenzie* contains what appears to be an eyewitness account of the action, but Carter had been on sick leave since April 1874 and did not return to duty until October. Historian William G. Tudor has traced Carter's account to versions by Lt. Charles Hatfield, and Carter's longtime correspondent, Sgt. John Charlton, both of whom where there, and to an unsigned article in the September/October 1885 issue of *The United Service.*[14]

Do such things invalidate the book? No more than Bernal Díaz's exaggerations invalidate his *True History of the Discovery and Conquest of New Spain.* If Carter believed he was chasing Kicking Bird, it is only because Mackenzie also was under that assumption. If his account is flawed, it is in his refusal to accept the facts, long after the facts became known. Yet, even John Gregory Bourke could be guilty of that at times.[15]

It is in his assessment of Mackenzie that Carter rings most true. He admired Mackenzie as an outstanding commander but did not try to hide his quirks and shortcomings. Bourke perpetuated an image that Crook himself strove to project—genial, caring, popular among officers and men, and self-effacing—when in fact, he was just the opposite. In Carter's writings, we see Mackenzie as autocratic, overbearing, foul-tempered, and not well liked among officers and men. He was a man who never allowed himself to become close to his troops, but shared their travails far more willingly than Crook. He was a man who led, rather than ordered. As a commander, he made very few mistakes and when he did, he learned. He believed that the most successful action was one that achieved the desired results with the least casualties. If not loved, he certainly was respected. In short, Bourke has presented us with an icon; Carter has offered us a human being.

Perhaps the great reason that Bourke has held up much better than Carter is his ability as a writer. In listing *On the Border with Mackenzie* among his

[14] William G. Tudor, "Was Carter with Mackenzie at the Palo Duro in 1874?" Paper presented at the annual meeting of the West Texas Historical Association, Alpine, Texas, April 4, 1992.

[15] Charles M. Robinson III, *Bad Hand: A Biography of General Ranald S. Mackenzie* (Austin: State House Press, 1993), 91; Carter, *On the Border with Mackenzie*, 123. Bourke never could accept that, operating under Crook's orders, Col. Joseph J. Reynolds had attacked a camp of neutral Cheyennes in Montana on March 17, 1876. Despite all evidence to the contrary, he went to his grave insisting that Reynolds had attacked Crazy Horse's camp, upholding Crook's version of events. See Robinson (ed.), *Diaries of John Gregory Bourke*, 201–202.

Basic Texas Books, John H. Jenkins wrote, "Carter's narrative is poorly written, his ego is a bit trying at times, and he almost bursts with what we now call prejudice. On the other hand, he pulls no punches in this outspoken narrative, and the reader always knows where he stands."[16]

Carter's prejudice may be another factor. As Bourke spent more time among the Indians, he grew to respect them and their culture. He also believed government policy was largely responsible for Indian troubles. In a moment of frustration, he wrote, "it matters not whether the grievances of our Indians be true or false, exaggerated or under-estimated, the fact that the word of our Government is mistrusted by every tribe on the continent cannot be denied and is a black blot upon our national escutcheon."[17]

Carter expressed frustration of a different sort when, in 1905, he watched Mackenzie's old nemesis, the Comanche chief Quanah Parker, riding in President Theodore Roosevelt's inaugural parade "with other 'good Indians,' most of whom had dipped their hands in many a white settler's blood on the once far off borderland of the West." He noted that Quanah "was reputed to be the wealthiest Indian in the United States, through the generosity of the Government." Such statements are a little too biased for modern "political correctness," but as Jenkins observed, Carter "had watched his old fellow Indian Campaign officers struggle in vain to get pensions, while the Indians they had fought were given land and aid." It also must be remembered that Bourke had many years to mature on the frontier, while Carter's career was cut short by his injury. Early in his career, Bourke likewise would have been satisfied to see the Indians extinguished from the face of the earth.[18]

This may account for why Carter's work has not carried over into modern times, but does not explain why it did not see wider circulation in his own lifetime. Whereas Bourke could expect publication in popular magazines like *The Century* (which also published Mark Twain), as well as in scientific journals, most of Carter's work essentially was self-published in limited printings that account for its rarity today. The answer in part can be attributed to the character of the two men, and in the circumstances in which

[16] John H. Jenkins, *Basic Texas Books: An Annotated Bibliography of Selected Works for a Research Library* (rev. ed.; Austin: Texas State Historical Assocation, 1988), 65.

[17] Bourke, Diary, XXVI, 19.

[18] Carter, *On the Border with Mackenzie*, 214; Jenkins, *Basic Texas Books*, 66; Robinson (ed.), *Diaries of John Gregory Bourke*, 7–8.

they found themselves. Bourke was a born publicist with a gift for self-promotion who answered directly to a publicity-hungry general. Crook surrounded himself with newspaper reporters and associated with the high and the mighty, which Bourke used to his advantage. His position as a general's aide-de-camp sent him on errands for Crook, in which he often developed his own contacts. Indeed, their falling out in 1886 could be as much attributed to Bourke's no longer needing Crook and wanting to expand his career as to any other reason. Carter, on the other hand, served under an officer who was uneasy with people, whose fame at the time was more regional than national, and whose associations outside the army were limited.[19] Additionally, Carter's primary duties were restricted to his company and his regiment. His early retirement for disability forced him into the anonymity of the white-collar civilian labor force, and others filled his place as Mackenzie's star rose.

Finally, as Jenkins noted, Carter's work was poorly written. Although Dykes called him "a rather experienced writer," by 1935 when *On the Border with Mackenzie* first was published, the fact is that any writer can gain experience publishing his own work. That does not necessarily make him a good writer, whose work merits a commercial house absorbing the cost of publication. *On the Border with Mackenzie* was submitted to commercial houses, and, according to Dykes, one suggested he "secure the services of a professional writer 'to whip the manuscript into shape for publication' and intimated that after this was done he might be interested in issuing it." Carter "indignantly" rejected the idea, which is a shame, because it might have been published in sufficient quantity to be easily available today.[20] As it stands, the original 1935 edition was published by Eynon Printing Company in Washington, and in such limited numbers that copies rarely appear on the market. When they do, they are very expensive. One must assume this was a family arrangement, because one of Carter's granddaughters had married an Eynon.[21]

[19] As a student and a cadet, Mackenzie was gregarious and had many friends. During the Civil War, however, he underwent a personality change, possibly due to a visible physical impairment suffered at Petersburg in 1864. See Michael D. Pierce, *The Most Promising Young Officer: A Life of Ranald Slidell Mackenzie* (Norman: University of Oklahoma Press, 1993), and Robinson, *Bad Hand.*

[20] Dykes, foreword to Carter, *On the Border with Mackenize*, x–xi.

[21] Ibid., xi.

Foreword

The work was reprinted in 1961 by the Antiquarian Press of New York, with the inclusion of the six pamphlets from which some of the chapters were drawn. While not as rare as the 1935 edition, it nevertheless is scarce. In the 1980s, J. M. Carroll & Company of Mattituck. New York, reissued the 1935 edition in a limited printing of three hundred. With this reprint by the Texas State Historical Association, Carter's work finally will have the availability it deserves. For all its faults, it is, as Jenkins noted a "basic Texas book," essential to any study of the Indian Wars of the Southern Plains, as well as for its insights into Mackenzie. If, as sometimes has been said, Bourke is Boswell to Crook's Samuel Johnson, then Carter must be Bernal Díaz to Mackenzie's Hernán Cortés.

CHARLES M. ROBINSON III
San Benito, Texas

THIS STORY has been compiled from the diaries, journals and memoranda of an officer of the Fourth U.S. Cavalry who served with General Mackenzie in most of his Indian campaigns. He was his Field Adjutant on Mackenzie's first Indian Expedition in 1871, and as his Acting Adjutant and confidential adviser assisted him in his plans for his great raid into Mexico in May 1873, which resulted in quiet along the Rio Grande border for many years, and a joint resolution of "Grateful Thanks" from the Texas Legislature convened in special session for that purpose by the Governor of that State.

Accompanying this story are many photos for reproduction, very valuable now as the negatives (wet plate) have long since been destroyed, showing the various border posts; Indian village life in their skin lodges or "tepees"; hunting camps; drying buffalo meat; many noted chiefs, now dead; etc., etc.

Some of the most prominent members of the U.S. Geological Survey and of the Cosmos Club of this city, and who are more or less familiar with the recurring Indian outbreaks in the southwest, are urging me to publish this material, in order that the present generation of Texans, of the Indian Territory (now Oklahoma) and along the Rio Grande border, may know something more of the hardships, privations and sacrifices which our little regular army made in those days to free the settlers from marauding bands of savages and to secure the peace and prosperity of that part of Texas which is now one of the richest and most populous sections of the United States in minerals, oil, cotton, etc., where during that period that section was overrun with Indians, buffalo, wolves, jack rabbits, prairie dogs, sage brush and cactus.

R. G. CARTER, Washington, D.C., April 1935

THE DRAGOON BOLD

"Oh, the dragoon bold, he scorns all care,
As he goes around with his uncropped hair,
He spends no thought on the evil star
That sent him away to the border war.

"His form in the saddle he lightly throws
And on the moonlight scout he goes,
And merrily trolls some old time song
As over the trail he bounds along.

"Oh, blithe is the life a soldier leads
When a lawless freedom marks his deeds,
And gay his path o'er the wildwood sod
Where a white man's foot hath never trod."

Preface

✫✫✫

The railroad—that great civilizing agency—the telegraph, the telephone, the automobile, the airplane, the radio and the many marvellous inventions of man have wrought such a wonderful transformation in our great Western country, that even now the American Indian has really become a race of the past—a "Vanishing Race"—and history alone will record the deeds and career of this strange and almost extinct people.

With these almost miraculous changes has come the extermination of the buffalo, and pretty much all of the wild game which, in countless numbers, freely roamed the vast prairies.

Where there nomadic red man and his migratory companion, the bison, lived and thrived but a comparatively short period ago, are now populous towns and cities, railroads, schools, ranches, great farms with immense yields of wheat, cotton, oil gushers, etc., and all the factories, mills and appliances of modern civilization.

It is my purpose in offering this work to contribute from my diaries, journals, itineraries, and illustrations, before they are lost to view, whatever has occurred in my experience, covering a period of years, in that Far West, in the expansion and peopling of which I was merely one of the actors, as an officer of our little Army which was so closely identified with that work.

This is by no means a history of the Fourth U.S. Cavalry. That I leave for abler hands. It is simply a brief narrative of events during the campaigns of that regiment under the leadership of that "beau sabreur" of the Cavalry, General Ranald S. Mackenzie, who, General Grant declared in his memoirs, was "The most promising young officer of the Army,"—from 1871 to 1876 in Texas, the Indian Territory (now Oklahoma), on the "Staked Plains" (Llano Estacado) and Old Mexico into which has been woven a few sketches of personal adventure, hunting and incidents peculiar to the frontier life of a Cavalry subaltern, in camp and garrison, on the march and in bivouac, at a time when the Western border was ablaze with Indian wars, and no "Artist-on-the-Spot," or "Our Special Correspondent" were on hand to give a vivid or realistic picture of that life. Mackenzie's part in the "Winning of the West" has never been, as yet, fully visualized, nor full credit given to the Fourth Cavalry for the part it took in the opening up of the Southwest, where credit was due. Doubtless had he lived much more would have been recorded of his busy life during the Civil War and on the frontier, than the writer is now able officially to transcribe, as many of his reports, letters and papers have either been lost or are almost impossible now to find.

History is defined to be "the recorded events of the past, that branch of science which is occupied with ascertaining and recording the facts of the past."

History deals with facts and history can only be reliable when it is written by persons not interested in the outcome of the treatment to be given men or events dealt with.

What we now call propaganda is and has been too often mistaken for historical facts. There is no doubt but that much of what goes as history would have been differently recorded if the writer had had access to the facts or had not mistaken propaganda for facts, but better still have been a personal and active participant.

So far little attention has been paid to the facts having to do with the history of West Texas, while every phase of the history of the older portions of the State have been dealt with. This section has a history all its own just as fascinating and colorful as any other part of Texas; probably more so.

During the period prior to and including the years 1870–1873 while there had been a continuous Indian warfare on the border east and west of the 100th meridian, and north, including parts of the Texas Panhandle, in which units of our little regular army had been involved, all of which has been made a matter of record for years, and during which many lives were lost, ranches burned, women and children captured, and cattle and horses stolen, it was not until 1874 that the War Department resolved to place enough troops in the field, operating along converging columns and under some of its very best officers of tried experience, for the purpose of subjugating or annihilating those wild bands of

Comanche, Kiowa, Arapaho and Cheyenne Indians, who up to this period had absolutely refused to go into a Government reservation and become Agency Indians.

For many years West Texas had been given over to the red man and no settler dared to go west of the 100th meridian unless under the very guns of the forts temporarily placed at strategic points as a line of defense. The columns sent into the field during that period, 1874–1875, were under General N. A. Miles, operating from the North; Lieut. Colonel ("Black Jack") Davidson operating West from Fort Sill, I.T. (now Oklahoma); General Ranald S. Mackenzie, Fourth U.S. Cavalry, "than whom there was no more effective fighter in the entire army," operating from Fort Concho towards the North and West; Col. G. P. Buell and Lt. Col. ("Beau") Neill operating in cooperation with General Mackenzie near the Fort Sill reservation in the Indian Territory, while Major Price was operating from old Fort Bascom, N.M., towards the East.

Thus there was placed in the field some 2,000 men for the purpose of crushing or subjugating these savages, who broke treaties and promises, because they were enraged at what they declared was the encroachment of the whites on their lands and the slaughter of buffalo on what they considered their own hunting ground—4,000,000 alone having been killed by the buffalo hunters north of Texas, to say nothing of the millions killed in Texas.

Many battles took place in the Texas Panhandle among the canyons and breaks of the Staked Plains. Until finally, after their villages and supplies had been taken and burned and all of their ponies captured and killed, leaving the Indians afoot on the high plains in midwinter, they were compelled to go into the reservation and surrender or starve. And thus the way was cleared and West Texas was at last relieved from further savage incursions, burning, pillaging and capture of women and children, and that region was made open to settlement and rapid development made possible.

The officers and men of our little army freely offered their lives and actually cleared that vast region giving it to civilization forever. One writer states, "It is to be hoped that the services and sacrifices of these men will at least be remembered by the people who occupy this country and enjoy its benefits."

That section alone freed from the ravages of the Indians by our various campaigns, but particularly that of 1874–1875, is larger than all New

England, together with New York, New Jersey and Delaware. This work will deal only with the Mackenzie column to which the writer was attached for this hard and perilous duty, and of which, it is believed, he is now the only surviving officer.

R. G. CARTER,
Captain, U.S. Army, Ret'd.
Formerly Fourth U.S. Cavalry

Army & Navy Club,
Washington, D.C.,
October 29, 1931

Introduction

***

The writer was born at Bridgton, Maine, October 29, 1845, but in 1847 removed to Portland, Maine, where he received his early education in the public schools of that beautiful "Forrest City"—the home of Longfellow—on Casco Bay by the sea. His father was a prominent journalist, lawyer and jurist for more than 60 years. He was then editor of the leading Whig paper of the state—the *Portland Advertiser*—and was associated with the Washburnes, Morrills, William Pitt Fessenden (Secretary of the Treasury under Lincoln), Hannibal Hamlin (his cousin, who later became vice-president of the United States with Abraham Lincoln), Neal Dow, James G. Blaine, who succeeded him as editor of the *Advertiser*, and many others in the formation of the Republican party of that state. As a delegate to the first convention of that party in 1856 for the nomination of John C. Fremont, he and Blaine occupied the same room and bed at the old Continental Hotel in Philadelphia.

Becoming wearied of politics, Judge Carter removed to Massachusetts in 1857 and resumed the practice of law. The writer's education being then incomplete, he was, at the age of 15, about to enter Phillips (Andover) Academy to prepare for college or business, when the demon of Civil War broke out and changed the entire course of his future life. At the age of 16, the youngest of four brothers, he entered the service to fight for the preservation of the Union. One brother entered the regular army and the others enlisted as volunteers. Although their father was then, on account of his military experience (having been a Cadet at West Point for two years—1832–1834), Chairman of the Military Committee of the Massachusetts Senate, and in daily conference with the great war governor, John A. Andrew, and could have secured commissions for all of them for the asking, but on account of their extreme youth and lack of experience, all declined, preferring to remain in the ranks where they felt they could perform more efficient service.

They covered all of the principal campaigns and battle from the first Bull Run in 1861 to the surrender at Appomattox Court House, April 9, 1865—one brother commanding "B" Company, Third U.S. Infantry, at the former battle, while another, the eledest, was a sergeant in the First Massachusetts H.A. (Fourteenth Massachusetts Volunteer Infantry) at the surrender. It is also a well authenticated fact that these two brothers were both on duty at the same day at either end of Long Bridge, examining all passes of officers and soldiers crossing the Potomac River.

The writer came from a race of soldiers. He has the military records of 34 ancestors on the paternal and maternal sides who fought in every war that this country was engaged in, including "Unigrets," King Phillips, (one ancestor, Major Mason, being credited with having killed the great Narragansett chieftain), both sieges of Louisberg, Acadian Expedition, French and Indian Wars, the relief of Fort William Henry, Siege of Oswego, Lord Amherst's Expedition to Crown Point, etc., up to the Revolution, in which both paternal great-grandfathers fought—one with four sons, as a Captain, and the other, as a Colonel, with two sons. Among these ancestors was on Colonel David How (or Howe), cousin of Tabitha Hough (How or Howe), the wife of Colonel Josiah Carter, the writer's great-great-grandfather, a Colonial and Revolutionary soldier, who had been in the garrisons of Sudbury, Leominster, and Lancaster, Mass., when the latter was burned three times, its inmates massacred and women and children carried into captivity by Indians. Colonel Howe built at Sudbury the celebrated "Red Horse Tavern," made famous by the poet Longfellow as "The Wayside Inn." It was maintained in the possession of himself and descendants for nearly 150 years, and has been recently bought by Henry Ford, the automobile builder, to be restored to its original form and converted into a museum.

The campaigns and battles of the Civil War have been graphically portrayed by the writer in a volume of 509 pages entitled "Four Brothers in Blue—or Sunshine and Shadows of the War of the Rebellion—a true story of the great Civil War from Bull Run to Appomattox," and is compiled from all of the letters written home by these four brothers and carefully preserved by a loving mother for future reference. They do not follow the diary form but are broken up into a running narrative or sketched story.

The year of 1865 found this young soldier fresh from the battles of the Army of the Potomac, now a veteran, entering West Point as a cadet. His father and a brother had been there before him, the former in the class of 1836 with such distinguished soldiers as Generals Meade, Hooker, Meigs and Haupt. His roommate had been A. P. Crittenden, nephew of Senator John J. Crittenden of Kentucky. He had resigned from the army, had studied law, and was practising in San Francisco, when he was killed by one Laura Fair, a California adventuress on the Oakland ferry boat. The writer's brother was in the class of 1861 and was a classmate of General Custer, killed in the battle of the Little Big Horn, June 25, 1876; Alonzo Cushing, killed in the assault by Pickett upon his battery "A" Fourth U.S. Artillery at the "Bloody Angle," Gettysburg, Pa., July 3, 1863; Colonel Patrick O'Roarke (140 N.Y. Vol. Inf.), killed on Little Round Top, July 2; and Lieut. G. A. Woodruff, killed at the Bryan House near Ziegler's Grove, the next day.

West Point was therefore a hallowed spot, a cherished memory for the young soldier just graduated from the old Army of the Potomac and with his just pride in the record of battles fought on the fields of Antietam, Fredericksburg, Chancellorsville, Gettysburg, etc., for the preservation of the Union, he transmits the same as a heritage to his children and to the readers of these lines. Moreover, his ancestors had been there and at Newburg in the Continental line during the disaffection of Benedict Arnold and his treasonable plot to surrender West Point to the British for a sum in gold. Almost the first thing the writer saw when attending Sunday service in the old cadet chapel, and always pointed out to all new cadets, was the black tablet on its walls, and next to such names as Knox, Wayne, Greene, Lafayette, and Pulaski, with no name upon it—a perfect blank—to indicate to the cadet just about to enter upon his studies and following his graduation, a life long and honorable career, how odious was and will ever be, that act of Arnold's black hearted treason for mercenary gain.

Colonel 4th. Cavalry.
Commanding Post.

CHAPTER I

The Wedding Tour of An Army Bride

GRADUATED from West Point June 15, 1870; married September 4, 1870; assigned by a War Department order to Troop E, Fourth U. S. Cavalry, then stationed in Texas, with headquarters in San Antonio. What next? Why, a "Wedding tour or 'tear' by an army bride"—of course. This long and rather eventful journey, of over 2,000 miles from Boston, Massachusetts, to the far off western frontier or extreme border of Texas, was our goal and our "reveille," or awakening to army life on the border, and ultimately of putting this young battle-disciplined soldier and his unsophisticated bride on "The Fighting Line" for the further advancement of civilization all along the southwest border from the Rio Grande to Kansas, and from a line of rude posts already established or being built to the easterly limits of New Mexico and Arizona, then almost uncharted territories. This vast area comprising the state of Texas and Indian Territory, much of it now included in the state of Oklahoma, and covering the great unexplored region of the "Staked Plains" (Llano Estacado), and the "Panhandle" was then infested by numerous bands, large and small, of the nomadic and hostile tribes of Comanche, Kiowa, Cheyenne and Arapaho Indians, intent upon securing their rights under the many treaties which the Government had been making with them; with predatory bands of Lipans and Kickapoos, the latter having left their reservations in Kansas and gone into old Mexico during the Civil War; while to the North and East were the civilized and semi-civilized tribes of Cherokees, Chickasaws, Choctaws, Creeks, Osages and Delawares of the Indian nation— which had many years before been transported from their homes in North Carolina, Georgia and Alabama.

1

The following official letter from the headquarters of the Fourth Cavalry was our only guide, and on September 12 we started:

"Headquarters Fourth U. S. Cavalry,
San Antonio, Texas,
August 22, 1870.

Second Lieutenant Robert G. Carter,
Fourth U. S. Cavalry,
Bradford, Mass.

Sir:

I have the honor to acknowledge the receipt of your personal report of the 8th instant, and to inform you that your Company (E) is stationed at Fort Concho, Texas, 215 miles distant from here.

Your route is, via New Orleans and Indianalo—the latter by stage; thence by stage to Fort Concho, three times a week.

I presume you can get a horse at the station of your Company.

Very respectfully,

Your obedient servant,

(Signed) JNO. M. WALTON,
2nd Lieut., 4th Cav'y,
R.Q.M. & Act'g Adjutant."

Our journey was via the old "Panhandle Route," through Cincinnatti; Louisville, Ky.; Holly Springs and Humboldt, Tenn.; Milan, Grenada and Jackson, Miss.; to New Orleans; thence across the Gulf of Mexico to Galveston (we found we could not go by Indianola as the official letter had indicated), and from there partly by stage and by rail to San Antonio, where we could take a stage to Fort Concho—running tri-weekly, if it ran at all.

It took six days at that period to make the trip from Boston to New Orleans. The luxurious, palatial dining and drawing room and observation cars, the buffet cars and stateroom sections, barber shops, libraries, etc., etc., had not then been installed. Each passenger, if he was more or less opulent, carried a huge lunch basket or capacious hamper filled to the brim for the entire journey.

Note:—Lieut. Walton was retired in 1879 and was for many years a distinguished citizen of Philadelphia, being for nearly thirty years in the Common Councils and Comptroller of that city.

Failure to thus provide meant getting out at dingy, dirty stations at all hours, when a stop was made, and eating hasty, greasy, indigestible meals, or go without, trusting to luck or the generosity of a neighbor in the next section.

Sometimes, if the train had been delayed by "washouts," or culverts and bridges had been carried away, or, as occurred once or twice, a collision with a cotton freight train took place, no stops for food were made.

We got coffee or tea whenever or wherever it could be obtained. On one occasion the bridegroom got off at Humboldt, Tenn., to get a pitcher of coffee. It was early morning. When he re-appeared the train with the nervous bride had disappeared. After frantically scouting about and making numerous inquiries of the yard men, it was found that the train had gone around a curve for about an eighth of a mile and was backing in on another track. The bridegroom had the tickets and all the money either possessed. They were only separated a few moments but "great was the joy" of their reuniting.

Much time had been spent in trying to persuade the newly-made bride that the best course for us to pursue in this whole matter would be to leave her in New Orleans and for the bridegroom to precede her to Fort Concho, get everything in readiness for her comfort, then to return for her. But the plan suggested to no purpose; with her it was *"now or never,"* after a rather long and lingering engagement of three years. A quarantine at New Orleans of six weeks on account of an epidemic of yellow fever was pleasantly spent with the bride's father who was then living there and was a Customhouse officer, but not without considerable anxiety as people were dying almost daily all about us. It is recalled that an old paymaster (Col. George Febiger), then stationed in New Orleans, long since dead, upon learning that we were just from New England and consequently unacclimated, said to me one day, "Young man, my advice to you would be to go

Texas is 900 miles North and South and 1,500 miles East and West.

around the corner to the nearest liquor store and get four
gallons of good whiskey and stimulate daily during the
time you may be compelled to stay here.''

This was the old-fashioned idea of preventing the disease among those who were suddenly exposed to this terrible and generally fatal scourge.   But we had no fear of
it, and merely adopted a strictly quiet life and diet, keeping out of the sun, remaining indoors at night, and being
regular in our habits.

On October 28 (Wednesday) after a most delightful
stay in the beautiful ''Crescent City,'' we took the train
from Algiers, across the river, for Brashear City, where
we changed to the ''Morgan Line'' of steamers for Galveston.   This was called the ''Berwick Bay'' or ''inside''
route.   This was the first time our Northern eyes had
ever seen sugar or rice culture, and this ride of 85 miles
proved exceedingly novel and interesting.

The entire country seemed one large plantation, cut up
and intersected by almost interminable irrigating ditches.
The Chinese coolies in their native dress, transported us
in a degree to a foreign clime.   The rank vegetation,
everywhere about us; the new, strange foliage of the
trees; the long miles of swamp, thickly studded with live-
oaks, with their long, gray Druidical beards swaying in
the bright sunlight like huge veils; all this tropical growth,
this new land was instructive, calling up new thoughts and
ideas.   It was a constantly shifting panoramic view.   Our
steamer was the ''City of Norfolk.''   The trip across the
Gulf of Mexico, although a new and most interesting one,
was practically devoid of incident or adventure.   The sea
was smooth.   We watched the sea gulls follow the steamer
and greedily swallow the crumbs and offal which were
thrown from the tables into the water.   There was the
never-ending stretch of blue peculiar to the waters of the
Gulf.   At night we watched the intensely phosphorescent
light flashing amidst the yeasty foam as the steamer

ploughed her way in the bright starlight of a soft and beautiful tropical night.

At 6:00 A. M. the following morning we found ourselves nearly in over the shifting bar of Galveston. This bar had been in charge of the Engineer officers of the Army for many years. Extensive dredging operations had been conducted at great expense, as also a great breakwater then under construction, the completion of which in later years and until the great hurricane—which put it out of business, added to the city's commercial prosperity.

Soon spires began to appear, one by one, and as the sun lifted its head from the far off Gulf, and the low, flat island rose like a mirage and hung apparently suspended in mid air, it recalled to our minds pictures of Venice and the incomparable Adriatic Sea.

Upon landing the usual rabble of hackmen was met, who demonstrated before we reached the train, on the other side of the city, by a pitiless extraction of ten dollars for the transportation of our quartette, that the Texas "Jehu" of that period was not so very far behind or any different from his New York brothers, in fact we thought him a little ahead.

Taking the train in the sand—which seemed to make up this curiously located city—from a dirty, dingy, pine-built depot, we found ourselves—after paying eighteen dollars apiece in gold—on the G. H. & H. RR., bound for Columbus on the Colorado River, where we were to take a stage for San Antonio. This proved to be a very long, hot and terribly tedious ride. We crossed the bridge which seemed to interminably span the waters of this Texas Venice, connecting it with Virginia Point, and soon got further and further from the cool sea breezes. We now entered upon prairie after prairie, mile after mile over an unsettled country, and the further we rode the more they stretched out and the more there seemed of them.

First passing through some small herds of cattle, we

continued through herd after herd, each larger and larger, until it seemed to have rained cattle from the dark ages to the present time, and all that one could seem to refer to as a comparison—over this vast stretch of grazing land, were the locust flights of our Biblical teachings. They were the famous "long horns," which we had read about in such Texas literature as we had picked up on the trains. As the expanse of prairie grew almost limitless, so increased proportionately the vast masses of cattle. We seemed to literally wade through them as the train slowly proceeded, they merely giving us the right of way through courtesy. We realized this more fully years later when we tried many times to pass on the trail countless thousands of buffalo as they blocked our way to some camp we were trying to make many hundreds of miles away.

The day was hot; the cars were filled with an assemblage of whites and blacks. Once four cowboys or "punchers" entered; their six shooters were strapped to their hips; they wore flannel shirts of every hue and color, with collars open at the neck. Wide sombreros were upon their heads and huge Mexican spurs jingled on their heels. Pulling out a very greasy pack of cards, they opened up a very lively game of "seven up" or "California Jack," and soon the car was filled with their loud talk and boisterous laughter. There were no "Pullman" or "Drawing Room" cars. All this frightened the brides into a very Quaker-like silence and their eyes were never taken from those belts and formidable looking "guns." The "boys" left at a station further on.

Reaching Harrisburg, after passing through Richmond and several small "burgs," none of them boasting of more than a few ranches, a cattle pen or corral and a dozen or more loose swine of the razor-back species, comfortably waddling and grunting in the oozing mud or hog wallow—we changed cars and continued on, being jostled and jolted along. The country now became more rolling and there were frequent fringes of timber to relieve the eye and the monotonous stretch of prairie. The same brown mass of cattle, seemingly endless, still continued however, and pen utterly fails to give anybody a clear conception of their countless numbers. We ascertained that a recent heavy rain and flood, evidences of which we had seen along the route, had overflowed and broken through the banks of the Colorado, and it was reported that the town of Columbus was nearly all under water. A construction or repair train had just come in; it was now late in the afternoon. The train hands said that we could go no further, so we made our preparations to tarry for the night at a rather inhospitable looking place called Eagle Lake. We saw neither eagles or lake. It consisted, like many other small places which we had passed through, of one ranch, with the usual low, broad piazza or porch extending about the entire house, and a few sheds or outbuildings. Sheriff Goode lived there. There were at least 50 people—Irish, Germans and negroes from the construction train—besides all of the passengers from ours. What was to be done with us? After a hearty meal of fried chicken, biscuits, dried peaches, etc., Mrs. Goode proceeded to solve the problem and make the best possible distribution for the night, not a very easy task as we could plainly see. Of course, the men disposed of themselves in rows on or about the long porches and on the floors of the empty attics. Mrs. Goode knew that we were two bridal couples journeying to San Antonio and the frontier. It was suggested that our brides should sleep on the floor with the women from our train in a separate attic or ranch loft, while we, the bridegrooms, should "spread down" with the men. This hardly conformed, however, with our previously conceived ideas of a "bridal tour" or "tear," and the brides naturally objected to such a solution, their fears getting the better of their judgment, and "when she wont, she wont," etc., etc. The next best, and really the only other alternative, was that our quartette should sleep in one of the lower rooms on the first floor, with two beds in it. After some demurring but knowing that it was "Hobson's choice" they (the brides) consented, in the belief, perhaps that really there might possibly be quite a touch of romance to it (the "Wedding tour") and work in as a sort of novelty to our enforced predicament.

This room had three low windows, which, as the night was sultry, were wide open, and all looked out upon the open porch well filled with the men from the construction train. After much tactical maneuvering one bridal couple going in first, followed by the other, and with tallow dips—which were lighted and blown out at opportune moments—all managed to settle down to bed for a much needed rest, for the ride from Galveston had fully tested our mental and physical strength. But now occurred a most laughable—really ludicrous—incident. Lieut. O— and his bride, who had accompanied us on this journey— occupied a bed diagonally opposite to ours. He had scarcely retired when his bed gave a sudden groan, then a dismal squeak, and began to come down one slat at a time, until in his desperate efforts to see what was the matter the mattress gave a lurch and a slide and with the last slat and a terrible rattle deposited the uncomfortable couple on the floor, with a noise that could be heard all over the ranch. The men on the porch, sleeping within a few feet of their bed, immediately set up a loud shout. It was taken up inside, and soon there was an uproar of rude, noisy, but good-natured laughter, sandwiched with remarks and jokes at the expense of the discomfitted "tenderfoot" bridal pair. This, of course, brought in Mrs. Goode to the rescue with candles, followed by two strapping negro wenches with hatchet, axe, boards, nails, etc.

Lieut. O— set to work, with his black assistants to nail cleats on the side rails to hold up the short or attenuated slats. In the meantime Mrs. O— had been stood up in a corner, well wrapped in a blanket. The two wenches giggled and rolled their eyes about the dimly lighted room, while we, the other bridal couple, were striving to smother our laughter under the bedclothes. Huge cracks opened into all of the adjacent rooms, giving every one a full view, while the windows were lined with curious heads. Finally came the explosion. As the helpers were about to leave the room, one of the wenches turned to Lieut. O— and said aloud, so that all could hear, "Ain't yo shamed of yoselbs, sleepin' all togedder in one room? Yah! Yah!!" This was the signal for a grand shout from all the guests and involuntary lookers-on. It was a dismal joke, however, for the sensitive brides. There was little sleep that night on account of the heat, mosquitoes, bedbugs and the rare novelty of our situation. Bright and early the next morning we chartered an old, brokendown, ancient vehicle—long ago devoid of all paint or beauty, and called in Texas "a hack," and were soon on our way to Columbus on the Colorado.

The dimly defined road was badly gullied; mud, sand, stumps and "hog-wallow" holes predominated. Our team consisted of an old faded, worn-out mule, hitched up with a small, scrubby, bony shadow of a horse or pony—that had once been black but was now faded out to a dirty, rusty brown. Our driver was a small negro boy, about fourteen years old, and as black as an ink bottle. The mule's name was "Maria," and the skeleton pony enjoyed the euphonious name of "Zeke." Crack! Crack! went the black snake whip, and "Get up you, 'Ria," "You, Zeke," were the oft repeated ejaculations of our small sable Jehu driver, much to the amusement of our observant brides—one of whom had been a school teacher in or near Troy, N. Y., while the other had but recently graduated at one of the oldest female seminaries in Massachusetts. We rolled along, now uncomfortably striking a stump, and nearly jerking "Zeke" out of his patched-up, disjointed harness, now hub deep in black "doby" mire, to the utter discouragement of her muline ladyship who, with ears laid back and nose thrust out almost parallel to her body, was trying to see which was the toughest, her well-ridged hide or the boy's black snake whip.

We were kept in a perfect roar of laughter, which so astonished our small driver—who had become well hardened to this sort of thing—that, with our "chaffing," left him hardly knowing whether to be indignant or moderately amused.

After a continuous series of mishaps, during which we had several breakdowns and had repaired our "hack" and harnesses several times, we arrived at the ferry—a distance of about 12 miles from Eagle Lake—opposite Columbus, where we embarked upon a boat of "Ye olden style," navigated by one man by means of a rope and a creaking windlass, block and tackle. We crossed. Remounting our conveyance we moved through a deep cut in the red soil and on to the Columbus House, the latter selected on the recommendation of our now rather communicative boy driver. It was a low one-story and a half frame house with double porches in front, dingy in appearance, devoid of paint, and otherwise rather uninviting. The chambers were small, close and uncomfortable, and the beds—well— they proved to be already thickly populated. Notwithstanding the present high posted bed and tester, with mosquito bar over it and the windows, we could with difficulty see out of our eyes in the morning and most of the night was spent in repelling frequent attacks of our hungry pests. The food was greasy and unpalatable, consisting of the everlasting fry, with a dessert of "fruit"—which meant dried apples or peaches, except on one occasion, when we were treated to a genuine sweet potato pie— floating in vinegar—which highly amused our amateur cooks—the brides—who, upon first inspection had pronounced them "just a delicious peach pie." While eating our meals the brides were somewhat startled at first, but later became reassured when several "razor-backs" came under the dining room and loudly scraped their backs against the floor, accompanied by many squeals and grunts of satisfaction after each visit and nearly jostling the food from the table. The stage company would carry but one trunk. We had two and a chest; all excess baggage had to be carried by weight, payable in gold. The big trunk and chest with our most useful belongings, could not be transported. We arranged, however, with Captain Hodges, the military storekeeper, at Columbus, to store our surplus baggage, to be shipped to us at the first opportunity, which he assured us *would be in a few days.* Only articles absolutely necessary, therefore, were placed in our brand new leather army trunk. The bridal trousseau—there was no help for it—must be left behind. It was hard to convince the uninitiated brides, or to preach faith as a guide. When the question came—"What shall we do when we are presented at Fort Concho and San Antonio" our answer was necessarily short and crisp, for we were now under Uncle Sam's orders—"Well, don't know! Can't help it!" etc.

The weather was still sultry; the stage road thick with dust. There were six passengers inside the Concord coach; finally increased to nine, and we had 230 miles of staging.

Among the passengers was a pale, sickly, tired-out looking German woman, who carried a weak, worn-out, crying baby. Her fat, ill-natured, cross-grained, good-for-nothing, beer drinking, sauer-kraut eating husband was loath, in fact, absolutely refused to do anything to assist the mother by holding the baby, notwithstanding our oft repeated hints and strong suggestions to that end. Had we not relieved and strengthened her occasionally with a little brandy, which we happened to have, it is doubtful if she could have survived the trip. The ride was long, hot and very tedious, only relieved night or day by the changing of horses, stopping for meals and the beautiful scenery which we frequently enjoyed after crossing the wide, monotonous prairies.

A Texas Prairie

The country, the trees, flowers, grass and surroundings were all new to us. We were, at all times in the midst of a lovely landscape, literally travelling over flower prairies. Flowers of every hue and shade were on all sides as far as the eye could reach; they were almost numberless; we counted many varieties one is familiar with among our Northern wild flowers and cultivated gardens, and then they seemed to have but just begun. They grew in immense beds or vast patches—here the most vivid yellow and brightest scarlet, then the deepest crimson, often shading off as they became mingled to a beautiful purple, blue and white. There was an almost limitless stretch of yellow sunflowers, or helianthi, painted cups, yellow indicus, purple lupines, California poppies, verbenas in huge beds, the delicate little sweet peas clambering up the long grasses; marigolds, scarlet flox, passion flowers, even the little innocent field violets with their faint azure hue, and lilies with their delicate white tendrils and soft shadings. There was the beautiful little sensitive plants whose leaves shrank up and folded at the touch, however light, of the human hand, and whose round, fuzzy balls of rich crimson —with fragrant perfume—was most entrancing to eye and nose.

Such brilliant surroundings in nature, such gorgeous grouping of colors, gave the ground the tints of the clouds during one of those summer sunset skies—which artists delight to contemplate but have scarcely the courage to delineate on canvas. The background of rich live oaks, post oaks and pecans, broken up into shady glades and openings amidst which were the emerald green of the various grasses, all fading away into the serene blue of a perfect Southern sky, seemed to steal away one's senses and almost leave us in a land of dreams.

Myriads of gaily-colored butterflies and other tinted insects, hardly less beautiful than the flowers themselves,

flew over and about us. The ever changing colors of this
vast and most charming picture, the glancing light of a
tropical sun, the vast solitude—with its almost painful
silence and undisturbed restfulness—all were new sensa-
tions and far exceeded our expectations or preconceived
ideas of a Texas prairie.

For the first time in our lives we saw large droves of
wild turkeys, whose feathers, as they swiftly darted along
the roadside and in and out of the chapparal, flashed and
glistened with almost a metallic lustre.

Again, a herd of deer crossed the road in front of the
stage, sometimes quietly but more often in alarm, and
bounding at the fastest speed; frequently we came upon
them feeding in the live oak openings and but a few hundred yards from the stage road.

Before reaching Gonzales, about 3 o'clock in the morning, one of the horses was taken sick. We were in the
midst of a long, open, rolling prairie. It was dark as a
pocket. There was nothing we could do but to wait for the
driver to go into Gonzales and return with another horse.
Our horse had blind staggers. In the meantime he was
bled and a huge plug of tobacco was thrust far back into
his mouth. This caused intense nausea and a relaxation
of the nerves, which soon brought him out of his attack.
It was not, however, until about daylight that we resumed
our journey.

Gonzales is on the San Marcos river. There was nothing to especially distinguish it from the other towns we
had passed through except its history in connection with
several battles while Texas was struggling for its independence. It had its usual public square, surrounded by
a collection of shops, houses, a court house and a hotel.
The nearly vacant street at that hour was a type of most
main streets in a sparsely settled country.

Upon reaching "Sweet Home" we were regaled with a
delicious dinner of wild turkey, vegetables, nice wheat
bread, and some small strawberry or Mexican tomatoes

which were most refreshing and gave a very wonderful flavor to the name of this most attractive and *home-like* place which is in Levaca County. Our route lay near the historic town of Goliad, where the brave but unfortunate Fannin and all of his command were massacred by the Mexicans during the Texas Revolution. It is said that the prisoners were shot by lot. Ten white and ten black beans were placed in a sack. The unfortunate men who drew the black beans were taken out and immediately executed by shooting.

We passed through Sequin on the Guadaloupe River and other small places which were once peopled by the Mexicans, who formerly owned the land but vacated when Texas fought for and won her independence after many bloody battles over this very ground we were now traversing. We had a lunch basket and frequently during the long halts we ate by the roadside, and when the stage was pulling over the long, black, waxy bottom prairies we got out and walked to stretch our legs, picking the brilliantly variegated flowers that everywhere dotted the long grass, getting in again when the stage overtook us.

San Antonio

Our entree into the old city of San Antonio de Bexar, or "Santone," as the natives called it, was on the afternoon of November 3. It was like coming from a desert into an oasis We could not see the city until we were right upon and entering it, owing to the almost interminable stretches of mesquite chapparal which entirely surrounded it on all sides.

As the stage deposited us, hot, dusty and intolerably dirty after our long and uncomfortable side, at the inviting doors of the old Menger House, we felt that refreshing feeling of calm, cool repose which one feels after such a weary trip.

Our journey was over, or a part of it, perhaps the worst. We could not see what was before us. It was just as well

that we could not. There was everything to delight the
eye at the Menger after such a ride over miles and miles of
boundless prairie. A sort of Oriental softness and comfort seemed to make up our surroundings. Cool fountains
threw their sprays and splashed in the little courtyard
or "pateo"; here were ornamental trees, plants and flowers, all waving a welcome to our tired bodies. The brides
thought they had at last come into a sort of Paradise.
Baths refreshed our outer persons, while good food calmed
and satisfied our inner selves, for, our stomachs, considering that we were a bridal party, had been a decidedly neglected part of our systems.

Here were roses of every color. The oleander did not
grow in little Yankee pots and tubs, but were large trees
whose dark green waxy leaves and immense pink blossoms
with exquisite perfume mingled with the orange, magnolia,
fig, mulberry and huge banana plants, with other beautiful
trees and shrubs.

We stayed in San Antonio three days. There was much
to be seen and done in this quaint old town with its jumble
of mixed races, costumes, languages, its buildings, missions, etc. It had for us a most fascinating attraction.
Its population numbered about 8000. There were no railroads. Its remote situation was strangely impressive; its
delightful old residences were embowered in shaded gardens, near which ran the San Antonio River with most astonishing windings and curvings, flashing here and there
in the shadow and sunlight until one was mystified with its
capricious moods and bright glimpses. The city is essentially Spanish in its origin, having been settled about 1730,
by several Castilian families who are said to have emi-
grated from the Canary Islands, although the original Mission of San Antonio de Valero dates from 1715, when
Spain established her occupancy of Texas.

There were two squares or public plazas, in one of which,
near the Menger House, is the famous Mission of the
Alamo, the history of which probably every school boy is

familiar with. Evidences were still seen of the hacking
and battering it had received in several battles, and since
its heroic defense by Travis and his handful of men in
1836, against hosts of men under the Mexican general,
Santa Anna, and its connection with the fall of that gallant and honest statesman, Davy Crockett and his comrades, Benham and Bowie, it has ever been an enduring
monument to their daring deeds and unsurpassed bravery.
It was now used as a Commissary storehouse by the U. S.
Government. We rode out to the Missions, which are
down the river and reached by winding roads, in and out
among the trees and by the banks of the stream. There
were three—San Juan La Espada; San Juan, or, as it was
then known, San Jose; and La Purissima, all consisting of
buildings made of rough blocks of limestone covered with a
creamy-gray stucco, which here and there was chipped off
and crumbling. Each church, convent and other buildings
were arranged about a courtyard. The decorations, for
that period, were probably chaste and magnificent, and
were plainly visible. They consisted practically of rude
heads of saints, colossal figures and mouldings, and small
scroll work, with flowers, etc. Much had been somewhat
defaced by vandalism. Aside from the religious associations and recollections of the priesthood and the sacred
superstition of that period, the architectural style, the
carvings, sculptuary, images, etc., would delight many an
antiquarian in search of past art. There was to us, however, a sort of melancholy feeling of decay, of lost strength
and departed wealth that counterbalanced all else.

The next day was spent in shopping, buying a few articles of furniture, moss mattresses, made in sections for
convenience in packing, etc., for our use on the far-off
frontier, and penetrating to the limits of this quaint old
Spanish city.

A Proposition

Col. J. J. Reynolds, 3rd U. S. Cavalry, Brevet Major General, U. S. A., assigned as Commanding the Department of Texas, sent for us and we were informed by him that we could leave our brides in San Antonio—where they would be hospitably cared for—while we travelled by stage to Fort Concho, where we could prepare quarters for them, when he would order us back to temporary duty; or, we could report at once to Captain and Brevet Lieut. Colonel Eugene B. Beaumont, for duty in driving some 400 half-broken broncos, which had been bought by the Chief Quartermaster of that Department, for assignment to the Fourth and Ninth Cavalry regiments at Forts Concho, Stockton, Davis and Bliss. We were told that it would require a 15 day march through a wild unsettled country, infested by numerous bands of predatory Indians, and if we wished our brides to accompany us they would be furnished with a comfortable spring ambulance for the journey. Wherever possible they would have the shelter of ranch houses whenever they might be found. At all other times they would of necessity camp with us and we would have to furnish whatever might be required for their comfort on the march except the tents, as the Government issued those always to officers when on duty.

The two plans were at once submitted to the brides. Their decision came quickly. They thought it would be— "Oh, so lovely, romantic, charming, delightful!" They didn't want to stay in that "lonely old city of San Antonio among so many strangers," etc. Well, that settled it—for hadn't "we just been married, and weren't we on our bridal *tow-er?*"

The March to Fort Concho

Colonel Beaumont was very glad to have us for duty. The ambulance or "spring wagon," with four mules, was furnished the brides, while we were permitted to select

two of the unbroken bronchos for our own use. Packing
our small accumulation of movables into the wagon—our
trunks with the bridal trousseau not yet having arrived—
we started on November 5th for the far off frontier—our
future home for years to come, where children were to be
born, and all of the cares, dangers and unseen perplexities
of life upon the extreme verge of civilization were to be
endured by this unsophisticated bride, and with as little
knowledge of what she had got to encounter in that as yet
untried life as a little child. Troop "A" of the Fourth
Cavalry, Colonel Beaumont's Company, with its first lieutenant, William A. Thompson, and Lieutenant Jewett of
the Tenth Infantry were ordered on duty with the escort,
now consisting of five officers, including ourselves, and
about 60 men. All were well mounted, armed and equipped
for the long journey.

Winding through the curiously planned and irregularly
built old city, in and out its narrow, roughly paved streets,
and dense chapparal of mezquite, we soon struck a dim
stage trail, known as the "Concho Road," and stretched
out for Leon Springs, our first stopping place or camp,
where we penned the horses in large corrals for the night.
The brides were *penned in a ranch,* and it was a well venti-
lated one too. On the 6th we reached Boerne, a German
settlement, and camped four miles beyond on Big Joshua
Creek. Colonel Beaumont when passing through this settlement introduced us all to Mrs. Brady, a great favorite
with army people, who generously furnished us with plenty
of milk for our lunch, which singularly enough to us was a
very great rarity in Texas at that time as all of the cows
were out on the great cattle ranges with their calves, and
the cattlemen did not take the trouble to keep any milch
cows at the home ranches. This night the brides were
under canvas for the first time in their lives—a new experience for them. They were, however, made very comfortable about the rousing campfires. After supper was
had on the large mess chest, we all sung songs to Colonel

Beaumont's accompaniment on his guitar. The mules made their hideous groans and wee-haws, the horses in the pens neighed their shrillest neighs, and the brides unanimously voted that it was a "jolly wedding tour" and "romantic of course." In the moonlight all was wild and weird. On this day's march we passed through Comfort, a small settlement. On the 7th we started early. A part of the troop formed on both flanks of the herd and it was allowed to "string out" and follow the "bell mare" without which more or less confusion would have occurred, while the rest of the command followed in rear. Next came the four mule ambulances, and then came the rear guard composed of the best and most reliable old soldiers, for there was much risk as we were now approaching that part of the country where small parties of Indians were in the habit of raiding and stealing horses from the ranchmen scattered about this section of the country, besides burning ranches and capturing women and children.

The country along the route was wild and picturesque and was mostly rolling until we came near the streams which were heavily wooded with fringes of timber, mostly pecans, cottonwoods and hackberries. The prairies were dotted with the everlasting mezquite, one very singular feature of which was that on many of the limbs, as though grafted there, appeared large bunches of the English mistletoe with beautiful wax-like white berries on sprigs or small branches, which we gathered in large quantities as we rode. This hybrid, or fungous growth, was not the only peculiarity of this wonderful tree, for we ascertained that it could be utilized for a greater variety of uses even than the palm trees of the East. It is closely allied to the gum-producing acacia in its botanical habits. They are trees of an irregular or scrubby, thorny growth and bear a thin, feathery-looking foliage, not unlike the peach tree, the leaf being long, narrow and much smaller. The fruit, or more properly speaking the pod, is long, curved and somewhat compressed, containing a sweetish pulp in which the seeds or beans are lodged. It is very nutritious and much used by the Mexicans in feeding their cattle and is readily eaten by cavalry horses. A sort of beer is said to be manufactured by Mexicans and Indians, as also sugar, and a meal for making cakes. A gum exudes where the bark is cut, which hardens upon exposure; this resembles in looks and in its characteristics, the gum-arabic of commerce; dissolved in water it makes an excellent mucilage. It is supposed by some naturalists to be analagous to a bean fed to the horses in South America, and to the food of Saint John the Baptist in the wilderness. The sapwood is light in color, while the heart is of a reddish brown and very hard. It furnished nearly all of the frontier posts of Texas with the fuel they then used. It is said to possess astringent qualities not unlike that of pure tannin. The roots when dug and used for fuel are superior to the tree itself and give a heat equal to coal and leaves a solid, glowing charcoal ember that lasts far into the night and is unexcelled for cooking purposes. So much for this most wonderful, though uncouth, insignificant, straggly looking tree.

We passed through almost countless prairie dog villages, which we had never seen before, the inhabitants proving such a novelty that the brides amused themselves nearly all day watching their cute movements, antics and ludicrous tumbles into their mounds. A large greyhound belonging to the troop, named "Blue," would chase a little fellow—who had been out visiting a neighbor—towards his hole, always a second too late however, arriving just in time to see the twinkle of his tail, and hear his squeaking bark as he dove out of sight.

Occasionally the shadowy form of a coyote or a large gray wolf, or "lobo" could be seen skulking into some ravine or break; sometimes in small packs, and in the distance a herd of antelope. Lieut. Thompson was quartermaster, caterer and general forager for the command. He could not be excelled. When we made camp every afternoon, there was always plenty of beef, frequently a turkey or chickens, always plenty of tomatoes, corn, lima beans, bread, butter and coffee—oftentimes a large tin bucket of delicious wild honey or some nice fresh eggs. Lunch of biscuit and breakfast bacon, sandwiches of ham or chicken and fruit was put into the ambulance for the brides, and at noon or lunch time, if everything was progressing favorably, we rode alongside and all chatted with the brides as we ate, the latter always insisting that it was "just one elegant picnic" and "wedding tour."

Colonel Beaumont with his jet black hair and moustache, soldier's slouch hat, riding pants tucked into his boots, pistols in his belt, and his off-hand, soldierly way of putting things, favorably impressed our as yet uninitiated minds—particularly the brides—especially at night when in the moonlight he stalked in to the camp fire where the group was sitting, with his spurs jingling, and with dark, solemn face, told us that now was the time for Indians to be roaming about the country, and "vigilance must be the price of security for our scalps tonight," etc. He could sing a good song, several of which he had himself composed; tell a good story, and his hand was always ready to strum an accompaniment on the guitar, or add to our comfort or that of the brides, or "girls"—as he called them—in any way. One of his choice songs composed by himself, follows:

BURNSIDES BLOW UP

1. Our troops were all marshalled in battle array
   With Ben Butler on the right to show them the way
   But he couldn't make the rifle and to cover up the blame
   Sent Gilmore to the rear in dishonor and shame.

Chorus

Boom go the mortors and bang go the shells
Boom go the "Parrots," bang the "light twelves"
Rattle go the kettle drums, we're off for the wars
Hurrah for Gen. Grant and our glorious Stripes & Stars.

2. Then the gunboats and monitors their shots did fiercely pour
    Such another cannonading you never heard before
    While Sheridan and Wilson tore up railroads and pon two
        little occasions
    Got most essentially chawed up at Reams and Trevillian
        Stations.

Chorus

3. Then Ambrose, "the Faithful," bethought him 'twould be fine
    To surprise the Rebel Army with a small powder mine
    To blow up their batteries higher than a kite
    Charge upon their rifle pits and put them all to flight.

Chorus

4. The mine was exploded along about daylight
    Up went rebels, cannons; it was a horrid sight
    The darkies they pitched boldly in but quickly they came out
    Instead of "Johnny Reb" our troops were put to rout.

Chorus

5. What Gen. Grant will do next I cannot really say
    No doubt he'll pitch into the Rebs when he finds a way
    But if he wants to lick 'em, then just one man we lack
    Let him recall our hero, the gallant "Little Mac."

Chorus

(*Last line of chorus*) Hurrah for "Little Mac" and our glo-
    rious Stripes and Stars.

Note:—I wrote this song at Petersburg in 1864 just after Burnsides mine was exploded. They never believed in the project at Army Headquarters and it only had a
half-hearted support. If it had I think it would have been a success.—E. B. B.)
Air: "Sailors Hornpipe" or "Hoist up the flag, long may it wave."

GEORGE HENRY

A Melancholy Ditty

Oh! listen to me, white folks,
And a story I will tell;
It's about young George Henry,
And I knowed him mighty well.
He swings a graceful whip, boys,
And he is bound to shine
Like a high-salaried driver
On the Denver City Line.

Chorus

With a rip-up, and a skip-up,
And a whoop-de-doo-den-doo;
With a rip-up, and a skip-up,
And a whoop-de-doo-den-doo.
He swings a graceful whip, boys,
And he is bound to shine
Like a high-salaried driver
On the Denver City Line.

As he was going 'long Delaware Street
The other afternoon,
And just as he was passing
The Kansas St. saloon,
He spied a nice young woman,
The finest ever seen;
She had just arrived that morning
From the Jersey Quarantine.

With a rip-up, and a skip-up
And a whoop-de-doo-den do;
With a rip-up and a skip-up,
And a whoop-de-doo-den-do;
He spied a nice young woman,
The finest ever seen;
She had just arrived that morning
From the Jersey Quarantine.

Oh! where are you going, young woman, he said.
And she gave him a look that almost killed him dead.
She handed up her band-box
And then got up herself;
Which so surprised George Henry
That it almost took his breath.

Chorus

With a rip-up and a skip-up,
And a whoop-de-doo-den-doo,
With a rip-up, and a skip-up,
And a whoop-de-doo-den-doo.
She handed up her band-box
And then got up her self;
Which so surprised George Henry
That it almost took his breath.

He thought he'd caught an heiress
Or a Southern Lucy Neil,
Just like the French Captain
Or the Maiden of Mobile.
"The sun is very hot" remarked she
"Just gimme part of your umbreller;
"For my name is Phyllis Dinah,
And *I peddles sarspariller.*"

Now when George Henry heard this news,
Which by no means could possibly be wuss
His hair, it all turned yaller,
And he tumbled right off that buss.
They bathed his head in vinegar
To bring him up to time,
And now he drives a mule team
On the Denver City Line.

Chorus

With a rip-up and a skip-up,
And a whoop-de-doo-den-doo,
With a rip-up, and a skip-up,
And a whoop-de-doo-den-doo.
They bathed his head in vinegar
To bring him up to time,
And now he drives a mule team
On the Denver City Line.

Note:—This song was partly recitative. Col. B. was a great mimic, and his rendition of this ditty with the accompanying facial gestures and contortions were highly amusing to the two brides who joined in the chorus with much animation.
—Wilkes-Barre *Times-Leader*, Thursday, Aug. 17, 1916.

COL. BEAUMONT DIES AT HARVEY'S LAKE SUMMER HOME TODAY

One of the Most Brilliant Military Figures in the Civil War Passes Away—a Graduate of West Point, He Achieved Renown as Famous Cavalryman.

Lieutenant Colonel Eugene Beauharnais Beaumont, U. S. A., retired, died at the summer home of his son, Andre A. Beaumont, at Harvey's Lake, at four o'clock this morning. Col. Beaumont was born on the second day of August, 1837, in Wilkes-Barre and was the youngest son of the Hon. Andrew Beaumont and Julia A. Cole, his wife.

Col. Beaumont received his appointment to West Point through Hon. Henry M. Fuller and was graduated in May, 1861. Upon graduating he was appointed a second lieutenant, First Cavalry. During the first battle of Bull Run he was aide-de-camp to General A. E. Burnside and was highly complimented in the report of that officer.

He served with the Army of the Potomac in 1861-62 as aide-de-camp to General John Sedgwick on the upper Potomac, in the Shenandoah Valley and on the Peninsula. In 1862-63 he was aide-de-camp to the General-in-chief, Major General H. W. Halleck. In May 1863, he joined the Army of the Potomac at his own request and was ordered to report to Major General John Sedgwick as captain and aide-de-camp and served with the army during the campaign of Gettysburg, particularly in the battle of Rappahannock Station, Mine Run, Wilderness, Spottsylvania Court House and Cold Harbor. After General Sedgwick's death he was ordered by General Grant to report to General J. H. Wilson and was in the battle of White Oak Swamp and all the operations and fights of the division around Richmond. In the raid for the destruction of the Danville and South Side Railroad and the campaign against Early in the Shenandoah Valley. In October, 1864, he accompanied General James H. Wilson to Nashville and was appointed assistant adjutant general of the cavalry corps of the military division of the Mississippi.

Battle of Nashville

He was actively engaged in the organization of the corps and highly complimented for his efficient services. He participated in the battle of Nashville and in the pursuit of Hood; the fight at Hollow Tree Gap, Richland Creek, Little River, Pulaski, and in other skirmishes. He was with his corps in the march through Alabama and Georgia, taking part in the battles of Montevallo, Ebenezer Church, storming of Selma, capturing of Montgomery, Columbus and Macon, Georgia. *This march was one of the most brilliant and successful of the war.* He received Jefferson Davis at Macon on his arrival as a prisoner after his capture by Col. Pritchard. In April 1866, he took command of Troop A, Fourth Cavalry at San Antonio, Texas; was engaged in scouting and other duties, commanded a battalion of four troops in the fight at Palo Duro Canon, September 28, 1874, Red River, which resulted in the destruction of numerous camps and the capture of 1700 horses and mules, and the defeat of a band of Comanches. He was on duty at West Point as instructor of cavalry from 1875 to 1879; was promoted major of cavalry November 12, 1879, and joined General Mackenzie's expedition against the Uncompagre Utes at Fort Garland where he took command. In 1882 he organized and led a second expedition into the Uncompagre country and later was stationed at Forts Wingate, Bayard, N. M., and Bowie and Hauchuca, Arizona. In October, 1888, he was detailed as acting inspector

general, Department of Texas, and served there until 1892. He
was promoted lieutenant colonel of the Third Cavalry, January
14, 1892. He was placed on the retired list at his own request
May 16, 1892, and has since resided in Wilkes-Barre. During his
active service he was in over thirty engagements and pitched battles. He was appointed major and adjutant general of volunteers, October 20, 1894; brevetted lieutenant colonel of U. S. Volunteers for gallant and meritorious services during the campaign in
Tennessee; brevetted colonel of U. S. Volunteers for gallant and
distinguished services in battle and capture of Selma brevetted in
regular army captain for gallant and meritorious services at the
battle of Rappahannock Station; brevetted in the Regular Army,
Major for gallant and meritorious services at the two battles of
Selma; brevetted in the Regular Army, Lieut. Col. for gallant and
meritorious services during the war. He was awarded a medal of
honor by Congress for gallant and meritorious services at the battle of Selma. He was a member of the Loyal Legion, Sons of the
Revolution, Society of the Army of the Potomac, Society of the
Sixth Corps and the Society of Mayflower Descendents.

Distinguished Father

Col. Beaumont's father, the Hon. Andrew Beaumont, represented Luzerne County in the General Assembly, and in the Congress of the United States from 1832 to 1836. He was the son of
Isaiah Beaumont, who served in the Continental Army and was
wounded at the battle of Princeton. Isaiah was descended from
William Beaumont, who came to this country from Carlisle, England, in 1643, and settled in Saybrook, Conn. He married Lydia
Danforth, daughter of Nicholas Danforth, deputy governor of
Connecticut. Their son Samuel married Hester Buckingham,
whose father, the Rev. Thomas Buckingham, was one of the found-
ers of Yale College. The wife of Isaiah Beaumont was Fear
Alden, who was a grandson of John and Priscilla Alden.

Col. Beaumont's mother was Julia Colt, second daughter of Arnold Colt, who was one of the most enterprising pioneers of
Wyoming Valley. His ancestors came to this country from Col-
chester, England, and settled at Hartford, Conn. He traced his
ancestry to Sir John Colt, a peer of England.

Col. Beaumont was married September 18, 1861, to Margaret
Rutter, daughter of Nathaniel Rutter, of Wilkes-Barre, who died
April 22, 1879. On December 20, 1883, he married Maria Lind-
sley Orton, of Lawrenceville, Pa., who died November 19, 1901.
Four years later he married Mrs. Stella S. Rushing, a sister of his
second wife.

Col. Beaumont is survived by four children and twelve grand-
children, Natalie Sedgewick, widow of General George A. Forsythe, U. S. A.; Hortense D. Elliott, wife of Captain Charles P.

Elliott, U. S. A.; Eugene B. Beaumont, Jr., of Lawrenceville, Pa., and Andre A. Beaumont, of this city.

The funeral will be held on Saturday at an hour to be announced later from St. Stephen's Church.

Note:—The foregoing obituary sketch was taken from the Wilkes-Barre *Times-Leader* of Thursday, August 17, 1926, which makes the following eulogistic comment on the death of Colonel Beaumont: "One of the most brilliant military figures in the Civil War passes away—a graduate of West Point, he achieved renown as a famous cavalryman."

Lieutenant Thompson was a jolly, rolicksome fellow, full of good humor but somewhat of a tease. He delighted to ride up to the ambulance and with mischief lurking in his eyes, which were large and of a roguish blue, tell the brides that near a certain tree we were now passing, only a few weeks ago, "a whole stageload of people had been massacred by Indians, scalped and mutilated," which would cause them to cry out and to grasp with nervous strength one of the smallest sized Smith and Wesson pistols with which one of them had armed herself at the beginning of the journey and which would not bruise a man at fifteen feet, or, at night he would suddenly grasp his Colt '45, if a horse snorted or jumped, and wisely exclaim "Indians must be about camp to cause that animal to make such a noise." His most tantalizing joke, however, was when upon our arrival in camp in the early afternoon he would seize a demijohn of huge proportions, crook it over his elbow, and winking to the bridegrooms—one of whom he knew never drank—would call out aloud, "Come on over and wash the alkali out of your throats." This would cause one of the bride's eyes to snap, and the other to grow serious at such wicked temptations.

Every two hours, or when the horses grew restless and troublesome in driving, we halted where the mat of mezquite grass was plentiful and letting them spread out over the prairie, gave them an opportunity to graze and fill up. During this time we put a herd guard on, to prevent surprise, dismounted, unfastened or uncoiled our 30 foot lariats, and lying down in the soft, thick grass, perhaps in the slight shade of a mezquite bush, we took our "dolce-far-niente." We now seemed to be deeply lost to all about us in the utter stillness of nature, and sometimes were roused up only by the "forward" of the trumpeter's call. Our road, a mere dim stage trail, from San Antonio to Concho, when on the open prairie—extended always through immense patches of yellow, blue and red flowers, intermingled with the luxuriant grasses.

The mornings were pretty cool as we generally started soon after daybreak; the weather had been mostly delightful. The crossings of the streams were made by sending a man in first to ascertain the depth and general direction of the ford, the rate of flow, or if there were any quicksands, etc., which were liable to "bog down" the animals. A man on each bank would now determine the course for the horses to take, and then with the "bell mare" leading, with men on the flanks as guides, and a gentle pressure by the men closing up on the rear, they were gradually forced across. We met with but few accidents. The water frequently came into the ambulance, causing the brides to become a little nervous and to exclaim—"Oh! Oh!!" Then they would be cautioned to stand or crouch upon the seats so that they would not get wet. Sometimes a stray horse would be crowded off the ford into the current and deep water, compelling it to swim to regain the ford. On November 7 we crossed the Guadaloupe River about noon; it was "booming." We safely crossed the horses in a very rapid current, but lost two lead mules from one of the wagons through the carelessness of a young Mexican teamster who allowed his lead and swing mules to get off the ford. The brides crouched on the seat, with several men in the ambulance to weight it down so that the rush of water would not overturn it. When they saw the drowned mules cut loose from the team and go swiftly down the torrent, their great ears flapping like some huge aquatic plants on the surface, they thought they had never seen anything so "distressing" and yet "so irresistibly comical."

On November 9 we camped at Hunter's Ranch on the Perdenales River and at night Lieut. Thompson and the bridegroom went turkey hunting, going mounted, and taking a guide and a dog for retrieving, but the turkeys had recently changed their roosts and we did not get a bird. Lieut. Jewett, however, tried to make up the loss by shooting a sand-hill crane, a bird only eaten by Mexicans and negroes.

The following morning we passed through old Fort Martin Scott, where many of the old officers of the army had been stationed before the Civil War, and the town of Fredericksburg, where Colonel Beaumont was well acquainted. It was a German or Alsatian settlement and bore the appearance of thrift, enterprise and contented prosperity that all of these older towns did in Texas, having fine farms, good schools, newspapers, bakeries, breweries and all of the comfortable surroundings of the native American towns.

We got some most excellent beer here and camped four miles beyond the town at "Teally's" ranch, on "Six Mile Creek," having loaded forage on our wagons and procured necessary supplies in Fredericksburg for the men and our own mess. The brides were again in tents, and there was music by the entire troupe. On this night Colonel Beaumont sang, "George Henry" (see p. 22). On the next day we crossed the Llano River and camped at Keller's ranch.

On the 12th we passed through Fort Mason, another old pre-Civil War post where many of the old dragoon officers had summered and wintered, when the Indians used to come down more into the lower settlements and where several companies of the Fourth Cavalry had at one time been stationed. We penned the horses in a large field at Crosby's ranch near the San Saba River. It rained all day and during the night, which was black, and we herded the horses in this immense field, letting them spread out when they became uneasy. About midnight as the bridegroom, who was "officer of the herd guard," was

sitting near a small spluttering campfire, close to a fringe
of chapparal, and congratulating himself on the good behavior of the herd, and how successful had been our
"wedding tour" thus far—free from serious accident,
presence of Indians, etc.—when suddenly there came a
hog out of the wet bushes into the glare of the firelight
and near a small bunch of horses arching their backs to
the rain. The razorback gave a loud grunt, rather a
snort, of surprise at seeing so many strangers near his
stamping ground. The nearest horse shied, gave a loud
note of alarm and ran with a sudden plunge into the small
herd; they "flushed" and bolted for the middle of the
field. In an instant the entire herd thundered off in the
darkness, crashing and plunging over each other and perfectly wild with terror. The bridegroom rushed for his
horse (a broncho selected from the herd), which was unsaddled and staked out near the fire, and jumping on his
wet back rode quickly towards the break, which we had
made in the post and rail fence to let the animals in, to
see if it was up or guarded. Colonel Beaumont was already making a break for the same point, shouting, "Men,
get into the break quickly!" The field was soft, muddy
and slippery. The bridegroom's horse, while going at full
speed, perfectly crazy to join his friends in the herd, suddenly planted both feet in a mudhole up to his knees and
stopping quickly, shot him over his head in a perfect catapult into the inky darkness. In a moment the horse had
joined the stampeding herd. They tore up and down and
around that pen all night. We could do nothing to stop
them, but deploying along the entire length of the fence
we kept them from dashing against it. Luckily every
panel held firm. At daylight they had become exhausted,
actually "pumped out." We remained in camp all day
on the 14th. They drove as meekly as kittens all the next
day along the trail. Even the cowboy yodels or soothing
songs of the flanking herders or "trail drivers" failed to
disturb their quiet or to accelerate their pace.

The brides were comfortably quartered in Crosby's ranch when the roaring of the stampeding herd awakened them and it was a night of anxiety for them since, without anybody to inform them, they supposed for a long time that our camp had been attacked by Indians and their suspense was not relieved until daybreak. A number of the men insisted that instead of a hog it was really Indians who had first flushed the horses and afterwards kept them running about the field, in the hope that they would break out. But the writer soon quieted that story, as he witnessed the first break, and as no shots were fired, a razorback hog was the criminal.

We rode on this day about 22 miles, the longest drive yet, without seeing a ranch house, and penned the animals at Taylor's ranch on the San Saba River. The horses were again quiet and with the brides again in the ranch no excitement occurred to mar their "wedding tour." The next day we crossed the turnings and twistings of this beautiful little stream three times, passed the settlement of Menardville, where the road turned off to Fort McKavett, and stopped at Coughlin's ranch. One of these crossings of the San Saba River was named "Peg Leg" after a man with a wooden stump who had lost his leg. We ascertained that this man, well-known among Texans as "Peg Leg," was Thomas William Ward. He was a soldier in the war which achieved the independence of Texas and was a hero in the battle of San Jacinto. He was an Irishman without the vivacity and good nature common to his race, but his bravery and loyalty made him popular. At an anniversary of San Jacinto his leg was blown off by a cannon and after that he wore a wooden substitute. It was a long and straight limb, without any joints whatever and he swung it around in great fashion.

In course of time Ward was made Consul to Panama. While he was there an American was put in prison. Ward heard of the outrage. His patriotic blood was stirred, and he sent a note to the Governor, demanding that the

American be released. This was a matter, of course, for the Minister and not the Consul. No attention was paid to the demand, and Ward grew furious. "I sent you a note," he wrote to the Governor, "some three hours ago, politely seeking the release of an American from prison. No reply has been received. This is to warn you that if he is not set free by 4 o'clock this afternoon the United States sloop-of-war, Mary, which is in the harbor, will bombard the town." Long before 4 o'clock the man was set free and "an apology had been rendered." "We ought to have such people nowadays," was the later comment of a prominent senator from the "Lone Star" state, "and the enthusiasm which stirred 'Peg Leg's soul."

We had to leave sixteen of our horses at this ranch (Coughlin's) as they were completely worn out and could go no further. Here a detachment of the Fourth Cavalry, under command of Lieut. D. A. Irwin, met us to assist in getting the horses in. We remained here a day and on the 18th went to Kickapoo Springs—a notorious Indian passway and rendezvous for their raiding parties. On the following night we herded the horses on the open prairie, every precaution being taken to guard against surprise or stampede. The brides were again under canvas. We now went on to Lipan Springs, where we were compelled to remain another day, nursing the strength of the worn out animals, which, unused to driving without shoes, were now very foot-sore.

Indian depredations had been committed here but very recently and all had to be on the alert that night. We were now nearing the end of our destination, and on the 20th we started out for our last leg of the journey, heading for Fort Concho—our station to be. On this day we got our first taste of a Texas "Norther." The dark clouds had been gathering all day, and soon it began to blow a steady wind, increasing to a cold, icy gale right in our faces. At all halts we were obliged to kindle huge fires of the dry mezquite and dodge around it at every point of the compass to avoid being scorched or burned. Coming as it did directly after a warm, soft day it was more difficult to start our sluggish blood, but in the hospitable welcome which we received at the post the brides were soon made to forget their temporary discomforts.

We had seen our first herds of buffalo on the prairie all along our route of that day. We were soon to become better acquainted with this strange and now almost extinct animal.

General Alvin C. Gillem of the Eleventh U. S. Infantry, and colonel of that regiment, a veteran of the Civil War, now commanded Fort Concho. Lumber was very scarce at this post for building purposes and although, in expectation of our arrival, a hospital tent had been framed for us and a stone chimney commenced with a fireplace, there was such a scarcity of material that it was still unfinished and we had to fall back upon the hospitality of Major W. W. Webb, Captain of "E"—the troop to which the bridegroom had been assigned, and other kind friends for a few days until we could complete our house, move in and get settled.

To add to our discomfort it continued to be bitter cold and we were unprepared for it. But, worse than that— for the bride—there wasn't a servant to be procured at that post for "love or money."

On November 23 both officers of the troop, Captain Webb and Lieut. G. A. Thurston, were ordered to San Antonio for a month, and the bridegroom was left in command of an old troop, a few days after his arrival at a strange post and with new, strange duties to perform, to move, settle, build, etc., etc., and no chest with our camp rugs, curtains, table furniture, etc.—all of which had been procured before leaving the North—by advice of a brother then stationed in Texas—knowing the almost priceless value of such things on the remote frontier.

Canvass Quarters

Fortunately on the second day after moving into our as
yet unfurnished and very primitive tent quarters, an officer of the Eleventh Infantry, Lieut. George Lott, who
was just starting north on a leave of absence, loaned us
a colored boy about 15 years of age, who had been taught
to cook, and he managed to take care of the meat and
vegetables, etc., while the bride attended to the pastry,
desserts, etc., although she had never had any experience
in that direction, but had fortified herself with either Har-
riet Beecher's or Marion Harland's cookbook before
starting out on this long "wedding tour" to the far off
frontier.

We hung our gray blankets at the sides of the well ven-
tilated tent to keep out the wind; made a dressing table out
of a barrel, covering it with a gaudy chintz, bound with
red; covered a rude, wooden "bunk" with a chintz valance
all about it in order to hide the butter keg, the commissary
box, and the boards stowed away for furniture, etc. These
articles, with a camp chair or two, loaned to us by Major
Webb, completed our worldly goods until those left behind
in our large packing trunk and chest at Columbus should
arrive. On a shelf over our heads at the head of our bed
was our box of groceries. A seventy-five cent looking
glass hung over our dressing barrel, and our dining tent,
store tent, etc., were things of the dim future.

But finally we got straightened out by duplicating some
of our most necessary things—such as crockery, glassware,
etc.—which we already had back in our trunk and chest—
at Veck's store at San Angelo across the North Concho
River. The fire burned brightly—*when it didn't smoke,*
and the kerosene student's lamp threw a bright glimmer
upon the circle. It was "home" and the bride was contented and cheerful. It would, however, have amused a
northern housewife to have seen "Cato," our skillful (?)
colored boy cook, dip out soup with a cup, and rush our
plates out to be washed, to be used later for our desserts.

Still, with canned commissary goods, and flour, macaroni, beans, rice, cheese, salt mackerel, lard, coffee, butter, sugar, canned fruits, jellies, etc., we existed, and quite reasonably—beef being but 3¾ cents per pound, with liver, oxtails, kidneys, brains, soup bones, etc., thrown in.

Rattlesnakes were seen among the rock piles and amidst the prickly pears. Tarantulas lurked under every cactus or shrub. Centipedes brought forth their interesting broods under every building, and scorpions of various sizes were found, but less frequently than either of the former. Terrible sand storms were of frequent occurrence and so violent as to fill the air for thirty feet or more with blinding dust as far as the eye could reach, sifting into every house and tent and filling everything of the food kind with grit. It was then that the bride ate her "peck of dirt." The Texas women wisely remarked to the bride when questioned about the climate, "Why, Lord bless your soul, gal, nobody can die in Texas, and consumption has never been heard of here."

Courts martial, Boards of Survey, guard duty, police duty, etc., filled in the time pretty fully.

On December 10th the Indians came within about 16 miles of the post and ran off some stock and a detachment was sent out after them, but the raiders escaped. Again on January 14th another command under command of Captain William O'Connell, one of our best old Irish soldiers, started in pursuit of a party of Indians who came in a half mile from the post, near San Angelo, and ran off 16 horses. Gen. Gillem, who had been transferred to the First Cavalry, then in California, left January 14th to take command, and Major (Brevet Major-General) John P. Hatch, our senior major, assumed command of Fort Concho.

On the 8th of February, Troop "A" with headquarters arrived from San Antonio, bringing with them *our long lost trunk and chest.* This was a very happy day for the bride, for, after going to a garrison hop, and a bridal reception in improvised costumes, she could now enjoy at least the unpacking of the hidden and unused bridal apparel or trousseau. We dragged out the tent rug, crockery, china and what little silver we possessed, and having secured the services of old "Aunt Mary," a colored cook also loaned by one of the absent officers (Major Webb), we enjoyed what little time we had to stay to the utmost of our limited canvas house and resources.

One day word was sent around that the butter was limited but that each family would be issued eight pounds, and that we could have what tea we desired. A hint was also dropped that there would be no supply or "bull" trains the remainder of the season. Our base was Bremond on the Texas Central Railroad, hundreds of miles distant and our supplies came by slow Mexican relays. The bride, thinking possibly that we might run short of provisions, purchased *ten pounds* of tea, a *kit of salt mackerel,* dried apples ad libitum, and other quantities in proportion. The bridegroom immediately applied officially to have *his canvas quarters extended.*

The Brides' Buffalo Hunt

About February 20th, General Hatch proposed that we take the ladies out to a buffalo hunt. The animals were grazing within sight of the post near the Twin Mountains.

An ambulance, with an escort of 15 men, was furnished, and in the early morning we started. It was our first buffalo hunt although we had seen them in large numbers at a distance on our last day's march into the post. Riding out on the Fort Stockton road a few miles, and sighting a few small herds, we soon came upon countless thousands— the vast prairie was black with them. As soon as they sighted us, several huge fellows nearest to the road made a rush to cross it, directly in front of the ambulance. The brides screamed with excitement, rose up on the seats and shouted to us—"Why, don't you go after them?" Clapping spurs to our horses we were soon among them and riding alongside. It was new and novel sport. Pushing up to a huge bull the bridegroom fired in quick succession five shots, three of which took effect, but it only stopped him temporarily, for he turned as quick as a flash, his shaggy head and long beard bristling, his small eyes, almost hidden in the thick dense hair, and charged. Luckily the bridegroom was mounted on a well trained buffalo horse, which quickly turned to avoid the blow. Upon firing again, this time bringing him to his knees, one more shot laid him out dead, and his tongue was soon hanging to the pommel of the saddle—a first prize, and we were conceited enough to imagine that the killing of that one buffalo classed us as a great hunter, although frankness leads us to confess that the bridegroom—as most amateurs do when chasing buffalo for the first time—barely escaped shooting his own horse in the head.

The brides thought it rare sport and they could sit and see every movement. The immense herds worked off, however, until finally lost to view. It was found impracticable for the ambulance to follow, the ground being too much cut up by breaks and arroyas.

We proposed to have a day's sport, however, so leaving the party, we struck out for the game, keeping to the leeward as much as possible. The bridegroom had not realized up to this time what the sport was until this moment. Somebody shouted, ''Cut out a young cow from the herd and run it.'' That was easier said than done. We started to do so. After a hard run and a young two year old had been separated or ''cut out'' from the herd, the race began. It was through mezquite chapparal, over smooth, then rocky ground, in and out of ravines, now almost up to the animal, again by his doublings to get back to the herd, left way behind. Shots were fired in a stern chase to cripple him. He was hit twice in the hind leg, but he only gave a quick, sharp jerk of the tail, and rolled, scrambled and tore on faster and faster. That two year old was run nearly twenty minutes, or, until the rider's horse was almost exhausted or ''blown.'' Several times in going through the

thorny, thick mezpuite chapporel, the bridegroom was
struck and almost dismounted by the branches, but—we
must have that buffalo! Drawing a second Colt '45 and
taking a diagonal cut when the animal was seen to curve
and try again and again to rejoin the herd—to which all
buffalo were very much attached from birth, recognizing
but one leader and one cow mother—we ran right upon
him, gave him one shot that stopped and then another that
killed him. One gigantic leader was wounded and took
refuge in a water hole, swimming about as unconcernedly
as though he had always lived there. Twenty carbine balls
were fired into him before he gave up his life. We had not
then, of course, learned to range up alongside his left flank
and place one bullet, ranging forward, behind the left
shoulder—as "Buffalo Bill" did when filling the contract
for beef with the Union Pacific Railroad—that one shot
killing instantly and resulting in the saving of ammunition.

The men had scattered out in every direction. The
herds which, when we started were immense, had now
split into hundreds of small ones, and each choosing a bull
leader were going in as many different directions. The
cracking of carbines could be heard all about us, and far
off in the distance men could be seen going up a gentle
slope where the sunlight and shadows seemed ever chasing
each other. A puff of smoke and down went a buffalo,
then another and another, until the fast waning light
warned us that we must recall the detachment. We had
killed about twenty-five, the bridegroom's share being a
bull, a cow and two young "two year olds," which seemed
pretty good for a novice, and yet we could put on our hats
without the use of a shoe horn.

Our ammunition was running low, and although we
struck many large herds before reaching the stage road,
where we had left General H— and the ladies, prudence,
on account of Indian parties that might be lurking about,
compelled us to deny the men further hunting. We arrived
at the post a little after dark—our horses loaded with

meat, and wagons were sent out the next day to get the remainder for the garrison—the rule of those days, and
before the slaughter of the buffalo and their extermination
by "pot hunters" for their skins began—was to kill only
as many as were necessary for the use of our garrisons or
commands in the field to eke out their rations.

The huge buffalo heads were scalped and after proper
treatment and tanning of the skin were used for door mats
in our tents, which, the bride thought were "useful" if
not "ornamental."

We had many hunts after this. Our horse herds grazed
towards the "Twin Mountains" and oftentimes it was
with the greatest difficulty that we could prevent their
being stampeded into the post by these buffalo herds.

When serving a turn as officer of the guard it had been
the bridegroom's custom to inspect the relief posted at
the stables, Quartermaster's corral, and the commissary
storehouse, about midnight, and as the latter was near our
tent he often stopped in to get a cup of hot coffee, which
the bride had ready for him, before returning to the guard
tents.

One night as he reached the back door to the main, or
hospital tent, a terrific explosion took place inside that
tent, which sent the red coals out of the door in every
direction. As he sprang in, everywhere about the floor, on
our bed, and in the folds of the canvas, the hot coals had
been scattered. In a few moments the tent would have
been in a blaze. It was the work of a second to seize the
cover on the bed and shake it out the front door; to fill a
pail of water from a barrel outside, and extinguish the
flames. Not, however, without some damage in the way of
numerous holes in the canvas. There were no engines or
fire extinguishers at that date within hundreds of miles.
The bride was much frightened. There was only a temporary panic. No fire alarm had been given although the
report had awakened the garrison and they came swarming out.

Upon examination of the fireplace, it was evident that it had been caused either by a cartridge having been placed for mischief in the wood, which the guard house prisoners were in the daily habit of sawing, splitting and delivering along the quarters—or confined steam in the porous limestone used in laying the bottom of the fireplace, which was found to be split and pieces of the stone shivered off. Had it occurred when I was absent, a serious fire, but without much loss of property, although with more fright to the bride, might have resulted.

On Sundays there was no chaplain; no church or service, and we were compelled to commune strictly with nature. By March 1st the thermometer ran up to 85° in the shade, and several times to 95°, but it was a dry heat and it was not so prostrating as 80° at the North.

In the little town of San Angelo on the opposite side of the river, fights were frequent at night, and drunkenness of daily occurrence. One of our trumpeters of Troop "B" (King) was, while in a Mexican jacal one night, so poisoned that his life was despaired of for several days.

The First Scout

March 4th. The Fort Griffin stage came in and reported that it had been attacked by a small party of Indians, the passengers barely escaping. A Mr. Hicks, post trader of Fort Griffin, was aboard the stage and vouched for the story.

Major Rendlebrook ("Old Joe") and the bridegroom were ordered out in pursuit. In less than 30 minutes we were ready with the mules packed and on the road.

We examined the stage road for 20 miles until we had passed the "Lone Tree." A few pony tracks had been discovered but no trail, although the passengers had said that the stage was jumped about nine miles from Fort Concho. Taking a northwest direction we marched all that day and camped that night upon an unknown stream, probably a tributary of Dove Creek. It was the bridegroom's first scout. He had been told that Major Rendlebrock would, as an old and experienced Indian campaigner, give him all of the "points" and act as his instructor. As we were about to make camp, the old veteran instructor in cavalry scouting and Indian fighting—a German officer in the Fatherland army before coming to the United States—asked me, "How you put dis command in camp, eh?" The bridegroom not wishing to be caught the first time on such an interrogatory, and putting on a bold face, briskly replied, "Why, Major, I would picket the horses close to camp, with a small herd guard on to prevent surprise or stampede." "Oh, no!" said "Old Joe," "what you do for de animals at night so close to camp and wid no grass, eh?" I had not thought of that in my strong desire to huddle them in close to camp for protection against Indians who might be hovering about. But I never forgot after that, to put the animals far enough out to graze them until just before dark with a vigilant herd guard, and then draw them in for protection on good grass near camp at night.

In the morning our German instructor said, "Now, Carter, we go oop dis walley (valley), and we catch boof-a-lo, and mebbe catch trail same time, vat you say, eh?"

As we wound out of our camp many wild turkeys were started up by some dogs which we had taken along with the column; they would run hard for a few moments, then taking wing would make a long, straight flight into the valley below, where they would stick their long necks in the grass like their ostrich friends, completely winded and too frightened to move, and they were soon easily secured.

We were now in the Colorado Valley; it was literally packed with countless thousands of buffalo, feeding on the now green and nutritious mezquite and grama grasses.

Our supper at night consisted of broiled wild turkey thighs, larded with bacon slivers, and buffalo sweetbreads, with "doby" biscuits and coffee, and with appetites like wolves, sharpened by our long day's ride in the keen, bracing air, we would not have exchanged that meal for one of *"Delmonico's" best*.

Late in the afternoon we had quite a scare. We had seen several Indian ponies, evidently dropped on some previous raid. Secreting the command, several of the best men were sent across the valley to secure them. After a long chase, they succeeded in capturing the ponies, but not before we had seen them start up several times and alarm a large herd of buffalo.

At night the men had not come into camp; it grew quite dark and still they were missing. Major R— now beginning to feel quite anxious, and not wishing to discharge any carbines as an alarm, directed that they be signalled by torches made of the long, dry sedge grass, then lighted and raised on sticks, which our party vigorously waved. This "took the trick" as the Texan vernacular indicated, and they soon came into camp leading four, thin, gaunt, sorebacked ponies, evidently abandoned by Indians a moon or two before.

We slept the sleep of tired "troopers," rolled up in blankets, booted and spurred, with a saddle blanket on the saddle for a pillow, pistols ready at hand and the horses securely "side lined" and "staked out" with a "herd guard" on.

As we were quietly marching the next morning, having given up any thoughts of discovering the trail, which had probably scattered among the hills on the first day, we dismounted and led up afoot over the steep bluffs to the tableland or Mesa above.

The buffalo could be seen hurrying and scurrying from the large to the smaller valleys where they could be safer from our intruding column. First came the old black bearded fellows, the bull leaders, then the younger bulls, and following, the cows with the wee, little humpbacked, long-legged, grotesque looking calves, bringing up the rear—the latter most unwillingly assuming the rolling, stiff-legged gallop which the frightened leaders persisted in maintaining.

The grass was springing forth in great green luxuriant mats; the mellow sunlight lying warm and soft all over the land; the broad, sweeping shadows, in patches here and there; the mounds, buttes, conical peaks and the abrupt, washed-out valleys; all gave one a grand opportunity for the study of nature and the surface geological formations all about this beautiful Colorado valley. Here were the Morraine Terraces and we were then upon a Lateral Terrace skirting the entire course of the valley we had been winding through.

At a period ages remote, this whole fair land had unquestionably been under water, and we now were silent witnesses—where the foot of white men had scarcely ever penetrated—of the unseen agency of some great power—invisible and unseen—the powerful hand of God Almighty—the Creator of all things seen and unseen.

Our camp at night was on Dove Creek, and we had to be extremely careful not to bivouac too near the trails of buffalo leading to water, for fear of a stampede.

We reached the post at 1:30 P. M. on March 7, after an unsuccessful scout, coming in near the old sawmill. We had learned a great deal from our old scouting master, or Indian trailing instructor, but *the bridegroom had not been very forcibly impressed by his zeal or persistence in following any trail had he found one,* but rather a tendency to *looking after his stomach* and the *flesh pots* of a perfect Eden for hunting among the numerous buffalo and antelope herds, the droves of wild turkeys, innumerable coveys of quail, prairie chickens and fat Highland plover. "The Wedding Tour of an Army Bride" had ended.

Our work on the frontier had just begun.

Note:—From 1865 to 1892 it is of record that 823 battles, engagements and actions, with some unrecorded, had been fought with a relentless savage foe by our little regular army in their efforts to "Win the West" and to advance civilization on the border. A large majority of these conflicts took place in Texas—both before and after her Independence.

After being married for fifty-three years and two months and at her death in November, 1923, there appeared the following eulogy of the bride in the Army and Navy Register of Washington, D. C. This was copied far and wide, one paper—the Boston Evening Traveler, publishing it as an editorial.

A PIONEER ARMY WOMAN

There died on November 24, 10:45 P. M., at the Walter Reed Hospital a most remarkable little woman of the pioneer days, the days of the "Covered Wagon." In 1870 she made a bridal trip with her husband, Captain R. G. Carter, U. S. Army, retired, from Boston, Massachusetts, to Fort Concho, Texas, to which he had been assigned after graduation from West Point that year, and which was then one of the extreme frontier posts on the Western border of Texas—then habitated only by a few hardy settlers, ranchmen and cowboys, and Indians, buffalo, wolves, prairie dogs, jack-rabbits and rattle snakes.

After reaching "Santone" (San Antonio) by boat, rail and stage, she marched 15 days with her husband, who was assigned to the duty of driving 400 unbroken Texas horses (broncos) over this expanse of wilderness—at the end of which she took up her abode in a wall tent. She had four children. Two daughters were born at Old Fort Richardson, Jack County, Texas, located on Lost Creek, a small tributary of the West Fork of the Trinity River. One of these daughters was born in a wall tent during a howling "Norther," and the tent was held down by men at the guy ropes; the other was born in a rough pecan picket jackal plastered with mud, infested with scorpions, centipedes, tarantulas, ants, etc. She made one march of 30 days with two babies through this wild, savage country, swarming at that period with hostile bands of Comanche and Kiowa Indians, the camp being picketed at night. She was a devoted wife and mother, always hopeful, brave and cheerful, a model army woman and mother of the old

Frontier Days. She was the mother of Mrs. A. H. von
Bayer of Wheeling, W. Va.; Lieut. Col. Robert D. Carter,
U. S. Army, and Mrs. H. C. Hilgard of St. Louis, Mo.
All of her surviving children were with her at the last
moment and one grandchild, Carter Dexter Hilgard. She
was in her 77th year and had hosts of friends, both in
the army and among the citizens of this city, especially
of the Mt. Pleasant district where she had lived for many
years.

General Charles King, U. S. Army, the distinguished
military novelist and writer, added the following graceful
and eloquent tribute.

(COPY)

St. Johns M. A.

Delafield, Wis., Dec. 4, '23.

My dear Carter:

With heartfelt sympathy and sorrow I have just read the sad
tidings of the death of that wonderful little Army heroine, your
devoted wife.

The story of her early experiences in the wilds of Texas, as told
in the Register, will be read by thousands of Army folk as something almost incredible today. Indeed, even in war time, very,
very few encountered such hardship, peril and privation, very few
suffered as she did and survived.

The history of your own career in the Civil War and in the old
4th Cavalry is almost without a parallel but, to my knowledge and
belief, hers stands unrivaled.

I hardly dare intrude upon your grief and desolation but could
not let you believe that among your host of friends my wife and I
were not grieving with you in so deep a sorrow.

Faithfully yours,

CHARLES KING.

Captain Robert G. Carter,
U. S. Army, Retired.

When the writer was National Commander of "The Order of Indian Wars," at its 21st annual meeting, General
Charles King was called upon to address his companions
of the Order. The following extract appeals to us as a
fine tribute to the memory of both those who survive, and

those of the regular army who have passed on, who composed that "little fighting army of the plains."

"It is all a memory now, but what a memory, to cherish!
A warfare in which the soldier of the United States had
no hope of honors if victorious, no hope of mercy if he
fell; slow death by hideous torture if taken alive; sheer
abuse from press and pulpit, if, as was often inevitable,
Indian squaw or child was killed. A warfare that called
us through the cliffs and canons on the southwest, the
lava beds and labyrinths of Modoc land, the windswept
plains of Texas, the rigors of Montana winters, the blistering heat of midsummer suns, fighting oftentimes
against a foe for whom we felt naught but sympathy, yet
knew that the response could be but deathless hate. . . .
A more thankless task, a more perilous service, a more
exacting test of leadership, morale and discipline no army
in Christendom has ever been called upon to undertake
than that which for eighty years was the lot of the little
fighting force of regulars who cleared the way across the
continent for the emigrant and settler. Who, summer and
winter, stood guard over the wide "frontier"? Whose
lives were spent in almost utter desolation? Whose lonely death was marked and mourned only by sorrowing comrade, or mayhap grief-stricken widow and children, left
destitute and despairing? *There never was a warfare on*
the face of the earth in which the soldier (officer or man)
had so little to gain, so very much to lose. There never
was a warfare which, like this, had absolutely nothing to
hold the soldier stern and steadfast to the bitter end, but
the solemn sense of soldier duty.

"Yet, as it had just that one inspiration, so has it had
at least one compensation that we may hold and cherish.
In no other warfare that I ever heard of were officers and
men so closely drawn together—wearing the same rough
garb, sharing the same rations, or lack of them—sometimes the same blanket, facing the same peril and enduring the same hardship, there grew up between the rank

and file and their platoon and troop leaders a sense of
comradeship and sympathy that years of garrison service
or long campaigning could never have brought about.''

THE MAN WHO HAS WON

I want to work by the side of the man
    Who has suffered, and seen, and knows,
Who has measured his pace in the battle line,
    And has given and taken the blows
With the grace of a gentleman,
    Who has parried and struck and sought and given
And—scarred with a thousand spears—
    Still lifts his head to the stars of heaven
And is not ashamed of his tears.
I want to grasp the hand of the man
    Who has been through it all, and seen,
Who has walked with the night of an unseen dread
    And stuck by the world machine;
Who has bared his breast to the winds of dawn,
    And thirsted, and starved, and felt
The sting and bite of the burning blast
    Which the mouths of the foul have dealt;
Who was tempted—and fell—and rose again,
    And gone on, trusty and true,
With God Supreme in his manly heart
    And his courage burning anew.
I'd give by all—be it little or great—
    To walk by his side today,
I'd stand up there with the man who knows
    The clash and shock of the fray;
Who has gritted his teeth, and clenched his fist
    And gone on doing his best,
Because of love for his fellow men,
    And the faith in his strong man's breast.
Oh, I'd like to walk with him,
    Hand in hand, together to journey along;
For the man who's fought, and struggled and won,
    Is the man who can make men strong.

                            —Author Unknown.

CHAPTER II

A Frontier Line—Border Posts

SHORTLY after the Civil War when the hostile Indians became more and more threatening and aggressive, and their murderous acts and numerous raiding and plundering excursions so serious as to compel the Government to adopt more vigorous measures to control them, or, about 1867, it became necessary to establish a line of forts, or, more properly speaking, posts—for none of them were enclosed works or even stockaded enclosures—to guard the extreme Western Counties of Texas, then impossible to even survey or to settle on account of this ever increasing Indian menace.

The security and safety of this entire outer line, and the protection of its settlers, was the work cut out for a part of our little regular army as a police force—and it proved, in more ways than one, a most strenuous, almost herculean task. Prior to the Civil War Forts Mason, Martin Scott; Camps Cooper, Cobb, Hudson, Colorado, Lancaster, etc., had been established. The outlying posts and sub-posts, so far as they can now be recalled, which were built, rebuilt and occupied after the Civil War, were Fort Richardson, the most northerly, located in Jack County, on Lost Creek, a small tributary of the West Fork of the Trinity River, and about 7 miles from its mouth. It was built by the Sixth U. S. Cavalry and occupied Nov. 26, 1867, and abandoned May 23, 1878, having fulfilled the object for which it was built. It was used as an Indian School for a short time afterwards. Originally a five company post it was expanded by extending its lines of officer's and men's quarters by tents to accommodate ten or more companies. It was about 450 miles northwest from San Antonio. This post was named for Brig. General Israel Richardson who was mortally wounded at the battle of Antietam, Sept. 17,

1862. Forts Belknap and Phantom Hill were established
in Nov. 1851. On Oct. 28, 1852, Fort Chadbourne was laid
out and occupied by Co's A and K-8 U. S. Infantry. Next
came Fort Griffin in Shackleford County, located on the
Clear Fork of the Brazos River. It was about 370 miles
northwest of San Antonio. It was originally a part of
Maxwell's Ranch; was named "Camp Wilson"; was abandoned and was then rebuilt by Lieut. H. B. Mellen of the
Sixth Cavalry and occupied July 29, 1867—abandoned
about 1879. It was named for Gen. Charles Griffin, the
original Commander of the famous West Point Battery
(afterwards Battery "D" Fifth U. S. Art'y) who later
commanded a brigade, then the First Division of the Fifth
Corps—A.P.—and finally, after Gen. G. K. Warren was relieved at Five Forks, the Corps at Appomattox C. H. He
died of yellow fever at Galveston in 1867. Next in the line
came Fort Concho, Tom Green Co.

Then came in this frontier defense line the posts of
Forts Stockton, Davis, Bliss (at El Paso), McKavett,
Clark (the last three built after the Mexican War), Mc-
Intosh and Inge. There were several sub posts or intermediate stations, located at different periods—more for
rapid communication, by courier between posts, than to
fulfill any practical offensive or defensive purpose. The
principal ones were "Bothwick's Station" on Salt Creek—
about half way between Fort Richardson and old Fort
Belknap, an abandoned post on the Brazos River—"Camp
Wichita" near Buffalo Springs, between Fort Richardson
and Red River station—and "Mountain Pass"—between
Fort Concho and Fort Griffin. There were then no railroads running into San Antonio—the "Sunset" Route
from Indianola being uncompleted. There were no railroads between the posts—and the roads connecting these
posts with the outside world were the dim stage roads—
mere trails—starting from San Antonio as a center, and
running as the "El Paso Stage Line," with its branches, a
distance of nearly 900 miles to that town on the Mexican

border. Four horse Concord coaches started from San
A— but long before the first post was reached (McKavett
being the nearest) they were replaced by small two seated
Concord mail wagons which carried the driver and an
Infantry guard. The "relays," or stage stations were
about 20 miles apart, and if the mules were wild and unbroken—as they usually were--they were led out blind-
folded and "hooked into" the stage, the driver mounted
to his seat and took the lines, while the two blinded mules
were held, and at a signal from him the blinders were
"jerked loose," and the mules keeping the trail made the
run to the next station when this method was again repeated. Our mail was tri-weekly, unless the water courses
were high and "booming," and then, with all stages and
wagon trains "water-bound," it was a "gamble" if we got
one mail a month, mounted couriers often-times being sent
out to meet the stages and bring in the mail pouches on
their saddles. Frequently our food supplies ran very low
on account of the slowness of the Mexican freighters or
"bull whackers" who, with their two-wheeled Carreta
loads with a "trailer" and 6 or 8 pairs of steers or "bulls"
yoked by the horns (a method which would drive a yankee
farmer crazy), would often go into camp by a stream for
ten days, forgetting in the meantime to see if the water
had all run out so that they could again begin their long
journey. "Manana" or "por la Manana" was the Mexican "bullwhacker's" watchword. Indianola on the Gulf,
550 miles away, was our first base and Bremond on the
Texas Central, its terminal (it had not then reached Del-
las), was our second supply base—and the "Katy" (M.K.
& T.R.R.) had not reached the Red River—but was
"hooked up" somewhere north of Atocha, I. T. Later, our
bases were shifted to Hemstead, Corsicana, Dennison,
Sherma, etc., nearer points.

Brief History of Concho Land

The history of the great Concho region had its beginning
long before the Pilgrim Fathers saw Plymouth Rock; many

years before the English heard of Jamestown. Unreliable tradition accredits Cabeza de la Vaca and his followers with having passed through the domain of Concholand during their wanderings in 1535-6; reliable history records the fact that two Franciscan Fathers visited the Conchos in 1580, more than 100 years before the French pioneer, LaSalle, mistook Matagorda Bay for the Mississippi and erected a fort at Dimit's Point on the La Vaca. It is a strange, thrilling story of these two fathers, too lengthy for repetition here. An invitaiton had reached them at Paso del Norte, asking them to visit one of the East Texas tribes of Indians and there establish a mission. They responded and in their travels they came to the country of the Yojuanes, where they tarried several months expounding the holy faith to the Indians and baptizing a large number of their children. They explored the surrounding country and made a very correct map thereof, the same which is yet preserved in the Archivo General in the City of Mexico. On this map are outlined two rivers, the one on the north they gave the name of "Concha," the Spanish for Conch, or shell, and to the river on the south, they gave the name "Perla," the Spanish for pearl. Hence on that old map, one may see the "Dio de las Conchas" and the "Rio de las Perlas" in the clear outline. While here, they found many pearls in the Rio de las Perlas, and hence the name bestowed upon that stream.

Some of these pearls were sent to the Viceroy of Mexico; some were sent to the Spanish Monarch in Spain; while, according to tradition, two of the largest and best were sent to Rome to adorn the Papal crown. Studying the narrative of these two missionary Fathers, one is led to the conclusion that the town of this tribe, the Yojuanes, was located at or near the confluence of these two rivers, the Rio de las Conchas, now the North Concho, and the Rio de las Perlas, or South Concho, but there is nothing on the map they made to confirm this conclusion.

Reckoning from the date of visitation of these early missionaries, two hundred and eighty years were added to the roll of centuries past before any permanent settlements were made by the white race in Concholand. True, it was often visited by trappers, hunters, rangers and surveying parties. Captain Shropshire, an aged veteran and ex-ranger, living in (1914) at North Angelo, was a member of Burleson's (father of Ex-Postmaster General in President Woodrow Wilson's cabinet) Rangers and with that company spent several weeks on the Conchos in 1852. In 1862, the Chisholm ranch was established in the Concho country and the year following, the late Frank Tankersley* effected, so far as I can understand, the first permanent settlement in Concholand.

How San Angelo Got Its Name

As at all newly established military posts, a village sprung into existence along the north bank of the North Concho, opposite the post. It would be interesting to note the beginning and growth of this frontier hamlet made up mostly of jacals, sod and picket huts "shacks," "dug-outs" or "shanties," later to give place to palatial

---

*(A town near old Fort Concho was named "Tankersley"—after him—one of the early pioneers of that country. John Warren Hunter of San Angelo—who died in 1915—a newspaper and magazine writer on border history and pioneer reminiscences writes in the San Angelo Standard of Feb. 18, 1914, as follows:
Lieutenant Carter, the now Captain Carter U. S. A. (retired), was well and favorably known to the early pioneers of Concholand, and his memory is yet cherished by the survivors of the Old Guard. During his long term of service on the Texas Border, he became familiar with every trail made by savages and outlaws; mastered every phase of Indian ruse, signs, signals and strategy, and in the course of time, he became a terror, not only to the Comanches, but to evil doers of every description. His courage and prowess was aptly voiced in the remark of the late Frank Tankersley, who, on a certain occasion in the early 70's was asked about an Indian raid then being made in the country and who it was that led the squad of the Fourth Cavalry that had gone out that morning. "That was Lieutenant Carter," replied Mr. Tankersley. "The Indians have a day's start on him, but he'll follow their trail to the jumpin' off place, and when he comes up with 'em and gets through with 'em, the ground will be tore up, the bushes bit off, an' blood, hair, livers an' lights will be scattered all round." Such was the estimate set upon the gallant Lieutenant Carter of the Fourth Cavalry. Nor was this estimate confined to any particular locality but it became state and national in scope, to the extent that he was awarded the Congressional Medal of Honor for "Most Distinguished Gallantry in Action with Comanche Indians," and the "Grateful Thanks of the State of Texas for prompt action and gallant conduct," etc., by the State legislature in joint assembly, besides two brevets—one for "Specially Gallant Conduct."
Captain Carter and three of his brothers served in the Army of the Potomac throughout the four years' war and is the author of "Four Brothers in Blue," a copy of which he has kindly sent me and I find it one of the most thrilling narratives of soldier life it has ever been my good fortune to possess. Nothing, however, the scholarly soldier has ever written will command greater interest in Texas than his "Reveille and Taps, or "On the Border with Mackenzie," when the work comes from the press and the distinguished author may feel the assurance that Texans will exhaust the entire edition, and I may safely say that it will find its way into no less than 1000 homes in San Angelo.
The writer is indebted to Mr. Hunter for much of the historical knowledge of Fort Concho, San Angelo, and the settled regions in that country since the old Indian days.)

residences and metropolitan business houses, schools, churches, hotels, sanitariums, etc. It would be interesting to mention the names of all the brave, energetic men and women who were among the first to erect their modest homes where San Angelo now rears its (comparatively) magnificent proportions, many of whom have passed to their reward, while others are yet spared to reap the golden harvest of their early privations, but all this must be left to the consideration of the future historian.

Up to 1870, '71 or '72, somewhere along about that time, the little village across from Fort Concho, with its population of 30 or 40 people, mostly halfbreeds, had no name. In the post it was mentioned as "Over the River," and among the inhabitants of the little settlement it was spoken of as "Over the River." Bart DeWitt owned the land on which San Angelo now stands. I think he lived at that time in San Antonio. . . . He was a very near friend of the late W. S. Veck and family. DeWitt's wife was named Magdelina, and she had a sister who was then a nun in the Ursuline Convent in San Antonio, and was known as "Angela." Mr. and Mrs. Veck lived in a little picket hut on what is now (1931) Oakes Street; near where George Richardson's office and warehouse now stands. While visiting this home one evening Mr. DeWitt mentioned to Mrs. Kate Veck the importance of bestowing a name that would convey a meaning upon the growing village, and the absurdity of allowing it to be continually known as "Over the River." He suggested calling the new town, "'San Magdalena" out of respect to his wife. Mrs. Veck objected to this and called DeWitt's attention to the fact that his sister-in-law, Angela, a most lovable character, was then a nun in San Antonio, and on account of her many virtues, the town should be named for her, to which DeWitt readily agreed, and Mrs. Veck then said, "The town shall be called San Angela!" And so to this highly esteemed lady belongs the honor of having bestowed a name upon a town which today bears the regal title of "The Queen City of the Conchos." But the government did not take kindly to the name offered. There was something about the orthography "San Angela" and its gender, that lacked euphony in the ears of the Postal Department, and as a result the terminal "a" in Angela was dropped and an "o" substituted, making it read "San Angelo," and this to the satisfaction of all parties interested.

San Angelo was, at the period of which we write, a small settlement with not more than twenty or thirty settlers—mostly cow men and half breed Mexicans. There was one general merchandise store known as "Vecks." It is now a large town with about 25,000 inhabitants. It is the County seat of Town Green County, has two railroads running into it, and another being, or has been, completed to Topolobampo on the West Coast of Mexico. From a cow country it is now, as stated, quite a cotton center, with schools, churches, modern hotels, up-to-date stores, newspapers, a modern Sanatorium, water works, a Chamber of Commerce, etc. Its growth has been little short of marvelous. During the Indian outbreaks there were no wilder or more unsafe sections of Texas, or on the entire border to live in. Fort Concho now (1931), is about the centre of the town, and it's parade is a park.

Fort Concho

The establishment of a military post on the Conchos and its occupancy by United States troops for a period of nearly fifteen years, becomes a part of the history of San Angelo, and for that reason a brief history of Fort Concho becomes necessary and highly relevant in this connection.

In 1866, a commission was appointed by the Secretary of War, to visit all the frontier posts of Texas, which had been abandoned by the U. S. government at the beginning of the Civil War. This commission, accompanied by an escort consisting of two companies of cavalry, left San Antonio in June or July, 1866, and came by way of Fredericksburg, Fort Mason and Fort McKavett, and thence across to Spring Creek, where they remained in camp several days, prospecting, as per instructions from Washington, for a suitable location for the erection of a new army post. The result was the selection of the delta formed by the junction of the North and South Concho rivers, and on this point of land, chosen on account of the abundance of wood, water, good range for cavalry horses and its advantages from a strategic standpoint. However, the post was not built exactly on the site chosen and recommended. Early the year following, December 4, 1867, the first contingent of troops—five companies of the Fourth Cavalry—arrived and pitched their tents along the Concho. The officer to whom was delegated the task to survey and plot the new post, decided that the site chosen by the commission and approved by the Secretary of War, was unsuitable, and on his own volition he selected the present site on which old Fort Concho stands, made his survey, establishing his metes and bounds, sent in his report, and was later tried by a military court and was said to have been dismissed from the army.

As stated, five companies of the Fourth Cavalry, commanded by Col. John P. Hatch, were the first troops stationed at Fort Concho. The new post was given a multiplicity of names. It was first called, in 1868, Camp Hatch, later it was known as Camp Kelly, the construction department or quartermaster, called it Fort Griffin. Finally there came an order from district headquarters at San Antonio, emphasizing the fact that the new army post should be known then and thereafter as Fort Concho.

The foundation of the first building was laid on the first day of January, 1868. It was abandoned June 20, 1889. It was intended for a ten company post and for a number of years all supplies had to be brought by wagon transportation from Indianola, 550 miles, and San Antonio, 230 miles distant. The nearest town was Fredericksburg, 160 miles away, a German colony, which

reaped largely of the benefits accruing from the building
of the new post. It supplied in a great measure the stone
masons and lime burners; hay camps along the Concho
plains were operated by sturdy Germans, German contractors furnished vast supplies of grain and breadstuffs
and German ox and mule trains lined the road from the
coast to the Conchos. The cost of the building of this
post has been estimated as high as three millions. I do
not assume to say that those figures are correct, but after
all, the expense involved was immense. For two years,
two saw-mills were operated on the San Saba, 65 miles
away, for the production of lumber and shingles employed in the construction of the post buildings. This material was hauled on government wagons, drawn by government teams, driven by government teamsters who were
paid $40 per month and rations. The shingles sawn from
oak, elm and pecan timber, may be seen today on the dilapidated roofs of a number of the buildings in old Fort
Concho, placed in position more than fifty years ago.
When completed, Fort Concho was one of the most beautiful and best ordered posts on the Texas border. Its
arrangement was artistic and every feature bespoke comfort and convenience. On the south side of the ample
parade grounds stood the officers' quarters, tasty, elegant,
imposing; on the north, the commodious and handsome
barracks; on the east the commissary and quartermaster's
buildings, while the west side of the grounds was closed
with an ornamental fence with a large gateway in the
center.

It bordered upon the "Staked Plains." Countless
herds of buffalo grazed between the Twin Mountains and
the post, much to the alarm of our horse herds—a mile
or two out—which were frequently stampeded by the
huge, ungainly beasts much to the disgust of the Commanding Officer and the Officer of the herd. The great
grey lobo wolf and coyote came nearly to the back doors
of our tents in their ravenous search for offal at the beef

corral nearby, the latter frequently tipping over our garbage barrels. Their blood-curdling howls, especially the latter—which is first a sharp bark, followed by a succession of sharp, staccato yelps running into each other and ending in a sort of long drawn out quavering howl—were, at times almost indescribably melancholy, and awakened us at all hours of the night, which caused the newly-made bride to sit up in bed and shrink back in alarm. The flat, treeless prairies were a vast prairie dog village, interfering even in our pursuit of game, and from behind nearly every bush or patch of prickly pear, the jack, or mule-eared rabbit with ears aloft and vibrating with nervous energy, got up with a startled bound and disappeared in an instant, leaving nothing but a cloud of dust and a most vivid recollection of a misty, shadowy form behind him. Herds of graceful antelope were daily seen near the "Twin Mountains," a few miles away; their white spotted flanks flashing in the sun one moment, the next disappearing in the dun or neutral tint of the everlasting prairie. The whistling quail could almost be shot from the back porches of the officer's quarters; prairie chicken and Highland plover were killed from an ambulance while crossing the river to San Angelo, or riding upon the road to the stage station at "Ben Ficklins" or Bismarck, while on the streams wild duck, curlew, greenwiged teal and the magnificent trumpeting white swan abounded. Upon all the pecan timbered creeks wild turkeys swarmed, and were brought in by the wagon load requiring but a nights still-hunting with shot guns at their numerous roosts. Hunting was therefore unsurpassed. Fishing rewarded the angler by the slightest exertion upon the Main and North Concho Rivers. Our plans had been matured for many an expedition to this realm of flesh pots and land overflowing with game, this hunters paradise, when lo! the advent of this new Colonel, Ranald S. Mackenzie, upon the 25th of February, 1871, sent rifles and shot guns to the rear to rust in their covers for many

a month until that larger and more troublesome game
"Lo, the poor Indian" should be sought and conquered,
for the peace and quiet of the settlers on the entire intermediate border.

The Border Ablaze

The entire border was ablaze, and the stories that these
wretched settlers brought in from time to time of murder, rapine, burning, pillaging and plundering was almost
heartrending. We were kept in an almost constant state
of alarm and preparation for active work, and seldom a
week or a month went by (these alarms generally occur-
ring at the full of the moon) that we were not in the saddle scouting after these thieves, marauders and murderers, and always handicapped by the number of hours it
took to bring the news of a raid to the post, and for us
to reach the scene of operations, as well as by the fact
that the Indians always had fresh mounts from their loose
herds or "caviards" which they always drove loose on
the flanks, and which they could use as relays every 20
miles or more, while we were absolutely confined to our
one Government horse or mule whose speed and endurance
was always limited by the distance traveled and the start
which the raiders would invariably have of us. This,
without explanation, was always an enigma to the average
citizen or member of Congress far away from the scene,
and comfortably ensconced in an office chair, beside an
open grate with a good cigar and a tall high-ball or a
mint julep to suck through a straw at the Capitol or "The
Willard." "Why can't our army officer, on fleet, well
groomed horses overhaul Indians in a hundred mile chase,
mounted on scrubby, scurvy ponies or "Cayuses"? The
reason is herewith given in brief.

Most of the settlers, cattlemen and ranchers had moved
into the near posts for protection, abandoning their
ranches, except a few of the more daring, and it was with
these that we kept in close touch and communication for
news of the frequent bloody Indian incursions, and thiev-
ing raids for horses and cattle.

CHAPTER III
The March to Fort Richardson

ON the 25th of March, the headquarters and five companies of the Fourth Cavalry were ordered to proceed to Fort Richardson about 230 miles North-east, and relieve the Sixth Cavalry, which was then under marching orders for Kansas; and on the 27th the column was filing across the Concho River past the little settlement of San Angelo, on the road to the Colorado River. There were the usual scenes and laughable incidents attending the departure of a Cavalry column. Unmanageable pack mules, which had kicked their packs loose from the old saw-buck pack saddles (the Arapahos not then being in use) and scattered their loads of coffee, flour and bacon upon the parade, had to be secured and repacked; a vicious horse disciplined, the condition of some unsteady soldier examined, who, liking liquor, not wisely, but too well, had imbibed too freely of Mexican mescal, or the *insinuating* a guardiente. But at last the hearty cheers of the assembled garrison were given and the column splashed through the clear waters of the sparkling stream and stretched out on its long march. "Mt. Margaret," named after the most accomplished, loving and devoted wife of one of our favorite Captains, E. B. Beaumont, was passed—the Colorado was reached and forded in the midst of a cold, driving rain storm, which made our fires of drift cottonwood at that nights camp more acceptable than usual, and the glowing embers of the mesquite, heaped up in the mess kettles, which we used as stoves, more necessary for those *better halves* who—notwithstanding the many frowns and incredulous smiles of our gallant, yet *unconverted,* bachelor Colonel—had chosen to share the fortunes of their bold trooper husbands upon the Indian border. Our next camp was at old Fort Chadbourne a small, two company post on Oak Creek, built shortly after the Mexican War; surrendered in 1861—re-

occupied—then abandoned. A prairie dog village was
spread over the parade ground—their sharp, squeaking
barks and comical antics seemingly expressing their disgust at having their wise town councils broken up by an
uninvited and noisy intrusion. We had seen many buffalo
since leaving our camp the night before, and hundreds
now grazed near this night's bivouac, some on the parade.
Several years before (shortly after the Civil War),
Colonel Beaumont had been stationed here with his Co.
"A." His wife and infant child were with him as companions.

The Buffalo Stampede—A Thrilling Adventure

Lieut. P. M. Boehm—Beaumont's first Lieutenant—was
on duty at Chadbourne with his troop—one day Col. B—
being absent from the post, hunting, Mrs. Beaumont, as
was the custom of many an army woman in those days—
whether in camp or on the march—attached a lariat to the
waist of little Natalie, her daughter, then beginning to
walk, and fastening it to a stout stake or picket pin, she
was allowed to play about the quarters, in sight of her
mother. She had a thirty foot radius in which to romp.
Thus securely "staked out" for safety, and where she
could at all times be seen, there was little thought of fear,
for Indian depredations had been less frequent since the
post was established. Immense herds of buffalo were
grazing as usual a mile or two away; they had approached
no nearer while the company was stationed there but, as
their sharp cut trails to Oak Creek for water—had led
in this direction before, this low plateau upon which the
post was located had evidently been their favorite grazing
ground. All was quiet, and there seemed to be no cause
for apprehension, when suddenly something alarmed the
herds; crazed with fright, and with a noise like the roaring of a tornado they came rushing toward the post, converging as they ran; other herds joined in the terrific
stampede; the ground fairly shook with the shock of the
thousands of maddened animals. Mrs. Beaumont heard

the ominous sound and stepped to the door believing it to
be the rolling of distant thunder. At a glance she took
in the situation; she saw the countless thousands of immense beasts heading for the parade and her little one
directly in their path. She felt powerless to act. By
getting in their path she would only sacrifice her own
life. Not a moment was to be lost, however—Boehm had
also heard the noise; had seen the herds rapid approach,
and seeing her imminent danger, was rushing hastily for
the child—who, unconscious of her danger, was busily
picking flowers at the end of her lariat. The shaggy
monsters were even then thundering upon the parade.
Any hesitation for an instant and she would be trampled
into a shapeless mass by the frenzied brutes. A mesquite tree stood near the picket pin with limbs low down—
Boehm reached her by a few bounds; and instantly pulling the picket pin and drawing in upon the lariat as he
ran, gathered the child in his arms and springing into
the tree, desperately clung to it with the little girl until
the many thousands of animals almost brushing them—
had passed. He shouted and waved his arms; they divided at the tree as they plunged and tore along, thus
saving the lives of both. A false step, an uncertain movement, and they would have been crushed and trampled to
atoms. It was a *thrilling moment!* A *narrow escape!!*
She (Natalie B) married Gen. George ("Sandy") A. Forsythe the hero of the bloody fight for eight days with
Roman Nose' band of 700 Cheyenne Indians in September, 1868, at the Arickaree Fork of the Republican River
(now called "Beecher's Island"). Forsythe was wounded three times; lost nearly half of his 50 scouts and his
Lieut. (Beecher) and Surgeon (Mooers) were both killed.

The Blockade—Buffalo vs. Bulldog

The next day we experienced a fearful storm as we
passed by "Pulpit Rock" and "Church Mountain," and
camped on "Bluff Creek." Here "Old Aunt Mary"—

under cover of a bank—baked a large wild turkey in a
"Dutch oven" to a turn—although drenched to the skin.
On the 31st, a wild a boisterous day, we wound through
"Mountain Pass"—a narrow gorge or break about a mile
in length to which we descended from the immense high
mesa or divide we had been traversing to the plain below.
Here the Indians had been frequently in the habit of am-
bushing parties and attacking the mail stage. It has
precipitous sides, covered with a dense growth of bushes
and scrub trees. Just the place for an ambuscade; but
we went through safely exercising the usual caution.
Shortly before a detachment of the Ninth Cavalry had
been stationed at the cut on the North side. As we
emerged, an almost endless prairie stretched out before us,
and again we were literally moving through almost un-
told numbers of our bison friends. On the right and left
of the stage trail the vast plain was dotted with herd upon
herd clear to the horizon their dim bodies contrasting
strangely, yet attractively, with the vivid green of the
short, velvety grass and our little column of blue-coated
troopers, and where a buffalo now would be as rare a
curiosity as the *Ichthyosaurus* of past ages. Behind was
the white canvas-topped wagon train, and ever chasing
each other in and among the herds and over the rolling
sweep were the alternate flashings of cloud and sunshine,
and the shadows cast by the mountains we had just left.
It was a spirited scene, an animated picture. As the
command wound along the trail and our strong scent was
"carried down" the fresh wind in their direction, the buffalo commenced to raise their heads in alarm. The old
leaders of each herd seemed to give them a warning, and
immediately the whole mass was set in motion. This had
been repeated several times during the day. It does not
appear to be generally known, even among the naturalists
and writers on the habits of animals, that the buffalo,
when alarmed, would always cross the trail of his supposed enemy and get to leeward, but they would *never*

pass to the rear of that enemy, or of a moving body—
whether of a wagon train, pack train—Cavalry or Infantry
Column or a train of cars.* Crowding with a reckless
and resistless brute energy, each herd, therefore, with its
chosen leader, gradually worked along towards the head
of our leading company, until at length it brought them
in front of the entire command. Our march was blocked,
and we were compelled to halt to bide the time of our
beast companions. Further progress was utterly impossible. Mackenzie, becoming somewhat impatient at this
suddenly enforced blockade, because our camp for the
night had already been selected, and we still had many
miles to march—seized a carbine from one of the men
and dismounting, attempted, by firing at the heads of the
herds to break them and swerve the immense throng from
its headlong course, now so crowding upon the advanced
company as to become positively dangerous, the horses
showing great fear and becoming almost unmanageable.
He fired several shots. The nearest herds swerved; but,
now contrary to their instincts, came roaring down beside
and *parallel* to *our mounted troopers.* This was a little
too much, even for well-trained disciplined Cavalry soldiers, and the men, in their intense excitement forgetful
of orders, and contrary to custom, commenced a rattling
fusillade from their saddles. The buffalo veered off, but
not until several had been killed and wounded. The men
were sternly ordered to "cease firing." One gigantic
bull, a leader, was nearest; he was badly wounded. As
was the case on nearly all marches of troops changing
station on the frontier, many dogs of all ages, sizes, colors
and degrees of character and temperament—always an un-
desirable accumulation at every frontier post, the men
raising them for companions and pets—had, under protest, accompanied the column on its march. At the Colorado River, many of the most worthless curs were drowned

---

*Upon mentioning this fact one day to the Superintendent of the National Zoological
Park at Washington, D. C., he confessed that he had never heard of this absolutely
fixed habit or instinct of our buffalo or American bison.

when fording it, or left behind, but there were still several remaining and it was these that had turned the buffalo
down the column.   There was among them a large, white
English bull-dog, weighing about seventy-five pounds, belonging to the regimental band.   He was a powerful brute,
and had been trained to pull down beeves at the slaughter
corral at Fort Concho—seizing them always by the nose.
He was, withal, a prime favorite with the soldiers, notwithstanding his ferocity.   The pack of mongrel dogs
were in full cry after the stampeding herds of bellowing
beasts as they rushed and tore along the column with
their peculiar stiff-legged, rolling gait.   But "King," the
bull-dog, singled an immense wounded leader, who had
now slackened his speed and was faltering in his tracks.
He sprang at his head with great courage, fastened upon
him, and the battle commenced with the mounted column
as silent spectators.   It was a most novel spectacle.   The
bronzed troopers; the great shaggy beasts thundering by;
the white-topped wagon train closed up and halted; the
fleeting shadows and the almost limitless stretch of surrounding prairie and vast solitude.   The bull went down
upon his knees, but so great was his strength that he
quickly rose and whirled the dog in great circles over his
head—"King" had been taught *never to let go*.   The entire command now watched with almost breathless attention the apparently unequal struggle, expecting to see the
dog crushed to death.   Down went the bull again on his
knees, this time not from any weakness, but to gore the
dog; rising, he would stamp his feet in rage, then shaking
him for a while, he would resume swinging and snapping
him like a whip cord through the air.   The foam, now
bloody, flecked the long, tawny beard of the bison bull.
His eyes, nearly concealed in the long, matted hair that
covered his shaggy head, flashed fire, and his rage knew
no bounds.   The dog, which had begun the fight a pure
white, had now turned to a spotted crimson from blood
which had flowed from the buffalo's wounds, mixed with

alkali dust—and still his brute instincts, tenacious courage and training led him to hold on. Had he let go for *a moment*, the crazed bull would have gored and trampled him to death before he could have retreated. The bull was now, however, growing perceptibly weaker; he rose to his feet less often. He could no longer throw the dog in circles above his head. The blood stained "King" to a more vivid red, and begrimed with froth and dirt, he had lost all semblance to his former self. All were looking for the struggle to end. The suspense was beginning to be painful. Impatience was already displayed upon the men's faces—when suddenly Mackenzie shouted. "Kill the animal, and put him out of his misery!!" It was a *merciful* command. Two men stepped forward to the enormous beast, now on his knees swaying and rocking to and fro—the dog still holding on—and placing their carbines behind the shoulder to reach a vital point, fired. He gave one great quiver, one last spasmodic rocking, and spread himself upon the vast prairie dead. *Not till then did "King" let go!* So great had been the courage of this favorite dog in his fearful struggle, that months after when a post order, annually issued for all our dogs—an accumulative nuisance at all frontier posts—to be exterminated—"King," the white bull-dog belonging to the Fourth Cavalry Band was exempted by a *special paragraph* for his *"gallant conduct."*

Fort "Phantom Hill"—The Legend

Our camp on April 1st was on "Dead Man's" Creek near old Fort Plantom Hill which was about one mile south of the junction of Elm Creek with the Clear Fork of the Brazos. This fort was, like Fort Clark, Texas, one of a series built in the years following the close of the Mexican war. It is said that Major, afterward Gen. George H. Thomas of Civil War fame, established it. On approaching the spot from the river valley on the north he took it to be a high hill covered with magnificent trees, commanding a fine view of the surrounding country, and as he judged

an ideal location for a fort. As he drew near, the hill sank
into a gentle slope, and the trees dwarfed themselves into
small shrubs as the mists lifted and the mirage which he
had been looking at disappeared.   The low mesquites had
spread out high in the shimmering air like a ghostly phantom. Although he had been deceived by the appearance of
the mirage, plenty of wood and water were near at hand
on the Clear Fork, together with logs and stone suitable
for building; so he decided after all to establish the fort
here, which, he said, ''We will call *Fort Phantom Hill.*''
The barracks had been huge log houses with heavy stone
fireplaces, and included a stone house for the officer's quarters, a stone commissary store house and a stone powder
house or magazine.   During the Civil War a large force of
Texas rangers under Col. Buckner Barry marched to the
post and demanding its surrender it was given up without
a fight, as only a small garrison then occupied it.   The soldiers vacated the post and they and the rangers camped
nearby.   That night the buildings were set on fire, by whom
it was never definitely ascertained, and all the log quarters
were destroyed.   The post was never rebuilt.   As we
passed through it on our march the officer's quarters still
stood; also the old magazine, and the walls of the commissary store house—the latter being two feet four inches
thick.   Some twenty stone chimneys mark the ruins of the
post, which for many years has been a noted land mark,
and their tall white stone columns, outlined weird and
ghost-like against the sky, like giant specters certainly suggest phantoms.   Many years ago, according to Gen. Randolph B. Marcy, father-in-law of Gen. George B. McClellan
and who, with him, surveyed a route about 1851—two for a
Southern Pacific Railroad—in a very interesting little book
which he published shortly after, a dreadful massacre occurred at this spot, and with the many legends attached
to it, many apparitions seem to have been associated with
the place from a time prior to the establishment.   Two
years later the writer camped on this same spot when en-

route to Fort Clark near the Rio Grande River, and that
night in 1873 the tall, white chimneys standing like monuments to mark the spot, made the flesh creep at their naked
ghostly shapes when thinking of the bloody tragedy enacted here.*　By some writers it is claimed that Gen. Robert E. Lee built this spot, and by others that Gen. Marcy
built it.

*POEM

OLD FORT PLANTOM HILL

To the Veterans of the Blue and the Gray

On the busy Texas border, on the prairies far away—
Where the antelope is grazing and the Spanish ponies play;
Where the tawny cattle wander through the golden incensed hours,
And the sunlight woos a landscape clothed in royal robes of flowers;

Where the Elm and Clear Fork mingle, as they journey to the sea
And the night-wind sobs sad stories o'er a wild and lonely lea;
Where of old the dusky savage and the shaggy bison trod,
And the reverent plains are sleeping midst drowsy dreams of God;

Where the twilight loves to linger, e'er night's sable robes are cast,
'Round grim-ruined, spectral chimneys, telling stories of the past,
Thereupon an airy mesa, close beside a whispering rill,
There to-day you'll find the ruins of the Old Fort Phantom Hill.

Years ago, so ran the legend, 'bout the year of Fifty-three,
This old fort was first established by the gallant soldier Lee;
And to-day the restless spirits of his proud and martial band
Haunt those ghostly, gloomy chimneys in the Texas border land.

Then once every year at midnight, when the chilling Northers roar,
And the storm-King breathes its thunder from the heights of Labrador,
When the vaulted gloom re-echoes with the owls—"whit-tu-woo!"
And the stealthy coyote answers with his lonely long "Ki-oo!"

Then strange phantoms flit in silence through that weeping mesquite vale,
And the reveilles come sounding o'er the old Mackenzie Trail,
Then the muffled drums beat muster and the bugles sadly trill,
And the vanished soldiers gather 'round the heights of Phantom Hill.

*It was on this long march that the writer, when acting as Quartermaster during
these four weeks between Fort Richardson and Fort Clark, learned from an old California "Forty-niner"—a teamster—how to "cross-lift" a wheel and prevent a wagon
train not only from *going to pieces*, but literally from *lying down* on this dry, treeless
plain.　It is extremely doubtful if there are many if any Cavalry officers living today
who even know what the term means, to say nothing of being able to practically apply
the principle in an emergency.

*These verses were copied from "Ranch Verses"—loaned to the writer by Cadet Walton
H. Walker, 3rd Class U.S.M.A. upon the occasion of his visit to West Point at the
reunion of his class of 1869—and after a visit to the grave of Gen. Ranald S. Mackenzie in the Cadet Cemetery June 16, 1909.

Then pale bivouac fires are lighted and those gloomy chimneys glow,
While the grizzled veterans muster from the taps of long ago,
Lee and *Johnston* and *Mackenzie, Grant* and *Jackson, Custer* too,
Gather there in peaceful silence waiting for their last review;

Blue and gray at length united on the high redoubts of fame,
Soldiers all in one grand army, that will answer in God's name.
Yes, they rest on heights of glory in that fair—celestial world,
"Where the war-drum throbs no longer, and the battle flags are furled."

And to-day the birds are singing where was heard the cannon's roar,
For the gentle doves are nesting 'midst those ruins of the war.
Yes, the mocking-birds re-echo; "Peace on Earth, to men good will,"
And the "swords are turned to ploughshares" in the land of Phantom Hill."

Fort Griffin—Ladies Visit the "Tonks"—Salt Creek Prairie—"Dead Man's Cross"

We arrived at Fort Griffin on April 4. It had a mixed garrison of the Fourth and Sixth Cavalry and Eleventh Infantry. As we approached it one could see it for miles, being well located on a hill, but it was now in a dilapidated condition. On the flat below the Post, between it and the Clear Fork, lived the Ton-Ka-way Indians who were enlisted by the Government and employed as scouts, they furnishing their own ponies, and being armed, paid and rationed by us. An officer of the Army had charge of them and when in the field with troops, an officer from the command was detailed to command them. They proved to be very valuable as scouts. Many years ago they were a powerful and war-like tribe. The Comanches were their implacable enemies, and on one occasion, becoming jealous of their friendly feeling for the whites, they fell upon them and massacred so many that the remnant fled to the protection of a military garrison and later were located at Fort G. They were the implacable enemies of the hostile tribes. Some of our ladies were anxious to go into their village and observe some of their customs, mode of living, etc. Their curiosity seemed to have been soon gratified for they came stampeding back into the post shortly afterwards. Something very mysterious must have occurred for we could never get any of them to enthuse over the

"Tonks" or to describe anything that they saw or heard, and for many years the reticence of that self appointed, investigating feminine committee of the Fourth Cavalry was a great mystery and a subject of much conjecture.

Crossing the Brazos River at a bad ford on April 6th, we passed through Old Fort Belknap. It was built by the Fifth Infantry in 1855, but was now abandoned, its tumble down quarters, originally a four company post, was now occupied by squatters, and mule tenders of the El Paso stage line. It was no longer of any importance. It had been re-occupied by the Sixth Cavalry in 1867. At night we camped at Salt Creek, 14 miles from Fort B, and crossing 12 miles of prairie the next day camped at some water holes at the edge of the timber, about 16 miles from Fort Richardson. Salt Creek prairie was a famous pass-way for Indians coming in or going out of the country. On our march this day we passed "Dead Man's Cross" where four men had but recently been killed by Indians. There were other rude head boards marking the last resting place of some "freighter," cow boy, or rancher who, in passing along this dangerous stretch of stage road, had sacrificed their lives in encounters with the Indian raiders and murderers. We had occasion to pass these markers for the dead, of which there were 21, many times during the next few years.

' *Fort Richardson—The "Life or Death" Ride* '

The next day we found Major A. K. Arnold's battalion of the 6th Cavalry awaiting us, Col. James Oakes commanding the regiment having proceeded on his way to Kansas with headquarters and the balance of the command. Our accommodations this night were very limited and crude, most of the Fourth Cavalry going into Camp outside of the post, and the bachelor officers most generously tendering their quarters to our ladies—who, spreading mattresses upon flea infested gunny sacks or burlaps upon the warped floors of the pecan log huts tried to wear out a night of undisturbed (?) rest and imagine themselves in a state of comfort and regal luxury, at the Waldorf-Astoria or some other palatial hotel. Before midnight the writer was ordered to conduct the empty train back to Fort Griffin, starting at daylight. After a sleepless night, because of his wife's illness which had begun back at our camp on Salt Creek prairie, the wagons were "pulled out" on the road. The return to Fort G. was without special incident. On turning the train over, and starting back for Fort R— on the 16th, we had got as far as the 16 mile water hole or "The Chimneys," and were just going into camp. The writer's horse (the only one with the escort, which was made up of a detachment of Infantry) had been unsaddled, when a Cavalry detachment of one Corporal and three men rode in hastily and delivered the following note. It was from Fort G— which I had left at 3 P.M. only a few hours before. It was 7 o'clock, with enough twilight to read—

FORT GRAFFIN April 16, 3 P. M.

DEAR CARTER:

I am exceedingly sorry that you will receive bad news by the bearer of this. I most sincerely hope that you may find Mrs. C— better upon your arrival. Corporal Petri Co. "E" 4th who missed you on coming in (taking another road), tells me that Gen. Mackenzie ordered him to tell you to take a non-commissioned officer and three men, with the best horses and *hurry through, leaving the train;* also to tell you that Mrs. Carter is *very sick.* You told me this morning that you would be the only mounted man, so I have got the Colonel to send three men to escort you, in case that you have not one. Praying that you will find Mrs. C— out of all possible danger, at the same time reminding you that you cannot argue that she is dangerous.

I am, your friend,

W. E. REESE,
2nd Lt. 6th Cavalry,
Acting Adjutant of the Post.

The writer knew what such a message from Mackenzie, sent by couriers 80 miles from Fort R— meant. They had almost killed their horses in delivering it, as Mackenzie had directed them to spare nothing within human power to reach me. There was no time to lose; watering and giving

Note:—Reese was a classmate—Class of 1869 U.S.M.A.

the horses a thorough "rub down," and hearty feed—
while they were being saddled, a hasty programme or plan
was worked out. The writer's animal was a medium sized,
half-bred dark-brown troop horse belonging to Trumpeter
Keleverer, of Troop "E," which I had taken for this trip.
He had been shot in the head with bird shot at Jefferson,
Texas, during the "reconstruction days," in a raid after
desperadoes. He was a quick, nervous, jerky sort of an
animal, with nothing especially to distinguish him beyond
any other troop horse except that he was particularly well
gaited—had an easy covering lops—quick trot—would
"fox gait" and was a *very fast* walker.

   "All ready, Corporal?" "Are your men good men; and
fit to ride for their lives?" "Yes, Sir!" "Mount then
and follow me as far as possible in all of my gaits!" It
was 16 miles that I had come to "The Chimneys." That
in about four hours. There were 64 miles yet to cover
before daylight the next morning. It was eight o'clock.
I "led out." I had talked with a mail stage driver that
morning at Fort G— who had been shot in the arm by
Indians at the gorge at Salt Creek only a day or two before. They had thrown a lariat over his head, from which
he had disengaged himself, and cutting one of his mules
loose as he reached the edge of the prairie, had escaped by
making a run into nearby timber with the result as noted,
a bad flesh wound. We had to pass that same spot
shortly after midnight. At a fast walk—trot, single foot,
lope, and gallop—and over rolling country, the night being
dark but starlight, the Brazos river was reached at midnight. It was as "dark as Erebus." The ford was not
visible. It was a quick sand ford but not a dangerous one.
Throwing the reins on his neck, the horse was allowed to
negotiate it. The silence of death reigned about this wild
spot, only broken by the splashing of our horses, as we
plunged in where the ford ought to be, trusting to our
horses instinct, and their swimming if they slipped off.
Half swimming and wading through the black, murky

waters, the swift current rippling against the horses'
flanks, and the treacherous quicksands causing them to
sink at every step, at last, we gladly emerged from the
stream, and scrambling up the bank, ascended through the
gloom, the "steep" leading to the ruins of *"Old Belknap."*
We had pushed over this distance at a terrific pace, over
thirty miles in about four hours. "The horses can't hold
this gait much longer, Si-r-r!" respectfully suggested the
soldierly Corporal. I knew and felt that this was true,
but, we had traveled *half the distance,* and we *must go
through.* Not a sound could be heard on the midnight air
except the clattering of our horses hoofs upon the hard,
stony ridge. We gained the plateau, upon which the abandoned post stood. Its dark, spectral shadows loomed up in
the misty blackness like huge ghosts in our path. We had
no guide. Little had been seen of the post as we had
passed through a few days before. The writer determined
to skirt it for fear of shots from the few settlers and stage
"mule whackers," its only inhabitants. It was dangerous
"riding around loose" in that country after dark, so we
stretched down the "nine mile slope" to Salt Creek. My
nervous animal, as we neared the Creek, seemed almost
instinctively, to accord with my feelings and thoughts. He
jumped at every sound of the crackling twigs under his
feet; nothing seemed to escape his keenly awakened intelligence or notice. The burned trees and blackened stumps by
the roadside near "Borthwick's Station," now abandoned,
were just outlined in the blur of the night, closely resembling the forms of men, and as we moved swiftly by them at
a swinging gait, he repeatedly shied, and his snorts of
actual terror made the air ring again and again. We were
now close to the gorge, the worst Indian pass-way in the
whole region about. The wounded stage driver's story at
Fort Griffin and his narrow escape from roping and death
was in my mind. It had been given to the Corporal in detail, and he was on his guard. Moving through the darkly
shaded cut, the branches of the trees almost touching the

water, we could not see a hand before our eyes, but trusting to the animal's instinct, and giving him the spur, a loose rein, and with hand on "six shooter" poised for instant action, we dashed into the deep ravine, across the cut or gorge, and up the hill upon the broad prairie beyond. A mile further on giving the command to "close up" and "dismount" the first time we had been out of the saddle since leaving "The Chimneys," we loosened the girths, rubbed down our horse's backs, turned the saddle blankets, removed the bits, and grazed the horses for about ten minutes on the lush grama grass—wet with dew. Again, "cinching" and mounting we pushed on. We came upon a camp of Mexicans on the right without waking them. Their steers or "bulls" were "turned out," and "belled." Their huge "Carretas" loomed up like buffalo in a "mirage." The embers of their fires were visible for some distance. Our presence was unknown to them, and we could have easily killed every man. We clattered by the rude headboards of the victims who had sacrificed their lives but a short time before. Again we saw freighters on the left. They had heard us. My shouting alone saved us from their rifles. Jumping in haste from about their camp fire and behind their wagons we saw the glint of their rifle barrels just in time. Dashing into the timber, we were on a very narrow, rough and indistinct road, just 16 miles from Fort Richardson. Dismounting to find the trail by the hand touch, the Corporal here rode up and declared that his horses were exhausted and could go no further. Halting just long enough to give him directions about saving them if possible, and determined to make it in alone, the writer pushed in through the pecans and oaks. There were no 20 mile relays as Archibald Forbes, the English War Correspondent once had in his famous 120 mile ride in 24 hours in Zululand. The animal begun to flag—and I now begun to use, but moderately, the "quirt" and spur— to which he cheerfully responded—several times the road had to be found by hand touch. But now the moon began to rise—and the way was clearer. The loud "too-hoot-too-h-o-o-t-t of the owls, the loud crashing of the pecan limbs heavily loaded with their weight of wild turkeys—and the loud gobbles g-o-b-b-l-e-s of the big gobblers, made the blood fairly dance and tingle in the veins. It is in the early, cold grey hours of the morning, with man or beast, the sick or well, that natures forces flag, the spirits ebb, the strength fails, the heart groweth sick and exhaustion ensues. *Both of us were nearly at that point.* At about the last notch. The early streaks of dawn were approaching. A light touch of the braided Indian "quirt"—a slight tick of the persuading spur, and the courageous little fellow snorted and took the lope Can one wonder at the undying affection of the humane Cavalryman for his noble horse? Reaching the brow of the hill overlooking the town of "Jack" (Jacksboro) nestling in the valley on the north side of Lost Creek, one could see it and the quarters and stables beyond in the fast quickening daylight, throwing fantastic shadows all over the land But there was no time for romance and without halting to admire the picture, I dashed down the slope, splashed through the creek and a few moments later flung myself from the noble little animal at the door of my "jacal," and half staggering, and crawling into the little picket hut where, but a few days before the stern necessities of a soldier's duty had obliged me to leave the sick and, in a sense, unprovided-for wife, I fell exhausted upon the floor.

The limbs were numb and cramped, and refused their functions. All was darkness before my eyes. I could scarcely speak. Old Dr. John F. Hammond said, "She is saved!" It was 4 o'clock—sixty-four (64) miles had been covered in just 8 hours, and 80 miles in twelve, on a *single horse;* the 16 miles at little less than an ordinary marching gait. The ride for "life or death" was ended! The Corporal's horse died—the men's horses were foundered and rendered unfit for service—but, by care and good treatment, turning out to *graze* without *grain feed-*

ing, very little water until cooled off—a vigorous rubbing down, etc., the *"trumpeter's brown horse"* of Troop "E"—with his shot-scarred face, lived to carry the writer on other weary miles march and through many more adventures with Mackenzie and the gallant troopers of the Fourth Cavalry. Sometime later the writer measured the distance between the two posts with an odometer. It was 80 miles and a few hundred feet. As the writer was acting directly under verbal instructions of Gen. Mackenzie, sent by courier to Fort Griffin to intercept him if possible on the road, and no post or regimental order was issued covering such a ride, since it was not necessarily a military duty to be performed under orders—no record was made of it, for the post or regimental files.

Gen. Sherman Inspects the Line

Gen. Sherman was now daily expected on his annual tour of inspection of the frontier posts. The writer was enjoying as much as he could (?) that enviable (?) triplicate or quadruplicate role of Post Adjutant, *acting this* and *acting that,* which is generally thrust upon a newly attached officer, for the empty honors resulting it is supposed. In addition he was commanding detachments, taking his "tour" as officer of the day, attending "stables," drills, Boards of Survey, Courts, etc., etc. One day he was startled with the announcement that he was to select 15 men from the regiment and proceed on the road to Fort Griffin until he met Gen. Sherman and escort him into the post. In the meantime two gun detachments must be made up at once to fire a salute in honor of the Commanding General from the 3-inch ordnance guns of which, paradoxically as it may seem, we had two. It was not believed that there was a man in the post who had ever fired one of these guns, or who had ever drilled in a "gun squad." Going to the First Sergeant the question was asked: "Sergeant, any artillery soldiers in the Company?" "No, Sir!"—and so on one company after another was visited until finally at "F" Co. the **Sergeant** said: "Sergeant Foster and Corporal Charlton have both served one enlistment in Light Battery "K" of the First Artillery, Sir!" "Sergeant Foster, have you ever served in the Artillery?" "Yes, Sir! Five years in the First!" "Can you drill a gun detachment?" I could scarcely have offered him a more complete insult. The old soldier straightened himself up and with an extra roll to the "r," replied, with pardonable pride, "Yes, Si-r-rr! I think I *ought to know how!*" with strong emphasis on the *"Know."* In a short time he and Corporal Charlton were drilling two fine looking gun squads at the 3-in. rifled guns. After this one need never despair of getting any kind of service from a garrison of old soldiers. On May 17, therefore, with 15 carefully selected men the start was made. I had the four big black mules from the post water wagon, and my instructions were to tender these fresh mules for use on General Sherman's ambulance; also to offer the use of Mackenzie's quarters to him. It was a warm day. We had reached Rock Station when I heard the cavalry escort coming along at a spanking pace followed by Gen. Sherman's ambulance. I mounted my men, saluted—and upon being ushered to his side was as cordially greeted by the "Old Man" as though I was his *"long lost brother;"* was presented to Gen. Marcey, former Chief of Staff for Gen. McClellan and his father-in-law, Colonels Tourtelotte and McCoy of his staff and Col. Myer of the Q. M. Dept. Gen. S— declined the mules— saying, that his were comparatively fresh and fast—and in his brisk, breezy fashion said: "That is kind in Mackenzie to tender the use of his quarters, but I have got plenty of canvas and we will pitch our tents right behind and close to him." Your horses look warm. It would be too hard on them to try and keep up with us. If you will put us on the right road, you had better come in at your leisure. I appreciate it just as much—and I will thank Mackenzie personally for his kindness in sending

you and such a fine looking detachment out to insure my
safety." I was thinking about the salute. Reluctantly
acquiescing, without divulging to him the dual role I was
personating, after I had ventured to suggest that I could
keep up with his spanking mules, at which he wisely shook
his head—the honor of firing a salute to the General of
the Army was thus lost and we arrived crest fallen enough
at the post about dark, too late to notify the gunners of
the "slip" in the programme—and those guns *were not
fired*. The General (S—) was not inclined to think so,
but it was well known that the numerous raids about the
country in recent months had been committed by the Fort
Sill "reservatio Indians;" and, after receiving the calls
of respect from the officers of the garrison, he gave a
delegation of Jacksboro's best citizens an opportunity of
stating their grievances. This party was composed of
W. W. Duke, R. J. Winders, J. R. Robinson, W. M. Mc-
Connell, Peter Hart and H. H. Gaines.

All had a most bitter story of cruel wrong and murder
to relate, displaying a number of scalps, some of them female, which had been recovered from bands known to be
the Ki-o-was and Comanches from the reservation and pe-
titioned him for assistance in recovering their stolen stock
and punishing these savages.

In July, 1870, Captain McClellan of the Sixth Cavalry,
while on a scout towards the Little Wichita, not far from
where the small settlement of Henrietta was burned that
year, and near where the present town is now located, discovered a large body of Indians, estimated at about three
hundred, who, seeing that they outnumbered him about
six to one, proceeded to attack him. This was said to be
a war party of Kiowas under one of their principal war
chiefs, "Kicking Bird." McClellan dismounted his men
and seeing the overwhelming odds began retreating slowly, the men fighting between their horses, which were led
by No. 4, leaving but three fourths of the men engaged.
The Indians divided into three parties, one party fighting

at a time, the others relieving each other in the attack
while the balance endeavored to outflank and surround our
line.   The heat was intense, our men had no water, and, as
it was on an open prairie there was no shelter.   The action lasted about eight hours and several times the Indians had McClellan's men practically surrounded.   Having reached the West Fork of the Trinity and night coming on the Indians discontinued their offensive and withdrew having suffered a heavy loss.   By their not renew-
ing the attack the next morning it was apparent that they
had had enough.   Captain McClellan's loss was two men
killed, who could not be taken from the field as he had no
ambulance; fourteen wounded, some severely, including
Dr. Hatch, his surgeon; and eighteen horses killed and
abandoned, besides some of the pack mules.   During the
night he sent a courier into the post for medical aid and
ambulances, and at dawn the next day, July 12, resumed
his march into Fort Richardson.   These Kiowas were
armed with breech loading rifles and only one man was
wounded by an arrow.   It was positively ascertained that
this war party was from the Fort Sill reservation.   A
classmate of the writer's, Lieutenant H. P. Perrine, was
in this action.   Several of McClellan's men who distinguished themselves in this action were awarded medals
by the War Department and "Jim" Doshier, the post
guide, by his coolness, bravery, skill and good judgment in
advising Captain McClellan as to the ground, positions to
take, line of retreat, etc., was also awarded a medal.   He
had been on the frontier a long time and knew every land-
mark from Jacksboro to the Red River.   Cool, self-reli-
ant, modest, sober, tireless, he was a most competent and
thorough guide and a brave, intelligent man.   Many men
who hung around frontier posts and called themselves
"guides" were frauds and were not only of no value to
our scouting columns but became a drag and a nuisance
because they had no more knowledge of the country or the
habits of Indians than many of the cattle men who had

been rounding up cattle in the near vicinity of the post. "Jim" Doshier was not one of this kind; he was a *guide in fact*. We shall have occasion to refer to him later in this story. All of these facts were communicated to General Sherman by the delegation from Jacksboro, as convincing proof of these constant outrages which were being committed by the Reservation Indians who were being fed and fathered by the Government.

CHAPTER IV

A Most Horrible Massacre—Sa-tan-tas Capture

GEN. SHERMAN was inclined to be very incredulous and shook his head in such a manner as to cast doubt upon the pleadings of these poor harassed settlers who had been expecting so much from him.

On that very night, the night of deliberation, of doubt and uncertainty, almost of despair and what was believed by the Jack County ranchers and cattlemen to be an almost hopeless appeal, a wounded man, Thomas Brazeale, hobbled into our post hospital with a horrible tale of massacre and atrocious butchery on Salt Creek prairie. His wounds were dressed, and in the morning Gen. Sherman, who visited him, listened again with almost an air of incredulity of the man's simple story of the bloody struggle. He, with R. A. Day and Charles Brady, alone had escaped, and in almost a miraculous manner; the balance, as he thought, had been killed. Twelve men, belonging to Henry Warren's corn train of 10 wagons had been intercepted by a large war party of Indians at a point about four miles from where I had met Gen. Sherman—Rock Station—and on the open prairie near the edge of the timber. Having been, as stated, a sort of *"Pooh-Bah"*, Post Adjutant and *"what not,"* the writer was sent for and directed by Mackenzile to take down from dictation some letters and dispatches which Gen. Sherman wished to rush off without delay. There were no shorthand sharps, no telephones, typewriters nor broadcasting radios—no stenographers, automobiles, airplanes, chain-lightning-writer-artists or "Scribes" in those days. It was a *first experience.* There was no declining or "backing out." There was nobody to fall *back on. It was an order!* It looked like a hopeless task. Many times it has been wished that those stenographic (?) notes might have been preserved for some museum or library. We started. The "Old Man" was as

80

considerate as his vibrant nature would permit. His delivery was like a catapult. All sorts of dashes, signs—abbreviations were made—which the Sergeant-Major and myself in trying to transcribe later could hardly decipher or translate the meaning of. The substance was as follows: Gen. M— was directed to send out a strong force at once to the scene of the massacre, and ascertain the truth or falsity of the man's story. If it proved true, he (Mackenzie) was to send couriers through to Fort Griffin, and with the two companies there to cut the trail, and to prepare to move out with his entire command upon it, and to meet him (Gen. S—) later at Fort Sill, I. T. Letters were also rushed out to Dept. Headquarters, and to Fort Sill, all by runners, couriers or mounted messengers, as we had no other means of communication.

The report proved not to have been exaggerated in the least and in a perfect deluge of rain, such as had scarcely ever been known in Texas before, flooding the parade to the depth of several inches, Gen. Mackenzie with four companies (A, B, E and F) arrived on the scene. It was supposed that this war party of Ki-o-was under Sa-tan-ta, their principal war chief, hearing that Gen. Sherman was coming that way had planned to intercept and capture him, and then hold him as a hostage for a heavy ransom, but this story he (Sa-tan-ta) always most strenuously denied to us in broken Spanish during the period—June until November—that he was held a prisoner at Fort Richardson.

There could be nothing more appalling, heart rending or sickening to the human senses than the spectacle which was witnessed when our command reached the scene of the Salt Creek Prairie massacre. The poor victims were stripped, scalped and horribly mutilated; several were beheaded and their brains scooped out. Their fingers, toes and private parts had been cut off and stuck in their mouths, and their bodies, now lying in several inches of water and swollen or bloated beyond all chance of recognition, were filled full of arrows which made them resemble porcupines. Their bowels had been gashed with knives and carefully heaped upon each exposed abdomen had been placed a mass of live coals, now of course, extinguished by the deluge of water which was still coming down with a torrential power almost indescribable.

One wretched man, Samuel Elliott, who, fighting hard to the last, had evidently been wounded, was founded chained between two wagon wheels and, a fire having been made from the wagon pole, he had been slowly roasted to death— "burnt to a crisp." That he was still alive when the fiendish torture was begun, was shown by his limbs being drawn up and contracted. The grain sacks had also all been cut open and contents dumped upon the ground, where it was found, littered and scattered in every direction. Some distance from the wagons dead mules, piles of corn soaking in the water, harnesses, and other evidences of the fearful struggle were to be seen. Here and there a hat, an Indian gew-gaw and a plentiful supply of arrows and other debris of the fight were spread about the rain-soaked ground. There were seven men killed, the names of whom have never been published before and are herewith given: S. Long, N. J. Baxter, Samuel Elliott, James Bowman, James Elliott, James Williams and John Mullen. Forty-one mules had been cut loose from the wagons and run off by the retreating Indians—the others had been killed. The balance of the men, some of them wounded, escaped into the timber, and later came into Fort R—. Taking the trail, Mackenzie attempted to follow it. It was but an *attempt,* for the powerful rains that fell daily in quick succession, pounded every vestige and obliterated every sign until there was no trace remaining, and rendered it impossible to more than take the general direction which led through the Wichita swamps and across the Big and Little Wichita Rivers and Red River towards Fort Sill.

Sherman, the Optimist

Gen. Sherman made a tour of the post—nervous, quick, snappy, inspiring, smiling and magnetic as was his custom. As post adjutant the writer walked at his side. Entering the pecan picket quarters of the men, he shook hands with the old Sergeants; gave a hearty greeting to the men here and there; commented on what he saw in the kitchens; sampled the soup, etc., then turning to Mackenzie, with his eyes twinkling, he said with much emphasis: "Now, Mackenzie, let's go and see the ladies." They seemed to be nearest his heart. He knocked at each cabin door and became, if anything more voluble. He spoke cheery words to the wives, shook hands with the children, patting them upon their heads; praised all for their courage, patience and devotion in sharing the toil and isolation of their soldier husbands at this far off frontier station remote from the centers of diversion and the pleasures of life, but laughingly recommended "early marriages" for all, saying: "I did it myself—why shouldn't you all do it. It's the best thing for young officers. It steadies them up," etc. In short by his warm, inspiring, sunshiny presence he made everybody feel that he had their best interests at heart; shared in common all of their hardships and privations and that he and they were a part of the great whole—the little regular army which then at that period was so vital in promoting the advancement of civilization on that extreme verge of the United States. William Tecumseh Sherman, the versatile general of our little regular army, was a confirmed and most consistent, smiling optimist. His success was largely due to that essential quality in a great commander. His memory for faces was amazing.*

After expressing his gratitude to the writer and scribe for his efforts to connect a long handed letter dictated with chain lightning speed—into a shorthand stenographic (?) report—he left the post as the command departed, pleasant, smiling, jerky, volubly chattering, as was his cus-

---

*Five years later Gen. Sherman was delivering the diplomas to the graduating class at West Point. The writer was there with Henry W. Lawton (killed in P. I. December 1899). Gen. S— greeted him most cordially—Lawton started to introduce us. The "old man's" eyes twinkled; he looked at me a moment with one of his quibbical expressions, and then said: "Carter—Carter! why I know him—how are you Carter—you saved my scalp on Salt Creek Prairie in 1871!"

tom. Somebody ventured to remark that his scalp might
be in some danger, but the fine old soldier grimly smiled,
and patting the Winchester that lay across his lap, called
out as the Dougherty Ambulance shot forward with his
armed Infantry escort and with a Sherman twinkle in his
eye—"Oh, No! I have sixteen shots here myself!" For
16 days the command swam, waded and struggled through
the swamp-overflowed bottoms of the Wichitas—the Ki-o-
was all the time spying upon its movements. One morning it was found that an Indian had dragged himself during the stormy night through the mud and water to within a few feet of the camps; had slipped or cut the lariat
of one of the horses, but becoming alarmed, had made
off—leaving his knife and moccasin tracks as ample
proofs of his stealthy bravado.

Gen. Sherman's Peril—and Nerve—an Unwritten Chapter

Mackenzie's command reached Fort Sill on June 4, having left the corn train at the scene of the massacre on May
19, when he had dispatched a note to Gen. Sherman reporting the frightful condition of things as he had found
them.

In the meantime Gen. Sherman had arrived at Fort S—
Sa-tan-ta's Ki-o-wa war party and murderous raiders
closely following in—no sooner had they arrived then they
began boasting of the massacre.

Lawrie Tatum, then the Quaker Indian agent at Fort
Sill, told General Sherman that he thought he could find
out in a few days if they were reservation Indians who
had committed the massacre and what Indians they were.
Four days later the Indians came in for rations. Before
issuing their rations, Tatum asked the Indians to come
into his office. He told them of the tragedy in Texas and
wished to know if they could tell by what Indians it was
committed. Sa-tan-ta said, with much show of bravado,
"Yes, I led in that raid. I have repeatedly asked for
arms and ammunition, which have not been furnished. I

have made many other requests which have not been granted. You do not listen to my talk. The white people are preparing to build a railroad through our country, which will not be permitted. Some years ago they took us by the hair and pulled us here close to Texas where we have to fight them. More recently I was arrested by the soldiers and kept in confinement several days (referring to his arrest in 1868 by General Sheridan shortly after the fight by General Custer with Black Kettle's band of Cheyennes on the False Washita). But that is 'played out' now. I want you to remember that. On account of those grievances, a short time ago I took about a hundred of my warriors to Texas, whom I wished to teach how to fight. I also took the Chief Se-tank, Eagle Heart, Big Tree, Big Bow, and Fast Bear. We found a mule train, and killed seven of the men. Three of our men got killed, but we are willing to call it even. It is all over now, and it is not necessary to say much more about it. We don't expect to do any raiding around here this summer; but we expect to raid in Texas. If any other Indian claims the honor of leading that party he will be lying to you, I led it myself.'' The other chiefs mentioned were present, and assented to the correctness of the statement made by Sa-tan-ta. Tatum went to General Grierson's quarters and requested him to arrest all of these chiefs on the charge of murder. General Grierson sent for them to come to his quarters.

Gen. S— upon hearing of this immediately consulted with Col. Grierson, who was then commanding the Tenth Cavalry and the post of Fort Sill, and directed that a council should be held at Gen. G's headquarters at which all of the chiefs with Horace P. Jones and Matthew Leeper, Jr., respectively post and agency interpreters should be present. Gen. Sherman had taken the precaution however, to have two reliefs of the guard, fully armed, concealed in the house behind closed shutters to windows low down and fronting directly on, and commanding the en-

tire porch—with carbines at a half cock held at the closed
blind slats, the muzzles were within three feet of the
hearts of the hostile savages. Every Indian, as soon as
he should arrive, was to be carefully covered. All were
awaiting developments—the crisis. It was a thrilling moment—Sa-tan-ta (See-ti-toh—"White Bear"), Ouirl-Parko
(Lone Wolf), Se-tank, and Big Tree with the sub-chiefs,
stalked upon the porch—with their pigeon-toed gait, and
with blankets closely wrapped about their forms although
it was warm. Concealed beneath them were their bows
and loaded rifles or carbines and pistols. Sherman was,
notwithstanding his usually excitable and voluable manner,
even more imperturbable than the Indians. It was a
great game that was about to be played. There was no
"show down of hands," as each narrowly watched the
features and movements of the other. They were like two
sets of fighters or gladiators with the stage set. The men
behind the blinds, noiseless and with bated breath, in command of a nervy officer of the Tenth Cavalry (The *"Brunette's"*), closely watched for the signal which, upon any
sign of treachery, was to be snapped off by the "Old
Man"—when a blizzard would have launched the last murderous Indian into eternity. Through Jones, the Post Interpreter, who spoke Comanche, the Court spoken language of the Ki-o-was and other tribes, Sa-tan-ta and his
Indians were charged with the murder of the teamsters on
Salt Creek Prairie, and then of having come in and glee-
fully boasted of it. Sa-tan-ta, who was the spokesman for
the chiefs, flatly denied the accusation. Upon the absolute evidence of the deed being then produced, and upon
the chiefs, whose motions were now being narrowly
watched—showing a hesitation or slight wavering—Gen.
Sherman at once ordered all of them to be seized and
taken to the post guard house—there to be placed in double irons.

Then came the crisis—which all had been awaiting with
almost breathless, tense anxiety. The Indians quickly

threw back their blankets almost as one man—and as if they had rehearsed it—and started to use their weapons—and some to string their bows. With Indians it took but an instant—which quicker even than their own movements, like a flash, Sherman gave the signal—Bang! open went the blinds like clock work—and with them came the simultaneous click of two score carbines to a full cock with every trooper's finger ready to press the trigger—the open windows filled with "brunettes" ("Buffalo soldiers") with every eye squinting down the barrels—and a death look and meaning in every face. This was too much even for the nerves of Sa-tan-ta and Lone Wolf—two of the most celebrated and to be feared, bloodthirsty Indians along that entire border South of Kansas. They knew that in a moment every one would, while Gen. Sherman's hand was raised, be shot into eternity—Sa-tan-ta gave a half shout or yell of surprise—Lone Wolf gave a loud, sharp *Ugh!!* sprang from the porch, before he could be seized, and making a running jump, cleared the railing, and bounding over the ground like a frightened deer, followed by some of the sub-chiefs, Big Bow among them, reached the flat below the post where all of the Indians were gathered to await the result of the council, and giving the signal and mounting a pony in waiting for him, the entire tribe swept out of the post in one wild rush, their pony's lariats dragging and the garrison firing upon them. In this running skirmish one or more Indians were killed or wounded. Sa-tan-ta, Se-tauk and Big Tree were seized, ironed and conveyed to the guard house, where they were secured.

Gen. Sherman waited a few days for our command to come in and then wrote the following characteristic letter—which has never been published even in his memoirs or family letters. The writer had his Sergeant-Major make a personal copy for future reference when copying it into the Letters Received book—it explains itself.

GEN MACKENZIE Com'dg, Fort Richardson, Texas.

GENERAL :—

I have now waited a whole week here, and have not heard one word from you since your note of the 19th, written at the corn train 22 miles from Richardson. So I have written you, Satanta, Setank and Big Tree, three of the principal Kiowas, are now here prisoners in double irons and strongly guarded, ready to be delivered to you or to a Sufficient Guard that you may send for them, to be held by the military till tried and executed by regular process in the Criminal Courts of the locality where they committed the murder in question.

The Agent of these Indians, Mr. Tatum, asked for their arrest, as he is fully convinced that for a long time his Indians have been raiding in Texas, that his humane efforts have been fruitless and he now not only consents to, but advises severe measures.

We tried to secure a fourth but some young warrior took the alarm and fled, firing their arrows at some soldiers between the Fort and the Agency, who returned the fire and killed one dead and wounded another, which stampeded all those who are about the Agency. At that moment about a dozen were counselling with me, Gen'l Grierson and others as to my judgment in Santanta's case some of whom cocked their guns and strung their bows; but we had a guard present who aimed their guns and *we came near having a row.* I also demanded that 41 good mules should be brought in.

They are now doubtless at their camps, on the Wichita, debating peace or war, and you should take all due precautions, as soon as you have a guard to take care of your property at Richardson.

All the Cavalry in Texas should operate towards Red River and Fort Sill; communications should be opened with this place via the Ferry at Red River Station—so that you act in concert. If parties of Indians attack soldiers or citizens, they should be followed into this Reservation till they realize that if they persist in crossing Red River they will be followed back. I think, however, that the Kiowas and Comanches of the Reservation in the arrest of Satanta, Setank, and Big Tree, will realize this and if my orders for their trial and execution in Jack County be not revised or stayed by orders from Washington that property on your frontier will henceforth be more secure. Satanta says many of the mules of the train were killed and wounded; that in the attack he lost three of his warriors killed and three badly wounded, and that the warrior here killed makes seven, so he says *"we are now even,"* and he ought to be let off—*but I don't see it.* I have written Genl. Pope to let Grierson have the rest of his Regt. here, so that he also can patrol Red River from Cache up to the Wichitas and keep up communication with you, and you should dispatch north the remaining two companys, of the Sixth Cavalry—for the Indians foiled here—may turn for revenge north to the Arkansas.

Not hearing of you by tomorrow morning I shall renew my journey to Fort Gibson, arriving to attend the Indian Council at Ocmulgee next Monday. If you get this in a week or ten days write me at Fort Leavenworth—send copy of this to Gen'l. Reynolds and one under cover to me for record at Washington.

(Signed) W. T. SHERMAN, *Gen'l.*

For versatility, resourcefulness, military sagacity and wisdom, sound common sense, strategical and tactical combinations and grand strategy, celerity of movement and a complete mental grasp of the major and minor problems of war, General Sherman had but few equals; none surpassed him. His march from Savannah, Ga., to Raleigh, N. C., and battle at Bentonville with General Joseph Johnston in 1865 has rarely, if ever, had its parallel in the history of war. It affords today and will for all time to come, to the professional soldier and to the military student, the most perfect example of the movements of a great army in the field, overcoming, as he did, almost insurmountable obstacles in his path, but always with morale and discipline unimpaired, ever ready for instant battle.

CHAPTER V

*The Captive Chiefs Conveyed to Texas—"Death Chant"
and Killing of Se-tank—An Acrobatic Corporal*

UPON the arrival of the worn and mud-bedraggled command at Fort Sill on June 4th the Indian prisoners were turned over to Mackenzie, and on the 8th, handcuffed and leg ironed, were placed in the wagons for transportation to and trial for murder at Jacksboro, under the written instructions from Gen. Sherman already quoted.

Lieut. George A. Thurston of Troop "E" had charge of the train guard that day, and Sergeant Miles Varily, a tall, fine-looking old Scotch-Irish Sergeant of that troop, with full reddish blonde beard and steel blue eyes, rode with several men of his troop in rear of the two wagons in the first of which, on the floor, was seated Se-tank, the oldest principal Chief of the Ki-o-was. A Corporal and two men were seated on either side of him, their backs against the side of the wagon, with loaded carbines between their legs. It was a hot day and the wagon sheets were all loosed and thrown back for air, giving an unobstructed view of the prisoners. Upon leaving the post Se-tank would have killed himself had he not been grasped by Big Tree and restrained until he could be placed in the wagon. He then drew his blanket closely over his head, thus concealing his face and all of his movements, and began most dolefully chanting a wild, weird death song as was their custom. The Ton-ka-way Indian scouts flanked the train on both sides—all the while the wily old scoundrel was desperately but quietly and noiselessly slipping his handcuffs, skin and all. When near the Cache Creek ford or crossing (which was near the Indian Agency), he suddenly gave a piercing yell, flung off his blanket and jumped to his feet; at the same time, drove at the corporal with a big scalping knife which in some mysterious manner he had concealed in his legging—and stabbed him, although not seriously. The corporal dropped his carbine, flung himself over the side of the wagon by a very agile back somersault to the ground, which would have put to blush the most skillful circus ring performer. Se-tank seized the carbine, his wrinkled face lighting up with savage joy, and springing the lever, leveling it at the same time at the nearest guard, he expected to wipe out the entire wagon load, but Providence, or, perhaps the wisdom of a careful old soldier here intervened. A cartridge having already been thrown from the magazine into the chamber of the carbine (a seven-shooting Spencer), the *second one jammed*.

Corporal John B. Charlton, Troop "F," Fourth Cavalry, was riding with Sa-tan-ta and Big Tree in the wagon immediately following the one containing Se-tank. There was some confusion. Charlton took in the situation at a glance. His wagon closing up suddenly on the one ahead containing Se-tank, the lead and swing mules were forced out to the side of the road, thus leaving an open or full field of fire ahead. In an instant his carbine was at his shoulder, and with its bark Se-tank crumpled down in a heap with a shot through his breast. It did not kill him. With an almost superhuman effort he rallied, recovered himself and sat up in the wagon, still working the lever of the carbine. Charlton fired a second time, the shot again taking effect through the breast, but going clear through him and hitting and slightly wounding the teamster on the nigh wheel mule of the team ahead, who, when Se-tank's war whoop first sounded, imagined that the *entire Kiowa tribe was about to ride his pet mule.* Se-tank went down again, never to rise. His career was ended. Thus perished the Kiowa chief whom the Quaker agent, Lawrie Tatum, characterized as the "worst Indian on the Fort Sill reservation."

Lieut. Thurston, who, as has been stated, was officer of the guard on that day, had told the writer before his death that Sergeant Varily fired the shot which killed Se-tank, and it was so recorded by me and printed. Fifty years

later, a story which I had written for the National Tribune
of Washington, the official organ of the G. A .R., happened
to fall into the hands of Corporal Charlton, whom I had
never heard from since 1876. He wrote me. In the correspondence which followed, in which I cited Sergeant Varily's brave conduct, the Corporal made the following statement. It is undoubtedly true. Sergeant Varily if following in the rear of the two wagons could not possibly have
shot through both wagons and killed the chief without killing or wounding some of the party in Corporal Charlton's
wagon—all of which the latter shows by a rough but very
accurate diagram, giving the positions of the chiefs in the
wagons, with the mules pulled out to the side of the road,
etc.

Corporal Charlton, after his discharge in 1876, and after
roaming about the world to Alaska, Australia, South America, and Mexico, married and settled down as a stock raiser
in Uvalde, Texas. He died March 5, 1922, and is buried
in the post cemetery at Fort Clark, Texas. He was one of
the finest soldiers the writer ever saw either in the volunteers during the Civil War or in the regular army. He
was the "bravest of the brave." We shall refer to him
often in this story.

STATEMENT OF JOHN B. CHARLTON
EX-SERGEANT FOURTH U. S. CAVALRY

Captain, there is a little error in your story of the killing of
Setank which I have long wished to speak of but somehow could
never bring myself to do it until today. Not that it is of any
importance, but you may be interested to hear of the events of that
day as I saw them.

The day Se-tank was killed Corporal Robinson ("D" Troop)
and I were Corporals of the guard. I don't remember who was
Sergeant, possibly Sergeant Variley. Lieut. Thurston was officer
of the day. Two wagons loaded with grain, beds full, even with
sideboards, were drawn up to one of the Company quarters (at
Fort Sill). In a cellar beneath these quarters Big Tree, Sa-tan-ta
and Se-tank were prisoners. The guard house had not then been
built. General MacKenzie, Colonel Grierson and several more officers had assembled there to see the Indians brought out. Corporal
Robinson and I were with the wagons. When the prisoners were

brought out to be placed in the wagons Se-tank started toward Colonel Grierson with hand extended presumably to shake hands, but Big Tree and Sa-tan-ta caught him and forced him into the wagon.

Corporal Robinson and Private Cannon were placed in one wagon to guard Se-tank, while Private Beals and I were put in another wagon to guard the other two Indians. Just before we started the interpreter (Horace P. Jones) came to me and said: "Corporal you had better watch that Indian in the front wagon for he intends to give you trouble." I asked him how he knew. He replied: "Because he is chanting his death song now."

The command started and the wagons followed close. I don't know who was in command of the column as General MacKenzie remained behind.

I was sitting near the back of the wogan on the right with my carbine loaded and between my feet. Big Tree set on my left and a little to the front; Sa-tan-ta sat to the front facing me with Private Beals on his right. Each wagon had six mules attached with the driver riding, as you no doubt remember, the near wheel animal. (See rough sketch of position of wagons.)

When we had reached a point about a mile out on the Fort Richardson road, about three hundred yards from the Agency on Cache Creek, I heard a commotion in the front wagon. Looking out I saw Corporal Robinson turn a back somersault out of his wagon, and following, without ceremony, came Private Cannon. Both had left their guns in the wagon. Se-tank, with both hands free, had picked up one of their carbines and was trying to work the lever. I immediately threw my gun up and fired at him and he fell over. Big Tree placed his hand on my arm and said "No bueno!" but I threw another load in my gun. Se-tank in the meantime had raised himself to a sitting posture and was again trying to load the gun.

He had his right side toward me then and I fired quickly, the ball passing entirely through him.

Lt. Thurston *rode up* and asked what the trouble was. On investigation we found that Se-tank had slipped off his handcuffs beneath his blanket, taking much skin and some flesh in the process; had drawn a concealed knife and struck at Corporal Robinson before he (Robinson) knew that Se-tanks hands were free. The knife inflicted a slight wound on Robinson's leg. It. must have been one of my shots which struck the teamster after the ball had passed through the body of Se-tank.

Trumpeter Oxford came up and asked: "Who killed Se-tank?" I told him "I did but am afraid I'll catch ——— for doing it." A few minutes later General MacKenzie overtook us. "Who killed that Indian?" he asked. "Corporal Charlton," replied Oxford.

General MacKenzie then ordered me to search the other two

Indians for concealed weapons which we did but found nothing. He ordered the body of Se-tank left by the roadside.

No doubt the old rascal had intended to kill Colonel Grierson had the other two Indians not stopped him.

He had two shots through him, one in the center of his breast and the other through his breast from the side.

(Signed) JOHN B. CHARLTON.

Uvalde, Texas,
January 12, 1921.

It is the writer's belief that the foregoing statement of John B. Charlton, Ex-Sergeant of the Fourth U. S. Cavalry, is absolutely true in every respect. All of the sailent facts as to the manner of the killing of Se-tank, one of the principal War-Chiefs of the Ki-o-wa Indians—then a prisoner, and enroute to Fort Richardson, Texas, for trial for the massacre of seven (7) teamsters of Henry Warren's Corn Train, by the Civil Authorities under instructions of General W. T. Sherman, Commanding General of the Army, are substantially as they were related to the writer by Lieut. George A. Thurston, Fourth U. S. Cavalry (later Captain Third U. S. Artillery), who, on that occasion, was officer of the day. He stated that it was Sergeant Miles Varily, Troop "E," Fourth Cavalry, who was Sergeant of the guard on that day, and the members of the guard riding in the rear of the wagon which contained Se-tank, who fired the shots which killed that Indian. The writer did not see the act, but having gained his knowledge from Lieut. Thurston who was supposed to be an eye witness of the act, it was, and always had been the writer's belief that Varily killed Se-tank.

After reading John B. Charlton's statement it is now the writer's belief that he was in error; that Lieut. Thurston not only did not see the shooting (Charlton says he *rode up* upon hearing the shots) but that without questioning Charlton he took Sergeant Varily's statement as true and this credited him (V.) with an act which Charlton's statement now clearly shows could not have been the case.

The writer is now very glad to be able, nearly 50 years after the occurrence, to correct the error contained in his booklet, "Massacre of Salt Creek Prairie," published in 1919, and give the credit which is plainly due, and where it properly belongs, viz: to this brave, distinguished and gallant soldier—John B. Charlton.*

George Washington, a Caddo Indian, rode by the side of the wagons as they left the post. While on the journey Se-tank said to him: "I wish to send a message by you to my people. Tell my people that I am dead. I died the first day out from Fort Sill. My bones will be lying on the side of the road. I wish my people to gather them up and take them home." He was buried by the soldiers at Fort Sill. The Indians were told that they might take him up and bury him at their own camp, which they declined to do. Sa-tan-ta also sent back the following message: "Tell my people to take the 41 mules that we stole in Texas to the agent."

Se-tank's body was placed by the roadside for burial, but our *observant Ton-ka-way* scouts coming along about this time, *accumulated* his scalp as a rich prize and a much valued addition to their war trophies. The command moved on as though such an incident had never occurred. During this march of 123 miles from the Fort Sill reservation, Sa-tan-ta and Big Tree were closely guarded. At night pickets and outposts were thrown well out to prevent surprise, as it was surmised that the Ki-o-was, upon learning that their chiefs had been taken to Texas, there to be tried for murder, would follow and attempt their rescue. Herd guards and strong sleeping parties were posted and every precaution taken to prevent a stampede. The wily chiefs were spread out upon the ground, a peg driven at each hand and foot and they were then securely bound with rawhide.

In the Wichita swamps where huge mosquitoes swarm in countless thousands and to a size that would have shamed a New Jersey "green head" or "Galley Nipper," and

---

*See "The Old Sergeant's Story," published in 1926 by Frederick H. Hitchcock, 105 West 40th Street, New York City.

which, drawing blood every time they bit, drove the entire command for refuge into the smoke of the green log fires about the bivouac, the position of our two prisoners can be at once pictured to the dullest imagination. The loud, sharp grunts, or Ug-g-g-g-h-h! and long drawn out exclamations and strenuous efforts to escape these thirsty bloodsuckers, sounding strangely on the midnight air. Notwithstanding prisoners and guard slept—or attempted to—in the dense smoke, the latter with long gauntlets and mosquito nets ingeniously made of hoop skirt wire and drawing strings so that it would balloon out from the face when lying down, all were more or less punctured and mutilated before an early reveille called all again into the saddle.

Corporal Charlton, shortly before his death, wrote me, however, that one night while in charge of them, being unable to withstand the appeals of these chiefs in their absolutely helpless condition, and notwithstanding the cruel, barbarous treatment which they always accorded their prisoners, he unsnapped their handcuffs, and although leaving them still confined to the ground, placed boughs in the hands of the sentinels placed over them to brush off the pests which were biting their faces and hands. "This," he writes, "for *humanity's sake.*" The heart of such a soldier always relented on the side of humane treatment.

The Ki-o-was were stealthily dogging our rear, closely watching for any opportunity which might offer itself for a possible rescue of their favorite war-chief. Sa-tan-ta's second and last message, sent in by the Caddo Indian Geo. Washington, already referred to, who had accompanied Mackenzie as far as Cache Creek, was: "Tell the Ki-o-was that I may never see any of them again, but I now wish them to be at peace with the whites." As proof that no value whatever was to be attached to such a message, Sa-tan-ta after being once released through the efforts of the "Indian Ring" was caught raiding with his Indians, and again made a prisoner.

Satanta, the Savage—A Dramatic Scene

It was a bright, warm day on the 15th of June when the bronzed, weather-stained and wearied troopers of the Fourth Cavalry rode into Fort Richardson, with the prisoners closely guarded by our faithful Ton-ka-way scouts. They had been given ponies to ride. The rest of the garrison with the band, turned out to greet the command. The impression made upon the garrison will never be forgotten, for Sa-tan-ta, the celebrated chief of the Ki-o-was, whose name had been a terror to all the settlers and the entire Kansas and Texas frontiers for so many years, was now really a prisoner of war. As the column halted, every eye was upon him. Every man, woman and child had heard of his reputation for bloody, almost unspeakable deeds.

He was over six feet in his moccasins, and, mounted upon a small pony, he seemed to be even taller than he really was. He was stark naked, from the crown of his head to the soles of his feet, except for a breech clout and pair of bead embroidered moccasins. Owing to the intense heat he had allowed his blanket to slip to his saddle and about his loins. His coarse, jet black hair, now thickly powdered with dust, hung tangled about his neck except a single braided scalp lock with but one long eagle feather to adorn it. His immense shoulders, broad back, deep chest, powerful hips and thighs, contrasted singularly with the slight forms of the Ton-ka-ways grouped about him. The muscles stood out on his gigantic frame like knots of whip cord, and his form proud and erect in the saddle, his perfectly immobile face and motionless body, gave him the appearance of polished mahogany, or, perhaps a bronze equestrian statue sprinkled with dust. Nothing but his intensely black, glittering eyes and a slight motion of the eye lids betokened any life in that carved figure. Every feature of his proud face bespoke the disdain with which he regarded the curiosity of the crowd—the despised white race—now gathered about headquarters to gaze at the famous savage chief. His feet were lashed with a raw hide lariat under his pony's belly; he was handcuffed—and disarmed and helpless, he was indeed a picture of fallen, savage greatness.

Big Tree, his companion, was much lighter in color, smaller in stature, and much inferior in his general appearance. His features were quite regular, and his nose more aquiline. There was something in his face, however, that betokened the crafty sneak, and he lacked nobility of manner and expression. He was more interested in the noisy hub-bub about him, and when the band played, he frequently turned his head to watch them and hear the music—not so Sa-tan-ta; his head never turned nor a muscle moved. Big Tree had a single feather to ornament his scalp lock, and, like Sa-tan-ta, he also was naked.

The captives were turned over to the officer of the day, and after a hearty cheering and joyous greeting to the dust covered and bedraggled command, after their month of wearisome marching and exciting adventures, quiet once more reigned. A strong guard was placed at the guard house to prevent the incensed people of Jacksboro from killing the red handed murderers, as the nervous hitching of their six shooters about on their belts showed anything but a strong love for their red brothers—for some of the murdered men of Henry Warren's corn train lived in Jacksboro and went out from it on that eventful May day to their frightful death on Salt Creek prairie.

The writer was Post Adjutant and was in frequent conference with the Sheriff of Jack County and the District Attorney as to the security and safety of the Indian prisoners—pending their trial—and the manner by which they could, without too great risk, both be conveyed to the Court House—when that day should arrive. The guard house was within a few yards of Lost Creek, the opposite side of which was fringed with a dense chaparral making it comparatively easy for a few determined ranchers or cow boys to conceal themselves and pick off the prisoners the moment they emerged through the doors of their cell. Frequent threats had ben made to that effect. The District Attorney's name was S. W. T. Lanham. He was from Spartanburg, South Carolina, and lived in Weatherford about 40 miles from Fort R—. Many years after the trial he became a prominent member of the Texas bar of the firm of Watts, Lanham and Roach of Weatherford; was elected to Congress (about 1896-8), and later (about 1902), became Governor of Texas, serving several terms. Governor Lanham's son, Fritz Lanham, now (1924) represents his father's district in Congress. One of the counsel appointed to defend the prisoners was Tom Ball. He also became prominent in politics and was elected to Congress from Brackettville or Jacksboro, serving in the House of Representatives about the time Gov. Lanham did. He was at one time a candidate for Speaker of the House. Associated with Ball was J. A. Woolfork of Weatherford.

Sa-tan-ta's Trial—The Cow-boys' Verdict

In accordance with Gen. Sherman's letter of instructions herein quoted, the two chiefs were regularly indicted for murder in Jack County, Texas—and on July 6—they were removed from the Post guard house to the County Court house in the square of Jacksboro for trial, being very heavily guarded.* The day for Sa-tan-ta's trial for murder had arrived. This trial was one of the most impressive and picturesque—yet most ludicrous acts of legal jurisdiction ever witnessed by the hardy settlers and cow boys of Jack County and was, the writer believes, the first instance in the United States when an Indian Chief was regularly indicted and tried for murder by a legally drawn jury under a civil process. The Modoc war had not then occurred—the trial of the Modoc chiefs taking place nearly three years later.

---

* At one of my conferences with the District Attorney, Mr. Lanham, and at my suggestion, a screen, composed of two reliefs of the guard—about 20 men—was placed between the manacled prisoners and the guard-house as they emerged, so that nobody could shoot from the chaparral without killing or wounding some of the guard. The distance across Lost Creek to the Court House was somewhat more than one-quarter of a mile over a mere trail.

The town of "Jack" was swarming with men, all intent upon seeing *justice* done Texans, the state and the *red man*. Accompanied by the Fort Sill interpreter, Horace P. Jones, who had come down with the command—and the counsel who had been assigned, the blanketed chiefs with clanking chains walked into the little frame Court House. The jury had been empannelled; the district attorney bustled and flourished around. The whole country—*every man armed to the teeth,* tried to crowd in. It was impossible; so they surrounded the Court House, and listened almost breathlessly through the open windows.

Two long, dingy-wooden benches, well whittled and worn held the jurors, who, in their shirt sleeves and with *"guns"* in their belts, nervously hitched about in their seats, and uneasily regarded the extreme novelty of their situation. Inside the prisoners railing sat the stolid chiefs, closely wrapped in their blankets. The charge was regularly read. The interpreter's plead "not guilty" for the prisoners, then Ball, their counsel, opened up and in a spread eagle, but eloquent speech, referred to the numerous wrongs that the noble red man, "my brother," had suffered, wherein he had been cheated and cheated and despoiled of his lands, driven westward, westward until it seemed as though there was no limit to the greed of his white brothers.

If he had been guilty of acts of violence toward the aggressive race which was driving him out that was but the excusable retaliation, which merely human instinct, nay, even the instinct of the worm that turns, required of him.

Warming up to his task, he now threw off his coat, as it was an intensely hot day, and discoursed about the times of the Aztecs, Cortez and the Montezumas, and pictured Gautemozin lying calmly upon a bed of coals, as upon a couch of roses. Here he displayed considerable historical lore. But when he spoke of the majestic bird, the eagle, that emblem of our national freedom, and urged that the great chiefs be allowed to "fly away as free and unhampered," we turned quickly to watch the jury. Every cow boy juror had been industriously whittling the bench with his hunting knife and squirting tobacco juice at a crack. But the words of the counsel having been interpreted to the chiefs, their frequent grunts of approval and delight at what they supposed meant immediate release, now sounded loudly over the court room. We noted an immediate change. They all hitched the "shootin irons" or "wee-pons," which were strapped to their hips, to the front, rolled their shirt sleeves a little higher, immediately ceased reducing with their sheath knives the proportions of the jury bench, and now closely watched for further developments and more oratory. Gen. Mackenzie, H. P. Jones, the Fort Sill interpreter, and Brazeale, the wounded freighter, were the witnesses for the prosecution.

The District Attorney was really an able advocate and lawyer, and he grew eloquent over the enormity of the chiefs crime, as he rapidly painted the cold-blooded massacre, and the cruel murder of the poor, white teamsters upon Salt Creek prairie. As he pictured the scene, the bloody chiefs victims lying cold and stark, the charred remains of one who had been slowly roasted alive chained to the wheel, every brow on that jury grew black, every juryman settled himself in his seat, gave an extra hitch to the gun on his belt, and we all saw the verdict plainly written on their faces, from the foreman to the very last man of the twelve *"tried and true."*

The after piece of the other counsel for the defence had no perceptible effect. He took off coat, vest, collar and necktie, rolled up his shirt sleeves, and advancing up to the foreman, an old gray-headed wrinkled frontiersman, shook his fingers at him and gesticulated in the most emphatic, even violent manner. It was of no avail. The doom of the noble red man was sealed. The jury was briefly charged. It retired to a corner of the same room—a few moments of hurried consultation and angry head shaking, and they were back again in their seats. It was extra quick work.

"Have the jury agreed upon a verdict?" "We have."
"What say you, Mr. Foreman, are these Indian Chiefs,
Sa-tan-ta and Big Tree, guilty, or not guilty, of murder?"
With a most startling emphasis, the grizzly old foreman
shouted so that everybody could hear him through the
open windows of the crowded square: *"They are! We
figger 'em guilty!!"* It was a *unanimous verdict.*

This trial took place in the State Court at Jacksboro,
viz., the District Court of Jack County, Texas. Big Tree
was tried on July 5, 1871, and Sa-tan-ta was tried on July
6, 1871. Judge Charles Soward was the presiding judge.
The same jury passed upon both cases, and it was composed of the following members: T. W. Williams, Foreman;
John Camron (or Cameron), Enent Johnson, H. B. Verner,
S. Cooper, William Hensley, John H. Brown, Peter Lynn,
Peter Hart, Daniel Brown, Lucas P. Bunch, Jim Cooby.
The number of the case is 224, on the criminal docket of the
District Court Clerk at Jacksboro. They were sentenced
to be hanged Sept. 1, 1871. Agent Tatum immediately requested that the Indians be not executed, and independent
of his principles against capital punishment, had given
reasons for thinking that it would have a better effect on
the Indians of the agency to imprison them for life. After
the trial Judge Soward wrote Agent Tatum that he would
request to have the sentence commuted. Under this pressure Gov. Davis felt compelled to accede to this request,
which was done. They were sent to the state penitentiary
for life. It seemed remarkable to the agent that Gen. Sherman,[*] Colonel Grierson and the Judge on the bench should
all so heartily cooperate with his views and judgment in
connection with the disposal of those Indians. General
Sherman assured him that so far as his influence and authority extended he would have his requests carried out.
It had a most wonderfully sobering effect upon the Kiowas
and after a conference with Colonel Grierson and the inter-

---

[*]General W. T. Sherman in a letter written July 29, 1871, from St. Albans, Vt., to
Colonel McCay of his staff, states, however, that he "thinks Satanta and Big Tree
should be hung, for the *effect will be salutary in the highest degree.*"

preter, H. P. Jones, it was agreed that they had never been so effectually subdued before. Their repeated outbreaks, however, after this, notably in 1874, and Lawrie Tatum's determination to punish them after each offense ultimately proved to be the downfall of this humane but stern Quaker Indian agent.*

We held these chiefs as prisoners at Fort Richardson until the following October or November. During good weather they were taken out of the post guard house for air and exercise. The writer either as officer of the day or guard, frequently had them under his charge. During these periods, in their walks about the corrals and "Suds-ville" (laundress' quarters), their leg irons and handcuffs were never removed, except on one occasion when Sa-tan-ta contracted a genuine, and pretty bad case of "guard-house itch," and then his handcuffs were unsnapped to permit him to scratch his ankles and apply some kind of soothing salve prescribed by the post surgeon. They were then transferred to the State Penitentiary at Huntsville, where, a year later, they were released at the earnest solici-tation of Indian Humanitarians for a short period on their good behavior. This was in September, 1872.

Sometime after the "Massacre of Salt Creek Prairie," about January or February, 1872, a rude monument was erected on the site, four miles from Rock Station, by Cap-tain (later Brig. Gen.) Wirt Davis and his Troop "F" of the Fourth Cavalry. It was made of oak by the quarter-master at Fort Richardson and hauled in sections by the troop to the spot. Captain Davis superintended its plac-ing. It was pyramidal in shape and about 8 feet from its

---

*Many incidents of this period (since the notes from my diary were transcribed) will be found in "Historical Sketch of Parker County, Texas," by H. Smythe, St. Louis, 1877, pp. 248-288, giving details of what took place at General Grierson's quarters at Fort Sill during the arrest of Sa-tan-ta and Big Tree; their trial at Jacksboro; ex-tracts from the argument of the District Attorney, S. T. M. Lanham, and Sa-tan-ta's reply; many very interesting extracts from the journal of Gen. R. B. Marcy, former Inspector General of the army, who accompanied General Sherman on his tour of in-spection in 1871: also the correspondence of General Sherman, Judge Worsam, Gov. Edmund Davis, Lawrie Tatum, and Mr. Hoag, Commissioner of Indian Affairs, re-garding the commutation of Sa-tan-ta's and Big Tree's sentence—that of death—to im-prisonment for life, and their subsequent occupation at the Huntsville penitentiary up to the date of Sa-tan-ta's suicide and Big Tree's release.

peak to base; the latter about 4 feet on each side. The plinth was 6 feet in width and 2 feet high. It was painted an olive color. This box covered the entire grave and bore the following inscription: "Sacred to the memory of seven brave men who died while defending their train against 150 Kiowa Indians. S. Long, N. J. Baxter, Samuel Elliott, James Bowman, James Elliott, James Williams, John Mullen." "May 17, 1871." This inscription was printed in black paint.

O. L. Torney, of Kaufman County, Texas, who was familiar with that section of the country, saw this monument in January, 1880. He states that it was then "badly warped and the inscription was almost defaced." It is not known whether any steps have ever been taken to replace this memorial, as Torney states that "every inch of farming land in that section is now under cultivation, and possibly there is a corn field now where these brave men were buried." A later report states that there is now (January, 1922) "nothing but a sand bank there and a board bearing the number '7' to mark the number of men in the grave," but, which, the writer says, "is liable to be taken for the corner of a land survey and be lost when the old timers pass away."

CHAPTER VI

Pursuit of Kicking Bird

*A Campaign in the Texas "Bad Lands" Against
the Ki-o-was*

SHORTLY after the horrible massacre of the seven (7) teamsters of Henry Warren's corn train on Salt Creek Prairie, near Jacksboro, Jack Co., Texas, on May 18, 1871—under instructions from Gen. Sherman in the letter already quoted—steps were taken to pursue and punish their murderers, known now to be the reservation Indians, who had fled from Fort Sill upon the arrest by order of Gen. S— of their principal chiefs, Sa-tan-ta, Se-tauk, and Big Tree—and now led by Ton-ne-un-co—"Kicking Bird" (literally an eagle striking with his talons), who, so far, had refused to come in.

Preparations went on very rapidly for the inauguration of an extensive and offensive campaign against all hostile Indians—Comanches as well as Ki-o-was—who were known to be off the Fort Sill reservation. All of the troops of the Fourth Cavalry at Laredo, Brownsville and San Antonio—"C," "L" and "M"—were ordered up from the Rio Grande on the 29th of June. Troops "B," "E" and "F," were sent out by slow marches to Gilbert's Creek, a small tributary of the Red River, to establish a base and a camp of observation near its mouth from which to scout up and down the river—watch all the movements of the hostiles, but especially to get in touch with and locate Kicking Bird's migratory village if possible. Extensive requisitions were made on "Whaley's" Ranch, at the mouth of the Big Wichita near Red River, for forage, grain, etc. On July 16 and 17 troops "G" and "I" came in from Fort Concho, also "K" from McKavett, "L" from Brownsville, and "C" from Laredo, and were sent into camp about a mile from the Post, towards Weatherford in Lost Creek Valley. The weather was extremely hot and the Post was overcrowded with newly

arrived officers and men, and ample time was given to
form new acquaintances and friendships and to meet the
new Colonel, as this was the first time so many Companies
(10) of the Fourth had assembled since the Civil War.*
Here we saw, for the first time, Henry W. Lawton whom
Mackenzie had had transferred from the Twenty-fourth
Infantry, and was now a First Lieutenant of "C" Troop,
Captain John A. Wilcox, just in from Laredo. He had
very dark brown, almost black, bushy, wiry hair, brushed
up and stiffly back, a la Pompadour—dark brown eyes,
and immensely long, English "Dundreary" whiskers and
moustache. He stood 6 feet 4 inches in his stocking feet.
He was rather restless, quick spoken, energetic in his
movements, and full of life and fire; in fact, what could
be better expressed as—"A live wire, and as hard as
nails." He was in no sense a drill master, tactician or a
theoretical strategist, and he wore soldier's riding boots,
blouse, re-inforced riding pants and a soldier's black campaign hat with no *"Montana peak" or dents.* He seemed,
at first glance, diffident, retiring, and rather reserved or
reticent in manner; a little stiff, upon first acquaintance.
But the writer, with whom he lived and messed at various
periods for nearly two years, never saw his equal for active energy, and chain lightning movements as a Quartermaster, or quick and comprehensive grasp of complicated
situations in an emergency. There was never a better or-
ganizer of men, or a better all round, rough and tumble
field soldier. Lawton had a disgust or supreme contempt
for, and absolutely disregarded the conventional methods
and red tape (and no one knew better than he how to cut
that) slowness of a "cut and dried," thumb-rule" book
soldier, whether it was a young West Point Martinet or,
of the trained service-school, War College type who, without ever having had campaign service, is ever ready to ex-
pound his theories and "how it should be done" by book,
but, who has never had any field experience to test it out.

---

*Lawton, "the Regular."

All of the theoretical and experimental problems, worked out ahead of time to fit into all situations in the field during a campaign, or, battle conditions in time of war, he scorned—and he became positively explosive—if they in any way conflicted with some simpler method which he, with the rest of us Civil War men, not only had seen done many times in that way as a vital practical problem in an emergency, but who was even then, solving the same or, sometimes even worse problems in these strenuous operations against such a foe, as we were now dealing with. He was generally in the *right* place at the *right* time to do the *right* thing in the *right* way with no wasted effort or lost motion.

He faced the most difficult and intricate problems as they presented themselves, and overcame all obstacles as he found or met them, by sheer force of will power, iron nerve, physical strength, wonderful resource and quick mentality, combined with plenty of good, horse sense. While men were sitting around in their saddles or by the roadside studying how this or that could be properly solved by some Service School or War College rule, pins stuck in a map or by the game of *Krigspiel*—Lawton would brush all aside, and shout, "Take hold here men, *with me,* and we'll soon have this d—d thing straightened out." The writer once heard an envious, jealous graduate of West Point of high rank make the sneering remark—"He (Lawton) was a mere 'rough-neck' wagon master." But, nobody who ever saw Lawton poised for action could ever doubt his ability, or the methods that he and the other Civil War men of the Fourth Cavalry employed in applying their practical experience gained in that war, which, while it may not have been in point of numbers the *greatest* war in the history of the world, will always remain the one great struggle of the American people, and the *greatest military effort* of *the United States,* besides having a much larger percentage of losses for the numbers engaged and the areas occupied, than in this re-

cent great World War—with its millions of combatant and
non-combatant participants—Lawton made his own rules
and fitted them to the problems and situations as they
came up to be solved, and he wasted no time in discus-
sions. If he was confronted with a condition he never
looked at it as a theory to be figured and argued over. It
mattered little to him if a book contained an abstract principle by which to work out some complicated problem, so
long as he knew, in the time given him, that *he had no time
to look it up,* and that he would have to apply good, sound,
common, horse sense, all the resources of a fertile brain—
and his practical experience to it as a concrete proposition. He had but little book knowledge of the Art and
Science of War and was never seen by the writer to read
a book on strategy. He believed more in a thoroughly
practical application of actual experience in all things, particularly in field campaigns and operations against as wily
a foe as he and the rest of us knew the Indian to be, and
less in the perfection of drill and much of the useless,
unnecessary grind that has become such a fad in our present Army. On one occasion Mackenzie sent a courier or
Indian runner to Lawton with orders to "hook up" his
train and be at a certain point on the "Staked Plains" at
daybreak. He had to make a night march. A hundred
Infantry soldiers had been assigned to him for escort duty.
His route lay across several bad creeks and over a "sand
hill," "Shin oak" country. Just before daybreak he had
reached almost a sheer bluff over which he had to pull
his train to make good Mackenzie's expectations and to fulfill his orders. He knew he had to "make good." An
officious, dapper Infantry Officer went up to him and said,
"Colonel (he was a brevet Lieutenant-Colonel), you will
have to *double up your teams to make that pull!*" Lawton brusquely brushed him aside and replied, "Yes, that is
the rule, but *double up* h—l—all the mules in my train
couldn't pull an empty wagon up that place; they couldn't
even pull your hat off!" There was not an instant's hesi-

tation—his orders came like a shot out of a rifle. He
shouted to the Wagon Master—"Sergeant, 'unhook' all of
your mules—get out the picket rope—be quick!!'' And to
the "doughboy" officer—"Loop that rope over the wagon;
run the ends to the front; man the pole and the two rope
ends with all of your men; when I give the word start
them together and 'snake' it over the bluff!!'' This was
repeated with each wagon. Every wagon was soon over
the bluff and at Mackenzie's disposal at daybreak. Some
intensively-trained, theoretical student officer, with no field
experience, but with some cut and dried rule from one of
his text books, would have sat down on the trail and figur-
ing on the weight of each load would have carefully com-
puted how much each mule or man should advantageously
pull, and how many mules or men it would take to move
the given number of loads in a given time. *The writer
has seen it done.* He had also seen Lawton's rule for
pulling loads in an emergency thoroughly and successfully
worked out in the withdrawal of the Army of the Potomac
at Chancellorsville, May 6, 1863, when a brigade of seasoned veteran Infantry in which he was serving swung
the two partially submerged bridges at United States
Ford, and with the assistance and under the direction of
Engineer Officers, dismantled, stripped and loaded them
on to the wagons, and then with cables bent on and the
poles manned, the entire train was hauled over the bluff,
under cover of thirty guns on the heights above, in thick,
gluey mud where the mules could not pull an empty wagon. Just preceding Mackenzie's campaign against Dull
Knife's band of Northern Cheyennes in the Big Horn
Mountains in November, 1876, Lawton had returned from
a tour of recruiting duty in Boston and had reported at
Camp Robinson, Neb. Mackenzie had made him R.Q.M. at
once, and in half an hour he was, after being greeted most
enthusiastically by the entire command, deep in the calcu-
lation of the amount of hay it would require to feed the
horses of blank companies for six months, and from that
time he hadn't an idle moment. He was busy **day and**

night, frequently up all night, with no rest, of course, on
Sunday.   Once on an urgent call when he was getting supplies ready to send to Gen. Crook, a courier came in just
after dark.   His (L-s) wagons were distributed among
all the companies with poles off, and coupled out for logs.
He got them all in and coupled up with poles, bows and
sheets on; issued arms and ammunition to the teamsters;
loaded and billed 81,000 pounds of stores and moved his
train at daybreak.   It is doubtful if such a feat has ever
been equaled or surpassed in the history of our little
Army.   He knew every part of a wagon, and could repair,
almost build it.   He knew every part of a harness—all of
the many eccentric habits of the festive, wee-hawing Army
mule, the parts and workings of a portable saw mill; could
set it up, repair, and operate it on time better than almost
any other live Quartermaster in the Army at that period
of our sphere of usefulness.   The one secret of Lawton's
reputation and success as a soldier is the fact that he was
unusually endowed with plenty of good, sound, common,
horse sense and thinking capacity.   It is generally an in-
herent quality.   That is what some of our *would-be* theoretical soldiers do not possess.   Unfortunately for those
men that deficiency is impossible to replace or ever ac-
quire either at West Point or at any other school where
soldiers are supposed to be turned out.   The writer was
the last one of his friends to see him in Washington, going
with him at his urgent request to the train (Federal Express) from the War Department in General J. C. Breck-
inridge's carriage after he had bade good-bye to General
Miles and other friends.   He had just come from the
White House where he had had half an hours conference
with the President (McKinley) at the latters request—the
substance of which he related to me in strictest confidence.
The latter told him that he was to go over to the P. I. and
relieve General Otis in Command of the Division.   *He gave
him full instructions.*   Somewhere between that White
House and the Philippines, during his 55 days trip via the

Suez Canal, some generous-hearted and disinterested friend (?) played a trick on him (by whom it will probably never be known), and when he arrived he found that his orders had been changed (probably cabled over his head), and he found himself without a command. But—"De-Mortuis Nil Nisi bonum"—his fame rests secure in the hearts of his loyal friends, even while those disloyal ones flourished for a brief period, flared up—flickered and were *snuffed out to be forgotten*. So much for Lawton, the Army of the Potomac, mules, etc., by way of diversion from the campaign after Kicking Bird's bunch of bad Ki-o-was Indians. But as the French say, "Revenous a nos Moutons!" (Let us return to our subject.) Jacksboro had been practically deserted during the Civil War, but was now made up of a population peculiar to a frontier settlement, consisting of cattlemen and ranchers who had fled in from their ranches to the protection of the Post, and a miscellaneous collection of Mexicans, negroes, discharged soldiers, gamblers and saloon keepers—occasionally increased by a roaring, rollicking gang of cow-boys on a spree or "big jag" who, when they had become well saturated with "Tangle foot," spent their time, especially at night, in riding up and down "Jacks" only street—screeching and yelling like a lot of wild Indians and firing their six-shooters at saloon windows and many other imaginary enemies. They were only cooled off by a night's reflection in the guard-house. When we first arrived these orgies had been of almost nightly occurrence, but after Mackenzie had sent over one or two warnings and then proceeded to apply force by bagging them and confining the worst ones, in which the better element of "Jack" cordially co-operated, there was little to complain of. At Fort Richardson there were 10 sets of officer's quarters, 5 frame and 5 picket. The former were one and a half story cottages with broad porches in front and rear ceiled and plastered, each containing 4 rooms. The picket quarters contained but one room; were set on the ground; had no porches; were unceiled, with rough "parabolic" floors, and

large, stone fire places, where one might freeze his back
and roast his face during a ''Norther.'' When the dried
chinking dropped from the picket partitions, which were
plastered with a thick, red clay mud, an arm could be
readily thrust through into the neighboring officer's room,
and any noise above a whisper was easily heard in the adjoining quarters. Tents were used for an overflow.
These extended along the line on both flanks from the center. In these picket huts made of the intractable green
pecan which, soon after exposure to the weather, warped
out of shape so that nails could only be driven by boring—
a New England farmer would hardly stable his animals;
the bachelors of the Sixth Cavalry had used them for *dog
kennels.* Up and down the rough, log walls, and through
the large cracks and knot holes of the floors, crawled the
many legged and varieagated centipede of unknown dimen-
sions. About our Army cots at night, gambolled the spor-
tive rats and mice in blissful happiness. The repulsive
tarantula, whose coarse haired form bristled with venom-
ous rage, greeted our astonished gaze. An occasional scorpion comforted one now and then with their poisonous
stings. Swarms of the most agile fleas, a legacy from the
dogs of our departed comrades of the Sixth, pitted us like
small-pox. Through the cracks o'er-head we could see the
stars of Heaven. Sand and hail, during the ''Northers''
sifted down upon our uncovered heads, requiring the services of a broom on the beds and dinner table before we
could comfortably sleep or eat. Here, at 8:00 A. M., June
21, 1871, at this far-off Palatial(?) frontier Post, upon
the extreme verge of civilization, amidst the blare of the
trumpeters morning call for ''guard mount,'' and the inspiring music of the Fourth Cavalry band when ''beating
off,'' was born a young life, a soldier's child who, compelled by force of circumstances later, to leave these
scenes behind, was destined in after life, in blissful ignorance of her birth-place, no mark of which now exists, to
gaze with wondering eyes on a picture of her early home,

and to listen with eager ears to the tales and adventures of border life, when savage Indians lurked about the Post, hostile bullets sung over the picket hut, and arrows hurtled about the heads of this devoted band of officer's and soldier's families posted there for the advancement ant expansion of the civilization of our country.

The contract price for beef was from 3½ to 4 cents per pound, with soup bones, liver, heart, brains and kidneys "thrown in." By an understanding between the contractor and the cattlemen whenever we were scouting or campaigning inside the cattle ranges, and before we struck the buffalo herds, we were free to kill as many steers as we needed for fresh meat with which to supply the command. We hung the hides in the trees out of reach of wolves. The cattleman came along, took down the skin, recognized his brand, took it in to the nearest Post, and the claim voucher was promptly paid by the Quartermaster at the contract price. This proved a very great convenience to us, and was a sufficient source of revenue to him. It was a "gentlemen's agreement" and was never violated. Milk was very rare and hard to obtain. In summer it was 10 cents and in winter 25 cents a quart. Butter was 40 cents in summer and 75 cents a pound in winter, and almost impossible to obtain. Eggs, chickens, etc., proportionately high. Fresh vegetables were rarely obtained and commanded at all times enormous—almost prohibitive—prices. Irish potatoes ranged from $5.00 to $8.00 per bushel. We rarely ever saw any, but supplied them imperfectly by a soggy sweet potato brought from Eastern Texas and of a greyish color, which we soon tired of. Apples or any fruit came from Arkansas and were worth their weight in gold, generally $1.00 per dozen. The writer *never saw an apple tree in Texas.* It was a very busy garrison, and the writer as Post Adjutant—although the illness of his wife still hung over him like a hovering shadow—rarely sought his bed until the "wee small hours," and then only to "turn out" again to the lively beating of the Infantry drummers

and the blare of the Cavalry trumpeters ''sounding off'' an
early ''reveille.'' There were Boards, Courts, papers galore. Hobbles, side lines, picket pins, packs, panniers,
saddles, bridles, carbines, pistols, lariats, ordnance and
ordnance stores, etc., etc., etc. All had to be looked after,
besides the thousand and one other details in an expedition of this kind. But of all the busy men, our great Quartermaster was the busiest. He never seemed to eat or
sleep; he was here and there, and at all places at all times.

On July 28 ''G'' and ''I'' Troops were sent out to the
Little Wichita and, with ''A,'' ''C,'' ''D'' and ''H'' were
placed under the command of Capt. N. B. McLaughlin, our
senior Captain, and a Brevet Brig. General. He was directed to bridge the stream if necessary and prepare the
crossing for the passage of the train. A mounted inspection for the field was made of the entire command. The
writer had been designated as Field Adjutant. On the
morning of August 2nd ''L'' Troop was ordered out to the
West Fork of the Trinity River to await the arrival of
Gen. Mackenzie and headquarters, and at 8:45 P. M. he, the
writer, Lieut. P. M. Boehm with all of the Ton-ka-way
scouts, whom B— commanded, rode through the bright
moonlight, across the silent prairies, under the brilliant
stars to the camp of Captain ''Clint'' B. Powers on the
West Fork. The low fires of his bivouac glowed in the
shadows of the pecans and post-oaks surrounding and
skirting his camp, as we rode among the sleeping forms,
and without waking them we quietly rolled ourselves in
our blankets, with feet to the blaze, and without tents, were
soon fast asleep with the tired troopers. Such is the sudden transition from affluence to poverty—or, rather, from
a good bed in a picket house, to a soldier's couch upon
Mother Earth. It was near this Camp in which we now
were, that one of those singular, and almost unaccountable
incidents occurred, which even the victim himself was
never able to fully explain.

Gen. J. B. Fry in a little work entitled ''Army Sacri-

fices'' graphically relates this incident, but, as the writer
had it direct from the officer himself at Fort R— and we
were now on the spot, it will bear repeating here. Lieut.
H. B. Mellen, Sixth Cavalry, was stationed at Camp Wichita, near Buffalo Springs in December 1870, and had been
ordered in to Fort R— on Court Martial duty; upon arriving at the West Fork of the Trinity, which was much
swollen by recent rains, he attempted to swim the stream
on his horse. A severe ''Norther'' was blowing and it was
freezing. In ascending the opposite bank, it gave way, and
horse and rider were precipitated into the icy flood. Although a powerful swimmer and a very strong man, en-
cumbered as he was with heavy clothes, overcoat, boots,
pistol, etc., he found it impossible to swim, so struggling
and drifting with the stream he soon found out that he
was on the same side of the stream from which he had
started, and managed to crawl out. He now lost con-
sciousness, and only recovered to find his faithful horse
standing over him. He attempted to rise and mount, but
found that both of his feet were frozen in his heavy boots
and his legs were benumbed and powerless. Again and
again he made the attempt, but his efforts were fruitless.
He lay in this condition for about 48 hours, without food
or drink, and slowly freezing to death. He was finally and
almost providentially rescued by a party of hunters who
heard his horse whinny. The thermometer registered 10
degrees below zero. A party started out from Fort R—
to his relief; several were frost-bitten, including the surgeon. Mellen was delirious, and it was with the greatest
difficulty that he was rescued and taken into the Post. He
lost his left leg, below the knee, and most of his right foot,
but thanks to an iron constitution and indomitable pluck
and good nursing, he entirely recovered, and was for many
months an object of special care and pity at Fort R— while
the writer was stationed there, being rolled up and down
the officer's line in a wheeled chair. He was retired and
died at an advanced age a few years ago.

Lieut. Boehm, by Mackenzie's special permission, was wearing a *white* sombrero hat with a low crown and very wide brim—such as the cow-boys of that period affected. It had no Montana peak. We all envied that hat. It was softer, cooler and more comfortable than our black campaign hats. Without launching a "Round Robin" letter at headquarters, it was suggested to the writer, as Adjutant of the Expedition, that he should go to Mackenzie and plead that all should procure and wear the same kind and color. The answer was snapped out: "No! Boehm is in command of the Indians. As such he is outside the marching column, a sort of 'free lance,' and somewhat of an independent and picturesque character." We must all wear "uniform black hats." "Could we pack any buffalo robes on the mules to use in event of cold weather?" "No that was a *luxury* he did not intend to indulge in himself." "Were any tents besides the "dog tents" for the men to be carried along?" "No! myself, my *Adjutant* and my Interpreter ("Mat" Leeper), are to share one wall tent fly, and then only in bad weather will it be pitched; two or more officers are to have the same, all to be painted a dull, lead color," etc. We never saw Boehm go sailing by with his miscellaneous bunch of Ton-ka-way Indians wearing his big, soft, wide-brimmed white hat that we did not sigh and almost bark our disappointment and disapproval of his *ununiform* head covering flapping in the breeze, often calling out—"Hey there 'Peter,' 'Are you the Old Man's pet?'" "Where did you get that hat?" (This was long before that phrase became so popular later.) "How much did you pay for it?" etc.

Our march from the West Fork was through a blackened, burnt-over country, entirely bare of grass, all the way to Buffalo Springs. There had been no rain since May 19—the day Gen. M— led our Cavalry column to the scene of Sa-tan-tas massacre of the teamsters on Salt Creek prairie. The ground was parched, dry and baked. There were great fissures or cracks to be seen in every

direction, and no water was to be had on the road. Upon
arriving at Buffalo Springs where we expected to water
our suffering animals, the wells or water holes were found
to be literally choked up with dead cattle, in every stage
of decomposition, and a pestilential odor was already in
the hot, suffocating air. We could not drink the water.
Halting but for a few moments, we pushed on across the
black, sooty prairie, until we reached Camp Wichita, an
old sub-post of the 6th Cavalry, but now abandoned and
rapidly falling to decay. The water here, although very
bad, and highly impregnated with sulphur, and the salts of
many other minerals, mingled perhaps with *one* or *two*
putrid, and decaying animals at its source, was better than
nothing, or, to use our phrase "beat nothing all to pieces"
—which little saying is often the soldier's only consolation.

We were all soon too busy, however, with preparations
for camp to mind such trifles, and, after a hearty supper
and the solacing weed, *which took the taste out of our*
mouths, no more was thought about water that night.
There came a time, however, a little later, when the "ghost
would not down" . . .   ,

Water was found in the "water holes" and "arroyas"
along the line of the next day's march. The country was
a rolling prairie with here and there a small belt of Post
Oak timber. We saw McLaughlin's trail, and passed
through the little abandoned settlement of Henrietta, consisting of two or three old broken-down, partly burned
ranches, which the Indians had raided but a short time
before our arrival at Fort Richardson, resulting in the
killing of several settlers. Shortly after crossing a big
"slough" of the Little Wichita, which had been filled with
brush and bridged, we struck McL's command, all busy
constructing a bridge across the main stream. It was finished at 8:30 the next day, and the entire command crossed
safely. Shortly before we had started from Fort R— an
officer had asked the writer to loan him Mahan's Civil
Engineering as he expected to act as Engineer Officer for

McL's command and would probably have to construct this
bridge over the Little Wichita.. I tried to persuade him
that he would not need it, as the book did not deal with
makeshifts, emergencies, or exigencies, but with *permanent* or *semi-permanent* bridges and structures where
plenty of material was available and *time was no object.*
There he would find very little material, and the bridge
would be but a temporary makeshift. So it proved. It
merely required that a man's wits, common sense and resourcefulness should supply the rest. It consisted of two
heavy cribs made of green logs, notched and fitted, and
filled with the largest stones to be found in the vicinity,
which were secured with considerable patience and labor—
these to load down the cribs. Then two long stringers
were thrown across, having to be spliced and secured. A
roadway of small tree trunks were laid on which were
pinned and lashed. The approaches were of corduroy,
earth and stone. It was a problem of well directed labor
with *axe, pick* and *shovel* and a few ropes instead of cut
and dried engineering. The wagons were run over by
hand; the mules were swum across. In returning several
weeks later and attempting to ford the stream, a young
Mexican teamster ran his wagon off the ford, upset it, and
the mess chest containing my valuable (?) Mahan's Civil
Engineering went to the bottom, and when fished up it was
found to be pulp. However, it was no great loss as it was
of no practical value on a campaign. From bank to bank
was 30 or 40 yards, with moderately steep banks.

Our progress, after crossing was slow, for a deep ravine
lay directly across our trail which the wagons could not
"head," and several long halts were made to water, etc.,
during which the "camp strikers" and cooks amused themselves in true *"Old Virginny"* style by dislodging an ancient "possum" from a tree near by and later, cooked and
tried to eat. As we approached the Big Wichita the country became wilder and more broken, and upon arriving at
the river it was found that the train could not cross with-

out much hard labor in cutting down the banks and repairing the ford. A large detail was placed at the disposal of the Quartermaster, while the balance pitched a nice camp just in time to avoid a heavy rain which continued and threatened far into the night. With a stout duck tent fly, painted a lead color to blend with the landscape and attract less attention from the enemy spies, this thrown over a horizontal pole placed in two crotched stakes driven into the ground and sides pinned down, and with plenty of wood for a blazing fire, we fared pretty well. Deer and wild turkeys were plentiful, and the "Tonks" kept the "Big Chief," as they called Mackenzie, and the mess the writer was running, well supplied. We had not yet reached the Buffalo Country. Most of the wagons crossed during the night, and at 8:40, after waiting but for a short time, the last of the train (25), pulled up the bank and ready and saddled, we mounted and struck out for Gilbert's Creek to join the balance of the command there and complete our march of Concentration. A big fire broke out in our camp soon after leaving it, and the writer was directed to return and put it out. It proved a very hard job even with the strenuous use of saddle blankets, etc. In returning to overtake the command, grass was passed through, the top of which could not be reached from the back of a horse 16½ hands high. At 1:45 P. M. Gilbert's Creek was reached, where we found "Mac's" command in fine shape. The 10 Troops of the Fourth were immediately organized into five squadrons, while the two companies of Infantry were detailed as guard for the wagon train and supply camp wherever located. At 6:15 A. M. the next day we broke camp and headed at once over a big "divide" for the crossing of Red River. There were about 90 *green* pack mules, and we had no professional packers, and only the "saw-buck" pack saddle. The Aparejo pack was not then in use by our army. The experiment was tried the first day of driving them in one herd, with a pack herd officer to steer them. It did not work out. They crowded the

trail and refused to "string out"; a few got frightened at
the unearthly clattering of pans, kettles, etc., and started
to run. Their loads collided, and for the next ten minutes
there was an indescribable mass of mules' ears, heels and
tails, iron mess-pans and kettles. It literally rained clouds
of flour, sugar, bunches of coffee and hard bread, etc., all
over the prairie, and as the animals at once scattered during the panic produced, it took a long chase before the re-
fractory brutes could be brought to faithful allegiance
again. It was a long, hot, hard day's drive; many of the
men became prostrated with heat, and one Infantry officer
succumbed to it, and had to be sent in to Fort Sill, from
which he was unable to rejoin. We were compelled to
camp on the South side of the river, the mules were so exhausted. About midnight when the camp was buried in
deepest slumber, the trumpeters loudest "Tra-ta, Tar-a-
ta-a-a-a-!" rang out in the air.

The Alarm—Driven Out by Fire—A Narrow Escape

The alarm was sounded and the command sprang to its
feet, to discover rolling in upon it a perfect sheet of fire.
The long, coarse sedge or cane grass which we had passed
through on our march from the Big Wichita was in a mass
of flames, the fire probably set by Indian spies lurking in
our rear. It was a magnificent spectacle, far surpassing
or completely overshadowing the many distant prairie
fires we had seen at Fort Concho or Fort Richardson.
Great forked flames seemed to leap to the very sky, as
though to lick up the stars of Heaven, and countless thousands of floating sarpks were carried up in the air by the
wind and almost obscured the horizon. As the breeze
freshened we could see the flames driven forward at a
fearful rate of speed, and could now distinctly hear the
tremendous and ominous roaring. The other fires had
been *far off;* this was *near to.* We didn't gaze long at the
magnificence of such a spectacle. In a few moments it
would be in among the mules, horses, the wagon train, and
into our very bivouac; nothing could save us from a stam-

pede, perhaps destruction, unless we could pull into or across the sands of Red River. The commands came in rapid succession: "Pack up!" "Stand to horse!" "Mount!" and "Forward!" It was a comparatively easy matter moving the Cavalry into the bottom; not so, however, with the wagon train. It was only by the greatest exertion that it was pushed and dragged into the sand bed of the stream. It was a grand sight as we looked over our shoulders in the sandy river bottom. The stillness of night was only broken by the noisy wagon train and the roaring of the swiftly approaching object of terror which now glared brightly over the long column strung out in the gloom. The "black snakes" cracked, making the air resound, while the constant "We-e-e-haw-w-w-ing" of the mules could be heard for miles. All night the train struggled in the yielding sand, under that Prince of Quartermasters, Lawton, but our little army did not feel quite safe until "sun up," and it was announced that all were safely across, over the sand dunes, and we were stretching across the country towards Otter Creek. After leaving the bluffs of Red River, and a hard march over numerous sand hills, we struck rolling prairie covered with rich mesquite and crossing a slight divide, a march of 14 miles, we camped on West Cache Creek, seeing many buffalo and antelope, some of which the "Tonks" and the hunters killed. The grass was in great abundance, but the water was vile. It had been churned by the buffalo until it was thick and muddy, and nearly the color of pale chocolate. We had been passing through an almost continuous prairie-dog village all day, hence the Indian name of Red River. "Keche-a-qui-ho-no." We were continually winding in and out among the mounds, and frequently when the sun rose and warmed the earth, a sharp rattle, or whir-r-r-r, and a quick jump of our horses, warned us to keep a sharp lookout for the rattlesnake friends of the dogs, who had now crawled out and lay coiled and lazily basking in the heat of "Old Sol." We frequently saw owls on the mounds. It seemed quite probable to us that this strange trio of bird, reptile and rodent form one and the same "happy family," the mutual offices of which, or economy in nature, is not so well understood, and it has long been a disputed point by both naturalists and hunters. There was great hunting in this region, and in this dry, hunger-producing air, many a princely potentate with weak and dyspepsia-tortured stomach would have grown green with sheer envy could he have seen the troopers of the Fourth Cavalry gather about their camp fires and eagerly devour a rib roast of buffalo well larded with bacon, a sweetbread, or steaks from the saddle of a fine antelope or deer, topped off with a succulent El Paso onion, some "doby" biscuit and black coffee. Oh, boy!!

Otter Creek—The Tenth Cavalry

Heavy timber could be seen the next day about noon, and at 2:45 P. M. the command rode into the grateful shade of the trees that lined Otter Creek. The "old Radzminski Trail" was crossed during the day. Gen. B. F. Grierson was found to be about two miles below with most of the Tenth Cavalry, of which he was the Colonel. Lieut. W. H. Beck was his field Adjutant. Our march had been about 25 miles, and the train did not arrive until 8 P. M. owing to many halts to load buffalo meat for the command, heading ravines and the intense suffering of the mules for water. Visits were exchanged between officers of the two regiments; the command was stripped down for scouting, and a Supply Camp was located here and placed in command of an officer (Lieut. H. Sweeny) who had become disabled on account of sickness. All unserviceable animals, "plunder," etc., was left behind, and as soon as Grierson and Mackenzie had made a personal reconnoissance of the country and had conferred together for a co-operative expedition, the two commands with their pack-trains at once moved on divergent trails in search of Kicking Birds Ki-o-wa village.

The two Fort Sill interpreters joined us here, H. P.

Jones, the Post interpreter, going with Grierson; Matthew
Leeper, the Agency interpreter, with Mackenzie, joining
our mess. We headed for the North Fork of the Red River
and crossed it three miles from Camp. It was a "shin
oak" country and over prairie burned off, baked and dried
by the long drought. Leeper said that Kicking Bird might
be on Rainy Mountain Creek, a fine stream, having its
source in the Wichita Mountains.

A Reminiscence of the "Indian Ring"

As we left our camp in the early morning of Aug. 17
and again moved in and out among the sand hills and "shin
oak," where our progress was on the basis of "two steps
forward, and one backward," and along the sand bed of the
North Fork, a courier overtook us with mail, sent out by
Lieut. Henry Sweeney, Fourth Cavalry, from Otter Creek.
Mackenzie, after reading one official letter seemed much
agitated but, although the writer was his Adjutant, we
rode all day in silence and to the day of his death he never
revealed its contents, leaving me to the solace of mere conjecture. Of course subsequent action by him always led
me to believe that it was an order from Washington limit-
ing his operations and confining him to ascertaining Kicking Birds whereabouts, but to make no offensive attack on
him. It was, at that time, a mere surmise. All our movements from then on seemed strange in view of the real object of our expedition. I really never knew the contents
of that mysterious communication until Dec. 19, 1903 when
Lieut. Colonel (later Brig.-General) S. M. Woodward, who
had been Grierson's Regimental Adjutant, told the writer
at the Ebbitt House in Washington! Gen. Woodward died
in April 1924.

It is extremely doubtful if any officer of the Fourth Cavalry ever saw this communication. Woodward said that
the authorities ("Indian Ring") at Washington, fearing
that Mackenzie, acting under the instructions contained in
Gen. Sherman's letter of May, had for his object or avowed

purpose the attack of Kicking Bird, whether he was on or
off the reservation, and thus precipitate the war they were
seeking in every way to avoid, and ignoring Sherman's
instructions, had an order sent to Fort Sill directing
Grierson, as the senior officer in rank, to assume command
of both columns, so long as the Fourth Cavalry was operating in the Indian Territory, in order to hold Mackenzie
in check and avoid such a calamity. He (Woodward) as
Adjutant received it, and forwarded it by mounted courier
to our camp at Otter Creek, with instructions to place it in
Mackenzie's hands "pronto" wherever he might be. It
was this courier from Sweeney which overtook us that day,
which so disturbed Mackenzie and caused him to alter all of
his plans. It accounts now largely at this late day for his
reticence and chagrin. It also accounted for Kicking Bird
getting inside the Fort Sill reservation so hastily, when,
later, we were so close to his village, and when Grierson
under positive orders to avoid war with the hostiles, at all
hazards just then, no matter where they might be, upon
discovering their whereabouts on the Sweet Water, sent
Jones, the interpreter into their camp and, without notify-
ing Mackenzie, warned Kicking Bird to "get in." For
this act Mackenzie never quite forgave Grierson.

The "Gypsum Belt"—"Bad Lands"—A Bitter Taste

On the 17th buffalo and antelope were seen all day on
both flanks, and we began to traverse a very wild country
with many very singular and remarkable Geological features, and it soon became evident that we were now fast
getting beyond the range, known either to the *"Tonks,"*
Old Dozier, the *"guide,"* whom we had taken out with us
from Jacksboro, or the *"Interpreter."* Many old deserted
Ki-o-wa and Comanche villages were passed through, and
shortly after 1:00 P. M. we struck what by our maps,
which were poor, we supposed to be the Salt Fork of the
Red River, but which, later, proved to be Marcy's Creek.
The writer was engineer officer and was running the
courses by the pace of his horse and an old prismatic com-

pass. Its banks were thickly lined with reeds, and willows, and tall, rank sedge grass. The water was so perfectly vile and nauseating that one was made sick as soon as it was drank. After a bath in the stream, the body, before one could dress, was at once crusted with gypsum which was removed with difficulty. There were many bluffs about us, and ever in the distance, the picturesque peak of Mt. Webster, which, rising nearly 800 feet above the level of the plain, was named by Generals Marcy and McClellan, his son-in-law, in 18552—in their survey for a Southern Pacific R. R. route. Marcy and other writers say of this mountain and the Wichita group—"one cannot leave these mountains without regret." They were right. We were now on the edge of the Great Gypsum Belt of Texas. The country was broken up in every direction, being absolutely impassable for wagons, and nearly so for pack mules. If there were any worse *"Bad Lands"* in the Dacotahs, Wyoming or Nebraska, where the writer had never served, some of those men who had wandered among them, ought to have had a chance, by way of comparison, to flounder and browse around in some of the Texas gypsum gulches, ravines, arroyas and small canons.

Everything was raw, rank gypsum. We had some corrective fluids with us, but it was our coffee that we could not seem to remedy. Neither Citric Acid, lime juice nor brandy corrected that. The more the stuff was boiled the worse it proved. Our camp the next night was worse than ever—for after gaining a high divide, ever passing through the countless herds of buffalo, and winding about at almost every point of the compas, we struck the dry bed of a stream, supposed by our maps—which were so imperfect as to be almost useless—to be the Elm Fork. Here the water was more bitter than ever; gypsum held in solution, thoroughly impregnated with buffalo essence (excrement and urine), and so warm and nauseating as to make not only the men, but the animals at once sick. There was no grass, and no water except this vile stuff. A green scum was over all which had to be scraped aside.

Buffalo had wallowed in and stirred it up until it was thoroughly churned; the hot sun had thoroughly *cooked it,* and when drank it had to be sifted through the teeth to avoid being strangled with buffalo hair. Drinking Coffee made of this wretched water was like trying to force warm Epsom salts down the throat. We tried lime juice and citric acid cocktails, with a dash of brandy, but still, above all, came the nauseating odor and taste of this vile compound, this double distilled, concentrated essence of buffalo-gypsum liquid. Our surgeon was now so weak and sick, from chronic diarrhea and bowel trouble that he could scarcely sit on his horse; several of the men were being carried along on horse litters. The lips of the officers and men in the entire command were so cut by the alkali that the blood was trickling down their chins, only remedied by a thick smearing of camphor ice on the lips, and goggles had to be freely used to protect the eyes from the reflected glare of the sun. Our canteens were thickly crusted with the salt. This Gypsum Belt extends across the country for many miles. It is the most extensive deposit of this Salt in North America. The water when drank creates a feverish thirst, constantly increasing, and violent cramps with vomiting and purging. Our animals begun to grow weaker, and many died. We were in this Gypsum Belt for ten days—just "sloshing" or, as the British officers termed a period of our unproductive "intensive training" during the World War, just "slogging along." Most of this period was so hot that one could not touch the barrel of a carbine or pistol without blistering the hands. One night when we were all sicker than ever, and a good deal of profanity had been slyly indulged in out of hearing of the "Old Man"—and he was about the sickest of all—he said at the Camp fiire, "Gentlemen, we shall all have a new stomach when it gets thoroughly coated with a crust of gypsum," and measuring on his finger added, "I think my coating is now about *that thick!*" Taking a swallow of our coffee concoction he started into the bushes to dispose of it and later, when some one slyly and dryly asked

him "what was the matter," with a sickly smile, intended
for a *cheerful laugh,* he replied, "Oh, *heap* sick! *heap*
sick!!" In the generosity of his heart, however, when he
saw Capt. "Clint" Powers' white, sick face come into the
group, he quickly beckoned the writer aside and in a
hoarse stage whisper said, "You have got the only brandy
in the command, you brought it out for me; let's give it
to poor Powers; we will not need it," and calling an orderly said, "Here, orderly, carry this bottle to Captain
Powers with the compliments of the Adjutant!" It was
a bottle of Old New Orleans Sazerac brandy—"Umpteen"
years old—sent to me by an indulgent father-in-law by
express from New Orleans just before we had started on
this campaign. Powers was then known to be tuberculous,
and going in before the command, went on home and died
shortly after of this disease in his native state. He was
a Cavalryman "Par excellence," a prince among men, a
noble, generous, cheerful soul. We lost a soldier when
he departed.

About 8 o'clock one night when sitting by the embers of
of the camp fire, chewing the bitter, gypsum cud of reflection and wondering what we were going to accomplish in
this mess of gypsum bluffs, gypsum streams, buffalo wallow holes, etc., and when we were to ever get out of it,
among the loose herds nearby we saw and heard two or
three horses apparently rearing at their lariats and play-
ing as they sometimes did. All of a sudden a quick rush
was heard across the creek, where the second and third
squadrons were, and then a noise resembling rolling thunder, and, in an instant, the camp was in an uproar.

The horse herds were stampeding. Every man was on
his feet in an instant. Although carefully "staked out,"
and secured with "side lines," the horses came rushing
by like a whirl wind. In the darkness that enveloped the
camp, in spite of the orders to "get to your horses, every
man," they disappeared in the gloom of night.

Lieut. Boehm, with our Ton-ka-ways, adopting the Indian method of following and "circling" them back,

jumped on their ponies, bare-back, and galloped out with the thoroughly panic stricken herd. They were mostly of "C" Troop (Wilcox's). After following them closely for several miles, a portion of them was "cut out" and recovered, but the herd swerving just at this moment and Boehm's horse stopping with a jerk that almost threw him back on his haunches, the herd thundered off in the darkness and B— reluctantly abandoned further pursuit. A detail was sent out after them at daylight under Lieut. W. C. Miller, the command following shortly afterward. We came to where Boehm's horse had swerved. It was within a few feet of a gypum cliff, nearly 100 feet high and *was an almost sheer, perpendicular wall.* There were many officers of that command who, knowing that we could not be very far from Kicking Bird's village, our Indians having seen signs and trails of them just before entering the Gypsum Belt, believed for many years that the hostiles had stampeded Wilcox's horses that night. On March 31, 1908, the writer was talking at the Ebbitt House, Washington, D. C., with the surgeon who was with us in that bivouac, and whose tent was but a few yards from ours, the nearest to the horse herds on that side of the creek. He related the following facts. He had never dared give them out before, at least while *Mackenzie lived.* He declared that it was he who caused the stampede. On that night, becoming somewhat desperate and wishing to be comfortable and get a good night's rest, having been made sick by the intense heat and drinking the filthy poisonous alkali water from the buffalo wallow holes, he stripped off his outer clothing and putting on a *long, white night shirt,* which he had carefully packed on the mules in the pannier containing his medical supplies, lay down in his blankets to get one *good night's blessed sleep.* Having occasion to get up shortly after, and step out of his tent, the horses nearest to him in Wilcox's herd ("C" Troop), upon seeing this nocturnal ghostly apparition loom up so near them and, *having never seen a night-shirt before,* became frightened and ran into the main herd.

The panic was soon communicated to the balance and away they all went with the result as already related. Capt. Wilcox, with the balance of his troop, was ordered into Otter Creek. The trail of a small party of Indians was crossed this morning, and Lieut. Miller, who had been sent out after the stampeding horses, gave chase with the "Tonks." As he with our scouts were going up one hill the hostile Indians were coming up the opposite side of another hill, with a deep ravine between; neither were aware of the near presence of the other until brought almost face to face. They fled; he pursued, but upon the waving of a white rag by a "Tonk," they halted. Miller with the "Tonk" advanced and met them. They were Ki-o-was, but refused to tell where their village was. They were fantastically dressed, painted and ornamented with beads and feathers. They soon set off at a run. It was a stirring scene. We wondered then why he (Mackenzie) did not pursue and capture some of them and hold them until Kicking Bird's hiding place was divulged. The "Indian Ring," Grierson and Mackenzie, held the secret. The reason has been given, but then we were in blissful ignorance of the official ban which had been placed upon him, or of the most wily and diplomatic "side step," and "double cross," our partner in this game of "hide and go seek" (Grierson), had played upon his friend (?) Mackenzie. Later, under a flag of truce, Mackenzie held a parley with this same party of Indians, somewhat increased, but, although every effort was made by him to obtain some knowledge of Kicking Bird and his village nothing was gained from the rascals, and they were allowed to depart, much to the disappointment of the command and the utter disgust of the loyal Ton-ka-ways, who, considering them as enemies, and their lawful prisoners—knowing no more than we did of what had been going on behind the scenes—doubtless itched for their scalps and the plunder which comes with success in Indian Wars.

The Night March—Ludicrous Scenes—Mule "Cussing"

Towards night Power's squadron was sent out to observe several Indians who had been seen hovering about us all day spying our movements, and to discover their village, if possible. At night Mackenzie determined to "pull up" and make a night march, join the detached squadron, and thus throwing the hostiles off the scent make a vigorous search for their concealed camp.

A "Tonk" was sent in from the reconnoitering column for a guide, and, a *"night-march"* it was!

One who has never made a night-march in an Indian Country with a cavalry column over a rough country will hardly appreciate its real significance, or even begin to know what it really was by any description that could possibly be made for, when trying to enlarge upon such a subject as this, all human descriptions are futile, and the imagination fails to grasp its full meaning. Each pack mule was led by a trooper in rear of his company. Our course was a little West of North, by the North Star, varying frequently to conform to the rough and hilly country. A ravine, "arroya," or huge "break" was soon reached. A halt resulted, in order to find an outlet. Where the banks were least steep for the pack mules and their precious burdens, the column marched "by file," and although a tedious process, it got along without much serious delay. Then came the mules. The first was pushed and slid down one bank and, as he advanced cautiously up to the other, he "halted" and "balked." The men closed in, and coming behind him with blows and curses, yells and whoops, that would have put a Comanche to the blush, urged *pushed* and *strapped* him along. The packs stick in the narrow defile; off come kettles, pans, bags, sacks, etc., etc. The mule kicks and lashes, brays and squeals; the things fly, the men fill the air with *their opinion of that mule,* until it grows, well—not blue, because it was a dark, *moonless night*—but *sulphurous* to the extreme, and the men pull and tug, but "no go!" The mule is backed down

the ravine, and after widening the gap a little and cutting
down the bank, his load is picked up (all in blackness,
dark as Erebus), and he is finally pushed, and *half lifted*
over the crest. Another poor victim is reluctantly dragged to the scene; all the time the men unloading themselves of all the spite words residing in their systems.
The Adjutant had been sent back to help them, not to
swear, but to "speed up." Ninety mules passed through
at least 8 or 10 of these constantly recurring breaks and
ravines in this manner during that night. Nearly all of
these arroyas extended so far that it would have required
a march of many miles, and entirely out of our course, to
have headed them, and during such a dark night next to
impracticable. Scarcely a sound was heard along the line
of march except the "clanging" of the packs, or, an occasional "cussword" from some man leading, until the next
ravine, or "slough of despond" was reached, when the
scene was reenacted. There was a succession of halts and
rapid closing up, owing to the column at the head keeping nearly at the same gait after crossing, and, by the
rear, in their unavoidable delays in "stringing out."
Just before dawn, but light enough to distinguish objects,
a huge cougar or mountain lion went bounding by the
head of the column, causing the horses to shy and snort
with fright. As soon as it was broad daylight it became
necessary to go into bivouac on account of the great strain
upon men and animals. We found ourselves about a mile
from the missing squadron, and soon moved and joined it.
It was estimated that *we had marched but about 7 miles
the entire night*. The march was resumed at 2:05 P. M.
The "Tonks" were on the flanks and reported the North
Fork in sight. Several halts were made to ascertain our
bearings. The men and animals were suffering greatly
from weakness, and many were giving out. At dark finding no water nor a place for a camp, so rough and broken
was the ground, all dismounted and made preparations for
leading the mules on another night's march, but at 9:30
P. M. the animals became so exhausted that Mackenzie de-

cided to halt and make a "dry camp." The squadron with
the pack train having become lost, it was sometime before
they knew we had gone into camp and then only through
signal lights or flares, improvised out of torches of dried
grass, and displayed or "flared" by the command. As
soon as day broke, the column pushed out, without breakfast, in search of water. About two miles from camp the
"Tonks" signaled, and we found a water hole *filled with*
rain water. Although every effort was made to keep it
clear, all rushed in, men and animals. The former said all
they could say in their stoical faces; the horses whinneyed
and the mules wee-ee-haw-w-w-ed. It was soon a filthy
mud puddle; no amount of hard talk, harsh commands,
pursuasion or threats could check it; nothing but summary
punishment on the spot which, considering the circumstances the General did not deem justifiable. It could, of
course, all have been avoided by posting a guard over it in
advance as we always did during the Civil War. When
the mud in our canteens had somewhat precipitated, we
made rain water punches, out of the almost priceless citric
acid, lime juice and sugar.

Nearing the Village—Fresh Trails

We now began tracing up the course of the North Fork.
Indians signs and fresh trails of hunting parties were seen,
and the "wickey-ups" with piles of fresh shavings where
they had made their arrows for killing buffalo—which
swarmed ahead and on our flanks, and their countless numbers of sharp cut trails led in every direction, presumably
towards water. The leaves of some of the "wickeys"
seemed still green and fresh, a little curled, and, later in
the day as we crossed the bed of the North Fork, about one
mile below the mouth of McClellan's Creek, it was evident
by a little incident that occurred here, that the Ki-o-was
were not far away. So intent upon procuring fresh water
was the entire command that upon dismounting, they commenced digging small holes in the sand. The "Tonks"

some distance off were doing the same, when a small party
of Ki-o-was came up behind and nearly succeeded in stampeding their ponies. The "Tonks" gave chase, but lost the
hostiles in the breaks back of the river. Now our faithful
allies began to get wise, and their "Mebbe So, Yes!" and
"Mebbe so, No!" and "Mebbe so now catch 'em!" "Mebbe
so no catch 'em!" became a spirited quotation among us.
We crossed the trail of the Tenth Cavalry for the first
time. Shortly after going into camp Mackenzie went out
on a reconnoissance, and did not get in until quite dark.
Fearing he might have got lost, signal torches of dried
grass were made and waved. We had now begun to strike
"Aqua-pura" and both canteens were washed clear of all
traces of gypsum and filled. They were called "life pre-
servers." We were now in the wide valley of McClellan's
Creek, and following it up for several miles the next day
came upon an old trail; while examining it, the "Tonks"
rushed up and reported a fresh one near by. We soon
reached it and swinging out, came to where a blanket had
been dropped, then some ash cakes (or hard "pone"), corn
meal, etc.—all in hasty flight.

The False Washita—Scene of Custer's Fight

The trail led over dry, wiry buffalo grass and notwithstanding every effort, the signs soon became too dim to follow, and after spending several hours trying to regain it
we went into camp near the remains of an old village on
the banks of an old "back water," or "Slough" of some
stream, supposed to be the False Washita, and if correct,
we were not far from the scene of Gen. Custer's fight in
1868 with Black Kettles band of Cheyennes, and the Confederated tribes of Sa-tan-tas Ki-o-was, the Comanches and
Arapahoes.*

The squadrons were separated and camped over a very
large area in the valley in order to get sufficient grazing
for the horses. The water was stagnant and foul with

---

*Here Black Kettle was killed; also Major Elliott, Seventh Cavalry, and Capt. Albert
Barnitz desperately wounded. Custer's command was in great peril.

green scum, and had been used by the buffalo until it was sickening even to look at, and much worse to smell, to cook with and drink. A terrific thunder storm struck us at night and blew down the camp. All got thoroughly drenched, and to add to our misery, the coffee, made from the poisonous gypsum water, had nauseated and purged the men so that alarming symptoms of either poison or cholera morbus had seized many, leaving them almost too weak in the morning to mount their horses and continue the march. The writer was one of the victims. Our surgeon, Capt. Julius Patzki (now a Colonel, Medical Corps, U.S.A.) was almost too sick himself to prescribe or care for them. An amusing incident occurred this night. Mackenzie had been extremely nervous and unusually irritable and irascible during the entire campaign; he was very exacting; he had not slept much, nor taken care of himself. He was "burning the candle at both ends," the flame flaring up and dying down with a flicker, later to expire. He had spared no one, especially the interpreter and the writer, who were nearest to him at his beck and call. Neither of us had had much sleep or rest. We had been called up at all hours of the night. If a mule clanked his chain or a horse jumped or snorted, up on his elbows sprang Mackenzie. We, the Fort Sill Agency Interpreter ("Matt" Leeper, and the writer) had both resolved this night, by mutual agreement that whatever happened, we would not respond to his call, but would feign sleep to the last limit. When this torrential storm was at its full height, with thunder, lightning and almost a tornado of wind, the tent fly with buckets of water in its sag came down with a bang. The heavy ridge pole fortunately truck between Leeper and Mackenzie and deluged the latter with about a barrel of water, the entire wet, heavy fly lying across our faces. Mackenzie plunged around, shouted for his orderly and then to us. Leeper kicked the Adjutant from under the weight of soaked canvas and he (the Adjutant), responded. Neither stirred. The orderly removed the debris from

Mackenzie's face and body, disentangled us from the wreck, and then Mackenzie, resting on his elbows asked us "how in the name of Jehovah and the angels we could both sleep in the midst of such a howling storm," and "it would always remain a mystery" to him. "General," said Leeper, "I am always a very heavy sleeper in the field—it takes more than a storm like that to wake me." I thought that was a good enough answer for both and said nothing, leaving him to infer that I had the same peculiar habit. It had seemed so absolutely necessary that we should get some rest, being nearly exhausted, that we felt compelled to enter into this cold-blooded conspiracy in the belief that the "ends justified the means." But these trifling drawbacks were not allowed to detain us except for sufficient time to dry out our clothes in the morning, and about 12 m. we crossed a small divide, and again descending in a course about southeast, came into the valley of, and camped for the night on the Sweet water. So that on two successive nights, we tasted of two extremes, the *bitter* and the *sweet,* for this was pure water, with a slightly sweetish taste.

The following morning Boehm with the "Tonks" were in the lead as usual and were devoting their best energies and utmost skill in trying to strike a trail that led to the village. All day we saw columns of smoke which McCord, the Ton-ka-way chief, said were made by the Ki-o-was signalling our approach to their camp. As we were about to halt for the night, a hostile Indian was seen by the "Tonks" who, whooping and yelling, gave chase, and after a long run succeeded in capturing him. He proved to be a Lipan. As nobody could speak his language, which consisted of a series of gutterals, we could get nothing out of him. Ton-ka-way "Johnson" said he was one of a hunting party from Kicking Bird's Camp, and mistaking our scouts for his own party, ran into them; also that he (the Lipan) indicated that the Ki-o-wa village was nearby but he would not give the direction. Our best scouts were sent out but without gaining any information. We had quite a reception of the "Tonks" about our Camp fire that night and their dusky faces shining in the ruddy light of the blaze, as each smoked his hand rolled cigarette in a circle about the captive Lipan, with Mackenzie and a few officers carelessly lounging about, and above the bright canopy of stars, formed one of those truly wild, border groups worthy of the pencil of an artist. Johnson professed to speak the language of the prisoner, as his mother was a Lipan, but it was evident, from the expression on his face, which we carefully watched, that he did not comprehend the full meaning of the hostile, nothing but a few signs. He was a handsome Indian. His beautiful white teeth shone like pearls, and his eyes, which denoted an expression the depth of which is rarely seen in a human being, glittered in the strong, flickering light like two diamonds. Occasionally he smiled at the blank, immovable faces of McCord, the chief, and Johnson, and then his hands swept once more through the graceful motions of the "sign language;" his eyes glittered again until all were fascinated into a statue-like group about the half reclining form of the captive savage.

Kicking Bird's camp proved afterwards to have been about 9 miles up the stream (Sweet water), and had our march in the morning been in the opposite direction, we should have reached it in about two or three hours. It was not far from where Fort Elliott (named for Major Elliott) was later located. Did "Providence" or the "Indian Ring" change our course? "Quien Sabe!" Cutting off a big bend of the North Fork, near the mouth of the Sweet water, we struck out across a "shin oak" and sand-hill country for about 8 miles, the command marching afoot. Buffalo, deer, antelope, turkeys, quail, and almost every variety of game was so abundant that the camp "strikers" had spent most of their time away from the column hunting. Strict orders had been given on this day, however, that there would be no shooting of game on either flank of the marching column. This order applied to the "Tonks" as well, but, unfortunately

they had not as yet been informed of it, having started
ahead as usual before breaking camp. A shot was heard
and the Adjutant was directed to *"bring in the culprit."*
After a ride of a mile or so, "Old Ton-ka-way Henry"
was discovered to be the guilty hunter, and he was told in
Indian jargon—the only way we had of making ourselves
known to them—"Mackenzie heap want Henly!" "Mebbe
so catch 'Big Chief'," etc. The old fellow refused, however, to understand, and would not go in to the column.
The Adjutant, not wishing to go back empty handed, after
exhausting all of his persuasive power but without avail,
seized the pony's bridle, with the intention of leading him
in. Instantly, in a rage at the prospect of being dragged
in, the Old Ton-ka-way sought his carbine, while the Adjutant reached for his six-shooter. It began to look serious
owing to the difference in our "Mother tongues," and, in
the midst of the mix up, the pony's bridle gave way.
Finally, the writer, spurring his powerful horse, and seizing Henry by the shoulders, and plying the "quirt" to
his pony, the obstinate Indian was half dragged and
driven across the intervening space to the head of the
column where, upon arriving, a glance at his woe-begone
face at once started a half suppressed shout of laughter
from all in the command. Henry was *good* after that.
The heat was almost unendurable; there were no sun
strokes or heat prostrations, however, as every man was
compelled to have a wet sponge in his hat, and an extra
canteen of water to keep it moistened. But it was with a
great sigh of relief that we halted in the afternoon and
went into camp in a wide valley or canon, everywhere
surrounded by high gypsum bluffs, which rose about us in
stately magnificence. The bluffs, with here and there a
detached mound, butte or dome, with contrasting colors,
presented the widest variety of most curious shapes, closely resembling monuments, vases, urns, and spires or col-
onnades. As we left the endless monotony of the surrounding plain and descended into the gorge or canon by rough
and precipitious paths, we saw gurgling from the cone-like

apertures, clear, cold, crystalline streams, and near them
gypsum of every form and variety. Much of it was in
the form of clear, translucent blocks of selenite which we
picked up and carried back to Fort R— where they did
service as paper weights and table ornaments. It is said
that where the cleavage is perfect it has been used for
window glass by the Mexicans. The gypsum, cropping out
of the red marl of the bluffs, and the conical mounds of
different colored earths, seemed to be of every hue, from
the pure white of the selenite, with foliated structure,
through every shade of pink and rose to a dark ox-blood
red, and the pale shades of apple and sea green. Early
in the morning, as the rays of the sun caught upon the
outcropping mineral, in its native purity, it certainly presented the most beautiful sight that we had yet seen in this
wild Gypsum Belt of Texas. The cliffs seemed to be transformed as by magic into solid masses or mountains of silver, dazzling the eye by the brilliancy of their flashings.
Turn whichever way one might, that cañon of gypsum,
with all its ramifications, seemed to be the perfect embodi-
ment of the Arabian Nights Tale of our youthful reading,
and the inevitable production of Alladin's Wonderful
Lamp.

Here in this great solitude of nature we found our deepest study spread out before us, and gathered "Sermons
from the stones," "books from the running brooks," and
"God in everything." With all these evidences of an unseen, Divine power about us. In these magnificent temples
made with His hands, we gathered inspiration, and from
this self communion, added to that breadth of knowledge
and experience which come not in the life of every man,
even when traveled, fully educated and intellectually developed. There is lacking just this period and kind of
journey and travel to round out some men. A close communion with the innermost recesses of nature. Hardships,
dangers, privations and sacrifices—quiet conceits, remove
selfishness, filter the dross, purify and elevate, and make

all mankind akin. It has been said in ecclesiastical circles, and among churchmen and theologians that soldiers and sailors lack the true essence of religion in their makeup; or, at least they are not only not enthusiastic over religion and the salvation of one's soul, but are inclined towards atheism and infidelity. This is not true. Most professional soldiers and sailors are neither atheists nor infidels, and discard everything looking to a belief in annihilation or that "death ends all," always holding fast to the hope of a future and better life and the immortality of the soul with all it conveys. Yet, by such close contact with nature and "Mother Earth" and sleeping perhaps for years under the canopy of heaven and the myriads of Star or planetary worlds, which God in His Infinity and mystery of life has set in the firmament, they accept pretty largely the theory of the *God of Nature* and leave the mere theology of religion with all the various beliefs, creeds, etc., etc., to be taken care of by religious quacks and scientists who are lacking in their own service experience. Perhaps this is the belief of an agnostic. Leading up over the bluffs with difficulty and scrambling out upon the prairie, we were kept busy crossing many difficult breaks and arroyas. It had rained but once since May 19 on Salt Creek Prairie where we had found the bodies of Henry Warren's freighters almost covered with water and it was now August 29th. It began to rain at dark, but merely in a light drizzle, and only continued four hours. The peaks of Mts. Webster and Scott were discovered, and we concluded that the General, abandoning any further idea of trying to locate Kicking Bird, seeming now to be somewhat indifferent (this without our knowledge of the orders from the War Dept. which he then had in his pocket), had decided to work his way in by short marches to the supply train at Otter Creek, which proved to be the case. He was very close-mouthed and uncommunicative. Our camp was on the Salt Fork. The horses were giving out and on August 31st ten horses and 2 mules were abandoned. The gypsum

water, heat and constant wear and tear had been too much
for them.

The Mule Regulator—An Atrocious Deed

"Mike" Wright, a colored field-cook for Captain Wilcox,
and discharged soldier of the Ninth Cavalry, was reported
this day to have cut out his mule's tongue because he could
no longer carry him. Upon investigation it was found to
be true. He was immediately called, placed in arrest and
after receiving a severe reprimand from Mackenzie, which
had about as much effect upon him as bird shot against the
side of a battle-ship, he was told to report himself to the
officer of the guard in command of the rear guard, to
march afoot, under its charge into Otter Creek, a distance of over 20 miles, over sand hills and "Shin Oak."
Having been a soldier although reckless and known to be
somewhat of a straggler and desperado, it was never
dreamed that he would disobey the order, or do otherwise than to literally carry it out. "Mike" was sent to
the rear, went up to a recruit while the command halted
and casually said to him, "General Mackenzie has just sent
me to tell you that he wants your horse and that you are
to walk." Not quite understanding and somewhat
amazed, the man stared at the rascal, but the audacity
and refreshing coolness with which the message had been
delivered, completely disarmed and dismounted the recruit trooper, while "Mike" *deliberately mounted the
horse and started,* apparently, for the head of the column
to turn him over, but instead of doing so, rode him nearly
all day well out on the flank, just out of sight and reach
of the soldier, the officer of the guard and *also General M.*
before the trick was discovered, and the poor recruit rein-
stated. It is, perhaps, to add that "Mike" Wright, our
estimable (?) *mule regulator* and "Camp Striker," not
only covered the remaining distance afoot, and under close
guard, but spent the time of stay at our next camp either
"tied up" or "walking a ring" with a 30 pound log
nicely balanced on his shoulder, besides receiving a fur-

ther summary punishment for his atrocious crime. In a
desperate attempt to solve the servant problem, permission having been given me to employ him, I secured, a
year later, the services of this desperado as a cook. He
swaggered about my picket shack with a '45 strapped to
his hip. One night he invited all of his male cook friends
to a banquet. After appropriating all of my available
canned goods and sundry prune pies which he had made,
the crust of which could scarcely be cut with an axe, he
wound up in the early morning well "lit up" with a profound "jag," and going to Major J. K. Mizner's quarters,
threatened to *exterminate* him. He was reported to have
shot two men in cold blood when a soldier, but by some
miracle escaped punishment. Upon Major K's complaint,
Mackenzie directed me to notify the officer of the guard to
arrest and confine him in the guard house. "Mike," instinctively feeling by their near presence that he was
wanted for *"high crimes and misdemeanors,"* fled upon
their approach. The last ever seen of this terror of the
garrison of Fort Richardson was on the Fort Griffin road,
running like a deer, the guard far in the year, and "Mike"
occasionally turning in his flight to apply his thumb to his
nose to show his utter contempt for them and his absolute
disregard for the "law and order" which they represented. Boehm was sent into the supply camp to get forage for the command, while we remained in camp. On
Sept. 1, when we finally reached our old camp at Otter
Creek we found that General Grierson with the Tenth
Cavalry, had returned, gone into Fort Sill the day before,
leaving Captain Lewis H. Carpenter in command of their
camp. They had found the Kiowas, and acting as he supposed under the orders placing the two commands under
him. Grierson had slyly *anticipated* all of our plans and
wants by warning Kicking Bird of our approach and had
succeeded in safely stampeding him and his Indians into
the Fort Sill reservation. We were literally dumped into
the sage brush with tent flies, "dog" tents, few conven-

iences or comforts, and living practically on bread, bacon
and game.

Carpenter's Dinner—The Dessert

Mackenzie and the Adjutant rode over to Carpenter's
Camp to make an official call. He died a few years ago as
a Brig.-General, retired. He was a Philadelphian, was a
handsome man, and had a fine record.* It was a beautiful
camp in an open grove near the stream, and it had all of
the luxuries and comforts—in which we were most woefully lacking—including tents, arbors, kitchens, streets, and
convenient sinks or latrines. He invited us to dinner.
Mackenzie, after looking over this Tenth Cavalry "outfit,"
seemed to reluctantly consent after Carpenter had a second
time most cordially and urgently pressed the invitation.
Carpenter was certainly a "camp artist." Between two
new, clean, white wall tents, contrasting most cheerfully
with our old worn painted tent flies, a floor had been laid;
new, clean flies were stretched over it from the tents. A
table of clean, smooth boards was stretched on trestles
with a *real table cloth on it,* and *real, truly comfortable
camp chairs drawn up to the same.* We were seated with
a Chesterfeldian wave of Carpenter's hand, and a courteous: "Be seated gentlemen." A dapper "brunette" soldier waited on the table. The dinner was served on *real
dishes,* and in *courses,* from soup—fish out of the stream,
wild turkey, quail, and buffalo sweetbread entrees—down
to desert, and that was the piece de resistance. This consisted of *prune pie.* When the pie was served Mackenzie's
face was a study. It had been one of amusement and ill-
concealed astonishment all through the meal After we had

*Captain Louis H. Carpenter, Tenth U. S. Cavalry, was the officer who was sent out
from Fort Wallace, Kansas, in 1868 to the rescue of General George A. Forsythe
("Sandy") and his command of enlisted scouts who, for several days, had been besieged on a small island in the Arickaree Fork of the Republican River ("Beecher's
Island") by a large band of Cheyenne Indians under Roman Nose. Forsythe had
been hit three times and was desperately wounded. Lieutenant Beecher, Third U. S.
Infantry, had been killed, the surgeon (Moeers) mortally wounded and about fifty per
cent of the scouts either killed or wounded. The entire command was subsisting on
putrid horse flesh. It was a ride of 90 miles. "Jack" Stilwell, one of Forsythes most
trusty scouts, had crept through the Indian lines by night to report the disaster, and
Carpenter arrived just in time to drive off the Cheyennes and save the lives of the
survivors.

mounted our horses and were out of earshot of Carpenter's regal camp and well on our way to our own forlorn bivouac, this amusement took shape. Turning to the writer and snapping his amputated finger stumps with more than usual vigor, he emphatically exclaimed: "prune pie! Well, I'll be d—d! *and in the field;* what do you think of that?" One could hardly interpret his tone and manner as supreme disgust and contempt or simply astonishment at such a departure from custom when on an Indian Campaign. But certain it was that it made a most lasting impression upon him, for several times he would repeat: *"prune pie!" "prune pie!"* Well, I'll be ——!! What do you know about *that?"* until we reached our sage brush dump, unsaddled and resumed our normal conditions. He never forgot Carpenter's sumptuous dinner on Otter Creek, and in later years, his admiration for the man who could furnish prune pie with so much courtesy and true hospitality when out "gunning for Indians" never abated. I related this incident to Carpenter many years later much to his amusement.

One night during this stay at Otter Creek when all were sitting around the camp fire, old McCord, Chief of our Ton-ka-way scouts, came over and made a complaint to Mackenzie that Boehm (he called him "Bim") was holding back their rations of sugar, coffee, pork or bacon, flour, etc. "Mebbe so him. 'Bim,' he keep um short 'lations." Mackenzie listened closely and then said to the writer: "Send for Mr. Boehm and we will investigate this matter!" Knowing full well what B's statement would be and that it would prove in every way satisfactory. Upon his arrival the old Chief in his Indian pigeon jargon repeated his complaint. Boehm showed clearly, of course, his method for issuing rations to the entire band of "Tonks," explaining that when three days were issued and the Indians ran short of game and were hungry they would often eat the entire amount for breakfast, relying upon their luck on that day to kill a buffalo, a deer or some antelope.

This was repeated to McCord, but he could not be made to understand that an issue for three days must last for that period and not be eaten at one meal, and turning angrily to Mackenzie he said: "Oh, him 'Bim'—he heap lie; he heap go to h—l; him heap d—n——!!" All laughed except Boehm and McCord. But when Mackenzie told McCord that Boehm was "heap bueno" and that his Indians must make "lations" last three suns—holding up his fingers in groups of three and counting three times. So great was McCord's faith in the "Big Chief"—Mackenzie's sword and his promises, that he arose from the camp fire smiling—shook hands and said "how" to Boehm, and stalked off to his camp perfectly satisfied and contented.

Here we received a copy of a letter from Lawrie Tatum the Quaker Indian Agent at Fort Sill.

Fort Sill,
Office of the Kiowa Agency,
8 mo—12—1871.

Colonel Grierson:

Yesterday, the Ki-o-was brought in and delivered to me 38 good mules—some of them very good—and one horse, which, with two previously delivered, makes 41, the number required of them. I accepted them in full for the mules stolen by Sa-tan-ta and others in the recent raid."

"Kicking Bird, on behalf of the Ki-o-was said they intended to cease their raiding and follow the example of the Caddoes. They appeared to be sincere, and I hope it will continue. From what they said I suppose they are on the reservation near the West line. . . . The Indians said he (Mow-wi) had moved, and the water where they had camped had dried up. . . . I hope H. P. Jones learned from the Indians where he is and can give the necessary information. The ponies stolen from the Ki-o-was by the Sioux, and returned here to be delivered to them, have been turned over to them and Kicking Bird thinks it will have a very good impression."

Respectfully,
(Signed) Lawrie Tatum,
Indian Agent.

Copy respectfully furnished Colonel R. S. Mackenzie, Fourth Cavalry, for his information.

(Signed) B. H. Grierson,
Colonel 10th Cavalry Commanding.

Headquarters Troops in the Field
Otter Creek, Aug. 14, 1871.

Kicking Bird through the persuasive influence of the "Indian Ring" having suddenly became a *"good Indian,"* there was nothing to do but to go back to Texas, moving the command by slow marches to conserve the strength of our horses. Capt. McLaughlin messed with several of the "youngsters," forming quite a large mess. It has been surmised that all was not quite harmonious there. One day he came over to headquarters. After sitting sometime, dinner was announced. It was *very informal.* There was no style. We were camped in the sage brush, and our table was a rubber blanket or poncho; our chairs were cracker boxes. He seemed glad to accept our invitation to dine, and with a readiness rather unusual. The conversation lagged. Finally the bluff old soldier blurted out, "General, I am going to break up my mess!" "Why so?" was the inquiry. "Oh, I can't stand those youngsters any longer!" What's the matter?" "Well, they have got a notion that nothing is good to eat but what they themselves prefer, giving no consideration to anybody." "What do you mean?" Then the old man "ripped out." "For the past two months those people have had nothing but liver, kidneys, brains and *"buffalo frys,"* served up in every conceivable style for breakfast, dinner, lunch and supper. Every time I say a word, they reply, "Oh, General, come now, you'll learn to like them shortly; don't get mad over such trifles;" but McL. replied, "I haven't learned to like such stuff and never shall, and d—n me I am just going to leave them to their buffalo *'delicacies',"* and he stalked off to join another mess.

Major Mauck was now directed to proceed with all of the command except "C," "E" and "I" Troops to some point near Fort Griffin and establish a large grazing camp, and to continue the expedition later. On Sept. 6, therefore, we broke camp; the command separated, and headquarters with the above named troops and "C" company of the Eleventh Infantry, proceeded leisurely until we struck the old trail for Fort Richardson. We found the country had all been burned over, but there still remained enough grass for our small command by camping with judgment. There was, however, but little water and the prairie was baked hard with great wide cracks and fissures across our trail. Our old guide, Dozier, was a curious "Customer;" he had accompanied us on the entire trip without knowing any more about the country after he had gone about 30 miles from Fort R— near which he had a ranch, than our junior sub-altern or a "camp striker." He was, nevertheless, a good, wholesouled, old fellow; hard working, brave and conscientious. He had been driven from his own ranch into Jacksboro, and had been engaged in a number of skirmishes with the Indians, and was with Captain McClellan's command of the Sixth Cavalry when he had his desperate fight with Kicking Bird's band in 1869, near where we were now marching and in which he showed great gallantry. Henrietta on the Little Wichita was burned at that period. His remarks were dry and original; his stories had the peculiar freshness and twang of all Western frontiersmen, and it was a novel treat at times, as we sat about the camp fire and listened to some of his quaint sayings, much to the amusement of Mackenzie with whom Dozier had become a great favorite, as had Horace P. Jones, the Comanche Interpreter at Fort Sill. Riding along one day at the head of the column, it being very hot and dry as usual, although a little overcast, the General said, "Well, Dozier, shall we have any rain to-day?" The old guide squirted at a stick over his horse's shoulder, spat out his dry quid, cocked his "weather eye" at the sky, and noticing the slight gathering of clouds, said, in a strong, nasal twang and with great deliberation, "Well, General, I shouldn't much wonder if we did have a *leetle chunk* of a sprinkling of a rain afore night." Our visibilities were at once started and it was all we could do to hold in, when the old man added, "But, I'm not so plum sure of it nohow," which capped the climax, and we went off with an explosion of laughter at such a choice "chunk" of wisdom, although in his innocence, he never mistrusted the cause, for we immediately "turned it off," and never referred to it afterward. We found the bridge at the Little Wichita intact, but at night we had scarcely rolled into our blankets (the writer slept with Mackenzie) before an intense itching and pinching sensation warned us that we had bivouacked directly upon an extensive ant heap in the semi-darkness and our clothes and bodies were completely alive with the little pests. We tried to brave it out, but finally concluded that the ant had indeed "come to the sluggard" and we would have to "pull up stakes"—which we did—shaking out all of our clothes, and found another spot and that priceless blessing, sleep.

Our night at old "Camp Wichita," near Buffalo Springs, among the ruins, proved spectral and gloomy, and glad indeed were we when morning broke, and the General announced that we would "cut loose" from the command and he, Dozier and the writer preceding it, were soon moving out for a 40 mile ride into the post. We arrived at 5:40 P. M. riding through a severe and drenching thunder storm, and were received with such a welcome as only soldiers and their families, on the extreme verge of civilization, know how to give one after a long six weeks absence.

The expedition from Aug. 1 to Sept. 1 had been a failure for reasons already given, much to Mackenzie's mortification and chagrin. He had planned to seek Kicking Bird's village and attack and punish him for the massacre of Salt Creek Prairie; to drive him in and compel him to keep on the reservation. On that days march from Otter Creek, when the courier overtook us with dispatches, and he was so agitated, was the beginning of a bitter disappointment which seemed to possess his soul and disturb his peace of mind. The writer was busy for several days making out maps, filling in his itinerary and making out reports. On the 19th we were again ordered to proceed to Fort Griffin and prepare for a new campaign, this time against the wild Comanches of the "Staked Plains." Mackenzie had been completely foiled by the machinations and plots of the "Indian Ring" in Washington, and the "double cross" methods of an over zealous Colonel of the brand which that Ring relied upon to block the game, and for the political or military preferment he could secure by such work. The Tenth Cavalry laughed over it, declaring that it was not a "trick," but a "pardonable joke."

The next year (1872), the writer saw Kicking Bird and all of his Sub-Chiefs at a big Council in the Agency Building on the Fort Sill reservation. Two years later he was poisoned by the enemies surrounding him who were jealous of his fast growing friendship and power with the whites.

R.G. Carter, Captain U.S. Army, Ret'd.
Formerly Fourth U.S. Cavalry –

CHAPTER VII

TRAGEDIES OF CANON BLANCO

The Texas Panhandle

IT IS more than sixty years since these tragedies occurred. There are few survivors. The writer is, perhaps, the only one. This is written in the vague hope that this chronicle of the events of that period may possibly prove of some lasting and, perhaps, historical value to posterity.

The country all about the scene of these tragical events —the Texas Panhandle—was then wild, unsettled, covered with sage brush, scrub oak and chaparral, and its only inhabitants were Indians, buffalo, lobo wolves, coyotes, jack-rabbits, prairie-dogs and rattlesnakes, with here and there a few scattered herds of antelope. As cited in the preface, the railroad, that great civilizing agency, the telegraph, the telephone, the radio and airplane, and the many other marvelous inventions of man, have wrought such a wonderful transformation in our great western country that the American Indian will, if he has not already, become a race of the past, and history alone will record the remarkable deeds and strange career of an almost extinct people. With these miraculous changes has come the total extermination of the buffalo—the Indians' migratory companion and source of living—and pretty much all of the wild game that in almost countless numbers freely roamed those vast prairies. Where now the railroads girdle that country the nomadic redman lived his free and careless life and the bison thrived and roamed undisturbed at that period— where are now the appliances of modern civilization, and prosperous communities, then nothing but desolation reigned for many miles around.* It was, indeed, a most

---

*Extermination of the buffalo, absolute defeat of the Indians and their control on the reservations, an orderly, organized settlement resulting in the laying out of towns, the establishment of schools, churches, libraries, etc., driven wells for a permanent water supply, a well-regulated system of irrigation—all these factors have effected this wonderful transformation. But, subduing the Indians, most difficult problem of all, was of the first importance to solve, and our little Regular Army solved it.

149

desolate land! In the expansion and peopling of this vast country, our little Army was most closely identified. There is no exaggeration in the chapter—"Winners of the West." In fact, it was the pioneer of civilization. The life was full of danger, hardships, privations and sacrifices, little known or appreciated by the present generation. Our only water was obtained from the buffalo wallow-holes—stagnant, warm and nauseating, odorous with smells, and covered with a green slime which had to be pushed aside—or from the Brazos River, the Double Mountain Fork of the Brazos, and their many small tributaries, all strongly impregnated with gypsum, which was but a trifle better. The Indians carried all of the water they used, in crossing the Staked Plains, in buffalo paunches packed upon the mules.

Where populous towns, ranches and well-tilled farms, grain fields, orchards and oil "gushers" are now located, with railroads either running through or near them, we were making trails, upon which the main roads now run, in search of hostile savages, for the purpose of punishing them or compelling them to go into the Indian reservations, and to permit the settlers, then held back by the murderous acts of these redskins, to advance and spread the civilization of the white man throughout the western tiers of counties in that far-off western panhandle of Texas.

THE OLD MACKENZIE TRAIL*

Stretching onward toward the sunset,
    O'er prairie, hill and vale,
Far beyond the Double Mountains
    Winds the old Mackenzie Trail.
Ah, what thoughts and border memories
    Does that dreaming trail suggest;
Thoughts of travelers gone forever
    To the twilight realms of rest.

---

*This and other poems are by Wm. Lawrence Chittenden, the "Texas Poet" of Anson, Texas, taken from "Ranch Verses." published by G. P. Putnam's Sons, 1893, 6th ed., 1900. They were given me by Mrs. Walker, of Belton, Tex., whose son, Walton H. Walker, was a cadet at West Point in 1909. She seemed to be very familiar with many events included in these pages.

Where are now the scouts and soldiers,
　And those wagon-trains of care,
Those grim men and haggard women?
　And the echoes whisper—Where?
Ah, what tales of joys and sorrows
　Could that silent trail relate:
Tales of loss, and wrecked ambitions,
　Tales of hope, of love, and hate;
Tales of hunger, thirst, and anguish,
　Tales of skulking Indian braves,
Tales of fear, and death, and danger,
　Tales of lonely prairie graves.
Where are now that trail's processions
　Winding westward sure and slow?
Lost! Ah, yes; destroyed by progress,
　Gone to realms of long ago.
Nevermore shall bold Mackenzie,
　With his brave and dauntless band,
Guide the restless, roving settlers
　Through the Texas borderland.
Yes! that soldiers' work is over,
　And the dim trail rests at last;
But his name and trail still lead us
　Through the borders of the past.

This is cited to show how the efforts of our gallant and hard-toiling little Regular Army of that period in aid of that far-off, wild, unsettled country—then absolutely closed tight to the white man—has borne fruit. But, alas! how little credit for standing as a bulwark for such a civilization and achieving such astonishing changes has been given to the men who accomplished it.

Cañon Blanco

Cañon Blanco in northwestern Texas, the so-called Texas Panhandle, extends through parts of three counties— Crosby, Floyd and Hale. Through it flows a small quicksand stream called Catfish Creek, and sometimes the canon itself has been called Catfish Cañon The butte at the mouth of the canon, where the creek joins the Freshwater Fork of the Brazos, was where two of these tragedies occurred.

Near here are the small towns of Blanco, Palo Duro, Floydada to the north, McAdoo a few miles east, and to the northwest, on the A. T. & S. F. system, are Canyon and Happy, while almost due north and about twelve miles from the Tule "Canon," which was an old Indian hiding place, is the considerable town or city of Amarillo in Potter County, at the junction of the C. R. I. & G., P. & S. F., and A. T. & S. F. systems. This town has not only been a rich and productive wheat center, millions of dollars' worth having been marketed annually, but it and the surrounding country to the south and southeast has become one of the greatest oil centers of the United States, if not of the world, the Ranger and Burkburnett fields during recent oil booms having made many millionaires, besides wrecking many would-be speculators.

In Cañon Blanco, Tule "Cañon," Quit-a-Que (*Keet-a-Kay*), and about the headwaters of the Pease River, there had dwelt for many years a nomadic band of savages, known as the Qua-ha-da Comanches (taken from Comanche-Kwaina, signifying "vagrant"). They were the implacable enemies of the whites, and this hatred had been handed down for many years.

The Comanches

The Comanches are divided into several bands the same as the Sioux, each band owing allegiance to and bearing social, economic and political relations to the tribe proper. There were the Cost-che-teght-kas (or buffalo eaters), the Pen-e-teght-kas (or honey eaters), the No-ko-nees (or wanderers), the Yam-per-i-cos (or root diggers), and last came the Qua-ha-das of the Staked Plains ("Llano Estacado"), the Chatz-ken-ners (or antelope users). The three first bands, broken up, are Moo-chas (or "Crooked Mountain" band), the Ten-na-was (or "Liver-eaters") and Tea-chatz-ken-nas (or "Servers"). The middle Comanches were the Yam-per-i-cos, and the southern Comanches were the Comanches proper*

This story deals entirely with the Qua-ha-da band, the famous Chatz-ken-nas, or antelope-users, of the Staked Plains. This band had, for many years, been isolated from the tribe, having refused to enter into the "Medicine Lodge" Treaty of 1867, by which the Comanches, Ki-o-wa, Apache, Cheyenne, and Arapahos were assigned to reservations, and until 1875, four years after this tragedy, were roaming outside of any designated reservation or abiding place. They were free-lances in a partially civilized region. Everything was open to their bloody and frequent incursions.

In 1836 the principal war chief of the Qua-ha-das was Peta Nacona (the "Wanderer"). It was then the wildest and most hostile band of the Comanche tribe, and the most inveterate raiders on the Texas border.

Parker's Fort—The Romance of Quanah

On May 9, 1836, a few days after the battle of San Ja-

---

*This information was given the writer in April, 1872, by Horace P. Jones, the post interpreter of Fort Sill, Indian Territory (now Oklahoma), who died a few years ago— a most intelligent, reliable, and valuable man. He was adopted by the Comanches; knew their language, both spoken and sign, and spoke it fluently; was often the only white man permitted to live in their villages for months at a time. He married a Comanche girl. He told the writer that these Indians had no knowledge whatever, either in the way of written history or other sources, of their origin, their language, rites, customs, ceremonies, religion, etc. What they knew, and this in a rather fragmentary, disjointed way, was from legends handed down from one generation to another, from made pictographs illustrating their war scenes, early ceremonies, etc. In collaboration with an officer of the Tenth Cavalry, Lieutenant Charles R. Ward, they began a Comanche dictionary that year (1872). But the work was abandoned; at least, the writer has never heard of its publication. The Agency Interpreter, Matthew Leeper, Jr., son of a former Indian agent at the old Camp Cobb Comanche reservation, who grew up and played with the Indian children, became an officer of the Fourth Cavalry, and years later an A. A. Surgeon in the Spanish-American War, now dead, also gave the writer much valuable information. Acting Assistant Surgeon, John M. Feeney, U.S.A., informed the writer in Washington, July 11, 1904, that he went to the Philippine Islands in 1899. While there he frequently heard an old packer from Arizona, by the name of Oynor, still there in 1904, say that he had been able to make himself understood by the Igorrotes and Maccabeebes in the Indian sign language which he (Rynor) had learned in Arizona and Texas. If this is true—and it has been substantiated by others—the ethnologists of this country, in their efforts to solve the origin of our North American Indians, can have little doubt with that as a basis. The Ki-o-was and Comanches told Horace P. Jones, the post interpreter at Fort Sill, that their ancestors had declared in their legendary lore, that their forefathers had come from the far North *on sledges* drawn by dogs, and when they reached the prairie country they had caught up the mustangs or wild horses and then became pony or foot ("dog soldiers") Indians. The Ki-o-was resemble very closely the Maccabeebes of the Philippine Islands in their color, shape of face, and in many other characteristics, except size being larger. It is possible that at some period these Malay tribes, who were fishermen, drifted from island to island, some becoming castaways, and came across Bering Straits, landing upon this continent; came south on sledges, caught the mustangs and then through climatic influences and environment grew larger in stature.

Captain Feeney said that his statement could be substantiated by Captain Augustus C. Macomb, Fifth U. S. Cavalry (now Colonel, U.S.A., retired).

cinto was fought, these Indians, under Nacona, raided
Parkers Fort, situated at the headquaters of Navasota
Creek—a tributary of the Brazos—near where the town
of that name is now located, sixty miles from the nearest
white settlement, and two miles from the present town of
Groesbeck, Limestone County, Texas. The post was occupied by six men and several women and children. The Indians shrewdly presented a white flag, and sent some of
their number to the post to say they were friendly.

One of the inmates, Benjamin Parker (who was the
father of Cynthia Ann Parker and the grandfather of
Chief Quanah Parker), let them enter the fort, believing
that they were friendly Indians and wanted to make a
treaty with the whites, but when he was within their power
they treacherously attacked and killed him and immediately
captured the fort.

It was a stockade fort, occupied by several families who
had just returned from the flight before the Mexican army,
commanded by General Santa Ana. After effecting an entrance into Parkers Fort by pretending to be friendly, the
Indians massacred all the men and some of the women and
children, carrying away captive Mrs. Plummer and her
son, two years old; Mrs. Kellogg; Cynthia Ann Parker,
then nine years old, and her brother, aged six. After leaving the fort the Comanches and Kiowas traveled together
until midnight. They then camped, brought their prisoners
together, tied their hands behind them so tightly as to cut
the flesh, tied their feet together, and threw them on their
faces; then gathered around with the bloody scalps they
had taken at the fort and commenced their war dance.
They danced, screamed, yelled, and stamped upon the prisoners, beating them with bows until the blood flowed from
their bruises, and the rest of the night the women had to
listen to the cries and groans of the little children. When
the tribes parted each of the bands took a captive.

Cynthia Ann Parker was claimed by the Comanche tribe,
and became their permanent captive. Nothing was heard

from her for many years, but in the meantime her relatives and friends and the Texas authorities did everything in their power to ascertain her fate and secure her release by ransom, if she was living.

In the autumn of 1860 the Comanches, in force under their chief, Peta Nocona, the father of Quanah Parker and the Indian husband of Cynthia Ann, raided through Parker and adjoining counties and inflicted great distress upon the white settlements.

But in December he was followed and surprised in his own camp on Pease River by a force of forty Texas Rangers and twenty dragoons of the Regular Army, in all sixty soldiers, under Captain Rose, of the Rangers. His camp was captured and many slain. The chief fled at full speed, with another Indian behind him on the same horse, and his wife, with an infant in her arms, on a fleet pony beside him. The captain of the Rangers, with one attendant, pursued. They soon overtook the chief's wife, who held up her child and stopped. Leaving her with his attendant, the captain pursued the two Indians on one horse, and, coming up with them, fired with his heavy revolving pistol, killing the hindmost. The same ball would have also killed the chief, but his shield hanging on his back prevented. The hindmost, in falling, dragged the chief from his horse, but he lit upon his feet and plied his pursuers with arrows, wounding his horse. The wound set the animal to rearing and plunging so violently that the ranger could not aim his weapon. Victory in the single combat seemed on the point of declaring for the savage. His well-directed arrows were sent rapidly; but a random shot from the Ranger broke his right arm and disabled him, both hands being indispensable to the use of the bow. The captain's horse becoming quiet, he shot the chief twice through the body, who then walked deliberately to a tree near by and, leaning against it, began to sing a wild, wierd song—the death song of his tribe, a custom in many tribes in the presence of certain death.

The captain's men coming up with an interpreter, the chief was summoned to surrender, but he answered by a savage thrust at the captain with his lance held in his left hand. It was plain that he would surrender only to death. The captain directed one of his attendants to "finish him," and the death song ended. The Indian who had been riding behind the chief proved to be a young female, but her sex was not distinguished in the flight, because she was covered with a buffalo robe with only the head visible. The woman taken with the child, the fallen chief's wife, was seen to be a white woman, and she had blue eyes. She wept incessantly and the captain directed the interpreter to tell her that they recognized her as one of their own nation and would not hurt her. She replied that she was not weeping for herself, but for her two boys, who were in the battle, and, she feared, were slain. She was sent to the white settlement, where she was speedily identified as Cynthia Ann Parker, who was captured when nine years old by the Comanches at Parkers Fort massacre in 1836. She was not reconciled to civilization, and had to be watched to prevent her escape. Her little child, named Prairie Flower, died, and in less than two years she died also and was laid beside her little barbarian. Of her sons, one died on the plains, but the other lived and became the famous chief, Quanah Parker.

This battle ground was but about twenty miles above the town of Vernon, on Pease River, at the mouth of Mule Creek and in Foard County, Texas.

There have been many wild newspaper stories and legends concerning the capture of Cynthia Ann Parker. One was that she was taken in 1790 on the banks of the Scioto River, near the present site of Chillicothe, Ohio, and that her parents were from Virginia, etc.

The story, as the writer relates it, is not only official but absolutely reliable, coming as it does from the gallant Ranger, who afterwards became a brigadier-general in the Confederate Army, and subsequently governor of the State of Texas. He died some fifteen or eighteen years ago, universally beloved by all Texans. While serving as governor he gave to Hon. John H. Stephens, M. C., all the particulars regarding her capture.

Quanah himself knew but little about the early life of his mother, or when and where she was captured.

Quanah was born about 1845. He grew up with the Qua-ha-da band, and on the death of his father, Nacona, rapidly rose to more or less commanding influence as principal war chief of that band, as well as in the Comanche tribe.

In 1871 the band was still out under Quanah, moving about from place to place, but generally near the headwaters of Pease River, their old stamping ground, the Palo Duro Cañon, in Cañon Blanco, and near the mouth of Mc-Clellan's Creek, a small tributary of the north fork of the Red River, although he was associated in these raids, reports of which were constantly reaching us, with Mow-wi (the "Handshaker") and Para-a-coom ("He Bear"), both subchiefs of the Qua-ha-da band.

After having accomplished this duty of stampeding Kicking Bird into Fort Sill, and hearing that the Comanches had been raiding down the country again, and had already secured many horses and cattle, and, as rumor had it, killed some people and captured women and children, among them a child five years of age, Mackenzie determined to pay his attention now to the Indians of the Texas Panhandle in their fastnesses, the breaks and small cañons of the "Staked Plains."

Camp Cooper—The Rendezvous

On September 19 therefore, we left Fort Richardson again for a new campaign. We concentrated and reorganized at old Camp Cooper on Ketumseh's Creek, a small tributary of the Clear Fork of the Brazos, about five miles from Fort Griffin, Texas. General Robert E. Lee built this post some years before the Civil War, and occupied it for some time. General John B. Hood and other generals in the Confed-

erate Army, saw their first service here. It was a former
reservation for the southern Comanches, and, at this period, was in ruins. On August 12, Lawrie Tatum, the
Quaker Indian agent at Fort Sill, wrote General Grierson
as follows: "I should be very glad indeed if thee and
General Mackenzie could get that little captive, and induce
Mow-way (Mow-wi) and his band to come into the reservation and behave . . . Mow-way does not appear likely to
bring in that poor little captive child of his own volition
. . . I did not get a definite idea of where Mow-way is."
. . . A copy of this letter was furnished to General Mackenzie, who then determined to definitely locate the Qua-
ha-das, punish them, and, if possible, bring in the child.

On September 25, eight (8) companies (or troops) of the
Fourth Cavalry (A, B, D, F, G, H, K and L), and two (2)
companies of the Eleventh Infantry (F and I), with about
twenty Ton-ka-way scouts, were in camp near Fort Griffin.
On that night a big band of Indians came in to Murphy's
ranch, about twenty miles from the post, and, it was reported, ran off a herd of one hundred and twenty cattle
and thirteen horses and two citizens, Stockton and James,
part owners of this stock, joined us at our camp, ready to
take up the trail of their animals, assist in punishing these
depredators and murdering thieves, and to identify, if possible, their brands, if secured. General Mackenzie had not
then arrived, and the settlers showed signs of anger at
Capt Wirt Davis, commanding camp, because. he would not
order out the command at once and take up the trail But
he had positive orders from Mackenzie to remain at this
camp resting the men and animals. Up to this period the
writer had been field adjutant and a general *"Pooh Bah"*
of the command—topographical engineer, etc.—but was
now attached, first to "K" Troop (his own troop having
been left at Fort Richardson), and later to "B" Troop
for duty, and to command it, as Captain Clarence Mauck
of that troop now commanded the squadron, then composed of two troops.

On the morning of September 30 the writer was ordered to take eight men and five "Tonk" trailers or scouts, proceed up the Clear Fork, and select a good camp for the command and some kind of a practicable road for the wagon train. Upon his return, on October 3, we moved out. The writer rode at the head of the column, directing the scouts in advance, and guiding it over the trail he had made to the bend of the stream.

The March for the "Panhandle"—The "Double Mountain" Fork—A "Close Shave"

We left our bivouac on the beautiful bend of the Clear Fork the next morning with about six hundred men and nearly one hundred pack mules, all in fine condition, although the horses were somewhat thin and worn by their long campaign since May. The Indian scouts, our faithful "Tonks," under Lieutenant P. M. Boehm, were far in advance, well fanned out, combing the country for trails, with a selected advance guard in close support if necessary, and to guard against surprise. All were cheerful, and our old song rang out, "Come home, John, don't stay long; Come home soon to your own Chick-a-biddy!" California and Paint Creeks, both quicksand streams, with rather steep banks and no regular fords, were crossed. Plenty of buffalo and antelope were seen on the flanks, but no hunting was now permitted. Other and different game was our objective. Mackenzie sent the writer to the rear several times to assist Lawton, our newly joined Regimental Quartermaster, in crossing these creeks and numerous "sloughs" or "arroyos," saying: "You men of the Civil War have had more experience in that work, in "speeding up" wagon trains, than my other and younger officers, and if you and Lawton can't make time I don't know who can."

Our next camp was but a few miles from the Double Mountains, which were in plain sight. Marching early the next morning we crossed the Double Mountain Fork of the Brazos, and at night camped near "Flat Top," or "Cot-

tonwood Springs.'' Here we found the vilest water, but
excellent grazing for the animals. We saw immense herds
of buffalo all day, and at night we were literally in their
midst, for they only moved off a mile or two for our ac-
commodation, and to avoid the scent of our command
coming down the wind. Only enough were killed to furnish
fresh meat for the entire command, as was our custom.
The writer was in charge of the guard that night. This included herd guards, ''sleeping parties,'' all camp guards
and picket outposts. Preparatory to midnight inspection
of all the posts, he lay down in a buffalo robe near the sergeant in charge of the picket reserve, to protect himself
from a cold wind that had now increased to a stiff gale,
making it difficult to hear any sounds outside the camp.
Suddenly, however, he heard above the din of the gale a
tremendous tramping and an unmistakable snorting and
bellowing. Placing his ear to the ground, he could hear it
plainer, and this time there was a heavy jarring. Throwing off his robe, he could distinctly see coming through the
darkness an immense, black, moving mass, which he knew
at once were the herds of buffalo. They were making directly for the reserve and our horse herds which had inad-
vertently been staked or lariated directly across the paths
or water trails leading to their usual drinking holes. There
was no time to lose, even to alarm the sleeping camp. The
writer did not dare to fire upon them to break the heads of
the herds, as that might alarm and also stampede the
horses, and besides orders had been given that no shots
should be fired now that we were in the enemy's country.
He jumped to his feet, shouted to the sergeant to rout out
his guard, and to carry their blankets forward and, by
meeting the mass, waving them, and yelling, to try and
turn them aside. The men acted promptly and effectively.
The immense herds of brown monsters were caromed off
and they stampeded to our left at breakneck speed, rushing and jostling, but flushing only the edge of one of our
horse herds, and were soon crowding down the banks to

the flats below, thundering off in the black gloom of night
with a noise that aroused every sleeper in camp, who supposed for a moment that our horses had broken away from
their lariats and had gone. As we watched their grotesque
shadows and brown masses troop off in the darkness in
countless hundreds, with a noise like the mighty rumbling
of thunder, making the ground fairly tremble with their
tramping, one could hardly repress a shudder at what
might have been the result of this nocturnal visit, for although the horses were strongly "lariated out," "staked"
or "picketed," nothing could have saved them from the
terror which this headlong charge would have inevitably
created, had we not heard them just in time to turn the
leading herds. It was a close shave, and might have
proved a sad disaster.

Duck Creek—The Unsuccessful Scout

Moving early we reached Duck Creek—no water on the
road and our trail was mostly over a rolling prairie thinly covered with mesquite, but thickly covered with dog
towns, populated by prairie-dogs, and immense herds of
buffalo as far as the eye could reach. The water in the
creek was clear, contained in large waterholes, all impregnated with gypsum, an improvement, however, over the
last camp. We discovered this day the trading stations
of the Mexicans with the Indians, consisting of curiously
built caves in the high banks or bluffs, the earth being
propper up or kept in place by a framework of poles, giving these subterranean abodes the appearance of grated
prison doors or windows, reminding us of the cave dwellers of Arizona and New Mexico. These trading stations
were now abandoned. At night, after much persuasion,
the "Tonks" were sent out to find, if possible, any signs
of the Comanche villages, it being Mackenzie's intention,
as soon as they, the "Tonks" returned, to make a night
march and surprise the enemy. Our Indian scouts were
very timid when sent out in a new country without an

escort or supporting column, for fear our own men might mistake them for hostiles, before they could be recognized, especially at night, and fire upon them.

Night March in the "Bad Lands" for a Surprise—The Barrier

Here we located our supply camp from which we could load the pack mules for mobility and quick movements in any direction, the two infantry companies to be left as a sufficient guard, and Lawton to control the supplies. Here the writer was directed to take a small detachment and scout to the head of the creek to reconnoiter for signs and, if possible, strike the trail of our "Tonks." It proved unsuccessful as our route was too far to the east. Upon our return the same day, Mackenzie announced his intention to strike out that night and make a quick march to surprise the hostiles. The wagons were therefore corraled or parked, the mules packed, and, without waiting for the return of the "Tonks," and under cover of darkness— about 7:00 p. m.—leaving our cook fires to deceive the enemy, we started. We had a pack train of about 90 mules.

After many trials, tribulations, and much hard talk verging upon profanity, and many bruises, we all brought up at midnight in a small box cañon or break, against the high and rocky face of an impassible wall, which, in the inky blackness of a starless and moonless night, we could not see our way clear to scale, and unable to find any way out, after many rather comical scenes, floundering among the ravines and arroyas forming this barrier, we bivouacked without fires until morning, the heels of the pack mules sharply defining our limits, and the companies hardly moving from column as they halted, for fear of inexticable confusion and injury by accident. Cold "snacks" were all we could obtain for "eats." At daybreak, or just before it was fairly light, we moved by a flank around the obstacle in the impenetrable darkness, which precipitous bluffs we found too steep to climb, and after a rapid and hard march over rough country of about five hours we eached the Freshwater Fork of the Brazos River about 9:30 a. m., the objective we ought to have gained at daylight. To our surprise the water was really fresh, and its name was not misleading. We unsaddled, built fires, and ate breakfast. Until now no signs of the missing Ton-ka-ways had been discovered; nothing was known thus far but what our march had been a success. Lieutenant Boehm recognized the spot as being near where Captain Carrol of the Ninth Cavalry and he had had a fight with this same band of Comanches the year before. A hasty reconnoissance revealed the brush huts or "wickey-ups," and remnants of lodges or "tepees" could be seen on high ground near the stream and to our left. In the early afternoon a squadron under Captain E. M. Heyl was sent out on a reconnoissance, while the balance of the command rested after their hard struggle of the previous night.

The "Tonks" Discover the Comanches

The "Tonk" scouts soon espied our column and came in, but while hastening along some ravines, on high ground, ran rather unexpectedly upon four Comanches, also busily intent upon watching our reconnoitering squadron, and our "surprise" (?) column. The "Tonks" gave chase, which, for a time, proved quite exciting, but the hostiles being better mounted soon distanced their pursuers and vanished into the hills. The scouts all looked the worse for wear, being fagged out, dirty, and with scalp-locks looking touzled and tangled. Having been without sleep or food since leaving our camp on Duck Creek, they were nearly famished and as ravenous as wolves.

They reported their belief in having discovered the trail leading to the Qua-ha-da village. At three p. m. the writer was detailed as officer-of-the-day, and immediately after the short ceremony of guard mount, word was passed along—"boots and saddle" never being sounded in an Indian country—for the command to "pack up." The column was soon in motion, and with a strong guard the writer followed in the rear with the entire pack train. The Fresh Fork was full of quicksands, and in crossing the train a number of the animals "bogged," which, fortunately, we got out upon dry land very soon, but not without hard work, and were just congratulating ourselves when, after marching about 2 miles, a shot was heard, and then another, either at the head of the column, or of the pack train, now strung out at some length.

The main column was alarmed. Mackenzie came galloping to the rear, and with some excitement inquired where the shots came from, fearing that Captain Mauck's squadron, which had been sent back to the camp we had left, as a "blind," had been attacked. Without waiting to learn the cause of the shots, he directed the writer to ride at a gallop to the head of the column and tell Captain Wirt Davis to countermarch the command, and move it rapidly to the rear. Mackenzie, upon meeting it, however, after having ascertained that a careless soldier of the rear guard had discharged his piece, caused it to move to the front again. Much valuable time had been thus lost. The country was rough with some foothills and small arroyas. Frequent halts were made and it was nearly dark before the command was straightened out and ready to go into camp.

The absent squadron was sent for, and under the shadow of some abrupt hills, scarcely one hundred yards from the stream, we went into bivouac. It was a "pocket valley." The horses were "staked out" with "cross side lines," picket pins securely driven, and the men allowed to make small fires, which, in the writer's judgment, was a grave error, as will be seen. The missing squadron came in after dark, and, not finding much room, crowded pretty close to the rear company, the horses being somewhat huddled upon their grazing ground—another unfortunate error.

We were in a narrow pocket, with a line of small bluffs or foothills close to us on one side, and a treacherous quicksand stream on the other, with a wily enemy always to be accounted for—an excellent camp in time of peace, or even an ideal theoretical camp in time of war—*provided no Indians were about.*

The Midnight Alarm and Attack—"Hell Breaks Loose!"

The pickets were posted by the writer, the necessary instructions were given, and, without taking his pistol off, loosening his belt, or removing his boots, but uncoiling his lariat and driving his picket pin close to his hand so that he could quickly seize it, his horse remaining saddled (the only one in the command), he lay down until time to inspect the posts. Nearby were Lieutenants P. M. Boehm and W. A. Thompson, and the two cattlemen, Stockton and James, already referred to, who were accompanying us to recover their stock.

It had been a most eventful day. Our thoughts were of the exciting incidents of the night march, the march at early dawn; reaching the Fresh Fork; the chase of the four Comanches by our scouts; the shot and rapid countermarch—but especially the poor camp we were now in. It was, in fact, a rapid review of this day's events, and we all made our comments.

It drew near midnight. All was still except the night noises of the horse herds grazing at the end of their lariats The fires which had been allowed (an error of indulgence to the men), and a few slumbering embers of the one nearest to us flashed up, sparkled and died down, and all was dark, almost inky darkness, when suddenly a yell, followed by a shot, rang down the valley; then a succession of unearthly, blood-curdling yells, a dozen shots in quick succession, one after the other, a rush, and, in an instant, our whole camp was aroused.

The camp was attacked! The rapid flashes of the carbines and pistols from the rear squadron, now in action, showed us, at intervals, that the ridge, or line of small

foothills which skirted our entire camp, was alive with
wild Indians, riding by at full speed, shaking dried buffalo
robes (raw hides), ringing bells, yelling like wild demons,
and by every other possible device trying to stampede our
animals.   The answering whoops of our Ton-ka-ways and
the loud bangs of carbines, with the shouts of the men,
could now be heard, mingled with the hoarse commands of
the officers, ''Get to your horses!''   For a few moments
all was uproar and confusion, but above all this din of
arms, yells, whoops of Indians and shouts of soldiers came
another sound, like the rumbling of heavy thunder, never
to be mistaken when once heard by a cavalry command,
which told us all too surely but sadly that all of our horses
were stampeding.   Upon them was staked almost our very
existence in this far-off wilderness.   Unless checked, their
total loss seemed inevitable.   Now came the loud commands: ''Every man to his lariat!''   ''Stand by your
horses!''—heard amidst all the tumult.

The scene beggars all description by tongue or pen.
There was no ''artist on the spot!''   At every flash the
horses and mules, nearly six hundred in number, could be
seen rearing, jumping, plunging, running and snorting,
with a strength that terror and brute frenzy alone can inspire.   They trembled and groaned in their crazed fright,
until they went down on their knees, straining all the time
to free themselves from their lariats.   As they plunged
and became inextricably intermingled and more and more
tangled up, the lariats could be heard snapping and crackling like the reports of pistols.   Iron picket pins were
hurtling, swishing and whistling, more dangerous than bullets.   Men, crouching as they ran, vainly endeavored to
seize the pins as they whirled and tore through the air,
only to be dragged and thrown among the heels of the
horses with hands lacerated and burnt by the ropes running rapidly through their fingers.   To one who has never
seen or heard a night stampede of horses, mules, or of
buffalo such a description would give no adequate conception of this midnight debacle.   This was tragedy number
one of Canyon Blanco.

The herds thundered off in the distance; the men secured all they could.

The hissing and spitting of the bullets sounded viciously, and the yells of the retreating Indians from the distance came back on the midnight air with a peculiar, taunting ring, telling all too plainly that the Qua-ha-das, Quanah's wild band of Comanches, had been among us.

We found them at last! Or, at least, *they had found us!* The tangled masses of horses, lariats, picket pins, and side lines were straightened out in the darkness as well as conditions would permit, and firing parties were thrown forward to the crest of the ridge. The busy hum of many tongues, all intent upon relating the adventures of this nocturnal visitation, sounded strangely upon the crisp midnight air.

Confusion gradually subsided; every endeavor was made to ascertain our losses in men, horses, etc. Companies were being hastily formed. The horses could only be saddled in the darkness by one man holding his struggling and thoroughly terror-stricken brute, while another man adjusted the saddle and bridled him (no easy task), and until the gray of morning a sharp watch was kept to guard against another stampede.

It was ascertained that about seventy of our best horses and mules were gone, this loss falling principally upon "G" and "K" troops, as the Indians struck their flank first. It is doubtful if either of these troops had any "sleeping parties" among their herds. General Mackenzie lost a fine gray pacer, which he prized very highly, and his adjutant, Lieutenant Lynch, also lost a very valuable horse.* The Comanches went almost over headquarters, as it was located directly under the ridge along which they rode, and where they first struck it.

When the alarm was first given, the writer frantically

---

*General Frank Baldwin, U. S. A., retired, told the writer on February 6, 1914, that when he was Indian agent at Fort Sill, Indian Territory (now Oklahoma), about 1876, and in almost daily conference with Quanah, that the latter told Mackenzie in an interview which he (Quanah) sought, that he would return to Mackenzie the gray pacer he had run out of our camp this night. This Mackenzie declined.

grabbed for his picket pin, only to see it whizzing through
the air into the darkness beyond his reach, and his horse
going like mad for the huddled herd of "F" troop. Following with desperate energy, knowing full well the value
of his efforts in that direction, he saw the lariat catch in
another; the horse jerked back; it held. His hand was
upon it. He drew in hand over hand, upon the terrified
animal. *He felt that he had drawn a prize.* The din and
uproar was at its height. Getting a half hitch on his
horse's nose and holding on with main strength, it was
found that his hobbles—a new pair—were unbroken, and
as soon as the tumult had somewhat subsided, the writer,
having been ordered to inspect the outposts, mounted him
as speedily as possible and unattended—for it was impossible to find a trumpeter—started to ascertain what damage the picket posts had sustained. It was early dawn.
They had been overrun. The nearest post was about
twenty yards outside of "F" troop's horses, and in charge
of a Dutch corporal, who told his story in a very broken,
brief, but ludicrous manner: "I vas lying down, sir, ven I
hears a shot. I shoomps up, dries to get my bicket pin as
de horses roosh py, and de next ding I knows de Injuns
dey ride all ofer me. I raise my carbine to my preast as
he broosh py me; he stagger, almost fall, and he deesap-
pear in de dark."

The Stampeded Horses—Attack and Chase

While the command was still saddling up, and as the
dawn was beginning to streak the east, the writer rode out
through the gloom and sage brush to the other picket
posts, crossed the Fresh Fork up to the saddle girth, pistol in one hand, bridle rein in the other, feeling at any
moment that the Qua-ha-das might be on the outskirts of
the camp to pick up loose horses. He saw the trail of the
stampeded horses, but neither saw nor heard anything else
until the last picket post on the bluff was reached. Their
story was soon told, and the direction of the frightened
horses going out. Cautioning them to give the alarm

promptly, he passed on. Reaching the most remote post
on the hill overlooking our camp, to gain which the river
had to be recrossed, he was about to question the pickets,
when a shot was heard (this shot was fired by Quartermaster Sergeant Morgan of "G" troop), followed by a
loud shout in the valley beyond. The writer galloped
rapidly up. Here, coming from different directions, also
at a gallop, he met two detachments of "K" and "G"
troops which had been sent out shortly before to hunt up
stray horses, and to find the trail of the stampeded herds.
They were commanded by Captain E. M. Heyl and Lieutenant W. C. Hemphill. All looked down the valley. A
dozen or more Indians were seen rapidly making off with
as many of our horses. In a moment we were dashing
after them. Although still quite dark their forms were
distinctly visible. The men scattered out somewhat in the
chase, the best and freshest horses of "K" troop leading.
We gained on them rapidly, were almost within pistol
shot, and a moment later the men began to open fire, when
suddenly the Indians abandoned the animals and disappeared in a ravine or arroya, crossed it, and rode out on
high ground beyond, toward a high bluff, butte or small
mountain, now clearly outlined in the quickening dawn of
day. Most of the men stopped short at the break or arroya, as there was an abrupt shelf or jump-off, quite difficult for any but the best horses to clear, but Captain Heyl
and the writer were close upon the Indians. We gave our
horses the spurs, jumped the ledge into the ravine,
scrambled out, and were again closely following them to
the open prairie, now gradually ascending until it seemed
to terminate in a smooth prairie ridge as we approached
the mountain or butte.

"My God, We Are In a Nest!"

We were now more than two miles from the camp in a
direct line, and more than that by the route we had come.
As we ascended the ridge, glancing quickly to the front,
there at the base of the bluff or butte could be seen in the

clear light of approaching day the ground fairly swarming
with Indians, all mounted and galloping toward us with
whoops and blood-curdling yells that, for the moment,
seemed to take the breath completely from our bodies.
But a scant dozen of our men had followed us across that
difficult arroya in the prairie, and the first, almost paralyzing, effect it had upon that little party can never be effaced
from one's memory. The picture is indelibly stamped
upon the brain.

It was like an electric shock. All seemed to realize the
deadly peril of the situation and to take it in at a glance.
For a moment the blood seemed fairly congealed, for we
realized what the ruse of the Indians had been and knew
now that their purpose had been to lead us into an ambuscade. We all drew rein on the ridge as one man, each
looked at the other, and then raised a simultaneous sound
of surprise. Captain Heyl was the first to speak: "Heavens, but we are in a nest! Just look at the Indians!" Although the writer echoed this sentiment, in his heart he
could not speak it. No words could express it. No act
could convey what we felt at that moment.

The writer had left his large, three-fourths thoroughbred, strawberry roan horse at Camp Cooper to be sent
back to Fort Richardson, as he was in poor condition, and
was badly mounted on an old sorrel troop horse the writer
had borrowed from Lieutenant Hemphill, and he was worn
out from the long summer scout. He had good pluck and
endurance, but in his weak condition was now blowing
fearfully from the long run, as he had been urged to his
utmost speed, and his legs were even now trembling under
me.

The scene had suddenly shifted. We were, in a moment,
confronted not with a theory, but a perilous condition,
really a most serious crisis. The supreme moment in a
soldier's life for quick decision and action had arrived.
The situation was taken in at a glance. Not a moment
was to be lost. The thought flashed over the writer:

Could we spur our jaded horses back to the ravine from which we had just come? The writer thought not. It was, at all events, a most hazardous and dangerous alternative, and extremely doubtful, in view of the fact that Indians are always mounted on selected and absolutely fresh animals taken from their big caviards or reserve herds. If we could check up their advance with our rapid carbine fire, until Mackenzie could hear our shots, we might gain it gradually, meeting in the meantime his (Mackenzie's) advance coming to our rescue. This was undoubtedly our only course to pursue, as there was absolutely no shelter or cover on the bald, open prairie where we now were. We were at least 3 miles from our camp of the night before; our horses were nearly exhausted from their long run. It would have been certain death had we all turned and sought shelter in the ravine or coulee we had just left, now some 800 or 1,000 yards as the Indians had already begun to move out in fan shape, had commenced circling and lapping around our flanks. Men in such position generally think and act quickly. They have to!

I waited a moment and then turned to Heyl, who was riding on my right, mounted on a large, powerful, and speedy black horse, full of fire and go (the horse), for some word of command. He seemed completely dazed, or momentarily paralyzed. He gave no commands, but simply stared. I shouted the plan that had so suddenly flashed over me as quickly and briefly as possible. He acquiesced by a nod of assent, and said (there was no time for conference as to details): "Yes, that is right! Deploy out on the run, men, and give them your carbines!" The order was then given for all of the men to move to the right and left, to deploy and dismount, and to fall back slowly, and without bunching, for the distant ravine. Heyl went to the right, more than a hundred yards, far out of reach of my voice, his seven men deploying under his direction, and, dismounting, opened fire. We had no trumpeter to sound any calls. Five men of Hemphill's troop "G" had, it

seems, followed me across the ravine and to this point.
They were Sergeant Jenkins, and Privates Melville, Downey, Foley, and Gregg. They were known to be about the
best, staunchest, most loyal, reliable men in the regiment.
I knew them all. They had been out on scouts with me.
I knew they would stand by me and implicitly obey every
order, and all die, if necessary. My confidence in every
one of them never wavered for a moment. They were
game to the core. They followed me to the left, deployed,
dismounted, and opened fire. Melville was on my left with
orders to keep that flank protected, always refusing to his
rear and left, and to allow no small parties to creep by and
get in his rear through the small ravines. Sergeant Jenkins also remained in that flank. I posted myself in rear
of the center and watched both of my own flanks, connecting as far as possible with Heyl. As we all opened a deliberate and steady fire upon the Indians, who were now
moving like a cloud upon us, and evidently intent upon
outflanking us, thus cutting off our only hope of the last
avenue of escape to the camp, and to finish our small detachment before help could read us, their line suddenly
recoiled and checked up.

The Fight, Retreat, and Death of Gregg—Tragedy
Number One

The well delivered fire of our little handful of men, covering now a considerable line, caused the savages to scatter out still more, to falter and hesitate, and to commence
their curious custom of circling. They were naked to the
waist; were arrayed in all their war paint and trinkets,
with head dresses or war bonnets of fur or feathers fantastically ornamented. Their ponies, especially the white,
cream, dun, and claybanks, were striped and otherwise artistically painted and decorated with gaudy stripes of flannel and calico. Bells were jingling, feathers waving, and
with jubilant, discordant yells that would have put to blush
any Confederate brigade of the Civil War, and uttering
taunting shouts, they pressed on to what they surely con-

sidered to be their legitimate prey. Mingled with the shouts, whoops, and yells of the warriors could be distinctly heard the strident screeching and higher-keyed piercing screams of the squaws, far in rear of the moving circles, which rose above the general din and hub-bub now rending the air. In the midst of the circling ponies we could see what appeared to be two standard bearers, but upon their nearer approach we discovered them to be two scalp poles gaily decorated with long scalp locks, probably of women, with feathers and pieces of bright metal attached which flashed in the morning light. There were also other flashes seen along their line which I afterwards ascertained were small pieces of mirrors held in the hand and used as signals in the alternate advances and retreats, deployments and concentrations, in place of tactical commands. These were carried by the principal warriors or sub-chiefs, acting, I supposed, as file closers, squad leaders, etc. They had no squad, platoon, or company line formations, and no two, three, or four Indians were seen at any time to come together or bunch. While a general line was maintained at all times, it was always a line of right and left hand circling, individual warriors with varying radii, expanding and contracting into longer or shorter lines, advancing or retreating during these tactical maneuvers. The scalp-pole bearers I took to be chiefs, or big medicine men, for they were arrayed in all the gorgeous trappings that savage barbarity is capable of displaying. It was a most terrifying spectacle to our little band, yet wild, grand, novel (to look back upon) in the extreme. No shouts or cheers from our men were given in response to the diabolical yelling and din of screeches of the Indians. They maintained a stolid, grim silence, one of determination to do or die to the last. Unfortunately Heyl's men were nearly all new recruits who had just joined us on this expedition. They had never been in a fight before; were all well mounted on comparatively fresh horses, and as with him (Heyl), who was mounted, as has been already stated, on a large, powerful, black horse, full of fine spirit and strength, the excitement of the chase having partially subsided, everything thus far having gone their way, their fighting ardor had as rapidly cooled, and, seeing the ultimatum of being surrounded and massacred, unless assistance arrived very soon, chose to trust to their horses' heels in an endeavor to escape, rather than to face longer the ferocious Qua-ha-das, whose wild yells, whoops, screams, and screeches now sounded so unpleasantly close to their ears.

This is just precisely what they did do. To my utter surprise and consternation, on my attention being called by one of my men—"Lieutenant, look over there, quick; they are running out!"—I saw Captain Heyl and his men "bunch," and with spurs in their horses' flanks, ride out of the fight at full speed.

Shouts, commands, threats, curses were of no avail. The moral effect of that wild, fancifully dressed, shrieking band of half-naked Comanches, drawing about our flanks and now beginning to close in with their arrows and pistols, was too much for raw men who had never been "tried out" under fire. To my utter dismay I was left a long distance in rear with these five men of "G" troop, a gallant, brave squad of men. We were still some hundreds of yards from the ravine toward which we had been slowly but gradually drawing when we first realized our critical dilemna. This was all done without any notice or warning being given to me by Captain Heyl. He had given no orders or instructions since we had first arrived on the ground.

At this movement by Heyl and his men, the Comanches gave an extra yell of supreme satisfaction, began bunching for a charge, and, making a sudden dash at us with some of the leading warriors, the bullets and arrows began coming in quickly, and to brush uncomfortably near us from every direction.

Knowing that it would be certain death should he turn,

try to join the panic-stricken, retreating party, and make
a run for the shelter of the arroya, the writer mounted his
men, cautioned them to kep well deployed, to cut off the
magazines of their Spencer carbines, reserving them until
the last moment, and to commence falling back—using
single shots—turning to fire, but on no account to turn and
run until they got the word. The order was carried out
to the letter. The Indians were poorly armed with muz-
zle-loading rifles and pistols, lances, and bows. We commenced moving to the rear, bending low on our horses,
several of which were struck with arrows. We faced
about as often as possible to fire and check them, hoping
every moment to see the head of Mackenzie's column come
out of the adjacent valley of the Fresh Fork. When we
finally faced the leading warriors, a bullet struck Downey
in the hand, cutting two fingers, as he was in the act of
working the lever of his carbine. With his hand streaming blood, his efforts seemed useless. The shell would not
eject. "Lieutenant, what shall I do?" I shouted, "Use
your hunting knife, and eject the shell with it!" The
brave man did it with his wounded hand, and firing a moment later, almost in their faces, dropped an Indian out
of the saddle. They were still afraid of our carbines.
Using them up to the last moment as single shooters, I
shouted, as we neared the arroya: "Now, men, unlock your
magazines, bunch your shots, pump it into them, and make
a dash for your lives! It is all we can do!" The Indians
recoiled as we delivered this volley, and several going off
their ponies caused some confusion, as we made the run.
Thank God for those Spencers! My affection for them has
never changed. It was not necessary that they should
carry one thousand or twelve hundred yards, but kill at
from five hundred down to twenty or thirty yards, in what
almost became a mix-up. The situation had been desperate from the first. It now seemed to be absolutely hopeless. I never expected we would reach the arroya. I felt
that our time to die had come, and many thoughts rushed

unbidden to the mind. Gregg was about ten or fifteen yards to my right and rear, after we gave them our magazines and turned, riding then on my right flank. He said: "Lieutenant, my horse is giving out!" I glanced partly over my shoulder, and saw that it was too true. He was on an old flea-bitten gray, and the horse was beginning to sway in that peculiar manner always seen in an exhausted horse. The Comanches, almost by intuition, also knew that he was in their grasp, and the leading Indians, having partially recovered from the blizzard we had pumped into them, and seeing the animal stagger and falter, rushed in to dispatch the unfortunate man.

A large and powerfully built chief led the bunch, on a coal-black racing pony. Leaning forward upon his mane, his heels nervously working in the animal's side, with six-shooter poised in air, he seemed the incarnation of savage brutal joy. His face was smeared with black war paint, which gave his features a satanic look. A large, cruel mouth added to his ferocious appearance. A full-length head-dress or war bonnet of eagle's feathers, spreading out as he rode, and descending from his forehead, over head and back, to his pony's tail, almost swept the ground. Large brass hoops were in his ears; he was naked to his waist, wearing simply leggings, moccasins and a breech-clout. A necklace of bear's claws hung about his neck. His scalp lock was carefully braided in with otter fur, and tied with bright red flannel. His horse's bridle was profusely ornamented with bits of silver, and red flannel was also braided in his mane and tail, but, being black, he was not painted. Bells jingled as he rode at headlong speed, followed by the leading warriors, all eager to out-strip him in the race. It was Quanah, principal war chief of the wild Qua-ha-das.*

---

*It had been the writer's belief for some years after this action that the chief who led the advance warriors was either Mow-wi ("Hand Shaker") or Para-a-coom ("He Bear"), but Quanah told General Frank Baldwin, U. S. A. (then a Captain Fifth Infantry), while acting as Indian agent at Fort Sill, Indian Territory, also Colonel J. F. Randlett, U. S. A. (then a Captain Eighth Cavalry), while acting as Indian agent at Anadarko, Indian Territory, that he not only led his Indians the night of the stampede, but also in the attack upon Heyl and the writer on the morning of October 10, 1871. The race pony's name was "Running Deer."

Quanah – Parker, Principal Chief
of the Northern band (Qua-ha-das)
of Comanche Indians which depredated
for years in the Panhandle-Plains Country in Texas.

In vain did we try to save the life of the doomed man. The writer turned, checked up his horse, shouting for the men to do the same. With a Smith & Wesson pistol he fired several shots at a distance of not more than thirty feet, but the wily chief was on the other side of Gregg, and guiding his pony by rapid zigzagging so as to make a shield of him, his (Gregg's) life was in danger from our shots. Our fire was effectually masked. Melville, at just this moment, was hit in the arm.

We dared not close with them, as that would, in a melee, be almost certain death. In vain did the writer shout for him to use his carbine. Alas! he did try, but, through nervous strain or excitement, his pull on the lever was too weak, and—the cartridge stuck.

Again the writer shouted, "Pull your six-shooter!" He reached for it. Too late! A flash! A report from the chief's pistol, now at Gregg's head—a fall—a thud—a tragic death—and his horse, now relieved of his rider, turned and ran into the Indian lines. *This was tragedy number two of Cañon Blanco.**

It seemed almost an age since we had first discovered the Indians, and they had charged out for us. But this had all occurred in a very brief space of time, much less than it has taken the writer to record it. It seemed as though General Mackenzie must have heard the firing and even then be coming out of the valley to our rescue.

Without stopping to scalp the fallen man or to finish us, as we naturally expected might now be done almost any moment, the Qua-ha-da suddenly whirled, and followed by his warriors—more than forty of whom were within a few yards of us—he rode rapidly toward the butte.

---

*Lieutenant John A. McKinney, of the Fourth Cavalry (killed in the fight with Dull Knife's band of Northern Cheyennes in a Cañon of the Big Horn Mountains, Nov. 25, 1876), told the writer that when he was at Fort Sill in 1872 the Comanches brought in a buffalo robe with a pictograph on it representing this scene. It was at the moment of Gregg's fall from his horse, and the latter running into the Indian lines. The writer was shown, firing at Quanah. Five Indians were shown dead on the ground, just the number they admitted they lost. The writer endeavored, later, to secure this robe, but could get no trace of it either through the two interpreters or the Indian agent. The flea bitten gray (almost white) which Gregg rode, and which ran into the Indian lines must be the "large white horse" mentioned in Mrs. Hooker's story of "*Star.*"

We were saved! With a loss of one man killed and two men wounded, almost at the edge of the ravine, into which a few moments before the recruits of "K" troop had so ingloriously fled in a headlong demoralized flight.

The Gallant Act of Boehm—Our Rescue

What had proved our salvation? What had caused this sudden turning of the band? Did the wily chief suspect a decoy to the ravine, there to be met by the command, cut off, and his warriors massacred? Did he suddenly discover the dust of the column coming out of the adjacent valley by the Fresh Fork? Or did he consider his vengeance satisfied, blood for blood, for the warrior killed by the corporal at the picket post during the stampede?

A loud shout, and the writer turned quickly. Looking to our left in the direction toward our camp, we saw in a moment the true cause for our rescue, and the mysterious conduct of the now retreating Comanches. For, over the little hill or knoll which separated this prairie from the valley down which we had chased the Indians who were running off our stampeded horses, only in a shorter and more direct line to our camp, came all of our Ton-ka-way Indians, with Texas, the squaw,* fantastically arrayed in all their finery, mounted on their war ponies, their carbines cracking, yelling with all their lungs, and kicking up such a dust that to the keen eyes of the wary Qua-ha-da chief indicated the rapid and close approach of the main column, which, coming up in his rear, would have pressed him between the ravine and the mountains, with a poor chance for escape.

Lieutenant Boehm had heard the firing; had rushed out in its direction; met the flying recruits, and, brandishing

---

*Mackenzie had given positive orders that none of the Ton-ka-way squaws should accompany the expedition. Notwithstanding this, Texas, a young squaw, had, in some unaccountable manner, smuggled herself on Lawton's train, and, mounted on a claybank pony which she had striped with paint so that it closely resembled a zebra, and decorated with feathers and red flannel, was now in the midst of the bucks, full of fight, yelling and screaming like a demon—a veritable virago.

a carbine, compelled them to return, together with many
stragglers from our chase belonging to the two troops; also
Captain H—— and Lieutenant Hemphill, and, in another
moment, waving on his "Tonks," the entire force, amount-
ing now to not over forty men, but, with the heavy dust of
a galloping column of over five hundred troopers close behind, were pressing the flying Comanches. Captain Heyl
did not assume command, neither did Hemphill utter a
word. Boehm said, "Bob, you take the left and I will take
the right of the line! Let's push them now. Mackenzie is
right in our rear." With our skirmish line well deployed
we moved forward steadily toward the butte of the Cañon
Blanco. A novel battle now ensued.*

In the rear of the Indian lines could be seen the squaws
now bringing up led ponies, keeping up their shrill, discordant screeching and screaming, and at the base of the
butte, or low mountain, the savages were spread out, and
circling here and there, looked like a swarm of angry bees,
so that it was almost impossible to estimate the number of
the moving mass with any accuracy, although we judged
that there might have been from three hundred to four
hundred—including the squaws.

They were heartily responding to the shouts and war
whoops of our scouts, sometimes interluded with most emphatic and regular old-fashioned, round cursing. Here
the real excitement and fascinating charm, so peculiar to
an Indian fight, began. It was one grand, but rather dangerous, circus. As before stated, an irregular line of

---

*"Peter" Boehm, as he was affectionately known in the old Army, enlisted as pri-
vate, general mounted service, and bugler, Company B, Second Cavalry, July, 1858,
discharged March 1, 1865. During the Civil War he was, for a long time, brigade
orderly trumpeter for General Custer. At the Battle of Gettysburg, during Custer's
great charge with the Michigan Brigade ('Wolverines") on the right flank, he sabered
and captured General Wade Hampton's trumpeter, at the time General Hampton was
cut across the face with a saber. For this act Custer had him (Boehm) commissioned
second lieutenant, Fifteenth New York Cavalry, and took him on his staff as one of his
aides. At the Battle of Winwiddi C. H. he rallied the brigade and drove the enemy
back several miles and was awarded the Cong. Medal of Honor. At the Battle of Five
Forks he was desperately wounded in the arm and leg while charging over the breastworks. His horse was killed, and falling pinned Boehm to the ground, where he was
picked up for dead. Appointed second lieutenant, Fourth Cavalry, May 1, 1816; first
lieutenant, September 27, 1866; captain, May 1, 1873; retired, March 1, 1876; Major,
April 23, 1904. He died in 1914. The writer a few years later had his remains transferred from Chicago to the Arlington National Cemetery, and on each Memorial Day he
plants a flag over his grave in loving remembrance of this gallant soul and generous,
faithful companion.

battle, or front, was kept up, always, however, in continual motion, every individual warrior fighting for himself— each, as he came around on the front arc of his right or left hand circle, whooping, or yelling, and brandishing his arms. This yell can hardly be described, but it approached a Yah-hoo   Y-a-a-h-h-o-o-o-o! and with the high keyed-up pitch.

At no time did our lines approach close rifle distance. Occasionally a Ton-ka-way would leave his circle, and, dashing straight to the front, would be imitated by a Comanche, both apparently bent upon meeting in personal combat, or a duel; but, as we breathlessly watched, expect- ing every moment to see the collision, they whirled, and delivered their fire, strongly reinforced by untranslatable Indian language—which we took to be serious name-calling —they darted back to their places in the ever-changing battle line.

This went on for some time. Occasionally a warrior could be seen to stagger as though about to fall; again, a pony was shot and fell, but instantly the wounded savage was hurried to the rear to be cared for by the squaws, who also brought up an extra pony, to remount the one whose animal had been shot, not forgetting to keep up their ear- splitting screaming, horrible screeching, and noisy exhibi- tion of courage.

Upon the sides of the mountain, or high butte, the In- dians could be seen gliding from rock to rock, and the puffs of smoke, from time to time, accompanied by the un- comfortable ping-p-i-n-g-g of the bullets close to our ears, told us that they had a lot of old target rifles in the hands of skillful marksmen on the summit. Their line was falling back rapidly, even before our small numbers. This was easily accounted for, as the dust of our main column was approaching nearer and nearer. The breaks or deep ar- royas and numerous ravines in the prairie were full of Indians, hastening to the level ground beyond, to guard against surprise, there to keep up the rapid circling, firing, and falling back as before. They had no idea of being caught in any traps, and the rapid movement of the galloping column hastened their steps.

Charge Up the Butte—The Shattered Leg—Tragedy Number Three

Upon a suggestion to Boehm that we rout out the Indian sharpshooters from the butte, we took about a dozen men from the line and started up. Captain Heyl remained below. Our route was up the sides, and finally along a narrow, steep, zig-zag path, either a bucalo trail or one used by the Indians. We hardly knew but at any moment we might be picked off by a bullet. Urging my horse to his utmost speed by voice and spur to lessen their chance, the writer came suddenly upon a sharp, projecting boulder, jetting over the narrow trail. He turned his horse's head quickly, thinking to avoid it. Too late! Just at that moment he stepped upon either a rolling stone, or slipped and stumbled, and the writer's leg struck the boulder with a crash that sounded like the crack of a pistol, and he was almost lifted out of his saddle by its force. The writer grasped the pommel, for it made him sick, and all was dark and swimming before his blurred eyes. He felt himself sway and stagger, then apparently fall down an interminable distance. The cold sweat came from every pore, and he became unconscious, but dropped himself forward upon the horse's neck as he lurched. It has always been a puzzle how he got up the side of the butte. His horse had carried his dead weight, and his arms were still tightly clasped about his neck, with the reins loosely dangling. Luckily, the Indians, upon our nearing them, had hastily galloped off, abandoning the position, and scattering in every direction. The writer remembered the cheering, seeing the big column come up, with Mackenzie at its head, knew that we were saved—and then all is blank. The cool air at the top of the bluff, a dash of water in the face by one of the

---

Note—I found later that my horse had been shot in the nigh or left fore shoulder causing him to fall on me and crush and lacerate my left leg.

men, and a drink of water from his canteen revived him
somewhat. The pain was intense, but, looking about him,
he could see the Indians still falling back; could hear the
cracking of the carbines, and shouts below, as the entire
command deployed into lines and rode through the broken
gullies and over the plain beyond. The Indians were being
continually mounted on fresh horses, while our own were
jaded and worn out by long and continuous marches, the
stampede, and the hard run of the morning. I traversed
the length of the butte slowly with my men and joined the
column where it shelved off, it having arrived just in time
to see the last Qua-ha-da rapidly disappear in the hills and
bushy ravines that ascend to and clearly define the plateau
of the "Staked Plains" or Llano Estacada. *This was
tragedy number three of Cañon Blanco.*

Slowly we turned, further pursuit at that time being
useless, and sadly retraced our march back over the
ground just fought over to where the body of Gregg lay
just as he had fallen when shot through the head by
Quanah. We hastily buried him under the shadow of
the butte at its southeast foot, with the simplest
form of a soldier's funeral, no chaplain being with
us, and after heavy stones had been placed over the mound
to protect it from the big wolves that swarmed all over this
country, without unsaddling, we went into a temporary
bivouac, and awaited further developments. Pickets were
thrown out to guard against surprise, and the horses were
allowed to graze under strong guard.

We remained here until about 2:30 p. m., the "Tonks"
in the meantime coming in and reporting a broad and fresh
trail leading up from the mouth of the cañon, which they
said undoubtedly led to Quanah's village. Up to this time,
in the excitement since the night before, I had neglected to
attend to my wounded leg, but now that the nerves had
somewhat relaxed, an intense pain warned me that, perhaps, it was more serious than I had supposed. It was
now badly swollen and stiff, and growing more so. I

called our contract doctor, A. A. Surgeon Rufus Choate, and consulted him. The boot had to be cut off. Slitting the boot leg down and removing all covering, it really presented a dreadful appearance. It was covered with clotted blood, black and blue, terribly swollen, with much laceration. The doctor, after a hasty examination, for the trumpeters were then sounding "boots and saddles," decided that the leg was not broken, but it might be a fracture, and considered it wise to put my leg in splints, which he did, using my boot leg and what material he happened to have on hand for that purpose. We had no ambulance or stretchers with the column, and there was no material at that place with which to construct a horse litter or a "travois," nor was there sufficient time. I mounted my horse; the command "Forward!" was given, and soon the column was moving around the base of the mountain and up the cañon to take the freshly discovered trail. It was impossible for me to go back forty miles or more to Lawton's supply camp on Duck Creek. Taking charge again of the pack train and rear guard, with instructions to afford whatever assistance to Lieutenant Vernou, now in command of the dismounted men, who had lost their horses, we moved out on the trail for the Comanche village.

The Pursuit—The Qua-ha-da Village and Ruse

These men were somewhat demoralized at the prospect of following afoot over many weary miles of plain, and through cañon, in search of our wily enemy, which had but a few moments before disappeared from our view on the horizon of the Staked Plains, and up the trail we were now on. A dismounted cavalry trooper is a much more demoralized man than a tired-out, straggling infantry soldier, since, from force of habit, he has learned to rely almost wholly upon the strength and brute courage of his faithful horse rather than in his own powers of endurance, thus subtracting to an important degree that factor of initiative so necessary in any soldier there in that country where our resources were so limited.

The saddles of our stampeded animals had all been concealed, or "cached," in some of the many small, bush-lined
ravines, or "pockets," with which the country abounded.
It was a hard march. Animals and men were very weary
from the continuous strain of the previous forty-eight
hours. By dint of hard talking, sharp commands, and
even threats, accompanied by strong appeals to their
pride, etc., we succeeded in getting the miscellaneous assemblage of foot-sore, chafed, blistered, mad, and dis-
gruntled grumblers, grouchers and kickers, and the sore-
backed horses and mules into camp, but it was at the expense of about every atom of our patience, strength, and
nerves, and only after these "fag-ends" had all been
urged and shamed into their last ounce of energy and patriotic ardor. We so informed Mackenzie that night.
We bivouacked without shelter, "cross side lined" our animals,* picketed the camp, and, with strong sleeping parties among the horse herds, we "turned in"—an almost
exhausted command.

Mackenzie must have diligently chewed the matter over
during the night (he rarely slept much anyway during an
Indian campaign), regarding my plight, and the condition
of these dismounted men, for early the next morning he
sent for me. I was asked if I wanted to go ahead with
the column, then moving out, or conduct these horseless
troopers by slow and painful marches back to Duck Creek.
He said, "I am told that your leg is badly injured, and the
doctor has put it in splints. These dismounted men can
go no farther with the column; they will only impede our
march in pursuit. An officer will have to conduct them
back, and this seems to be the only way in which you can,
by taking charge of them, get good care and treatment at

---

*The writer never saw this method of a "cross side line" used by any other cavalry
command. It is extremely doubtful if there are many officers living today who know
the full meaning of this term. The two leather hobbles are fastened, one on the nigh
fore, the other on the off hind leg, well below the knee and hock at the joint, connected
by a light chain, with toggle or swivel to prevent kinking or knotting, and a ring midway the connection, through which is passed the lariat. While it shortens the grazing
radius of the animal, on a thirty-foot lariat, the fulcrum of the lever operates to throw
the horse upon his nose or side whenever he lunger, plunges, or jumps back, without
injuring him or pulling the picket pin. When not in use it was carried with the coiled
lariat on the left side of the pommel or the saddle.

Lawton's camp. While it is true that I want you with me, I am looking out for your interest and safety. There is no ambulance with us to carry you should you become more disabled so that you can not march, and you had better go back. That is my advice and judgment.'' ''Is it an order, sir?'' ''No, sir, it *is not* an order, but, I repeat, I am considering your comfort and safety.'' ''Then, sir, if it is left to me, I go forward with the command!''

He added, ''Another thing—I have been told that Captain Heyl did not behave well in that action yesterday morning. I had him transferred to this regiment because of his ability, efficiency, and reported gallantry in action. What do you care to say about it? You were a close witness of his conduct.'' I hesitated. At that period I could not feel like making any statement that would absolutely destroy the future reputation and permanent career of any officer who had stood sufficiently high in the estimation of Mackenzie to warrant his transfer to the Fourth Cavalry. So I quietly replied, ''Well, General, if you have had him transferred on account of his previous good reputation as a gallant officer, I shall say nothing that might injure or destroy that reputation. I will merely say that under all of the circumstances of that affair, in my opinion he committed a *very grave error of judgment*, and you can draw your own conclusions!'' He never took any action in the matter. I never referred to it again to him. Captain Heyl never made any statement, or spoke of it, either to Boehm or myself, and it passed into regimental *''innocuous desuetude.''*

In the National Cemetery of Arlington there is a memorial over Heyl's grave. On it is a full-length bronze tablet reciting most minutely the details of every event of his military career—*except that one incident.*

It is not recorded. He could never allow himself to figure or to be included in that tragedy—the death of Gregg, and my almost certain destruction in Cañon Blanco through that act. This is conclusive evidence that whatever Mackenzie, in his deliberations, decided to do or not to do, Heyl himself knew and felt what that act was, and that he could have no justification in perpetuating it in bronze at Arlington, unless he perjured his own soul or perpetrated a fraud upon the two men then living who were witnesses of that event. The writer left Mackenzie to draw his own conclusions more than fifty years ago. The reader can draw his own now in view of this omission on the bronze tablet. Many years after this affair, Captain Heyl told General H. W. Lawton, when both were Majors and Assistant Inspectors General: ''Lawton, that day was the bluest moment of my military life. I was so dazed when I faced up to that horde of yelling, rushing Indians, with almost certain death staring me in the eye, that I simply lost my head and went into a state of *'blue funk,'* and the worst of it was, I could not help it!'' This Lawton frankly told the writer, with no reservations of confidential secrecy, in the winter of 1888-'9, while a guest for eight months in his house in Washington during that season.

Lieutenant C. A. Vernon went back with the dismounted men. The two columns separated, and were soon lost to sight as they moved in opposite directions. Everywhere, as we advanced up the cañon with its abrupt bluff faces, we saw evidences of its having been occupied by Indians for years, and scattered all along were many of the small ''wickey-ups,'' still intact, put up for the use of the Indian herders, usually half-grown boys and girls. Every few miles the cañon widened out into more or less broad valleys bounded by almost impassable bluffs. We also saw numerous ravines and sand hills, as well as many small herds of buffalo. Here and there the creek (Catfish) widened out, sometimes presenting a succession of small, but beautiful, ponds or lagoons, clear as crystal, out of which swarmed immense flocks of wild ducks and curlew, and occasionally a majestic swan, whose trumpet notes sounded strange to our hunters who had rarely, if ever, seen such game. All the following day we marched steadily along, without catching even a glimpse of Indians, although they were undoubtedly spying on our every movement from their secret hiding places. The stillness and utter solitude of this lovely valley was only disturbed by the constant tramp of our horses' hoofs, until late in the afternoon when our trailers suddenly discovered the long sought for village, or where it had been—for what apparently was a large buffalo lodge village had suddenly vanished.

They had "folded their tents and silently stolen away," everything indicating a hasty departure. A broad lodgepole and stock trail showed plainly out of the village, leading up the cañon. Our halt was brief, stopping only long enough to ascertain what was inside of the freshly heaped mounds of earth all about, which looked like small graves, and debris of every description. The "Tonks" laughed at this, and said it was done as a "blind" to detain us—to "pull the wool over our eyes." Continuing, we soon came to where the trail divided; it was confused, crossing and recrossing in every direction, and for the first time our sharp-eyed scouts seemed "at fault." After much parleying and time lost, they concluded that the wily enemy had "doubled" on us and gone back upon the same trail. Countermarching and moving down the open valley again, we found, much to our chagrin, that it was even so, and after marching on the "back trail" until dark we were compelled to bivouac not far from where we had first discovered the abandoned village. The following morning, soon after we were in motion, the "Tonks" signalled from the edge of the bluff on the plains above us that they had "picked up" the lost trail leading over the seeming impassable barrier. There was a long delay in scaling with horses the steep ascent, but, at length, after toiling over many rocky bluffs and floundering around in the "breaks" and "arroyas," all were over and out of the cañon upon what appeared to be a vast, almost illimitable expanse of prairie. As far as the eye could reach, not a bush or tree, a twig or stone, not an object of any kind or a living thing, was in sight. It stretched out before us—one uninterrupted plain, only to be compared to the ocean in its vastness.

This was the beginning of the "Staked Plains," or "Llano Estacdo," which we had been seeking, and over which we would now be compelled to trail Quan-ah's moving village.

It was October 12, and a cold, overcast, gray morning. Our elevation was over three thousand feet. The air grew sharp and penetrating. We were all clothed for a summer campaign on the low plains of Texas. A severe "norther," peculiar to Texas at this season of the year, was beginning to strike us upon this barren waste, which, by contrast with the warm, bright sunshine of the previous day in the sheltered cañon, chilled us to the very marrow.

A short, dry, buffalo grass grew upon this immense plateau, over which our keenest-eyed "Tonk" trailers, now dismounted, were endeavoring to follow the slightest "signs." We moved along cautiously, marching slowly until about noon. Fresh signs of the Indian ponies in the large "caviard," or herd of horses which the enemy was driving, were the only indications of the course to be taken. Lodge poles on the dry, stiff stubble gave no trail. Suddenly, however, the trail turned, and again went over the bluff into the cañon. This was unexpected, but, dismounting again, we led out "by file," slipping and sliding down the dangerous descent, until all were once more at the bottom, and again there was a confused lot of fresh trails—some leading up, others down, while still others led straight across the valley, directly at right angles.

Again, in our supreme disgust, we felt that we had been completely foiled. The "Tonks" scattered and rode rapidly all over the valley, and before the rear of the column had got fairly down into the cañon and closed up, they were waving us on. It had been found going out

again over the bluff, this time, however, on the opposite
side of the cañon. We were soon ascending for the second
time that day the steep, precipitous sides of the rocky bar-
riers. It was a singularly sharp trick, even for Indians,
done, of course, to blind us and to gain time in moving
their families of women and children as far as possible out
of our reach. Without our own Indian scouts to beat the
Comanches at their own native shrewdness, we would have
undoubtedly lost the trail and hopelessly abandoned the
task.

But now we found ourselves on a very broad and distinct lodge-pole and stock trail, leading in but one direction, and that to the west and northwest. We carefully
estimated that they had from two to three thousand head
of stock, and that the entire "outfit" was moving along
with them, with all the plunder incident to a stampeding
village. Could we overtake it, its capture was almost certain.

The "Norther"—"Hot Trail"—Night Attack— A Bitter Storm

The bitter cold increased, and on this high tableland,
with no shelter, the wind from the northwest swept through
our thin uniforms. Many had no overcoats or gloves, and
the suffering grew intense. But we consoled ourselves
with the thought that if Indians with their women and children could endure it, we certainly must.

The trail grew fresher and "warmer." We now
stretched out and moved more rapidly. We crossed numerous "carreta," or cart trails, made by the Mexicans in
trading with the Comanches. They were well defined and
headed toward the Pecos River. As we "rose" or "lifted"
a slight ridge in the almost level prairie, we observed, in
the far distance, moving figures, silhouetted against the
sky line, as of mounted men galloping along the horizon,
here as distinct as the sea line that limits the boundless
ocean. First, two or three, then a dozen or more, until
finally, on both sides of our now swiftly speeding column,

there seemed to be hundreds. The "Tonks" said they were the Comanches, and we knew ourselves that at last we were on the right track! We now had them! Or, at least, we thought we did. Everybody was elated. The writer had not thought of his smashed leg, with its pain and uncomfortable splints, for hours, so keen had become the excitement of this most absorbing chase, as the Comanches began to swarm on the right and left of the trail, like angry bees, circling here and there, in an effort to divert us from their women and children. Every preparation was made for a fight, for we firmly believed that, failing to throw us off the lodge-pole trail of their fleeing village, the red scoundrels had gathered all of their warriors for a determined resistance and a supreme effort should we overtake their families. We knew that it is then that an Indian will fight with all the ferocity of a wild animal, blind to everything except the preservation of his squaws and pappooses.

Their efforts were therefore now all concentrated in an endeavor to throw us off the lodge-pole trail in order to gain time for the squaws. But Mackenzie determined, upon the advice of the Ton-ka-way chief and our best Indian campaigners, to disregard this wily bait, and keep steadily on, knowing that we must now be very close to them or the Qua-ha-das would not make such warlike demonstrations in the face of our superior force. We also fully realized that by keeping after the lodges, the warriors would soon close in and fight to the last Indian for the rescue of the ones they held most dear. Our object was, therefore, twofold. We could secure the ponies later.

The Qua-ha-das now began to get excited when it was found that we did not chase out after them, and, as we hoped, they began to swarm in toward us. The command was closed up in columns of fours, the men "counted off" again, and were directed to fill their blouse pockets with both carbine and pistol ammunition, of which we had taken along an ample supply. Cautionary commands were given for squadron and platoon formation, deployment to the front, right, and left, fighting on foot, etc. The pack mules, always a source of anxiety in the emergency of a battle, so far away from our base (nearly 100 miles), as they carried all of our precious food in this far-off wild, were closed in and placed in herd formation; a squadron was detached to surround them and guard them from stampede while still rapidly in motion—a sort of hollow square. A strong line of mounted skirmishers were thrown out to the front while flankers rode far out on the sides of the now threatening Comanches.

The Ton-ka-ways—McCord, the head chief; Simoon, "One-armed Charlie," Jesse, Lincoln, Grant, "Old Henry," Anderson, Job, William, Buffalo (the "Beau Brummel" of the "Tonks"), and many others whose names can not now be recalled—slipped from their riding animals, caught up, from their pony herd being driven on the flank, their favorite war ponies, until then unused, stripped all superfluous loads from their saddles, and quickly began, in their rude, inartistic way, to paint and adorn their persons for the coming battle, which we now surely considered was impending. A small piece of looking glass, a puddle of saliva in the hollow of the hand, much red, green, yellow, and black paint (ochre), were quickly mixed and applied in reeking daubs. The cream, claybank, dun or white pony was plentifully striped. Head dresses, horns, much red flannel, and bright-colored feathers completed the "Tonk" ensemble. The whole operation did not exceed five minutes, but sufficiently long to excite the laughter of the entire column of brave troopers even at that critical moment, when all were expecting a battle. Our gallant allies then pranced alongside the column, posturing, moving their heads from side to side, brandishing their carbines, and evidently feeling all the pride of conquering monarchs, so self-conscious were they of the dignity which all this display of paint, feathers, gew-gaws, etc., gave them.

The afternoon was now on the wane. We began to see

ahead of us, although indistinctly, the dark, moving mass
of the fleeing village. The Comanches still swarmed about
our flanks. We came upon their fires, still burning, which
they had hastily abandoned upon our approach. Then we
struck a large lagoon of fresh water in a depression or
"sink" in the prairie, where we hastily watered. Pushing
rapidly on, we came upon lodge-poles scattered in large
numbers on the trail in their sudden flight, also many iron
and stone hammers, mortars, pestles, and all sorts of
strange tools of the rudest description. Puppy dogs of
the Indian half-wolf breed had been dropped by the
squaws. The men picked up several and carried them on
the pommels of their saddles. Great chunks of mulberry
wood and mesquite roots, used for cooking purposes when
crossing this treeless desert, were also to be seen all along,
and occasionally—what they never throw away unless hard
pressed—the dried buffalo skins of their "teepes" or
lodges. The chase had now grown "hot." The dark cloud
of fleeing Indians loomed up closer. Still the Qua-ha-das
dashed and circled about watching for a chance or vulner-
able point for attack in our compact fighting column. Sev-
real times we thought that they were bunching for a
charge, and our skirmishers and flankers grew more alert
and drew in closer.

It grew darker and colder. The wind whistled. The
air grew thicker and more hazy, and soon a cold rain,
mingled with snow and sleet, began to drive into our faces,
through our bodies, and into the very marrow. This was
the supreme moment—a crisis. This was the time to have
speeded up, made a sharp dash by a part of our command
among the huddled, frightened, and demoralized women
and children guarded for the most part only by old men
and boys, while the other and larger half could have engaged and easily defeated the warriors. Nothing worse
could have happened than a few men killed or wounded,
but we surely would have got the entire "outfit," stock,
women and children with all of their plunder, and made a

"clean sweep up." Everybody was looking for Mackenzie to give the order to "Trot!" "Gallop!!" and "Charge!!!" It never came. This time he leaned, it seemed, on the side of extreme caution, and lost, what the writer believed at the moment, the best opportunity the Fourth Cavalry ever had for capturing practically Quan-ah's entire village and "lay-out." Or, it may be (for we never asked him the reason) that he was guided by feelings of humanity, and the big risk which we all ran, so far away from our supply camp, had our losses been heavy in a fight with a band that had always been noted for its bravery and hard-fighting qualities. Personally, it is the writer's belief that the snow and rain squall, driven by a howling northwest pale, was the determining factor that influenced, to a greater extent than any other, Mackenzie's judgment at that moment. Let us see what occurred. The village, which seemed but a mile or more away, was at once shut from our view, and to our utter dismay the inky blackness of night was instantly upon us. It seemed as though a great black curtain or pall had suddenly dropped in front of our eyes, shutting off every object. We could hardly distinguish forms about us even a foot or two away. Had the trot and gallop been taken half an hour earlier, there is little doubt that we would have captured the entire village and pony herd, but the menacing attitude of the warriors just as the storm was about to strike us, partly, if not wholly, diverted the General from his true objective.

The horses were very thin and much worn. We had no fresh mounts to draw from as the Indians possessed. The men were terribly fagged and tired; but the *morale, fighting spirit,* and *confidence was intact,* and all they needed at that moment was the word to "turn loose" and finish those Indians then and there—what they had come for, marched so many weary miles for, and sacrificed so much to accomplish.

Perhaps Mackenzie's judgment and wisdom was best, and we might have met with a calamity or dire disaster.

"Quien Sabe." But, looking back through that long vista
of years it seems improbable, almost impossible, that we
would not have achieved a complete success had we been
given the command at the crucial moment before that black
curtail fell and forever shut out the fleeing village and the
"norther" that saved them. In discussing this campaign
later, it was with the keenest regret and bitter disappointment that the driving of this half-breed Qua-ha-da into the
Fort Sill reservation to become later a "good Indian"
could not have been accomplished then by the Fourth Cavalry, instead of its being delayed until more than three
years from that date, and then by converging columns
operating in four different directions.

We were at once dismounted. Mackenzie seemed to be
deliberating whether further pursuit was practicable, when
the storm, which had been gathering all day and had already begun, burst upon us with renewed fury, cutting
man and beast to the very vitals. It raged, sleeting and
raining alternately, freezing as it fell and coating us with
ice, which soon stiffened our clothes, and, as we could not
see an arm's length before us, all hope of striking the trail
was out of the question. The wind increased to a gale, and
whistled and moaned incessantly. We formed a large
ring, or defensive circle, with a radius of about one hundred and fifty yards, with the pack mules in the center.
The men held their horses. While in this position, and
awaiting further developments, a shot, then several, followed by a loud volley, greeted us, and the entire band of
Comanches dashed almost over our close circle and instantly swept off into the impenetrable darkness that enveloped us, their taunting whoops and shrill yells sounding
strangely to our gallant troopers as though to mock them
in their helplessness. The Qua-ha-das had evidently seen
the command halt before the storm broke upon us. The
gloom of night had suddenly shut us from their view, and
riding at breakneck speed in the direction where they had
last seen us, to ascertain just our position, if possible, had

accidentally stumbled upon us. All crouched down; the volley was returned; nobody was hurt, and the intense excitement this episode furnished us was soon over. Other difficulties confronted us.

A squadron under Captain Wirt Davis was hastily pushed out after their retreating forms, guided only by sound, and for a few moments the lurid flashes and loud banging of our skirmishers, rising high above the howling storm, indicated quite a lively fight, but, as the Indians fled, it soon ceased, and our men came in, having been lost at a distance of less than five hundred yards, and only guided back to the circle by a peculiar yell, rarely used by Indians except when lost, and now made by our scouts accompanying it and answered by those scouts who had been left inside the circle.

Every precaution was now made to shield men and horses from the piercing cold and the fury of the storm. Enormous hail stones had began to fall, pelting the animals so that they could only be held with the greatest difficulty, and bruising the men's bodies. "Tarpaulins" (canvas) were dragged from the mule packs; robes and blankets were fished out in the darkness and spread inside the circle, where they would do the most good, and keep all from perishing, and, half lying and squatting beneath these improvised shelters, we wore out the livelong night, one long remembered by every officer and man in that gallant command of the Fourth Cavalry. Pack mules and horses trampled, in their fright, near our heads and feet, and their continued moving and stamping, snorting, and wee-haw-ing made sleep out of the question among the men, who took turns by detail in holding on to the suffering animals. It was a bare existence, with nothing to eat since morning, and a bitter night to wear out. Mackenzie had no overcoat, and somebody wrapped his shivering form in a buffalo robe. Several wounds received during the Civil War had disabled and rendered him incapable of enduring such dreadful exposure.

It was with many misgivings that we thrust our heads out from under the close, heavy, lead-colored (painted) "paulins" in the sharp morning air. A beautiful day was ushered in. The frightful storm had spent itself, and was giving place to genial warmth and balmy sunshine. Without breakfast, we broke our "charmed circle," and, by early light, were soon on the trail, still plain and leading in the same general direction. There was little or no enthusiasm, however. The spirits of the column "flagged," for no living creature was in sight on that vast expanse. We knew, or felt, that the village had been moving all night, and it would prove a hopeless, stern chase—a long march, fruitless of results.

Soon a spy or two occasionally showed themselves on the horizon to watch our movements. A little later that wonderful phenomenon of the mirage was perfectly shown—

"Clear shining through the swimming air,
Across a stretch of summer skies." *

The Return March—Dead Comanches—Mackenzie Wounded—Tragedy Number Three

Mackenzie soon found from our maps that in a direct west course the Pecos River was far away. The nearest post (Fort Sumner) was in New Mexico. The animals were now suffering for water, and some were beginning to show clearly signs of giving out. Our "chow" or rations were growing slim. The Comanches, by that lucky storm— for them—still had a night's march ahead of us, so he prudently, but most reluctantly, turned back. There was nothing to cook our food with but buffalo chips (bois de vache), and with scarcely water enough to wet our lips. We made a dry camp at our impromptu bivouac of the night before; the next day, in a sort of melancholy procession, reaching the lagoon, where it was decided to fill up with fresh rain water, and rest the command. The men on this day's march had picked up hundreds of smooth, well-worn cedar

---

*The writer has since learned that this point is at or near where the present town of Plainview is now located.

lodge-poles which the Comanches had dropped in their headlong flight, to be used for fuel at our bivouac supper. It was a most singular sight to see a long column of five hundred troopers, each with two or three fourteen-foot poles raised righ in air over their shoulders. Mackenzie, who, at the head of the column, when his attention was first called to it, suspecting a joke, or that they were being carried along as relics, was about to seriously order them to be thrown away when somebody suggested their possible utility for fuel instead of buffalo chips, which scented our bacon and coffee. They reminded one of a traveling circus, rather than a well drilled, disciplined body of cavalry.

The writer had been riding all this time with his battered leg in splints and closely bandaged. Upon Dr. Choate's inspection this day, after removing the bandages, it was found that it was not only not broken or even fractured, but was terribly bruised, and the flesh badly crushed and frightfully lacerated. Bathing it freely in the soft water of the lagoon, carefully cleansing and rebandaging, there was experienced, but little stiffness or pain. This lagoon we found to be full of countless numbers of curlew and many white swan, but none were allowed to be killed.

Taking up the old route again the next day, there was absolutely nothing to relieve the voiceless march, so singular had become the effect of this mysterious silence of the Staked Plains upon the men. We leisurely dropped down again into Cañon Blanco, drinking in the quiet solitude and natural beauties of this Indian paradise. The "Tonks" were leading The men and horses, who had been resting all day, now half asleep, were suddenly startled by the cry of "Indians! Indians!!" which brought every trooper erect in his saddle All was soon organized activity. A healthy excitement ran through the bronzed column. Striking a trot, lope and gallop, all carefully closed up, and horses well in hand, we soon saw our advance scouts running at breakneck speed toward some small ravines, followed by the leading troop. The excitement grew intense. Two

Comanches had been discovered following our old trail up the cañon, dismounted and leading their ponies. When first seen by our "Tonks" they abandoned their animals and ran into some bushy ravines, our scouts closely pursuing. As soon as we arrived, all entrances were closed. The "Tonks" went upon over the bluff, thus cutting off their escape in that direction. Mackenzie directed the leading troop to open fire, while our Indians, by their fire from above, tried to drive them out into our command. The Comanches were game. They would not come out. Mackenzie ordered Lieut. Boehm to take fifteen dismounted men and drive them out. There were several openings into the ravines. Boehm divided his men, and worked several paths. Mackenzie, becoming impatient, dismounted and got in behind Boehm to direct him, the two Comanches firing all the time. Just then something happened. A sharp swish, a thud, and a spiked arrow buried itself in the upper, fleshy part of Mackenzie's leg. He hurried back to the rear and had the spike cut out and the wound dressed. Soon all firing ceased, and we knew that the two Comanches were dead. The "Tonks" came down from their high perches on the bluff overhead, where they had given the entire command one of the finest circus acts (with several rings) of lofty tumblings, somersaults, vaulting, standing on their heads, etc., it had ever been our good fortune to see in an Indian country, and, upon parting the bushes, found both Qua-ha-das. One was shot several times through the body, the other through the head. One had been shot in the hand while firing his pistol. The bullet had shattered the pistol butt. A bloody bow-string showed that he had used his bow later. With the strength necessary to draw the string, it must have proved very painful, and a clear test of the Indian's wonderful courage, tenacity, and stoical nature under such circumstances. One of our men, a farrier of Troop "H," had been shot through the bowels, and, in turning, was shot in the hand. *This was the fourth tragedy of Cañon Blanco.*

Note—Mackenzie never reported his wound—and that was the fifth tragedy of Canyon Blanco.

As it was getting late, we bivouacked near the spot. The "Tonks" entered the ravine, shot a few bullets into the Comanches' bodies, as was their custom, scalped them, ears and all, and then cut a small piece of skin from each breast, for good luck, or rather "good medicine"—such was the peculiar superstition of the Indian. This, dried in the sun, and placed in a bag, or attached to a string and worn next to the person of the warrier, acts as a safe guard against danger or sickness in any form. It was their "medicine" or "mascot." At night Dr. Rufus Choate, Lieutenant Wentz C. Miller, and two negro boys, field cooks, went up the ravine, decapitated the dead Qua-ha-das, and placing the heads in some gunny sacks, brought them back to be boiled out for future scientific knowledge.

The Boiling Heads—And Wounded Farrier

Shortly after midnight we heard the wolves, which had sniffed the flesh from afar in the keen night air, fighting, snarling, and howling like incarnate fiends over this horrible human feast.

A barbarous and tragical end to a barbarous band, who, while mutilating and heaping red-hot coals upon the nude forms of their writhing victims (as the writer had seen the preceding May at the massacre on Salt Creek prairie) in the peaceful settlements of Texas, during their numerous blood-thirsty raids, had danced for joy at the savage torture inflicted.

Before starting the next morning, a horse litter had to be constructed upon which to carry our wounded man. The poles were lashed to the pack saddles of two mules traveling tandem. Cross-pieces were lashed to them in rear of the croup of one mule and in front of the breast of the other. A head covering was made of a framework of boughs, over which a blanket or shelter tent was thrown. He was thus carried more than two hundred miles, and by the personal nursing and unremitting attention of our faithful and efficient doctor, Rufus Choate, he lived, although his bowels had been perforated.

On this day we had but just gone into camp, and were about to eat our dinner, when Miller shouted to Major Mauck and the writer, from a short distance up the cañon, "Come up, we have something good!" "What is it?" Miller replied, "Soup!" We had observed two camp kettles strung on a pole over the fire. Seizing our cups, never suspecting a joke, we reached the spot. When to our horror we saw the two Comanche scalped heads, with the stripes of paint still on their faces, and with eyes partly opened, bobbing up and down, and rising above the mess kettles, mingled with the bubbling, bloody broth. It was a gruesome spectacle.* With hands on our stomachs, we fled, directing "Bob," our valuable, able cook to transfer our dinner and all of our personal belongings further down the cañon, out of sight and reach of our esteemed ethnological head-hunters and skull boilers. A more sickening sight it would be difficult to conceive of. We were no longer hungry that night.

There was a night alarm about midnight. Some Indians who had followed our trail tried to creep by our pickets, which, as officer-of-the-day, the writer had charge of, and stampede our horses. They were soon driven off with the assistance of "F" troop (Wirt Davis). We moved slowly down the cañon, the animals getting weaker and weaker. Lieutenant Warrington was sent in to Lawton's camp on Duck Creek to direct him (Lawton) to move his train and meet us at the Fresh Fork. Here we camped near the scene of our tragedy of October 10. Many of our hardships for the time being were forgotten in complete rest, good food, and calmness of mind and body. We visited the scene of our action. Armfulls of arrows were brought

---

*One of these skulls proved to be of no value, as it had a bullet hole in it. The other the writer saw in October, 1885, in the Smithsonian Institute. Later he saw it in the National Museum to which it had been transferred. In 1890, he saw it again in the Medical Museum, where it had again been transferred. It bore the following inscription: "Skull of Indian chief, Texas. W. R. Choate (nephew of Dr. Rufus Choate), Smithsonian No. 42911; National Museum No. 3051." It was in the southeast corner of the gallery among the "Unknown Indian Skulls." In 1912, it had been again transferred to the Ethnological Bureau of the New National Museum. It has traveled some. It is hard to say when or where this Qua-ha-da Comanche skull will find its last resting place. As the word Qua-ha-da signifies "Wanderer" he may, like Tennyson's "Brook," "go on forever."

in, and all shuddered who had participated in the narrow escape, and loudly praised the prompt action and bravery of our noble, gallant "Peter" Boehm and the conduct of our faithful friends and rescuers, the Ton-ka-way scout allies. Upon going to Gregg's grave, it was found the earth had been dug up by wolves so that it was nearly uncovered. The region was scoured for larger stones with which to cover and anchor it down.

The wounded farrier of Troop "D" (Stiegel) who had been shot through the bowels, and whom we had brought down the cañon on the horse litter, was very low. The ball had passed completely through him, cutting the intestines, which, with the fecal matter, exuded from the hole in his back. Gas was also being emitted from the wound. No one believed he could recover. Our efficient, tireless, ever-persevering A. A. Surgeon, Dr. Rufus Choate, never left him for a moment. He not only devoted his professional skill to saving the man's life, but, as a nurse, his tireless care and attention, notwithstanding the long period of jolting over very rough ground, placed him on the road to a quick recovery and permanent cure. He could only retain liquid food, nourishment taking place by absorption. It was Dr. Choate's object, therefore, to afford this with the least possible strain upon his physical and nervous system. Buffalo meat, devoid of all fat or gristle, was converted into a strong beef tea by quick methods. Liebig's condensed beef was added to this hot "bouillon," and poured into him as often as possible, at least without nauseating.

His wound thus closed, while his strength was conserved, and in this manner his life was saved. It was one of the most marvelous recoveries—due to perseverance, skill and devotion to duty by an unselfish medical officer—known to us who had seen many deaths from culpable neglect both during the Civil War and afterwards. Two years later the writer saw this man, who had been discharged, working in the Quartermaster's Corral at San Antonio, Texas.

"Camp Misery"—The Doctor's Practical Joke on Mackenzie

Several horses died here. Others, too weak to move, had to be shot, and still more were broken down. Lawton arrived with forage and rations for the horses and men. Mackenzie, feeling confident that Quan-ah, finding that on account of the storm we had abandoned further pursuit, would turn back from the Pecos River and move to one of their old, well-known haunts on Pease River, determined to send a part of the command in further search of him, taking command himself, sending all disabled, dismounted men, and weak, sick animals into Duck Creek. On October 24 the two commands separated. After reaching Duck Creek, Mackenzie's wound proved too painful and he was compelled to come in, and joined us on the 29th. From this camp we moved to another, in a frightful storm of rain and hail. The "pull" through the sand and "shin oak" killed off more animals. The General was irritable, irascible, mean and "ornery." Nobody seemed to want to go near him even for sociability. Our esteemed A. A. Surgeon, Dr. Gregory, who had remained with the infantry at the supply camp, incubated a scheme or practical joke, however, which he confided to Lawton and the rest of us, by which he was going to "put one over" on the "old man." He would go and tell him that it was necessary for the preservation of his life for him to keep quiet and calm, etc. Otherwise he would be compelled to *amputate his leg*. He went to Mackenzie's tent. We watched him disappear. Shortly after we saw the doctor shoot out of the tent and make for his own, his face a deep scarlet. We could only guess at the result. We ascertained later, however, from him that with the conscious importance of professional skill, he took off the bandages, examined the wound, and with the utmost gravity told General Mackenzie that it was very much inflamed, and unless he controlled his irritability, he would be compelled to amputate the limb. He got as far as amputate when the General seized a crutch or big cane, and making for the doctor caused him to jump out from under the tent flap to save his own head from amputation. He did not repeat that advice. The joke fell flat.

From this camp the writer was directed to take command of all the dismounted and disabled men, sore-backed horses and mules, all the "tag ends," and proceed to Cottonwood Springs on the Double Mountain Fork, put them in camp and await the return of Major Mauck with his column from Pease River, while Lawton was ordered to take the supply train into Fort Griffin, load with half forage of corn, and return to our camp. This was carried out. The writer spent a lonely five days in the new camp. Thousands of buffalo darkened the prairie about us.

Besieged by Wolves—A Dose of Strychnine

Frequently on the march we came suddenly upon many packs of wolves of from eight to ten in number, dashing ahead of the column through the numerous breaks which cut our trail. They were hanging on the outskirts of the immense herds, waiting patiently for some young calf, or sick, or wounded buffalo left to die, which they soon feasted on. Many a bleached skull remote from the herds attested the untiring patience of these savage hangers-on to the interests of their ever-craving appetites. It was not so easy, however, to get the calves at all times, for the cow buffalo, unaided, was no weak fighter and defender of her young, and, when aided, as was generally the case, by a circle of young bulls, the cowardly sneak thieves were frequently tossed and trampled out of all shape. It was rarely the case, therefore, that a pack of wolves would go into a buffalo herd and make a desperate fight for a calf or a distressed cow. It was only when the helpless animals were abandoned that the wolves banqueted.

We gathered all the disabled animals and sick and wounded men, made a small enclosure, or breastwork, on three sides of a square, out of boxes, barrels, bags filled with earth, etc., pitched our tents, placed everything inside

and prepared for a defensive stay—a period of "watchful
waiting"—until the return of the Pease River column.

We had every reason to believe that the hostiles, eluding the column sent there, might seek and follow our trail
with a large body; if so, our little handful of men would,
it was feared, have made a feeble resistance if attacked.
At night the wolves came out of the "bottoms" and numerous coulees, arroyas, and ravines, in countless numbers
and besieged this camp. The sick and wounded became
very nervous, for in their boldness the ravenous animals
advanced to within a few feet of our tents in their eagerness for the meat which we had hung all about us in large
quantities for immediate use, besides the carcasses scattered here and there had attracted their scent, and in the
glare of the campfire their long, white teeth could be distinctly seen, as they tumbled, fought, and howled over
their canine feast. It came as an unpleasant episode in
our enforced imprisonment. No such number of wolves
had ever been seen or heard by us in that country. If
some came nearer than others, we charged them with large
fire brands, throwing them in their midst, whereupon the
brutes scattered in every direction. They dreaded fire.
About the third or fourth night, however, during which it
had been impossible to sleep, their number seemed to increase and double up. They became bolder than ever,
for now, outside the camp, they had but a few bones to
quarrel over, having picked them white, while our fresh
meat was still a very great temptation. The little A. A.
Surgeon, Dr. Culver, who had been with the infantry
column, and Lieutenant Spear of the Eleventh Infantry,
became perceptibly nervous, if not actually alarmed. We
played cards to divert our minds, but still the wolves gathered and crowded in upon us. We did not dare to open a
rifle fire upon them for fear our shots might attract any
Indian scouts that might, perhaps, be lurking about our
trail.

The doctor had a quantity of strychnine among his medical stores, and, at the suggestion of the writer, we used it all in poisoning a quantity of meat and scattering it here and there. We soon had the satisfaction of hearing their blood-curdling yells and howls while fighting for the poison. When morning came, we found them stretched out in every direction; some were dead, others were *wanting to die,* being in their last agonies after having gone to the stream to "water up," where we found their already bloated bodies. It was only a temporary cessation of hostilities. On the last night, not daring to sacrifice any more of our meat, which we might need, for we had no serviceable horses with which to run the buffalo, still in large numbers all about us, we tried the experiment of poisoning some of the wolf meat. They again congregated by thousands, coming out of the river bottom at dusk and remaining until the first streak of dawn. They sat upon the bluffs, gathered about the carcasses, and again set up noises hideous enough to cause the hair to stand upon end, but they would not touch the meat. They will not banquet upon their own kind unless driven to it by desperation, no matter how much the meat might be disguised. This lobo fraternity had been pretty well fed up. Again we could get no sleep, and once more resorted to firebrands. If one could control their nerves, the tumbling and stampeding of this vast throng would have been most laughable. But their terrifying yells had somewhat the same effect upon the doctor and Lieutenant Speer as the Germans in their campaign of frightfulness in the world's war. *The more noise, the greater the effect.* The writer had heard this noisy yelling in many battles of the Civil War. Thus we spent five days and nights in this wolf-besieged camp, with nothing to do, and nothing to see but that vast expanse of solitude and wilderness, the horizon of which was a constant mirage, except the immense buffalo herds which we could no longer reach except by still-hunting.

The March In—Snow, Sleet, Abandoned Animals

On November 6, the command from Pease River under

Major Mauck arrived in the midst of a dense, driving snow storm and "norther," it having snowed the night before to the depth of five inches and grown colder, and many animals having died at the picket line, their backs crusted with snow and ice. Many of his command were riding pack mules. They had been unsuccessful in their search for the Comanches. The animals, many of them, were mere shadows. They needed some corn for feed and fuel, so that we might save those that remained and get them in by short and slow marches. Lawton rolled in the next morning (8th) with his corn train. Both outfits had had a rough time. We commenced to feed full forage. The poor brutes could hardly stand up. With great caution, and amidst intense cold and much suffering among men and animals, we made our way in across California and Paint Creeks and the Clear Fork of the Brazos, and slowly into Fort Griffin, which we reached on November 12, singing the same old song with which we had started more than a month before: "Come home, John, don't stay long; come home soon to your own Mary Ann!"

The writer left thirty wolf skins under five inches of snow in that wolf camp on the Double Mountain Fork— enough to make eight large, fine robes—which he never saw again.

On the night of the 13th the "Tonks" gave us a scalp dance in their village on the flat below the post. They had divided the two scalps into eight equal parts. We did not stay long. It proved to be too warm in their small "tepees," and too "smelly," as they had stripped off in the dance down to their breech clouts, and later, when they discarded them, *was the time when we departed.*

On the 17th we were slowly marching across Salt Creek prairie toward Fort Richardson; when about halfway across, near the scene of the massacre in May, a storm of rain and sleet, which had been brewing all day, broke upon us. It blew a gale and toward night had changed to a driving sleet, hail, and snow storm, compelling us to go into camp. The men were much exposed all night trying to save the animals from perishing by using their saddle blankets for covers. Many died, however, during the night, and more men were mounted on the pack mules. Major Mauck, who was in command, decided, if we were to save the remainder, we must make a desperate effort to negotiate the remaining twenty miles, and that without delay. Breaking camp early, therefore, in the midst of the raging storm, the snow from six to eight inches deep, we "led out," the men dismounted, and the entire command floundered and staggered into the protection of the post-oak timber near Rock Station, fourteen miles from Fort Richardson, where we were somewhat sheltered from the pitiless hail and sleet which cut our faces like glass, and, after a short halt, pushed on, arriving at the post at three p. m., tired out, cold, hungry, and dirty. We had at last arrived "home," for that was what it seemed to us, after most of the regiment had been in the field since May 1. All were delighted to greet their wanderers, and, like all soldiers' hardships and sacrifices, they were all soon forgotten in hot baths, change of clothing, good grub, complete rest, and the warm congratulations of our friends and the love of anxious, devoted wives and families.

Commendatory Letters Confirm Statement

Following are letters from the late Major (then Lieutenant) P. M. Boehm, the late Major (then Lieutenant) W. A. Thompson, the late Lieutenant, Colonel (then Captain) John A. Wilcox, and others, voluntarily given in support of the writer's statement:

Boehm says: "I was present at the time the Indians made the charge, and I can vouch for the brave conduct and skill of Lieutenant Carter. I can not express in too great a sense the ability shown by this officer in covering the retreat, and holding his men in such a position as held the Indians back."

Thompson says: "Had it not been for your coolness, good judgment, and great gallantry that morning, the

chances are ten to one the whole command would have
been killed before we could have reached them. . . . Prompt
and decisive action and bravery held the men to their
work and saved the day. . . . The Qua-ha-da Indians are
noted for their great bravery and close fighting. I may
add that the part taken in this Indian fight by Captain
Heyl (late Fourth Cavalry) left the impression that all
the credit was due solely to Captain P. M. Boehm and
Lieutenant R. G. Carter (at which time both were Lieutenants of Fourth Cavalry, now retired.''

Wilcox says: ''Your personal bravery in the fight near
the Brazos River when the Indians partially cut off your
little detachment, and killed your sergeant, is well known
to all the old officers of the Fourth Cavalry. In regard
to the occurrences incident to the fight at Remolino,
Mexico. I was present and distinctly recollect your coming up and reporting that you had but recently killed an
Indian. I am familiar with your statement about the
packs being cut loose from the mules. . . . I distinctly recollect the 'captured Indian' you speak of being brought into
camp by the Seminole scout; his efforts to shoot Captain
Mauck and his being killed on the spot. Many discharged
their pieces, and you among the rest. I was standing
within ten steps from this Indian when he was shot. . . .
What you claim regarding yourself are undeniable facts.''

Vernou (now Colonel C. A. Vernou, U. S. A.) says:
''. . . As soon as some of the horses which had stampeded
the night before were caught and sent in from the front,
we heard from the men about the man of Troop ''G'' being
killed, and they told us of Lieutenant Carter's gallant behavior, and said if it had not been for his action things
would have gone pretty badly. . . .''

There also follows a letter from one of the oldest and
best First Sergeants in the Fourth Cavalry, later Ordnance Sergeant Joseph Sudsburger, U. S. A., retired, now
dead:

To Whom It May Concern:

This is to certify that I was a Corporal of Troop "B," Fourth U. S. Cavalry, which Lieutenant R. G. Carter commanded (being specially detached from his own Troop "E" for that purpose) in the campaign against the Qua-ha-da Comanche Indians from October 2 to November 18, 1872. On the morning of October 10, 1871, the Indians stampeded our camp on the Freshwater Fork of the Brazos River, Texas.

While I did not participate in the action which followed later that morning, I know that the statement of Lieutenant Carter is absolutely true in every respect. I had knowledge of all the facts. It was common report among all the enlisted men in the regiment that had it not been for the great skill, cool judgment, and most conspicuous bravery of Lieutenant Carter in the action of that morning, every man of both his own and Captain E. M. Heyl's detachment would have lost their lives. Private Gregg was killed within a few feet of him, and Privates Melville and Downey of Troop "G" were wounded by his side.

I have full knowledge of all the facts connected with the serious injury which Lieutenant Carter received that morning by the falling of his horse when making a charge upon a body of Indian sharpshooters posted on a rocky bluff; of his riding five days with his leg in splints when in pursuit of this band of Indians; and of his treatment for such injury by A. A. Surgeon Rufus Choate, when the command was moving out. I have seen him often since 1887, and known of his suffering ever since.

I was with the command when it made its great raid into Mexico, May 17-19, 1873, and was present when a Lipan Indian, who was decoyed into the burning Kickapoo Village, by a Seminole Indian scout and not disarmed, tried to shoot Captain Mauck, who commanded my troop.

I saw Lieutenant Carter and a Corporal of Troop "M" shoot the Indian down, the former firing first, his shot turning him around and backward so as to throw up his rifle at the moment of discharge into the air, when he fell dead. Lieutenant Carter, by his prompt action, saved the life of Captain Mauck, and the act was witnessed by many officers and men in the command who were standing around the captured prisoners in groups.

Lieutenant Carter was always regarded in the regiment as one of its hardest worked, most efficient, and bravest officers, not only by the commissioned, but by the non-commissioned officers and enlisted men. His constant and valuable services, tireless energy, and conspicuously gallant conduct during those years of continuous Indian warfare, and his uniformly firm but kind treatment of the men in his troop, afforded an example and incentive which stimulated them to their best efforts and made the Fourth Cavalry, under the leadership of General Ranald S. Mackenzie, second to none in the entire Army. It was the only cavalry regiment that ever received the thanks of a State for its services in driving the Indians from its frontier counties.

And when the Army Appropriation Bill of 1877 failed in Congress, and the officers of the Army were without their pay for a period of about six months, in a letter which General Sherman wrote to General Mackenzie, at Fort Hays, Kansas, which I saw, he stated that the entire Texas delegation agreed to vote for the bill, provided General Mackenzie with the Fourth Cavalry should be ordered back to the Department with headquarters at Fort Clark, Texas.

JOSEPH SUDSBURGER,
Ordnance Sergeant, U. S. Army, Retired.

Late First Sergeant, Troop "B," Fourth U. S. Cavalry.

Sworn to and subscribed before me, a Notary Public for the District of Columbia, at Washington, D. C., this 29th day of April, A. D. 1904.

THOMAS J. SULLIVAN,
(SEAL.) *Notary Public, D. C.*

Letter of Brigadier-General Wirt Davis, U. S. A. (then Captain Fourth Cavalry), now dead, follows. His reputation throughout the entire Army was that of being one of the bravest and most efficient officers in the cavalry service.

BALTIMORE, MD., *December 6, 1904.*

To Whom It May Concern:

This is to set forth that Troop "F," Fourth Cavalry, of which I was then the captain, was one of the six troops of that regiment, Colonel R. S. Mackenzie, Brevet Brigadier General, U. S. A., commanding, that took part in the expedition in October and November, 1872, against the hostile Qua-ha-da band (Quoina's) of Comanche Indians, and that I was present during the whole campaign.

About sunset on the 9th of October, 1871, the command encamped on the Freshwater Fork of the Brazos River, Texas. About 1 o'clock a. m. on the 10th of October, 1871, as the moon was setting, a considerable number of mounted Comanches, yelling and firing pistols, charged past our camp and succeeded in stampeding some horses and mules. At daylight several officers with detachments of men were sent out by Colonel Mackenzie to search for and recover the stampeded animals. . . . Captain Heyl's troop while hunting for the loose horses, had one of his men killed, but the Indians were assailed and driven off by Lieutenants Carter and Boehm, who, with their detachments, promptly and gallantly rushed to Heyl's relief. Colonel Mackenzie, when the firing was heard, ordered me to mount my troop (the horses were already saddled), and with him I proceeded at a gallop toward the scene of conflict. When we arrived there, however, the Indians had scattered and had fled up the Freshwater Fork of the Brazos toward the Staked Plains. Lieutenant Carter, while pursuing the Indians who had attacked Captain Heyl's troop, was badly injured by his horse falling and jamming his leg against a rock. The injury was a serious one, and it was so pronounced to be by Acting Assistant Surgeon Rufus Choate, U. S. A., who attended him. Although I was not an eye-witness of the mishap that befell Lieutenant Carter in the affair with hostile Comanches on October 10, 1871, yet I know that he was injured as described herein. Lieutenant Boehm, who was first lieutenant of my Troop "F," but who on that expedition was chief of scouts for Colonel Mackenzie, related all the facts and circumstances in the case to me in camp on the following day and subsequently often referred to the matter in conversation with me. It may not be irrelevant for me to state that Lieutenant Carter was known in the Fourth Cavalry as a *very energetic and gallant officer,* and his involuntary and reluctant retirement from service on account of disability in the line of duty was regarded by *many officers as a decided loss to the regiment.*

WIRT DAVIS,
Brigadier General, U. S. Army, Retired,
In 1871—Captain, Troop "F," Fourth U. S. Cavalry.

In a personal letter to Captain Carter, General Wirt Davis adds the following:

DEAR CARTER:

Enclosed with this is a statement concerning the affair on the Freshwater Fork of the Brazos River, Texas, and although *it is not as strong as I would like to make it,* still I hope it may help you in securing favorable action on your petition. I have read the brief very carefully, and it is a lucid and forcible statement of reasons why an enabling act of Congress should be passed authorizing the President to appoint you a Colonel, U. S. Army, mounted, to date from January 30, 1903. You certainly deserve consideration for your service in the War of the Rebellion and in the arduous Indian campaigns after that memorable war. I sincerely hope that you may be successful in obtaining special legislation for your relief.

The foregoing letters are from every officer of the

Fourth U. S. Cavalry now living who was with Captain Carter in the Indian campaign of 1871.

The Medal of Honor "Most Distinguished Gallantry"—
The Brevet "Specially Gallant Conduct"

The writer, many years after this affair, was accorded partial justice by being awarded the Congressional medal of honor, the officers of the Fourth Cavalry practically uniting in an endorsement on the following application made by Major P. M. Boehm, then Captain U. S. A., retired.

WASHINGTON, D. C., *December 13, 1893.*

To THE ASSISTANT SECRETARY OF WAR,
                    Washington, D. C.
SIR:

I have the honor to recommend and to request that First Lieutenant and Brevet Captain R. G. Carter, U. S. A., retired, may be awarded a medal of honor for conspicuous gallantry and bravery in action with Qua-ha-da Comanche Indians on the Freshwater Fork of the Brazos River, Texas, on the morning of October 10, 1871.

I have read Lieutenant Carter's statement and it is correct in every respect. I was present at the time the Indians made their last charge upon him and his little command, and can vouch for the *conspicuously brave conduct, skill,* and *good judgment* shown by Lieutenant Carter. . . .

If any distinguished honor is to be bestowed upon any officer engaged at the time herein mentioned, Lieutenant R. G. Carter is clearly entitled to it, as his act was entirely voluntary, he being officer of the day at the time, and on a tour of the pickets when he first sighted the Indians which he and the other officers chased with their commands until they met the main body.

I have the honor to be, sir,
                    Very respectfully, your obedient servant,
                              (*Signed*) P. M. BOEHM,
                              Captain, U. S. A., Retired.

This medal of honor was awarded the writer for *"Most Distinguished Gallantry* in action against Indians on Brazos (Freshwater Fork) River, Texas, October 10, 1871, in holding the left of the line with a few men during the charge of a large body of Indians, after the right of the line had retreated, and by delivering a rapid fire, succeeded in checking the Indians until other troops came to the rescue, while serving as Second Lieutenant, Fourth Cavalry."

Under the act of Congress of February 27, 1890, granting Indian brevets for gallantry, the writer was given the brevet of First Lieutenant, U. S. Army, for *"Specially Gallant Conduct* in action against Indians on the Brazos (Freshwater Fork) River, Texas, October 10, 1871," and later the brevet of Captain, U. S. Army, for *"Gallant Services* in action against Kickapoo, Lipan, and Mescalero Apache Indians at Remolino, Mexico, May 18, 1873."

Adobe Walls

Quan-ah made one last desperate effort to hold his Indians together, and through his influence and wily diplomacy succeeded in persuading all of the bands of the Comanche and Cheyenne tribes with about half of the Kio-was and other Indians to affiliate with him and make an attack upon an organized company of white buffalo hunters who he claimed were depredating upon the well recognized Indian lands over which the immense herds of buffalo grazed, and upon which the Indians then relied for almost their very existence in houses (skins for lodges), clothing, food, etc. He mustered about seven hundred warriors, and the campaign began June 24, 1874, with an attack led by Quan-ah in person with his confederated Indians against the buffalo hunters, who were strongly intrenched in a rude fort known as the Adobe Walls, on the South Canadian in the Texas panhandle. In addition to the thick walls, the hunters had a small field piece which they used with such good effect that after a sieze lasting all day the Indians were obliged to withdraw with considerable loss. Quan-ah, however, was implacable to the last, when four converging columns finally administered the death blow to him and his Indians, "the *Vanishing Race*."

Quan-ah as a "Good Indian"—His Reward—Another
Romance—His Death—Last Rites

Quan-ah lived, after "coming in," at the Fort Sill Reservation. To placate him, and keep him on the "good road," so that he might follow the white man and be a useful member of society, he was given land, horses, mules, and cattle, and a substantial two-storied house to live in. This house had a large star on the roof, to distinguish it, presumably from the other houses, and was about twelve or fifteen miles from the town of Lawton. He leased his land to cattlemen for grazing purposes, and, in this way accumulated a large fortune for an Indian. He rode in state (four-mule ambulance) with his squaws—of whom he had, it was reported, at one time seven—and twenty-two children. He came to Washington many times, and at Theodore Roosevelt's second inauguration, in 1905, the writer saw him ride up Pennsylvania Avenue in the inaugural column with other "good Indians," most of whom had dipped their hands in many a white settler's blood on the once far off borderland of the West.

On February 10, 1908, Hon. John H. Stephens, Member of Congress from Texas, offered a bill appropriating one thousand dollars for a memorial to Cynthia Ann Parker in Texas, offering the following as his reason: "In view of the *public service* rendered by this Indian (Quan-ah) to the white people on the Texas frontier, in *causing his tribe* to quit the war path and live on their reservation, and the further fact of the suffering of his mother for so many years as a white captive among the savages." This was done at the request of Quan-ah, then in Washington, in behalf of his mother, who had died about 1864, and his infant sister, Prairie Flower, both of whom had been buried in the Fosterville cemetery, near Poyner Station in Henderson County, Texas. This bill was passed on the Indian Appropriation Bill on the same day. Quan-ah then had ample means to erect this memorial.

The Texas authorities having refused Quan-ah permission to remove the bodies of his mother and sister, "Prairie Flower," to his new home, he, accompanied by C. W. Birdsong, Indian agent, and son-in-law of Quan-ah, on November 29, 1910, smuggled the bodies from their graves, and brought them to Cache, about twelve or fifteen miles west of Lawton, near Fort Sill, Oklahoma.

Quan-ah died February 22, 1911, of an attack of asthma and rheumatism, leaving three wives and fifteen children. He was reputed to be the wealthiest Indian in the United States, through the generosity of the Government. He was buried at Post Oak Mission Cemetery, near Lawton, on February 24, 1911. The reburial of his mother had been postponed for the following Sunday, and it had been planned that Quan-ah should perform the ceremony, but his sudden death interrupted these plans. At sunrise on the morning of his death, the real Indian burial ceremony began. Three times during the night, Too-nicey, the favorite of Quan-ah's remaining three squaws, arose and loudly called to the Great Spirit for her chief. At five o'clock, crying loudly, "This is the time I always build a fire for him," she waked all the family. At six o'clock, Marcus Poco, Chief Medicine Man of the tribe and preacher, conducted the "sunrise funeral," crying to the Great Spirit and to the white man's God to accept the spirit of the dead chief. The Indians chanted weird dirges. More than one thousand attended, including hundreds of Indians.

The body of Quan-ah was dressed in his buckskin suit of former days. At noon the funeral party wended its way among the hills of the Parker ranch to the little Indian cemetery, and the funeral service began. A. J. Breaker (or Becker), Mennonite missionary, conducted it after the manner of the whites. Following this, the Indians sang the "Swan Song," the Medicine Man again cried to the Great Spirit, and the body was lowered to the side of his white mother. In the coffin were placed a buckskin bag containing Quan-ah's favorite feathers, his war bonnet, trinkets, and jewelry. Among the latter was a diamond

brooch, valued at $450, the present of cattlemen who had
grazed their stock on the Comanche ranges fifteen years
before, and became rich.

Nacona, a town named after Quan-ah's father, is on the
M. K. & T. R. R., in Montague County, a few miles south
of Old Spanish Fort on the Red River.

Quanah, a town in the Texas panhandle, some miles east
of Cañon Blanco, the county seat of Hardeman County,
not far from the town of Vernon on Pease River, is named
for him, the latter town being near where Peta Nacona,
his father, was killed, and where his mother was recap-
tured by Captain Ross' rangers. Has anybody ever heard
or known of other county seats in the Texas panhandle being named for any officers of the Fourth United States
Cavalry, who risked their lives and sacrificed their health
and future happiness here on earth in more than one effort
to drive out that savage Qua-ha-da Comanche band and
open up that wild and desolate region to settlement, civilization, wealth, and all the material prosperity it now en-
joys, and which that wily Indian was seeking to prevent
by bloody incursions, burning, plundering, and savages
orgies?

Not until his (Quan-ah's) band was driven from the
fastnesses of the Palo Duro Cañon in 1874, his villages
were destroyed, and his ponies were captured and shot,
did he submit, relent, or repent. Then, seeing his ultimate fate, he "came in" and became a "good Indian."
Generous Government, indeed! Could a generous Government afford to do less for a "gallant officer" of the Army
who had almost sacrificed his life in an effort to promote
the settlement of that wild uninhabited, savage-infested
territory, and to advance civilization in that now richest
of rich countries, than it could later do for this murderous
savage, so suddenly become converted to the white man's
ways, but whose entire previous career had been devoted,
not, as Mr. Stephens declared when asking for a $1,000
memorial to Quan-ah's mother, in *"public service* rendered
by this Indian chief on the Texas frontier in causing his

tribe to quit the warpath and live on their reservation,''
but in burning, pillaging, plundering, ravaging, and murdering every man, woman, or child who attempted to settle
there. If Congress, through such a sentiment for a so-
called civilized (?) Indian, whose career had been marked
by an orgy of blood and rapine, some of the foulest, darkest deeds ever recorded in the annals of Indian warfare,
leaving always a trail of fire in his path, could bestow a
$1,000 monument* to honor the white mother who bore this
implacable half-breed Comanche, and give him a Christian
burial with imposing ceremonies (the writer has erected
his own memorial in Arlington from the amount which Mr.
Elihu Root declared a most generous Government had paid
him for his wreckage), it could certainly have done a simple
justice to the one officer who was so ready, for the sake of
peace and civilization in that far-off Texas panhandle, to
risk his life in what has, indeed, proved to be something
more than a mere story, a chronicle of events, or a calm
retrospect. It has become the supreme sacrifice, an almost
life-long heritage of a *real and truly great tragedy of
Cañon Blanco.*

---

*Since this was written Congress has appropriated an additional $1500 for a memorial to be erected in honor of Quanah Parker.

*Could Mr. Stephens have seen the Fourth Cavalry in the action at Palo Duro in 1874, he would have witnessed their method of "inducing" Quanah and his Indians to go into Fort Sill, and thereafter follow the "white man's road." It would certainly, in these days of a maudlin sentiment, have been a revelation to the average settler of the Texas panhandle.

CHAPTER VIII

On the Trail of Deserters—A Phenomenal Capture

THE year of 1871 had been so full of incidents and far reaching results for the Fourth Cavalry and its new Colonel, Ranald S. Mackenzie, that it is somewhat difficult to go back into the dim vistas of that period and select the one incident or absorbing event which would be either of greatest magnitude or afford the most thrilling interest.

This capture of ten deserters, however, under circumstances of more than ordinary importance, since it is believed to be the record capture ever made in the Military Department of Texas, or, perhaps for that matter, of any Military Department in the United States, came about as closely in touch with the writer's life as almost any other experience he ever had while serving as an officer of that regiment, including, as it did, terrible exposure, and unavoidable **hardships** and privations which are almost indescribable.

Like all of the other Cavalry regiments in our Army which were then doing about three-fourths of all the active effective work, the work that disables or kills, in the subjugation of the savage tribes in the United States, driving them into Indian reservations, and rendering it possible for the frontier border to be settled, and civilization to be advanced to a point where it could feel safe from raids and bloody incursions, the Fourth U. S. Cavalry, notwithstanding its high morale and almost perfect state of discipline, had its share of desertions.

Was Mackenzie a "Martinet?"

Mackenzie was not a West Point "martinet," as that term is generally understood in our army—but, from four wounds he had received, three in the Civil War, and one that year (already referred to but not officially recorded) in the campaign against Quan-ah Parker, the Qua-ha-da Comanche Chief, and almost criminal neglect of his own health, in his intensity of nature and purpose in prosecuting these arduous Indian campaigns, he had become more or less irritable, irascible, exacting, sometimes erratic, and frequently explosve.

This much may be said, however, it is certain that notwithstanding his physical condition, and his mental temperament resulting therefrom, he never sought to inflict an injury or punishment upon anybody unnecessarily, never became a petty or malicious persecutor, hounding a man into his grave, and when it became evident to him as well as to others that he had done any of his officers or men an act of injustice, nobody could have been more open, free and frank in his disavowal of that act, or quicker to apologize and render all the reparation possible in his power. This applied to any and all down to the last Second Lieutenant and private soldier in the regiment.

One man never knows another so well, even intimately, as when he is thrown closely in contact with or lives and sleeps and eats with him. The writer had done all with Mackenzie during a greater part of this period of 1871, having been his Post Adjutant twice during Gen. Sherman's inspection in May, at the time of the massacre of Salt Creek Prairie, and prior to our Expedition of that year, and his Field Adjutant on his entire campaign in his abortive attempt to strike Kicking Bird's band of Ki-o-was before he could be stampeded into the Fort Sill reservation from May 1st until Oct. 3 I had got to know him very well.

Causes for Desertion

Both officers and men had been under a terrific high-keyed pressure, a very great mental and physical strain, almost to the breaking point; were tired and dispirited because the results and the hard work performed had not justified their expectations and because they could not then see any immediate relief from the performance of such exacting duty. The pace had been a little too fast even for the Fourth Cavalry. Much of the spirit and enthusiasm

for such unremunerative work was at a very low ebb.
While it had not yet approached a complete discouragement, it was a condition of supreme disgust and contempt
at the methods employed. They felt that with the Government at Washington nullifying and rendering most of
their hard labor abortive, that success in those long, weary
and extremely exhausting Indian campaigns was not so
much dependent upon their absolute loyalty to duty and
perfect willingness to sacrifice themselves when necessary
in achieving results, as upon the paralyzing acts and influence of the "Indian Ring" in Washington and the ever
changing political cesspools of a politically ridden country.
They wanted to see the tangible results or fruits of such
terribly hard service and to feel that such hardships, privations and sacrifices as they had experienced, had not
been in vain or wasted by a gang of cold blooded, un-
scrupulous plunderers and grafters remote from the scene
of these border activities. We have but recently passed
through a similar experience with the same class, in fact
are doing it now. Like *"death and Taxes,"* we have them
with us always, especially in time of wars. It is then the
vultures abound. It is then we have the jelly-fish, spineless slackers, the pussy-foot pacifists, conscientious objec-
tors, chicken hearted shirkers "I didn't raise my boy to be
a soldier" shriekers and "let George do it" fighters, coming down to the secret renegades, traitors, and Bolshevist
anarchists to the bomb throwers. They have always been
the curse of this Nation, the natural result as a rule of
the "Melting Pot" that does not melt, breeding a lot of
mongrel curs and hybrids that should no longer be a part
of our American life. It is feared they will always be
with us.

Thus they reasoned and the propaganda poison spread.
These were some of the contributing, but not all of the real
causes that led to what soon became almost an epidemic of
desertions in the regiment. The last snow storm in which
they had floundered and wallowed into Fort Richardson,
seemed to have destroyed the last atom of patriotic ardor

and martial enthusiasm among even some of the best of
our Indian scrappers. The loss of Quan-ah Parker's village in the snow, sleet and hail of that black, awful night
on the solitary plateau of the "Staked Plains," when the
entire command came so near perishing, and the swiftly
moving mass of fleeing panic-stricken Indians was "so
near, and yet so far" had taken nearly all of the "gimp,"
snap, and live-wire spirit out of our hitherto bold Fourth
Cavalry warriors. Following this the terrible monotony
of the life without amusements or recreations of any kind,
no athletics or competitions; no libraries, infrequent
mails; no hunting except a few men selected on account of
their being expert shots (no ammunition then being issued
by the Government for that purpose); no theaters or con-
certs; nothing but the dreary monotonous grind of guard
and police duty, detached service, and the rather questionable pleasure they got out of some saloons and gambling
hells which generally landed them "broke" and subjects
for the guard house and disciplinary measures and more
forfeiture of pay, hard labor or other punishment. These
were the causes for the desertion epidemic. During this
period of unrest and discontent, however, on account of the
conditions described, there were few court martials, nearly
all corrective or disciplinary measures being applied by the
Troop Commanders through the First Sergeants, under
proper restrictions or limitations by the Colonel. "Knock
downs" and "drag outs" were not infrequent, and at no
extra expense to the Government. Sometimes the victim
of an unfortunate "jag" was got under control by a twenty-four hour sojourn in the "orderly room," a "dip" in a
water hole near by, the "boozer" being thrown in a few
times "by order," or, if he became too obstreperous, abusive or insubordinate, a "sweat box," a "30 pound log on
a ring," or a "spread eagle on the spare wheel of a caisson" was resorted to to fully control the habitual drunk,
shirker or malingerer, all with the knowledge of and under
the direct or indirect supervision of the Commanding
Officer.

On the 29th of November it was reported that ten men had deserted from one troop ("B"), and Mackenzie thoroughly aroused now by the frequency of these wholesale desertions, took immediate and decisive action.

Rock-Ribbed Orders vs. Elastic Verbal Instructions

About dark on this day Mackenzie sent in great haste for Lieut. H. W. Lawton and the writer and told us the situation; that he was going to send us out on this special trip in pursuit of deserters and to get ready as soon as possible. He would have a written order for us in a few minutes. We were generously informed that while it was not our turn on the detached duty roster for this service, yet, so and so was too sick, another had a cold, still a third was inefficient, and would never get results—and a fourth could not stand the gaff of a "Norther," etc., etc., *all so comforting and soothing* (?). We were, therefore, "It." We were to report to him in thirty minutes. We were each to select any Corporal in the regiment to accompany us. A black, and ominous "Norther" was brewing and it was then beginning to be bitter cold. We reported within the time given with our Corporals, and the following official order was placed in the writer's hands.

HEADQUARTERS FORT RICHARDSON, TEXAS

November 29th, 1871.

SPECIAL ORDERS No. 280

(*Extract*)

V.   Second Lieutenant *R. G. Carter*, 4th Cavalry, with a detail consisting of two non-commissioned officers and eleven privates of that Regiment, mounted, fully armed and equipped, furnished one day's rations and sixty rounds of ammunition per man, will proceed at Retreat this day, in pursuit of deserters under the *verbal instructions* of the Commanding Officer of the Post. The A. C. S. will turn over to *Lieut. Carter*, the sum of ($250) Two hundred and fifty dollars, subsistence funds, for the purchase of subsistence for the men of his detail. The A. A .Q. M. will turn over to *Lieut. Carter*, the sum of ($300) three hundred dollars, Quartermaster's funds, for the purchase of forage for the public animals.

By Command of Colonel RANALD S. MACKENZIE,

(Signed) W. J. KYLE,

1st Lieut. 11th Infantry, Post Adjutant.

Lieut. R. G. CARTER, 4th Cavalry.

The money was turned over to us by the Post Adjutant, Lawton receiving the same amount, and then turning to both of us Mackenzie said: ''In addition to those orders, I wish to give you special instructions for your guidance in this most important duty you are going on. I shall not expect you to follow them implicitly but to be guided by circumstances arising at the moment, and which, being on the spot you will know how to deal with better than anybody else, and to use your best judgment and wisest discretion at all times. You are to keep one Corporal with you all the time, taking him into your confidence so far as you may deem it necessary for your success. You are to go in different directions. Lawton is to go on the Decatur road, while you (the writer) are to follow the Weatherford road. You are to cover all of the intermediate settlements near and beyond those towns, seeking at all times the assistance of the Civil authorities and holding out to them the prospect of the Government reward ($30) for the apprehension and delivery to you of each deserter. The towns should only be entered at night and then with a deputy sheriff or other civil officer. It should be systematically and thoroughly searched. Should you find that these deserters have headed for the railroads, and you have traced them that far, and it becomes necessary, drop your detachment, leaving it in charge of one non-commissioned officer, while you take the other with you, continuing the pursuit, even if it leads to Galveston and New Orleans, or, even to New York,'' and then, hesitating somewhat he added, pitching his voice to a high key, and as was his habit snapping the stumps of his amputated fingers, ''I *don't want either of you to come back until you have accomplished results.* I want these men brought back and punished. Obey the *Civil Laws* and if they are not violated and you stick to the spirit of your instructions, I will cover all of your acts with a *''blanket order.''*

The writer suggested that Lawton and himself, and the Corporals whom we might select to remain with us whereever we went, should go in citizens clothes, since, if we had

to "cut loose" from our detachments, we would be able
to co-operate more effectively with the Civil authorities
when we might be acting as detectives about the large
towns, especially at night. To this Mackenzie readily
agreed, saying that it was an excellent and practical suggestion. He included this idea in his intsructions. The
writer had been at an immense conscript and draft rendezvous during the Civil War, among the worst classes of
"substitutes" and "bounty jumpers" ever known in the
history of our Army. They were deserters from every
Army and Navy of the world; had come over here for the
huge bounties paid under our vicious conscript laws, only
to desert, re-enlist and repeat the method again and again.
We frequently mingled with them in citizens clothes, got
their plans, and either thwarted them or caused their arrest and punishment. On one occasion the writer caused
the execution of two for desertion.

We thought that these instructions were very lucid, elastic, and they certainly were very wide sweeping, enough
so to satisfy the most exacting soldier. It looked like a
winter's job had been cut out for us and secretly in our
hearts we wished the trail might lead through the places
he named. Visions of Galveston, New Orleans and "Little
Old New York" loomed up very large and alluring, for
neither of us had visited those attractive "burgs" and
elysiums of pleasure for a long time. But the conditional,
or *"If"* clause in this interview caused us to dubiously
shake our heads with feeling of hope, it is true, but not of
elation and not unmixed with some dread and apprehension
for the future, hardly knowing what was before us in this,
to us, most novel frontier adventure. It was now nearly
dark, and wishing Mackenzie "Good Night," and stepping
out into the gloom of approaching night to face the drizzle
of a gathering "Norther," we (Lawton and the writer)
shook hands and separated, both busily chewing the cud
of reflection, inwardly cursing our reputed Civil War efficiency that had led to our selection for such "beastly"
service, and industriously trying to digest and assimilate

these most elaborate far-reaching and carte blanche instructions the "Old Man" had given us. While we felt that in a measure, we were free lances, all freebooters, with nobody to say "yea or nay," our own Commanding officers with no one to disturb our independence of thought and action (and with such limited means of communication at that period and under such conditions, one can easily see that no such limitations could be imposed as are placed to-day), we also realized the terrible responsibility so suddenly thrust upon us, and the great risks we ran in dealing with determined men wrought up to such a desperate pitch as they were by alleged acts of injustice, and hard and fast conditions under which they were serving. All this aided, as we felt these men might be, by other equally bad gun-men, all over and down through that country wherever we might trail them.

I had selected Corporal John B. Charlton of Troop "F" for my *civilian* companion. I considered him one of the best non-commissioned officers in the regiment. While he had a free, rollicking, reckless, dare devil spirit about him, he was easily controlled, and perfectly amenable to discipline. He was a very handsome, intelligent, active, energetic man of about 24 years of age, and was on his second 5 years enlistment, his first having been in the Light Battery "K" First U. S. Artillery. He was fully six feet, spare, sinewy, straight as an arrow, an athlete, one of the best riders, shots and hunters, and all round soldiers in the regiment. He had a straight nose, strong chin and steel-blue eyes, the glint of which when he was aroused looked dangerous when squinting down the sights of our old Spencer Carbines. He reminded me of that free, rollicsome, "devil-may-care" d'Artagnan, one of the "Three Musketeers." He probably had a past like many other enlisted men who entered the regular army after the Civil War. If so, for obvious reasons, we never pried into that past. He entered into the spirit and novelty of this new adventure with commendable zeal, energy, spirit and enthusiasm. I felt that I knew my man perfectly, and that,

under all circumstances, he would prove absolutely loyal
to all duty and be faithful to whatever trust I reposed in
him.

We were all well mounted, well armed, and had one
good, well trained pack mule to carry our grub. We both
had guides, the one assigned to the writer being William
Rhodes, a rancher, who had been driven in to the shelter
of the post by Indians, a very quiet, sturdy, honest and
reliable man who knew the country fairly well within a
radius of forty miles, but beyond that his knowledge was
no better than my own or any other man in the detachment, besides being one more man to feed and care for
after he had got beyond his bailiwick as a post guide. I
never took another guide beyond a fifty mile radius.

The Pursuit—A Howling "Norther"

At 7:15 we made the start, the writer taking the Weatherford stage road across the prairie, a mere trail. The
"Norther" which had been brewing broke with full force,
with alternate snow, rain, hail and sleet, a heavy gale driving it into our faces. We left the trail and rode into several freighters' camps, where they had sought shelter in
the timber, at great risk to our lives, to search for the
missing men but without learning anything. They had
immense roaring fires which could be seen for a long distance, but so great was their fear of Indians, that we found
them up and ready, rifle in hand and behind their wagon
bodies, determined to sell their lives as dearly as possible.
It was hard to tear ourselves away from these huge fires
and plunge across the interminable prairies in the teeth of
the increasing gale. We were none too warmly clothed,
the men and horses, hardly recovered from their year's
hard work, were beginning to show the effects and wear
and tear of such a frightful storm. Believing that we
should all perish if we continued the ride all night, and
Rhodes, the guide, agreeing with me, upon his informing
me that his brother had a ranch only a mile or two off the
road, directions were given to him to head for the ranch

by the shortest line so that we could secure the needed shelter. After a fearful struggle over several miles of an open stretch of prairie, breasting into the teeth of one of the worst blizzards ever recorded in Texas, we reached the ranch, the men and horses almost exhausted, and completely coated with ice. The ranch proved to be a low, one story log house, with several out-buildings, a ramshackly horse shed and corn crib. It was midnight. Several dogs announced our approach, and Rhodes aroused his brother. Ordering the men to unsaddle, blanket the horses with their saddle blankets, and to "tie in" under the "lee" of the buildings, the men to occupy the horse shed, Rhodes, the Corporals and the writer stalked into the shelter of the "shack." There was but one room with a large stone fire-place. Rhodes piled on the logs. The room had two beds in it. He and the writer, stripping off our outer frozen clothes, and hanging them up to dry in front of the blaze, occupied one bed—his brother, wife and infant child were in the other, while the two Corporals, with several large ranch dogs, curled up in their blankets on the open hearth. It was a "wild and woolly" night. When the baby wasn't crying the dogs were sniffing, growling, whining or whimpering over being disturbed by such an influx of strangers. We wore out the night with little or no sleep. When day broke it was found that the storm was still raging although the wind had somewhat abated. Feeding the horses liberally from Rhodes' corn cribs, for which we paid him generously and after a hasty breakfast, we saddled up and started across the prairie to find the road. The country was one sheet of glare ice. Our horses were smooth shod. At the road we met Sergeant Faber of Troop "A" with a small detachment returning from some duty and going into Fort R—. We learned from him that the deserters had been seen the night before in Weatherford, which was but a few miles away. We skated, slid and floundered along through the ice crust, a horse going down now and then until we reached a creek about one-half mile from W— when the command halted and was placed in bivouac, con-

cealed by heavy chaparral. Corporal Charlton was directed to get ready to accompany the writer at dark and
afoot for a thorough search of the town and to begin to
assume his role.

The Search—Amateur Army Detectives— The Corporal's Joke

We struck the town under cover of darkness, and proceeded to ''comb'' it, both heavily armed and with no insignia of rank on or about our citizens clothes or any indication that we were of the army. ''Now, Corporal, you
are to preserve your incognito. You are to deal with your
Commanding Officer as though we are simply two friends
or acquaintances on a night's drive through the 'slums';
there are to be no 'Yes, Sir!' or—'No, Sir!'—No deference
is to be paid him. Don't forget your part! You are to
be simply 'Green,' and the other party is to be plain
'Brown.' Have your guns handy, and at a given signal be
prepared for a quick pull on the trigger. These are all
the instructions necessary, except that you are under no
circumstances to be separated from me for a moment and
watch me all the time for signals.'' Charlton straightened
up, saluted, replied ''Yes, Sir!'' and that was the last
recognition of rank the writer got during this adventure.

All night long we plied our trade of amateur detectives.
No stone was left unturned. We worked the ''dives,'' faro
banks, brothels, saloons and questionable resorts, but without avail. The deserters had been seen but everybody
seemed mum and blind or deaf and dumb. They had been
paid off for several months, had scattered it, their money
liberally and had left the town. Nobody knew where. At
one *gilded dive* ''Green,'' becoming bold and watching his
chance, assuming the detective role with some slight show
of experience and with a most startling blase air said to
the bespangled proprietress—''Didn't you have a place at
one time in Jacksboro?'' ''Yes!''—''Well, then, you must
remember Brown, here,'' pointing a finger at me—''Oh,
yes!'' was the reply—''I remember him well, and that he

came often and I have often wondered what became of him.'' Anger came to the front at this joke but it had to be choked back; the instructions had been given. No frowns or even scowls or anything but a *positive order* would have disturbed the imperturbable musketeer Corporal, the d'Artagnan of our adventure at this point. The writer was married and had left his wife and child in the howling gale at Fort R—; and had never seen this ''Jezebel.'' His outraged dignity sustained a distinct shock. The Corporal was mildly rebuked later and it was passed by as part of the duality of character which Mackenzie had forced me to assume if success was to be assured. Nothing was accomplished by our night's work. At day break, sending the Corporal back to the bivouac of the command, it was ordered to meet me in town at once. Just as we were deliberating what the next move was to be, Sergt. Miles Varily of Troop ''E'' with a mounted detachment rode into town. He had been to Huntsville, Texas, where he had conveyed Satanta and Big Tree, the Ki-o-wa Indian Chiefs, who had been in confinement at Fort R— under sentence since July 6th, to the State Penitentiary where they were to be confined for life for the massacre of Henry Warren's teamsters on Salt Creek Prairie. Varily had met and talked with the deserters on the Bear Creek Road to Cleburne. He said they were all well armed and had declared that they would not be taken alive. This he gave as his reason for not arresting them with his small force. He knew all of them and had identified them as men of Troop ''B.'' They were in a two-mule freighter's wagon, with a low canvas top drawn down tight for concealment. It was driven by a medium sized, but stocky built civilian. At last there seemed to be a definite clue. They were evidently heading for Cleburn and Waxahatchie—perhaps Corsicana or Waco. I must overtake and capture them before they reached Cleburne which was forty-five miles distant, an all day ride. There was no time to lose. Placing Charlton in the road and the other Corporal with his men on both sides fanned out or de-

ployed for a mile or more, and combing all of the ranches
and small settlements, the writer pushed and directed the
search all of the way without any further developments.
Occasionally the detachments were signaled in to the road.
Cleburne was reached at dark after a terribly hard ride,
the storm still continuing, with a lull in the wind but growing colder. Securing the services of the Deputy Sheriff,
we made a thorough search up to one o'clock that night
but with no results.

A Sleepless Night—The Gettysburg "Johnny"

At 3 o'clock a. m. having sent the Corporal to bed and
placed the men in bivouac in the edge of the town, the
writer, having secured a small map of Texas, was seated in
front of a log fire diligently studying the situation. The deserters must surely be somewhere in the near vicinity.
They were certainly not in Cleburne. Where had they disappeared to after leaving Weatherford? Many roads and
trails led out of Cleburne, some towards the railroads. No
mistake must be made. A sudden inspiration seized me. I
woke up the Corporal. "Corporal, find me a two seated
carriage or conveyance of some kind with driver, 'rake'
the town, and get it here as soon as possible; rout out the
detachment and report yourself mounted to me at the same
time." "Never mind the expense!"

In about thirty minutes Charlton was there with a closely
curtained-in two-seated carriage, carry-all, or Texas
"hack," with two mules, and a *one-legged driver;* also the
entire detachment mounted. Amazement was on the faces
of all. What was the play? What was the game being
"pulled off" by the "Old Man"? "Corporal Charlton,
take your carbine and pistol and get in the front seat with
the driver," and turning to the other Corporal (Jones),
"You will take our two led horses—and follow this 'hack'
never losing touch with it but always remaining as much as
possible out of sight, about a mile or two in the rear, concealing yourself as much as possible by the timber. Keep
your eyes on this 'hack'—*one flash* of my handkerchief and

you will drop further back out of sight if it is open country; two flashes, and you are to come up with your detachment and our led horses at a run; remember, and always keep out of sight as much as possible." We moved out on the Hillsboro road. Inquiries were made all along but with no satisfactory results. We scoured the settlements, ranches and side trails but without avail. We had had a description given us, however, of a certain two-horse team with a number of men in it, which partially filled the bill. Feeling perfectly sure that they were breaking for the railroad, either at Corsicana or Waxahatchie, yet it was feared that we were on the wrong road. The driver of our conveyance, or "dug out," it seemed, had been a Confederate soldier, and had lost a leg at Gettysburg in the desperate charge of Longstreet's Corps on July 2nd upon the "Round Tops" and the "Peach Orchard." He had belonged to the Fifth Texas, Robertson's "Texas Brigade," Hood's Division, and strange to record had confronted the First Brigade, First Division, Fifth Corps, in which the writer had served on that fateful day, and in that death-strewn spot. He immediately *recognized an old enemy,* became extremely voluble, and insisted upon fighting the battle "o'er again," with many a story and reminiscence of his war campaigns, until, at length, he, not having been let into the secret of our plans, was so inclined to put in his time telling stories that we were in great danger of losing the object of an entire night's hard work. He even wanted to stop his mules to emphasize his points, when much to the "Johnny's" chagrin and to the intense amusement of Charlton, my d'Artagnan "Musketeer," the "lines" "by order," were turned over to the latter, while the writer having no whip, prodded the mules along with a sharp stick. *Time,* and then *Time,* was our one objective. We were not so sure of our direction. It was getting late and with our delays we were still some miles from Hillsboro. All was working well in our plans; the detachment was out of sight well to the rear.

We emerged from the cover of the timber upon a "hog wallow" prairie and from this high, rolling hill or divide, when descending to the valley of a small creek, saw ahead, two miles or more, a small train of wagons in the hollow, moving to head this small "branch." Talk about the thumping of one's heart!! Some intuition told me that my deserters were there; my pulse quickened perceptibly, and I almost shouted to the *"Jehu,"* who had been allowed to resume the "lines" but was slackening up to "keep busy," and to gather his animals for a rallying burst of magnificent speed. Now the train was seen to split, some going around, while *one low canvas-topped two-horse wagon* kept on the road for the "branch." Then I saw a number of men—six or eight—get out and try to wade across the stream. *They were the deserters!* of this I now felt sure. I said nothing but sharply touched the Corporal's elbow, jumped from the "hack" and running back a few yards gave the handkerchief signal "two flashes." The *detachment was in full view* on the high ground silhouetted against the sky. The Corporal had closed up too much while we were in the timber, and when emerging exposed himself to the view of the men in the valley as I had feared. They had seen him, and scenting danger made a wild break. The detachment came forward with our led horses at a gallop, but the deserters, having crossed the stream and scattered, were now heading for the fringe of timber, chaparral and brush which either skirted, or was near, the creek.

Once mounted I shouted for one Corporal to head off the main wagon train on the road and detain it and *hold it at all hazards* until my return. Taking Charlton we dashed for the stream. My powerful horse bogged; dismounting in water up to my waist, by careful management he was soon out on dry land. Charlton led. "Get after them now, Corporal, Open fire! Shoot over their heads and close to them, but not to kill." Finely mounted and one of the crack shots in the regiment, with carbine advanced, he was

in his element and "swung out" at a gallop for the men
who were trying to gain the bushes or chaparral in the
distance. He was an absolutely true type of the handsome,
graceful soldier and rider, with the close seat and the
American or cow-boy stirrup, and the resourceful, master-
ful, trained cavalryman of the days closely following the
Civil War. Bang! Crack!! Crack!!! went his carbine. As
I followed him I could see the dirt and dust sprayed over
the fleeing deserters. As the shots whistled and struck
about them, they instantly dropped to the ground for
safety and lay there until some men, whom I had recalled
from the detachment, had followed me and gathered them
up as prisoners. None were to be shot unless they resisted.
I gained the road to the brow of a hill overlooking the
country. After securing five with no resistance, and being
told by them that there were two more, a little darky near
by shouted, "Oh, golly Massa, dere dey go ober de hill,
way yonder." At least two miles away they could be seen
running, fairly flying. The Corporal and writer dashed
after them, and after a long ride and a diligent search in
the bushes, together with a few warning shots, we secured
them. With these men and the driver of their team we
returned to the train. I had not fully trusted the other
Corporal, on account of his seeming indifference, and he
had somewhat hampered my plans and movements, so I
felt anxious as to whether my orders to hold the train fast
had been obeyed. He had, however, stopped the train and
held the wagon master, and the whole "outfit" at the point
of his carbine, as in a vise.

The wagon master was a cool and determined fellow
with cold, gray eyes, and a pugnacious nose and chin; he
and his teamsters were well armed, their guns showing
conspicuously in their holsters or open belt scabbards. He
had been threatening the Corporal, and now, seeing no
insignia of rank on my citizen's clothes, he began to
threaten me with criminal prosecution as soon as he
reached Hillsboro for illegally holding up his train. Vis-

ions of Mackenzie's instructions relating to a *"violation of the civil laws,"* began to loom up large before my eyes. He saw my hesitation and becoming abusive began to be more insistent for the release of himself and men. Sizing up the situation at a glance, the bluff was made. "Look here, my man! We have found a wagon in your train filled with deserters from the United States Army. I am an officer of the Army and if you don't stop your abuse I will put you in irons and take you along to the civil authorities and turn you over on a charge of assisting them to escape." That quieted him.

"Are these all of the teamsters in your train? Produce every man who was with you when it was first sighted, or I will order my men to search it before you can go! Never mind your threats! *We are out for deserters."* He replied: "These are two men who joined my train a few days ago; they are citizens. I know nothing about them. They can tell their own story." The two men stepped forward in citizen's clothes unarmed and with no "set up" or the slightest appearance or sign of the soldier about them. The larger and older, told with a strong Irish brogue a very straight story; how they had "been working" their way along; had sought the train for "shelter," had "not been in the country very long," etc. The other was a mere boy. I was about to let them go with the train, none of the detachment or the deserters whom I had already secured being able to recognize or identify them, when my attention was suddenly attracted to the older man's face. It showed distinctly that a heavy beard *had but recently been shaved off, a*nd this as winter was coming on. I gave no signs, however, of having made this discovery, but said: "You teamsters can go but I shall hold these men. If they are not deserters, they can easily clear themselves, and will be released."

As I watched the older man's face, I saw him change color, but he maintained his nerve, replying that he would "prosecute me for false arrest and imprisonment," probably taking his cue from the wagon master, who, after more bluster and more threats of what he would do, disappeared in the distance and we never saw or heard of him again. It was a chance on the bluff. Loading the nine men thus accumulated into the old man's wagon, upon reaching Hillsboro, a few miles away, and securing the services of Deputy Sheriff H. A. Macomber, we and the prisoners were given a good meal at the house of the jailer, J. A. Purnell, the first any had had since leaving Fort R— and shortly after dark, the jailer leading with a lantern, the prisoners closely guarded, and the three citizens (?) loudly protesting in Chimmie Fadden's vernacular: "Wot 'tell!"—and then adding: "What's the use!" etc., the astounded ranchers of H— saw this strange procession proceeding to the county jail to give them protection from the howling, icy gale still blowing.

All jails in Texas were then made of huge square-hewn green logs, built up solid, and the outside thickly studded with sharp nails. Upon the outside a flight of rickety steps led up to a door heavily padlocked and barred. We entered by file, a sort of chamber or loft, about twelve or fourteen feet square. In the center of the floor was a large trap door with a ring in it. This trap being lifted a ladder was lowered down to the ground floor inside, and the prisoners were ordered to descend into this ground cell in which was but one small grated window, high up for air only. The ladder then being drawn up and the trap door secured, they were supposed to be safe, as it was eight or ten feet from the floor of the cell to the floor of the loft. In this Hillsboro jail, however, the ladders had been broken and had disappeared, so that the deserters had to be let down by hand, the little short old wagoner coming last. It was most amusing to hear this well paid old scoundrel's squeals and whining, and his piteous appeals for mercy as he hung dangling in mid-air through the "manhole" before dropping him the four or five feet to the ground. He kicked, squirmed and wriggled in his agony of fright; he moaned, groaned, grunted and sighed; begged, implored and prayed, in the most ridiculous man-

ner. All the time the deserters below him, realizing how
fortunate they were in being sheltered from the icy blast
of the "Norther" now howling around the corners of the
old log jail, were mocking, *"booing"* and sarcastically
commenting on the little man's lack of sand, grit and
courage.

Having heard much and seen little of these Texas jails
except the outside, and at a distance, my curiosity was
aroused to more closely examine one. The jailer tried to
persuade me not to take the risk. But after assuring him
that I had nothing to fear from these men in going down
among them as I knew every one, and handing him my pistols, he lowered me down, passing the lantern down after
me. After carefully examining this uninteresting hole
very carefully, however, I felt that my curiosity had been
amply satisfied and cheering up the "old man" much to
the amusement of the prisoners, all of whom seemed to
be contented with their blankets and a comparatively warm
shelter from the storm, telling one of the men to give me
a "leg up," I was pulled up by the jailer, all of the prisoners assisting and bidding me a most cheerful "goodnight." The next morning after "turning out" the deserters and filling them with a hot breakfast at the jailer's
where Charlton and the rest of the detachment with myself had spent the night, they opened up with a long and
very strange story. Peters, the spokesman for the deserters, declared that two detectives (?) or, as they called
themselves *"constables"* had followed them from near
Weatherford, on the Bear Creek road, and arrested them.
Instead of being armed as Sergeant Varily had informed
the writer, they (the deserters) had parted with all of
their carbines before reaching W— for a good round sum.
The pseudo detectives, therefore, found it a comparatively
easy matter, with their double barrel shot guns to persuade the unarmed soldiers to "throw up their hands."
They had even started to turn back to Weatherford, when
at the suggestion of one of their number negotiations were
opened by which they were released by the fake constables

but, at the sacrifice of all the "greenbacks" the entire party possessed. After this compulsory squeeze, the detectives (?) and their plucked friends parted company. The writer resolved, upon his return, to investigate this matter and if the deserter's story proved true, and they had all corroborated Peters' statement, to secure the arrest and indictment of these Border Sharks.

The march back was cold and bitter. We were more than 100 miles from Fort R—. No handcuffs or irons could be obtained and it was decided not to "rope them." Thick ice was in all the streams. Calling Peters, the most intelligent of the prisoners, to me, the writer laid down the law. "Peters, I am going to march you to Fort R— and I want no trouble; tell the men they shall be well fed and they shall have shelter whenever it is possible to obtain it. Corporal Charlton will be placed in direct charge of you, 'fall in' the men in the middle of the road in column of twos." Then turning to the men—so that all could hear me—I added: "You men must keep the middle of the road and obey all orders issued through Corporal C— by me, without any question or discussion. Any movement by you to bolt the trail, or to escape into the chaparral will only result in your being shot down. You can talk and smoke and have freedom of movement but you know both of us well enough to understand that there will be no trifling." At eleven a. m. we started and camped at the Widow Jewell's ranch, fifteen miles from Hillsboro. Placing the men in an open corn crib, assigning each a sleeping place and posting a man at the log door, he was ordered to "shoot the first man who left that position without authority from me." This was said loudly in the hearing of every man, and he was then asked if he understood it.

For the first time we now ascertained from the prisoners why they had so mysteriously disappeared from the map after leaving Weatherford and after being seen and talked to by Sergt. Varily on the Bear Creek Road, and why we got no trace of them the next night in Cleburne. It seems that just before reaching the town, upon the advice of the wily driver of their get-away wagon, they had turned off the Bear Creek Road and followed a blind trail to the right had reached the little settlement of Buchanan and bivouacking there that night, had come into the Cleburne-Hillsboro road again the next morning, shortly before I sighted them at the small creek or "branch" near H—. During all of that miserable night while we were searching the slums and dives of Cleburne, they were at a comfortable, blazing bivouac fire not more than three or four miles away, debating the probabilities of their being followed.

At the first opportunity I proved the two citizens who had been "kidnapped" from the train near Hillsboro to be deserters. While giving them the "third degree" in camp the first night after leaving H— they were thrown off their guard by my suddenly shouting—"Stand attention, Sir! when talking to an officer!" Which he did *instantly*. I then had them stripped and found Government shirts and socks on both of them. They then made a "clean breast" of it, declaring that they were recruits of Troop "K" and had been enlisted but two or three months; all of which accounted for their non-military appearance when it was decided to hold them on suspicion. It also accounted for the inability of any one, either in the detachment, or among the old deserters of Troop "B," to identify them. Turning out the prisoners in the morning they were placed in column and the order was repeated. "Shoot dead instantly any man who starts to leave the road without my permission." It had the desired effect.

Wherever I could find one they were placed in jail. In passing through Cleburne and stopping off to pay some bills, suspicion having been attracted to another man, I "rounded him up" and after some strenuous "Third Degree" questioning, he proved to be a deserter from "Troop F" who had preceded the others by a few days. I had now ten deserters, and the "old man" driver of the freight wagon. As we approached Weatherford, I began to give some thought to the two alleged detectives or constables (?), and ransacked my brain as to the method for their capture. The rascally old driver had, after much diplomatic persuasion, informed me that these men were really constables and acting detectives, and one was even then acting as Deputy Sheriff of the County, and lived just outside of W—.

While I was doubtful as to my power to arrest either, I determined to make a show of frightening them, and to report their case to the civil authorities for their disposal. I commenced a vigorous search. Riding into a ranch, pointed out by the prisoners, I inquired, "does Mr. Mason live here?" Being in citizen's clothes and alone, my mission was not suspected. "That is my name," said a man sitting in a chair on the porch. "I arrest you then in the name of the United States Government for accepting bribes of deserters from our army, and allowing them to escape. My men are outside in the road; don't waste any words, but come right along." To my astonishment, the man was so frightened that mounting his horse, which stood outside, and surrendering his gun, he preceded me to the road, where he came face to face with all of his accusers, who now seeing him under arrest, made bold to unmercifully taunt him with his rascality, shouting "Hey, Johnnie, where's my $10.00?" "How much of a pile did you pull out of me at Bear Creek (?)" etc., etc., much to the bogus detective's discomfiture and chagrin. They had now the "whip hand." He rode like a little kitten under charge of Corporal Charlton into W— when a complaint was entered and sworn to by all of the deserters, and he was placed under bonds for his appearance at the Spring term of the U. S. District Court at Tyler, Texas, where, some months later, the writer was ordered from Department Headquarters to appear as a witness against him and the second constable whom I captured in much the same manner as the first, but nearer Weatherford.

The old wagoner pleaded hard, saying that he had never been in such a scrape. It would "kill him to have to go to

prison,'' etc.—but, knowing that Mackenzie was anxious
to break up these wholesale desertions that were then taking place in the regiment, many of them with the secret
connivance and assistance of citizens, although it was
never discovered that any of them were *constables*, and
would endorse the most extreme measures I might make
to accomplish it, I promptly placed him under bonds and
left him in W— in charge of the civil authorities.

The Discovery—The Deserter "Squeals"

The streams were all frozen up. The weather was still
icy cold. So far I had been unable to get any trace, or
sure clue of the missing carbines which the men had carried with them when deserting, and sold. The deserters
refused to divulge their whereabouts except to hint that
they were somewhere between Crawford's Ranch and Fort
R—. At last I determined to use heroic methods. At that
date such methods were recognized as *legitimate*, if not
legal in bringing recalcitrants to their senses, instead of
resorting to the slow and laborious, as well as questionable methods of Court Martial. These methods were
legacies of the Civil War, and in the field, away from the
complicated machinery of Post Administration, and on
such duty and under such *wide open instructions* as Mackenzie had given us, I considered it absolutely necessary
to employ. I resolved to select the weakest minded man
in the group of deserters, and, in the presence of them, the
two corporals and the entire detachment, *"tie him up by
the thumbs,"* until he "squealed."

Such punishment was of almost daily occurrence at the
great Draft Rendezvous. This was done with the desired
result and I located the missing arms, the property of the
United States which I was out after, without further
trouble. This man was Crafts. Placing the deserters in
Mrs. Crawford's corn bins, the ground still being covered
with snow and ice and the weather bitter cold, I determined to send in a mounted courier or runner to Mackenzie. Writing a hasty message, a personal note on a piece

of soiled brown paper—a brief announcement of the capture was made, but reciting no details, also the condition of both the men and horses, "all nearly exhausted from cold and loss of sleep, the prisoners nearly barefooted, and with sore and blistered feet, chafed legs, etc., but plenty to eat; horses unshod. He was urged to "send a wagon, some handcuffs, ropes, rations, etc., to meet me somewhere on the road and without delay between Crawford's Ranch and Fort R—. I was proceeding slowly," etc. The wagon met me, but not until I was within a few miles of the post, and just as the prisoners were emphatically exclaiming that they *"could go no further."* They were bundled into the wagon, much to their and my relief, for these footsore and chafed cavalrymen, as I had seen them in October after being dismounted in the stampede near Cañon Blancho, were now in the same demoralized condition, and it is extremely doubtful if they could have been pushed any further afoot.

Hardin's Ranch—Two Viragos—The Search—The Threat

When Hardin's Ranch, sixteen miles from Fort R—, was reached, I bivouacked my men and taking Charlton proceeded to reconnoiter. I found two tall, gaunt, leathery, bony, unprepossessing, sour-looking females. With some hesitation, I approached my delicate mission or undertaking and began to interview them, using all of the engaging manners and suave (?) diplomacy I was capable of, which, as a soldier, so I have been told, has never been of a very pronounced character. It availed me nothing. To the inquiry as to whether any of the men were at home, and if any carbines had been left at the ranch by these soldiers when going down the country, the reply was curtly snapped out, "No!" They 'lowed they hadn't never seen no carbines; the "old man" wasn't home. I *politely* asked if I might "look about the ranch and premises." That stirred the gall of these specimens of the gentle, tender sex. "No! you can't!" Then I began a mild form of the "third degree" and bringing up the man who had, under pressure, "squealed" to identify the women and to make an even stronger statement as to the disposal of their carbines, we were met with nothing but repulses, followed by foul abuse, such as: "You blue-bellied Yankees better go away from here; if the 'old man' was here he would like you uns outen yer boots," etc.

I was not, at this point, inclined to spoil the reputation I had already acquired or sacrifice my good name, or make any slip by any "Violation of the Civil Law" now in full force in all parts of Texas in view of Mackenzie's explicit instructions on that point. Neither did I feel inclined to be beaten just at this stage of the game, the end of this frightfully exhausting and most momentous trip, or to be balked and bluffed by these two raw bone, belligerent termagants, and lose the fruits of my thus far assured success. I wanted to make a clean "sweep up" of my trip, and, in order to do so—*I must have those carbines,* now that I felt I was so close to them. So I swung around to other tactics, or rather *Grand Strategy.* "If you don't produce those carbines from their places of concealment, which I know to be here or about your premises, I shall be compelled to search your ranch."

This last shot hit hard. More and more abuse, coupled with more threats of what the "old man" would do to me.

The climax had now come. I could not see my way clear to bluff any longer. I felt that I must act at once and decisively. "Corporal Charlton, call the men at once. Search this ranch thoroughly. If necessary rip up the floors, and turn over the *'loft';* ransack all of the out buildings, but be careful that you do not injure these *ladies*" (?). "If they resist or try to use any guns, treat them as you would 'he' *men;* jump on them, and securely rope them and don't let them get 'the drop' on you. You take charge of the job and see that it is well done." His steel-blue eyes flashed. My musketeer Corporal "d'Artagnan" sprang at it with a relish. He had heard, and been the object of much of the abuse of these scolding viragos. The ranch was thoroughly searched, the "rough-neck" women offering no resistance except with their bitter

tongues which shot off the vilest sort of *"Billings gate."*
It was without avail. The carbines were evidently concealed at some point distant from the house.

As we were about to leave, the women, unconquered,
again spat out— "If the 'old man' wuz heah he would lick
you uns out o' yer boots." Here was a fine chance for
another bluff. I walked up to them, and in my most impressive manner gave here this decisive *Coup d'Etat.* "If
your old man doesn't deliver those carbines into Fort Richardson by 10 o'clock to-morrow morning, I will bring this
same detachment out here with a raw hide lariat and hang
him to that oak tree." They had seen me ransack the
ranch, they had known what that threat of hanging meant
in the reconstruction days among the "bad men," the
"gun men" and desperadoes of the far South West.
They showed signs of wilting and I departed, inwardly
cursing the luck which had deserted me at the last moment
and compelled me to make a raw bluff which I knew full
well I could not carry out or enforce in view of Mackenzie's *most strenuous official objections.*

Land the Prisoners—The "Old Man" Makes Good

Reaching Fort R— in a few hours and reporting to Mackenzie, the prisoners were "turned over" and I was just
seeking a shave, a hot bath, some good grub and a rest
from the dreadful "wear and tear" of one of the most
wearing and completely exhaustive duties I had ever performed, either during the Civil War or later, when Mackenzie sent for me. I was still in a very dirty and bedraggled suit of citizen clothes. I needed complete relaxation and rest from my week's gruelling trip during which,
with the exception of two nights, I had slept, or tried to
sleep "out in the open" in this howling icy "Norther,"
and with much responsibility pressing upon me. "Ask
the General to please excuse me until I shave, wash, and
change my clothes." Word came back at once. "Tell him
that Gen. Hardie is here and wishes to see him particularly. Never mind his personal appearance, come now just

as he is!'' It was virtually an order. So I went but in
a condition of wilted militarism. Mackenzie opened up
with a most cordial introduction to Gen. H— and the remark: ''Gen. Hardie, I want you to see what my officers
of *Civil War record*'' (I inwardly grew profane) ''can accomplish when they are sent out in weather like this to get
results under merely *'verbal instructions,'* and acting alone
under their own initiative, good judgment and discretion.
He has done far more than I expected of him and I am
extremely gratified.'' He continued with profuse congratulations, thanks and personal commendations.

''Congratulations''—''Thanks''—''Special Commenda-tions,'' Etc.—A Soothing Balm (?)

Gen. James A. Hardie, then an Assistant Inspector General U. S. Army, the one time friend and confidential Military Adviser of Abraham Lincoln, whom he selected to
send on that delicate mission to Frederick City, Md., to relieve Gen. Hooker from command of the Army of the Potomac just prior to the Battle of Gettysburg, appointing Gen.
Meade to succeed him, happened to be at Fort R— on his
annual tour of inspection of the frontier posts. After such
an introduction from Mackenzie, Gen. Hardie was very informal. He was a very handsome man, then about forty-
eight years of age. He was very courteous and had an exceedingly attractive personality. With the disparity in our
ages, he seemed, at that period, to be a very ''old man.''
He had served in the Mexican War, and died as a Brevet
Maj. General, Dec. 14, 1876. Placing both hands on my
shoulders he said: ''Young man, I am proud of you. General Mackenzie ought to be proud of having such an officer
in his regiment.'' ''I want to personally congratulate and
warmly thank you for the fine work you have done. It was
a duty of very great responsibility, and you should be
commended not only by the Department, but by the entire
Army. I believe it is a record that you should be very
proud of.'' In rehearsing my adventures to them, I came
to the incident at Hardin's ranch, and my encounter with

the two "Jezebels." Mackenzie flared up. "Didn't I particularly impress upon you in my *'verbal instructions'* that you must not *'violate the civil law'* in any way—I——"
Without waiting for him to finish his sentence, I replied: "Well, Sir! I have violated no civil law. I have hung nobody as yet, only made a huge bluff. You will see those carbines here to-morrow morning." The "old man" who was going to "lick me out of my boots" promptly at 10 o'clock, rolled into Fort R— *with all of the carbines.* I happened to be at the Adjutant's office. "Is the Gineral in?" "He is!" "I've brought in them guns!" After making a statement more or less satisfactory of how they happened to come into his possession, and after Mackenzie had "hauled him over the coals" for a "send off," the rancher departed, "a sadder but a wiser" man. I never got any *sweet looks* from the "ladies" after that when duty called me past that ranch.

Lawton came in a day or two later. He certainly was "out of luck." The deserters had not headed his way. He had gone farther than the writer. Way up into the Indian Nation (now Oklahoma), and not only had not succeeded in "bagging" anybody, but, most unfortunately, one of the best men in his detachment deserted, taking his horse, arms and entire equipment with him. After ascertaining what had come my way, he seemed to be much crestfallen.

A few days afterwards Mackenzie, upon hearing that another man of Troop "F" was known to be a deserter, and had been located rather vaguely as being in the "Keechi Valley" sent for me, and, after smilingly giving me as well as he was able, the location of the ranch and announcing that as I had been proved the *"champeen"* catcher of deserters, he was going to send me out after him. He trusted that I would not belie my "reputation." After a day's trip in fine weather I was able to definitely place him, and after watching the ranch all day surrounded it, and, without any trouble, captured him as he came in from his work in the field. My record now was: eleven deserters and three citizens, two of them Constables, with all the arms carried away from the post. Corporal Charlton had proved himself a very invaluable man. As a soldier he was wonderfully resourceful and active; in action he was intense, energetic and decisive. With his intelligence and good, horse sense, he would even without the complete education which some men have *without sense,* have made a good all round commissioned officer, a credit to the regiment and to the Army. It is a pity that we did not have more of his type with which to build up the army with practical men of his caliber—instead of having *so much over educated material.*

I had gained much valuable experience in the methods of unearthing rascality, and in accomplishing results, under dreadful exposure and hardships; many trials and difficulties.

Shortly after this the writer received a letter of thanks from the Department. As it is the only one that he ever received, and as he never expects to receive another, it is esteemed as a rare curiosity, and it is modestly added to complete the record and round out the story.

HEADQUARTERS DEPARTMENT OF TEXAS
Office of Ass't Adjutant General,
San Antonio, Texas, Jan. 4, 1872
Second Lieutenant ROBERT G. CARTER, 4th Cavalry,
(Through Headquarters, Fort Richardson, Texas)—
SIR:—

I have the honor to acknowledge receipt of your report of the 9th ultimo, relative to your pursuit of deserters under Special Orders No. 280, Fort Richardson, Texas, dated November 29, 1871,—which resulted in the capture of ten deserters.

The Department Commander desires me to express to you his *gratification at your success,* and his *special commendation for the zeal and ability displayed by you.*

The good conduct and faithful services of the enlisted men composing the detachment, and Mr. Rhodes, citizen guide, is deemed a proper subject for a letter of commendation to the Post Commander.

I am Sir, very respectfully, your ob't servant,

(Signed) H. CLAY WOOD,
Assistant Adjutant Gen.

In a garrison of ten troops of Cavalry and three Companies of Infantry—Mackenzie had not only carefully gone over the entire roster from which to select two officers upon whose experience and good judgment he could absolutely depend for the performance of a duty in which he not only wanted but expected and demanded decisive results, but he had revolved all the possibilities and probabilities of dismal failure had he selected any other than Lawton and myself.

It is hoped that the writer will neither be charged with petty conceit, undue egotism nor personal vanity in making these simple declarations of facts the absolute truth of which never was, nor ever could be gainsayed by any officer of that period in the Fourth Cavalry.

In this entire campaign after these deserters, success was dependent, not upon any study or knowledge of tactics, strategy, or any game of war, but largely upon good, common sense, sound judgment, almost intuition, a ready resourcefulness and quick, decisive action. It was practically outside of a theoretical conception of any war problem as we understand it, but included within the scope of its practical activities. No book has ever been written, or ever will be, which could begin to lay down any cut and dried plan of action, rules, or any fundamental principles in a case like this, or hundreds of other cases similar to the performance of such special duties, any more than a text

---

*Theodore Roosevelt in his "Letters to His Children"—pp. 87-89, referring to his son "Ted" entering West Point, says: "It would be a great misfortune for you to start into the Army or Navy as a career and find that *you had mistaken your desires* and had gone in without fully weighing the matter. You ought not to enter *unless you feel genuinely drawn to the life as a life-work.* If so, go in, but not otherwise." . . . "Mr. Loeb (Secretary to President Roosevelt) says he wished to enter the army *because he did not know what to do,* could not foresee whether he would succeed or fail in life, and felt that the army *would give him a living and career.* "Now, if this is at bottom of your feeling I should advise you not to go in. I should say *yes* to *some boys,* but *not to you.*" If all fathers had given as good advice to their sons who have been aspirants to that kind of military glory which would give them *"a living and a career,"* we would have been saved the mortification of "canning" some of our graduates of West Point during the world war, who having acquired the *"career"* were not worth the powder with which to blow them out of their O. D. (Olive Drab) uniforms.

book could have been written prior to 1914 on how to deal
with the German methods of conducting a war for the subjugation of the world by trench, barbed wire and dug-out
systems along the Hindenburg lines, etc. All the study of
a life-time involving such problems, or military knowledge,
would be of no avail to some men, whether civilians or soldiers, unless they possessed, at the same time, plenty of resourcefulness and horse sense and could readily adjust
themselves to the ever changing conditions of those same
problems. The factors never remain fixed or constant. It
is the same in battle and with the factors controlling it,
which accounts for the lack of success of many so called
soldiers by their failure to get away from fixed rules.
There is one word that seems to involve the main spring
of a soldier's action in all such emergencies and that is,
Experience, and the practical application of that experience
to all of the problems of life whether great or small, but
especially in puzzling situations like this, where the factors
are dependent on no fixed rules, are never constant and
therefore events so shape themselves in such rapid succession that without quick, decisive action based upon one's
resources and sound judgment gained by experience, the
dependence upon study of any books which might bear in
any way upon such conditions would not only prove a most
ridiculous farce but would be offering a premium on commonplace student soldiers, obtuseness and asinine stupidity.

There is such a thing in the development of a soldier
along certain lines for practical work, as *over education,*
as well as *over training.* In the one case he thinks he
knows so much that he cannot be taught any more, and is
apt, therefore, to eliminate entirely the element of common sense, the one factor for success upon which he must
largely depend, and to neglect to apply some of the most
simple and practical principles in his earlier education;
and, in the other case he may go stale, and lose much of
his spirit, enthusiasm and energy while waiting to test out

his knowledge in the real field of endeavor and practical experience.

All of our varied campaign and battle service, and experience and knowledge gained during the great Civil War and our practical activities in scouting and campaigning after wild, hostile Indians subsequent to that war entered into this chase and capture, as *military factors,* without which we would have been as helpless as two children.

Who could look ahead into that long, trackless, desolate hundred miles of thinly settled country, almost a wilderness, with small towns more than forty miles apart, in the midst of a bitter cold tempest of rain, snow, or War College papers and compositions upon obsolete campaigns and battles; or any extended use of war games, annual maneuvers or sham battles, etc., things that many of our young officers have been fed upon for years to fit them for great wars, emergencies, crises, etc., and predicted any success for either Lawton or the writer? Any experience (?) gained in such theoretical military knowledge as would fit into such a case would have been about as effective for Lawton and myself as our study of the Sanskrit and Chinese languages.

It was a problem based purely upon military experience gained by hard knocks and campaigns and in battles, seasoned up with plenty of good, sound horse sense, combined with our battle discipline and morale; courage, resourcefulness and powers of endurance entered, of course, as factors. These were our guides.

All these combined with the true military spirit were the determining factors in that strange adventure so far as they are able to guide us in this mysterious and complex game of life, or can enter into the human problems in which we engage and are ever attempting to solve to our satisfaction and credit. Such was the philosophy and logical reasoning of we two "hold overs" of the Civil War, as we plodded our weary way across the black prairies in the howling "Norther" in our pursuit of these deserters. Lit-

tle or no thought was given to the training received at the
Military Academy beyond a well nourished pride in its
motto of "Honor—Duty—Country." The balance was in
our pride as battle-service soldiers of the Civil War and all
of our knowledge and experience gained thereby—but especially so far as the writer was concerned to a short
period of service at a huge conscript and "substitute"
camp.*

Here he acted as a provost guard and as a young detective among many deserters from every Army and Navy
in the world, hardened and desperate criminals of the
worst description, intent on receiving a large bounty only
to desert at the first opportunity and enlisting at another
rendezvous, repeating this trick *ad libitum.* Here was real
human character depicted in its worst forms of iniquity,
depravity, greed, selfishness, low cunning, trickery, treachery, atrocity, and the most desperate crimes, not stopping
short of black-jacking, garroting, sand-bagging, robbery
and frequent murders. To mingle with them was to know
their types, their methods, habits, resources, etc. All this
knowledge was of incalculable value to the writer when the
plunge was made into darkness and depths of an uncertainty, of an adventure the outcome of which could be but
problematical or only to be guessed at.

All this applied to Lawton, who, although he was not a
graduate of West Point, had had the same campaign and
battle experience as the writer, and as Lieut. Colonel Commanding the 30th Indian Volunteer Infantry had developed in him all of the necessary elements at Chickamauga,
Missionary Ridge, Dalton, Resaca, Kenesaw Mountain, and
in his march with Sherman "from Atlanta to the sea,"
which, as essential factors would fit into our problem, and
which, many years later, he fully exemplified in the Philippines by his push, energy, iron will, resourcefulness, well-
balanced judgment in his campaigns, and characterized
him as the personification of an ever ready and perfectly

*Men who had been paid large bounties during the draft period to take the place of
men who were *long* on money, but were *short on gall*, and who had no stomach for a
fight of any kind.

trained, although not *intensively* trained soldier, the magnificent soldier without frills.

A Brief Summary—A Record "Round-up"

While this was not the concluding chapter, or the end of my dealings, either by way of experience or adventure with these deserters, or all that was likely to grow out of it, I felt that much of the burden had been lifted. The long chase in the howling "Norther." The novelty of our night at "Rhodes Ranch"—with seven people, including the crying baby, and the three dogs in a one-room "shack" to keep us from perishing; sliding and skating over the desolate solitude, wind-swept and ice crusted; the two long, weary nights among the dens, dives and slums of Weatherford and Cleburne with my optimistic, jovial, joking—Musketeer Corporal; the all night study of the map, the one-legged, *"Johnny driver"* with his friendly Gettysburg battle-field reminiscing that came so near losing me the fruits of a night's hard labor, and uncertainty of plans in the early morning at the latter town; the exciting, thrilling, almost spectacular capture of the men in the brush near Hillsboro; the bluff and threat of the wagon master; the novelty of a Texas log jail with its forbidding exterior and interior, but sheltering walls; the little, panic-stricken wagoner; the indictment of all the citizens implicated in their escape and temporary release under the stimulus of "blood money"; the "squealing" of Crafts on the concealment of the arms; the identification of the raw recruits; the encounter with the fighting termagants at Hardin's Ranch; the hasty return of the carbines by the "old man" who would "lick you uns outen yer boots"; the commendations and warm personal thanks of Generals Mackenzie and Hardie; the letter of thanks and congratulations from the Major-General Commanding the Department of Texas; all were now over, and I could at last, heave a great sigh of relief and, for a few days, at least, indulge in a brief period of well earned rest.

It is believed that this march of over 200 miles in the

dead of winter, during an unprecedented severe "Norther" (10° below zero) with sleet, snow, hail and ice almost thick enough to bear the weight of our horses, and for a part of the time in jeopardy of our lives—the capture of these ten (10) men with all of their arms and safe delivery into a military post, and the apprehension and indictment of the three (3) civilians for their share in the adventure—stands on record as the most complete and wide-sweeping "round up" of deserters, under all of the circumstances, ever known in the official Military Annals of the Department of Texas, if not the entire United States Army. At all events, in any way it may be summed up, it was a most remarkable and "Phenomenal Capture."

CHAPTER IX

RECOLLECTIONS OF AN INDIAN RESERVATION

An Army "Soft Job" (?)

CLOSELY following the 200 mile trip in December 1871, and the capture of ten (10) deserters during a sleeting "Norther," and their delivery with all of their arms at Fort Richardson, Texas, together with the arrest of the three civilians, who were more or less connected with their escape, and securing their indictment and order for trial before the U. S. District Court at Tyler, Texas, where the writer arrived too late to appear as a witness against them on account of delay in serving the subpoena through Department Headquarters, Mackenzie, on Feb. 29, 1872, sent for the writer again. This time, it was to offer him what in Army parlance is termed a "Soft Job." They came but seldom in the old days. Sometimes never in the lifetime of some soldiers.

He informed him that he (M.) was to be ordered to Fort Sill in a day or two as President of a General C. M.; that on account of the extraordinary and terribly hard trip in December after deserters, when it was out of his turn on the officers detached duty roster, he would like to have the writer take command of the Calvary escort, etc. It would not be an order but a request, and the time limit was unknown, depending on circumstances. The writer was to select his own escort. The offer was accepted. Starting on March 2nd with one of the best duty Sergeants in the regiment—Thomas Brown of Troop "L"—who died a few years ago at the National Soldiers Home, Washington, D. C., and 20 picked men of Troop "L," we made the march of 123 miles in fine weather and under most favorable conditions. There were five (5) officers besides the writer and two (2) ladies—Colonel Mackenzie and Major J. K. Mizner, Fourth Cavalry—Major H. M. Douglas and Captain G. K. Sanderson, Eleventh Infantry, Captain G.

B. Russell, Judge Advocate on the staff of Gen. C. C.
Augur, commanding the Department of Texas, Mrs. J. K.
Mizner and Mrs. G. K. Sanderson. All are dead these
many years. The trip was without special incident, except
on the first day, when, shortly after leaving our camp on
the West Fork of the Trinity, we came upon a dead Indian
lying nude and scalped in the middle of the trail where he
had been killed, we afterwards learned, by a party of settlers who had gone out the day before, upon an alarm after
a party of Indian raiders. This "scare," and such a repulsive sight, so shocked the ladies that we were compelled
at our camp on White Creek that night to exercisie more
than our usual precautions, and at all of our later camps
on their account, and to prevent stampede of our animals.

On this day Mackenzie had been riding in a Dougherty
ambulance; he was unusually nervous and irritable. Realizing fully the extent of this days "jolt," the writer was
particularly vigilant. A herd guard of one Corporal and
three men had been sent out to herd the animals and guard
against stampede or any Indian attack. They were in full
view of Camp, and instructions had been given Sergeant
Brown that one third of the entire detachment should remain saddled up until dark, or, until the herds were drawn
in and the herders relieved. Mackenzie, who had the stampede of October 10, 1871, by Quanah Parker's band of
Qua-ha-da Comanches on the Freshwater Fork of the
Brazos, still weighing heavily on his mind, a veritable incubus, came to the writer and said, "How many men are
out on herd guard?" Upon being told, he added, "You
must not neglect your duty! I told you that you were to
Command the detachment, and in your own way, and I
should not interfere with their control. I want no care
nor bother, leaving it all to you, but I see only two men
out there, where is the other man?" I replied, "Well,
General, I am responsible for those men, but shall hold
them to a strict performance of their duty. I personally
posted the men myself, and left them in charge of a good

Corporal. If one is absent, it is probably on account of sickness or for some good excuse. I will attend to it at once, Sir, but I don't care to be accused of neglect, or even have it hinted at. I know how to perform such duty, but if I am supposed to stand here and see that these men are herding the animals properly, I prefer to mount my horse, relieve them, and herd them myself, then you may feel perfectly assured that they are being well guarded, and are safe." He flared up, "Carter, I like you very much. You have never failed me, but"—snapping his amputated finger stumps with more than his accustomed energy— "Sometimes you get a little insubordinate and you must not talk to me in that way." "I shall not, Sir, unless you choose to reflect upon my performance of duty." As it was suspected, the Sergeant was already sending out a man to relieve the herder who had been taken sick. Mackenzie walked away. No further reference afterwards was ever made to this incident.

When the writer was placed on the retired list, however, Mackenzie wrote me the following letter.

My Dear Carter:

"I spoke of your case * * * to Gen. Sherman yesterday and will bring the matter up again before I leave. *You do not know how sorry, Carter, I am to lose you from the regiment. * * * Believe me to be, very truly, Your friend,*

(Signed) RANALD S. MACKENZIE."

Upon arriving at Fort Sill on March 7 in the midst of a howling gale and terrific sand storm we were most hospitably received and royally entertained by Gen. B. K. Grierson and the officers of the Tenth Cavalry, who gave us breakfast, lunch, dinner, dancing and picnic parties—the latter to the Signal Station at Mt. Scott.

We passed "Victoria Peak," and crossed Red River at Red River Station. The nights were cool, but we sat by blazing camp-fires and told anecdotes, and sung songs to the accompaniment of a guitar, or played whist on the tail board of a wagon. Passing by Bluff Creek, we made a short halt at Beaver Creek, a bold, running stream, to

catch some fish.   There was a ranch here but with no visible signs about the place for the support of its inmates.
When the "old woman," who was leaning over the apology
for a "worm" fence was asked what they lived on, she
blew the smoke from her well-worn corn cob pipe, and said,
"Last year, me and the old man 'crapped' it a leetle,"
meaning doubtless, that they raised a bushel or so of corn,
and lived mostly on fish from the Creek.

An Indian Reservation

Fort Sill is magnificently located on the Comanche, Ki-o-
wa and Apache reservation; its elevation above the sea is
1700 feet.   It is 123 miles North of Fort Richardson, about
190 miles South West of Camp Supply, 30 miles South of
Washita, and 45 miles North of the Red River.   The site
was selected by Gen. Sheridan in his winter campaign of
1868-9, and for many years served as a base of operations
against the confederated tribes of Comanches, Ki-o-was,
Southern Cheyennes, and Arapahoes, and had been their
reservation with the affiliated tribes of Wichitas, Keechis,
Wacos and Caddoes, and other semi-civilized tribes.   It
was occupied by Gen. Grierson with the Tenth Cavalry in
June, 1868, under the name of "Camp Wichita," although
it had been known for a short time previous as "Camp
Sheridan."   It was occupied as a post in January, 1869,
but the name was finally changed to Fort Sill on August
1, 1869, by Gen. Sheridan in memory of Gen. J. W. Sill,
who was killed at the battle of Stones River, December 31,
1862.   The reservation is in the form of a quadrangle,
nine miles in length by four miles in width.   Within its
boundaries are the confluences of the Cache and Medicine
Bluff Creeks, at the junction of which is located the Post—
the latter being an area of one square mile in the center
of the military reservation.   It is on a plateau of irregular outline sloping in all directions.   The Wichita Mountains in plain sight extend from the North-West corner of
the reservation Westward about fifty miles and give a
savage grandeur and beauty to the entire country about.

The intervening country is traversed by a network of streams, which rise in these mountains. The mesquite, oak, and hackberry abound. Buffalo, elk, bear, antelope, white-tailed deer, panthers, wolves, jack rabbits, wild-cats, otter, prairie dogs and raccoons were abundant. Thirteen kinds of game, besides trout, bass and other kinds of fish have been otained in one week, only a few miles from the post, on West Cache Creek. Buffalo swarmed the prairies, and quail and highland plover were killed in almost incredible numbers from the stage trail as we rode through the country. The two creeks, near the junction of which the post is located, are clear, limpid streams which empty into Red River, and are overlooked by a precipitous bluff, called Medicine Bluff. Most of this beautiful region, including the Wichitas, has long since been converted into a magnificent National Park, the natural features of which can scarcely be surpassed in wildness and grandeur on this Continent.

Medicine Bluff—Its Legends—And Traditions

Medicine Bluff was, unquestionably, the result of upheaval, though an earthquake alone could have detached it from the adjacent rocks. It is a mile in length, forming a perfect crescent, and rising at once from an immense fissure, now the bed of Medicine Bluff Creek, which flows at the base of the perpendicular scarp, a beautiful stream about twenty yards in width. In some places the Creek seemed bottomless, so that looking into its crystal waters, it has the appearance of a basin of ink, at the next moment an emerald green and again as it pursues its way and in more shallow spots become pure and parkling like a diamond. From the very brink of the creek rises the vertical sides of the bluff, three hundred and ten feet in height by actual measurement. The sides have the appearance of a trap-rock, and the strata stand almost perpendicularly. The surface of this face of the bluff is perfectly regular and smooth. A minute species of moss covers the sides with a garb of pale green, which might be easily mistaken for the rock. The largest portions of the face are perfectly bare, though at some places a few stunted cedars have found a lodgment in the crevices. From the rear the bluff presents three knolls, the center one being the highest. The steep sides are composed of fragments or rock, indicating that at one time they were made up of boulders. The disintegration, however, was of a character to admit of large quantities of bunch grass, and a peculiar variety of flowering cactus. This plant consists of one, two, and sometimes of eight or ten buds an inch or two in diameter, and flattened on top. The buds cluster upon a single root; are covered with a heavy mail of spines, and cannot be touched with impunity. The flower is of a purple tint; and formed a tuft in the centre of the ball. The course of Medicine Bluff Creek can be traced, wending its way from the mountains, across the intervening valley, and away down the broad expanse in the rear. Mount Scott, about eight miles distant stands before one with its pyramidal outline. Clouds sweep its rocky summit. It stands like a sentinel guarding the eastern gate to the Wichita Mountains. On the right a belt of timber defines the course of Cache Creek, which about two miles from the bluff unites with the Medicine Bluff Creek, the latter then losing its name. It is just below this junction that the beautiful Post of Fort Sill had been built, the site of which was selected by Gen. Sheridan in the winter of '68 and 9, and a short distance from it is located the Indian Agency where the Comanches, Kiowas, Kiowa-Apaches, Lipans, Wichitas, Wacos and other tribes on the Sill Reservation drew their rations. A more beautiful locality could hardly be imagined, wild, romantic and full of nature, as yet untouched by the hand of art.

Medicine Bluff has figured almost from time immemorial, in Indian history, Superstitions, and traditions, and has been held in the highest reverence by all the tribes who have dwelt or hunted in the vicinity, and by none more so than by the Comanches and Wichitas. The hill was considered to possess miraculous as well as mysterious influences. There the Great Spirit, often descended, and from the bluff looked over and cared for his people, saw that game was abundant, and that his children were prosperous and happy. Upon the summit of the principal knoll the Comanche Medicine men had erected a cairn of stones about six feet in height. Here the sick repaired, or were brought by their relatives or friends, and were left to the invisible and subtle power of the Great Father, and more especially those who were beyond the control of great medicine men of the tribes, were deposited on the cairn and left to be disposed of by the Great Spirit. If the sick had not offended the Spirit; they were suddenly healed and returned to their kindred. Sometimes they were transported bodily to the happy hunting-ground. But if they were notoriously bad, they were allowed to die, and the ravens descended from the air, and the wolf came up from the valley and devoured the body, and the bones were gathered up by the bad spirit and deposited in the land of terrors. Sometimes the Great Spirit descended upon the hill. Upon such occasions the immediate vicinity became suddenly lit up as by a great fire. The dews of night, the rain and the wind circled about the spot, but within the small spaces on the very summit, none of these agencies of nature trespassed, and the patient was thus sheltered better than if in his own wigwam. There are some remarkable cases narrated. One, for instance, of an old warrior, who had long lived among the women of the village. He had long ceased to hunt the buffalo, and had been turned out to await his time to join his fathers. The old warrior had struggled to the top of the bluff to die and be borne away by the Great Spirit. He had been absent three nights. Every night when darkness covered the face of nature, the awe stricken people of the village below observed a great blaze, as if a signal-fire had been built to alarm them. On the morning after the third night, a young man equipped as a warrior, was seen descending the bluff, and following the trail of the village. He looked about him with surprise. He approached the chief's

lodge and sat by the fire. The warriors, with their arms,
gathered around, gazed at him. No one recognized him.
All remained silent, expecting him to speak. Lighting his
pipe, decorated with beads and feathers of strange birds,
he handed it to those present, and each having smoked, he
told his story. When he reached the top of the hill, he
looked off upon the vast expanse which surrounded him,
and saw the village of his people. He could hear the children laugh, the dogs bark. He could hear his kindred
mourning, as if some one had been taken away from them.
He saw the buffalo and the deer covering the plain. He
saw the sly wolf lying in wait to pounce upon his prey.
When he looked around and beheld the young warriors in
all their pride and strength, he asked himself, why do I
live any longer? My fires have gone out. I must follow
my fathers. The world is beautiful to the young, but to
the old it has no pleasure. Far away to the setting sun
are the hunting grounds of my people. I will go there.
With this he gathered up all that remained of his failing
strength, and leaped into the air from the giddy height before him. He knew no more of the woes of life. He was
caught up in mid-air. He was transported into a smiling
country where game was without numbers, where there
was no rain, no wind, where the great chiefs of all the
Comanches were assembled. They were all young and
chased the buffalo and feasted. There was no darkness,
but the Great Spirit was everywhere, and his people were
continually happy. Beautiful birds warbled upon the
trees, the war whoop never penetrated those sacred realms.
The superstition of the savage was captivated and the
young warrior at once became an oracle and a "big medicine man" in the tribe. His counsel was all powerful, and
his abilities to cure was considered invincible.

The ancient customs of late years have been mostly
abandoned. The tribes have become scattered since the
rapid depletion of the buffalo. But the reverence for the
bluff is still fresh. The Comanches will not ascend the hill,

and it is rarely that an Indian of any tribe is ever seen to make the ascent.

The bluff has long been a famous place for suicides. The disappointed and disconsolate have resorted thither to terminate their miserable existences. Until very lately, it was a Comanche custom that when a young warrior was about to take the war path for the first time, he provided himself with a shield and proceeded to the highest point of the bluff for three successive mornings, and in the attitude of warding off an arrow or a spear, presented the face of the shield to the rising sun. The sacred surroundings of the place, and the sun, the emblem of the Great Spirit casting its rays upon the shield were supposed to possess it with supernatural powers.

Many years ago, says an old Comanche, so old, that he supposes himself the brother of one of the loftier peaks of the Wichitas, the Comanches were a great people. Their warriors were as numerous as the buffaloes, and as cunning as the wolf. They had immense herds of ponies and many villages; everybody feared them. But there were two warriors, braver than all the rest. They vied with each other in courting the dangers of the war-path and winning the scalps of their enemies. They were rivals in the hunt. They tried the strength and agility of each other in the village games. The warriors obeyed them alike. The children held them in equal awe, and the squaws coveted alike their favor. This equality was keenly felt by the great warriors, and each made in consequence, extraordinary efforts to accomplish something which would surpass the other. One day they were returning from an excursion into the enemy's country. As they rested to graze their ponies under the shadow of Medicine Bluff, one of the warriors, the younger, gazed upon the quivering height. For a moment he was wrapped in deep meditation. Suddenly the young warrior drew himself up to his full height, and, turning quickly, in all the pride of confidence, gazed boldly at those who were lounging about on the green grass. His

defiant manner startled his comrades, several sprang to
their feet. He exclaimed, "I am the great warrior of the
Comanches. No one equals me. I am like the mountain,
my deeds tower above you as the mountain does above the
plain, where is the Comanche who dares follow me?" As
he said this, he raised his shield in one hand and his spear
in the other. His rival, not to be out-done, approached
with proud and haughty tread. "You the great warrior of
the Comanches?" said he striking his breast. "Then you
are the buffalo that leads the herd, I am the old bull buffalo, driven away to die and feed the wolf. You ask me to
follow you, I will not follow you. I will go with you!"
All the warriors gathered around. They gazed with wonder upon their stalwart comrades, eager to see what fresh
act of courage was contemplated. The rivals arrayed
themselves gorgeously, mounted their favorite war-ponies,
which they had decorated with scalps and feathers. The
two warriors left their comrades who were surprised at
their singular conduct, and rode away without uttering a
word. The party watched them until they disappeared
over the adjacent hill. They now gathered in a circle, to
talk over the strange scene which they had witnessed.

The rivals crossed the rapid flood of the neighboring
stream. The young warrior now directed his steps towards the sacred summit of Medicine Bluff. When they
had reached the highest point, the younger, pointing to the
fearful brink not more than fifty feet before him, said to
the other, "You have followed me so far, follow me now!"
With these words, he gave a whoop, clapped his heels into
his pony's flanks, and plunged towards the precipice. His
companion, as quick as thought, fairly lifted his spirited
pony from his feet, and, with a responsive yell, planted
himself in one of those sublime attitudes calling for the
most desperate resolution, and followed his rival. The
edge of the giddy height was reached in a moment. The
courage of the young warrior failed. He reined his pony
upon his haunches. The other warrior saw the treachery.

He gave a yell of triumph and bounded off far into the trembling air. The warriors on the plain below heard the terrible yell. They saw their great leader leap from the awful height. He sat upright and in his fearful descent, was calm as if in council. He shouted, "Greater than all Comanches!" The warriors below hastened to the spot where the mangled forms of warrior and pony lay, and conveyed them to a neighboring hill, where the solemn rites of burial were performed. All night the wind moaned through the trees. The warriors sat in solemn council, and chanted their death songs. They cut their hair and painted their faces black. In sight of the bluff, the spirits of the warrior, and his stead were left, to take their flight to the land of the Great Spirit. When the war-party reached the village, the old men and women came out to re-joice. They were met with the wailing of the warriors, and saw their blackened faces. The scene was changed to mourning. The deeds of the dead warrior were spoken. The women nightly gathered in a neighboring valley to grieve for the loss of the great warrior. The young warrior wandered from village to village. The very dogs snapped at him. The name of his rival he heard in every wigwam, his own was an accursed word with the Comanche. He wandered a stranger in the world, unknown, but inwardly punished. A hunting party in pursuit of the buffalo, as was the custom, passing in the vicinity to visit the grave of the greatest of the Comanches, found the body of a warrior, half devoured by the wolf. The spear and shield, with the bow and arrows, identified the character of the person when living. The young warrior, disap-pointed and overcome with remorse, had come to die upon the grave of his rival.

At one point of the bluff, about fifty yards towards the right, is an enormous fissure or more properly, embrasure, about fifteen feet in width. Thirty feet in depth, and at least two hundred and fifty feet from the stream below. In the rear part of the bluff a small, sharp ravine leads directly up to this opening. The embrasure itself is exceedingly rugged, its sides being composed of boulders and huge fragments of disintegrated rocks, which look as if they were about ready to fall and crush everybody and everything beneath them. It would seem as if in the awful convulsion of nature which must have thrown the underlying strata into such an extraordinary position, this, being the weaker part gave away. In the process of time this fissure became filled, leaving but the embrasure described. The descent is almost perpendicular, in a direct line, but a few communicating ledges, and apparently winding paths, intersecting this apparent crack, makes it seem as if the descent were feasible.

This path was known among the Indians as the "Medicine Man's Walk," by means of which according to tradition, in the darkness of the night, a famous savage doctor, of the necromantic art passes from a cave in the bluff down to the stream below, or out upon the summit above.

Horace P. Jones—Comanche Interpreter—The Wolf Hunt

Horace P. Jones, who had a fine pack of well trained grey hounds, gave us many exciting diversions in the way of some lively coursing after Jack-rabbits, and bloodstirring runs after the lobos, or grey wolves, and coyotes, who, as night approached, came in near the post for offal at the beef corrals where meat was issued to the Agency and reservation Indians.

"Old Jones," the post interpreter and guide, had been a fixture of this, the old "Camp Cooper" and "Camp Cobb" reservations for many years, about twenty of which had been spent in close contact with the various tribes of Indians. Adopted early in life by the Comanches, he had married into the tribe, and had lived for months in the villages of the different bands, where it would scarcely have been safe for any other white man to have approached them. He spoke the language perfectly; knew the sign language accurately, and was well versed

---

*Much of this information and legendary lore concerning Medicine Bluff was given the writer in March 1872 by Thomas C. Batty the Agency school teacher.

in all their habits, customs, religious rites and annual dances. He had accompanied them upon their hunts and understood the peculiar habits of all the animals in that region about. He had seen the Wichita Mountains swarming with elk, and the prairies where the post of Fort Sill then stood, dotted with countless herds of buffalo. Up to this time he had never seen a railway car, steam engine, or any of the appliances of modern civilization. He was, however, unsurpassed as a hunter, and in his brown parchment-like face, stoical as an Indian's, there lurked a native shrewdness, and in the twinkle of his dark grey eyes, a gleam of honest intelligence that to-day would be a rarity in the sharp struggles and competitions for life. He had got together a large pack of grey hounds, of all colors and sizes, many of them of fine breed; had organized, drilled and trained them by the hour, until they compared favorably with any other pack of its size in the country. He promised us a wolf hunt, and on the following morning all of the Tenth Cavalry officers who could muster a speedy mount came to the "meet" arrayed in their best "outfit." There were about twenty followers of the dogs, but everywhere "Old Jones" was the center of attraction; all bestowed on him a respectful consideration. The great lank hounds whined, yelped, fawned and leaped about him with an almost human affection, they watched every movement of his almost immobile face, every motion of his correcting hand. In their eager impatience they bounded with most astonishing leaps in and among the riders and occasionally scattered to the right and left. The old guide's hand would then steal to the horn at his side, and winding one long, sweet blast, they came gamboling and dancing in to the sound of its notes like the children to the magic flute of the "pied piper of Hamlin." It proved an exciting day. Near the Indian Commissary were the large beef corrals where the beeves were slaughtered and the meat was issued to the various bands. About the middle of the afternoon the wolves commenced to sneak in for the "tid-bits," and before

dawn the following morning returned to the ravines and
"arroyas" that everywhere break up the country. We
were soon on the ground and had not long to wait. After
running a few coyotes we soon sighted a big lobo or grey
wolf, which, trying to avoid us, was vainly scrambling
under cover of a long ravine to secrete himself. The dogs
no sooner sighted him than they made a simultaneous
rush, "Old Jones" giving them a long loud halo-o-o-o-o!
and away went the whole "field." The villainous wolf's
bushy tail whisked and tore through the grass and bushes,
over the prairie, often across the abrupt breaks and
through dog villages. If the dogs could keep him in sight
he can generally be run down in a distance of from five
hundred to a thousand yards. It was a quick dash; he
was soon overtaken and brought to bay; but to my surprise the lobo, half crouching and facing them by quickly
turning and snapping, displaying his two rows of long,
sharp teeth to the best advantage, kept the whole pack at
a respectful distance. "Shoot him! Shoot him!" shouted
some. "No-o-o-o!" quickly replied the old guide. "You'll
now see the ra-a-a-al sport!" When the smooth-haired
grey hound is bitten or cowed by a courageous animal at
bay, he will rarely, if ever, seize his enemy or fight. A
large bull-mastiff was, therefore, kept with the pack, which
until now, we had not observed, for the purpose of coming in at the death, but unable to run with it. The guide
indicated the direction of his approach. The wolf, en-
circled by the pack, was held at bay; occasionally one of
the more courageous of the pack dashing in and grappling
with him, but only to retreat yelping a moment later.

The mastiff waddled up, for he is not a fast runner.
Waiting a moment or two for him to regain his breath,
while the pack worried the wolf, the guide gave the word
and the powerful brute seized the lobo with great courage. He was not killed, however, without a severe strug-

---

*Col. Theodore Roosevelt in his "Winning the West" asserts that the smooth haired
greyhound is a very courageous animal and will tackle the big grey wolf without hesitation. This has not been the writers observation or experience. The rough haired
Scotch-stag-hound—the Russian Wolf hound—or any of our rough haired greyhounds
will do so, but not so the smooth-haired dogs of Jones' pack. Jones willed this horn
to General Hugh L. Scott, former Chief of Staff, U. S. A.

gle in which all of the hounds joined. Sometimes a pistol shot became necessary. Our second wolf, a large one, did not prove such easy game, for, after a dash of several hundred yards, the dogs lost sight of him in a ravine, and it took the entire "field" sometime to beat him out, and when he was overtaken there were scarcely enough of the hounds to hold him. He bit one or two severely, and the packs assistant, the big bull-mastiff, not then being on hand he made a second, and even a third break, but as this made the sport a little more exciting, it was keenly relished. The mastiff again rushed in, and in a few minutes one could hardly tell one from the other, so closely intermingled were their forms, and obscured by clouds of dust, mixed with hair, cactus, and the debris of the ground over which the struggle took place. This hunt was finished just as the evening twilight stole about and into the valleys. Old Sol's rays lingering just long enough to give us sufficient light to see the wily old rascal's form almost lost in the dusky prairie and shadowy arroya. But, as the hungry riders were now tired, and it was yet a two or three mile gallop to the post we did not wait for the now pretty well worn out mastiff to do his finishing work, but mercifully decided the lobo's fate by a well directed pistol shot. Jones calling off his pack, almost every hound of which was holding on to a leg or some part of the wolf's anatomy which their fighting assistant had not already preempted.

A Wide-Awake Rabbit—Jack-Rabbit's Victory
(*Youth's Companion*, 1886)

We were told that just below the post Agency there was a "Jack" rabbit which had defied all attempts at capture by the officers of the post and Jones' fleet pack of hounds. Even "Old Jones" confessed himself as chagrined that his favorite dogs had so far, never been able to negotiate this misty apparition of a Fort Sill rabbit—and by way of excuse, declared most emphatically—"That 'Jack' is the fastest rabbit I ever see!" On the following day, after

the wolf hunt we were invited to join in a chase after this
fleet and cunning animal; so with about half a dozen grey
hounds selected for their speed, and Jones to steady them,
we started for the scene of many a discomfiture to man,
horse and dog.   The rabbit's burrow was near the Indian
Agency, upon a bald knoll barren of trees or bushes, and
with the exception of small tufts of bunch grass, was bare
of vegetation.   Here and there were low thick patches of
prickly pear that favored the concealment of this animal
whose mule ears blended with the large, round discs of the
cactus, and his dun body was easily hidden by the sun-
burned stalks.   At the foot of the knoll, skirting it in
every direction, about in a circle with a five hundred yards
radius from the burrow, was a swale or low meadow.
This bottom was covered with long, coarse grass or thatch,
having clumps of thick chaparral, or wild plum bushes
scattered here and there upon its surface.   We saw at a
glance why "Jack" was able to escape when pursued, and
told Jones so.   Greyhounds run only by sight; should the
rabbit get a sufficient start of the dogs to gain the long
grass or thickets in the swale, he was safe until he was
routed out when he could easily double back and run
swiftly for his burrow.   Then, should the dogs get near
enough, before he reached his burrow to cause him to
double again, he could again make a cover in some of the
numerous places that favored concealment.   Whether instinct alone prompted that rabbit to select that bare knoll,
with the rank growth surrounding it, would be hard to determine, but, certain it was, it was an ideal place of safety
for the cunning old rabbit.   The old guide drew a few
mellow notes from his horn, and his graceful dogs bunched
noiselessly around him eager for the run.   Dogs and men
now carefully approached the burrow, so as not to startle
the game too quickly, and thus give the dogs every advantage possible.   Luckily, the rabbit was out taking the
air of the crisp, bright morning.   He had evidently heard
the guide's horn, which had ushered in his victory so often,
and was ready for a race; for when we were within a hun-

dred yards of the patch which marked his burrow, we saw the little form, so familiar to the dogs, crouching near a bunch of grass. The tall, thin ears were vibrating with excitement. A moment later the muscular legs gathered for a run. Then there was a bound, a rush, and in a whirl of dust, that almost enveloped him, the rabbit was off!

Nothing was seen but his ears, the dust and a stub tail as he leaped over the cactus, and fairly flew along the bare, brown ridge. It was surprising to note the lightning like energy that pervaded this wonderful bunch of sinewy muscle and nerves.

Scarcely less quick did the dogs, led by "Old Brindle" and "Vic," gather and respond to the movements of the game before them. It was a whirl of five hundred yards. *How* "Jack" tore for the swale! *How* the dust, grass and horsemen were mingled, and yet that misty form of ears, legs and tail led the way.

It was as I expected. With a hundred yards the start, the cunning fellow reached the cover of the grass in the swale, and was lost to view. The dogs no longer seeing their game, stopped short in their tracks. There was a pause for a brief moment or two, and then the start was made to beat the rabbit out of the cover.

Not thirty yards from where we had halted, the old fellow's fan-like ears shot out like a streak of light, and again his active legs scratched clouds of dust. He now broke for his burrow, followed closely by the hounds. The dogs were not napping this time, and were plainly overhauling him at the three hundred yards stretch.

Yes! Old Brindle was close upon the bunch of dust, ears and legs, when suddenly, like the flash from a reflecting piece of steel or glass, those ears gave an *extra* vibration, the legs poised seemingly in mid-air, and then, straight as the flight of an arrow from a bow, the cunning rabbit shot at an angle of ninety degrees in the other direction, while old Brindle and the pack disappeared in the extra whirl of dust which "Jack" had flung in their faces.

Indian Councils

The writer attended all of the councils held at the Agency, where their needs were gone over and discussed; rations, annuity, allowances, etc. "Howed" with all the chiefs, and saw the pipe "passed." On the 18th we went to the Commissary, a mile below the post to see Kicking Bird's band draw rations, and on the 19th to see Tar-say's (the "Pacer") band of Apaches. On one of these days while many of the warriors and squaws, all blanketed, lounging about, waiting for the issue to commence, our attention was called by one of the interpreters to one or two young squaws who had edged up near the largest sugar bin, and were intently regarding its depth of saccharine sweetness. Suddenly one of them stooped over it, and quickly, a large lump of the damp, brown variety, weighing probably several pounds was seized and as quickly transferred beneath her blanket. One of the employees had seen her, however, and immediately grabbing the blanket, drew it aside, and revealed the tempting morsel. She immediately dropped it and ran out through the open door, not, however, without running the gauntlet of jeers and loud laughter of the "bucks" who had witnessed her discomfiture, and evidently regarded her detection as a good joke. The scene in and about the commissary on these days defies description. There were every variety of robes, skins and blankets, red, green, and parti colored; flour, bacon and sugar sacks, pan, kettles, and unnameable stuff, or "plunder" scattered all over the ground. The squaws' shrill voices, the half-breed wolf dogs, barking, snarling and howling, the papooses' heads showing over the tops of the blankets of the cradles around which they were wrapped, the bead-like, jet black eyes, always roving about only to dodge down again if watched too closely, all yelling and howling in chorus, the loud, immoderate laughter of the swaggering "bucks," all made a "Babel" of voices and noises from which nothing intelligible could be understood, and by which any man with weak nerves, would have been driven crazy in short time. Inside the

building, where the ration issue had begun, a chief, representing so many families, or lodges, stepped up, upon call,
to the clerk with a card or ticket, in due-bill form which
represented or certified to so many heads or persons drawing so much coffee, sugar, flour, bacon or pork. The clerk
entered the amounts in a book, the men shoveled it out of
great bins, and this was tediously repeated until all the
families of the various bands were issued to. It was soon
over, and shortly, the squaws, who do all of the work, were
packing, lashing, and screaming to the mules, the half-
breed dogs were expressing their joy by barks and yelps;
the warriors were mounting, and, after one of the most
indescribable scenes of confusion and ear-splitting noises
I had ever witnessed, the whole "outfit" was finally
streaming over the prairie on their way to the store where,
after exchanging pork, which they do not particularly like,
for other food, and completing their purchasing and bar-
tering they started back again for their villages on Rainy
Mountain Creek, and other locations in the Wichita Mountains. On the 26th upon going again to the Commissary,
this time Quirl-par-Ko, or Lone Wolf's band, was drawing rations. He was a notoriously bad Indian and was
credited with the murder of as many whites on the Texas
border as Santanta had been in Kansas. He had an unusually dark and broad face for a Ki-o-wa; prominent
chin, very thin lips, and small, but wide, almond shaped
eyes, with a sharp smirking expression, and an ominous
glitter about them. With this, there was an oily, sinister,
deceptive look, one would hardly know whether to take it
for a friendly or deadly meaning since there was always
that smirk, half smile, until there commenced that deep
glint of those treacherous eyes, and, then, there was no
mistaking their meaning. While in the Commissary some
dispute about his rations arose which at once brought out
the latent villainy of his nature. The "Uriah Heap" expression suddenly vanished, and a perfectly devilish look
succeeded. We were closely watching the old scoundrel's
face and every movement. We were all armed by advice

of the interpreter. He (Lone Wolf) accused the good old Quaker agent of disbelieving him and wanted to know if his "talk" was not "straight talk," intimated that the white man's tongue was "crooked," and sought the long knife in the belt concealed by the folds of his blanket. It was not until an armed guard was brought in that the wily old rascal's fur could be smoothed. He was, next to Satanta, the "Evil Spirit" of the Ki-o-was until, caught raiding again in 1874, he was captured and taken as a prisoner, with other desperate Indians to St. Augustine, Florida, where he died. Outside the door was a perfect pandemonium; one who had never seen an Indian village on the move could begin to appreciate any description which might be given. There were all kinds of ponies, and of all colors, bony, sleepy, and looking spiritless and forlorn as most Indian ponies do. There were pack mules, some with their packs on, other with them off, which the squaws were overhauling preparatory to starting again. There were dogs of all breeds, shades, sizes, degrees and complexions, but all of one disposition, which was to snarl and snap at everybody and everything. Some were lying down while others were squatted on their haunches; but the majority trotted and dodged about, here and there, seeing what they could steal, avoiding blows, and cringing to the ground, with their tails drawn tightly between their legs, they arched their backs, frequently showed their long white teeth, and continually indulged in a hideous noise, half bark, half howl. They outnumbered the Indians two to one. The squaws ranged from the grizzly, bony, sepulchral and leathery-looking hag or beldame, down to the young girl of 16 years, the newly made squaw of some aspiring warrior, but who looked to be at least 40, so rapidly does a nomadic life with its terrible exposure and hardships develop Indian women. They were dressed so nearly alike the "bucks" or warriors, except that their moccasins came up higher, with a long legging and with a half skirt of buckskin or dirty calico half apron in front, that it was difficult to distinguish them apart. They were

all unkempt, dirty, wretched, squalid and alive with ver-
min, as some of our ladies who, from curiosity had gone
too close to them, sadly experienced on one occasion.
Some had papooses strapped to their backs, but when dismounted these cradles were carefully set up in rows
against the walls of the building, and when some of the
fun loving soldiers in the garrison incurred the rage of
these mothers, by reversing those bundles so that the
heads would be down, there came near being a serious
knife stabbing tragedy. We also visited the old Quaker
Indian Agent, Lawrie Tatum,* and the school for the
Caddo, Keechi, Anardarko and Waco bands who were
semi-civilized Indians. This school was taught by Mr.
Thomas C. Batty who, in 1877, wrote a very interesting
book, "A Quaker Among the Indians," with an account of
his work in this school. The Post Traders Store was
visited almost daily. It was managed by Mr. ("Jack")
Evans. Here I saw many Indian Chiefs from their various camps near the post, among them Kicknig Bird, one
of the finest looking Indians I ever saw, whom we went
out after in August, 1871, when Satanta was captured
after the Salt Creek Prairie Massacre. He was poisoned
in 1874 by his own people on account of a suspicion that
he was becoming too friendly with the whites. I saw
Sa-lo-so, the son of Satanta, a fine looking young Indian
of about 18 or 20 years of age. He was shooting with a
bow against Evans with an air gun at a distance of 30 or
40 yards, and at a target made out of a flour barrel head
(hard wood) with about a 3 inch bull's eye, made with
charcoal. Sa-lo-so was using unspiked arrows, and I saw
him hit the centre four times out of five, and the last shot
split the barrel head into two pieces.

Other Indians we saw were White Horse, and Irmoke
both Ki-o-was, Lone Wolf, Ter-yer-quoip ("Horse back"),
a Nokony Comanche, A-sa-ha-by, a Comanche (Bird
Chief—"Milky Way"), A-sa-tu-et, a Pen-e-teght-ka Com-

---

*Lawrie Tatum also wrote an intensely interesting book entitled—"Our Red Broth-
ers"—in 1899.

anche, Tar-say ("The Pacer"), a Kiowa-Apache, Para-a-coom ("He Bear"), a Coch-e-teght-ka Comanche, Sitting Buffalo Bull, Iron Mountain, Big Bow, Tome-altht-to and squaw, the latter a daughter of Lone Wolf. Also a son of Lone Wolf who later was said to have been killed at the massacre of Howard's Wells (?). The names of others cannot now be recalled. The photograph gallery of Mr. Soule was visited and many fine pictures of the principal chiefs of all the tribes secured, all of which are now in good condition and highly prized. In addition to these a pair of "Three Point" (III) red, Comanche blankets were obtained at the Post Trader's ("Evans'") Store. They have been in use for 47 years, a part of the time as scouting blankets, in all sorts of weather, and the balance as covers for four children, and are, with the exception of a few moth holes, in a serviceable condition. These, with a few Indian trinkets, such as paint pouches, scalping knife scabbards, awl cases, bead embroidered, are the only possessions to remind us of the "Vanished days."

CHAPTER X

Our Wild Nomads—A Vanishing Race

THE writer's observations and impressions while on this great Indian reservation are chiefly confined to what knowledge he gained in his interviews with Horace P. Jones and Matthew Leeper, the former being the Post, and the latter the Agency Interpreter, and his almost daily contact with the various bands as they came in from their camps to draw rations at the Agency or to trade at Evans Post Traders Store, and these impressions deal entirely with the wild or hostile tribes of Comanches, Kiowas, Arapahoes and Southern Cheyennes, and not with the Wacos, Caddoes, Ana-dar-kos, Keechis, the semi-civilized tribes whose children he saw at the Agency School under Mr. Thomas C. Batty's watchful care, plainly but carefully dressed, with hair combed and braided, and with commendable eagerness to learn what they could of the white man's ways, and his "pursuit of life, liberty and happiness." While their Schools were visited several times during our stay and their mode of living in their comfortable Agency houses, their customs, ceremonies, etc., were intensely interesting. Our attention was more particularly attracted to the wild nomads, those plains Indians who, with the exception of a few stray bands, had been forced at last into the reservation, there too to undergo a process of winnowing, a change of habits, a gradual evolution, a transformation from their savage state to one of semi-civilization, and later an approach to the white man's full standard of civilization. This the writer never saw fully attained; but among the Cherokees, Chickasaws, Choctaws, Creeks, Osages and Delawares of the Indian Nation, who had been removed for nearly 40 years from Georgia, Alabama and Florida he saw it approximated, and on their magnificent farms with their black or chocolate "gumbo" soil, their horses, cattle, sheep and hogs, great fields of corn and grain, orchards of fruit, schools,

churches, and comfortable farm houses, nothing more
could seem to be desired. It was an ideal life. The one
element necessary for the existence of the nomadic bands
was the buffalo. He was the beginning and the end, for
when his extermination was finally accomplished, even
though it came about in the most profligate and shameful
manner, the problem was solved, and the wild Indian was
as good as conquered. The buffalo to most Indians was
almost the Deity. "Through the corn and the buffalo we
worship the Father," say some tribes, while others ask,
"what one of the animals is most sacred?" And the reply given was. "The buffalo." To the Indian the buffalo was the staff of life. It was their food, clothing,
dwelling, tools. The needs of a savage people are not
many perhaps, but whatever the plains Indians had, the
buffalo gave them. It is not strange, then, that the animal
was reverenced by them, nor that it entered into their
sacred ceremonies, and was in a sense worshiped by them.
The robe was the Indian's covering and his bed, while the
skin, freed from the hair and dressed, was his sheet or
blanket. The dressed hide was used for moccasins, leggings, shirts, and squaws' clothes. The dressed cow hides
were used for their lodges or "teepees," the warmest, and
most comfortable portable houses or shelter ever devised.
Braided strands of raw hide furnished them with lariats
and lines, as was also the twisted hair. The green hide
was sometimes used as a kettle in which to boil meat or,
stretched over a frame of tough boughs, gave them their
"corracles" or "bull-boats" with which to cross rivers.
The tough, thick hide of the bull's neck, allowed to shrink
smooth, made a shield which would turn a lance-thrust,
an arrow, or, sometimes, even a bullet. From the raw
hide, the hair having been shaved off, were made their
trunks or "parfleches" which served the squaws to carry
their small household belongings, gew-gaws and valuables,
the cannon bones or ribs were made into rough tools for
scraping and dressing the hides, while the shoulder blades,
lashed to sticks, made hoes and axes, and the ribs runners

for small sledges drawn by dogs. The hoofs were boiled to make glue for fastening the feathers and heads on their arrows. This was "lobbed" on sticks, and when cooled carried in their bow cases. When used it was heated in water or over a fire, and applied to sinews lying along the back, backed their bows, the sinews also furnishing thread and bow strings. The hair stuffed cushions and the pads on their saddles and cinches for the same. The horns furnished spoons and ladles, and ornamented their war bonnets. Water vessels were made from the lining of the paunch. The long black beard, in strands, was used to ornament articles of wearing apparel, and their shields and bow and arrow cases. Fly brushes were made from the skin of the tail dried on sticks. Knife-sheaths, bow cases, gun covers, saddle cloths, awl and paint pouches and many other very useful articles, such as "travois" when moving; all were furnished by the buffalo. Their saddle trees and bars were made from elm in several parts; each part was laboriously shaved down and fitted, the high pommel and cantle, to the bars, pierced by sharp tools heated red hot, and then carefully sewed with green deer sinew, a hair being used as a bristle instead of a needle, the several parts brought tightly together and the joints carefully glued with the "lob" stick, and rubbed down with their bone rubbers, and given a coat of Ochre paint. Their bridles were hair; no bits were used, a loop being formed just above the mouth so that free use could be made of it, and the animal was guided by the pressure of the rein on either side of the neck or the legs from behind the cinch. So perfectly trained was the Indian pony that he could be stopped in his own length while running at full speed, or turned sharply in the arc of a circle without even the use of the rein, thus giving the warrior free use of both arms for his bow, lance or other weapon.

A large lodge was generally used in common for all tribal ceremonies, although on one occasion the writer saw a scalp dance "pulled off" in an ordinary "teepee." The visitors formed a circle, into which the young warriors

stripped to the "breech clout" and adorned with feathers
and painted for the occasion, came bounding in. The
heat and steam from old rags, paint, ancient breech clouts,
etc., would have driven an Eskimo crazy for fresh air out
of his "Igloo." Kettle drums, consisting of a dressed
skin tightly stretched across a hollow log, kept up a most
monotonous long drawn out noise of "tom-tom-tom-tom,"
which with the low chanting or half singing of the young
bucks, and shrill screams and "Yi-Yis" of the squaws,
made a harsh, discordant noise, which, had we not been
determined to stay it out and see the entire ceremony,
would have driven us almost frantic. With a slow, halting hop, or dancing gait, the young warriors swept about
the ring, occasionally stopping in the center to "jabber"
or talk an almost untranslateable jargon. This went on
for sometime, new and fresh dancers going into the ring.
shortly, however, the squaws began taking their turn, and
then the fun began. At the termination of dancing of
each set, they became furious, their rage, manufactured
of course, for the occasion, became so emotional, so intense that each squaw flung the scalp she carried upon the
earth floor of the "teepee," and sitting down upon it
ground it into the earth with so much vigor that I expected
to see the trophy fairly torn to pieces. This was, I was
afterwards told, the most deadly insult that can be offered,
and was intended to express the keenest and most intense
disgust and hatred for their deadliest enemy the Comanche. The music grew louder, the "tom-tom" of the
drum more monotonous, the shouting, and wailing quicker
and more furious, until with one "grand finale" as many
as the ring would hold, jumped in and wound up the
dance with a perfect pandemonium of noises.

Indian Cooking and Eating

An Indian would rarely eat when on a raid or the war
path. This was not a human, but more of an animal instinct to avoid the danger of wounds in the bowels or
abdominal region so that they would heal quicker when

not distended with food. But, as soon as this emergency had passed, their animal instinct at once took another turn, and around the carcass of a freshly killed buffalo, or deer, a small family would never cease eating, gorging themselves, and displaying the most gluttinous appetites until nothing was left but the hide, hoofs and horns, even the entrails being stripped through the mouth, breast, liver, lights, and all parts devoured with the fierceness of wolves, and even the rich marrow dug out with their scalping knives, and eaten on the liver as butter, the former cooked in the coals to the point of burning, and then all burnt parts cut off, leaving the balance to be sliced like bread, to accompany the roasted ribs, sprinkling with salt if they have it. A wild turkey was bled, dressed or "drawn," a few feathers plucked out and it is also flung into the fire of red coals. When one would suppose that there was nothing left of the bird, the burnt, black mess was raked out, left to partially cool, then with a dexterous movement of the knife the skin is peeled or stripped from the neck downwards taking the burned feathers, revealing a white and tempting morsel to a hungry man. It was then cut and torn apart and eaten with nature's weapons much as any wild animal would perform the same ceremony.

They are very fond of wild plums (Chickasaw and Bullberry), grapes and berries, and many eat roots and bulbs. In cooking fish, they enclose them in clay or mud after they have been "drawn" and cleaned, to a depth of several inches, rolling them over and over for that purpose; then digging a hole, making a big fire in it, the fish is laid in the same, the earth pulled over, and hot coals scraped on top. When cooked the hard baked clay is knocked off with their knives, the skin coming off with the casing, and eaten with salt, although coarse and less succulent than a small *brook trout* they are nevertheless delicious to a hungry man who has been subsisting on salt food and tough buffalo meat.

The Family Life—Making of a Warrior

The Indian boys were as the apple of his eye. The girls are of little account; great pains are taken to teach and educate the former, but little or none the latter.

When infants, all are "papooses" and carried about on their mothers' backs in curious looking wicker baskets or raw hide cradles fastened to flat boards, the babies being fastened in by raw hide thongs; these cradles, when set up in rows against the agency buildings during issue day, present a most singular sight which attracts the average white man's curiosity at once.

When the squaws were moving, it was like a knapsack "strapped upon the back" and in cold weather, covered up with blankets, leaving but the smallest hole for breathing purposes, the restless eyes of the infant gleam through these openings like stars in the midnight sky.

The care which the squaw bestows upon her young, is, to the uninitiated, a singularly instructive and practical lesson, which has to be seen to be fully appreciated, and which might well be emulated by many a young white mother.

When the boy becomes 5 or 6 years of age, a small bow is placed in his hands, and he is at once taught the manly art of shooting at marks, from the *size of a man's heart* to his head; also he shoots at birds.

Here were his first lessons in killing men, although the writer is prone to believe that he inherits this trait, and drinks it in with his mother's milk.

He was soon placed on a pony and taught the art of riding the animal, subjected to all of the cruelty incident thereto which, at his tender age, such lessons impose; the criticisms of his older companions, his father, mother and all the young braves.

If he was thrown no sympathy or pity was shown; he was rarely hurt, however, and I have never known of an Indian boy being killed or seriously hurt by such a fall. They nearly always strike on their feet like a cat, and if he was in any way bruised, it was made light of and if he started to complain, he was laughed at and jeered by the girls and young squaws. Sometimes he was bound on the pony by a raw hide lariat; another boy held the pony with another lariat and he was circled about until he literally became a part of the animal which he strides, and soon his skill as a jockey at all races, of which Indians are inordinately fond, was unsurpassed.

Thus passed the boy's young life, riding and shooting. He learned to herd and, at full speed to drive or "round up" hundreds of ponies with speed and skill, which a dozen well-mounted white men would find it difficult, if not impossible, to do.

He came to young manhood at from 12 to 16 years of age. He was now considered a young brave; he had never done a stroke of work beyond chasing game, and nobody had asked him to; he had simply been taught to perfect himself in the art of riding, shooting, hunting and fishing about the village.

But as yet he had *killed* nothing human; no large game or made a name for himself and, until he had done this, he did not loom very large on the world's horizon and was of little account in the tribe. He could not become a warrior until he had stolen some horses, could show a scalp or had done some deed for which he could show positive proof. He might be ever so fine a horseman and marksman, a fine looking brave, but yet the squaws laughed and the warriors jeered at him.

He took his place in the raiding party, and when the savage yell awoke the unwary settler from his midnight sleep, the young brave was at full liberty now to earn his name. The reeking scalp upon his return testified as to his abilities, and he received the unbounded praise and warmest congratulations from his relatives and friends; but especially from the young squaws. He was toasted and fêted. How noble he seemed in the eyes of the young maidens of the village; what a bright destiny he had before him. A few horses now and he could compete with any in the village.

A name was now given to him. He was no longer a boy, he is a full-fledged brave and, a little later, after his first battle with the enemy, he might become a leading warrior in the tribe. He must be named.

For instance, "Poor Buffalo" went out hunting; found one lone buffalo, gave chase, killed it, but when he attempted to cut it up found it so poor and tough that his comrades laughed at him, and thus his name of "Poor Buffalo." "Pacer" takes his name from his long stride or shuffling, shambling gait. "Lone Wolf" and all, have acquired their names by trifling matters among their people. In the Sioux Nation a name can be changed an indefinite number of times, and, frequently after a battle, this new name takes place.

The name of "Swift Eagle" was changed to "Dull Knife," etc. This is generally done with a great deal of ceremony, especially if he is a great chief and has done daring deeds.

Habits, Customs, Dress—Decorations, Ceremonies, Etc.

In their habits, the Indians were filthy beyond all power of descriptions. While enjoying a swim for the sport it afforded them, or a temporary enjoyment, it never occurred to them to do it as a matter of personal cleanliness. The writer never saw an Indian wash his face, they rarely washed their clothes, and calico hunting shirt, leggins and breech clout, don't do full duty until, by decay and hard usage, they literally fall from them. They always wipe the grease from their mouths and hands upon these articles of wearing apparel instead of a cloth or napkin.

Their hair, especially that of the "bucks" or warriors, is a matter of great pride to them and daily about a village they could be seen carefully combing, greasing and braiding their scalp-locks, which are generally tied with red flannel, with otter or beaver fur braided in; the whole surmounted by one or more eagle feathers, and in battle, by elaborate head-dresses or war-bonnets of the most unique and fantastical designs.

When not worn the latter were kept in the nondescript band-boxes, parflêches, or skin trunks already described.

They carefully part their hair in the middle, and in gait, dress, manner of riding, etc., are precisely like the squaws, the latter's moccasins differing only in wearing it with a much longer legging.

This strong resemblance in dress, etc., frequently accounted for the fact that the women were often killed in battle by mistake, but, principally for another reason which will be explained further on.

The "bucks," with rare exceptions, wear no beards. The writer saw at Fort Sill an Apache Chief who had cultivated at the corners of his mouth two tufts of hair and had thereby earned the soubriquet of "Black Beard."

They carefully plucked all hair from the face with a pair of tweezers made either of bone or metal. They could frequently be seen with their backs up against their lodges vigorously despoiling themselves of the hirsute growth, and also busily engaged in the additional labor of relieving each other's heads of the superabundant swarmers of insect growth, which, strange to say, were not wasted, but in many cases, formed a part of their daily diet.

They used paint for decorative purposes, in large quantities, and were very vain of the methods they employed in their art. Black is their war paint, but olive green, red and yellow ochre predominate. With a head-dress of buffalo horns, or wolf head with grinning teeth ingeniously combined with feathers, or even with the full war bonnet of long feathers streaming down their backs and down their ponies' tails, they presented anything but a friendly or amiable appearance, especially when under a full run at their ponies' top speed they yell, whoop, circle about and launched clouds of arrows with deadly aim, or fired

their more modern breech loaders at some enemy, supposed or real.

Slinging his elaborately head worked bow-case over his
shoulders, he grasped his weapons, lightly swung himself
into the saddle and grimly proceeded to commit bloody
deeds.

This was the picture of the brave; the warrior, arrayed peacock-like for show and war; proud, conceited and
vain as a city dandy or fop.

He was lord and master; arrogant and egotistic. He
never worked but hunted and fought. How was it with
the squaw? Maturing early, she was, by centuries of savage custom, his willing slave; with merely a significant
look or nod from him, she proceeded, lariat in hand, to
catch his favorite pony, hobbled and grazing near by the
village; to saddle him or to pack the mule for the hunt or
war path.

Upon his return, with scarcely a word of greeting, the
game was flung down before her; she proceeded to unsaddle, and lariat in hand again to hobble and "turn him
out." Then the game must be dressed and cooled or cut
into long thin strips and flung over large frames to dry.*
Thus sun dried, the Mexicans call it "Collops," she
dressed and tanned all of the skins and the finest buffalo
robes one used to see in the markets were all the result
of her untiring industry.

Spreading a robe with the hair side down upon the
ground, she proceeded to stretch it by driving small sharp
pegs along the edges a few inches apart, then spreading
wood ashes upon the fatty, greasy surface and wetting it
down with water or some other kind of moisture, and waiting just long enough for the lye to neutralize the fat, she
began to "flesh" the hide with scraper or "flesher" made
of stone, bone or iron until it was entirely free from fat
and perfectly clean and white; repeating the process several times until finally, by a serious of poundings and
hand manipulations she worked it into the soft and flexible

robes which, after being tied up in large bales were shipped in by pack train to the traders and thence for sale on the markets.

The thread which she used for moccasins for her lord and master and herself, was made of deer sinew carefully and patiently stripped out fine by the aid of sharp knives.

Upon this thread all of their beads were strung; all holes through which the thread was carried for stitches were made with a rude awl of their own manufacture. This was carried in a small leather awl pouch which, together with their paint pouches for carrying paint, had flaps and were highly ornamented with variously colored beads in simple designs, sometimes fringed with metal pendants and strips of buckskin. These were carried upon their wrists by a buckskin thong and formed a part of their everyday outfit, as much as the old fashioned reticules and handbags of our mothers' and grandmothers' days.

The squaw was exceedingly, almost inordinately, fond of jewelry and nick-nacks, these of brass or silver rudely hammered out; also bright-colored blankets. In this she did not differ materially from her white sisters. Silver rings, pounded out of the Mexican silver coins, were upon their fingers, generally marquise shape; brass rings, sometimes numbering some 15 or 20, adorned their wrists and an equal number on the arm above the elbow, as an amulet. Large hoops of brass were in their ears, from which frequently depended long chains or loops of brass wire, upon which were strung pipe-clay ornaments or long tubular, colored beads. Gaudy colored flannels, red, yellow, green and blue, if she could procure them, were ingeniously made into differtnt articles of feminine apparel, and with the inevitable paint upon her face, thickly smeared on, and red flannel in her braid of coal-black hair, she was a singular picture of wild, savage, tawdry vanity.

When a near relative died, or was killed, off went all

of her finery; her hair was cut short and gouged in the
most shocking manner; she slashed her breasts and body
with her knife; black paint, which took the place of red
and yellow, was smeared upon her coppor-colored face,
and she at once became a revolting picture of hideousness,
painful to the eye and to every feeling of female beauty
or taste.

She literally grovelled in the dirt and covered herself
with sack cloth and ashes. Any deviation from a correct
life or being unfaithful to her marriage vows, was punished by her losing her nose which was cut close to her
face. The writer saw several of these cases before he
thought to inquire the true cause for such an infliction.

It was a terribly barbarous means of punishment or
retribution, being a disfiguration for life, and marking her
ever afterwards in the village of her tribe as an object of
supreme disgust, wretched indifference and neglect.

On the march when changing camp, which was frequently done, she carried the papoose on her back, tended
ponies, brought wood and water and prepared the family
meal. In battle, her post was in the rear, bringing up
fresh ponies to replace those exhausted, carrying off the
wounded and supplying ammunition, etc.; all the time keeping up a shrill, piping, high-keyed yell or screech which,
with the well defined whoops of the bucks, made such a
discordant noise or Babel of sounds as to seem like a
veritable pandemonium.

When cornered she fought with all the strength of her
savage nature and the desperation of a tigress, using her
bow and arrows and six-shooter with both of which she
was an excellent and most effective shot. There were few
or none of the "peace-and-order" loving members of the
pussy-footed pacifists of that period, or members of the
press, who often times referred to her as the "poor *de-
fenceless* (?) *squaw*," who would have cared to put themselves in her way under any conditions of battle, especially when she screamed in a perfect fury of rage. After

the fight she helped scalp and torture the wounded, shooting arrows into their bodies, cutting off fingers and toes, even when they were alive, and committing the most horrible and nameless barbarities and atrocities, too revolting for recital here.

This is the true reason why she often got killed when our troops got into close contact with hostile Indians. Not a gleam of pity entered her feminine breast. She was a cold-blooded, thirsty vulture, only intent upon her prey. As good as the warrior himself; fighting like a fiend with the same deadly weapons, and mixing in with the former, it was then rarely the case that more or less squaws were not killed and wounded in our attacks upon their villages. There was little or no time for false sentiment, courtesy or knightly gallantry in the face of a "gun" in the hands of an infuriated squaw intent on "getting" somebody. Their attachment or motherly instincts for their children was very strong, but no more so than the whites; it partakes, perhaps, and is more suggestive of the savage devotion and instinctive traits of the wild animal. The same animal instinct is seen in the white mother. It was while shielding and trying to convey their children from the village to a place of safety that they were sometimes accidentally killed or wounded.

Stoicism, Heroism, Powers of Endurance, Etc.

Much has been written of the stoical character, heroism and powers of endurance of the Indian. It is true to a certain extent, but few white men, however, have been given the opportunity of seeing them at close hand, and of knowing the true Indian nature in its changeable moods. It is not so much a part of their nature. Their abstinence, or power to go without food is remarkable, but it is generally instinctive, and in case of battle always self-imposed as the danger from a wound in the abdominal regions is much lessened when the stomach is comparatively empty. After the fight is over, however, their self control is absolutely gone, and their capacity for making

up the deficiency was not only unequalled by a white man,
but it becomes almost laughable. They gorged and slept;
gorged and slept again; and repeated it sometimes for
two or three days. Their gluttony, for that is the only
term at all applicable on such occasions, was simply dis-
gusting, for as has been stated before, they left nothing
of a buffalo or beeve but the hoofs, hides and horns when
satiating their ravenous hunger. They were compact,
bony and sinewy, making good runners, but were possessed of slight muscular strength, as compared to any
well devoloped white laborer, and made but indifferent
wrestlers, relying upon agility, trickery and treachery for
what they lacked in brawn and muscle or skill.

They were dignified, sedate and very reticent; painfully
shy or diffident, until some ludicrous incident occurred to
disturb this assumed trait, or some game proposed to attract their attention or excite their interest, when those
solemn, fixed, almost graven features, would relax, and
they would break out into almost immoderate laughter,
which sometimes became contagious with an entire group,
and they would behave like veritable children, running,
tumbling over, and all with never a thought of behaving in
an unbecoming manner or with a loss of dignity, etc., in
thus conducting themselves, or of the impressions which
it made upon white observers. This all came under the
observations of the writer one day when the Indians, without knowledge of his near presence, were indulging in a
rollicking game of *"leap frog,"* he being the only white
spectator. So there has been a lot of "bunk" written
about the unchanging or unalterable stoicism, so-called of
our average wild Indian.

After thus briefly referring to their powers of endurance, and other traits, etc., the writer is ready to declare
that he has never seen a white man who has lived in the
open, a man of average intelligence, whose constitution
had not been broken down by dissipation or disease, who
could not compete with and excel them in anything except
covering long distances afoot or in the saddle and shoot-

ing with the bow. The question has been often asked, is the Indian a cowardly fighter? The answer might be easily given by referring to an affair which occurred many years since, when a few Cheyenne braves at Bluff Creek, near Fort Robinson, Nebraska, fought a cavalry Command (Third) from their rifle pits until they were practically exterminated, including a number of squaws.

This, however, was an exceptional case and under most peculiar circumstances. The best answer is that they *were* and were *not* cowardly, depending entirely upon the point of view from which we looked on him as a *trained fighter,* and not a *trained, disciplined soldier,* under somebody's command and always amenable to punishment for misbehavior.

The wild Indian was always taught and carefully trained to employ stratagems of all kinds to entrap his foe, and all sorts of artifices, whether right or wrong, to defeat him, and never to fight unless he had a decided advantage both in numbers and position or was penned, all of which, from the white man's view point are evidences of cowardice, as this includes ambush, trickery, treachery, unfair use of flags or truce (of the real meaning of which the Indian knew but little or nothing); but when we knew how desperately these same warriors would fight when cornered and the stoicism and absolute disregard of death, when come it must, *it is impossible to say that he was a poltroon.*

There was this too, that made the Indians wary. One of the superstitions of the race was that a warrior who lost his scalp, entered not the "Happy Hunting Ground." This explains also why they fought so desperately to carry off their dead and wounded. The matter then of bravery versus cowardice rested largely upon a matter of *scalps combined with personal safety.*

The plains Indians rarely ever fought on foot, seldom except against lines of dismounted men. Their safety as to casualties urged them to always keep mounted, moving

and circling like a swarm of bees and never *"bunching."*
Their tactics under fire is difficult to describe; it was
rather meagerly attempted in the action with Quanah
Parker's band of Qua-ha-da Comanches at the mouth of
Cañon Blanco, October 10, 1871, when they assembled
their entire force for an open field fight with our command
of the 4th Cavalry. Their rapid swing out or rush into
a V-shape formation, and then fanning out to the front
from these two wings into an irregular line of swirling
warriors, all rapidly moving in right and left hand circles,
no two Indians coming together, and their quick exten-
sions, while advancing, to the right or left, and as rapidly
concentrating or assembling on the center, but without
any close bunching, and their falling back in the same
manner, sometimes in a fan-shaped or wing formation,
all was most puzzling to all of our Civil War veterans who
had never witnessed such tactical maneuvers, or such a
flexible line of skirmishers; all without any audible commands, but with much screeching and loud yelling.

The question has been frequently asked why Indians,
mounted on small, undersized, bony, scrubby-looking
ponies or "cayuses," could distance our cavalry troopers
on the best thoroughbred or half-bred American horses
which the Government could purchase.

Every Indian's wealth consisted, not in squaws and
household possessions, but in a large or small herd of
ponies; his property consisting of many head of stock, so
much cash. Many of these ponies were the finest short
distance race animals ever bred in this country. These
they generally rode when going into action. When raiding through the country he generally rode his poorest animals unless pursued, and drove from five to ten along the
flank, the half-grown boys herding them generally in one
bunch or caviard. After depredating and murdering in the
settlements, we will say within 20 miles of a Post or Fort,
the settler would flee to the post and give the alarm often
times afoot especially if all of his stock had been run off.

All was instant hustle. In an incredibly short time a command had started for the ranch to find the trail. It had taken the rancher more than five hours if afoot, and at least three hours if mounted, to bring the news to the garrison. It took nearly one hour to "saddle up," pack the mules with rations and get under way. A ride of from three to four hours to cover the twenty miles; seven hours consumed at the lowest.

No time was lost; the trail was fresh and off rode the command, not so very fresh after a 20 mile dash. The Indians had only stopped to scalp the dead, gather up the stock and head by the nearest route for their distant village. They went on the jump with experienced herders. They rode a pony 20 miles; took the saddle from his wet back; a fresh pony was brought up by a boy at a signal, the tired one joins the "caviard" and, with a few moments delay only, then went off again. All this long before the command had come up.

In this way they could cover in seven hours nearly 50 miles. They never stopped for food or anything until they had covered at least 100 miles, or felt that they were safe from pursuit and capture.

They went over rocky ledges, where the trail was completely lost, through streams where the trails was always obliterated, often crossing a river as many as twenty times a day; through timber and undergrowth where the hard and dry twigs gave little or no sign; over high prairies where the dry, sun-burnt wiry grass, springing back to its natural positions, as soon as the animals hoof had left it, and left no mark. And still on they went.

The command, starting from the ranch and covering 40 or 50 miles, had anything but an encouraging prospect. In fact it was practically a most hopeless task and everybody in it who had ever had any experience in following an Indian trail knew it. They covered the distance at as rapid a gait as possible and not break down the horses, feeling their way along the trail, 20, 40, 50 miles. Coming to the ledge, river or timber over which the trail led, a careful search had to be made for any mark or "sign" and oftentimes unless the most experienced Indian or white trailers or guides were along, it was completely lost.

The horses, travelling often from early dawn, although the best and of fine bottom and endurance, but without change, became weary, spent and "blown." What was the result? The Indians were seldom caught. They escaped four times out of five.

Almost Miraculous

Supposing that by good fortune, the best of *luck,* and through pluck and endurance, the command arrived in sight of the fleeing hostiles and prepared for instant action. Did he then catch them? No, never! What, never! Well, *hardly* ever! For the Indians then not being in condition for fighting, had a plan already worked out for just such an emergency for they were far from being stupid blockheads. They *scattered,* even if pressed too hard, they had to drop some of their over-ridden ponies and the stolen stock. They disappeared like a twinkling, like a covey of quail, generally in timber; or else, in some rocky gorge or box cañon, almost inaccessible, they ambushed our men and then made a desperate stand for a fight.

They could, having picked such a strong, defensive position, only be dislodged by a terrible loss of life, and it would have been almost as much as any officer's commission, even had he possessed the wisest judgment, to have attempted such a risk, and then been defeated, owing to his men and horses being exhausted, ammunition low, etc. If unsuccessful he and his command would have been called inefficient and cowardly, for in our country, *Success* comes to him who *succeeds* at *whatever cost.*

If by almost superhuman efforts and through the skill and heroic bravery of a gallant officer and his gun fighters and Indian scrappers, they ever were successful, and the Indians "wiped out," that officer and *those* daring men would have been called a cowardly set of murderers for killing or massacreing a small band of poor, inoffensive red men who, after all, *have only* raided into the peaceful settlements, killed and *tortured (perhaps burned alive) and barbarously mutilated a few, miserable white settlers, men, women and children,* and *run off* a *few horses to avenge the wrongs and perpetuate the memories of their grandfathers who were so badly treated by the Puritan forefathers of the early Mayflower stock.*

More often the "Peace Commissioners" were sent for to treat with those red handed murderers; to offer concessions, compromises, presents, anything, everything which through a system of double-faced hypocrisy, would induce them to come out of their hidden positions, surrender and be pardoned, only to repeat the process, *ad libitum, ad nauseam.*

The lonely ranch, with its bloody grave so freshly made; the scenes of terrible murder and savage torture were soon forgotten, until the border adjacent to our far-off, isolated posts were again startled by some fresh out break which only differed in kind, excelling if possible, all of the horrible atrocities of the previous one.

When the Indians scattered, what should be done? Should they be pursued singly or in pairs? That required the almost impossible task of hunting for individual trails. The *game* had gone over ledge, twig and dry buffalo grass; no one knew whither; to meet again, by some prearranged plan, at some point 40 miles beyond, at some lone peak, tree, butte or passway, all the country about which the Indians knew so well, and of which his newly arrived white brother was in doleful ignorance. The trail has been lost, and the command, gathering up a few sore-backed Indian ponies, and remounting their own broken-down animals, usually rode slowly back to the ranch; buried the dead, and from thence to the post a disappointed and baffled column of brave, hard worked, tired out men.

The advantage was always on the side of the pursued Indian. That was too apparent, and any argument on that point always seemed then and seems now unnecessary.

The country on that border which we had to traverse when in pursuit of these hostile savages, can be best summed up in the following little doggerel poem, said to have been written by a young graduate of West Point who had just joined his Regiment.

"HOW THE DEVIL LOCATED A CLAIM IN TEXAS, FOR A NEW HELL"

By a Soldier at Fort Brown (Brownsville), Texas

The devil in hell, we're told, was chained,
And a thousand years he there remained;
He never complained, nor did he groan,
But determined to start a hell of his own,
Where he could torment the soul of men
Without being chained in a prison pen.
So he asked the Lord if he had on hand
Anything left when he made the land.

The Lord said: "Yes, I had plenty on hand
But I left it down on the Rio Grande;
The fact is, old boy, the stuff is so poor,
I don't think you could use it in hell any more."
But the devil went down to look at the truck,
And said if it came as a gift he was stuck.
For after examining it carefully and well,
He concluded the place was too dry for a hell.

So in order to get it off of his hands,
The Lord promised the devil to water the lands,
For he had some water, or rather some dregs
A regular cathartic, and smelled like bad eggs.
Hence the deal was closed and the deed was given
And the Lord went back to his home in heaven.
And the devil then said: "I have all that is needed
To make a good hell," and hence he succeeded.

He began to put thorns on all the trees,
And mix up the sand with millions of fleas;
And scattered tarantulas along all the roads;
Put thorns on the cactus and horns on the toads.
He lengthened the horns of the Texas steers,
And put additions on the rabbits' ears;
He put a little devil in the broncho steed
And poisoned the feet of the centipede.

The rattlesnake bites you, the scorpion stings,
The mosquito delights you with buzzing wings;
The sandburs prevail and so do the ants,
And those who sit down need half-soles on their pants.
The devil then said that throughout the land
He'd managed to keep up the devil's own brand,
And all would be mavericks unless they bore
Marks of scratches and bites and thorns by the score.

The heat in the summer is a hundred and ten,
Too hot for the devil and too hot for men,
The wild boar roams through the black chaparral,
It's a hell of a place he has for a hell.
The red pepper grows on the banks of the brook;
The Mexicans use it in all that they cook.
Just dine with a "greaser," and then you will shout
"I've hell on the inside as well as the out."

Scalps—Scalp Poles—Bows—"Lob Stick"— Saddles, Etc.

The Indians, after scalping their victims, and mutilating them beyond all power of recognition, tanned the scalp in much the same manner as any hide or skin. It was then stretched on a small frame or circular hoop of round tough ash, willow or reed, with cross or diagonal pieces to keep it taut, until in proper condition (dried) to attach to the scalp pole (which is then their battle-flag) or on a raw hide shield or lance.

The bows were made of the Osage orange, or bois d'arc (wood of the bow), strung with twisted deer sinews, and strengthened on the back by strips of raw, deer sinew, glued and allowed to shrink on hard until it is almost like steel. The ends were then closely wrapped for several inches with fine sinew thread, to prevent them from working loose through usage and the weather. This, after being carefully glued and allowed to shrink, made the whole very strong and tough.

The arrows were made of mulberry or ash, tipped with wild turkey feathers glued to the shaft with bands of sinew.

On the other end was the spike 2 to 3 inches in length, made of ordinary hoop iron, sharpened on point and edges and afterwards hardened and tempered in both fire and water making them like steel. The other end of the spike after being roughed along its edges so that it would hold into the wood better, was entered into a cleft split in the end of the shaft, and then carefully wound with fine deer sinew along its entire length, then glued smooth.

They could throw these arrows with the most deadly accuracy from 30 to 50 yards, and at from 10 to 15 yards they could send a plain, unspiked arrow shaft entirely through a buffalo, and hit a mark as large as a door knob four times out of five.

The glue which they used was made from the buffalo hoofs and was then smeared and "lobbed" upon a smoothly whittled piece of mulberry, allowed to cool, and then carried in the bow case with the arrows for frequent use. By softening in hot water it was ready as a most handy and instant mender for almost everything. The writer has used this glue on pieces of furniture with perfect success.

Their saddles were generally made of the American elm, and were very tough and durable. They were made in three pieces, the bars or seat proper, the pommel and cantle, and they exhibited great ingenuity in making and putting them together.

The pommels and cantles were made high with but slight pitch, the bars (open seat) of moderate length but comfortable. The holes for sewing were made with a rude red hot awl; the joints were carefully and neatly brought together or sewed with deer sinew and the seams made close, often with no other tools than their knives, an awl and a stone hammer, over these seams a pigment was smeared to keep the water out, over this a frame was stretched of raw deer hide, first soaking it well and allowing it to shrink on snug and secure, a small soft bear skin was worn on the saddle as a pad. On the march they would live for days on sun-dried or jerked buffalo meat called by the Texas "black strap," and by the Mexicans "Collops" together with a little parched corn or an ash cake made of pounded corn with salt if they could obtain it.

When they shook hands, it was done in a hearty, good natured, but rather awkward or uncouth manner as though they were not used to it, accompanied always with a loud guttural "How! How now! Cola!!!" repeated several times as if to make up for the lack of energy in the hand shake. The *left* hand was used, the right hand scarcely ever, and the latter they would rarely ever take. This was explained thus. His early education taught him to distrust all such friendly approaches or manifestations; that all were enemies until they had proved their friendships; and the right hand must always be kept free to strike with knife or other deadly weapon. It guarded against treachery on either side.

Pipes—Presents, Etc.

They would rarely ever smoke a cigar when it was proffered, and did not enjoy it. They were not great smokers of the pipe using it only at their councils, but were inveterate cigarette smokers.

They smoked a red clay pipe and a cigarette made of tobacco rolled in the small, soft, inner leaves of the corn shuck which they generally carried in packages tied to their hunting shirts.

Sitting over a small fire, apparently absorbed in deepest meditation, with blanket drawn close about them, their keen eyes moving about, and taking in the slightest movement or noise, they would draw the smoke into their lungs until full, then expel it by a slow motion in great clouds from their nostrils and mouth.

They would sit this way for hours without a word, and only an occasional grunt, a perfect picture of savage contentment and happiness.

They were the most inveterate beggars, and woe be unto the individual who, through mistaken kindness, accepted a robe, bow or pipe, or other article of value as a present from them. An hour afterwards Mr. LO might be seen approaching the quarters with his squaw; sitting down he would pull out his role of corn shucks and by signs would soon make it known that he was out of tobacco. Pointing to his better half, he would strongly intimate and soon convince you that she was out of beads or a blanket he had taken a fancy to, a ring you wear; that an old vest (of which they always seemed fond) would not be unacceptable, and so on, until all of ones wits and tact had to be exercised to put the troublesome beggar off or to get rid of him as soon as possible.

His most unreasonable demands were, for the most part, acceded to, and before he left he had succeeded in convincing one beyond a doubt of his ability to more than make himself whole for the presents which he had so liberally (?) bestowed upon you.

This red brother was as capricious as the winds. A fine buffalo robe which he would not sell under ten or twenty dollars, which was generally his standard price to officers, although three dollars and a half to anybody else, he would readily part with the next day for a few yards of bright-colored calico print or a few beads for his squaw, costing not over sixty cents. His visits and presents always signified a "guid pro quo."

"Lo! the poor Indian whose untutored mind"
"Sees God in clouds and hears him in the wind."
—*Pope.*

OWED (ODE) TO LO! THE POOR INDIAN

'Tis said that "music bath charms to soothe the savage breast,"[1]
That may be so, but "Chuckway"[2] will do it far the best,
They like good bread, they like good meat; are very fond of grease,
But "their ways are not of pleasantness," nor are their paths of
    peace.
So hustle out your "Chuckway," and give them all you can,
You'll find they'll fondly stick to you, yes, even to a man.
No doubt they are fond of music, but let "Chuckway" be the call.
That charms the Savage, soothes his breast, and brings them one
    and all.
To post or camp, it matters not how poor may be the fare,
If Lo! can get enough to eat, he'll promptly be right there.

---

[1]Congreve.
[2]"Chuckway"—Kiowa and Comanche for food.

Their appetites are wonderful, they are always begging food.
They'll eat from "morn 'till dewy eve," and show no gratitude.
And when they are full up to the throat, for more they'll give
    a sigh,
And if they get it not, why then it's "How! good bye, good bye."
Then, they'll go and hide themselves like panthers in their lair,
And if you chance to pass that way, they'll gently raise your hair.
Their minds untutored to do right, they know not how to pray,
The Clouds and Winds don't trouble them, they steal both night
    and day.
Bedecked with paint, they go to war, with frantic, hideous yell,
Remorseless, cruel, vengeful, they are merciless as hell.
You'll never find upon this earth wherever you may go,
A meaner, dirtier, murdering thief, than you will find in Lo!

                    Poet—Lo!—rate.
                         J. A. W.
             (Colonel John A. Wilcox.)

We left Fort Sill on March 28. As we were leaving the limits of the post near the Indian Agency, a man came out of the store and handed Gen. Mackenzie a box of cigars. He proved to be W. H. H. McCall. He had had a record. He had been a Colonel and brevet Brig.-General of the volunteers during the Civil War. When Gen. Geo. A. Forsyth had his desperate fight with Roman Nose' band of Northern Cheyenne Indians on Sept. 17, 1868, on a sand island in the Arickaree Fork of the Republican River in Kansas, now known as "Beecher Island," McCall had been his most efficient and daring First Sergeant of the 50 scouts who had volunteered to go with Forsythe and when he (F.) was wounded three times and his little command came near being exterminated. Some years after we had seen this man at Fort Sill, and I had known "Wild Bill" Hickox, who was so long associated with "Buffalo Bill" and "Texas Jack" in their dramatic productions, "Wild Bill" was shot dead at a poker table by one Mc-Call. The writer queried whether it was the man whom he had seen at Fort S. and who, dying later, was buried at Prescott, Arizona, after leading the adventurous and checkered career of a border spirit, but ascertained that it was another man of the same name.

CHAPTER XI

The Army Witness
and
His Dramatic Adventures

THE unlooked for and the unexpected is generally happening in a soldier's life. The writer had somewhat expected to be summoned as a witness in the case of the citizens whom he had, really in violation of the law, arrested in December, 1871, for their criminal act in pretending to capture the deserters whom later he secured, but whom they released upon their payment of "blood money" which these citizen constables demanded, but weeks and months went by and the event had almost escaped the writer's memory, so busy had been that period. Upon the writer's return, however, from a month's trip to Fort Sill, I.T., where he had commanded the escort to the officers attending the G.C.M., for the trial of Lieut. R. H. Pratt of the Tenth Cavalry, who, years later was a Brigadier General and the kind, humane and most efficient Superintendent of the Indian School at Carlisle, Pa., the following post order proved somewhat in the nature of a surprise.

The Subpoena—An Unwilling Witness

It was accompanied by an order from Department Headquarters with a regular subpoena, to appear before the grand jury in this case, a copy of the order follows:

Headquarters, Post of Fort Richardson,
Fort Richardson, Texas, May 20, 1872.
Special Orders No. 121

EXTRACT

III   *   *   *   *   *   *   *

Second Lieutenant, *R. G. Carter*, 4th Cavalry, will proceed to-morrow, the 21st instant to Tyler, Texas, to appear as a witness before the U. S. District Court at that place. Upon being relieved from attendance upon the Court, he will at once return to this Post.

300

Corporal *Edward Broderick*, Company "I," and five (5) privates, 11th U. S. Infantry, fully armed and equipped, furnished with sixty (60) rounds of ammunition and twenty (20) days' rations per man, will accompany Lieutenant Carter as escort.

The Quartermaster Dept. will furnish one Spring, and one Army Wagon as the necessary transportation, and will transfer to Lieutenant *Carter* one hundred ($100.00) dollars Q. M. Funds for the purchase of forage for the public animals.

The A. C. S. will turn over to Lieutenant Carter Fifty ($50.00) dollars Subsistence Funds.

By Command of Lt. Colonel George P. Buell.

(signed) CHARLES A. VERNOU,
1st Lieut. and Adjutant, 4th U. S. Cavalry (?)
Post Adjutant.

Lieut. R. G. Carter,
4th Cavalry.

This order from Dept. Headquarters was at least three weeks old, and I felt that it would prove a useless journey. I determined, however, so long as I was compelled to make it, that I would take my family. Gen. Buell also urged me to do so. It was to be a long and tedious journey by marching of several hundred miles due East across the State. They had been under canvas for several months and concluding, that the regiment, under Mackenzie was bound to be in the field for at least the balance of the year, it would be a good plan for her to go to New Orleans for a visit to her father, which could be effected by stage from Tyler to the end of the railroad, thence to Shreveport, La., and then by boat down the Red and Missisippi Rivers to New Orleans. So the "canvas ranch" was broken up, all the valuable (?) household possessions packed, not a stupendous task, and on the morning of May 22nd the start was made, with a complete camping and cooking "outfit," with "Black Aleck" as cook, a driver, etc., a wall tent; canvas to fit for a carpet, trestle bed and two fold-up camp chairs, mess chest, with folding lids to unfold into a table, mess furniture, water proof rubber clothing; a small canteen to carry milk in for the baby; a larger one with heavy blanket cover to wet and swing in the ambulance in place of ice water, Commissary stores,

etc., etc., all had to be provided for our comfort, as we
should live in canvas during the entire trip. We made
comparatively short marches, passing through many small
settlements, ranches, towns and hamlets, now connected up
by lines of railroads, and along the main highways, camping at Weatherford, Bear Creek, Fort Worth on the Clear
Fork of the Trinity (then a small town of a few hundred
inhabitants), Dallas (at the Fair Grounds), Johnson's
Mills, Cyene, Kaufman, Prairieville, Canton, Mt. Sylvan,
etc. There were no duties to perform except to guard the
Government property and look after the family. It was
the loveliest of Texas months; there was no commanding
officer to report to, and we could move, camp whenever
and wherever we chose, and do whatever we saw fit. Stopping en route at Mrs. Crawford's ranch, about 20 miles
from Fort R., we arrived at Weatherford without accident.
Just as we were about to break camp at Weatherford,
however, a stormy, rainy morning, a sudden tornado, or
strong gust of wind, got under the canvas, and for a few
minutes, even with all of the men at the guy ropes, we
came near going up in the air like a balloon. The baby
was thrust under the trestle cot bed, upon a large buffalo
robe; blankets were thrown about both she and her mother, and shortly, the storm having spent its strength, we
were once more on the march.

One of the teamsters had the colic and his life was only
saved by pouring hot brandy down his throat, and rubbing him with pieces of blanket stripped for the purpose
and wrung out in boiling water. Sometimes we lost the
road, but with map in hand and a compass, after a few
miles lost distance, we regained it. Again, floods descended and we were compelled to remain in camp or cut
a new road through the overflowed, swampy bottom. A
whiffletree was broken when crossing a stream or bog.
The ambulance broke down once. Swamps, rivers, creeks,
and small streams and "Sloughs" were crossed. We
passed through a little *"groggery"* near the East Fork

of the Trinity River, enjoying the characteristic title of
"Slap Foot." Why it was not called by the more appropriate name of "Tangle Foot," a modest discretion de-
terred me from asking as the omnipresent six-shooter was
on the proprietor's hip, and the writer was not even armed
with a pen knife. As we approached one little settlement,
we sent out a "forager" to buy chickens, eggs, etc., the
former 12 cents a pound and the latter 10 cents a dozen,
he was refused because the settlers thought we were railroad people, and "dey wouldn't sell no poultry, and no
eggs to no 'ornery' rail-road folks, no, sah! dey didn't
want no rail-road folks, nor no rail-road *running* fro dey
diggins no how"!! Once the wagon took the wrong road,
going on to Canton. After waiting for it until dark and
having no tent to pitch, we had to secure shelter for the
night at a German ranch in Prairieville where we had intended pitching our camp. It proved to be hot and populated with so many bugs in and about the voluminous
feather bed, that we had to pull a corn husk mattress on
to the floor and with three persons to occupy it, try to
sleep as best we might. The wagon had gone off the road
in the darkness, had upset and broken our bed so that we
had to haul up for repairs. I always strongly suspected
that too much "benzine" caused this mishap. The timber
grew larger; pine forests began to loom up, it was the
season for that infinitesimally small spider or "chigger",
whose burning and itching under the skin became almost
unendurable, the omnipresent wood tick also clung closely
to us and the baby with a tenacity which was only ob-
viated by digging them out at night by the light of a "tallow dip" with sharp pen knives or needles which left scars
for many a day afterwards. Occasionally we met a
"camp-meeting" of colored people, who laughingly saluted
us with, "Morning, Sah!" "Mornin, Miss!" and replied
to our good natured jokes. The merry sand flea and the
musical mosquito at our camp in the forests added to our
comforts (?), and yet—it was a *happy trip*. On Sunday

the 2nd of June we arrived at Tyler, and upon finding that
the District Court (Judge Duval) had adjourned, and had
returned to his home at Austin, Texas, as predicted, my
journey had been for naught. I was too late, and the culprits were never tried. A good camp was sought outside
of the town, and plans made for the trip to New Orleans.
I decided to leave the detachment in camp and accompany
the family by stage as far as Longview, placing them on
the train at that point, then the terminal of the Southern
Texas Pacific R. R.

The One Legged "Johnny"—A Rail-Road Terminal— Am Arrested

On the 5th, we signalled the stage in the early morning,
and with no other passenger aboard rode the 40 miles,
passing directly through the old rebel-stockade which was
used as a prison camp ("Camp Ford"), during the Civil
War—a place filled with most interesting reminiscences—
many of which were related to me by the one-legged driver
who had served in the Confederate Army during that
period, having lost his leg at the siege of Vicksburg, being
in the Artillery and serving the guns. This man was a
most unique as well as eccentric character. I had put on
a suit of citizen's clothes and taken a small hand "grip"
for baggage, and had started without even placing my
written orders in my pocket, or carrying anything as a
means for identification. Strickly speaking, I took a short
"French Leave," which I was entitled to as my orders
had not limited me as to time of return to Fort R. As
will be seen, however, this neglect on my part, and too
much confidence in human nature, later, placed me in a
most embarrassing as well as humiliating position in which
the "peg-leg" stage driver played no unimportant part,
I seemed doomed, in all of the incidents connected with
the capture of the deserters, to run up against obstacles
in which some old Confederate cripple acted in the role
of mediator. A 40 mile ride landed us at the "Davenport
House," a newly-built pine lumber hotel or "shack"

planted low in the hot sand, and similar to all ranches or structures in new locations about the State. The town resembled an "old 49-er." Rude, unpainted weather-board shanties and saloons of the "dew-drop-in" and "hole-in-the-wall" order; cheap patched up canvas shops, temporary abiding places, and most startling signs, posters and grand announcements in charcoal and chalk made up the "mise en scene." Fleas, dogs, barkers, desperadoes and reckless adventurers predominated in this railroad town which had gone up in a night. Dog-fighting, drunkenness, knock downs and "drag outs" prevailed, and an occasional shot up the main street (?) warned the *wary* and *weary* traveler and sojourner in that delectable burg that he had better seek cover, as it was not safe to be out after dark in that unlighted Avenue—Le Boulevard de Longview. We were ushered to our room. It was not ceiled, lathed or plastered. Below, there were thin board partitions. The bed rooms had thin cotton sheeting (muslin) merely tacked upon the studding. Conversations had to be conducted in a whisper, as every noise in the adjoining room was plainly heard. The floors were uncarpeted, and through huge cracks, the rooms and their occupants were distinctly visible. The baby fell out of bed during the night; a wash bowl full of water accidently upset while vigorously endeavoring to recover her, the contents of which, running through to the room below, flooded two young girls out of their bed, and almost splitting with laughter we "Old soldiers" heard and saw them pull for the opposite shore with their beds and all its surroundings. A little later, long after midnight, a fellow whose foot board was against our head board and light cotton partition "turned in" with his boots on, and almost too full for utterance, and in the exuberance of his joy that the "tangle foot" was giving him, planted both feet with full force against said head board, and exclaimed with all the emphasis and enthusiasm of his Texas nature, "drunk again by ———, dr-u-n-n-n-n-k—hic—ag-a-a-i-i-i-n-n!!"

This he kept up for an hour or more, or, until Morpheus came to his and our relief. The following morning, after passing a sleepless and most wretched night, with noise and almost pandemonium reigning without, and this situation added to fleas, bugs, and mosquitoes confronting us within, as we left this palatial (?) hotel to take a train for Shreveport, a man stepped briskly up to me and, tapping me on the shoulder, rather too familiarly I thought, said with a rather peculiar emphasis, "I arrest you as a deserter from the United States Army," with much stress on the "United States" I thought, because, I suppose he was in some ways reminded of "reconstruction" days. Here was "a go!" I had but just recently been mixed with a whole lot of deserters when I myself was the dominant character. Here I was not *dominant*. I smiled in rather a perfunctory manner, and assuming a nonchalant air replied, "You have the wrong party, I am an officer of the Army." He rejoined, "But, I have followed you all the way from Palestine (not the Holy Land), and I know I have got the *"right party!"* This was one of the methods employed by some of the Civil authorities, after they felt sure that they had come into their own subsequent to the "reconstruction," of annoying us, and I merely smiled as though it was beginning to assume a huge joke. But this persistent fellow was a genuine, bona fide detective, for I then asked to see his authority. He was armed (I was not) and the $30 reward for deserters loomed up, as big as "Jumbo," and he obstinately persisted in enforcing his arrest. As before stated, I was not in uniform; had no orders with me; was without any commission or insignia to make good my claim, not the slightest thing to prove that I was an officer, and unless I could at once devise some makeshift by which to convince him, I was certainly in a dilemma. A sudden thought flashed into my fast wool-gathering brain, "Come into the office!" I stepped back into the hotel closely followed by my newly-found friend, who stuck to me closer than a

brother, and said to the clerk, "Who am I?" hardly knowing my own identity, *after such a night.* "Please show
this man the register." Then turning to the one-legged
stage driver, who, fortunately, had not started back on his
return trip to Tyler. "Please identify me to this detective. Where did you take me on your stage coming over
to Longview?" "Ah, come off!" said my ex-confederate
stage driver friend to my shadowing law officer. "He's
no deserter, you are on the wrong track." (The phrase
"Off'n his trolley," had not then been coined.) "He's a
Federal Army Officer." (With emphasis on the *Federal.*)
"I picked him up at his camp, and he came over with me
on my stage."

The active little detective turned several colors and at
once disappeared from the ranch. We proceeded by rail
to Shreveport. The family was placed on the Red River
boat for New Orleans.

The Return—The "Poem"—An Indian Scare

Upon returning to Longview I did not tarry there, but
taking the stage proceeded to Tyler. There were several
drummers or commercial travelers as passengers, and we
all rode outside with the driver. This one-legged "Johnny" stage driver was a most unique as well as an eccentric and very droll character.

As soon as he got warmed up and his tongue loosened
by "a little Old Rye," which one of the drummers happened to have, he kept us in a constant roar of laughter,
which, as a panacea to my wearied mind and body was
better than medicine. It was a tonic and stimulant combined, and I yielded myself completely to its restorative
effects. He had, according to his story, been "pressed"
or "Conscripted" into the Rebel Army. He had no heart
in the cause, because, like many other young boys of that
period he had no full conception of the principles involved,
or how serious, almost fatal the outcome might be. After
losing his leg in the early part of the war, he was compelled to serve in the water batteries at Vicksburg, which

made him mad. While there, he composed a lot of doggerel poetry, mostly concerned with the causes, or alleged
causes, for the war, its authors who did little or none of
the fighting, or who endured none of the hardships or privations of the great struggle. Much of it was about
"Jeff" Davis and the wretched experience of the rank and
file of the Confederate Army. Shortly after he obtained
a short furlough to go to Tyler, his home, and by advice
of some of his friends, consented on one occasion to recite these *"Patriotic"* (?) verses in a small hall which he
had hired for their amusement. This effort nearly cost
him his life. He had scarcely recited a dozen verses
(there must have been 40, more or less), when he was
seized, borne from the stage, barely saved his neck from
stretching on the limb of a tree, and after being im-
prisoned for several days, was sent back to Vicksburg
with many warnings. This poetical effusion we persuaded
him to recite to us as we rode along. It ran to that ex-
hilerating tune of "Skew Ball Sez I," to our intense
amusement, especially of one "drummer" who, I feared,
would roll off the driver's seat. It was one of the most
laughable travesties and pieces of witty satire on the entire war for Secession, mixed with many camp and trench
misfortunes of the writer of the verses that we had ever
heard. Unfortunately neither the name of our one-legged
friend, nor a copy of his verses were secured for preservation and future references. He pointed out the stockade
prison ("Camp Ford") near Tyler where the prisoners
from Gen. Banks' Army and those captured at Galveston
were confined; where they were hitched to ploughs and
compelled to cultivate the land to raise their own vegetables. A pack of blood hounds were kept to trail prisoners trying to escape. The now crumbling log stockades
were still visible.

The march back from Tyler was without special incident until we reached Weatherford. As we started for
Crawford's Ranch—about 25 miles from Fort R—we met

the settlers moving with all of their goods and chattels into Weatherford. They informed us that Indian raiding parties were very numerous in the country, and that only half an hour before my arrival a party of Indians had been seen in the timber which I was just about to enter. I halted, closed up the wagons; deployed three men ahead, on both sides of the road as skirmishers, and flanking the team with the other men, their old ''Long Tom'' Infantry Springfield breech-loaders ready for any emergency, we went through to ''Crawford's'' prepared for action. Citizens were met who were out ''running the trail'' of the party seen. * * * Arriving at the post on June 16 and being assigned to drilling, and ''licking into shape'' some 200 new recruits, I remained on this duty until July 9th when, as though I was never to be separated from these deserters, captured, and disposed of by sentence of a Court Martial to be dishonorably discharged, with forfeiture of all pay and allowances, and a sentence of from 3 to 4 years at hard labor in some penitentiary. I received an order to deliver them to the Governor of the State Penitentiary at Baton Rouge, La., which then received all military prisoners in the Military Division, undergoing sentence, since the Disciplinary Prison at Fort Leavenworth, Kansas, had not then been established.

Headquarters, Post of Fort Richardson
Fort Richardson, Texas, July 9, 1872.
Special Orders No. 164

EXTRACT

*   *   *   *   *   *

II Second Lieut. R. G. Carter, 4th U. S. Cavalry, with *two* (2) *non. com*-officers and seven (7) privates, 4th U. S. Cavalry and 11th U. S. Infantry (Cavalry dismounted), fully armed and equipped, furnished with one hundred rounds of ammunition and eight (8) days rations per man, will proceed to-morrow, the 10th instant, at *9 o'clock a. m.* to *Corsicana, Texas,* in charge of seven (7) military prisoners en route for Baton Rouge Penitentiary, La. On arrival at *Corsicana, Texas,* Lieut. Carter with one non-com-officer and four (4) men will proceed to Baton Rouge with the prisoners, turning them over to the *Governor* of the *Penitentiary* and taking proper receipts for same, on completion of which duty he will return to *this post*. Lieut. Carter's transportation will return from Corsicana, under charge of one (1) non-com-officer and three (3) privates, and Lieut. Carter on his return from Baton Rouge, La., will avail, at Corsicana, himself of the transportation that is now with the paymaster. The A.C.S. of Post will transfer to Lieut. Carter the sum of *seventy-five dollars* ($75.00) Subsistence funds. The A. A. Q. M. will furnish the necessary transportation.

By command of Lieut. Colonel Geo. P. Buell.

(signed) ULYSSES G. WHITE,
2nd Lieut., 4th Cavalry,
Post Adjutant.

(Endorsement)

Office of Post Q. M.
Fort Richardson, Texas
July 10, 1872

Transportation furnished on the within order for one (1) officer and eleven (11) men from Corsicana to Houston, Texas, Houston to Galveston, Texas, Galveston to New Orleans, La.

(signed) W. J. KYLE,
1st Lieut., 11th Infty.,
A. A. Q. M.

Just as I was leaving the post, one insane man (Lapp of Troop "E") was turned over to me. My route to Corsicana was via Crawford's Weatherford, Robinson's, keeping down the Clear Fork to Bear Creek, thence to Armstrong's Mills, 7 miles from Alvarado, thence through the latter to Hog Creek, 4 miles from Milford. Sergeant Petri of Troop "E" was in charge of the prisoners. They were handcuffed, but I took them off to permit them to bathe. Crossing Milk Creek at 7 a. m., camped about 2 miles from Corsicana at 6:30 p. m., July 14. Here I hit the railroad, and going by rail via Houston to Galveston, took the City of Norfolk (Morgan Line) there at 2:30 pm. m. July 16th arrived at New Orleans at 4:30, on July 17th, going by rail from Brashear City. Transferred the prisoners to the Jackson Square Jail, Capt. McCann. On the 18th they were transferred to the steamer Frank Pargoud and turned over to superintendent James of the State Penitentiary. Had a long talk with a young man, a former Cadet at the Alexandria, La., Mil. Academy before the Civil War, and when W. T. Sherman was Superintendent of the same. He related many very interesting reminiscences of Gen. S. I received the following receipt for the prisoners:

Received, Louisiana Penitentiary, Baton Rouge, July 19th, 1872, from Lieut. R. G. Carter, 4th Cavalry, the following prisoners: Henry Koept, Henry Loveland, Henry Evans, Charles Brown, Alvah Love, Harrison Fisher, Abram Yokey. Crime, U. S. Prisoners.

(signed) Geo H. Matta,
Clerk of Louisiana Penitentiary.

Matta, the clerk of the Penitentiary was a "Trusty," He had a past and was serving a sentence. His crime as now recalled, was embezzlement of money from the Government while an officer of the volunteers, either a Paymaster, Quartermaster or Commissary.

Upon reporting at Headquarters Dept. of the Gulf the following order was issued:

Headquarters Department of the Gulf,
New Orleans, La., July 18, 1872.
Special Orders No. 109

I. Second Lieutenant R. G. Carter, 4th Cavalry, having reported at these Headquarters, with guard (one non-commissioned officer and three (3) enlisted men in charge of seven military prisoners en route to the Baton Rouge Penitentiary), the Quartermaster Department will furnish Lieut. Carter transportation for himself, guard and prisoners from this City to Baton Rouge and transportation to return from Baton Rouge to Corsicana, Texas, for himself and guard.

II. Sergeant D. Maloney, Company "K," 11th Infantry, with one enlisted man having reported at these Headquarters en route to Washington, D. C., in charge of Private Andrew Lapp, Company "E," 4th Cavalry, an insane soldier, the Quartermaster's Dep't will furnish transportation for the party from New Orleans to Washington, D. C.

By order of the Department Commander.

(signed) W. T. Gentry,
Capt. 19th Infantry,
A. A. A. G.

(Endorsement)

Office of Ch-Qr-Ms Dept. of the Gulf,
New Orleans, July 18, 1872.

Transportation furnished Lt. R. G. Carter and party in accordance with this order hence to Baton Rouge and return.

(signed) Wm. B. Hughes,
Capt. & A. Q. M., U. S. Army.

A "Rough Neck" Driver—The "Rough House" Cure

I joined my family in New Orleans. We had had so much trouble with servants on the frontier, being able to secure only a worthless lot of field cooks. I advertised for one, and got her promise to accompany us on the day set. After much trouble and delay in hearing from my transportation which was to meet me, first at Corsicana and then at Dallas, the start was made for a return to Fort R— on Aug. 5th. The trip was a pleasant one and without special incident until we reached Dallas. Here I found that through some misunderstanding my transportation had returned to Fort R— leaving me no other alternative than to go into camp, and await its return. We arrived about midnight. Not being certain where my camp would be located and as it was too late to find it at that hour, especially with all of my impedimenta, we decided to go to the only hotel then in Dallas, the Crutchfield House. There was a perfect rabble of hack-men about the station. The driver asked me for the trunk checks, but said later, just as we were about starting, that he had so much baggage he would be compelled to leave a part of it behind, among it our own. I assented, provided he got it up to the house early in the morning, which he agreed to do. Upon arriving at the hotel I concluded, as a matter of precaution, and as we had some valuable things in one of our trunks, to take my checks from him, get up early and, as his livery stable was near by, have him call for them and transfer the baggage. This he readily *consented* to. He made no objection or remonstrance. I paid him and rid myself of that anxiety which I would have felt had I left the checks in the hands of a stranger and a not over prepossessing looking one at that. I was up at 4 a. m. I waited until after breakfast, and still he had not come. I went to his stable; he was not there. "Would not be there until 10 o'clock, lived at the other end of town," said one of the rascally looking "hangers on," lounging on a broken chair. I was getting restless, was impatient to transfer my family to camp. I went at 10, and still no driver. The loafers winked at each other and blinked. "He may be here at 12 o'clock," in a most significant tone, punctually at noon I was on hand, getting more and more angry. The driver was there, looking surly, and defiant. I knew trouble was brewing. This was to be the concluding chapter of my connection with the deserters. I had the receipt for them of the "Trusty" at the Baton Rouge Penitentiary in my pocket. The following conversation took place: "My baggage has not been taken to the Crutchfield House." "No, and I don't propose to take it!" "I paid you for it, and I have waited patiently for you to do as you agreed," I replied. "You took the checks from me last night, and now you can *get the trunks yourself!*" At this brutal insult and repudiation of his word, I flashed up. A half dozen Texans sat about *armed,* their guns showing in their belts as usual. I felt that I had got to finish up my deserters' adventure in about the way I had finished it up at Hardin's Ranch the preceding December. I replied to his insolence as follows: "Well, now, my friend, as you have chosen to pocket my money, to violate your agreement, and to make this insulting remark, I am an officer of the Army, my camp is about a mile outside of the town; you have put me to a great deal of trouble, inconvenience and some expense, and now I propose that you shall get that baggage, if I have to bring the command in here to see that it is done." A sudden thought seized the wily rascal. He would cause me more trouble. "Oh! well, I will hook up and take your baggage to the Crutchfield House." "Yes!" echoed all of his friends, sitting on their hams, "Take it to the Crutchfield." Knowing full well in their evil brains, that I did not want it there then after waiting from early morning to use it in my camp. I said nothing, however, but mounting the old rickety wagon, thoroughly aroused now, merely remarked: "I will go down with you." Mad all through at being thwarted in his rascally designs he said: "If you go down with me I shall charge you regular fare!" I made no reply, fully resolved upon my plan of action after getting him away from his armed gang. I felt that I knew my man. Before reaching the depot, however, the scoundrel, seeing perhaps, in my dilemma, a possible small "douceur" or "tip" looming up before him began to change his entire attitude and to begin a palaver saying in a most patronizing manner, "Oh! say, "Cap," I didn't mean nothin'. It's all right, why didn't you tell me that you were an officer in the first place?" I had not slept any the night before on account of fleas, mosquitoes, bed bugs and one or two "boozers" about the hotel. "It makes no difference, Sir, whether I am an officer or not, whether I am Gen. Grant or plain John Smith, the principle is the same, you agreed to do a certain thing, and you must do it." There was a "hole in the wall" booze shop at the station. "Oh, now, what's the use of getting mad, come over and take a drink." "No, Sir! I do not drink with such scum as you." I was thoroughly incensed. He looked rather startled. We were alone. At noon nobody was about. He seemed to realize that he was going it alone and the cowardly sneak began to wilt. The day was terribly sultry; the depot was of pine, and was located on a sand flat. The scalding heat was reflected from the boards and sand as from a furnace. He began to handle the baggage. I paced up and down the platform; would extend no help. The fellow began to get angry, then mad, and after loading two trunks and a chest, the latter loaded with a sewing machine and much other heavy material and weighing like lead, several times into his wagon, it refused to hold them unless they were loaded in a certain way. This method I suggested. I knew the fellow was a swaggering bully, but, finally he refused to load and reload that chest any more, and wet through with perspiration and thoroughly enraged at my cool indifference and refusal to help him in the slightest way, he *wouldn't budge an inch.* Here was a crisis. I

had got to employ plenty of bluff, the same kind of bluff I
had used at Hardin's Ranch when the "Old Man would
lick you uns outen yer boots!" I was out of patience, and
fighting mad. There was nobody apparently within half
a mile of us. I stripped off my coat with a jerk. My
training in early boyhood had been with the boxing gloves.
At West Point I had trained and rowed for my class in all
of the three mile races, in one as stroke oar, and after
riding in the saddle hundreds of miles, I felt physically fit
to tackle almost any man except a Sullivan, Corbett, Fitz-
simmons, a Jack Johnson or Jack Dempsey. I walked up
to him, and looking the great strapping rascal in the eye,
said, "If you do not go to work and put that baggage in,
and start for my camp, I propose to give you a thrashing
and even up for the money that you have of mine in your
pocket, and the trouble and annoyance you have caused
me." There seemed to be no other way to handle him
than through the police and the Courts and there was no
time for such delays. This threat had the desired effect
he immediately reloaded the baggage, although reeking
with perspiration, and started. "Cap," said he, "I have
driven hack in San Francisco, New Orleans, and all over
the country and I have never been treated *quite so rough
as this.*" "Then look out the next time who you try to
play your nasty tricks on." This maddened him again,
and he blurted out, "I shall take your trunks to the
Crutchfield House, where I agreed to, I haven't got to take
them to your camp." "No, Sir! you will not; this morning I wanted to use them there, but now I *don't* want them
at the Crutchfield. I have had enough trouble over them,
and you will take them to my camp, or I will thrash you."
I commenced to take off my coat again to suit my action
to the words, but he relented. Upon reaching camp, however, the tricky rascal, after going through the operation
for the sixth time of unloading two trunks, one a French
packing trunk that would weigh nearly 300 pounds, briskly
and most patronizingly said: "Now, 'Cap,' you won't mind

giving a poor fellow a dollar for bringing you over, will you?" "You confounded scoundrel! You have put me to enough trouble to-day, already! Sergeant, bring a raw hide lariat here and swing this man over the limb of that tree!!" The villainous hack driver stopped not on the order of his going as the Sergeant jumped forward to execute the order, but fairly whipped his bony beast along the road to the town, assisted by the jeers and laughter of the blue coated troopers, and a shout, "Don't get caught in your own trap the next time!" My experience with these merciless robbers and hard-boiled extortioners had, at various times been of rather a galling nature, and I determined to teach this one a lesson he would long remember.

Visions of Riches—A Lost Opportunity

Our stay in this camp was among the most unpleasant experiences I ever encountered in a long military career. Day after day went by, with no transportations in sight. One day a man came over to our camp in the grove, his name was Peak, he was a Kentuckian who had come into that country about 18 years before. His ranch was near by. The Southern Pacific R. R. was to run through his land. He had had it surveyed, platted and staked off into lots for sale. As he sat by my camp fire he held out some most alluring inducements for the sale of these lots to me at a merely nominal figure. Visions of riches loomed up before me. Alas! I was just back from New Orleans. My expenses had been very heavy in car fare, etc. In the language of the street, I was practically "dead broke." "Can't you borrow some money? This is the opportunity of your life. Just as soon as the railroad reaches here, these lots will begin to boom," etc., etc. He need not tell me. I knew and saw the one chance in my life to have made a small fortune while I was lying around in that hot, foul camp, idling, just doing nothing but curse the ill luck that kept me there. I saw no way of raising the necessary purchase money. He pleaded and pleaded in vain. It was of no use. When an officer of the army in those days, had, by chance, any money saved up, he lacked *an opportunity.* When an opportunity was offered him he *lacked the money* by which to seize and profit by it. Those lots there at that farm of Peak's, I have been told, are in the *center of the City* of Dallas, and where they could have been purchased *then* for a few hundreds of dollars, those same lots *now,* are worth hundreds of thousands if not a million or two. Alas! Alas!!

The Emancipated Slave—"Habeas Corpus" and Ruse

The men had nothing to do, not even guard duty, for there was nothing to guard but their tents. Luckily it was fine, but distressingly hot weather. They got restless. One died from acute cholera morbus from eating immoderately of hard, green peaches, orchards of fruit being numerous near by. Neither rubbing with hot flannels, and brandy given internally, nor the services of a skilled physician could save his life. A chapter of misfortune seemed to accumulate thick and fast. The very valuable bright mulatto cook and nurse (Rhoda Lewis), who had come to us through an advertisement at New Orleans, and for whom $45.00 in gold had already been paid in car fare, etc., was with us in camp. She had been thus far almost worth her weight in gold through her invaluable services and faithful loyalty. She had been a slave in Texas before the war, which had set her free. She had been married, had six children, and had left her *"no account man."* Her mother still lived somewhere in Texas, and one object in coming with us was to find her if she was still living. While at the "branch" or creek washing one day she accidently met, by a most singular coincidence, her former mistress. No sooner had this woman seen and recognized her, knowing her value, than she called her by name and at once not only determined to re-possess her, but set about doing so by every means she could bring to bear. She told her that if she went out to the frontier with us the Indians would kill and scalp her, etc. Finding this would not work, she soon persuaded her by

threats, etc., acquiring, or asserting the old mistress' power over her, to leave us, and on the following morning,
mounted on a raw-boned, ghastly, flea-bitten white horse,
and her cadaverous, freckled face almost hidden by a great
flapping, striped sunbonnet that looked like bed ticking,
she came with a wagon to get Rhoda's trunk. We refused under our agreement (only verbal, however), to let
her go. "Well! she 'lowed she'd see whether any Yankee
Officer could keep a *'poor girl'* from going where she
wanted to. I want you to understand my husband is a
"Jedge." Sure enough he was a "Jedge," and, as ill
luck would have it, a justice of that municipal district.
On that same afternoon, therefore, true to her threats and
promises, a deputy sheriff came back with her and served
a writ of Habeas Corpus on me reciting that "the said,"
etc., was "holding the said ———— against her will,"
etc., and took her from our camp. Here was a calamity.
Here was a case where I might have resisted the Civil
Law by placing sentinels about camp and calling it a
"U. S. Reservation," keeping her inside and refusing to
surrender her, but I was not sure of my ground, and we
had had quite enough trouble already. Upon leaving
camp I had told her to persist, even in the face of threats,
to assert her rights, and tell the "Jedge" that she was
under an agreement to go with me, and did not want to
stay there in Dallas. Securing an attorney and making a
return on the writ, also a statement being made to the
judge, who was really the woman's husband and had issued the writ at her request, and upon Rhoda defiantly
repudiating the woman in Court, and stoutly denying that
we were holding her against her will, also that she did not
want to stay in Dallas; the "Jedge" released her. It was
the only thing to do. He was not so obtuse that he did
not see at once that his wife had misrepresented the whole
matter to him, and he did not dare to do so flagrant, arbitrary and manifestly illegal a thing as to hold her for
his wife's purposes. But fearing that he might *change*

his mind, I decided to place the camp in charge of the Sergeant, and slipping into Dallas that night made arrangements to take the stage the next morning and to spend the night at the "Crutchfield" with the family. At 3 a. m. we *"flagged"* the stage and started for Fort R. an officer having come down with transportation for the paymaster, and relieved me. I gladly seized the opportunity of going myself as my sojourn in that town had been more than a "Jonah" to me. As night approached, and as the stage left a long prairie beyond Fort Worth, and entered the slight fringe of timber near Weatherford, the driver, who had been drinking, tipped over the stage in the middle of the sandy road. The writer had met Gen. George P. Buell, then Lieut.-Colonel of the 11th Infantry, as we stopped at Forth Worth to change the stage horses. He had a two horse open rig, and being alone had invited me to ride across to Weatherford with him. We were a mile behind and had not seen the stage when it tipped over. Upon approaching the spot, we saw in the dusky twilight, the stage upon its side in the road, the mules gone and, to our horror, the passengers nowhere visible. We got out our guns, Buell having a rifle, and commenced creeping upon the overturned vehicle. Visions of Indians, butchery, scalps, loss of dear ones, came flashing with cruel force upon us, but a shout from some one and we soon discovered the entire party of passengers sitting a little off the road upon a sandy bank off which the stage had toppled, and, by almost a miracle, unhurt. The mules, which were somewhat wild, had run off. The driver, after a long delay returned with some borrowed mules and after an hour or more or darkness, we proceeded on our way, this time with myself inside the stage. Remaining that night and the next day in Weatherford at a Mrs. Goodloe, who proved to be a fine landlady, and starting again on the stage the next day we arrived at Fort Richardson at 7:30 p. m., on August 23rd, after a very hard and rough ride of 40 miles. Most of the delay at Dallas, and unnec-

essary inconvenience, annoyance, expense, etc., of my return trip from New Orleans had been due to the ineffi-
ciency of Buell, in not arranging for the transportation to
meet me either at Corsicana or Dallas at the proper time,
and his absolute indifference in trying to communicate
with, or informing me by mail or messenger the causes
for delay, etc. Being left absolutely in the dark by such
derelictions, we could not know how to make our plans.
The long and monotonous march across the state and return as a belated witness on a fruitless errand; the encounter with the little detective who, having a greedy eye
on the $30 reward, had followed me from Palestine (not
the "Holy Land") and arrested me as a deserter at Longview; the rescue through timely recognition by the one-
legged "Johnny" and Post stage driver; the "lit up,"
"be-jagged" friend (?) at the "Davenport House" who
drove his feet nearly through the headboard of our bed;
the removal of the prisoners to the Baton Rouge Penitentiary, and the adventures at the Crutchfield House in Dallas; the Habeas Corpus case in that town at the camp in
the Fair Grounds; the emancipated slave and the escape
ruse at night; the stage tip over and rescue; all was over.
At last the incubus of the captured deserters, and all that
had grown out of it, had been brought to a successful end,
and one could look back upon it as a series of events, a
chapter of unusual and stirring, almost dramatic adventures, not likely to occur again in one's lifetime, even in
the army; and they surely never did.

CHAPTER XII

Pictures of a Frontier Garrison Life
Our Quarters—"Carter's Village"

THERE had been much trouble at the Post of Fort Richardson, now overcrowded with both cavalry and infantry for the projected Indian expedition, to procure quarters that would be habitable for the subaltern officers. There were but five sets of frame houses, all of the simplest construction; the doors, window (glass) frames and sashes, and most of the other material having been transported many hundreds of miles by rail, "bull train" from St. Louis, Mo., and other transportation across an unsettled country to the Post. These quarters were not for subalterns, but for the Field and Staff of the regiment. The balance of the quarters were rough pecan pickets, cut, sawed and hauled from near the Big Sandy, nearly thirty miles distant, and tents pitched on the two flanks of the officers' line.

Consent had been obtained to put up tents for the writer's quarters, the number of which was to be limited, and on the extreme right of the line. Our accommodations now consisted, therefore, of a "hospital tent," framed, and floored, attached to which in the rear were two "wall" tents, also framed and floored, leaving a narrow passageway between to a cook house, a few feet to the rear, which was also a "wall" tent. Behind the latter and attached to it was an "A" tent for a servant's sleeping quarters.

This entire "outfit" was called "Carter's Village." Mackenzie, when passing by it on his way to the Adjutant's office near by, would frequently stick his head into the upper half of the door, call Mrs. Carter to him and say, seriously she thought, but jokingly meant by him, "Look here, I told Carter he could put up some tents on the line, but I did not intend that he should use up all the canvas in the Army."

Two doors were in the large tent, in front and rear, the doors being sawed in two in the middle and hinged so that one-half or the whole could be thrown open for ventilation; the upper halves having full glass frames, which were curtained. All of these tents were lined on the inside with canvas, which concealed the rafters; this was white-washed to resemble ceiling. The tent flies were cleated down and strongly nailed on the outside.

The rear seams of the hospital tent were ripped up; the wall tents neatly joined and thresholds were fitted over the joints. One wall tent was used as a bedroom, the other either as a dining room or storeroom for our trunks, commissaries, odds and ends, etc.

A chintz curtain was neatly looped up to conceal the entrances to both, and could be closed or pulled aside at our convenience. Canvas was tacked upon the floor, over which was a red and black-figured wool rug. A small sized "air tight" wood stove kept us comfortable on cold days. The pipe, which was jointed, passing through the canvas top, was tinned around, where it passed out, to avoid fire, and wired outside to the tent pole to hold it firm. A center table with spread; a "student's" oil lamp; five fold-up camp chairs; a cheap rocker; a chest covered with chintz bound with scarlet braid; rude shelves covered with a few books and ornaments; a few photos pinned on to the canvas walls; a combination wash stand and receptacle for shoes, etc., made from a barrel, cut half way down in front, covered with a board, and the whole draped with chintz; a knock-down bedstead; towel rack; a barrel chiffonier, covered and artistically draped with our friendly chintz, completed the furniture and surroundings of a cavalry subaltern's frontier abode. This village was far preferable to the picket quarters which had been bequeathed to us by our Sixth Cavalry comrades and which were now infested with fleas, bedbugs, centipedes, mice, and occasionally a tarantula.

Domestic Troubles

One of the most serious problems which presented itself at this post, but common to all garrisons on the then frontier, was that of obtaining servants of any sort or at any price. Those who were in any way attractive, either white or black (and there were few that did not have some attractions in that desolate country for a soldier), married shortly after having been transported from the East at considerable expense.

We finally had to resort to a most worthless set of colored boys and discharged soldiers who, having floated about from one garrison to another and with the marching columns of troops on many an expedition and scout as field cooks, were self-instructed, or had simply been taught to broil a steak, boil a pot of coffee, and make yeast powder or "dobe" biscuit in the omnipresent "Dutch" oven. But they proved to be such a source of anxiety and nuisance that had it not been for Mackenzie's willingness to punish them (as "camp followers" he could do this) for some of their thievish, rascally doings, or misdoings, we would, at times, have been completely at their mercy, and this one perplexing problem would have proved a double burden to our already overtaxed resources and more difficult of solution than ever, especially with the advent of young children. Then it was that our prospects almost fulfilled the conditions of a tragedy.

We had brought "Old Aunt Mary" with us from Fort Concho. She was a legacy from Major Webb, who had first gone on a leave of absence, then had resigned from the service. Our first chief assistant to "Aunt Mary," who was now too old to "tote wood and water," make fires, nurse children, etc., was "John." We knew him by no other name, or his genealogy. "Aunt Mary's" peppery tongue proved to be more than a match for this lazy, shiftless, good-for-nothing fellow. One night he turned up missing; he had been given twenty dollars with which to purchase something at Eastburn's Store in Jacksboro,

across the "crick" (Lost Creek), and we at once suspected
that the temptation to enjoy an hour or two in some gilded
(?) joint in Jacksboro had been too great for his plastic,
yielding nature. At "reveille" he reported, without blush-
ing, being as black as an ink bottle, that he had lost that
twenty dollars when he crossed "de crick" and had been
hunting for it ever since. "Fo God, he had." About
twelve hours on a ring at the guard house with a thirty
pound log nicely balanced on his shoulder, soon convinced
him, however, that we considered it a clear case of pre-
meditated defalcation and misappropriation of funds,
which had been entrusted to him for an honest disburse-
ment, and that notwithstanding his glib story he was much
mistaken as to the manner of the loss. This he soon
humbly acknowledged, and a month's subsequent service,
but without pay and under close surveillance, gave him
ample time to reflect upon the errors of his ways, after
which he was discharged.

Another most valuable (?) cook was named "Jim,"
about whose genealogical descent we also knew nothing
more than we had about "John's." He had a very great
weakness for the "ardent," which used to mean before the
Volstead Act, "red-eye-whiskey," "tarantula juice" or
"white mule." He started in at any old time, night or
morning, and when bringing in the coffee or the biscuits
to the table, we never knew whether he was going to pour
the scalding beverage down our backs or slip the plate of
hot "dobe" biscuits into our laps. On one occasion when
he was unusually soggy and more "tangled up" than ever,
the remark was mildly ventured, "Jim, you are drunk!"
"Oh, no-o-o-o, hic-S-i-rrrr! Don-n-n't f-ee-e-l za-c-c-cly
w-e-ell th-a-ss-s al-l-l-l!" As he turned we saw the neck
of a familiar looking "benzine" bottle protruding from
his pocket. He was immediately persuaded out of the tent
and his further services were promptly dispensed with.

"Mike Wright" was another enforced makeshift. He
has been referred to before in "The Pursuit of Kicking

Bird'' as having cut out a mule's tongue on our march to Otter Creek near the Wichita Mountains, and then trying to avoid punishment for it under peculiar but rather humorous circumstances. There was no help for our distressing conditions. It was ''root hog or die.'' To a sick wife with a young baby in that hot climate and with no conveniences, no nurses, and waning strength, it sometimes meant serious illness, possible death, thousands of miles from one's family and friends.

Mike was a discharged soldier of the Ninth Cavalry; a shrewd but perfectly vicious type of a swaggering scoundrel and desperado, who had served a sentence for killing one man, and subsequently murdering a Mexican in cold blood. He was a ''good plain cook,'' however, so recommended when he had come in from the field, and we were pinched for a servant, help of some kind. It was a desperate endeavor to solve the servant problem. He had always carried a gun in his belt, everybody did, and it was truly a most comforting (?) spectacle to see Mike's burly form swaggering about the picket jacal of a kitchen, industriously engaged in concocting a ''prune pie,'' of which he was extravagantly fond, but the crust of which could scarcely be cut with an axe, or compounding a ''Chili con carne'' (meat hash and stew smothered in red chili peppers), and occasionally hitching his pistol to the front as though his memory or conscience was pricking him or in anticipation of some imaginary enemy about to waylay him.

One night he invited, without our permission of course, most of the cooks along the line, to an impromptu feast or ''banquet'' in our kitchen, where, without our knowledge, he had appropriated all of the canned commissary goods for a month's supply, and having made himself and his invited guests uproariously drunk or ''lit up'' with a most profound ''jag'' on some smuggled whiskey, he wound up in the morning near the quarters of one of our majors (J. K. Mizner) whom he threatened to kill on

sight. Upon Mizner's complaint to Mackenzie a guard
was sent for, but Mike, instinctively smelling or intuitively
feeling their near presence and movements long before the
corporal appeared from the guard house, that he was
wanted for "high crimes and misdemeanors," had pre-
cipitately fled. The last seen of Mike Wright, our most
estimable desperado cook and past and future murderer,
this terror to the Fort R. garrison, was darting across
Lost Creek like a startled deer, and up the slopes to the
timber that skirted the Fort Griffin road, the guard far
to the rear, turning occasionally to apply his fingers to his
nose and suggestively thumb them at his exhausted pursuers, to show his utter contempt for them and his absolute disregard for the "law and order" which they represented.

"Billy Boker" was another "good cook" but a rascally
thief who stole one of the writer's pistols belonging to the
troop and suddenly took a French leave, slipping off to
San Antonio.

At last we were without a makeshift of any kind. An
order had come from the War Department expressly pro-
hibiting the use of enlisted men as garrison "strikers,"
and it was generally against Mackenzie's principles to
permit the same. He had, however, on occasions of illness
and absolute distress among the families in the garrison,
permitted the services of soldiers, when they were perfectly willing, and were compensated by the officers em-
ploying them.

A "Dog Robber"

Strunck was a smooth-faced, fat, jolly, good-natured, German soldier of the writer's troop "E." He had picked up
considerable culinary knowledge and skill in the company
kitchen, where all of the men, in turn, were required to
serve a tour, peeling potatoes, making bean soup, washing
dishes, etc. He was neat, attentive and willing. He
cheerfully consented to cook for us. We were at the end
of our rope and Mackenzie had yielded to our desperate

appeal. It was Strunck's first appearance on the stage, however, in this new role. He was, at first, much embarrassed and could not readily get over the military barrier and the respectful attitude and replies which soon become second nature to an old soldier when addressing the commanding officers of his troop or company. When Mrs. Carter would say, "Strunck, is breakfast ready?" the old soldier would straighten up, click his heels together, and assuming the correct position of a soldier and "snappy" salute would reply, "Yes, Sir!" And when a little praise was bestowed by her, at our suggestion, as "Strunck, these biscuits are very nice"; "the coffee is splendid," the answer would be promptly given, "I'm glad you think so, Sir!" which would sometimes cause us to smile in his face. He never mistrusted the cause, but interpreted it as one of commendation, and his efforts to please us increased and his "Yes, Si-r-r-rs" and "No, Si-r-r-s" grew more rolling to her questions.

The difficulty of getting and retaining a good man from the company under any circumstances, however, was increased by some of the envious men and wags in the troop, who sometimes taunted these men who were thus willing to help out the officers and their families, and applied the humiliating epithet of "dog robber" to them, which often proved too much for their pride and they would apply to be sent back for duty with their troop or company.

Whaley's Ranch—"Weggeforth City," the Fake Land and Railroad Speculator"

Indian rumors were now of almost daily occurrence, and a week, sometimes a day, scarcely went by that one or more companies were not sent out to scout the country for these marauders. A white-faced settler, a cattle ranchman, would come galloping into the post, upon perhaps the only animal left him, and report that his ranch had been burned, his stock driven off, his hogs killed and his wife and daughter taken away to a captivity worse than death. On the 8th of May, Troops "E" and "L" were ordered to

proceed to Whaley's Ranch at the mouth of the Big
Wichita near Red River. He had an immense and fertile
ranch of about 600 acres; not a house was within fifty
miles. He raised grain for the military post of Fort Sill,
more than fifty miles distant. His only protection against
the Indians was in the laborers who worked on his land.
The Indians raided him regularly every moon, and drove
off his stock, sometimes killed his men, and frequently
gave him a narrow escape with his scalp. Only a short
time before our arrival, while ploughing, he was compelled
to drop his team and flee for his life to his building, which,
in a way, he had fortified by stockades against their attacks. The Indians severel times almost succeeded in cutting off his escape. But here he had stayed for years and
made plenty of money. He was a discharged soldier of the
old dragoons, and was a noble looking man, six feet two
or three, with a long, blond beard and a steel blue eye to
"threaten and command." But like all of his class, he
could not keep the money he risked his life to make. After
his crops were gathered and sold, poor Whaley sought the
nearest town, where he managed to leave his last dollar;
then back to his lonely, isolated home to plod for another
year, with bloodthirsty Indians ever on the watch to kill
him and rob him of every animal he had. Another sow-
ing and reaping, another wild carouse, and so on to the
end which came in a few years, but with all of his faults
he was brave, generous and unselfish.

As we left Camp Wichita which, before we relieved the
Sixth Cavalry in April, 1871, had been a sub-post of that
regiment, and proceeded to the deserted settlement of
Henrietta on the Little Wichita, which the Indians had
burned shortly before our arrival, we saw at some distance a party of men fleeing through some small valleys
as though for their lives. A low divide concealed all but
their heads. We thought they were Indians and immediately gave chase. They, thinking that we were a red
enemy, were trying to escape, and it was not until we had

gone some distance that we discovered our mutual mistake.

The command and this motley "outfit," a prospecting party, camped together that night, at their request for their protection. During the evening their leader, a middle-aged, voluble but mild-mannered German, one Weggeforth, came over to our camp and did the talking for the entire party. He earnestly requested us to go with him as an escort to his party, for which he offered liberal pay, but which of course we had to refuse, especially after he had informed us that upon application to Department Headquarters he had been denied the same.

He then unfolded to us a gigantic scheme, by which he was to connect Eastern with Western Texas by railroad, establish a large colony of Germans on one of the Wichitas, or Beaver Creek, and open up the mining resources of the whole region thereabouts. If we would consent to go with his party as an escort, we were each to be presented with a "corner lot" in the projected town, most elaborate plans of which he showed us on a very beautiful map which he had made, laid out in squares and circles, with a spraying fountain, etc., and we would be destined to become wealthy landowners in the future "Weggeforth City," named after our talkative friend, whom we ascertained, after drawing him out a little, was a very visionary oil speculator from Pennsylvania, who had sunk a fortune in oil operations.

We were highly amused by his "air castle" building, politely declined his bribe, and, the mosquitoes soon becoming intolerable, we changed the subject and suggested "turning in." We verily believed had we not broken up the conference in this way he would have talked all night. This project we later learned was widely advertised in the St. Louis papers, but as there was no water within many miles where his map showed us that the "City" was going to be located, and no oil then known in that region, we have never learned that the voluble Weggeforth put his squares, circles and fountains on the map of Texas.

We remained at Whaley's Ranch until the 16th, when

we were unexpectedly ordered in, having a very quiet tour of duty almost devoid of interest or excitement, and unbroken except by a detachment coming in from Fort Sill belonging to the Tenth Cavalry, and the appearance in our midst one day of a piratical looking individual, who answered very closely to the description of a noted cattle thief, but, having no evidence at hand we gave him the benefit of a doubt and let him go, after making him very uncomfortable by keeping a close watch of all his movements.   Whaley had an ice house and furnished us during our stay not only with the first ice we had had in Texas but gave us fresh vegetables from his garden, both of which proved to be a veritable Godsend.

Heavy rains had set in and raised the streams, and our progress back to Fort Richardson was very slow and made with much labor, making and repairing bridges, corduroying, etc., necessary for our march.

As we left the near vicinity of Buffalo Springs, another abandoned outpost of the Sixth Cavalry, on the 19th, our train, which was some distance in the rear but protected by a strong rear guard, was attacked by a party of about 25 Indians, who, not perceiving the guard, which was for a few moments out of sight in a break or ravine, dashed in upon it with a yell.   Upon discovering the train guard they fled into some timber with a hard, rocky bottom.* The column, upon being notified by a runner from the rear, turned back at a gallop, but failed to find any trace of the trail after it left the road, and, after a diligent search for two hours gave it up and proceeded into the post, which we reached at 4:30 p. m.

In the scattered pursuit after the Indians the men captured a young fawn, but a few days old, whose mother had been frightened off at our approach.   Our pets at Fort Richardson now consisted of a deer, two fawns, three

---

*This was near the spot where Captain McClellan of the Sixth Cavalry had had his fight with Kicking Bird's band of Kiowa Indians several years before. During a terrific thunder storm on this same day and while at a halt at this point, we saw a wagon train of settlers go into camp and drive their stakes for what later became the new Henrietta, now a prosperous railroad town.

brown bear cubs, a buffalo calf, three old bears, one coyote, two wolf pups, an eagle, two wild cats or kittens, and many half-breed wolf dogs which we had captured from Quan-ah Parker's village the year before, after they had been abandoned by the squaws in their flight across the Staked Plains.

Tent Mates

We had presented to us a mall half-breed Chihuaha and Polonne dog, black and white, and nearly hairless, as a pet for the baby. We named him "Tippy." He was long bodied like a Daschshund, had short, bandy legs, and was in every way a most unprepossessing looking animal, but as babies in those days had no toys and but few objects to interest them or with which to play, we viewed him as quite a valuable acquisition. He had no sooner become fairly domesticated in the tent and the baby had got him pretty well trained, when we were presented with another pet, also for the baby, but of quite a different character and species. This was from the men in the troop. He was a wee, diminutive brown bear cub, but a few days old. He had small, gimlet eyes and was all legs, head and hair. The baby loved both of her pets, but they neither enjoyed their own society, nor hers. It was some time before the two animals became real trusting (?) and friendly (?) and no sooner had this rather curious friendship been successfully cemented than the baby succeeded in effectually severing it, first by subjecting both of them to a most vigorous ear and tail pulling contest and lovingly removing both hair and fur but, when both were hungrily lapping and discussing a saucer of condensed milk which had been set for them in a corner of the tent, by creeping upon them unawares and selfishly appropriating it to herself.

When the puppy dog was in the way of housecleaning or culinary work in our rather cramped quarters, he was most unceremoniously swept out of the backdoor by "Old Rhoda," our general utility maid, cook and nurse, yelping as though his heart would break, while the hairy bear cub,

rolling over and over, shambled behind the stove or under
the bed, and the baby laughed until the tears fairly rolled
down her cheeks.

But, soon there came a change, not only between this
strange "Damon and Pythias" friendship but with the
trio. The cub waxed strong and grew large; his animal
instincts perceptibly developed; he no longer softly cuffed
with his little paw but stood upon his hind legs like a
wrestler or athlete and dealt real prize ring blows, which
were not only a genuine surprise to the dog, whom he daily
boxed out of doors, but to the baby whom he tumbled into
a corner with a roughness and a display of claws and loud
growls, accompanied by a scratching and biting, which no
longer smacked of play but a strong desire to "knock out"
everybody. He had, therefore, to be sent back to the
men's barracks for discipline with other pet animals,
where he grew to be an immense fellow, who had long ago
forgotten his former playmates.

So much for a cavalry subaltern's Texas home, while
we were doing this strenuous police guard duty in the
"Winning of the West;" where children were born and all
the pains, pleasures, anxieties peculiar to a life on the border made us a united garrison, with no pretence to wealth
or superiority, except as to nominal rank, and welding the
bonds which so firmly bound officers, soldiers and their
families together.

The Washington Land and Copper Mining Company

Previous to the Civil War some attention had been given
to the deposits of copper supposed to exist along the tributaries of the Brazos and the Wichita, but the last prospecting party had been driven back by the Indians, and for
several years no effort had been made to make any further search for them. In the summer of 1872, a party
made up principally in Washington and Baltimore, and
known as "The Washington Land and Copper Mining
Company," made their appearance at Fort Richardson and
camped directly in the rear of the Post. Their destina-

tion was at or near Kiwoa Peak in Haskill County, and
the country adjacent to the Double Mountain Fork of the
Brazos. It was composed of ex-army officers, scientists,
geologists, zoologists, etc., and an ex-Congressman and a
number of Texas employees. Many of these employees
had been hired at Jacksboro. The party had four or five
good wagons and teams, several new Dougherty ambulances and "hacks," and, including the mounted men, made
a total of about sixty in all. The personnel of some of
the principal men in this party was its distinguishing feature, and perhaps there had never been seen in that section of Texas in one small crowd so many unique characters. The real head, or acknowledged boss of the party,
was a Mr. Chandler of Norfolk, Virginia, who had been a
member of Congress from that city in the ante-bellum
days. Then came one Kellogg, an Oriental traveller and
author of several books on Egypt and the Holy Land; he
was an artist as well and made excellent water color
sketches of the beautiful scenery about the country. Pro-
fessor Roessler, sometime State Geologist of Texas, and
somewhat of an idealist and crank of any age; one Trout-
man, a professional photographer, who accompanied the
party in the capacity of "official artist;" W. M. Beard
was commissary, a fine, young fellow, and later speaker of
the New Jersey legislature and who achieved eminence as
a physician; Dr. Loew, chemist of the expedition, a droll-
looking little fellow with an enormous head and short,
bandy legs, and about four and a half feet in height. He
had a small pony yclept "Bismark," the little animal requiring the entire command to catch it each morning. He
had never seen the insect and animal life of Texas. He
had immense jars of alcohol in which to pickle the finds
we brought him each day, consisting of tarantulas, centipedes, scorpions, lizards, chameleons, rattlesnakes, horned
toads, etc. As he put each specimen or gift in the alcohol
jars, especially the horned toads, he would step back a few
feet, cock his head to one side, and exclaim, "How pe-c-o-

o-liar!'' The army officers who had been "mustered out" or "benzined" from the service for various causes upon the reduction and consolidation a few years previous, were a motley aggregation. Among them were Ballard Humphrey, formerly of the Ninth Cavalry; "Sam" Robbins and Satterlee C. Plummer, of the Seventh Cavalry; and one Micklepaugh, all oddities in their way, except Robbins, who was a fine fellow, both officer and gentleman, whose muster out few could ever understand. A little later, a little Hungarian Count, Count Victor de Creeneville, who had been attached to the Austrian Legation in Washington, and whose father was then on the staff of the Emperor Francis Joseph of Austria, joined the party. While he was at the post he was, by request of Lieut. (Later General) Charles King, the military novelist, in a note written to the writer from New Orleans, my guest at Fort Richardson.

Last, but not least, was the executive leader of the party, one Colonel McCarty, whose home was believed to be Galveston, but who had been picked up by Mr. Chandler in Washington upon his, McCarty's, representation of himself as being familiar with this region but who proved to be a bare-faced fraud and humbug, as he soon convinced all that he had never been in that section in his life. His claim to the title of colonel was based on his having served in a Confederate regiment as a sergeant and before the company dissolved he was voted to be the most heroic and altogether the most herculean liar within their recollection. Later he figured in many escapades, notably a diamond robbery and an alleged elopement with a daughter of General Daniel Sickles in New York City. He also told one of the party that he was a nephew of Barbara Fritchie and had witnessed the incident on which the poet, Whittier, had based his famous poem. He was a handsome fellow, and wore his jet black hair long and in true brigand style; a red silk sash was around his waist, and with black moustache and goatee, and mounted on a splendid black horse and a silver mounted Winchester rifle thrown across the pommel of his saddle, with large jingling Mexican spurs to complete his outfit, a bigger fraud never was seen. The company went as far as the Double Mountain Fork of the Brazos. The "adventurer" was reported to have "salted" the mines, the ore specimens, for which he had obtained in Austin, and, upon their return the entire party broke up in a quarrel, and McCarty and Satterlee Plummer having come together in a prospective duel, Plummer having invited his fraudulent friend (?) to meet him in the open prairie and fight it out with guns, which McCarty declined, while Plummer *had to be held,* and after distributing thousands of dollars worth of miscellaneous goods and trinkets, with which their generous but too credulous backers in Washington, Baltimore and St. Louis had loaded them, consisting of red flannel, calico prints, beads, paints, soaps, perfumery, hand mirrors, etc., etc., with which to trade to the Indians, all as presents to the officers in the garrison, they suddenly "broke up" and disappeared off the map; all except two, the Count and McCarty, to whom the writer refers in his *"A Midnight Council on the Fort Sill Trail."* Among other things they were to take with them was a howitzer with ammunition. The writer being detailed to fire a National salute on July 4th from our 3″ ordnance rifled guns, and suddenly running out of friction primers, was compelled to borrow them from McCarty. This gun, with several of the costly ambulances, one of which the writer later secured from the Post Quartermaster (Lieut. Ira A. Quimby of the Eleventh U. S. Infantry), besides many of the trinkets, were left at Fort Griffin. In June the party rolled out across the West Fork of the Trinity, meandered around the forks of the Wichita, turned south to Fort Belknap, then proceeding to Kiowa Peak, located twelve sections of land, returned to Fort Griffin and reached Jacksboro (Fort Richardson) early in September, where it was paid off and disbanded. The Count had his first buffalo hunt on one of the writer's horses, which he nearly killed; gave a magnificent banquet in Jacksboro one night to four of us, Captains Webb, Sanderson, Lieut. Parker and myself; promised to write an account of his "wild and woolly" adventures in Texas which, so far as is known, after a diligent search, he never did; and then accompanying the writer to Dallas to receive the Indian Chiefs, Sa-tan-ta and Big Tree, he took the train at D. for Galveston and nothing was ever heard of him afterwards.

While we held the 130 Comanche squaws, captured in Mow-wis camp in 1872, until April, 1873, things remained rather quiet. The ordinary duties of the post were performed, occasionally a little ripple of excitement was caused by a prisoner escaping from the guard house; the hay stacks caught fire, and the entire garrison, by forming a "bucket line" to the creek (there was no engine within hundreds of miles) and passing water, only successfully extinguished the blaze by cutting the great stack in two parts and covering the end of one half with wet "paulins."

On another occasion a man of Troop "B" (Burke) was killed in a house of ill repute in Jacksboro. The troop "turned out" at night and burned the obnoxious gilt-edged (?) palace. The night before the burning of the house some half dozen non-commissioned officers were holding forth in "B" Company's "orderly room." Sergeant John B. Charlton of "F" Company was one of them. When in walked Mackenzie, unannounced, much to their surprise and consternation. Pointing his finger at each of the men in his severest tones and biting off each word, he exclaimed: "Sergeant Charlton, Sergeant Bridge, Sergeant Graves, Sergeant Murray," etc., calling each by name, "I'll hold you men strictly responsible for anything that happens in town tonight." Knowing what this meant, they went to their respectivve quarters and "turned in." The citizens of Jacksboro, upon hearing a wild rumor that the garrison was to cross the creek and burn the town the next night, assembled from far and near, armed for the conflict, and by dark a great crowd had collected. About 10 o'clock, when the excitement was at its height, and the armed gathering of cowboys, ranchers, etc., were breathlessly listening for the advance of the enemy, the writer was sent for by Mackenzie and directed to take all but one relief of the guard, and proceeding to the town, to patrol it, arresting any soldier he might find over there. It was a delicate job, requiring some little diplomacy but more strategy, because, should the armed mob see a body of armed men advancing up the only street, they would certainly feel convinced that the rumor was true, and they might not only feel called upon to open fire but probably might impulsively do so.

After crossing Lost Creek, therefore, the men were deployed in a skirmish line and cautiously advancing as far as we could into the center of the town without being discovered, the line was halted, left in charge of a trusty Corporal and, preceding it until the writer met the armed crowd, immediately sought out one or two of the more prominent and level headed leaders, when our object was at once made known. The names of these men cannot now be recalled.

Assuring them that their town was safe and, while there was no proof in the rumor of the proposed attack, every approach to it should be well guarded, General Mackenzie's word, in addition, was given that all would be well. That was sufficient and they quietly dispersed. As the men were being collected from the skirmish line for a return to the post, an old frontiersman approached with all the generous hospitality which always distinguish their class, and said, "Now, Cap, let's take your boys down to ―――― and "set up" some old "red eye" tarantula juice, which meant a very liberal drunk for the officer of the guard and his men. Thanking him most profusely and in as polite a manner as possible, telling him that the "code militaire" would not permit of poisoning the men in that manner when on duty, he *"accepted the apology"* and the great raid on Jacksboro closed without further incident.

Lieut. McKinney

About this time Lieut. John A. McKinney joined the regiment from graduation leave. He was from Tennessee. He had marched from Corsicana with a large detachment of recruits. He was a fine looking young officer with dark chestnut hair and brown eyes, about six feet in height, slim and straight. He had been the Cadet Adjutant of his class (1872) at West Point and gave promise of being a valuable addition to the regiment. The writer was acting as Post Adjutant. Mackenzie, being anxious to see and look him over immediately upon his arrival, said to me on the day he was expected: "When Mr. McKinney gets here have him come into the office right away." This I did. Mackenzie greeted him very cordially and seemed to be very much impressed with his manner and general makeup, remarking, "He looks like a very promising officer." Soon after this he made the discovery that McKinney was in debt. He sent for him and McKinney confirmed the discovery. "Mr. McKinney, I understand you are in debt. I don't like to have young officers when first joining my regiment to be in debt. What is the amount?" McKinney replied, "Five hundred dollars." "Here is my personal check for that amount," said Mackenzie. "I do not want any note from you; pay it whenever you can conveniently, and keep out of debt." That was all that passed between them at that time. But he kept a close watch on him. A little later he saw that McKinney was drinking more than he should. He sent for the writer. "You are older than McKinney, and having served during the Civil War have had more experience; and should exert a good influence over him; without saying anything to him (McKinney) or to anybody—*not even to your wife*—I wish you to exercise a little supervision over him in as quiet a manner and as diplomatically as possible, giving him no offense or exciting his suspicion that he is being watched, etc.; *just look after him a little.*"

This I did, but about the time I imagined my efforts were proving effective, I discovered that the bride was treating him (McKinney) with a coolness, suspicion and frigidity that he (McKinney) could not but help observing, so I found it necessary to break my pledge to Mackenzie and inform her of the delicate mission which had been thrust upon me; that instead of leading me astray as she had feared, I was really acting as the good Samaritan and was gradually steering him along the paths Mackenzie had marked out. To make amends for her hostility and ice wagon treatment of the would-be convert, she made up one day two rather large fruit cakes, a great rarity on the frontier in those days, loaded with raisins, currants, etc. They proved to be rather heavy, soggy, and consequently, most indigestible. One she gave to Lawton who disposed of it that night. His ostrich-like stomach proved immune to the pains of indigestion. The other she gave to McKinney, who in trying to emulate Lawton's example, was seized with cholera morbus and was a fit subject for the hospital the following day. I always accused her of trying to kill or wreck McKinney through the kindness of an awakened conscience.

McKinney grew very restless in the post and on every occasion sought to go out on the many short scouts which we were being sent on from time to time. He wanted the freedom of the open plains, to hunt buffalo, bear, deer, antelope, wild turkeys, quail, upland plover, prairie chickens, etc., with which the country then swarmed.

He would ask the writer to plead with Mackenzie for the privilege of going with him that he might learn and gain from the experience of a two years' service. "No!" said Mackenzie, "I find when two officers go out together they do not accomplish as much as when they scout singly. I will give Mr. McKinney plenty to do all in good time." And he did, for on November 25th, 1876, he sent poor

McKinney to cut off some Cheyenne warriors of Dull
Knife's band that cold morning in Willow Creek Cañon of
the Big Horn Mountains, and McKinney fell dead, both he
and his horse being riddled with bullets, having run into
a nest concealed in a coulee or ravine lying directly across
his route. Mackenzie had grown to be very fond of this
handsome, gallant young Tennessian, and when his frozen
body, packed many miles on a mule, reached the nearest
station where it could be shipped to his home in Memphis,
Mackenzie testified to his admiration and affection for him
by weeping like a child. This was one of the saddest results of our Indian conflicts.

The writer has a quirt which McKinney had his company
saddler make for him out of a half picket pin for a handle
braided over with fair leather strips and fringed with the
same to the tip. Fort McKinney was named for him to
commemorate the event of his tragic death. One more
splendid young soul offered up in the sacrifice of "Winning the West," that civilization might advance, and the
development of that wild country by seekers of gold, cotton, oil, etc., might satisfy the insatiable ambitions of the
white man, then pressing on to and beyond the border already allotted to the Indian.

The Frontier Wedding

Our great quartermaster, Lawton, had a fine old Scotch
clerk by the name of Masterton. One bitter cold night,
with a "dry Norther" raging, we were all invited to his
wedding, which was to be in true frontier style, the bride-
to-be being a Jacksboro girl. We all went over in ambulances; only the sick and disabled were left behind. The
house seemed to be hermetically sealed and it had been
heated to the highest temperature possible by means of
air-tight stoves. It was *red hot*. Masterton had prepared
a great feast, all drinkables and nearly all of the eatables
had been shipped up from Galveston or San Antonio.
Everything went as merry as a "wedding bell." The old
fashioned custom of calling out the guests to the supper by

couples was adopted (the tables being loaded with food, including smoked buffalo tongues, wild turkeys, quail, highland plover, roast pig, etc., etc.), and when General Mackenzie's name with his lady partner (he was a bachelor) was called, it is related that one young officer seeing that Mackenzie was a little slow, diffident or bashful in starting, gave him a vigorous slap on the back and asked him why he didn't "move out" instead of "blocking the traffic." Those were the days before the hooting automobile. One officer lost his cap while crossing the creek on stepping stones on his return home at 1 a. m., while another never did know how he ever succeeded in getting to bed, and if so, how he came to persistently push his head up the sleeve of his night shirt while frantically endeavoring to pull it on.

Occasionally we had an impromptu "hop" in one of the men's quarters, designated and hastily cleared out for the purpose. An orderly from headquarters went along the entire line sometime during the day and simply announced that there would be "a 'hop' in Troop 'E's' quarters tonight." All were invited to attend except officers on duty and all the ladies were expected to bring something to eat. When supper time came it was almost amazing to see what the zeal, ingenuity, culinary skill and united efforts of the ladies of a frontier garrison could furnish. The tables fairly groaned with wild turkeys, venison, bear meat, ham, smoked buffalo tongues, quail, "cove" oysters, salmon salad, jellies and preserves of all kinds, rolls, coffee and, on one occasion, *real mince pies,* made with *real* apples brought from Arkansas by "bull train" and worth almost their weight in gold. The regimental band under the able leadership of Mr. Held furnished delightful music, and nobody cared whether the ladies dresses were "Worth's latest creations" or plain, unadorned Swiss muslins. There were few, if any, critics bold enough to express their views, and all enjoyed the change from our otherwise enforced monotony at those far off frontier posts.

A Tin Wedding

Lieut. Vernou had been married ten years. He and his wife were Philadelphians. He had, before entering the army, belonged to the all American Cricket Club, which played the British Cricket Club just before the Civil War. Invitations were sent around for a "tin wedding" and "fancy dress party," a "masquerade" to be given in honor of this popular couple. This stirred the little garrison to its innermost depths. How twenty ladies managed to keep their secrets and appear "incog" that evening was then, and always has been since, a mystery to all of the grumblers and "I-told-you-sos" of the regiment, who were "quite sure that the whole thing would leak out through the indiscreet tongues of the females."

The writer was kept busy for a day or two, covering an old flat cedar whiskey keg, something like the canteens carried by the Confederate soldiers during the Civil War, with blue paper, and cutting out numerous silver stars to paste on it for his wife, who was to impersonate a French "vivandiere," or "daughter of the regiment," and stuffing a fat pillow into the capacious stomach of a large figured calico suit, made all in one piece, and loaned him by Capt. E. M. Heyl, for a "Jack Falstaff," much to the amusement of the enlisted men, who roared with laughter as the old fellow waddled through the picket door of the brilliantly (?) candle illuminated quarters. The grumblers and skeptics had to take a "back seat" for each newcomer seemed perfectly oblivious to all others, and might have come from another world for aught any one knew or suspected, until the unmasking took place.

"Old Falstaff" got inextricably mixed up with "Folly" (Mrs. Wilcox), who, with her wand, bells and enticing manner completely captivated his Shakespearian highness, while "La Fille de Regiment," after dispensing sundry but harmless drinks from the "Star Spangled" keg, was carried off by a burly policeman (Lieut. U. G. White). The proverbial "Mr. Lo, the poor Indian" was beautifully scalped by a disguised "Cowboy," while the "Chinaman, "Allee Samee Melican Man," was vigorously "bounced" by "Erin Go Braugh" and the "Goddess of Liberty" actually "hobnobbed" with a "Confederate Brigadier."

The tin presents were of course somewhat of a failure, but when the supper came, the deficiency was more than made up and all heart burnings, if there were any, were stifled in the loads of good things provided entirely from the resources of the post, hundreds of miles from any railroad, telegraph or telephones (telephone then unheard of), and more than 40 miles from the nearest frontier settlement.

The companies, in turn, contributed to the winter's entertainment by their "hops," to which all the ladies and officers were invited to participate in and to partake of the hospitality which the hunters among the soldiers had so bountifully provided. It seemed as though every kind of game from buffalo to jack rabbit was there. The cake and pastry were generally set off by a huge center piece of frosting with pink letters of cochineal on top—"Troop 'C,' Fourth Cavalry, Christmas, 1872, Welcome!"

Theatricals were attempted, but proved to be a dismal failure. One one occasion at Fort Concho, the Adjutant of the Eleventh Infantry, essayed the difficult role of a lady, arrayed in a superb muslin dress with long train, sent from New York for the purpose, with wigs, "chignons," and all the necessary et ceteras of a ladies' costume to match. At West Point he had enjoyed the class name of "Carrie," but on this occasion he did not seem to fit into the role. When the time arrived for the lady to swoon in the play of "Box and Cox," give a slight shriek, and fall into the arms of the Sergeant-Major who had been selected and trained for the cast, an old major, one of our bluff scoffers and confirmed grumblers, took his lantern (it was nearly time for "tattoo roll call," the reports of which he was to receive), and with a rather loud, "Oh, hell! That's too much for me," moved out of the quarters as hastily as possible. There was the usual amount of "chaffing" and good-natured enjoyment over such impromptu affairs, which soon died out.

A "Club" was started at Fort Concho, called "The *Happy Family*," with a newspaper accompaniment, but after lingering a few months it died a very *unhappy* death, and no effort was ever made to resurrect the body.

On the 14th of November, 1872, a fearful "Norther" raged about the post and all over the immediate country and at Fort Richardson. The wind blew almost a tornado, the dust and sand in great clouds were banked up against the sky, and the cold, piercing wind caught every nook and crevice of our canvas shelter. The guy ropes strained, the tent frame shrieked and groaned, the canvas lifted and filled like the main sail of a ship at sea; the rug rose from the floor in great waves (as the tent was set upon small blocks for a foundation), until it made one dizzy and sea sick as tho' one were really upon the ocean.

Under these conditions of comfort (?) and palatial (?) surroundings, another wee stranger, our second daughter, came safely into the world, and the Department Commander, General C. C. Auger, being at the post, the happy father received his congratulations. During this period of suspense, uncertainty and doubt the writer had to send over to the First Sergeant of the troop for a detail of men to hold on to the guy ropes to prevent the wall tent from ballooning into the air and off into space. We faced a calamity, perchance a tragedy.

A Bucking Buffalo

A buffalo calf had been "roped" and brought in by the men. It was placed in the corral. It got to be nearly a year old. A detachment of recruits (now called "rookies") had arrived. Wishing to have a little sport with this fresh arrival, as a change from the usual "blanket tossing," etc., these recruits were informed by the "old

timers'' that the usual initiation or induction into army
life on the frontier was not to "ride the goat" but to *ride
the buffalo calf*. As soon as the fiat had gone forth and
leaked out that there was to be an exhibition of buffalo
"busting" at the corral, everybody gathered to witness it.
Many people have witnessed the modern high class "ro-
deos" with bucking broncos and trick riding of the mules
and burros in circuses, but this *buffalo calf riding more
than exceeded all of our expectations*. He was strong, and
for catlike activity and aggressive methods, neither the
bronco or mean mule compared to him. His hump made
him so elusive that the recruit had no seat at any time.
A camel would have been a luxurious rocking chair. By a
series of wild plunges, sky-rocket pitches, and catapults,
he (the recruit) seemed suspended in the air for a very
brief period then hit the ground with a cold, dull thud; he
had been thoroughly initiated. One after another of these
green recruits, who had never even been on the back of a
horse, mule, or burro, tried this bunch of spring spiral
motions, back jumps and outlaw curves. They met with
but one fate, a hard throw on the ground. They held onto
the hair of his hump; they dug their knees into his sides
and flanks; they lay down upon his sharp back, gritted
their teeth, and used all devices of nail and claw and brute
strength, but that buffalo calf *"had everybody going."*
Nobody was ever able to ride him while he remained in the
corral. When he became older he was turned loose into
the numerous herds near by.

The Nanny Goat and Her Fate

Captain Wilcox had a small daughter, Mary, about a
year old. Little or no cow's milk was obtainable in the
country. She was being fed on army condensed milk and
was, in that hot enervating climate, pining away for lack
of proper nourishment. So Wilcox prospected around the
country for a nanny goat, and having secured her and the
family having become attached to her, she was "turned

loose" to browse about the post, generally on the parade ground.

Now a Texas goat was no respector of persons or things; they feared neither God, man or the devil, nor did they care for the personal belongings or property of the dwellers in the picket jacals, the thresholds of whose doors were but a few inches from the ground with the doors generally open for air. Mary's goat was in the habit of making a daily inspection along the line, and whenever she saw a door open, in she went. After spilling over the water, ink, mucilage, etc., and chewing up about everything she could not otherwise destroy, she got on the beds, chewed up the mosquito bar and soiled the white counterpanes, and then she left for new pastures.

Our Senior Surgeon, Col. John F. Hammond, had entered the service in 1837. He was a South Carolinian by birth and while he was a mild mannered man, with a benign countenance and chin decorated with a long flowing and white silky beard, now designated as "spinach" by "flappers" and "cake-eaters," he could, when aroused, swear in more well-ordered and various choice phrases and faster than any doctor we had ever seen or heard, but *he never raised his voice.* He lived in one of the frame quarters. Here he had a laboratory where he, in his spare hours, conducted tests and worked out many chemical problems. His glass reports, test tubes, measuring glass, acids and fluids were piled up on his table.

One day Wilcox's nanny goat, on her daily inspections, espied Dr. Hammond's door open. In she walked and proceeded to wreck the place. She tipped everything off the table and practically chewed up and destroyed the good doctor's workshop, not to mention soiling the floor and creating as much havoc as though an earthquake or tornado had been present. The doctor cussed and cussed himself breathless. The next day Mary's goat turned up "missing." Nobody had seen it disappear, or knew where to locate her. Wilcox searched and inquired in vain. The

Nanny was gone. Weeks and months went by and still no trace of Mary's goat. Wilcox offered a reward. It was of no use. The goat never was heard of or ever appeared on the map again.

Many years afterwards the writer was in New York. Dr. Hammond was Chief Medical Director of the Department of the East. We went to call upon him. He was delighted to see us, for we had sometimes acted as a sort of buffer between the good doctor and the sometimes explosive, irritable nature of Mackenzie. We had about exhausted our reminiscences. Presently the doctor said, "Do you remember Mary Wilcox's goat?" Upon answering in the affirmative, he continued, "Did you ever know what became of her?" "No! I do not nor do I believe anybody ever did." "Well," said Hammond, "If you will never tell Wilcox until after I am gone, I will reveal the secret." The promise was made. "I killed her. *I gave her a pound, more or less, of Paris Green,* and had her secretly buried." "Blankety, blank her destructive hide," and then he cursed a long string of oaths in his softly modulated voice while he pulled his white flowing beard out straight. Years went by and Wilcox, his attractive wife and Mary, now a grown-up young lady, came to Washington. They were at the old Richmond Hotel. We called upon them. The conversation turned on the old days, reminiscences of the far off frontier posts, etc. "Wilcox, did you ever know or mistrust the fate of Mary's nanny goat?" "No, but I would give a great deal to know who could have put her out of the way. I never suspected. Do you know?" "Yes, I do!" Then I revealed the secret. Dr. Hammond was dead, and my pledge to the good old doctor was no longer sacred. Wilcox's only exclamation, after knowing that the good old doctor was among the missing, was, "I wish he were living so that I could go to him and get square with the blankety, blank old rascal for killing little Mary's pet!" Mrs. Wilcox and Mary laughed most heartily over this long concealed secret, and it is our belief that they fully forgave his (the soft-voiced medico) act, when urged by anger at the wreckage of his frontier laboratory to fill the nanny goat full of Paris Green, and devoutly wished that his spirit might rest in peace.

CHAPTER XIII

A Midnight Council On the Fort Sill Trail

and

The Scouts' Test

By Captain Robert Goldthwaite Carter, *U. S. Army*

SA-TAN-TA, principal war chief of the Ki-o-was, "the worst savage that ever infested the Kansas and Texas borders" in the '60s and early '70s—according to Gen. Sheridan's report—and against whose name almost numberless crimes had been recorded, had, by General Sherman's instructions, been tried for murder in connection with the Salt Creek massacre of May 18, 1871, near Jacksboro, Texas; had been convicted and sentenced to hang, but was now in the State Prison at Huntsville, Texas, undergoing sentence for life, his death sentence having been commuted to a life imprisonment, through the sentimental mush and gush of certain Pacifists (for we had them *then* as we have them *now*) posing under the name of the "Quaker Ring." Several efforts had been made to secure the old scoundrel's release on his promise—of which he had given many—of good behavior. His last savage atrocity was the burning alive of one of the wounded teamsters in the massacre cited. At last success crowned the efforts of those maudlin Indian sentimentalists, and this bloodthirsty Chief was once more heading for liberty and freedom through an order from the Commanding General Department of Texas, that he should be conveyed under a suitable guard to Fort Sill for a grand "pow-wow' with certain Commissioners who were to meet all of the Southern Reservation Indians at Fort Sill for that purpose.

The Order

On September 4, 1872, therefore, after Sa-tan-ta had been in the Huntsville Penitentiary nearly a year, and upon receipt of this order, my troop "E," Fourth U. S.

Cavalry, was directed to proceed to Dallas, Texas, to receive him and Big Tree, and convey them in double irons to Fort Sill, I. T., to attend this big "pow-wow," consisting of these Peace Commissioners, all of the Confederated bands of Comanche, Ki-o-wa, Cheyenne and Arapahoe Indians then on Fort Sill Reservation, and then to return them to Dallas where they were to be turned over to the U. S. Marshalls and taken back to Huntsville.

The Hungarian Count

Accompanying us for protection, as escorts had to be furnished to all parties leaving our posts for the railroads, were the paymaster, Major "Jim" N— and his wife, who always accompanied him on his pay trips, and were now returning to San Antonio; a certain Colonel (?) McC., late of the Confederate Army (?) and who had but recently been connected with a bogus Land, Copper and Silver Mining Company which had broken up in a row, in which Satterlee C. Plummer, an ex-army officer ("benzined" out) had challenged the Colonel to fight a duel and as promptly been refused; and a Count (Austrian-Hungarian) Victor de Greeneville, a Cavalry Officer, whose father was attached to the Emperor Francis Joseph's Staff—he himself was attached to the Austrian Legation here in W. and then had become a member of this fraudulent company. He had been recommended to be my guest at Fort Richardson, Texas, by General Charles King (then on General W. H. Emory's staff in New Orleans) and had been staying with me for several weeks.

The Bogus Colonel and Guide (?)

Colonel McC. was a character. He was such a blow hard and windjammer, that with his black hair, worn a la "Buffalo Bill," and black eyes and moustache, and his bold, impudent, brazen air, he was a study, but, as will be seen, he came down from his perch before we got through with him. He boasted that he could drive a nail with his rifle off-hand shooting. It was a magnificent silver-mounted rifle, English make, with pistol adjustable breech, presented to him by *some nobleman in England,* so he declared. He wore a full fringed buckskin suit—made for him in New York—probably out of the funds he had been squandering of the bogus company. His leggins met a pair of very handsome heavily-beaded deer-skin moccasins. He carried an Indian braided quirt, with handle profusely inlaid with silver. A Mexican sombrero, with crown and brim heavily embroiderd with silver, covered his flowing black hair. In his belt, also inlaid with silver knobs, were two holsters, in which he carried two heavy steel-barrelled English revolvers. Suspending from the holsters were two buffalo tails, and from his silver-mounted saddle and bridle were several more. Take him all in all he was a magnificent looking animal—a veritable *"peacherino"*—who would have made Bill Cody, "Wild Bill," "Texas Jack," or any other genuine border man, look like "30 cents." The paymaster, having finished his pay trip, began drinking heavily; the Count was inclined to follow suit, but one day before reaching Dallas his conduct and language was so bad at the mess, especially in the presence of Mrs. Nichols, that I had to call him one side and *gently* (?) admonish him. I told him that he must cease his "roystering" in the presence of Mrs. Nichols. It was not customary in our Army. It was not gentlemanly or dignified and that he must *"cut it out"*— *"Pronto."* He took it kindly. From that time his behavior was that of a little gentleman, which he was by *birth, breeding* and *education* except when he had too much old "tarantula juice," old "red eye" or "Mexican Mescal." He did not repeat the offense. We camped at Crawford's Ranch on the 4th. Upon our arrival at Dallas, on the 7th, after camping near Weatherford on the 5th and near Johnson's Station on the 6th, we were surrounded by a curious crowd at the station where we prepared to camp for the night. Colonel McC. was the center of attraction and admiration on account of his impos-

ing dress and appearance, and furthermore after he had
announced that he was our *"Guide."* We then began to
guy him and take the stiffening out of him. "He! a
Guide? Oh, Lord, no! He has never been in this country
before! We are just 'towing' him along so that he will
not get lost and be safe from any loose Indians or Rangers
he might run up against to pick him up. He is *no Guide!!*
He is simply to look at." *All this in his hearing.*

The Chiefs Arrive

Remained in camp. That night, shortly after midnight
(Sept. 8), the troop—every man a gun fighter—was
marched over to the station, which was surrounded to
keep the crowd back, as our "Guide" (?), with a limber
tongue, had *"blabbed"* the object of our duty in D. The
Indians did not come. The next day after wiring the
Civil authorities, and being told that there had been some
mistake as to the hour of our arrival in D, we were assured that the Indians, under guard of a heavy sheriffs'
or Deputy Marshal's posse, would be in promptly at midnight. We repeated the march, and as soon as the train
rolled in at 8 a. m., Sept. 9th, we saw through the windows Sa-tan-ta's stalwart and familiar form, heard the
clanking of their leg irons, and very soon we had en-
circled them with our armed troopers, pressed back the
crowd, and had them secure in tents under a heavy guard.
The next day (Sept. 9) all Dallas came streaming out.
They were all shunted off on Colonel McC., on whom we
had now bestowed the title of "First Class Guide," which,
in his vanity, conceit and egotism, seemed to be to his
taste and to greatly please him. So, without seeing the
Indians, who were not permitted to exhibit themselves,
everybody was well "fed up" by the "Guide," who, as
official *"buffer,"* told them many most thrilling experiences of his life on the frontier among the Indians, hair-
breadth escapes, etc., etc. His tongue never ceased.

"Pard" Crosby, Our Newspaper Correspondent

Here a fine young fellow joined us on this day (9th). He was a New York Tribune correspondent. His name was Crosby. His father had been a Governor of Maine. He was a graduate of Bowdoin College. He requested permission to accompany us to Fort Sill. After looking him over rather critically, we assented. He proved to be not only a fine gentleman, but a most valuable acquisition on our trip. He had been a newspaper correspondent during the Civil War. He wore a high silk hat and carried an *enormous umbrella,* which, as we were "pulling out," with the Indians seated in an ambulance which we had brought along, we not only persuaded him to *furl*—although the sun was hotly beating on our heads—and to strap to his saddle, but he also consented to buy a big, black, soft hat for comfort, and transfer his dress beaver hat to Sa-tan-ta's head, who, after admiring it, set it on his long braided scalp lock and wore it from that day on as one of the most priceless adornments of his person during the entire trip, one of the first acts in dressing every morning being to carefully adjust that hat by the aid of a small round looking glass which all Indians use when they are obtainable, to see where to paint, and braid in the otter fur or red flannel strips, always a part of their every day dress.

A Night of Horror—"Jim Jams"— and The Paymaster's Attempt

The night of the 9th had been a very trying one. In addition to our anxiety regarding the safety of the Indian prisoners, as there had been many armed bunches of cowboys and bad gun men about our camp all day, the danger of their being shot by some of these swaggering, reckless and irresponsible men was now as imminent as it had been the year before at Jacksboro before and during the day of their trial for murder, when the writer, as Post Adjutant, used the entire Post guard and himself as a screen between the prisoners and the guard-house, which was so near the chaparral that it afforded complete shelter to any rancher who might lie there and shoot the Indians with perfect safety.

About midnight, the Count, much excited and distressed and out of breath, came running to my tent and said that Mrs. N. had told him that Major N. was out of his head; that he had a pistol in his hand and was determined on killing himself. Slipping on my clothes and going to their tent, I found N. with a most wicked looking Derringer in his hand and moodily soliloquizing to himself thusly: "Life is one great fraud! It is a grand Calamity!" and, hiccoughing a few times, would continue repeating these words with thick tongue and maudlin voice, adding: "What is man? In his infancy he is *an angel;* in his boyhood he is *a devil;* in his manhood he is everything from *a bug or a boll weevil up.* When he first comes into the world everybody wants to *kiss* him. Before he goes out everybody wants to *kick* him. If he stays away from church, he is *a sinner.* If he doesn't give he is *stingy* and *a tight wad*—O-h-h-h, this is a h—l of a world, and *I want to get out of it.* It is nothing but *fraud, fraud, fraud!!!"* And I thought of Abraham Lincoln's favorite poem and its application. "Oh, why should the spirit of Mortal be Proud?" But there was no time to drop into poetry, for in the meantime N. was placing the muzzle of this wicked looking gun to his head and *snapping* it, but there was no report. It was not loaded. There was no time to lose. This was a case of genuine *"Jim-Jams,"* pure and simple, or delirium tremens in its worst form. I had had a similar case on my hands the previous April when on the march to Fort Sill, commanding the escort to the Court which was to try an officer there for calling his Commanding Officer disrespectful names, etc. I threw myself upon this madman; took the pistol from him by force, anchored him down by main strength; got some bromide from Dr. Wolfe, our esteemed A. A. Surgeon, who was accompanyus (who, by the way, was always given these soft (?)

jobs), gave him a *he-man's* dose, and as soon as he was quieted down and the little Count was somewhat reassured, and stopped his antics, I went back to bed. The next morning before we started, N. and his wife and the Count left us by early train for San Antonio and New Orleans and the writer never saw either of them again.

Denton Creek and the Fort Sill Trail

We camped the night of September 10 on Denton Creek. We had been reading Mark Twain's "Roughing It" and we had already given Crosby the name or sobriquet of "Pard" and detailed him as principal forager of the command, a role which he filled most faithfully and creditably, going out daily on the flank of the column, leaving the road and coming back in the early afternoon loaded down with chickens, ducks, eggs, wild honey, milk, etc., etc. It was a drizzly night. The coyotes yelped and barked, the owls hooted and screeched, the night noises of grazing horses, the jangle of chains had quieted down, the rain, now a dripping drizzle, was lulling us to sleep. It was midnight, A sharp challenge rang out. We heard the rapid beat of horses' hoofs on the trail where it turns off from Denton Creek to Fort Sill. At the challenge, the rider halted, dismounted, and in a few moments the Corporal brought in a man who proved to be a messenger or courier who had been sent from Fort Sill with a note from the Commanding Officer there, and with imperative orders to intercept our command somewhere before we turned off, or as soon thereafter as possible. He had killed one horse and had borrowed another from a rancher whom he knew, and knowing the road or trail had struck our camp in ample time. The note was from Major George W. Schofield (brother of the one time Commanding General of the Army) and was substantially as follows:

To the Officer Commanding Escort to Kiowa Chiefs:

This is to inform you that there are some 3,000 or more Confederated Indians here and in or about the Fort Sill Reservation today, or will be by the time you are expected to arrive with the

prisoners under orders of the Department Commander to deliver
them here at this Post. They are all well armed and are sullen,
ugly and war-like. I have five troops of Cavalry (10th) aggre-
gating nearly 300 men; with your troop there would be about 360.
To bring Sa-tan-ta, their principal War Chief, here in irons
and expect to take him back to the State Penitentiary, without
trouble, probably a desperate fight, would be almost impossible.
Stilwell will tell you so. I beg, therefore, in spite of your positive orders to the contrary, not to bring them here on the Reservation, but to take them to the present terminal of the M. K. & T.
R.R., where the Commissioners—Capt. Alvord, formerly of this
Regiment among them—will meet you there with other hostile
Indians, some of whom are destined for Washington.

Very respectfully, your obedient servant,

(signed) G. W. Schofield,
Major, 10th U. S. Cavalry,
Commanding Post.

By Scout "Jack" Stilwell

After the note was read and the writer had remarked,
"I hesitate about taking full responsibility under these
conditions, and, in view of my orders." The conversation
quickly turned on, "Shall the order to deliver the prisoners
at Fort Sill be complied with?" The writer felt that on
his own judgment, and under all the circumstances, he
would most emphatically say, "No!" It was finally determined to put it to a vote. "But before we vote I will
ask that Mr. Crosby, who is to go with us and has proved
himself to be a man of good judgment, be permitted to
cast a vote. I also wish to ask the scout, Stillwell, some
questions, and that he, too, be permitted to vote on his
judgment and personal knowledge of the situation."

The Doubtful Result

This was a hard problem to solve. There could be no
"snap judgment." It required not only deliberate
thought, but good common horse sense.

The writer knew well the strict military interpretation
which is always placed on such orders and the necessity of
obeying them to the letter in almost any case, or, in any
case except that of dire emergency, yet it was his firm belief that it was not for the writer to exercise his own judg-

ment or pass too hastily upon conditions then existing at Fort Sill, based upon Major Schofield's fears, which were very difficult to determine at that moment, because while they were probably fully known to him, those same conditions could not well be known to us many miles away on that trail. The writer also felt that if all that note of Major Schofield's conveyed were true, we might have to fight our way out of the Fort Sill Reservation; perhaps, sacrifice our entire command.

There were a few brief moments of hesitation. I also felt almost afraid to ask that "Pard" Crosby might have a vote, for I feared he might vote "Yes!" because, as a newspaper man he might be inclined to want to see a sort of romantic finish to our otherwise tame and, up to this time, rather uneventful excursion, without counting the cost or the tragedy of such an unlooked or rather unsought for encounter, a sort of spectacular staged fight in which, of course, he would not dream of being a participant, or, at least an actual combatant (which is usual with newspaper men and war correspondents) in order to write it up for the New York Tribune. So I addressed myself to the scout. But before I questioned him I looked him over for I was then unfamiliar with his career, as most of us were, and there may be many now who never heard of this fearless scout and border pioneer.

Stilwell's Personality

He was a very boyish, modest, quiet-appearing and soft-voiced man, and, in many ways, as he stood in the flicker of our campfire, he reminded me strongly of that character, "Nick of the Woods" or the *"Jibbenainosay"* of my early boyhood days, that old Kentucky border scout, so accurately depicted in the drama of that title of the early '60s when one of our greatest tragedians, Joseph Proctor, took the part of "Wenonga," the "Black Vulture." Stilwell was of medium height, slim, rather sallow complexion, light chestnut-brown or candy-colored hair, very deep-set, penetrating grey-blue or steel-blue

eyes, a firm jaw and sharp nose. When he handed me the
note it was without comment. When asked his name, he
quietly replied: "I am called 'Jack' Stilwell." He displayed a slight disappointment in his manner that we did
not seem to know him. I had never seen or heard of
him. This unobtrusive, plainly dressed and soft-voiced
man who stood before us this dark, drizzly midnight at
Denton Creek on the Fort Sill trail, apparently holding
our lives in his hands by a simple Yea or Nay vote, was
then *the* "Jack" Stilwell who was an enlisted scout; had
been in one of the most desperate fights recorded in our
Indian Wars with General George A. Forsythe ("Sandy")
at the Arickaree Fork of the Republican River, September 16, 1868, now called "Beecher Island, an action with
Roman Nose and 900 superb Cheyenne warriors, in which
50 scouts, including Stilwell, were entirely surrounded on
all sides for eight days until Forsythe was wounded
three times, Lieut. Beecher killed, the surgeon mortally
wounded, more than one-half of his scouts killed and
wounded, all of the horses killed, and the survivors—in
rifle pits scooped out of the sand—were eating the dead
horses, piled up in front for breastworks, seasoned with
gunpowder.

Stilwell's Daring Act

Under these most desperate conditions Stilwell under-
took (offered) to crawl out, run the Indian lines, and seek
relief at Fort Wallace some 90 or 100 miles distant. He
made two trials, being driven back on the first, before he
succeeded. Old "Pet" Troudeau, an old frontiersman,
went with him. The two men crawled over the breastwork of the dead horses at night and waded the river to
the enemy's side. They reversed their moccasins and wore
their blankets about them in Indian fashion to deceive
them. Believing the river would be well-guarded, they
struck a course over the bald hill, crawling on their
stomachs and sometimes on their hands and knees, they
made only three miles before dawn that day. They saw
Indians on every hand and frequently were compelled to

lie still. The three miles brought them to the top of the divide between the Arickaree Fork and South Republican, and then they concealed themselves in a washout or the head of an "arroya," where the banks had been overgrown with grass and wild sunflowers. They left no trail behind them and were satisfied that they would not be discovered. From over the hill they could hear firing all day, which told them that their scout comrades, whom they had left, still held out.

When darkness came they started South again. During the night they saw two parties of Indians in front of them, which greatly delayed their progress, and at daylight found that they had only reached the South Republican. They also discovered to their surprise and chagrin, that they were *about half a mile from the Sioux and Cheyenne Village.*

At sunup they hastened to cover under the river bank in the tall grass of a kind of bayou or "slough" and there they lay in the water all day without moving. Indians frequently crossed very near. Once some warriors stopped not 30 feet from them to water their ponies and they heard them talking about the white men on the Island and how soon they would be starved out. They could hear the tom-toms in the village nearby as the squaws mourned their dead, and saw them carry out several bodies to bury on the scaffold coffins. That night, almost crazed by the mental worry the noises of the day had caused them, they managed to cross the South Fork of the Republican, and the morning of the fourth day found them on the prairie near the head of Goose Creek. The Indians seemed to have been left behind, and the boy (Stilwell was only 19) and the man (Troudear) concluded to travel by day. It pretty nearly cost them their lives, for about 8 o'clock in the morning they saw coming towards them the advance guard of what they afterwards found out to be "dog soldiers." Fortunately, the Indians had not yet discovered them. It was necessary to hide and hide quickly. In looking for a place to conceal themselves on the open plain

they accidentally discovered some yellow weeds growing
about a buffalo carcass. The weeds were not tall enough
to conceal them so they crawled to the carcass intending
to break off the stems and cover themselves. The buffalo
had evidently been killed the winter before, for the skeleton was intact and covered with the sun-dried hide.
While one of the enemy scouts was sitting on his pony
not fifty yards away, occurred the "rattle snake" affair
which has been so widely published. The two scouts had
crawled into the carcass, the dried skin, intact, completely
concealing them. Several of the enemy came near it,
some either sat on it or leaned against it. *There was a
rattle snake in the carcass,* and he had, upon being disturbed, crawled around, but not coiled, but made it exceedingly uncomfortable for the two scouts who seemed to
be usurping his home. They could not move a hand nor
fire a shot to kill the snake on account of the nearness of
the Indians. They could only lie still. Stilwell finally
spit a mouthful of tobacco juice on his head and into the
snake's eyes by a well directed shot, and the snake *vacated*
or *"vamosed"* at once.

But this was not the "last straw" to the camel's back.
Trudeau broke down completely after the Indians had become satisfied that there were no white men near. He
seemed to go "loco," as the plainsmen term it, with both
men and animals, and to have lost his mind and want to
shoot his revolver and sing. Stilwell kept him quiet until
dark, when he persuaded him to go to the nearest stream
and drink. This water did wonders for him, and they
travelled on as rapidly as possible.

The fourth day was foggy, and they could travel by
daylight without being seen. About 11 o'clock, when they
were about exhausted, they saw, coming out of the thick
haze of the Denver wagon road, on which they were traveling, two mounted men. They could not tell whether they
were Indians or not, but they had horses and the worn-
out scouts needed the horses. They had come over 80
miles on foot in four days. When these horsemen drew

near, Stilwell discovered that they were soldiers and caused Trudeau to put up his gun he was determined to use in case they should prove to be the enemy. The soldiers were two couriers on the road to Colonel Carpenter's command (then Captain Louis H. Carpenter, 10th U. S. Cavalry), lying at Lake Slater, some 60 miles from where Forsythe was besieged. As soon as Carpenter got the news of Forsythe's critical condition, he responded promptly, marching with two or more troops to F's relief.

Trudeau never recovered from the strain of that dreadful trip, but died the next Spring and was buried at Fort Sill, I. T. Stilwell's youth stood him in good stead, and he lived to make a name that has been handed down to the present generation, among those who knew him. His name really was "Giles," but he was always called "Jack."

This story of Stilwell, most of which has been recited many times in newspapers and magazines, is here recorded merely to show the kind of a man the writer had now got to deal with in the Midnight Council on the Fort Sill Trail. I am indebted to General N. A. Miles, U. S. Army, for much of this information concerning Stilwell's almost tragic adventure and subsequent career, but he (E) told me much himself regarding the horror of his day and night struggle to get into Fort Wallace and secure relief for "Sandy" Forsythe's command. He (F) also gave me many personal incidents, as did also Colonel Carpenter, but as they are not connected with this story of "A Midnight Council," such incidents are reserved for some future period. He was the friend of "Buffalo Bill" (Cody); saw "Wild Bill" assassinated, and comforted "Texas Jack" (all of whom the writer knew personally) in his last hours when he was dying of consumption. He was for several years a Post Scout at Fort Sill.

After all of the Indian troubles had become a thing of the past, Stilwell's occupation as a scout and "gun toter" and Indian fighter was gone. He gave up his life as a scout, his cattle raising and ranching, and *studied law.*

Brilliant scout and Indian fighter as he was, he made a
brilliant and successful lawyer, and his arguments before
the Courts of Arizona, Texas, Wyoming and Oklahoma
will long be remembered for their wit and clear compre-
hension of the law. He was appointed a ''Judge,'' and
about 1902 or 1903 died near Eagle Mountain, Kansas,*
of ''Brights disease,'' mourned and beloved by all the
friends who ever knew this ''bravest of brave men'' of
the Western frontier in the days that ''tried men's souls.''
(See ''My Life on the Plains,'' by Gen. Custer, pp. 128-
134.)Upon Carpenter's approach, the Cheyennes, having
met with a most frightful loss at the hands of the scouts,
and Roman Nose, their principal Chief, having been killed
early in the action, withdrew from the field. This was one
of the most daring and successful feats recorded in the
annals of our Indian Wars, not excepting some of ''Buffalo Bill's'' finest acts.

The Scout's Decisive Vote

As we sat up in our blankets, the rain pattering upon
the canvas, I said to him: ''Stilwell, have you seen or read
the contents of this note, or had any conversation with
Major Schofield relating to it?''

''No! Sir. I have had no talk with the Major, nor do
I know its contents.'' I read it aloud to him. ''Did you
have any knowledge of the substance of this note, or did
you guess at what it contained?'' ''Yes!'' he replied. ''I
suspected, of course, that it had something to do with the
delivering of those Indians and that it was a most important message, because I was directed to intercept you at
all hazards, and, if necessary, to sacrifice my horse, and it
is about what I supposed.'' ''Now, Stilwell, what is your
judgment on the conditions at Fort Sill?'' He spoke slowly and deliberately with a slight, soft drawl, but most emphatically, and a flash in his steely eyes. ''Gentlemen,''
said he, ''I ain't no soldier, but I have been in some pretty

*Some accounts state that ''Buffalo Bill'' took him to his ranch on the Platte River
where he died, at Cody.

tight spots in my life. As sure as you take these Chiefs into the Fort Sill Reservation you will be taking *very big chances* on getting them out again according to your orders. It will mean a big fight with all of the odds against you, perhaps a massacre. My best judgment and advice would be, unless you fear taking too much risk in disobeying your orders, *not to take them there,* but to heed the warning of Major S— who is not panicky, but is on the ground and knows fully all of the conditions he is up against and which you will have confronting you. I know the mood of all those Indians pretty well, and I believe Major Schofield's fears are correct.'' He voted an emphatic ''NO!!''

It was then for ''Pard'' Crosby to vote as his newspaper judgment might possibly have influenced him. He voted ''No!'' It was unanimous. *Our action then was a deliberate and positive disobedience of our orders.* I then decided to leave the trail and head North.

At daybreak, Stilwell, having consented to accompany us, we switched off the Fort Sill trail, and headed for Gainesville, where we wired our action, and received an answer from the Department Commander, General C. C. Augur (a classmate of General Grant's), fully endorsing, or most heartily approving the wisdom of our decision, ''Since you know the situation.'' We headed for Red River, camping that night, September 11th, near Montague, having crossed Elm Fork.

The Indians, instead of becoming excited, tried to maintain their habitual expression of stoicism, but a mere glance at their faces, that almost inscrutable mask which is generally meant to completely conceal their feeling, was sufficient. On it was an air of surprise, of chagrin and genuine disappointment, as they saw us turn off from the Fort Sill Trail and head more to the North and East, towards Red River, instead of West in the direction of the Reservation.

Sa-tan-ta's Signs of Recognition

Sa-tan-ta had raided through this entire country for
many years with his war parties of Ki-o-was and, often
as we rode along the trail, between Denton and the Red
River, especially near Gainesville, we saw the old red
scoundrel point with his hand to some distant peak, prominent butte or lone tree, and with the sign language and
guttural tongue call Big Tree's attention to them as he
recognized these landmarks so long identified with and so
familiar to them along this dangerous Indian passway.

First-Class Guide

Stilwell was a crack shot. We determined to give our
"First-class Guide" (McC.), a "heavy jolt" and "set
back." One evening when we had pitched camp early,
we told McC. that while we much regretted it (?) now that
we had with us a *real, truly, genuine, bona fide* guide and
scout with *a record* (although we had not then known of
Stilwell's part in Forsythe's fight) we should have to
"break" or demote him (McC.) for, unless he could surpass or equal Stilwell's shooting, who could kill a sand hill
crane while flying, we would have to reduce him to "Second-class Guide," while Stilwell would hereafter be known
as "First-class." He did not dare to accept the challenge
to shoot with Stilwell, and from that time on this blus-
terer and bragging "hot-air artist" meekly accepted the
new order of things as legal and unquestioned, all of
which drew from Stilwell a quiet smile.

The Rejected Meal

One day after having exhausted our mess chest of its
store of canned goods, et cetera, and having become somewhat tired of bacon and the usual camp fare, we proposed
that the next ranch we came to we would go over and
have a real, "first-class, square meal" of fried chicken,
eggs, wild honey, etc., with all the ranch trimmings of
fresh vegetables, etc. "Pard" Crosby was detailed to go
over and arrange terms, generally 50c per plate flat. He

soon came back and to our dire consternation and disgust announced that as soon as he had made it known that our "outfit" was a command of U. S. Cavalry travelling with Indian prisoners, they *"'lowed they would feed no Yankees no how!"* Then the "Second-class Guide," wonderfully subdued since his demotion, piped up and declared that he would go over and fix it up "all right," would tell them that he had been a Colonel in the Confederate Army, we were his friends, and that would be sufficient, etc. When he came back and announced with great glee his pronounced success and that we were all to go over to the best dinner the ranch could afford, his astonishment and humiliation was most painfully shown on his face when we declared we would decline. "Oh, h—l." You do not think we would feed with that rancher under those conditions do you? What do you take us for? We flatly refuse to accept such terms." I added, "It is beneath our dignity, contrary to our pride and an insult to our patriotic endeavor as officers of the U. S. Army, whose only crime was in an effort to preserve the Union, for him to take advantage of his service to the Confederacy. We will eat right here. You can go if you wish. We kept this country on the map when it was about to be destroyed, so that these ranchers could own and live on their ranches in peace, plenty and prosperity, and so that he too could go along with us as our guests, in a sense, and we could not lower or sacrifice our standard or principles by such a compromising proposal." McC. could not be prevailed upon to go, so great would be his embarrassment in eating alone with his new found food purveyors, so he concluded to eat his "chow" as usual, off a tin plate from our rude, improvised mess chest.

September 12th we camped near Gainesville. Wired Department Headquarters our action. Passed through Gainesville on the 13th and reached the Red River at Preston on the 14th.

Ford Red River

We crossed the Red River at Preston by fording it, the Indians seemingly enjoying our methods, but still showing a somewhat perplexed air over the course we were taking and what the outcome was to be. Proceeding through what was then the Indian Nation (now Oklahoma) we made slow marches with our prisoners through the towns of the Cherokee, Chickasaws, Choctaws, Creeks, Osages, and other semi-civilized tribes, across the Blue River, where we saw the old earth works built there during the Civil War by General Ben McCollough and his Texans and red-skin Confederates, many of these Indians having divided, some going with the Union, others with the Confederacy, on to "Boggy Depot." We followed Jessie Chisholm's cattle trail.

The Indian Nation

The Cherokees seemed to be the largest, best formed and altogether the best type of Indians we saw. Many of those types were peculiar and most striking owing to the intermingling or intermarriage of these tribes with their former slaves whom they had taken with them when they were removed from their old homes in the '30s, with their consent, in Georgia, North Carolina, South Carolina, Alabama and Florida, to their new lands west of the Mississippi River. They were, for the most part, large, big-boned, straight, with both negro and Indian racial features very prominent, swarthy, copper, black, black eyes, high cheek bones, thick lips, flat nose, and long, crinkly black hair which they wore straight with no effort at scalp-lock adornments of any kind. They were dressed like the whites, with civilian clothes, and most of those I saw about their ranch houses went unarmed. They spoke fairly good English, or Indian—pigeon to us—turning occasionally to speak their own dialect to their family friends.

Civilization vs. Barbarism

I was naturally curious to compare these quiet, peaceful, industrious farmers and herders with the hostile Comanches, Kiowas, Cheyennes and Arapahoes, those uneasy, restless wandering nomads of the plains who had, for so many years, been giving our little regular army so much trouble, and holding back the tide of immigration to a point where it was not only at a standstill, but was actually receding from the line of frontier counties in terror at the ravages which had been committed by those blood-thirsty savages.

These red men had once been fierce warriors who, with rifle, tomahawk and scalping knife in hand, had burned, pillaged and murdered all along the Western lines of the Atlantic border states, but now they were revelling, so it seemed, in the fat of the land, with no thought but peace and comfort on the magnificent farms which fronted on the roads along which we were now marching with one of the worst Indians who had ever burned a white man at the stake, or scalped a screaming woman for her long hair with which to adorn his shield or scalp pole. And such land!! It was clear, dark, mahogany-colored, deep loam, where corn, oats, alfalfa, and all the fruits and vegetables of the earth could be raised, and such fat horses, cattle, hogs and sheep as these copper-colored ranchmen possessed could be seen in no other country on earth. It was veritably a land "overflowing with milk and honey," and its tenants genuine lords of all they surveyed and now rich in oil gushers.

After leaving the cotton-wooded banks of the river, we rode through peaceful and flourishing settlements, and by the detached houses and small and large farms of these civilized Indians. Everywhere there were signs of independence and genuine thrift. The dusky owners with their half-breed wives gathered by the roadside to see us pass, while our two savage Chiefs from the Texas Plains gazed with equal curiosity from the sides of their curtained Army ambulance. But no words passed between them. In a measure, these two types seemed as wide apart as the two poles of the world.

The cattle, huge haystacks and carefully cultivated
fields were strong evidences of what the right kind of
civilization will accomplish over barbarism and its twin
friend—idleness. And we saw ample evidence of thrift,
energy, happiness and positive luxury, among the many
rich farms that abound in the Blue River country. They
were well-fenced in by the Osage Orange or bois d'arc
hedges; were ditched, irrigated, where it was necessary,
and cultivated to perfection; raising tobacco, wheat corn,
potatoes, rye, oats, and a variety of blue grass not dis-
similar to the celebrated blue grass of Kentucky.

Arriving at New Boggy Depot we camped at the edge
of the settlement and that day, thinking that we would
astonish our stomachs with a change in our rations, we
dined at the only ranch hotel in the place. Seated at our
table was a very fine looking man with a very handsome
daughter to whom we were introduced. He proved to be
a full-blooded Cherokee minister and was dressed in a
clerical garb—long black frock coat and vest, with white
collar and white lawn tie, all of which quite put to shame
our old sunburnt, dust-begrimed and spotted, soiled
weather-worn uniforms. He spoke excellent English,
grammatically, and conversed with us on many wide and
interesting topics. He seemed to be a refined, cultivated
man, and his daughter, who, it seems, had just returned
from some Eastern school or college, was a ladylike, educated and attractive girl, and yet these Indians were direct descendants of the wild tribes that once infested the
Atlantic border states, including those states named, and
drenched with the blood of our best officers and soldiers,
costing the Government millions of dollars to subjugate
them and remove them. How was this removal accomplished? Through the bravery and peace-producing influence of our little regular army, wholesome force and restraint, with, it is true, some bloodshed, and the saga-
cious wisdom of a great soldier, General Andrew Jackson.

It was a task accomplished with very great difficulty,
having been most strenuously opposed by all of the super-

fine humanitarians of that period, including Clay, Webster, Calhoun, by the entire Whig Party, and even by the Supreme Court of the United States, which rendered a decision in favor of the treaty rights of these Indians.

Jackson, nothing daunted, stood by his policy, because he fully understood the necessity for such a step to the country and more thoroughly understood the Indian character than any other man. John Marshall said: ''He has rendered his decision, now let him enforce it!'' Jackson, however, was so strong and popular on other grounds, that he was able to carry out his policy, and the last vestige of these tribes was conducted across the Mississippi in the closing year of his administration and the first year of Van Buren's. (General Charles Floyd, Wm. G. McAdoo's grandfather, Commanding the Georgia State troops, conducted the Cherokees from that State to the border line.)

It was one of the best and most farsighted strokes of practical statesmanship that the country ever experienced. There were no more Indian troubles East of the Mississippi. Our now flourishing states on the East bank, were then sparse settlements, and the presence among them of powerful Indian tribes was a constant source of danger and trouble, a condition similar to that which existed later for so many years among the settlements, comparatively new, in the great Southwest.

The little regular army proved to be the greatest conservator of peace and practically the best friends these savage warriors ever had. Peace commissioners, compromises, annuity presents nor all of the trickery, slippery talk, treachery, treaties (the obligations of which the savage mind never fully grasped or comprehended and, because he did not, he never kept), nor soft persuasion, could ever effect what a decided, wholesome application of real restraint and *active force—which one warrior compelled from another*—eventually accomplished.

General Scott understood this perfectly when sent by the President to remove the obstinate Cherokees, and he

performed the delicate task with such a universal and considerate humanity that it elicited universal commendation. But his much praised humanity and the splendid
achievement of his task by mere *moral suasion* would have
been impossible had he not had at his back an army of
disciplined regulars reinforced by volunteer State troops,
specially raised for the occasion, and large enough to be
irresistible.

His proffers of kindness were listened to and heeded,
because it was clearly seen that he had ample power to
compel the submsision of those whom he advised. Kindness from a warrior, *with such a force,* and accepted; but
civilian commissioners—a lot of spineless, jellyfish and
pussy-foote d"lounge lizzard" pacifists, depending upon
mere philanthropy and soft persuasion, backed up merely
by a *moral force*—would have been despicable, and despised and disregarded. As the saying goes with a
trained soldier, *"It never gets nobody nowhere."*

The Pullman Special—A Wild Scene

As soon as I neared Atoka Station, then the terminus
of the M. K. & T. R. R., I sent Stilwell in to find the Indian Commissioners. Upon his return the Commissioners
came rushing out, much excited; begged me to halt, take
off the leg irons and handcuffs from the prisoners and
hold them in the brush that night, the plan being to break
the news gently to Lone Wolf and the other hostiles that
Sa-tan-ta was so near, in order not to stampede them so
that they (the hostiles) might refuse to go on should
Sa-tan-ta not be released to go with them on his parole.
It proved to be a most bitter, cold night with temperature
way below freezing, and with no tents and the two prisoners short of blankets for such weather, it proved, even
with small fires, a most uncomfortable and chilling experience for all. The loud grunts—"ug-gh-h-s"—of Sa-tan-ta
sounded strangely on the keen frosty night air. Thick ice
formed on the miserable "slough" we had bivouacked on
and we lay curled up and huddled until daybreak, when

still another message came from the frightened Commissioners—this time to bring the entire "outfit" up. What was our surprise to know that they had come in a "Pullman Special." We, ourselves, had not seen a train for several years. What was our amazement, also, to meet my old friend from Fort Sill, Horace P. Jones, the old Comanche Post Interpreter, whom I had met there and hunted with the preceding March and April. He had never before seen a train of cars or been in one, and his effort to suppress his excitement and preserve his usual Indian stoicism was ludicrous to behold. Captain Alvord (formerly an officer of the 10th Cavalry), Lone Wolf, and many other Chiefs with their squaws and papooses, were all huddled in a sleeper with a temperature that almost sickened us after coming from our ice cold night-bath in the brush. The Indians had all shed their blankets and robes, and they and the squaws and children were pretty close down to their breech clouts and Mother Nature. Their excitement, and the loud noises, a genuine hubbub or Babel of sounds, almost deafened us. Many of these wild Indians had never seen a car and their wonder and amazement knew no bounds. They touched, examined and smelt of everything. The cars were redolent with the fumes of old paint, ancient perspiration, neglected persons, and bad smelling breech-clouts. This stale sweat, decayed rags, buffalo robes, saturated with powerful creosote odor of smoke from long use in the tepees, all combined to cause a feeling of nausea and a strong impulse to get into the open air as soon as possible. Therefore, for what seemed to be for our protection or safety—at least for our physical comfort—we fled from that Pullman car into the cold air, which, full of frost and ozone, soon revived us.

They all seemed to be delighted to see Sa-tan-ta, whose irons had been taken off before he was allowed to meet his old fellow murderers. While they did not "eat him up," their manifestations of joy that he, with Big Tree, were to be their fellow passengers on an Indian picnic to

St. Louis and Washington to see the "Great Father," was
clearly apparent, although their demonstrations were not
expressed in the same terms as a white man's. This
whole scheme seemed to be a wild and unwise junketing
trip, full of folly and ill-timed judgment and attended, of
course, with the usual enormous expense and, as afterwards shown, productive of no good results in benefits to
them or to the Government. They were taken to St. Louis,
Washington, New York, were feasted and feted, taken to
theatres and operas, et cetera.

Bidding farewell to our New York Tribune friend,
"Pard" Crosby, who had been our loyal companion and
friend, and to Colonel McC., our faithful guide (?), we
turned back on our old trail, glad to be relieved of our
troublesome Indian prisoners with all the resultant responsibilities. Both the Count Victor deC. and "Pard"
Crosby assured us that they were going to write up a description of this trip, the former, his impressions of
America in a book, the latter, in a special newspaper article. Diligent search among newspaper files and in libraries have failed to discover any such work of theirs
and, so far as the writer knows, this is the only circum-
stantial account of our fateful adventure.

The return trip to Fort Richardson was without incident since we returned by our old trails and roads. We
missed the volubility of the little Hungarian Count, the
brazen-faced effrontery of our bogus scout and guide (?)
Col. McC., the good common sense, wisdom and quiet
modesty of Stilwell, the daring boy scout who had saved
"Sandy" Forsythe's life when Roman Nose and his horde
of Cheyenne warriors had him hemmed in on the sand spit
in the Arickaree Fork, and whose intelligent summing up
of the threatening conditions on the reservation as we sat
in our blankets that stormy night on the Fort Sill trail,
and emphatic, decisive vote, had possibly averted a desperate fight, if not a bloody massacre, had he not so providentially intercepted us, after his breakneck ride. "All's
well that ends well!" and so had the "Midnight Council,"

fraught as it was with so many human probabilities. Many years afterwards, when the writer had written a story for the Youth's Companion, entitled "The Cow-Boy's Verdict," relating the events connected with the celebrated trial of Sa-tan-ta, July 6, 1871, at Jacksboro, referred to in this story, he received the following letter as a sequel to the same:

LIEUTENANT R. G. CARTER: Niles, Michigan,
Dear Sir: March 19th, '88.

Your story in Youth's Companion, "The Cowboy's Verdict" has brought so vividly to my mind the subject of your sketch as has also the sketch of your subject. I think the likeness a very good one although it has been over fifteen years since I've seen the original. When I was going to the Frontier of Texas, as a bride, with my husband, an officer of the Army, then quartermaster of the 25th Infantry, when leaving St. Louis we found that we had as distinguished traveling companions, the noted "Sa-tan-ta" and "Big Tree" occupying the stateroom of our coach, with the U. S. Marshals who had them in charge. The car part of the journey was uneventful excepting the severity of the weather. When reaching Red River, going over the bridge, the very first time that a passenger train had attempted the feat, there taking the stage at Dennison for McKinney to make the gap in the road—with thirteen passengers—*Indians on the best seats*, about two o'clock in the morning a drunken driver managed to tip over the coach so that we were all hurled down a deep ravine among sagebrush and frozen clay. I then heard for the first time those frightful "Ug-g-gh-h-h-h's" from one who was perfect in the sounds of all the letters. Before we left the car at Dallas these Indians gave me their autograph that they had learned to write while prisoners. I write to ask if you know that these Indians were taken to Huntsville twice; if not, then your dates and mine do not correspond. I can think of no other reason why they would have been on the road at that time. It is a story that I've often told my children of these Indians, but had never heard what became of them. Have known many Indians since, although none are so treacherous looking as the Apaches. Excuse me for addressing you and writing at such length, although I do not think that I am writing to a stranger, but a brother officer of my dear husband, and I am still in search of all Army news, although I have been away now over five years."

Very respectfully,
(signed) MRS. JENNIE QUIMBY.

P. S. My husband was Captain H. B. Quimby, 24th Infantry, stationed at Fort Snelling at the time of his death."

Again, when Sa-tan-ta was released in 1874, on his promise to travel the "White Man's Road," he was caught red-handed raiding outside of the Fort Sill Reservation and, upon being returned to the Penitentiary to complete his sentence, committed suicide, October 11, 1878, by throwing himself from an upper gallery to the pavement below and dashing his brains out, upon Governor Roberts' refusal to give him another parole. He was buried in the cemetery of the Penitentiary.

The Story's Lesson

It is the writer's belief that this story fully illustrates the utter futility of holding an experienced officer, one of intelligence and common sense, trained and more than once tried out, to any "hard and fast" rules or "cut and dried" programs, in any case like the one cited here, if all the responsibility for absolute success is to be placed upon him, his initiative and full individuality and personal equation must be given to him to be used at his own discretion, having, of course, full knowledge of all conditions, where a life or death problem hangs in the balance. He is on the ground, knows the situation, and all of the factors governing it, and he should be left free, within certain prescribed limitations, to work it out his own way instead of being bound down to some red tape order, which, as in our own case, *might and probably would have led to a most frightful disaster and massacre.*

In the forword to a book, entitled "Cricket, a Little Girl of the Old West," written by Mrs. Forrestine Cooper Hooker, and published in 1925 by Doubleday, Page & Company, she writes:

"This story of a little girl of the Old West could have never been written had it not been for the things she remembered, stories told her by her father, by her mother, and later by her father's friend and comrade, Captain R. G. Carter, Fourth U. S. Cavalry, now retired, who not only shared the hardships and dangers of those bygone days, but also through disobeying his orders, prevented the massacre of the people in the garrison, including the little girl herself.''

She was the daughter of Lieut. (later Brig. General) Charles Cooper, 10th U. S. Cavalry, stationed with his family during that period at Fort Sill, I. T. (now Oklahoma). In her book, "Cricket," she practically tells this story in Chapters XIV, XXVIII, XXXII, XXXIV and XXXIX, and many other incidents relating to the early days at Fort Sill.

CHAPTER XIV

Capture of Mow-wis Comanche Village and the Comanche Squaws

EARLY in the summer of 1872 General Mackenzie determined to make another expedition to the scene of our operations in 1871, on or near the headwaters of the North Fork of the Red River. The Lee family had been recently massacred about 16 miles from Fort Griffin, a few miles beyond Old "Camp Cooper." White Horse, a Ki-o-wa Chief, who belonged to Big Bow's band, is said to have committed the deed; also, that later he was connected with the massacre of Howard Wells in 1872. He stated that he "captured a train, killed 17 people and lost one of his warriors. * * *" He was "followed by the soldiers (9th Cavalry) and killed one man." Lieut. Vincent, Ninth Cavalry, was killed. The command was organized and equipped, as on the previous year, at Fort Richardson. It left Fort Richardson on June 14. The trails were mostly along those of the preceding year, via Fort Griffin, crossing at the big bend of the Clear Fork, Paint and California Creeks, thence to the Double Mountain Fork, Cottonwood Springs, and the Freshwater Fork of the Brazos where the supply camp was located. From this camp it scouted to many points and across the Staked Plains to Posts Sumner and Bascom, N. M. The command was composed of Troops A, D, F, and L, Fourth U. S. Cavalry, and Company I, of the Twenty-fourth Infantry, with two acting assistant surgeons of the Army, Doctors Rufus Choate and Wolf, in all 12 officers and 272 enlisted men. From this supply camp the command marched across the plains to Forts Sumner and Bascom, New Mexico, without seeing any large body of Indians and without incident of any note. Water was obtained at a few waterholes en route; the marches were slow and the animals were kept in good condition on good grass and with some short forage which was taken along in a

few wagons and on the packs.   Upon its return on September 2 and after a few short scouts, the command moved
with the pack train on September 21st to the Salt Fork
of the Brazos at a point about longitude 101°-30', without
anything worthy of mention.   Captain J. W. Clous, Twenty-fourth Infantry, was acting Engineer Officer.   On the
29th, with the cavalry companies, in all 7 officers and 215
enlisted men, and about 20 enlisted Ton-ka-way Indian
scouts, under the command of Lieut. P. M. Boehm, the
march was taken up for McClellan's Creek, a small tributary of the North Fork of the Red River, named after
General George B. McClellan, who later commanded the
Army of the Potomac, and who, with his father-in-law,
General Randolph B. Marcy, had made a survey of that
country in 1851-52 for a practicable route for the Southern
Pacific Railroad.   A trail was picked up which seemed to
lead up the creek to a large Indian village.   This was
reached in about 20 miles at a point about four miles
above the forks of those two streams.

After marching down the stream two miles, two fresh
trails were found by the "Tonks," one of two horses and
another of one mule.   Judging that the trail of the mule
led in the direction of a camp of Indians, it was followed
at a rapid gait from about 1 o'clock P. M. by our trailers,
urged and assisted by Captain Wirt Davis of Troop "F."
The Ton-ka-ways soon lost it, however, and a halt was made.
Captain Wirt Davis (later Brigadier General) had observed that along the creek there were many wild grape
vines loaded with grapes.   The Indians are inordinately
fond of them.   Dismounting from his horse he soon discovered that a pack train had been in the near vicinity
and from the loose grapes near the heavily loaded vines
they were probably from some nearby Indian village.   He
soon found the trail, and from the scattered grapes dropping from the packs followed it by a rapid march to within a short distance, about 3 or 4 miles to and in full view
of the village, located in a beautiful valley along the creek.
The column was closed up and after a brief rest and for-

mation into a compact column the order was given for a
charge on the now unconscious camp, with Troop "F"
leading.

The command moved off at a gallop. Sergeant John B.
Charlton, who had killed Se-tank, the Kiowa Chief, at
Cache Creek near Fort Sill, in June 1871, and whom the
reader will recall was with the writer that same year
when the ten deserters had been captured near Hillsboro,
Texas, was the junior sergeant of this troop, and was
closing up the rear. It was about 4 P. M. At the command "Right Front into line!" which brought the rear
four nearest the Indians, Charlton drove straight through
the village in the face of a very severe rifle fire. Every
man went down of that four, either killed or wounded—
one shot in the stomach, two shot in the neck, while the
fourth was shot through the thigh with an arrow. All
of the casualties of that troop occurred in Charlton's four,
while he came out unscathed. He had killed the Indian at
close range who had shot the first two. He was recommended for a Medal of Honor by his troop commander
but, even as late as 1921—nearly 50 years afterwards—
when an attempt to secure it for him while he was still
living—then over 70 years of age—through some techni-
cality of the law it was denied him. This often occurred
when distributing awards to gallant and deserving soldiers, especially if there was nobody to look out for them,
and in the meantime those whom one could look upon to
testify to their knowledge of the facts extending back to
those periods, had passed over the river.

The village was captured after a brisk fight of about
half an hour. The Indians had all been driven out or
killed and a herd of about 800 ponies were "rounded up"
and captured, approximately 50 Indians were killed; number of wounded unknown. An effort was made to head
off the escaping Indians at the lower end of the village,
but it was too late and but few of the warriors were captured. About 130 squaws and children were secured. The
village, with its accumulated stores of meat for winter

use; everything except a few choice robes, was destroyed.
It proved to be Mow-wis village, consisting of over 250
lodges. There was no resistance to any extent, and that
at only one point where three companies, A, F, and I were
engaged from time to time—F company being engaged
from the commencement to the close more continuously,
"D" being sent after horses. When driven to bay in the
ravine, and fighting the bloody and desperate battle which
was so characteristic of Indians when cornered, Mackenzie sent "I" troop, Captain N. B. McLaughlin and Lieut.
Charles Hudson, to head off any that might attempt to
escape at its head. The troop was too late, however.
Many had already passed out, but this force was enabled
to pour an enfilading fire down their place of concealment,
which soon finished the battle.

A curious incident now occurred. The pony herd was
taken about a mile from the burned village and with the
Indian scouts, our allies, the Ton-ka-ways, all under Lieut.
P. M. Boehm. All felt secure under such a guard and
under such a vigilant officer as Boehm from the Comanches who, it was surely surmised, would lose no time in an
attempt to recover them. The "Tonks" had picked from
this big herd the finest racing ponies for their own use.
They, this big bunch of captured ponies, were herded in
a roomy pocket or "sink" in the prairie. They (the
guard) felt so safe that all or practically all but a few of
the herders had rolled themselves in their blankets and
fallen asleep.

The Comanches, as soon as darkness set in, returned and
began, as was their custom, to circle the camp, firing in
occasionally and keeping up a yelling and whooping. Increasing these circles wider and wider, about midnight
they "cut in" on their captured pony herd and making a
rush they not only drove it before them but captured all
of the "Tonks" ponies, including Lieut. Boehm's horse.
The next morning in they all came, one Tonk leading a
small, forlorn looking burro, packed with their saddles,
every one afoot, looking sheepish and woefully dejected,

the butt and ridicule of the entire command. No effort
after that was ever made to hold a herd of wild captured
Indian ponies. *They were all shot.* Only 50 captured
ponies and mules were left. The "Tonks" had been permitted to select what they wanted to encourage them.
They felt much chagrined at their loss.

The command was moved some 2 miles from the village
after dark, and on the following day marched nearly 18
miles, rejoining our trains the second day after the fight
near the Freshwater Fork of the Brazos. General Mackenzie commended many of the officers in his official report
of this action for gallantry and recommended several enlisted men for Medals of Honor, and states his losses. He
cites the affidavit of Polonio Citiz, one of the captured
Mexicans, who recognized a large number of the Indians
as those who had wintered in 1871 in that part of Texas
known as Mucha Que; that of Francisco Nietto, who stated
that he was captured with his father's wagon train between Fort Duncan and San Antonio; also that of José
Carrion, a teamster and blacksmith, who recognized a mule
belonging to a train which was captured at Howards
Wells, Texas, in the spring of 1872. All of the officers
named were mentioned in G. O. No. 99, Headquarters of
the Army, November 19, 1872, and the men were all
awarded Medals of Honor by the same order. They were
forwarded November 23, 1872. General Augur, Commanding Department of Texas, in referring to Mackenzie
marching across the Staked Plains in August, 1872, says
in a letter or report: "This is the first instance within my
knowledge where troops have been successfully taken
across the "Staked Plains."

Sergeant Charlton tells the story of this action with
Mow-wis band in more detail and other events of the campaign are more particularly noted; all of which came under
his own knowledge and in which he was personally concerned and a most active participant.

Leads Charge on Indian Village

"I think I told you once before how we came to discover the Qua-ha-da Comanche Indian camp (Mow-wi's) on the North Fork of Red River, September 28, 1872. The troops had been two days, without food and during our march we came suddenly on a vineyard of wild grapes. General McK. allowed the men to dismount and feast, when McCord with his eagle eye discovered the trail of three Indians on the opposite side of the grape patch. He reported to General McKenzie and Major D—— went with McCord to discover their camp about a mile away. We immediately mounted, formed fours and started for the attack at a gallop. My troop ("F") was second in column. After a ride of about half a mile we came to a "draw" and looked down toward Red River we saw we had plenty to do. Hundreds of horses were in view and were between us and the camp but we could see both plainly. The herders were trying to rush the horses into camp to mount the warriors.

I was Junior Sergeant that day and was in charge of the rear column of "F" Troop. When we reached the edge of the camp we received the order "Right Front into line!" This threw me on the right of the company. I had in my set of fours Privates Rankin, Beals, Kelly and Dorst.

Kills a Comanche—Helps a Wounded Comrade

Now, Captain, the hottest part of the fight took place on our immediate front, proved by the fact that the only casualties that day were in my set of fours. Rankin was shot in the stomach. I thought he was killed when I pulled his blouse open and saw where the bullet struck him. I put my blouse under his head and left my canteen by his side. The bullet did not enter his stomach, however, but went round him and lodged near his spine. Dorst was shot through the neck and died at once, strangled on his own life blood. Kelly also was shot through the neck and died three days later. Beals was shot through the thigh with an arrow. I, alone, came off unscathed, but I *got the Indian who shot Kelly and Dorst.*

Recommended for Medal of Honor

We made a grand clean up, capturing 127 squaws and 3,000 horses.

We made the attack about three o'clock and fought them until sun-down. Burned their camp and then went to the sand hills and made a dry camp about a mile from our battle ground.

The Indians, evidently feeling for their squaws, attacked us again during the night but with no success though they put up a pretty hot fight until daylight.

The next morning the squaws were mounted on bare back ponies and the command started for our wagon train (at Cañon Blanco) 75 miles away.

When we reached there the squaws were placed in a corral and we made a dry camp. The Indians attacked us again during the night but did no damage.

Lt. Boehm had charge of the pony herd, that is the horses captured from the Indians. He took them about a mile from camp thinking by placing them in a convenient *"draw"* (sink in the prairie) to be able to hold them in case of an attack. The Indians fought us for about thirty minutes, but found the Old 4th more than ready for them, so they quit and went for Lt. Boehm and his pony herd. They got every horse he had and some of ours. The next morning he came in with the saddles piled on burros when we gave them the grand laugh.

He and his men said they saw the flashes of our guns that night but heard no shots, so thought the light was caused by men lighting their pipes with flint and steel, which would have been some smoking as there was a continual blaze of fire around the command for thirty minutes.

*   *   *

During all this time of marching and fighting we were given only one meal a day and that about noon. My troop lost two men killed and four wounded. "A" troop lost one killed and three wounded.

We went to supply camp and rested a week, supply camp being situated somewhere near the scene of the stampede and that terrible night of the storm in 1871. After resting a week "F" and "H" Troops were sent to Fort Griffin; the other Troops with Headquarters and the squaws went to Fort Concho.

"Maybe So White Man's Flesh"

Speaking of General King and the mule meat reminds me of the time when I ate far worse. This happened just after this fight with Mow-wi's band on North Fork of Red River. The men (of the command) had eaten nothing since the night before and it was then about two o'clock in the afternoon. We found a plum patch and General Mac-Kenzie allowed the men to dismount and *shrink their stomachs on wild plums*. It was here Major Davis found the Indians' trail. The camp proved to be about three miles distant. The fight lasted about two hours and as you know we captured 130 squaws. The men were very hungry and as there was plenty of dried buffalo meat in the camp we proceeded to "fill up." On one rope I noticed some very nice looking meat lighter in color than the other. After eating a quantity of it and not being able to decide what it was I gave some of it to "McCord" (Chief of the Ton-ka-way Indian Scouts) and asked him if it was pork. He tasted of it and said: "Maybe so him white man." This was too much for soul and stomach of "white man" to stand. I had been very hungry a short time before and could have kept it down, but it wouldn't stay down and I didn't feel clean for several days.

Takes Command of Scout Detachment

Once a detail was sent out scouting under Lt. ———. They were attacked by Indians out-numbering the men "two to one." This officer *ran—unqualifiedly ran*, begging his men to follow him and "not to fire a shot for fear of angering the Indians.'' Charlton rode beside him and said: "Lt., if we stop and make a stand they will run." "No! no! we can do nothing but try to out-run them," —— said. Charlton then *took command* and also chances of being tried for disobedience of orders, made a stand with the men, who were more experienced in such warfare than this young untried officer, and drove the Indians off. This officer came to him afterwards and asked him to not say anything about this at the Post, and Charlton told me that he never did.

Rescues Wounded Comrade

Again—it was on the return march of Gen. MacKenzie's command from North Fork of Red River campaign. The Indians had been harassing the troops all day and the scouts were kept on the skirmish line continually. All roll-call that night a man was reported missing. Charlton and one other man were sent back to search for him. He was seen last about a mile back from where the command encamped for the night. He was riding in a very feeble manner as he was wounded and could barely keep his seat in his saddle.

It was dark when the two men left in search of him. I do not know if they were mounted or not, but I do not think they were from what follows.

An Indian Dog Den

They dared not call him because of the possible nearness of the Indians. They spoke in undertones and occasionally ventured a soft whistle. On their right was an arroya or water course with numerous smaller gullies running into it. Creeping cautiously along one of these small channels, straining their eyes in the darkness for a sight of the wounded man, they had the misfortune to step on a dog and some half dozen puppies. There was at once an uproar. Charlton and his comrade became separated in the confusion following and neither dared call to the other so Charlton went on alone. He did not then just understand the presence of a dog in that vicinity but after crawling on his hands and knees for some yards he came in sight of an Indian camp, but he could form no estimate of the size of the camp in the darkness. The Indian dog was still barking viciously at intervals. Charlton was suffering from thorns in the palms of his hands. His knees were cut and bruised from stones. One shoulder had come in contact with a thorny bush and the sleeve of his blouse was full of thorns. He had an abdominal rupture, an old wound, that gave him great pain in crawling, but he went on and found his man.

Now here was a problem. The wounded man was unable to walk. Charlton dared not walk upright and no more did he dare call his comrade to come to his assistance, but he was equal to the occasion though it took every ounce of physical strength he had to manage it. He first felt of the man's wound to see if he was bleeding. He then wrapped his head and shoulders in his own blouse and rolled him as gently as time and place would permit, down over brier and stone to the bottom of a gulley out of sight of the camp. He got the poor fellow on his back then and by making a slight detour of the dog den he found the other man, and the rest was comparatively easy but he suffered a great deal of pain from his hands and knees and the rupture for several days.

Mortal Combat with a Comanche Indian

One more incident occurred on this same scout. In the next few days Charlton, McCabe and two Ton-ka-ways, under command of Lt. Peter M. Boehm, were scouting some three or four miles from the command when they came suddenly upon four Indians sitting on a grassy plot holding their horses. The Indians made a spring for their horses. Three succeeded in mounting, but Lt. Boehm shot the horse from under one of the three before he got away and then the two of them engaged in battle in which the Indian was killed, but not until several shots were fired. The two mounted men were followed by McCabe and the two Ton-ka-ways. The fourth man was left to Charlton.

My husband told me many times that this Indian was the most magnificent specimen of manhood, and the bravest that he ever encountered. He said that he was fully six feet, four inches in height, broad of shoulders and with a bold-straight-to-the-front look from his eyes, different from the usual shifty look of the savage.

Receives an Arrow Wound in Leg and Bullet in Hand

When he saw his horse was gone, he turned deliberately and took aim—not at Charlton, but at Lt. Boehm. This may have been because the other Indian was his son or brother or it may have been that because of some incident in the past he knew Lt. Boehm, and had an especial grudge against him. Before he had time to fire, however, Charlton shot him, not fatally, but this caused him to turn his attention away from Lt. Boehm. Now Charlton's horse would not stand firing. He could not dismount without fear of losing him, and every time he lifted his gun the horse plunged or threw up his head. The Indian kept a string of arrows in the air continually. One of these pierced Charlton's thigh, midway between hip and knee, going through the saddle leather and pinning him to the saddle. The Indian had exhausted his supply of arrows and began using his rifle. One shot struck Charlton's left hand, removing parts of two fingers. The bullet being turned after striking his hand, by the iron handle of his quirt. Charlton was not idle during this time, but his horse gave him lots of trouble. He told me that all through this fight he felt the keenest admiration for this Indian's bravery. One shot from Charlton's carbine shattered the Indian's hips and lower spine, but he laughed, tossed his black mane from over his eyes and kept on firing. He never weakened until he was shot fatally, that is, through the head. His body was then examined and he had nine bullet holes in him, any one of which would have killed an ordinary man.

Kills Indian—Saves Lieut. Boehm's Life

Lt. Boehm had two holes through the crown of his hat that were not there when the fight started.

The Indians were all killed but Charlton was the only man wounded. When he reached the command, his leg was so swollen that his trousers had to be cut away. He could not dismount until the doctor lifted his leg away from the saddle, cut off the barb of the arrow and removed the shaft. His hand too was in a bad shape as the bullet mashed his fingers against the iron of his quird, ripping the flesh to the palm and leaving the bare bones exposed. *Lt. Boehm never knew that Charlton saved his life that day.*

"Captain Carter, this is all I will attempt at this writing. I am not a writer and I realize there are many gaps in this narrative, but I have no written date and, womanlike, my memory did not retain anything but the exciting parts. If there is anything further you wish me to add to this,* I will gladly do it, if I can.

The abdominal rupture my husband suffered from was the doctor's cause for rejecting him the last time he re-enlisted at Ft. Sill when Gen. MacKenzie asked him to go after Mow-wi. He was never able to lie face downward on a bed without the greatest discomfort, so it was only youth, splendid health, and a spirit of loyalty to a comrade that ever enabled him to crawl over ground that he could not see and carry that wounded man out of that arroya.

Among the dead after the action were found several Mexicans and half-breeds, probably captured years before and held as prisoners by the Comanches. There was also found a white man.

(*Note.—It will thus be seen that the "Old Sergeant" killed three Indians: Se-tank, principal war chief of the Ki-o-was, June 6, 1871, at the Cache Creek Ford, near Fort Sill, I. T. (now Oklahoma) while attempting to escape; a Comanche Indian, September 28, 1870, in the action on McClellan's Creek near the North Fork of Red River, when charging upon Mow-wi's Village; and the third in mortal combat a few days later, the Sergeant being wounded by both arrow and bullet in the deadly duel. He also, on the same day, saved the life of Lieut. P. M. Boehm, one of the best officers of the regiment, besides rescuing a wounded comrade from almost certain death or capture by a savage foe. He was recommended for a Medal of Honor for the action on McClellan's Creek and also for the action of the Palo Duro Canon, which is now near the present town of Blanco in the Panhandle of Texas.

About 1844 a man had been appointed to the U. S. Military Academy by the name of Thomas F. M. McLean. He was from Missouri. His name in the Corps of Cadets, however, on account of his shaggy shock of hair, which bordered on the red or sandy, rough features and uncouth ways, had given him the sobriquet of "Bison" or "Bise" McLean. He did not graduate on account of being deficient in conduct and shortly afterwards he turned up in California as a sharp and exceedingly dangerous type of a desperado; that type which later the San Francisco Vigilantes drove out of that city after hanging and summarily dealing with a lot of them. McLean was finally run out of the state into New Mexico or some of the territories, but so depraved had he become that the occupation of cut throat and desperado grew to be too risky, so he joined a band of Comanche Indians and became in time a sort of sub-chief or leader among them. General John P. Hatch, who was a Major General of Volunteers in the Civil War and a most gallant soldier, graduated from the Military Academy in 1844 and, later, was the senior major of the Fourth U. S. Cavalry and colonel of the Second Cavalry. He had been at West Point for a short time with "Bise" McLean and knew his features well. He related the following story to the writer about the time of our action with Mow-wi's band of Comanches on McClellan's Creek, where the body of this white man was found.

"While serving in Texas, shortly after the Civil War, about 1867-8, I happened to be in or near the town of Fredericksburg just after a raid had been made upon that town by a war party of Comanches, * * * and upon walking up the street I met a man who seemed to be a stranger in the place and we gave each other a quick and steady glance. I felt sure when I passed the man that I had seen him somewhere in my long service in the army. I stopped and turned after he had gone by me, but he had suddenly vanished. The same impression had evidently been made upon the stranger and he had quickly darted in behind some houses. In an instant the coarse shock of red hair,

the large features and awkward gait of "Bise" McLean
flashed across my mind.   There was no mistake; it was he!
I ran up and down; inquired of this and that one about
the town, but nobody had seen which way he had gone.
The troops of the Fourth Cavalry, nearby, sent to discover and punish the raiding party, were at once put in
motion to scour the country, but the trail of "Bison" Mc-
Lean was never discovered."

In the battle near the mouth of McClellan's Creek, September 29, 1872, and in the discovery of the renegade
white, we thought the problem had been solved.   That
man had a thick shock of red hair and the unmistakable
features as described by General Hatch who, after the
incident was related to him, leaned strongly to the opinion that "Bise" McLean had met his death at the hands
of the Fourth Cavalry.   So far as is known nothing has
ever been heard of him since.

On the march into Fort Concho one wounded Indian
died, the springless army wagon having jolted the life out
of him, as he was found bolt upright, stiff and immovable,
against the side board, after being 24 hours on the way.
A squaw, however, who gave birth to a child in another
wagon as it jolted over the prairie and down into and out
of the arroyas, arrived at the post in fine condition, none
the worse for the wear and tear of such a dreadful trip
under such circumstances.   Their fortitude, powers of endurance and wonderful powers of recuperation were almost marvelous.   Not one word of complaint; not one sign
of pain was apparent in voice or face.   The babe died, but
the young squaw lived.

They remained in the corrals at Fort Concho all that
winter, well sheltered and fed, and in good health; in the
meantime negotiations were being strenuously conducted,
not only for their release but the release of Sa-tan-ta and
Big Tree.   The release of the former was effected about
April 1, 1873.   They were escorted by a detachment of
the Eleventh U. S. Infantry over that trackless country to
Fort Sill.   Two squaws escaped and came in a week or

two afterwards, not much the worse for wear although they travelled over many miles of country and subsisted on roots, birds and animals which they caught. They waded or swam numerous streams and creeks en route.

Captain Robert McClermont, Eleventh U. S. Infantry, commanded this escort. He was a character, a product of the old school of soldiers. In his early service he had been thrown with General Grant, either as an enlisted man in the same regiment (Fourth Infantry) or in the same garrison. In relating incidents connected with Grant's early life as a young officer, McClermont always referred to him as "Lyss." The writer was stationed with him at Fort Concho during the winter of 1870-1. This was a most hazardous trip at best. It proved so to McClermont. His route lay for over 450 miles along a dim trail running through numerous small settlements which had been raided by Indians, and fathers, husbands, sweethearts killed, while the women and children, after plundering these outlying ranches, had been carried into captivity and to a fate worse than death. It was customary to shoot an Indian on sight. His route lay through Jacksboro, from which less than two years before the seven teamsters of Henry Warren's corn train had ventured out from their homes to a horrible death on Salt Creek Prairie at the hands of Sa-tan-ta and his Kiowa Indian raiders. In approaching this town he heard that the white people had congregated there to intercept his train. He, therefore, sent the wagons loaded with the prisoners around while he drove his ambulance into town, waiting apparently for the train to follow. He found there nearly a thousand armed citizens, many of them drunk, not only determined to prevent the return of the Comanche Indian women and children to their people, but to wreak their vengeance if possible. Strange to say that during that winter the Indians had been unusually quiet, raiding but little. It is their belief that their people being captives would have been all punished by death—as they treat their own prisoners—by way of retaliation, had they continued their excursions for plunder and scalps. McCler-mont, after waiting in Jacksboro for some time designedly, drove back to see what had detained his train, leaving the drunken mob in anticipation of soon seeing them. The prisoners were well on their way, clear of the town. Thus, by strategy, he conveyed them safely beyond danger.

The Fort Sill Indians manifested strong attachment by their demonstrations of delight on meeting children, wives, relatives and friends. The prisoners reported that they had been *well fed* and *kindly treated*. The chiefs wanted to shake hands with Captain McClermont, and some of them gave him the warm salutation of a Comanche hug.*

About July, 1872, it was arranged to have a meeting of the civilized Indians at Ocmulgee and try and induce the hostiles to cease their raiding. It was held at old Fort Cobb, I. T., July 22, at which some of the Kiowas attended and a few of the Comanches. Lone Wolf demanded the release of Sa-tan-ta and Big Tree as a condition for their remaining *good* and travelling the *"white man's road."* Also, that all military posts should be removed from the Indian Territory, and their reservation lines extended from the Rio Grande to the Missouri River. The talk of Lone Wolf did not suit Kicking Bird. Little came of this council and the hostiles still remained defiant.

About six weeks after this council there was another very important one held by Capt. H. E. Alvord, who had been a former officer of the Tenth Cavalry, and Prof. Edward Parish of Philadelphia, who had been appointed a commission to look into the condition of the three agencies, Cheyenne and Arapahoe, Wichita and affiliated bands, and the Kiowa and Comanche tribes. Soon after they arrived at the Kiowa and Comanche agencies, Prof. Parish was taken with typhoid fever and died September 9, 1872. The Cheyennes were out hunting and were not present. The commissioners were authorized to promise the release of Sa-tan-ta and Big Tree, but before Prof. Parish was

*The Comanche prisoners from Fort Concho, Texas, under escort of Captain Robert McClermont, 11th U. S. Inf., arrived at Fort Sill and were turned over to Indian agent, J. M. Haworth, June 10, 1873.

taken sick the commissioners had given the subject much
attention, and decided that their release "would be highly
detrimental to the interest of the Government" and it
was not mentioned to the Indians. The Indians were collecting at Fort Sill in large numbers and were in a very
ugly mood. It was very difficult to get a suitable delegation of the Kiowas to agree to go to Washington. However, their consent was finally obtained with the promise
that if they would go *they should see Sa-tan-ta* and *Big
Tree,* and these prisoners were to be brought from the
State Penitentiary at Huntsville, Texas, to Fort Sill, I. T.,
and, after meeting the Indian delegation there, were to
proceed with the commissioners to St. Louis and Washington. Captain Alvord reported this meeting (not at
Fort Sill or St. Louis but at another point) as "proving to
be a most impressive and affecting occasion." * * * "All
believed it would result in good." Shortly after the prisoners had been temporarily released and returned to
Huntsville, the delegation went to Washington, where "the
Kiowas were promised the release of their chiefs, by permission of the Governor of Texas, at the end of six months,
upon good behavior meanwhile of the whole tribe and other
fixed conditions." Agent Lawrie Tatum opposed this, believing that "the effect on the Kiowas of the release of
Sa-tan-ta—a *daring* and *treacherous chief*—was like a dark
rolling cloud on the Western horizon," and he resigned
March 31, 1873. Much correspondence went on between
the Interior Department and Governor Davis. Meantime
the Indians had done but little raiding except Lone Wolf,
who led a raid into Texas and Mexico. One of his sons
was killed on this raid by Lieut. Charles Hudson of the
Fourth Cavalry who was following in pursuit. Sa-tan-ta
and Big Tree were finally released conditionally again in
1873, but were detained in the guard house until the Governor could come to Fort Sill with the final terms to be
given at a council. This council took place October 6,
1873. In the meantime both chiefs were to be kept confined in the guard house until these terms were accepted.

"All must answer roll calls and the absentees noted." The Indians were morose, surly, defiant. They finally plotted to kill the Governor if the two chiefs were again placed in the guard house. They had arranged for certain braves to be on their horses in a position to shoot the Governor and the guard when the two chiefs should be taken to the guard house, and two horses were ready for the prisoners to mount and flee. They (the chiefs) were finally released but *not pardoned*—a sort of parole—and on condition that any further raiding by the Indians would mean their immediate arrest and delivery to the Governor for their return once more, and this time for good, to the penitentiary. This continued until the following year when both were caught red-handed either in some raid or in the affair at Adobe Walls in 1874 and were returned once more to Huntsville, where Sa-tan-ta—who had been put to work cane seating chairs—committed suicide on October 11, 1878, by throwing himself headlong from a gallery to the pavement below after having had his parole revoked by Governor Roberts of Texas. He was buried in the prison cemetery, after the Kiowas, upon receiving notice of his death, refused to take any action as to his burial among his people.

CHAPTER XV

To the Mexican Border
For the Good of the Regiment

ON December 11, 1872, while acting as Post Adjutant of Fort Richardson, I was informed by Mackenzie that I would be relieved from duty that day by Lieut. H. W. Lawton and placed in command of Company "A" during the absence of its captain, who was on recruiting service, and the first lieutenant, who was soon to leave on the same duty. This, I was told, was for the "good of the regiment." A young, inexperienced officer had been assigned by a War Department order to this Company and was already then at the Post for duty. I was transferred by a Post Order, which later was confirmed by the War Department, in spite of my most earnest protest. The young officer referred to was assigned for duty to my own Company, "E." As "A" Company had been stationed in San Antonio for a long period its morale and discipline had become somewhat lax and I expected trouble from the start. In this I was not disappointed. With the exception of one sergeant (Shields), the non-commissioned personnel was poor, way below the regimental standard. The First Sergeant proved to be a professional gambler who, soon after pay day, managed to accumulate most of the men's money. There were, besides, two or three notoriously bad men whose influence over the balance of the Company was a most disturbing factor and not only well known among their companions but throughout the entire regiment. One had served a sentence, shortly after the Civil War, at Ship Island for mutiny, and then was a general prisoner in the guard house at Fort Richardson for murder; another who had served in the Navy for one or two terms, a great, strapping fellow, had a reputation as a prize fighter and reckless bully. I was told that I had been assigned to command this Company for the purpose of regulating, disciplining and restoring it to its former high standard in the regiment. This, while complimentary was certainly not a pleasing prospect or an attractive job. Lieut. Thompson left on December 14th and my disagreeable work then began.

There were 16 general prisoners in the guard house, all having been tried by a General Court Martial and under sentence for various offenses—among them one for desertion and the ex-mutineer and murderer, whose strong personality seemed to dominate his companions in misery. Strange to relate he had been educated for the priesthood. By some strange fortune, unknown to us, he had, probably for the love of excitement or adventure, drifted into the Army. After serving for 33 years and promoted through all of the non-commissioned grades, he finally went to his death at Santiago de Cuba in the charge upon the block house at San Juan Hill.

For several days, whenever the officer of the guard had marched on duty, these prisoners, confined by themselves, and led by this man, had been in the habit of soaking stale, dry loaves of bread in a barrel of ice water which had been placed under the grated window of their guard room, and when the new officer of the guard's back was turned a good shot from the window generally hit its mark; the wet mass then dribbling down the back of the neck to the discomfiture and loss of dignity of the innocent and unsuspecting victim. General Mackenzie determined to put a stop to this sort of guard house amusements. Certain forms of punishment which had been adopted in extreme cases during the Civil War had not then been abolished by order of the War Department. These were carrying the log, a "spread eagle" on the "spare wheel of the caisson," "tying up by the thumbs," the "sweat box," "walking a beat inside a barrel" suspended by the shoulders, and a placard thereon with "Coward," "Skulker," "Deserter," "Malingerer," etc., etc. Mackenzie had given us wide latitude and our own discretion as to how these guard house culprits should be punished.

Mutiny of the Guard House Prisoners

On December 17, as I marched the new guard to the guard house, I just missed an icy, soggy loaf of bread thrown from the barred window. I "turned out" the 16 prisoners, gave them the "Third Degree;" nobody would turn informer or "squeal" upon his "pal" or "buddy." I ordered them on the ring with the log. Under the inspiration of the convicted mutineer, all refused to take it. I had a lance sergeant on duty. He lacked nerve and was a spineless, mealy-mouthed pussy-foot. Taking the matter in hand personally, with loaded rifles, I forced the mutineers inside, procured ropes, tied all up by the thumbs, and then with loaded revolver in hand, and sending a messenger to Mackenzie detailing the occurrence and my action thereon, held them there until his arrival. He approved of what I had done, but directed that due precaution be taken that the feet of the mutineers should be on the floor so that no injury might result.

About noon, shortly after their dinners had been brought to them from the company kitchens, the sergeant rushed to my tent with the astounding news that all of the prisoners who had been tied up were drunk; were threatening to make a rush for the gun stacks of the guard and after seizing them were threatening to kill anybody who interfered with them. It is presumed that whisky had been smuggled into the guard house in camp kettles which contained their coffee. Instantly I had the two reliefs fall in, the stacks broken and the guard house surrounded; then with two or three of the best men with loaded rifles in hand I jumped inside. I had dealt with desperate "bounty-jumpers" of the Civil War. The two ring leaders were noisy, shouting, and threatening. I ordered the sergeant to bring a bucket of ice water, from a barrel setting outside, with a tin pint cup. Filling the cup and dashing it in the face of the mutineer, who was calling me all of the abusive names in the English vocabulary, and repeating it every time he shouted his vile terms, I soon

had him drenched, sobered and pleading for a cessation
of this novel treatment. He was completely cowed. I
gave the same medicine to the deserter and he was soon
begging for mercy and both promised if they were temporarily released and given dry clothing they would be
quiet and give no further trouble. This was done and
peace once more reigned. No more soggy, water-soaked
loaves of bread were ever thrown at an innocent and unsuspecting officer of the day or officer of the guard at old
Fort Richardson. I had learned this water cure form of
punishment at a great conscript camp during the Civil War,
where conscripts, substitutes and ''bounty jumpers,'' with
thousands of dollars on their persons, the worst class of
criminals ever assembled together on this continent, had
been rendezvoused for transportation to their regiments at
the battle lines of the Army of the Potomac at the front—
there to desert, to go into hospitals, anywhere to keep out
of battle. They were thieves, thugs, malingerers and cow-
ards. During the time I commanded this Company I had
the man, who had been a sailor and has been referred to
as a huge, overgrown bully and mischief maker, leading
the weaker men into all sorts of trouble, confined in the
guard house for insulting and mutinous language, and
later tried by a General Court Martial and sentenced to
hard labor for a long term. I reduced or ''broke'' the
first sergeant for gambling, neglect of duty and conspicuously undermining the morale and discipline of the men.
I had, besides, been making many reforms tending to
straighten it out and putting the Company into such shape
as I knew General Mackenzie desired when he had me
transferred to this Company against my wishes and the
reasons he had given therefor.

There had been rumors for sometime that the headquarters of the regiment were to be changed to Fort Concho, and on December 28th General Mackenzie with Companies ''B'' and ''L'' departed for that post. Colonel
William Wood, commanding the 11th Infantry and head-

quarters of that regiment, was transferred on that date to Fort Richardson.

The Epizootic

About January 1, 1873, the Russian influenza, or, as it was called then, the ''Epizootic,'' which had begun to make its appearance in the United States the preceding September and began spreading from the East to the South and West, struck the frontier posts in Texas. In October all of the horses on the car lines in Boston were so disabled that oxen were used to haul the passengers about the city and for the transportation of merchandise. I had about 100 horses and mules. Printed rules for the treatment of this disease were mailed from the Quartermaster Department in San Antonio.

Several of our companies were caught out while on a scout for Indians and the horses disabled for service. There was much inflammation about the eyes, nose and throat. The only exercise permitted was being ridden to water. They were led into a large hospital tent, pitched for the purpose; a nose bag partly filled with boiled oats was fitted about their noses. A thick, yellow secretion was thus kept flowing from the nose. A warm solution of carbolic acid was used for a wash. Hot bran mashes were fed to all the animals and in a few days (by Jan. 6) all were pronounced fit for duty. Only one animal was lost. A post mortem revealed his lungs badly congested, and his death was probably due to *over steaming*.

During this period a ''wet norther'' prevailed with a cold drizzle. It was reported that Lieut. Warrington lost 17 horses while en route to Fort Concho. We learned of the death, at Philadelphia on the 29th of December, of one of our favorite ladies in the regiment, Mrs. C. A. Vernon. We also learned that Col. Beaumont and family were at the end of the railroad (M. K. & T.) and would arrive in a few days under an escort in command of Lieut. John M. Walton who had gone to meet some recruits for assignment to the 11th Infantry.

Colonel Beaumont arrived January 25th and many of my most disagreeable duties in an attempt to straighten out and discipline this Company were now over. The only excitement we had at this period was on January 29th when one of the great haystacks caught fire and it took the entire garrison to put it out. It was only accomplished by cutting it in two, covering one half, and with a double bucket line to the creek, keeping the other half saturated with water. On February 4th I bought from Lieut. Ira Quimby, Quartermaster of the 11th Infantry, for $200 one of the Dougherty travelling ambulances which had broken down and been abandoned by the Land and Copper Mining Company, which has been referred to in a previous chapter. It had been thoroughly repaired and was as good as new. About February 3rd two companies of the 11th Infantry (Captains Jackson and Sanderson) left for Fort Sill. Lieut. McKinney and myself rode out with them on the Fort Sill road towards the West Fork of the Trinity River for several miles. Some of these friends we never saw again.

About March 1st rumors came that we were to move to Fort Concho and join headquarters there and soon orders came for us to start. Major Alfred E. Latimer was to go in command and it included A, B, C, and E companies and a detachment of K company. There were to be nine ladies besides numerous children.

The writer had been designated by Major Latimer as Quartermaster of the moving column on this long march, notwithstanding that he had a wife and two children and there were a number of single officers available for this duty. Such a protest was, however, unavailing, as Major Latimer insisted that he wanted me and no other. He was old, in poor health; had a fistula which made riding in the saddle painful and a real hardship. All this made him irritable, irascible and difficult to please or satisfy. He felt the responsibility of his duty and magnified the dangers of a march with such a command through an Indian country to such an extent as to increase the labors of

a Quartermaster to a degree which soon became not only
burdensome but almost intolerable. I would be away
from my family all day, not seeing them from sunrise until
long after the command had gone into camp, and with accidents and innumerable breakdowns not until long after
night had "set in." He always addressed me in a very
querulous tone of voice as "Mr. Quartermaster," after
expressing his fears about the dangers which he always
seemed to assume were lurking about camp; the weight of
the loads in each wagon, the condition of the animals, our
next base of supplies etc. The distance was approximately 500 miles.

The "Ramshackle" Wagon Train

Our wagon train consisted of a lot of broken down,
crazy, "ramshackly" wagons which had been gathered
from all over the Department of Texas and which were
from the effects of a dry climate for many months of the
year, in the last stages of a consumptive decay. They
could not carry full loads without collapsing. But our
little major, with his disabling fistula, insisted upon my
crowding them and keeping up full loads. We were allowed but five wagons to a company. Many of the officers,
on finding that they would be compelled to sacrifice their
personal property, "chipped in" and purchased some old
private wagons of the "schooner" pattern. We were informed that no government ambulances would be allowed
for the transportation of our families or the company
women (wives of soldiers, laundresses, etc.), and most of
us were compelled to buy in "open market" some of the
most stylish (?) turnouts to be obtained at low rates in
that section (Jacksboro) of Texas. Colonel Beaumont had
somewhat anticipated this event by purchasing and bringing with him from St. Louis a most unique vehicle on the
barouche order which had seen many years service in that
burg or some other city, and which fairly took off the
shine from our less pretentious "layouts" until, at some
later date, we got into the Nueces Cañon, when we turned

the tables on him by lashing him up with enough wet rawhide, an ample supply of which we had carried along for such purposes, to start a tannery, wherever his city-bred hack had started its joints and threatened to collapse. When this collection of wagons, company carts and carriages had been pulled out for inspection on that eventful day of moving, it was not a train for any Quartermaster to be very proud of; at least I was not proud enough to express it publicly to my brother officers.

A "Dougherty"

Our travelling carriage or "Dougherty" ambulance has been referred to as one I had bought of the Land and Copper Mining Company. It had been fully repaired, repainted and revarnished, was nearly as good as new and comfortable as possible for our purposes.

It was intended for two or four mules. A driver's seat was in front, under which was a box for wrench, oil can, ropes, lariats, halters, lashings, tools, etc. A drop curtain shut this off from a leather cushioned seat facing to the rear, and still further in rear was a third seat, also cushioned with high back. These cushions were so arranged as to slide into the space between the two seats, and the cushions to the backs were made to slide down and replace them, thus making a cushion mattress the full length and width of the ambulance, and where two persons could, when all of the side and driver's curtains were dropped and fastened, lie down and sleep if necessary in stormy weather when it was not practicable to pitch a tent. Under the cushion of the rear seat was fitted a commodious receptacle for odds and ends, and a convenient commode or toilet. A strong but light trunk rack was placed behind for a medium sized trunk, thus obviating the necessity of unloading a trunk from the wagons every night at the end of a day's march. Loops and hooks were arranged at the sides for hanging carbines, pistols, shawl straps, canteens and rubber and woolen wraps, etc. A convenient box under the second seat held rubbers, shoes, lunch basket, etc.   A heavy rubber boot was in front for the driver and all the curtains—side, rear and front—had small, rectangular lights.   Brakes and lock chains were attached for safety in descending hills or rough descents.

Sometimes a pole broke, a tire got loose, or a single-tree gave way.   With plenty of wet rawhide lashings we were generally able to wrap the broken parts.   These, after shrinking in the dry air, brought the split or break together as with bands of iron.

On March 3rd I had gone to near Rock Station with loads of forage where we expected to camp the next day, and after unloading them returned to Fort Richardson.   It was a long march and a busy day.   Had met Lieut. John M. Walton who was returning from a sick leave.

Early on the morning of the 4th, after our invalid Major had been lifted into his saddle, the trumpeter called the companies together.   Many last farewells were said, perhaps forever.   Many last lingering looks were given to the birthplaces of the children, to the quarters which had sheltered us for two years, to the parade, corrals, to "Sudsville," and to the many et ceteras of that rude frontier post which some of us were never to see again.

The final command was given and the five troops splashed across Lost Creek and wound slowly over the prairie on the Fort Griffin road, followed by the motley array of ambulances and "outfits" containing the women and children.   All of the soldiers' wives, laundresses and camp women were in the wagons on top of the loads.   Lastly the black snakes cracked.   "Pull out" was given, and the long train of white, canvas-topped wagons followed out of "park," in rear of which came a small rear guard.   We were bound for—

The Rio Grande

Besides Mellie, Bessie, black Rhoda (cook, nurse and general utility servant) and Aleck, the driver on the front seat, the ambulance contained "Tippy," the tiny half

Polonne-Chihuaha Mexican dog, now separated from his little wee brown bear cub and tent playmate.

On March 4th we camped at about 3 P. M. at the place where I had unloaded the forage on the previous day. It was a bright, sunny, warm day and the march had been a pleasant one.

On the following day we crossed Salt Creek Prairie, passing the scene of the bloody massacre by Sa-tan-ta and his band of murderous Kiowas in May, 1871. The bones were yet visible; the debris of the burned wagons, the corn still lay scattered about and the entire route was still marked by stones or stakes defining the last resting place of some poor dead settler or cowboy—a melancholy reminder of the uncertainty of life in these lonely, silent solitudes.

At night the wagons and ambulances "corraled" in a circle or rectangle, the wagon poles pointing inward. The horses were "staked" or picketed out, tents were pitched and supper prepared by the cooks. Camp guards and pickets were posted. The camp fires glimmered, and early to bed the tired troopers and women and children went to prepare for the morrow's march. The animals champed, the sentinels watched, the coyotes howled and the camp quietly slept. One of Col. Beaumont's children (Hortense), had an attack of colic during the night and the writer was called upon to furnish some Jamaica ginger for her relief.

There is more or less confusion on the first day's march; on the second, order reigns. The "pack up" and "boots and saddles" are sounded and in the fresh air of a Texas spring morning, we again moved. Shortly after we left camp at the Salt Creek crossing, "Tippy," the little pet dog of the children, was killed. In trying to jump from the ambulance his foot slipped, he went under the wheel and was crushed to death. The last we saw of the little fellow was when Aleck held him up by the hind legs like a rabbit, and with darky curiosity was inspecting the real cause for his death, while Rhoda was exclaiming, "Sure's you born, Miss Mary, dat am a low down shame.'' There was no time for much emotion or grief on such occasion, but we echoed the sentiment as we rode away from the sobbing children to join the train on its day's journey.

Old Fort Belknap was soon reached; more forage was loaded in the convalescent wagons, and again was the picturesque scene of fording the quicksands of the Brazos River re-enacted. Shortly after crossing and passing ''Widow Georges'' ranch, camp was made at the ''Eight Mile'' water hole, but there was precious little water in it.

Colonel Beaumont with his wife and three children and my own family made a group of nine. Our tents were pitched alongside. About our crackling mesquite log camp fire we reminisced of the Civil War, after which he played the guitar while we sang, ''I dreamed I dwelt in *marble halls,*'' and then all retired to sleep in *canvas walls.*

Our marches took us to Fort Griffin across the Clear Fork of the Brazos, which we reached on the 7th. Colonel George P. Buell, 11th Infantry, was in command. Here we remained until the 11th. While the wagons were being repaired our command was being hospitably entertained by the garrison. The ladies and children visited about the post and the village of the Ton-ka-way Indians, which was down on what was known as ''The Flat.'' This later became a notoriously bad place, a rendezvous for desperadoes, gunmen, gamblers, cattle trailers, buffalo hunters, etc.

Resumed our march on the 10th at 8 A. M. and after moving about 20 miles without incident, made a good camp. We were now on the Fort Concho road. On this day I picked up a Mexican boy on the trail and believing that he might assist Rhoda in her duties about camp, turned him over to her for instruction.

It was beautiful, balmy spring weather, the prairies were alive with quail, upland plover and prairie chickens. The cooing notes of the wood dove rang out its plaintive wail; buffalo and antelope were everywhere plentiful and frequently a prairie-dog village was seen with its singular squeaking occupants. Their antics were the delight of the children all day. A jack rabbit, with its long mule ears, would get up from his prickly pear and brush bed, and with a startled bound or two would disappear in the cloud of dust which he had kicked up.

Everywhere about us stretched the green flowered, almost limitless expanse of prairie. Our camp on the 11th was four miles beyond Fort "Phantom Hill," near the scene of the massacre, the tall white chimneys of the ruins still standing like monuments to mark the spot, or at night to make the flesh creep at their naked, ghastly shapes when thinking of the bloody tragedy enacted here. General Marcy in his explorations in this region gives an excellent description of this old army post.

Buffalo and antelope had been killed by the hunters of the command; all had been loaded into the wagons and distributed to the companies, and the appetizing smell of many a fry and roast greeted our nostrils as we waited hungrily and impatiently about the fires.

It had been a hard day for the wagons. Several wheels had dished and spread out on the ground and small saplings were being used under the axles as drags. Sometimes a pole broke, a tire got loose or an axle gave way, letting the loads to the ground; then the loads had to be shifted to the other and stronger wagons. We carried rawhide lashings which we soaked and wrapped the broken parts with, and these, after drying and shrinking brought the split or break together as with bands of iron or a welding. When the wheels got dry we threw them into the creek or waterhole at night, which swelled the felloes and spokes, making them temporarily strong and tight for that day at least.

A detail of men was sent ahead to remove the larger stones from the trail, so that the dry and creaking wheels would not strike them and crush to the ground. But, notwithstanding all our efforts many an overstrained, worn out wheel "dished" and spread out before our eyes upon the road. Sergeant John B. Sharp, was my wagon master; he was 6 feet 4 inches—a giant in strength and a man of most remarkable powers of endurance and capability. Sharp had brought along as a teamster an old California '49er. When we were about at our wits' ends and had about used up our spare parts, lashings, saplings for drags, etc., he suggested the "cross lift." This was entirely new to both Sharp and myself. It has already been described in another charter. Although the wheel "wabbled" and shrieked and groaned, and was always "out of dish" there was no way of getting away from this novel make shift. It was a comical sight to see a dozen or more of these mended wheels in a train rolling along and clumsily shifting to almost every point of the compass.

We had to lay over at "Phantom Hill" one day for repairs as many wagons had been unloaded miles back on the trail and their loads sent out for while the command was resting for the night.

All this with the irascibility of our fussing little Major with his disabling fistula was most wearing upon the Quartermaster. We moved through "Mountain Pass" and by our old landmarks "Pulpit Rock" and "Church Mountain."

Word had been sent ahead to Fort Concho for forage to meet us at Fort Chadburne, and as we rolled up to the little abandoned post, buffalo, prairie dogs upon the parade, and many an intruder in and about the decaying buildings scampered at sight of our strange caravan. It was no wonder for no animal had ever seen in that country such a yee-yawing, patched-up train.

In the Army and Navy Courier for February and March, 1927, published at Fort Sam Houston, Texas, edited by Colonel Martin L. Crimmins, U. S. A., retired, historian, is a very interesting incident connected with the early occupation of Fort Chadbourne taken from the unpublished memoirs of General David L. Stanley, U. S. Army, who, as a young officer, had been stationed there in the winter of 1854-5. "Soon after joining, the Comanches caught two soldiers (mail carriers) near the post and tying them to a tree, burned them alive. A short time after 40 Indians came into the post for a council. They were surrounded by soldiers and several Indians were killed.'' (Note—Letters were found upon these Indians which it was believed had been taken from the mail carriers whom they had murdered.) "Lieut. George B. Anderson and myself occupied one room in the unfinished hospital. One very beautiful bright moonlight night in September, we were awakened by some strange noise like some one groaning and calling, and going out we found a soldier by the name of Mattock, who was just being helped to the hospital by a soldier who lived with his wife near the creek. Mattock had been over the creek to the hut of a Dutchman who sold liquor. Having filled up he was on his way home, happy no doubt, and at the crossing of the creek which was in deep banks, five or six Comanches waylaid him and as he passed commenced shooting at his back with bows and arrows. Mattock shouted and ran until he met the soldier who lived in the cabin and who brought him moaning and crying out to the hospital. * * * Mattock had fourteen arrows in him; he bristled with them like a porcupine. Three of these arrows had gone so far through him that the surgeon extracted them by cutting the feathered part of the arrow and pulling them through the man's body. In two weeks time Mattock was walking around, and his only disability was finally from a superficial wound which had fractured a nerve. Assistant Surgeon Eben Swift, who treated this man, said he feared a truthful relation of this case would result in his being put down as a "Munchausen." Assistant Surgeon Swift was the father of Brig. Gen. Swift, U.S.A., retired, a graduate of West Point, Class of 1876. The latter related to the writer a few days since in the Army and Navy Club the sequel to the foregoing story. He was born at Fort Chadbourne, May 11, 1854. He was a small child when his father was ordered to San Antonio. A cavalry scout went with them to their first camp. That same day of their departure, upon the arrest in the post of some

Comanches by the soldiers, several of the former were
driven into the quarters his father had just vacated, and
killed there.   Later the Indians followed the escort and
fired into the camp but were driven off.   His father
saved the arrows which he had extracted from Mattock.
He was ordered to old Fort Randall.   At the opening of
the Civil War in 1861, upon being ordered to Council
Bluffs, Iowa, and from thence to Hannibal, Mo., the freight
car in which the family was travelling was set on fire by
the Confederates and those Comanches arrows, so long
packed away as surgical curios, were burned.

The favorite "water team" of the Fourth Cavalry had
been dispatched to our relief.   It was composed of eight
magnificent gray mules, and accompanied by our indefatigable regimental quartermaster, Lieut. H. W. Lawton,
with his six feet four inches in his stocking feet, it was a
sight for sore eyes and cause for heartiest congratulations.   Our cup of happiness now seemed so full, and our
confidence in the team so great that we overloaded that
wagon in our anxiety to relieve the "scrub" teams.   In
descending the hill leading to the river, crash went a
wheel, and the "water team" wagon had to be patched
up to correspond with the others.

As we emerged from the Colorado River, which we had
to ford, the ladies, already in camp and the entire command gathered to see the train pull up the bluff.   The
banks were cut down, the whips cracked; the teamsters
shouted, yelled and cursed blue streaks—which the mules
readily translated into pure Anglo-Saxon—and at dark the
last mule and a tired quartermaster retired to rest in the
quiet camp.

The Mexican, whom we had picked up on the road as a
camp helper, was found missing the next morning just as
we were leaving camp, and Rhoda discovered as her tent
was being taken down that somebody had managed to abstract, or subtract from under her pillow $35—all of her
hard earned wages.   She naturally suspected the Mexican.
Upon being caught and brought back it was found that he

could not speak a word of English, and when poor Rhoda, in her grief and rage over her loss poured out the vials of her wrath and called him a "low down greaser," thief, etc., not a word of which he could "sabe," one could hardly refrain from laughing at his dull, stupid face and her virtuous wrath, but, finally, mustering what little stock of the pure Castilian I had not forgotten, to my accusation he would only answer by a most profuse "No le habe! No le habe!!" A search of his clothes failed to reveal the lost money. Some of the men who took down her tent may have taken it from under her pillow.

As we were about to pull across the North Concho River on the 18th, having camped the night before on a creek near Mt. Margaret, a fearful storm approaching, a cloudburst struck up. The river was soon "booming." General Mackenzie, Lawton and others came down to see the train pull across. There was no time to lose if I wished to cross the last wagon and save my reputation. Any delay meant leaving half of the train on the North side. The bluff was steep and now muddy and slippery. Doubling up the teams and stations Sergeant Sharp on the rise while I remained at the foot, both armed with "black snakes," by plenty of application of the latter, intermingled with plenty of lung exercise and many cuss words from the teamsters, etc., all were safely over and "corraled" before dark, and after receiving hearty congratulations from Mackenzie and the spectators I sought shelter and dry clothes after the complete soaking I had undergone.

We remained here several days refitting the train for our next march via Fort McKavett for Fort Clark. It will be recalled that at Fort Concho were the 130 Comanche squaws and children which had been captured on Sept. 28, 1872, in the action with Mow-wi's band on the North Fork of the Red River.

On the 19th all of our ladies with most of the children went to visit the prisoners in the corrals, much to the delight and profit of the Indians, who not only received pres-

ents of food and candy but had the privilege of holding
the little white papooses in their arms, stroking our baby's
long, light blonde hair and always exclaiming "bueno!"
"Mucho bueno!!"—which was generally their most enthusiastic expression for the superlative whenever anything especially pleased them or appealed to their strongest emotions. The result on the part of the ladies was,
however, not so profitable as will be seen later.

A "hop" was given us here by Chaplain Badger. Upon
asking to be relieved from any further duty with Major L.
as quartermaster of the marching column, Mackenzie pri-
vately arranged it so as to retain him for duty at Fort
Concho and to place Captain Clarence Mauck in command,
his company joining us here for duty on the Rio Grande.
And on March 20th we resumed the march. Dr. Rufus
Choate, our reliable and indefatigable acting assistant
surgeon, accompanying us, with Lieutenants Miller, Hudson and Wood. We had now 65 miles to march. Our
first camp was at Lipan Springs and breaking camp at
8:30, marched to Kickapoo Springs the following day.

As we arrived at Fort McKavett, that beautiful little
post on the San Saba River, the next day, we encountered
another terrific rain storm, which drenched us to the skin.
Lt. Col. (Brevet Major General) A. McD. McCook, of the
Tenth Infantry, commanded the post. He was a distinguished officer of the Civil War and had proved himself
to be a most genial host. General Mackenzie joined us
here from San Antonio and General McCook prevailed
upon him to permit us to remain over for a day or two.
Lieut. Jewett, my old friend of the Tenth Infantry, who
had accompanied us on our first march from San Antonio in 1870, tendered us his set of quarters, as his wife
was then absent at her home in Wisconsin.

General McCook, in behalf of his regiment, gave us "an
old fashioned frontier hop" or "baille," with a great dinner and all the trimmings. Everybody well enough to
"turn out" attended. It was a revelation how the ladies
managed to secure so much finery in such a short time,

but we always suspected that most of it was borrowed from their generous hostesses of the Fort McKavett garrison.

After the hop a party gathered in the house of the Adjutant, Lieut. Gibson. It was a convivial party. The song of the "Little Brown Jug" was being sung. Woman's curiosity prompted our better half to cross the next yard and see and hear what was going on. It was still raining. Gibson's two dogs saw the intruder. They made a break for her and she only escaped them by shutting a gate in their faces and beating a hasty retreat into the borrowed quarters—her curiosity well satisfied.

General McCook wore at the "baille" a great white Mexican sombrero, presented to him by the citizens of Matamoras, with his name heavily embroidered with gold and silver bullion on the brim, and as he danced "La Paloma" with our better half, and that ten gallon hat perched far back on his ears, he looked the part, a genial frontier host and true gentleman.

Generals McCook, Mackenzie and Lieut. Miller accompanied us on our next day's march and stayed in camp that night. The regimental quartermaster, Lieut. Gregory Barrett, had sent out forage by Lieut. Budd of the 9th Cavalry. We camped on a small creek, running into the South Llano, about 16 miles from the Post. Cold night, a "Norther" blowing.

A Mean Quartermaster

General Mackenzie directed me to make an early start the next morning. It was drizzling. I had warned our better half to be ready when the men were at the guy ropes to take down the tent, so that I would not be delayed. Colonel Beaumont had all that he could attend to in looking after his own family, although he had generously done much for my own. All was ready. The men were at the sides of the wet tent. A last little touch to the hair was being given in front of the little glass hung on the tent pole. Mackenzie was watching for me to "pull out" the train, so that General McCook could see how the Fourth Cavalry did the job. I was in a dilemna. What should I do? That tent had to go in the waiting wagon. Could I do a *mean act* or should I receive a reprimand from him? I shouted to the corporal, "Let her go, Corporal!" Down came the wet canvas on her head, wetting her face and hands. She darted or rather scrambled from under the flaps and with tears streaming down her face and with mortification in her voice, exclaimed, "You are the meanest man I ever knew in my life!" All that day the accusation haunted me and I chewed the cud of bitter reflection, but trying in the meantime to justify my apparently mean act by the exigencies of the service, and the warning which I had received from Mackenzie; also, my desire to maintain my reputation as a zealous, efficient quartermaster, at least until I should have reached Fort Clark, the end of our journey. I believed, however, that she would not understand all this—how could she? And that ample apology would have to be made for such an apparently mean act, before her righteous anger could be sufficiently appeased. Upon arrival in camp after a hard day with numerous breakdowns, exasperating delays, etc., and too dark to see her face as I met her, I was much amazed when she rushed at me and throwing her arms about me she anticipated any shame-faced apology I was prepared to make, by acknowledging her own fault. She was never dilatory after that.

The Travelling Tent

Our tent, a wall, was strongly pitched. It had on the ground, a square piece of canvas of the size of the tent; over it was spread a bright red and black figured, warm-looking rug, a relic from the "Land and Copper Mining Company," which had been presented to me when that Company had become defunct and had broken up. A small cast-iron conical stove, cast in three sections so that it could be telescoped, was set up in a small soap box filled with earth, which, when emptied each morning, served to contain it. The funnel, also conical and in several pieces, telescoped to one foot in length.

A small light fold-up bedstead, with bedding consisting of three pieces of moss mattress, for convenience in packing, and two heavy red 3 point Comanche issue blankets, completed, with two light folding canvas bottom camp chairs, the furniture of our travelling house. The stove funnel was carried through a slit in the seam of the tent, around which was wired a tin for protection for fire, about 9 inches square. Bessie, the baby, slept with Rhoda in an "A" tent pitched in rear of the wall tent. Mellie, 17 months older, slept on a leather army trunk. This was moved up to the side of the bed. Her mattress was a folded buffalo robe. A flannel lined wildcat skin robe was her cover. Candles burned brightly in the tent. A blazing fire of dry mesquite was in front of the open tent flaps, while a freshly dug mesquite root—which burned much like charcoal and held all night—warmed the inside. A rope slung from rear to front pole held all of the wraps and kept them dried out for use in the morning. Such, in brief, was our travelling soldier's home in the wilds of Texas when on the march, of which house, bed, carpet, stove, trunk and all of our belongings could be stored away in the wagons in less than 20 minutes when aroused by an early reveille for the day's march.

A mess chest filled with compartments, was arranged so that the outer lid turned back on its hinges upon a leg fitted with a hinge for a support. This formed one leaf, while a similar inner cover, also on hinges, unfolded in the opposite direction, forming the other, making a little table sufficiently large for a small family.

A Dutch oven for baking bread, coffee pots, fry pans, tin plates and some common unbreakable dishes formed the culinary department. Cooking always took place in the open air over open fires, and also eating, except during unusually stormy weather when the mess chest was pulled inside the tent flaps. When the storm raged without, and the rain pattered upon the canvas roof, the children were warmly sleeping, one under trusty Rhoda's care. They were not alarmed by the noisy coyotes or the dismal howling of wolves, neither did they know of the Indians stealthy tread, for the vigilant picket beyond the camp and the sleepless sentinel inside, closely watched and guarded them from all harm.

When camp was reached great care was had to prevent them from straying among the close chaparral and dense cactus which skirted it and thus be lost to view, and for this purpose a 30 foot rope or horse lariat was attached to their waists, to the end of which a 12 inch iron picket pin was attached which was driven firmly into the ground. Often they fell and pricked their hands on the thorn strewn ground, but they were safe. Milk was carried for them in canteens when it could be obtained at ranches, and kept cool by wetting blanket covers and hanging the canteens to the side of the Dougherty to swing in the breeze. Condensed milk was substituted for the mess when the genuine article was not obtainable. The command moved and camped early so as to avoid the heat of the day.

We met nobody on the road day after day except occasionally a party of wild, rollicking "cowpunchers" starting off for a "round up," with their lariats coiled at the pommels of their saddles and big branding irons, their lower limbs cased in "chaps" to protect them from the thorns while riding through the dense chaparral.

As we crossed the tortuous, winding Nueces River, ten or twelve times in one day, now over a dry, rocky bed, again through a clear, limpid, smoothly flowing stream, then across a rough, brawling, but not dangerous torrent, we frequently came to small shelfs, benches or *jump offs,* two or three feet perpendicular, which, being difficult, sometimes impossible, to cut down, the wagons had to drop over. On one occasion on "B" Company's wagon, which was loaded to the bows, with the sheets unloosed, was a light Concord buggy belonging to Major Manch, perched higher up. A soldier with reckless bravado sat in it. We all watched this wagon when it dropped with a dull thud into the rocky bed, expecting to see the man and buggy pitched half across the stream, but strange to say, aside from throwing him forward against the dasher and giving the whole "outfit" a good shake up, it rolled safely over to the opposite bank.

The cañon opened out with low mountains all about us, now in a beautiful sunny valley with fleeting shadows here and there, now through a wold, rocky gorge with the tree crowned precipices, again entering a little glen or dale, but always by the side of or crossing this beautiful running stream.

This march of 500 miles was made and after 27 days of almost constant travelling, the two baby sisters, without cold, and with only a few cactus thorns in their hands, and the usual number of "chiggers" under their skin, were safely landed in their new home in blissful ignorance of the many dangers and hardships through which they had passed.

As we approached the South the country grew more green and beautiful and after crossing the South Llano River we traversed a fine rolling and well watered country. We now came to the cañon of the Nueces. It was rough, rocky, narrow and dangerous at times owing to cloud bursts and swollen torrents. Our camp on the night of the 28th was in a live oak grove at two ponds, just below which a small stream gushed out and spreading out formed the head of the Nueces. Hills surrounded us on all sides. It was a bright moonlight night and a beautiful camp. On the 31st we were still crossing and recrossing this beautiful stream and along a hard road which had been built but a short time before by the 24th Infantry, and, at places, seemed to have been hewed out of the solid rock. When it became narrow, ropes were placed over the wagons, men were placed at them on the upside and thus they were eased around the slides and curves. Our camp this night was on the West Fork of the Nueces. Here we began to find many species of cacti. The water was so clear that the men were shooting fish with their carbines in the river, which were plentiful.

After a 16 mile march passing through masses of prickly pear and cactus of every variety, and over an open country with the Las Moras mountains to the right of the road in full view, we arrived at the Las Moras Springs.

Fort Clark

The column rode into a spacious live oak grove at the base of the hill where Fort Clark was located. The ground was dry, baked and intolerably dusty and dirty by having been used for a camp for a number of years. A large detail was soon at work cleaning up the ground and after sprinkling down the dust with an improvised watering cart, it proved to be a most delightful camp in spite of all the dirt.

The post was now commanded by Lieut. Colonel (Brevet Major General) Wesley Merritt, the ''Boy General'' of Sheridan's old Cavalry Corps of the Army of the Potomac during the Civil War, and we were compelled to remain in this camp until the companies of the Ninth Cavalry, which now occupied the quarters, should move out. Two of my classmates, Hughes and Gerhard, were here.

We remained in this camp until April 11. On the 10th it was rumored that Secretary of War, W. Belknap, and General Sheridan, would arrive from San Antonio and that General Mackenzie would accompany them. An escort was sent out on the road to meet them on the 11th and at 6 P. M. all of the Fourth and Ninth Cavalry officers called to pay their respects.

The Big Baille

There was a ''hop'' at night given by the officers of the Ninth Cavalry in honor of the arrival of the distinguished guests and of the Fourth. It began just after tattoo roll call.

All was bustle among the ladies in camp. Finery, almost forgotten, was dragged from the remotest corners of the trunks. Owing to our early morning starts and the lack of conveniences at our many halting places or camps, hair that had long been neglected and more or less tangled, snarled and filled with alkali dust and the accumulations of long travel, had to be taken down, washed, dried and combed. It was Rhoda's job in our family. Her first exclamation was, "Laws, Miss Mary, you ought to see your haid!" "Well, what is the matter, Rhoda?" "It's just plum full of 'em!" The horror of the situation suddenly crept upon the family and explained, to some degree, the itching that had been experienced to a noticeable degree since leaving Fort Concho. That matinée one day with the Comanche squaws in the prison corral at Fort Concho had now borne fruit and had reached the climax. "What shall I do, Rhoda?" "I'll fix um," said Rhoda. Making a strong solution with black plug tobacco, she soaked the hair in a basin, then using plenty of lard the trick was done, or partly so. The strong tobacco caused intense nausea, the lard caused the hair to tangle into an almost uncombable mass, the result of which was to compel Rhoda to use shears to cut out most of the under mass, wait all of the rest of the time to dry out the balance, to cover up the gouges and make the head presentable. Upon making a careful canvas of the camp it was soon found that all of the ladies who had visited the prisoners at Fort Concho proved to be in the same predicament, but mustering up all the pent up courage they had and without disclosing the awful secret to the officers all went to that hop except one, and our better half, with that dark secret under her hair danced La Paloma, this time with General Sheridan and promenaded with the Secretary of War.

On the 12th the Secretary, Generals Sheridan, Mackenzie and Merrit had a prolonged conference over the Mexican situation which had been growing more and more tense. An inspection and review of the 4th Cavalry was had at which the writer acted as Adjutant and that same day both of our distinguished visitors departed for San Antonio.

On the 12th four companies of the 9th Cavalry moved out of the post into camp with us, which crowded the ground, and on the 14th we moved into the post. Lieut. D. F. Stiles of the 10th Infantry generously volunteered to give up his quarters to myself and family. They consisted of a 10 foot hallway running through a captain's set of quarters, which had been partitioned to make two small rooms. These were the old original quarters made of squared logs in 1852 by the 1st Infantry. On either side of this hall were Capt. John Craig and Lieut. Joel T. Kirkman, both of the 10th Infantry.

I was now securely installed in my new home at Fort Clark, until our next move with Mackenzie, which was his great raid into Mexico and which forms a chapter by itself.

General C. C. Augur,

(Copy)

Washington, D. C., Feb. 5, 1873.

"Headquarters Army of the United States,

Comdg. Dept. of Texas.

General:—

The President wishes you to give great attention to affairs on the Rio Grande Frontier, especially to prevent the raids of Indians and Mexicans upon the people and property of Southern and Western Texas.

To this end he wishes the 4th Cavalry to be moved to that Frontier, and it will be replaced by the 7th Cavalry to be drawn from the Department of the South. The 7th Cavalry is now scattered but it is believed the whole can reach Louisville or Memphis by or before the 10th of March. And if the Red River is up as it ought to be at that period of the year, the Regiment will be at or near Fort Richardson in all March. Its strength is now reported 1021 enlisted men, and the horses are believed to be in splendid order. This Regiment can replace the 4th in North West Texas. The 4th, as soon as it is safe to move, should march to the Rio Grande, and the ninth can be broken up into detachments to cover the Western Frontier and road toward New Mexico.

In naming the 4th for the Rio Grande the President is doubtless influenced by the fact that Col. MacKenzie is young and enterprising, and that he will impart to his Regiment his own active character.

I have the honor to be,

Your obedient servant,

(Sgnd) W. T. Sherman,

General."

Official copy furnished General Sheridan for his information.

Wm. D. Whipple,

Asst. Adjt. Genl.

CHAPTER XVI

The Mackenzie Raid
Into
Mexico
Fort Clark. Its Location

FORT CLARK, Texas, is situated in Kinney County, latitude 29° 17′ North, longitude 23° 18′ West, at an approximate elevation of 1,000 feet above the sea. It is 125 miles west of San Antonio de Bexar, and 45 miles north of Fort Duncan, at Eagle Pass, opposite Piedras Negras, Mexico, on the Rio Grande River.

Its location is on a rocky ridge of limestone, at the foot of which is a magnificent live-oak grove. Amidst its cool, inviting shadows, bubbling and sparkling from a clear and crystal pool, a series of beautiful springs, called the Las Moras (the Mulberries) emerge into a smooth and narrow, but sluggish stream. It forms the source of the river or creek bearing the same name, which, flowing on some eighteen or twenty miles, mingles its waters with the "Rio Bravo" or Rio Grande, our International Boundary Line.

Clark was an old infantry post in 1852, which had been built by the First U. S. Infantry, just after the Mexican War. In May, 1873,* it had not been rebuilt, and the delapidated and limited quarters, many of them rude log huts, proved anything but inviting to the wearied troopers of the Fourth United States Cavalry, just arrived from Fort Richardson, one of the line of extreme Western posts, and now bivouacked among the delightful live-oaks re-

---

*This story was first published in "The Outing magazine (Poultney Bigelow, Editor) in 1886. It was illustrated by Frederick Remington, R. F. Zogbaum, Kelley and other artists. It has long been out of print. The plates for illustration were destroyed. It has now been revised and rewritten at the urgent request of many of the writer's friends and brother officers of the army. As reconstructed it contains many additional incidents and details not before included in the original story.
Since then the private correspondence of General Mackenzie has been secured by the writer, giving the negotiations with Mexican officials for the release of the Indian prisoners, etc., and how very strained were our relations with Mexico.
The story was also reprinted in 1921 in the Uvalde Leader-News, of Texas, at the urgent request of an old sergeant (John B. Charlton) of the Fourth U. S. Cavalry, who was a stock raiser at Uvalde for many years after his discharge from the army, and who died there in March 1922. It was also published in the National Tribune, Washington, D. C., by special request of its editor, in 1929.

ferred to, waiting for the Ninth Cavalry to vacate the post.

The heat during the first hours of the day was almost overpowering, but in the early afternoon a cool, refreshing breeze from the Gulf of Mexico, sprung up, tempering the air to a soft balminess, and from that time until midnight all of the garrison lived out of doors, under the low, broad, vine-covered verandas or porches—built about all the quarters—from which our te-na-jas or water coolers (for ice was unknown) swung from their blanket covers in the air. The evenings were particularly fine, warm and dry, requiring no outside wraps.

We were, indeed, in a tropical climate. The water from the deep springs was cold and delicious, and the water cresses, everywhere in the greatest abundance along the banks of the Las Moras, furnished us with a crisp and delicate salad for our morning and evening meals.

Le Boulevard de Brackettville

Opposite the Post, beyond the creek, on a low, flat piece of land, almost in the mesquite chaparral, is a small town named Brackettville, the county seat of Kinney County, the exact counterpart of Jacksboro, near Fort Richardson, the ulcer of every garrison, an inevitable fungus growth, sometimes improved, but scarcely ever eradicated without much care and trouble.* Its composition varied somewhat, but there were the inevitable adobe houses, Mexican ranches or "shacks," huts, "jacals" and picket stores, profusely plastered with mud, used for whisky shops, gambling saloons, etc., Mexican "greasers," half-breeds of every hue and complexion, full-blooded descendants of the African persuasion, low down whites and discharged soldiers, with no visible occupation, composed the population, and at night a fusillade of shots warned us that it was unsafe venturing over after dark on the one, crooked, unlighted and wretched street—Le Boulevard de Brackettville.

---

*Lieut. H. W. Lawton (later Major-Gen. of Volunteers), R.Q.M. Fourth Cavalry, begun reconstructing it that year.

The Cavalry "Baille" and Inspection

On the 11th of April, the Secretary of War, General Belknap, and General Sheridan arrived, which created no little stir in camp, for we did not then know the object of their visit. The command was carefully inspected, and at night a brilliant "Baille" or "hop" was given by the Ninth Cavalry, partly complimentary to our distinguished guests, and especially in honor of the arrival of the Fourth Cavalry. Gen. Wesley Merritt commanded the post of Fort Clark.

On the occasion of this inspection, by direction of General Ranald S. Mackenzie, then commanding the regiment, I acted as regimental Adjutant. It was a mounted field inspection, and the Secretary and General Sheridan reviewed the Command. They both expressed great satisfaction, and Mackenzie seemed much pleased, for the regiment was then, after several strenuous Indian Campaigns for some years past, at the full maximum of its field efficiency in horses, arms, equipment and rigid discipline. Its personnel in enlisted men, especially in its non-com-officers, some of whom had been officers in fighting volunteer regiments during the Civil War, could not have been excelled in any army in the world.

Later (about 1888).

Gen. H. W. Lawton, who had been Regimental Quartermaster (later killed in the P. I.), told the writer at the War Department, when he was a Major and Assistant Inspector General, that the Inspection Reports for years had placed the Fourth Cavalry at the head (No. 1) of all the Cavalry regiments in the U. S. Army in general merit.

The regiment left Fort Richardson, March 4, 1873, the headquarters having been transferred to Fort Concho, Texas, a few weeks before. We arrived at Fort Clark, April 1, after a long, hard and very tedious march during which I acted as quartermaster. Prior to these dates and for some months before receiving our orders to relieve the Ninth Cavalry on the Rio Grande, the Indians and Mexicans had been raiding across the river in both large and

small marauding bands, plundering and killing the settlers
and ranchmen, and running off their horses, mules and
cattle. A Joint Commission was then in session at Eagle
Pass, near Fort Duncan, trying to adjust claims amount-
ing to millions of dollars made by the ranchmen. There
had seemed to be more or less indifference or indecision
by Gen. Merritt, then commanding the Ninth Cavalry, in
dealing with these murderous cut throats, bandits and
thieves.

The Mysterious Conference

A few days after our arrival, there was an important
conference at Gen. Merritt's quarters between the Secretary of War, General Sheridan and Mackenzie. I was
not present, but later Mackenzie told me the substance of
it, when I was so suddenly called into his confidence. It
was almost word for word, from my subsequent notes, as
follows: Gen. Sheridan started it:

"Mackenzie, you have been ordered down here to relieve Gen. Merritt and the Ninth Cavalry because I want
something done to stop these conditions of banditry, killing, etc., etc., by these people across the river. I want
you to *control* and *hold down* the situation, and to *do it
in your own way.*.. I want you to be bold, enterprising, and
at all times *full of energy,* when you begin, let it be a
campaign of *annihilation, obliteration* and *complete destruction,* as you have always in your dealings done to all
the Indians you have dealt with, etc. I think you understand what I want done, and the way you should employ
your force," etc.

Mackenzie, for the moment, was completely obsessed by
Sheridan's manner, and of his complete confidence, not
only in his initiative, but will to carry out any plan he
(M.) might make.

"Gen. Sheridan, under whose orders and upon what authority am I to act? Have you any plans to suggest, or
will you issue me the necessary orders for my action?"

Sheridan, much to Mackenzie's amazement, replied in

his most impressive, vigorous, vehement manner. He pounded the table as he spoke and gestured. "Damn the *orders!* Damn the *authority.* You are to go ahead on your own plan of action, and your authority and backing shall be Gen. Grant and myself. With us behind you in whatever you do to clean up this situation, you can rest assured of the fullest support. You must assume the risk. We will assume the final responsibility should any result."

The Nocturnal Visit

The regimental headquarters with "I" Troop were daily expected from Fort Concho and pending their arrival and the Adjutant, Lieut. Leopold O. Parker, I was summoned rather unexpectedly one night, by Gen. Mackenzie, who came to the door of my quarters. I was Officer of the Day, and, with my sash on and sabre unhooked and lying across a chair, was waiting for midnight so that I could inspect my guard and patrol the town of Brackettville to quell any disturbance that might occur among the mongrel crowd that, in those days, generally infested a border town. It was nearly 12 o'clock.

Mackenzie was very intense in speech and action. He said, "Is Mrs. Carter abed and asleep?" The question rather startled me, but upon answering in the affirmative, he continued: "What are you going to do now?" I answered: "I am about to inspect my guard, and then patrol B." "Very well! As soon as you have performed that duty, and without letting anybody know where you are going, I wish to see you at my quarters as soon as possible!"

Upon arriving at his house, about the only frame building then in the garrison, I found him *very nervous* and *uneasy.* I felt that he had something very important on his mind, or in his system, which he was feeling compelled to get rid of. I was inwardly guessing whether I was to be made a victim of some charge he was about to spring upon me, and ransacking my brain as to what I could pos-

sibly have done, and whether I had better plead guilty in
advance. There was evidently a great mystery incubat-
ing. He frequently arose before stating his business,
looked about the rooms, and, going outside, walked around
the quarters and closely watched to see that there were no
listeners.

He then, in strictest confidence, informed me that
through some renegade Mexicans and half-breeds he was
possessed of certain knowledge with reference to the Indians who, just previous to our arrival at Fort Clark, had
raided up the Nueces Valley, and committed the massacre
at Howard's Wells in which an officer of the Ninth Cavalry
had been killed. He had ascertained their exact locality,
number, etc., their trail, with stolen stock, led back across
the Rio Grande, and he should immediately commence
preparations for an expedition against them. He proposed to punish them for the past, and check their raids
in the future. At this interview, he gave me in detail all
that had passed between the Secretary of War, General
Sheridan and himself, at their conference in April. He
had selected three guides to do the scout work, etc. One
man Ike Cox, the post guide, a reliable and trustworthy
man, the others were half breeds, Green Van and McLain,
both first class men, who knew the country even better
than Cox. Both owned ranches along the river on the
American side, they, with Ike Cox, had lost some of their
stock. They were sent over the river some time in advance of our move, to the villages of these Indians, some
60 to 70 miles in Mexico, to ascertain their numbers, and
to locate all the accessible roads, routes and trails leading
to them, especially for rapid night travelling, with nothing
but the stars for points of direction. These fine scouts
and guides were absolutely faithful, truthful and trustworthy and did their work most thoroughly. Relying
upon Gen. Sheridan's declaration of absolute support,
Mackenzie said he should not hesitate to take the risk.
It *"was make or break!"*

Confidential Adviser

At his dictation (no telegraph stations, automobiles, air-planes, radios, stenographers or typewriters were available at that period) I wrote a detailed letter to the department commander, the nature of which it might not be proper or wise for me, even at this late day, to divulge; and having enjoined the strictest secrecy upon me until the expedition had proved a success or failure, I left his quarters at daybreak a very much burdened soldier—for *my wife* was included in the sacred pledge he had exacted. I was a *marked man* for four weeks. I was, in the meantime, shown a reply from department headquarters, authorizing the necessary supplies, on requisitions which I had made out on that night, for an expedition, the destination of which was known only to Mackenzie and myself.

Preparations went steadily on until about May 15th. Horses were carefully shod, pack animals and saddles overhauled, ammunition obtained in large quantities, sabres ground, etc. The companies were sent singly, or two or more together into grazing camps near the Post; some at Piedras Pintos, Turkey Creek, etc. This was for the ostensible purpose of recuperating the horses, which had been somewhat reduced in flesh by long marches, and to allay suspicion among the officers and men, or in the town of B. as to Mackenzie's ultimate object he might have in view. Here the men were drilled and subjected to the most rigid discipline; target ranges were laid out and carbine practice given every day; company, platoon, and every movement in column and in line, mounted and dismounted, was thoroughly worked out, especially rapid fighting on foot and to the right and left. This dispersion of the command would also admit of its movement without disclosing the object to prying eyes about the Post, who, interested in the stolen stock, closely watched the garrison. Besides there were many Mexican spies who professed to be living in Brackettville and engaged in business. As the town was but a few hundred yards away, it was easy for them to cross the creek and lurk about the post, especially at night.

McLain, the Scout, had been in the Indian villages, had reported his knowledge gained to the General, and all was now nearly ripe for the start. Upon more than one occasion I felt that Mackenzie had doubted my good faith, or, at least that, for some reason or other, his suspicions had been aroused.

A Burdensome Secret

At "stables" one evening, he beckoned me to him, with an impatient snap of his finger stubs (he had lost parts of two during the Civil War). "You have told L— the secret I reposed in you!"

"I beg your pardon, sir, but I have not!"

"You have, then, told your wife!"

"You are mistaken, sir, I have not told a soul, unless in my dreams. Why do you doubt my absolute loyalty and sincerity?"

"Well, but L— says *he* knows that *you* know, and says he can find it all out through *you* or your *wife,* just where this secret expedition is going."

"Yes, but Gen. Mackenzie, *that* is an entirely different matter. He *has not* found out a thing through me, nor will he. Of this you can absolutely rest assured!"

And yet L— was his *trusted* assistant, making preparations in detail to go—where, he knew not.

The "L" here referred to, was H. W. Lawton, then a First Lieutenant, and regimental quartermaster. During the Spanish-American War he became a Major General of volunteers, and was killed at San Mateo, P. I., Dec. 19, 1899. He was a great favorite of Mackenzie's, not only on account of his splendid war record, having been mustered out of the service in 1865 as a Lieutenant Colonel, commanding his regiment (30th Indiana Vols.) at the end of the Civil War, but particularly because of his intense energy and purpose, and exceptional ability as a Quartermaster, both in construction work in a Post, and in the field, where his knowledge, practical common sense and resourceful makeshifts made him especially valuable to a man of Mackenzie's peculiar temperament, methods and demands. I had, however, been especially warned not to reveal to him the object of our expedition or its destination.[*]

Lawton was then unmarried. He would, however, and generally at the wrong time—and this was generally known throughout the old Army—indulge in a weakness, and when in this condition grew *very loquacious* and *confidential*. At all other times he was always singularly *reserved* and *reticent,* sometimes painfully distant. At such times—when he grew talkative—Mackenzie always deemed it wise not to confide any of his campaign or military secrets to L—especially now when he was taking so much risk—even jeopardizing his future career—and when so much depended on absolute secrecy for his probable success.

While Gen. Augur, commanding the Department of Texas, knew, and possibly through Gen. Sheridan, the probable object of this expedition, neither Lawton nor, as I have stated, any of the troop commanders had the slightest clue. All they knew was that "an expedition is being prepared to take the field," etc.

I was especially directed to see, in as quiet a way as possible, that all sabres in the Command were ground to a *razor edge.* This stunt was a very great "puzzler" to all the old Captains, especially to Wilcox, O'Connell, Beaumont, Davis, and McLaughlin, who in some of their "kicks" and "grouches" against such a "fool proposition," came near "spilling all the fat in the fire," and some doubted my authority for such an almost *"unheard of"* thing, for we had never, thus far, *carried such encumbrances as sabres on an ordinary Indian Campaign.* But

---

[*]In a book recently published by Dorrance and Co. of Philadelphia (1929), General James Parker. U.S.A., retired, states that Lawton was not only Mackenzie's "right hand man" but his *"confidential adviser."* *It was not so*—as is here shown.

I finally carried my point, by quietly quoting that well
worn old Army phrase, "It is *by direction* of the Commanding Officer." All this time I was *acting as Adjutant.*
Most of the officers quizzed me, Lawton among the rest,
and generally he was the most strenuous, saying, *"I ought
to know."*

My Company was Troop "A," commanded by Captain
E. B. Beaumont brevet Colonel U. S. A., who had graduated from West Point in May, 1861, served as a staff officer on Gen. John Sedgwick's Staff, commanding the old
Sixth Corps; and was with him when he was killed at
Spottsylvania C. H. May 9, 1864; also on Gen. James H.
Wilson's Staff when he commanded the Cavalry troops
of the Western Army (Military Division of the Mississippi) which rode through the heart of the Confederacy
in 1865, and captured Jefferson Davis. Beaumont was
given personal charge of him (D.) after his capture. He
was one of the finest types of an "all around," efficient
Cavalry soldier I have ever known, and has been especially
referred to in the Chapter, "The Wedding Tour of an
Army Bride," et seq.

The Alarm—"Pack Up"

Our camp was upon the Piedras Pintos (Painted Stones)
Creek. I had just returned from a moonlight tour among
the luxuriant chaparral, everywhere about our delightful
camp, after an unsuccessful search for mescal and aguar-
diente (brandy) peddlers who, knowing that the men had
been recently paid, had ventured forth from the slum
depths of Brackettville to sell them this vile liquor and
thus demoralize them. I was Officer of the Day. I had
inspected my guard, and was lying by the side of Col.
Beaumont, half drowzing, when the loud clattering of
hoofs were suddenly heard, causing both of us to sit up
in our blankets, and Major Clarence Mauck rode hurriedly into camp from Fort Clark and gave orders from
Mackenzie to "pack up" and "saddle up" immediately.
He got up from a sick bed to carry this order. It was be-

tween 2 and 3 A. M. Col. Beaumont turning to me, said: "What is the meaning of this—where are we going?" I quietly replied, "Quien Sabe?—perhaps across the Rio Grande." He asked me no further questions. There had been no time given to say farewell to our families. We had not seen them for a week or more. All was soon busy preparation. Crackling camp fires were at once started so that we could see to pack by and, at early dawn, led by Ike Cox, the Post guide (McLain and Green Van being with Mackenzie), we filed out of our comfortable camp and marching rapidly across country, arrived about 8:30 o'clock at our rendezvous on the Las Moras, and dismounting, awaited the arrival of Gen. Mackenzie, with two troops from Clark, and troop "M" from Fort Duncan which, having lost its way, did not arrive until nearly 1 P. M. This was May 17, 1873. An hour later, the entire column of six companies, A, B, C, E, I, and M, and a detachment (20) of Seminole Negro, or half-breed enlisted scouts under the command of First Lieutenant John L. Bullis, Twenty-fourth Infantry, nearly 400 men, were moving slowly for the ford of the "Rio Bravo." There was no immediate need of haste for our object was to delay crossing the river until after dark.

In this extreme Southern latitude, the sun now high in the heavens, beat down with terrific force upon our heads. There were no sun strokes or heat prostrations, however, for we had before found it necessary to protect our heads with wet sponges fitted into the hat of every officer and man in the Command, and all were now provided with them. The heat was scalding, almost stifling. Several short halts were made, and at the last one, shortly before dark, at the ford near the mouth of the Las Moras where we were to cross the river, Mackenzie briefly explained the objects of the expedition, the probable results, the possible risks every officer and man would incur in our invasion of Mexican soil. If wounded, capture might mean hanging, the death of a felon, or, with back against a wall, his body riddled by Mexican or Indian bullets.

This talk had not, however, yet released me from my burdensome secret, for the fact that he was acting without *orders* or *authority* from our Government, or that he was taking the precious lives in that column over the Rio Grande, with merely the *implied permission* which Gen. Sheridan had given or *suggested* to him at their conference in April at Fort Clark, he *had not disclosed in the talk at this last halt,* and, as will later be shown, such disclosure came about purely by accident. I was still pledged to secrecy, and it weighed heavily upon me.

All officers in the Command believed implicitly that he had those orders from the War Department, and nobody thought then of asking any questions or suggesting otherwise. His conference with the Secretary of War, Sheridan and Merritt in April had disarmed all suspicion. Only Mackenzie and myself in that trusting command knew to the contrary, and the possible outcome of failure or disaster from any indeterminate or unforeseen cause. He (Mackenzie) had revolved all these chances in his own mind, and doubtless had carefully canvassed pro and con all probabilities and possibilities.

He had told me on the night I had spent with him writing letters, making out requisitions, and assisting him in his plans by suggestions, etc., that he expected he might be placed in arrest and tried by Court Martial for what might possibly prove to be a wrong interpretation of Sheridan's hints and strenuous urging, and his dismissal demanded, but he should, nevertheless, rely most implicitly on Sheridan's assurance that in whatever action he took both he (S.) and Gen. Grant would back him up to the utmost limit, and he did not fear that should the Country be aroused through International complications or a hostile press, either Grant or Sheridan would permit him to become the *"scape goat."* They were not that kind of men, and he knew both to be his warm friends. Gen. Grant refers to him in his personal Memoirs as *"The most promising young officer in the Army."*

The Start—Ford the Rio Grande

Notwithstanding the spectral ghost of a gibbet or a blank firing wall before our eyes, and the already tired condition of those who had then marched over twenty miles, all were in excellent spirits and full of hope and confidence. The river was reached shortly after eight P. M., sufficiently dark to cross without being seen. We waited for some time in the middle of the stream, the water being about up to our saddle girths, for the head of the column to gain the opposite bank, which, steep and treacherous, retarded its advance and had to be cut down. Our reflections were only disturbed by the murmuring of the water and the impatient splashing of our animals. All talking was ordered to cease. A low "forward!" We stemmed the swift current and a few moments later scrambled over the low but steep bank, into the dense canebreak that borders the stream above and below the ford. We debouched from the chaparral upon open ground. It was now too dark to distinguish anything but the dim forms of the moving horses and men. We were indeed upon the soil of Mexico, and without further delay, the start was made for a night's ride upon the distant Indian villages.*

"Terreno Desconocido"

West of Fort Clark and the Rio Grande in the Mexican Republic, lies the Bolsón de Mapini, a dreary, almost waterless waste of mountains and trackless deserts. Secure in this wold region the Apaches for three centuries defied the efforts of the Spanish troops, necessitating the presence of large garrisons on the route from New Mexico via Chihauha to Monterey, to protect the settlements and supply escorts for trains and travellers. So little was known of this desolate region by the whites that it appears on

---

*Five miles southeast of the Las Moras is the town of Quemado, Texas, and opposite is Moral, Mexico, southeast of Tunenez. Somewhere between Quemado and the mouth of the Las Moras the column crossed going in. It is called the "Sycamore Ford." Neither the Mexican Int. R. R. nor the G. H. & S. A. R. R. had been built in 1873, and there were no defined roads or trails. We either followed blind mule trails or those the guides made from their knowledge of the country.

the maps as Terreno Desconocido (Unknown Land) and
a remnant of the once powerful Apaches dwelt among its
mountains, but had changed the scene of their depredations to the soil of Texas. They had a good market in
Mexico for their stolen horses, mules and cattle. This,
however, is in strict accordance with the laws of compensation, for it is not much over a quarter of a century since
powerful bands of Comanches and kindred murderous
thieves, whose villages lined the banks of the Llano, San
Saba and Concho Rivers, plundered the frontiers of Mexico and found a market in Texas. Fredericksburg, a German frontier settlement about 75 miles northwest of San
Antonio, was a regular horse mart and there were then
living old citizens of this little settlement who had witnessed the return of bands of plunderers exulting in their
fine show of horses and scalps of women and children and
whose savage, drunken orgies have chilled the life blood
of the peacefully disposed citizens of those Texas border
towns. Detailed maps of this Unknown Land were non-
existent. Joined with the Apaches were bands of Lipans
and Kickapoos, all actuated by deadly hostility to the
Texans. Issuing from their mountain retreats, they traveled by night across the plains and mountains, hid by day
among the numerous ravines and cedar brakes, and then
suddenly swooping down upon some unprotected ranch,
cruelly murdered the wretched inhabitants, drove off the
stock, and sometimes carried off the helpless women and
children into captivity. Small parties drove off the horses
and mules from different parts of the country, and, assembling far out on the ''Staked Plains'' where few white
men had ever dared to venture, and where lack of water
made it dangerous to penetrate without a guide, they
rested and leisurely retreated into Mexico. Of the period
of which I write, their broad stock trails crossing the more
narrow buffalo trails were everywhere visible.

The Kickapoos were, if possible, the most relentless towards the Texans, by whom they were wantonly attacked
while peacefully emigrating during the Civil War from

their Reservation in the United States. The Texans, it is reported, were routed with great loss, but, from that day Texas was considered fair ground for Kickapoo raids and all murders there as justifiable retaliation. Rumor has it that the Texans refused to recognize a flag of truce of the Kickapoos, and killed a squaw by whom it was carried. To the credit of the Texans, it is also said that the command to a large extent were opposed to interfering with the peaceful march of the Kickapoos, who were committing then no depredations, but the hot headed young men insisted upon fighting and fired upon the flag. It is to be hoped that the latter bore the brunt of the fight and the well merited punishment which the Texans, it was reported, duly received.

These affiliated bands of Indians then, Kickapoo, Lipans, Pottawottamies and Mescalro Apaches, were the ones we were to attack and punish as soon as we should arrive within striking distance of their far distant villages.

The Night Ride In Mexico

At about 10 o'clock the head of the column emerged from the dense cane break and chaparral, and interminable river bottom, and winding through a rocky ravine ascended to open rolling ground, when the order to trot was given, and away sped the somber troopers, startling the dwellers in the lonely ranches when the dull thunder of tramping hoofs rose and fell as the rapid human torrent poured across plains or plunged into ravines. Lights disappeared from dwellings as if by magic, and perhaps many a devoted mother clasped her babe to her breast in mortal terror at this unusual and ominous roar at the dread hour of midnight.

The night was soft and warm. The moon rose, but, partially hidden by a light haze, shed an uncertain light upon the moving column. The gait increased. We rode rapidly, going where—we knew not—led by the half-breed guides on their fox-gaited beasts. They knew the importance of reaching the villages by daybreak, as planned, in order to surprise the enemy; also had measured the distance, and spared not their horses.

Our gait, therefore, was constantly changed, increasing from a fast walk to a "trot out," then a slow gallop or lope, again to a pushing trot and a rapid fox-gait, in speed between a walk and trot. Sometimes the dust so obscured the column it was with the greatest difficulty the rear companies could be "closed up;" every break or arroya would string the animals out "by file," which required later, a gallop to close up on the advance.

The Dilemma

The file closers or duty sergeants were kept busy. It was now becoming painfully evident, however, that our pack mules, no longer in sight, could not keep up such a speed and would so impede our progress before morning as to make our arrival on time uncertain, for it was ascertained that the train had sagged so far behind that it was then several miles to the rear. The mules had been heavily packed, and such a rapid gait had proved too much for them. We were then using the old *"Saw-Buck" pack saddle,* the Aparejo not yet having come into use. The more experienced packers of a later date could, by readjusting the loads, and lightening them, or even cutting them down to half rations, have avoided much of this condition which was now becoming serious, for a column such as ours, scheduled to attack at daybreak, can only move as fast as its *slowest unit,* and this slowly *impeding unit* was the *slowest mule* in that pack train.

It has been said that only the Lord or a *"mule whacker"* could inspire fear and speed in a pack mule. Lieut. George A. Thurston of my old Troop ("E") had charge this night of the pack train and whatever rear guard was with it, and Thurston was neither the Lord nor a mule driver, but faithful, *loyal* and *slow.* It was, besides, more than probable that this serious situation had not yet occurred to him, and he was doing his "level best." It suddenly dawned upon somebody's brain, too, that there was an ever growing danger that the Indians or Mexicans, or both, upon discovering our trail from the river, might cut it at almost any moment, and get, not only our food packs but all the mules if in sufficiently strong force to attack the rear guard.

Captains Wilcox and Mauck came to me at this moment, between 12 and 1 o'clock, and urged me in the strongest possible manner, and this request was at once vigorously backed up by Beaumont and O'Connell, to ride to the head of the column and suggest that the "packs be cut loose," presenting this problem in all its dangerous possibilities to Mackenzie. "You know him better than the rest of us," was the appeal. "You have been his Acting Adjutant and confidential adviser in the preparations for this expedition. You know how to reach him," etc., etc. All this was re-echoed by all. No time was to be lost. Mackenzie thus far seemed to be in blissful ignorance of such a situation or of its possible results.

I felt that it was a *bold suggestion,* to sacrifice all of our precious and much needed rations at the outset of an Indian raid, or invasion of foreign soil. But I also felt that what they stated was true and knew that such action was absolutely necessary and at once. I hesitated, and they saw it. I knew that even before we had started how nervous, irritable and irascible Mackenzie had been. However, there was no time to lose, I must risk it. I rode up the length of the rapidly pushing column at a hard gallop, mounted on a 3/4 thoroughbred silver roan horse that nothing could tire. He was in the "pink" of condition. I passed C, B, and I Troops, and reached General Mackenzie. The guides on each side of him were tense, every muscle set. As I surmised when I asked him, there was an explosion. Up to this hour he was absolutely ignorant of any difficulty in the rear, or that all was not going well. I *modestly* opened up the subject. Well! for about a minute one would have known that something besides the pack train *had* "*turned loose.*" But my *persuasive* language, after he had somewhat exhausted his vocabulary, soon became convincing, and I was rewarded with—

"Cut the Packs Loose!"

"Yes! tell the troop commanders I'll halt, and give just *five minutes* to 'cut the packs loose'. Tell the men to fill their pockets with hard bread."

Time was very precious. At Mackenzie's suggestion, I went to the rear, the entire length of the column, shouting this order, and then on back until the pack train was reached. I urged Thurston forward. The mules were fast becoming exhausted with their heavy loads and moving at such a pace. I helped him to close up, and supervised the cutting off of the packs and filling the men's pockets with hard bread. The knives flashed, and the mules, freed of their burdens, trotted along like kittens the remainder of the night. But, although we had no further trouble with them, now running loose with the column, they had already, by this delay, prevented our reaching the villages at daybreak, and attacking at that hour; also the probable capture of many Lipans who, it became known later, had gone out hunting in the mountains at a very early hour, before our arrival.

We again moved forward—not always on an air line, but along the path of least resistance—our general direction being Southwest. Sometimes when crossing a ravine, and when the rear was delayed, the only general guide we had was the almost blinding dust ahead, through which the moon's rays faintly glimmered. Sleep almost over-powered us, and yet, on, on we went. Conversation had long ago begun to lag. Nothing was heard save the ceaseless pounding of the horses and the jingle of the saddle equipment. It seemed as though the long night of fatigue, discomfort and thirst would never cease.

The gray of early dawn slowly crept upon us. Then the first faint gleam of daylight streaked the horizon. When day breaks upon the prairie nature appears the personification of death—cold, dreary and hopeless. The

faces of the troopers are pallid and corpse-like; but when
the glorious sun pours its golden flood of light upon the
plain, the earth smiles and life and hope return.

A dazed, exhausted feeling had begun to steal over our
weary bodies, and we seemed sustained only by the exciting novelty of the occasion, and hope of success. For the
first time we ascertained that the guides, even with their
accurate knowledge of the country, and their unerring
skill and judgment had, notwithstanding our tremendous
gait, during the night, miscalculated the distance, and we
were still some miles from the villages. They had not
made sufficient allowance for our delay through the exhaustion of the pack mules. It was now suggested to the General to increase the gait to a swinging gallop, but even
now the pace was beginning to tell upon our animals, and
his judgment was opposed to it. He dared not *wind* or
"pump them out" before making the final charge which he
had planned at the decisive moment. The pace was
slightly increased, however, and mile after mile sped
rapidly by. It was a "killing" gait. At the head of the
column, as the daylight gradually increased, the half-
breeds, Green Van, McLain, and our sturdy old Post
Guide, Ike Cox, could now be seen constantly plying their
braided quirts, and with their heels vigorously helping
their beasts along, never swerving a hair from the general
direction taken the evening before. Those tireless guides
had seemed, from the start, full of dash and daring, and
were fully inspired with the spirit of the enterprise, now
so dependent upon their loyalty, skill, indomitable energy
and powers of endurance. Mackenzie and his Adjutant,
who had joined in time to accompany him, rode with the
guides, all followed by a small escort of selected orderlies.
Then the Seminole negro enlisted scouts, with ebony faces,
flat noses, and full lips, but the characteristic high cheek-
bones of the Indian, their long, black, crinkly hair plentifully powdered with alkali dust. In the rear, the men, in
column of fours, their bronze faces also covered with dust;
their slouched hats, of every conceivable shape, plentifully

sprinkled with the same. Their features, haggard with
loss of sleep, and the strain of the all night ride, gave them
a kind of hard, desperate appearance that would remind
one of pictures in our boyhood days, of brigands in their
raids for plunder and ransom money. An occasional
laugh, the nervous, shifting movements in the saddle of
these leg-weary troopers to relieve the aching limbs, the
short, dudheen pipe to console the tired frame and empty
stomach. All went to make up a picture such as was not
the good fortune of any "Our Artist on the Spot" to witness, much less to faithfully interpret.

On, on, we rapidly sped!

The exhilarating breezes of the Santa Rosa Mountains
now clearly visible, cool, dry and life-giving, gave us new
strength and action. We now commenced winding down
into a lovely valley, daylight streaming all over the land,
and soon had the satisfaction of hearing tinkling bells and
seeing several pony herds which scampered off at our approach.

The Rey Molina

Immediately after we struck the rocky bed of a stream,
thickly skirted with chaparral and small trees. Large,
round stones washed clean and smooth, and thrown to the
surface by many a flood, somewhat impeded our progress
at every step. The stream, a mere thread, soon became a
series of water holes or pools, from which man and beast
now drank in pleasurable companionship, washing the
dust from their long parched throats. This was the Rey
Molina. We were now close to our objective—our mission
of death. *"Dismount!"* was now the command; this with
no bugle calls. We slipped from our horses and shifting
the saddles word was passed along to re-cinch or tighten
the girths. A *rapid inspection of all arms was made.*
We were making ready for the charge, we were in the bed
of the stream, concealed by its banks. It was broad daylight. The sun tipped the mountains with its golden
touch. The blue azure of a cloudless Mexican sky, a calm

and peaceful day was full upon us. It was an inspiring sight as the column, again in motion, wound its way under cover of the fringe of bushes, toward the object of its terrible task. We were rapidly approaching the Indian village. All talking ceased, and the clatter of the horses' hoofs upon the stones, the jingling of spurs, and the rattle of equipments grew almost painful.[*]

Prepare to Attack

The column was rapidly but silently closed up, every man in his place. As we debouched from the dry bed of the stream, and were beginning to wind around the base of a hill, we saw hurried preparations made ahead which indicated our very near approach to the scene of conflict. Men began earnestly to look at their weapons, and quietly prepare for the fight. Runners from the front traversed the length of the column with hurried orders which were repeated in low commands to the men. They were now fully alert and as steady as clocks. The pack trains were "turned out," "fours" were counted, file closers and all non-commissioned officers were cautioned in their duties. We commenced to descend a long slope, upon which, scattered here and there were thick patches of prickly pear, many cacti of every variety, and the ever present Spanish bayonet and mesquite. At the foot of the slope we could now clearly see the huts stringing out a long distance, and the general outline of an Indian abiding place. As the fringe of chaparral grew thinner, the lodges burst suddenly upon our view. We listened almost breathlessly for the cracking of the carbines in the advance. The head of the column, now lost to view, again reappeared, this time at a gallop. An order was now passed hurriedly to the rear to "form platoons," to "prepare to charge," to hold the horses *"well in hand,"* and "not to scatter out."

---

[*]The Rio San Rodrigo, just west of Remolino, on which Cabaceras is located, may have been the stream which we called the Remolino, which we crossed just before making the attack. The mountain range west of Remolino, which we called Santa Rosa, is designated as "Serreas Del Burro," although we could distinctly see the more distant and higher peaks of the former.

The Charge!

A shot, followed by another and a third, then a front line volley, and the grey horses of "I" Troop (McLaughlin's) in the lead could be seen stretching down the slope upon the villages, now in full view. "Left front into line!" "Gallop!" "March!" rang out from front to rear—"*Charget!!*" And then there burst forth such a cheering and yelling from our gallant little column, as that Kickapoo village never heard before. It was caught up from troop to troop and struck such dismay to the Indians' hearts that they were seen flying in every direction. The distance was nearly a mile over fairly open but rough ground. Our reserve ammunition was neither carried on the pack mules, with a possible loss by stampede, nor in the saddle-pockets on the horses, as was done by Custer in the battle of the Little Big Horn, and captured by the Indians when the dismounted men became separated from their mounts, but on the persons of the troopers *safely stowed in the pockets of their blouses.* Although it was an uncomfortable burden, Mackenzie, as a successful Indian fighter, never took any doubtful chances in action with such a slippery enemy who always took advantage of any culpable errors.

Our formation for the charge was in column of platoons. The order was for the leading platoon to deliver its fire by volley, then to wheel to the right, turning back and up the length of the villages again; each succeeding platoon to do the same from the front to rear of the column, and then reloading and falling in rear, still continue following down the length of the three villages. The leading platoons of "I" Troop were to pursue the fleeing Indians out on open ground, through and beyond the lodges. As a boy of seventeen, on the Gettysburg Campaign, I had witnessed the battle of Upperville, Va., during the Civil War (a running fight from Aldie, Va., to Ashby's Gap) between the Cavalry Corps of the two armies (about 25,000 men) under Generals Alfred Pleasanton and J. E. B.

Stuart, on June 22, 1863, the First Division (Griffin's of the Fifth Corps) in which I had served, having been detached from the Army of the Potomac for the purpose of supporting the Cavalry of that Army in this battle. I saw many charges of fifteen miles of country during that day, but I never saw such a magnificent charge as that made by those six troops of the Fourth U. S. Cavalry on the morning of May 18, 1873, at Rey Molina, Mexico. As has been stated, we had been drilling our men every morning at Fort Clark and in our camps in platoon formation and in column of fours at all gaits in dismounting and fighting on foot, and, barring casualties, liable to occur in any action, and the breaking up of tactical units incident thereto, their drill and execution thereof was as well nigh perfect as human effort could devise. Their carbines and pistols were clean, well lubricated, and were in workable condition with ejectors functioning.

The Fight

The sudden charge proved a complete surprise. The leading company was soon among the grass lodges. Carbines were banging, rifles were cracking. The men were incessantly cheering and scattering in pursuit. The warriors were yelling and flying in every direction, many half naked, from their huts. It was a grand and impressive sight. Sharp and imperative commands alone held the men in ranks, or kept them from dashing individually into the villages. Over mesquite bushes, rocks, prickly-pear, and the long, dagger-like points of the Spanish bayonet, dashed the mad, impetuous column of troopers. Here could be seen a horse gone nearly crazy and unmanageable with fright, and running off with its rider, who was almost or wholly powerless to control him. Small, mesquite trees had to be avoided, and what with controlling the men, dodging obstacles over rough ground, and handling our horses, a more reckless, dare-devil ride we never had.

Soon the rear companies struck the villages, and, dismounting and "fighting on foot" were closely engaged. It

was short work. ''I'' Troop was pursuing the flying warriors across the low, swampy ground, everywhere cut up
and intersected by irrigating ditches, and covered with
fields of grain, corn, pumpkins, etc. On the left were the
pony herds, and stolen stock, the former seemingly as intent upon getting away as their masters.

Mackenzie, remembering Sheridan's injunction to make
this a campaign of ''annihilation'' and ''destruction,''
gave the necessary orders for that work to be done.
''Fire the villages!'' The dismounted men, already told
off for this purpose, making torches of the long pampa
plumes and other rank grasses, ran in and quickly fired
the tepees or grass lodges, which being made of coarse
rushes or grasses, with walls about four feet high and
roofs heavily thatched and as dry as tinder, flashed up,
roared and burned like powder. The fierce crackling of
the flames mingled strangely with loud reports of carbines, sharp crack of rifles, cheers and yells. The destruction was complete.

War's Sad Spectacle

Taking a part of ''A'' troop, by Mackenzie's order, I
struck across to the left for the herds, now stampeding in
the distance, and, after much hard riding through the
chaparral, which everywhere skirted the villages, expecting momentarily to be ambushed by small parties of Indians who had fled in that direction, I succeeded in rounding up most of the animals, and started back. As I approached the small stream bordering the smouldering
lodges, riding at a rapid walk, one of the men shouted,
''Look out, Lieutenant, there are Indians under the bank!''
Turning quickly, I saw, under a large, overhanging bunch
of flags and long grass, what appeared to be the form of
a large Indian in the act of pointing a weapon. It was
about 30 yards and nearly concealed. I was the only officer who had brought a carbine. I had no gun scabbard;
it had been strapped to the saddle, but was now loose.
Raising it and firing immediately, the Indian fell. The

men then opened fire which was replied to from the bushes. Dismounting shortly after and ordering "Cease firing," I approached the bushes and, parting them, witnessed one of those most singular and pitiable spectacles incident to Indian warfare. A small but faithful cur dog was at the entrance of what appeared to be a small cave far under the bank of the stream, savagely menacing our advance. Near him, almost underneath, lay stretched the dead body of a gigantic Indian, and behind him seemed to be more bodies. It was necessary to kill the dog before we could proceed further. The men reaching in, then drew forth two small children, respectively two and four years of age, badly shot through their bodies. One was dead, the other nearly so. Opening the bush still further for more revelations, way in the rear we saw the form of a young squaw, apparently unhurt, but badly frightened. Her black, glittering eyes were fastened upon the group of blue-coated soldiers with a fascinating stare, not unlike that of a snake, expressing half fear, half hatred and defiance. We made signs for her to come out, but, as she refused, she was quietly, and without harm, dragged forth. We thought this was all, but almost covered up under the immense flags, we found still a third child, a girl of about twelve, badly wounded. It was one of those cruel, unforeseen and unavoidable accidents of grim-visaged war. They all had weapons and had fired upon my party. Gathering up our prisoners, we found that we had some forty or fifty, with nearly two hundred ponies and horses, most of the latter being branded stolen stock.

Only nineteen warriors were reported by Gen. Mackenzie as killed. He would never report as killed only those that had been officially counted. But many more were counted by several officers at various distances from the villages, and in out of the way places where they had fled for safety, especially in water holes and under the banks of the stream concealed from view. Mackenzie did not go over the ground himself. The exact number will never be known. There must also have been many wounded, but, as was usual in an Indian action, *none were found.* They had probably been carried to places of safety or, perchance, were burned up in the lodges when the latter were destroyed.

Among the prisoners was old Costilietos, Chief of the Lipans, who had been caught by a lariat thrown over his head by one of our Seminole scouts, as he was darting through the bushes. Another prisoner was brought in, but, through some neglect, he was not disarmed by his captor and nearly ended the life of one of our Captains.

A Close Call

This was Captain Clarence Mauck, who died some years later as a Major of the Ninth U. S. Cavalry. After returning with the prisoners and ponies which I had captured, I dismounted, and stood within the circle of quite a group of officers and men, within a few feet of Mauck, Wilcox was near me, also O'Connell with two or three of his men on the other side of Mauck, none of us more than ten or fifteen feet apart. My Spencer Carbine, with a cartridge in the chamber, and at a half cock ready for instant action, was resting on my right toe. I was facing the Lipan Indian which the Seminole had just brought in, and watching his face and every movement. The moment I saw the look of rage at what he had witnessed come over his face, I feared trouble. As soon as he had recovered from his amazement and apparent stupor and fairly realized, by the blazing villages, prisoners, women and children standing under guard, etc., what had happened and how he had been duped, with a defiant whoop, he brought his rifle down like a flash upon Mauck.*

A Captive's Tragic Death

As I saw him raise his rifle, I as quickly brought my carbine to my hip with a rapid motion, and cocking it (it

---

*There were found in the lodges, some of which were searched before being destroyed, many contracts made by prominent Mexicans with these Indians, for the regular delivery of so many horses and head of cattle at so much per head. These papers clearly established the guilty acts of these parties, and there is but little doubt that the Mexican Government had full knowledge of these transactions. Some of the horses we captured had the brand of "Ike" Cox, our post guide, on them.

was already at a half cock) and pointing it at the Indian
without aim, fired at the moment he had begun to press
his trigger.   He gave a loud, piercing yell, threw up his
gun, which went off in the air, and toppled off his pony,
dead before he touched the ground.   Corporal Linden of
Troop "M," so O'Connell told me, at the same distance
on the other side, had observed the motion of the Indian
at the same time, had fired, and the report of his carbine
immediately followed mine, his shot striking and whirling
the Indian around.   For a brief moment Mauck's deadly
peril seemed to paralyze all who had witnessed the scene.

Success would have been too dearly purchased by the
sacrifice of so gallant and efficient an officer.   But our
Army records will show scores of noble soldiers who, after
years of usefulness to their country, have ignobly died in
much the same way in action with these savages, notably
Gen. Canby.   Mauck had quickly dodged behind his horse's
shoulder, but it would not have saved him from the Indian's rifle.

Thrilling Incidents

There were many thrilling incidents and adventures
during the fight.   Captain McLaughlin, that sturdy and in-
trepid old soldier, whose troop led in the pursuit, shot at
and wounded an Indian, who fell and permitted McLaughlin to ride up to him.   What was the Captain's astonish-
mment to see the Indian rise up, deliberately level his rifle
and make a close shot at his head.   But a miss is as good
as a mile.   The next moment he fell by McLaughlin's six-
shooter.   Another had his pony shot from under him.
Quickly jumping from his body and running at full speed,
he overtook and leaped up behind a mounted Indian and
rode off under fire.   Some of the men's horses bogging in
soft ground just at this moment, they both escaped.

Sergeant O'Brien, of "A" Troop, a grey and grisly old
Irish soldier who knew no fear, was pursuing an Indian,
both afoot.   He (O'B.) had fired and missed, when the
savage, thinking he had no time to reload, turned suddenly,

and, whirling a heavy, brass-bound tomahawk, threw it with such precision as just to graze the Sergeant's head. Walking deliberately up to him with his carbine, throwing in a cartridge quickly, as he advanced, from the magazine into the chamber, O'Brien said, "I have you now, you old *spalpane!*" and shot him dead at fifteen paces.

Sometime prior to this action, Mackenzie had bought a dark bay, Kentucky thoroughbred colt, about three years old. He was a magnificent animal, but he had a *bad, glaring-blue, crazy eye.* One day when Mackenzie was riding him near Fort Richardson, Texas; the colt bolted with him into some post oak timber, knocked him out of the saddle, cut his head badly, scratched his face, ran into the Post, and Mackenzie never rode him again. When we made the charge upon the Indian villages, Mackenzie's "striker," Matthews, a discharged soldier of the Ninth Cavalry, was riding him, and with a *snaffle bit.* The mad rush proved too much for the blooded colt; he ran as though he was in a race; absolutely uncontrollable.

Away off on the flank of the madly charging column Matthews could be seen clinging to him like a monkey. No trained jockey ever rode such a race. The colt bounded over the mesquite like a frightened deer. He went over and through everything; jumped the widest irrigating ditches, and, going nearly a mile from the flaming lodges, gave one last leap into the air, broke his heart, and dropped dead in his tracks, Matthews flying over his head like a rocket into the soft earth, badly bruised but no bones broken. It was a most thrilling sight in full view of the entire command.

Without unsaddling, but staking the horses out with watering bridles, and a strong herd guard and, remaining just long enough to treat the wounded (one mortally), to amputate an arm and set a leg; to construct horse litters or travois, and assign the prisoners to ponies for the ride back, we prepared for the return march.

Fire and Desolation

Ruin and desolation now marked the spot—a cyclone could not have made more havoc or a cleaner sweep up— and danger lurked in the homeward path, for a few hours' march distant was a town and well settled district of Mexicans and Indians which, as soon as this invasion became known, would send their rancheros to avenge the insult to their territory. Mackenzie thoroughly understood the situation, but, confident in the excellence of his troops carefully and deliberately made all these arrangements for the transportation of the wounded and prisoners.*

We started. Beyond the Kickapoo village, about one-fourth of a mile, was that of the Lipans. Still further beyond, to the west, in the distance, stretched the Santa Rosa Mountains, whose peaks were now bathed in the mellow sunlight, seeming only a few miles distant, towards which many of the Kickapoos and the Lipans fled when they first became aware of our hostile approach. Mackenzie, when first informed of the relative strength of the Indian villages, was told that he would be compelled to make his main attack upon the largest—the Kickapoo village. While it was still uncertain when the command would reach its objective, and some time before the charge was made, the guides, who were perfectly familiar with the location of the villages and the lay of the land, strongly urged him to divide his force, sending a part around the Lipan village in the direction of the mountains, thus cutting off their escape in that direction, while the remaining companies made a vigorous flank attack upon the Kickapoos. But the General, who was strenuously opposed to dividing a command when about to make an attack, and especially now that he was engaged in an invasion of foreign soil, and having left his food supplies on the trail, and in the strong belief that the Kickapoos were more numerous, would not listen to the guides' advice. It must be borne in mind that Mackenzie's wise decision and sound

*The location of this place is accurately shown on an official Mexican map, obtained at the Pan-American Union Headquarters, Washington, D. C. This was Saragossa. We were in the State of Coahuila.

judgment was made more than three years before Custer
made the fatal error at the Little Big Horn in adopting
such a risky plan of approaching and attacking a numerous enemy, above all, a wily, tricky, shifty, evasive,
mobile bunch of Indians who would not, or *did* not play
the game fair, to the extent of working into any cut and
dried programme, prepared in advance by a white strategist whose war games they always ignored and despised,
and continually held up to contempt and ridicule. This
division of the Command *might have worked out.* At all
events, the guides thought so, and said so later, when it
became known that nearly all of the Lipans had escaped,
before they could be reached over the swampy approaches
to their stronghold. Again it might have proved a dis-
astrous Custer Massacre, for like that gallant Cavalry
leader, we had no base to fall back on in case of an unforeseen crisis. In a raid into "No Man's Land," *fore-
sight* is better than *hindsight.* The sun was now high in
the heavens, the heat had become more intense.

The Hated "Gringos"

We mounted and commenced our retrograde march.
Our course lay through the little Mexican settlement of
Rey Molina. It is in the State of Coahuila. Everywhere
we met the black, malignant scowls of El Mexicano. It
was a novel and most astonishing spectacle for them to
behold a body of United States Cavalry, with Indian prisoners, swiftly traversing their territory for safety beyond
"El Rio Bravo." We felt that their hatred forboded evil
before reaching American soil. Their occasional exclamations in muttered almost incoherent Spanish, such as, El
"Gringos," indicated anything but a friendly spirit to Los
Americanos.

It was a scalding day; not a breath of air stirred. The
heat hung over the earth in tremulous waves, parching
and roasting our little command, until in our already
wearied condition we could seem to bear it no longer. Had
it not been for the numerous lagoons met with frequently

during the day, our sufferings would have become intense, almost intolerable. Our trail had been discovered going in, and the results of our raid had been communicated by rapid runners or couriers up and down the river. Even then the "long roll" was beating from Piedras Negras to the upper fords of the Rio Grande for volunteers to gather and intercept our march. It was ascertained that a few miles away was a town or another Mescalero Apache village (Zaragoza), a well settled district. These Indians, long resident in Mexico, were sworn allies of the Kickapoos and Lipans, and were capable of sending many warriors against us.

The Return March

As darkness settled about us our anxiety increased, which, added to the exhausted condition of the men and animals, left us in no very cheerful frame of mind, or prepared for our long night ride and a possible fight in ambuscade. *We did not feel safe,* and we fully realized that the worst was before us, this interminable night of gloom and uncertainty. The moon, yellow and tropical, but dazzling bright, rose and illuminated our trail, now glittering with myriads of dew drops that everywhere flashed like diamonds under our horses' feet.

Night of Agony and Horror

We wearily rode on. The heavy, overpowering clutch of sleep was upon every officer and man. This was the third night that many of us had been absolutely without sleep or rest. The Indian prisoners were heavily guarded in rear, and our Seminole scouts stealthily hovered on our flanks, to guard against ambush and surprise, while our advance guard and selected scouts slowly felt their way ahead. It was a *long, long* night. Everywhere the men drowsed and swayed in their saddles. Officers, obliged to forego even *this luxury,* were on the alert to keep them awake, and at every halt, to urge them to renewed efforts. Men became alternately depressed, excitable, irritable, morose and quarrelsome, and, lying down during a halt, with arm through bridle rein, could, with difficulty be roused, and the officers had to be constantly on the watch to prevent their being left behind; to keep them from coming to blows, and to bring them back to a condition approaching the normal.

However, notwithstanding their state of almost utter exhaustion, and when it seemed that a surprise attack might be necessary to restore the mental balance and morale of those whom we had hitherto regarded as our very best Indian *scrappers,* yet, while their spirits were at this low ebb, there was latent a certain Esprit, and both their morale and discipline were found to be perfect whenever they could be aroused to a full realization of their *sense of duty* and warned of the imminent danger of a possible ambush or surprise. This was most remarkable, for our nerves were nearly raw, and almost worn threadbare.

We felt that the entire command had expended about every ounce of energy and strength. Many men in the command, under all of these existing conditions were subjects for a close study of the psychological changes which those forty-eight hours of physical suffering and loss of sleep had wrought upon the mental faculties and traits of all.

These conditions made the strain on the officers almost intolerable on account of their much greater responsibilities for the success of this last stage of our expedition.

Threats and persuasion seemed alike to have lost their effect. It was seldom, however, that we used anything more than the mildest force, such as pushing them upon their feet at our short halts, and shaking them. No blows were struck nor weapons used.

Sleep was the one relief sought for, and uppermost in their minds. They seemed to care for little else, nor considered for a moment their peril if left behind, and their sure fate if dealt with by a sullen, revengeful body of merciless savages.

Woe betide any sleeper who might be caught off his

guard, for the rear was being dogged by raging, cruel foes who had their homes and kindred to avenge. We read of the execution of Chinese criminals by sentinels keeping them awake with bayonets until death relieved their sufferings. All night long the officers rode the column, seizing the men by their shoulders and shaking them into an upright position in their saddles. The eyes seemed strained out of our heads. The tension was so great that our heads seemed full to bursting. The physical pain endured cannot be conceived or described by tongue or pen. Only the imagination or the experience of those dreadful hours could be the full realization of our agony. The imagination pictured all kinds of tangible objects to our over-strained minds. Now in the bright moonlight a huge boulder loomed up before our bewildered eyes. Again, we were passing through hamlets and large towns, all commenting upon the extravagant illumination which the people had resorted to. We were at all times dodging and stooping to avoid imaginary objects which, to our dazed senses seemed real, and for many years afterwards were declared to be tangible. One man, wandering from the column a short distance, while it was at a halt, to enjoy an undisturbed rest, and eluding our vigilance, awoke only to find the column gone, and a Mexican standing over him. He jumped up, fired at the enemy, ran through the chaparral, and, following our trail until morning, finally crossed the river and joined the command. Such was our mental condition, one of hallucinations and bewildering fancies or mental impressions; our minds bordering upon the insane.

Prisoners Lashed on Ponies

Towards morning the Indian papooses or children, in some cases mounted with the squaws by twos and threes upon the ponies, began to be troublesome by falling fast asleep and tumbling off on the trail, which occasioned frequent short halts in order to have the rear closed up for safety. They were finally lashed on with lariats. Several times the Seminoles in the rear and on the flanks came in and reported the enemy in sight. At these times word was passed along, and renewed efforts were made to keep the men waked up and up to their fighting pitch.

But we were not attacked.

The Irish Captain's Peril and a "Life Preserver"

About 2 o'clock, when everything seemed darkest, most dreary, almost hopeless and it seemed more than probable that we might not get through without serious disaster, and had reached the lowest possible ebb, a mere chance, or factor of safety, on account of the approaching exhaustion of officers, men and animals, the most *critical* and *alarming period* of that almost endless night, word was passed along to me that our old Irish Captain, O'Connell, was in distress. I went to him. He seemed to be in a most desperate condition, almost in a state of collapse, but still sitting upright in his saddle. We were at a halt. There was no time to ride to the head of the column and try to find our only doctor, Acting Assistant Surgeon Donald Jackson, a very valuable and efficient Contract Surgeon. Nor was there time to construct a travois. We had no ambulance or stretchers. Taking in the situation I determined at once to take what I firmly believed to be the only chance, and, in the writer's judgment, a very doubtful one, and a very grave risk. I had, when we left our Piedras Pintos Camp, packed a small, flat cedar keg filled with whisky on a troop pack mule. It held about six pints. It was painted a sky blue, and was bespangled with small silver paper stars, having been used at the tin wedding celebration in honor of Lieut. and Mrs. C. A. Vernon, the year before at Fort Richardson, Texas, previously referred to, by my wife, who had impersonated a French Vivandiere (Daughter of the Regiment) when all had gone in costume and were masked. When the packs were cut off about 1 A. M. the previous night, I had *personally attended to the saving of this valuable piece of property,* and distributed its contents among several officers, among them Beaumont, Mauck and Wilcox, that alert, practical, efficient and sturdy Troop Commander, I filled my own canteen. *So far I had not sampled it.*

I gave our fine old soldier a big slug of this whisky, and *then stayed with him* to see that he did not fall out of the *saddle* from weakness. He was an absolute "teetotaler" of the *Volstead type.* After repeating the dose several times later, he got across the river, and I shall always believe that it was the result of my *prescription.* It proved to be a "Life Preserver." At all events it firmly convinced the old man, for he always declared: "Ca-a-ther, you saved me life!" He entered the service about 1851 in the Old Dragoons; was a Corporal on duty at West Point with the Cavalry detachment; was commissioned later in the Fourth Cavalry—and did magnificent service during the Civil War, especially in the great charge at Lovejoy's Station, Ga., where he was wounded and his horse killed. He died a few years after the Mackenzie Raid, of paralysis, at Oakland, Calif., always declaring, in the last letters ever received by the writer, that those nights of horror were directly responsible for his death, and that it was the greatest ride ever made by him during his entire service. His condition that awful night was one of complete mental and physical breakdown, bordering on a collapse or apoplexy.

Green Van's Ford—Death—Strange Scenes

Hour after hour dragged its seemingly slow and never-ending length along until fifteen had passed. The gray of dawn found us still dodging about the winding path and trails and roads among the mesquites leading to the river. Soon would be disclosed the welcome waters of the Rio Grande which must be passed ere rest could be hoped for. At daylight the heavier timber that skirts the river was seen. Descending from the ridge which bounded the valley or bottom of the stream, the weary column wound by shaded roads bordered by almost interminable, dense thickets until a Mexican ranch with a clearing to the river

was passed, when, without the formality of "by your
leave," the farm gate was opened, and following a narrow
path, we were soon upon the banks of the stream, and the
horses buried their noses in the waters of the wide, rapid
river.   We had made many tedious halts in the dense chaparral and cane brakes. The long, interminable night of
horror, of night-mare, had passed.

I looked about me, scenes which neither pen nor tongue
could describe were everywhere about. Scenes which no
"Artist-on-the-spot" could ever vividly portray nor "Special Correspondents" accurately describe. Some of the
men were fast asleep low down on their saddles with their
arms tightly clasped about their horses' necks; others were
drowsing and swaying or nodding bolt up right. Some,
by persistent efforts to smoke and talk, barely held their
drooping eyelids from closing. The condition of the prisoners, although ludicrous, was pitiful in the extreme.
They had been riding, lashed on the captured ponies,
doubled up and by threes. The children, half naked and
streaked with dust and sweat, deprived, by being bound,
even of the privilege of lying down upon their ponies'
necks, were fast asleep, their black heads and swarthy
skins presenting a striking contrast to the blue-coated
troopers who surrounded them. Here was a child of but
five or six years. By custom, his head had been shaved
smooth, except a tuft or stiff scalp-lock, a crest running
pompadour from his forehead over back to his neck. His
face was painted in parti-colored stripes. His *infantile
warrior spirit had given away.* Young though he was, he
fully realized that he was a captured prisoner of war, in
the hands of a hated white man, and separated, as he believed, forever from his Indian home. The tears had
coursed down his face, over the paint and sweat, and the
dust adhering, gave him a very ludicrous, yet strangely
touching expression. His rigid form, bolt upright, but
added to this strange, impressive spectacle. All faces
wore that dull gray, ashy, death-like appearance, indica-
tive of overworked nature and the approach of exhaustion

and physical collapse. The appearance of the gallant troopers and our faithful Seminole scouts, their hair, faces and clothes white with alkali dust—all exhausted, but rigid and alert for the order which would send us into the ford—only accentuated the picture, one never to be forgotten in a lifetime.

At last, *at last,* we had accomplished our almost super-human task, reaching the goal of our terrible mission and returning to the Rio Grande. The agony of those dreadful nights was over, and we almost felt like shouting our long pent-up joy, and heaving a great sigh of relief at this final ending of our hardships and sacrifices, the almost endless and long drawn out pain, and at the nearly perfect results of our objects and purposes.

Men and horses seemed to draw new strength from the refreshing waters. It took some time to get the wounded on the horse litters across. One man died at the river. A low "forward' and all pushed with animation and renewed spirits across the ford. At last the rear of the column stood upon American soil, and we gave vent to our feelings with a soldier's—Amen!!

The Eastern bank was soon climbed, and the welcome order to go into camp given. The saddles were stripped from the jaded horses for the first time in forty-nine hours, and while our breakfast was preparing, the men thronged to the river to bathe. Our feelings can better be *imagined* than *described*. We had crossed at his ford, and were bivouacked upon the land of Capt. Green Van, described elsewhere in these pages, a rancher of considerable notoriety along this line of the Rio Grande who, with undaunted courage, had volunteered to guide us on this hazardous expedition, and who now, of course, would travel with his life in his hand, as the Mexicans would surely turn upon him for revenge.

Soon after our crossing, our great quartermaster, the indefatigable, tireless, resourceful Lawton, came in by previous arrangement with a supply train loaded with plenty of rations for the men and forage for the animals, besides luxuries galore for the officers, and shortly after, man and beast were busy trying to recuperate from our long fast on cracker dust and water since the evening of the 17th. There was feasting all day. Green Van, too, to show his generous hospitality, brought down to our bivouac from his ranch, in several buckets, some *new Mescal*, a very potent Mexican drink, a sort of rum with a weedy taste, fiery and throat burning, distilled from pulque, a dirty looking, yellowish-brown beer, brewed from the Maguey plant, which grows luxuriantly everywhere in that country. As soon as Mackenzie learned that some of the Troop Commanders were going to issue it, he ordered that it should all be spilled on the ground for, on our empty stomachs, and in our nervous and strained condition, he did not think it a proper kind of stimulant to be served to an exhausted command.

Threats—A Defensive Line

Our stay here in this bivouac was one of continuous excitement and soon shots were heard across the river, and threats were shouted across that the Mexicans and Indians were gathering to attack us that night. In a few hours we observed large bodies apparently getting ready to carry out this threat. They were very profane and boastful, and we certainly seemed in some danger of a dash across the ford. Our position was on a small plateau or tableland, a short distance back from the river, almost completely surrounded by dense cane-brakes. Mackenzie sent the horses back some distance for safety, "tied them in," placed a sufficient guard over them, thus releasing for the fighting line, the horse holders (number 4). He then placed all the best sharpshooters (in those days they were our skilled buffalo and bear hunters, no ammunition having then been issued for target practice) on the line of the river and as close as possible to it, covering the ford, which was a narrow, diagonal one, and could only be crossed by file. It had deep water just above and below it. They were entirely concealed by the tall, dense chaparral which extended back for some distance from the bank of the river. He then deployed the balance of the command some yards in rear; all concealed. They were armed with the 7 shooting Spencer Carbine, Cal. 50, Smith and Wesson's Revolver, Cal. 45, which had just been issued, and sabres, which, as before stated, had been ground to a sharp edge when we left Fort Clark.

The Mexicans and Indians, yelling and shouting, hurling oaths and abusive language and swearing vengeance, were then invited to come across. *They never came!!*

We heard nothing more of this boastful, gasconading rabble. Not an Indian or Mexican cared to *wet his feet in the waters of Green Van's Ford,* or "bump up" against the troopers of the Fourth Cavalry who had given them such a "clean up" at their villages on the Remolino.

After making all of these dispositions and safeguarding our front for the night, we calmly awaited further developments. In a semi-circle, our line unbroken, and with pickets thrown out, and selected sleeping parties in the brakes for quicker action, as was our custom when in contact with Indians, we turned in for sleep. The field proved to be an immense ant-heap. The little pests attacked, bit, persecuted and tortured us until early morning, when we moved to a more secure spot. The writer *had not closed his eyes for four nights.* Early on May 20th, we took up the march for the post.

After leaving Green Van's Ford, we made a march of only a few miles, and bivouacked back from the river in open ground, but surounded by dense chaparral.

Illegal Order—Mackenzie's Threat—The Retort

That night there gathered about Mackenzie's camp fire several of the officers of the command. Of all that number no one survives beside myself, after a period of over 61 years. There were present Captains N. B. McLaughlin (a Brigadier General of Volunteers during the Civil War); John A. Wilcox, who became a Lieutenant-Colonel, U. S. A.; Clarence Mauck, who became a Major of the Ninth

Cavalry; Eugene B. Beaumont, who became a Lieutenant-Colonel, U. S. A.; besides Mackenzie, his Adjutant, Leopold O. Parker and myself. I instinctively felt that something was coming. Col. Beaumont, in the course of a general conversation, mostly dealing with the incidents and adventures of this raid, suddenly asked Mackenzie if he had had any orders or authority for taking his command over into Mexico, especially after telling us of the risks we all (officers and enlisted men) ran, etc. Mackenzie replied that he had not. Beaumont then said: "Then it was illegal to expose not only the lives of your officers and men, in action, but, in event of their being wounded and compelled upon our withdrawal, through force of circumstances, to be left over there, probably to be hung or shot by a merciless horde of savage Indians and Mexicans.

Mackenzie replied: "I considered all that." Beaumont continued: "Your officers and men would have been justified in refusing to obey your orders, which you now admit as being illegal, and exposing themselves to such peril." To which McLaughlin, joining in, added: "Beaumont is right! and had I known that you had no orders to take us over the river, I would not have gone!!"

Mackenzie flashed up, and in a very firm, crisp and decisive voice, replied: "Any officer or man who had refused to follow me across the river I would have shot!" His father had hung Midshipman Spencer, son of the Secretary of War, at the yard arm of the U. S. Brig Somers many years before, for mutiny on the high seas, for which he (Mackenzie) was tried. His son had, perhaps, his father's act in mind when weighing the probabilities of such a contingency—the refusal of any officer to obey his orders to cross the Rio Grande.

McLaughlin who, a few years before, during the Reconstruction days in the South, after the Civil War, had killed Baker, a noted desperado, near Marshall, Texas, and was then, with the exception of Capt. Wirt Davis, probably the best pistol and carbine shot in the Army, snapped out sharply: *"That would depend, Sir,* upon who *shot first!"* Mackenzie did not reply to this. There was absolute silence for some minutes. Some of us thought that most always the time or acid test of obedience to an illegal order under all the circumstances of such a raid, and the dangers which confronted us, is, *Success!!* I *knew* that *Mackenzie knew,* that if he didn't *succeed,* his *reputation* and *career* were gone forever. I also knew, for he had told me, that he had *counted all the costs,* especially this last one. But here was one cost in which he had already been challenged. What the result might have been in McLaughlin's refusal to obey Mackenzie's orders to cross the river, one is left to conjecture. While, at times, he (Mackenzie) was irascible, irritable and difficult to deal with, mostly on account of his many wounds (and who could be a saint with four of them?) Mackenzie was one of the few officers of that period who was always ready and willing to assume the gravest responsibilities, and he would never hesitate to take the initiative while awaiting definite orders.

This he always expected of all his officers when assigning them to any duty and he generally gave them explicit verbal instructions as to the duties he expected them to perform, relying upon their *common sense, good judgment and wise discretion,* following such instruction. This was at a personal conference. He never pinned them down to it, however, as a binding order intended to cover all of their acts. *He trusted his officers.* These instructions were always given with the proviso that they should always act within *legal bounds,* and never exceed them in any manner that should be harsh, arbitrary or beyond the meaning of the term "an officer and a gentleman." But, he wanted something done, results. Then he would issue a blanket order covering those acts. I never knew him to permit one of his officers, when in the performance of any duty under these verbal instructions or orders, to be made a "scape-goat." He would back them up to the last limit. The writer had several proofs of such loyalty. Mackenzie never "went back" on any officer, especially of the old Fourth Cavalry, to save *"my official reputation"* or for the mistaken notion of the "necessity of self protection" and a desire to "soothe his wounded pride." *Justice* with him was inseparable from his professional duties and honor.

The silence soon became painful, and great was the relief when first one and then another withdrew from the flickering light of the mesquite bivouac fire, and rolling ourselves in our blankets sought relief from such a terrible condition—the *first in four long nights*—in the slumber of exhausted men, who soon forgot the turmoil and strife of war only to resume it again on the fateful morrow.

Anxious Families

We arrived at Fort Clark about noon on the 21st, there to meet the anxious garrison, who had purposely been kept in ignorance of even our destination and, after a terrible suspense, now rejoiced at our return. Up to that moment no member of our families had the slightest inkling of our whereabouts, or when, if ever, we would come back. The garrison had been full of rumors of disaster; the command "had been surrounded, and cut to pieces," or was "retreating before overwhelming numbers" and "was in extreme peril," etc.

There was little sleep for the anxious wives at Clark. The slightest noise would bring pale, frightened women to the doors of their quarters to learn the cause, and the careless soldiers were anxious for their absent comrades.

A Tropical Storm—The Alarm

On the 24th, General Mackenzie, hearing well founded rumors that a large body of Indians and Mexicans were making threatening demonstrations on the opposite bank of the river, took two troops of the regiment and scouted in the direction of Villa Nuevo and other points, and returned on the 26th without seeing or hearing anything of the enemy. Our scouts, however, reported during the day, that we might expect an attack almost any time.

The night of the 26th closed in very dark, and with every indication of one of those terrible tropical storms, accompanied by wind and lightning. All was gloom and inky blackness. The eye could distinguish nothing a foot away. The anxiety all over the garrison was very intense. Everybody during this suspense, felt nervous and "jumpy." Pickets had been thrown about the entire post for the night and all the camp guards doubled. Ladies and children gathered in groups on the porches of the quarters and breathlessly discussed the chances of coming battle and all the attendant horrors of Indian massacre and retaliation. The hoarse boom-boom of the thunder now sounded, one peal and crash after another; the incessant flash of the lightning following, glared about the little plateau, bringing out the buildings with startling clearness one moment, only to be succeeded by black, impenetrable gloom the next. It rattled, boomed and roared in angry succession. It was such a night as would set an Atheist to thinking whether there was really a God in Heaven who now controlled the elements, and if one was prepared to meet this Unknown Power.

The entire garrison, in their intensely nervous condition after an almost interminable suspense during our absence, was deeply impressed with the awful sublimity of the scene, when suddenly a carbine shot, another and another in quick succession, rang out, and a spluttering, rattling and cracking by the pickets, caused all to start to their feet. They seemed to be instantly electrified, and the ladies and children, with blanched cheeks, rushed together and began to huddle for protection. The "long roll" on the drums of the Infantry, vied with the rattle and boom of the thunder. The bugles of the Cavalry sounded their loudest "Assembly." Every blinding flash showed the gallant troopers pouring out of their barracks in the dreadful storm, carbine in hand. Officers, with a last word of cheer to the companions of their lives in this far off wild, beyond the pale of civilization, buckled on sabre and pistol and hurried to their companies now "falling in" to the music of the trumpeters and drummers. A few moments and every man was under arms and in ranks. We awaited further developments from the pickets who had now "ceased firing" and were maintaining a most provoking silence. In a moment or two, however, it was ascertained that one of the pickets—"jumpy" like everybody else—had fired at *a hog,* disturbed by the storm, and was, of course, followed by a fusillade from the others. His shot had started the entire line. All of the officers were immediately called to headquarters, where they were cautioned and given verbal instructions to be carried out in event of another such alarm or bona fide attack.

One set of stone quarters was designated for all ladies and children to assemble at in case of further alarms. The citizens of the town were notified, and thus ended the Mexican scare. The suspense was over. The attack never came. This Raid resulted in the Mexican Government coming down from their "high perch," and instead of covering up and concealing these high handed, brutal murders, atrocities, and wholesale robbery along the river, it consented to negotiate an International Treaty by which either country could pursue bandits, horse and cattle thieves and armed desperadoes operating on either side of the line, or, as it was called, a "hot trail" across the border, and punish them. At this date (1925) it is my belief that such treaty of 1873 has never been abrogated.

Quiet and peace reigned for many a day. For years one could have almost heard a pin drop along that line, so wholesome had been the effect of our punishment of these marauders and scourges on this border of the Rio Grande.

Grateful Thanks of Texas

So elated were the people of Texas over our success, especially along the border counties, that about May 25, Governor Edmund J. Davis called the State Legislature into extra session by a special proclamation, and the following Joint Resolution was passed by both houses of the same, a copy of which was transmitted to the headquarters of the Fourth Cavalry, but to my knowledge, through some inadvertence, it was never published in any regimental order, nor was a copy ever furnished to the officers who so loyally risked their lives in this great and daring Adventure. Nor was its existence known by them for a long time. Many years afterwards some of us, upon learning that such a Resolution had been passed, sent to Austin, Texas, and, upon application to the Adjutant General or the Secretary of State of Texas, we were furnished with certified copies of this valuable testimonial, duly authenticated by the Commanding General of the Department of Texas. It is given herewith in full. To my knowledge, it has never been printed before for publication.

It is the only instance, within my knowledge, in the Military History of the United States, when a Cavalry Regiment of our Army ever received the "Grateful Thanks" of a Sovereign State through its Legislature convened in special session by its Governor for that purpose.

JOINT RESOLUTION OF THE LEGISLATURE OF THE STATE OF TEXAS

Whereas:

Reliable information has been received that General Ranald S. Mackenzie of the U. S. Army, with the troops under his command, did, on the 19th day of May, 1873, cross the Rio Grande into the Republic of Mexico, and inflict summary punishment upon a band of Kickapoo Indians who, harbored and fostered by the Mexican authorities, have, for years past been waging a predatory warfare upon the frontier of Texas, murdering our citizens, conveying their children into captivity, and plundering their property, therefore:

Resolved; By the Senate of the State of Texas, the House concurring, that the *Grateful Thanks* of the people of the State, and particularly the citizens of our frontier, are due to General Mac‑kenzie and the troops under his command, for their *prompt action* and *gallant conduct* in *inflicting well merited punishment upon these scourges of our frontier.*

Resolved; That His Excellency, the Governor, be, and he is hereby requested to forward a copy of these Resolutions to General Mackenzie, and the officers and troops under his command.

Adopted May 25, 1873.

(Signed) LEIGH CHALMERS,
Secretary of the Senate.

Approved:

(Signed) E. B. PICKETT,
President of the Senate.

Approved:

(Signed) M. D. K. TAYLOR,
Speaker, House of Representatives.

Approved: May 30, 1873.

(Signed) EDMUND J. DAVIS,
Governor.

Department of State
Austin, Texas

I, James P. Newcomb, Secretary of State for the State of Texas, hereby certify that the foregoing is a true copy of the original Resolution as passed by the Legislature of the State of Texas.

Witness my hand and official seal of office in the City of Austin, this 2nd day of June, A. D., 1873.

(Signed) JAMES P. NEWCOMB,
Secretary of State.

SEAL
OF
TEXAS
A true copy.

(Signed) COLON-AUGUR,
A. D. C.
Department of State,
Austin, June 2, 1873.

C. C. AUGUR,
Major-General, Comd'g. Dept. of Texas.

General:

I have the honor to transmit herewith certified copy of Resolution passed by the Honorable Legislature of the State of Texas, tendering thanks to General Mackenzie for services rendered the frontier citizens of Texas.

Respectfully,
(Signed) JAMES P. NEWCOMB,
Secretary of State.

A true copy.

(Signed) COLON-AUGUR,
A. D. C.

A Record Ride

It is the writer's belief, and it is on record that this was one of the greatest long distance rides ever made by a Cavalry Command of the U. S. Army, under the *same* or *similar* conditions, i.e., *distance* and *hours* marched, viz., *160 miles* in *32 marching hours,* part of the time with a loaded pack train, and, on the return march with captured women and children (the latter having to be lashed on the captured ponies to prevent their falling off), two desperately wounded men on travois (one of whom died at daybreak as we reached the ford), and a large bunch or caviard of captured stock driven loose on the trail.

General Charles King in recording some of these long distance individual and column rides, gives the distance marched by our command as *145 miles.* He does not state, however, where he got the figures. They were not given in my magazine article of 1886 in the Outing Magazine. As he was an officer of the Fifth U. S. Cavalry, and cited the long distance march of General Merritt with that regiment to the relief of Major Thornburg in 1879, during the Ute uprising, and apparently to contrast it with the ride of the Fourth Cavalry, and as he was not with us nor kept any itinerary or record of our march, and the writer *did keep one,* it is left to the reader of this statement to judge of the accuracy of the writer's record when compared with one made many years after by an officer who did not have the figures which have always been in my possession, and was not a participant in the "Mackenzie Raid."

The following is a transcript from my diary and itinerary of that march, as are all the foregoing statements of facts:

From our grazing camp on the Piedras Pintos to Captain Wilcox's camp on the Las Moras:

From 3:30 A. M. to 8:30 A. M., May 17, 1873, 5 hours...................... 20 miles

From Capt. Wilcox's camp to near the Rio
Grande River, 2 P. M. to 6 P. M. (slow on
account of heat), 4 hours................   12 miles
From the river to Rey Molina, 8:30 P. M.,
May 17, to 4:30 A. M., May 18, 8 hours....   58 miles
From Rey Molina, Mexico, to Green Van's
Ranch on the river, 1 P. M., May 18, to 4
A. M., May 19, 15 hours................   69 miles
_____
Total miles marched....................   159 miles
Total hours marched....................   32 hours

As Green Van's ranch or ford, was about 25 miles above
the ford at or near the mouth of the Las Moras, which we
used when going into Mexico, our return march was some
ten or twelve miles further in reaching it.

Our halt in Mexico after the action, was from 7 to 8
hours, and from this time we had left our grazing camp
on the Piedras Pintos, about 17 hours, or a total of 49
hours, during which we *did not* unsaddle.   The distance
gone over during the action, or about 3 miles, in rounding
up the stolen stock, capturing ponies in scattered herds,
etc., is not counted in the total miles actually covered, except in adding to the aggregate, to make it up to an even
160 miles in 32 marching hours, or one (1) mile added to
a grand total of 159 miles.   This is the minimum, and a
very conservative estimate.   This differs only slightly
from Mackenzie's report, which gives the distance from

Wilcox's camp to Rey Molina................   70 miles
From Piedras Pintos to Fort Clark......   8 miles
From Fort Clark to Wilcox's Camp.......   12 miles
Return from Rey Molina................   70 miles
_____
Total miles marched....................   160 miles
My diary gives distance from Piedras Pin-
tos Camp to Fort Clark as................   7 miles
and from Clark to Wilcox's Campas......   12 miles

As we did not go through Fort Clark (the nearest route to Wilcox's Camp) but went a mile or two out of our way, to avoid being seen by Mexican Spies about Brackettville, the actual distance is estimated at full 20 miles, which is a very moderate figure.

From the Rio Grande to Remolina, 8 hours on the first night's march, we averaged at all gaits, mostly at a trot and slow gallop, 7¼ miles per hour, increasing our gait considerably at 1 A. M., after the packs had been "cut loose." This includes a halt made to close up the pack train, cut the packs from the mules, and distribute hard bread to the entire command—officers and men.

On the return trip from 1 P. M., May 18, to 4 A. M., May 19, when we reached Green Van's Ford, or 15 hours, with several halts, owing to the condition of the women and children (prisoners) our average was about 4 3/5 miles per hour. Besides, we were driving along loose many captured animals, ponies and horses stolen from ranches along the river.

The expedition was, with one exception, an entire success. The villages had been destroyed, and the Indians and Mexicans had been terribly punished. This, with our casualties at a minimum. The only error committed—and it was so vital that it nearly jeopardized or seemed to imperil the safety, if not the lives of the entire command— was in overloading the pack mules so that their gait and speed could not be adjusted to the fastest moving unit of the column, the fox-gaited beasts of the guides. In the judgment of the writer (but this is *"hind sight"*) half loads, which would have meant half rations for the entire command, both going and returning, would have resulted in completely regulating the speed of the *slower,* with that of the *faster* unit. As it was, we were behind our schedule, always liable to miss fire in time of war, however it may work out in the cut and dried programmes of sham "war maneuvers" and "sham battles." We missed making a complete bag of the game, and as a result, fed on cracker dust and water for nearly thirty-six hours. The error was in favor of kindness to the men in indulging full stomachs.

There were no "Union men" in the Fourth Cavalry; no "mess hall" or "silence" strikes for *thicker soup,* and no "lock outs." There were no "insubordinations" or "mutinies" promoted by dangerous propaganda. The so-called intensive training and every day incessant drill, especially in sultry weather was never attempted, because it was never found necessary. The discipline in the Fourth Cavalry was perfect, because it was *constant* and *unremitting* and based upon absolute *fairness* and *justice.* The men were marvelously obedient to *such* discipline and training, punishments were generally administered in the Company under the strictest supervision and control of the most experienced officers and non-commissioned officers of the Civil and Indian Wars. Under these conditions, the regiment was always ready for a "fight or a frolic."

Owing to long, continuous Indian campaigns, when the hardships were of the most unusual character, and the command saw no human habitations for months, nothing but Indians, buffalo, wolves, jack-rabbits, prairie dogs, sage brush, cactus and alkali, and the long drawn-out monotony of desert sand, "shin oak," and "bad lands," there were some desertions, but, compared to more recent dates, they were at a minimum and therefore practically negligible. We had few courts-martial. Gen. Sherman once wrote: "Too many Courts-Martial in any command are evidence of *poor discipline* and *inefficient officers.* The Captain can usually inflict all the punishment necessary, and the Colonel *should* always."

We had simply a straight out Cavalry Command— "hand picked"—the best soldiers that ever straddled a horse, dependent upon *nothing* nor *nobody,* for morality, sobriety, morale, efficiency, good conduct, bravery, and all that goes to make up a first class, true blue soldier of the old days, except proper, reasonable training and the necessary rigid discipline that makes for good service, a personal supervision by *well trained, experienced company officers* and "crack-a-jack" non-commissioner officers.

These red blooded troopers did not have to be "mollycoddled," daily indulged with "lolly-pops" from the canteens, etc., or entertained and "fed up" with "Church" and "parlor socials" and "cabaret shows" and dances, etc., etc., to keep him from becoming homesick, losing his morale and deserting, although he was possessed of the same sentiments, the same feelings, the same longings, and all the natural traits and characteristics that make up our present *volunteer* regulars, our National Army and selected draft soldiers of the World War, who have so gallantly upheld the honor of their Country and its flag in that long, wearisime, sanguinary struggle.

With this Command of our little regular army, on this terrible Raid, it was all *"No Man's Land,"* a veritable "Terreno Desconocido."

There was nothing but slow, tri-weekly mails and courier service, good, brave men hardened down to their best form; drilled, *but not over drilled, disciplined to perfect obedience,* trained, with morale, spirit and enthusiasm unimpaired by becoming stale through *long, unnecessary, so-called "intensive training;"* horses, no scrubs, trained hard, plenty of *bottom* and *endurance;* good weapons, always ready for instant action, at *short ranges* and close *"in-and-in"* fighting and personal combat.

Added to these conditions, there was only needed, a bold, enterprising, resourceful, but above all, a commanding officer with *nerve, daring, iron will, "guts" and quick decision,* the man who commanded a veteran Cavalry division under Sheridan at Appomattox and whom Gen. Grant declared was "the most promising young officer in the Army," a reliable, active Adjutant, an experienced and *tireless* Quartermaster, with the invaluable services of reliable, trustworthy, loyal guides, to accomplish such an apparently impossible and hopeless task as this great Mackenzie Raid into Mexico.

The first United States troops to arrive were two companies of the First Infantry, accompanied by an advance and rear guard or U. S. Mounted Rifles. The post was named after Major John B. Clark. The site of the fort was held as an encampment or cantonment for nearly four years before the erection of anything like permanent quarters was begun. It is known that the present headquarters building was constructed in 1857. This date stands out in relief above the East entrance to this day.

A great procession of officers and men have passed and repassed at Fort Clark during the long period of its occupancy. It is interesting to note that the First and Second Dragoons and the Mounted Rifles became the First, Second and Third Regiments of Cavalry. After the ordinance of secession was passed in Texas over the protest of Gen. Sam Houston, Fort Clark was one of the eighteen Federal posts surrendered by Gen. David E. Twiggs to the Texas Commission in February, 1861. On March 10 of that year, it was evacuated by the Federal troops, being shortly afterward occupied by Texas volunteers under command of Lieut. Col. John B. Baylor. During this period post records disappeared for the period 1852-1866.

The "Dutch Battle Ground"

One of the incidents of the Federal evacuation was the sudden conversion of the post-surgeon and the hospital steward to the Confederate cause. The records show treatment for about everything that can befall men, women, and children. Here were brought the Confederate wounded from the so-called "Dutch Battle Ground," near the upper Nueces. The old post cemetery, now no longer used, offers solemn suggestion of the violence and bloodshed of the Mexican Border. On entering the walled enclosure one is impressed with the number of graves marked "Unknown." Out of the 146 graves, 102 hold the dust of persons whose identity had been utterly lost. This may be explained in part at least by the traditions that all white people found dead upon the plains within a radius of many miles were brought here for decent interment.

"From the headstone erected in memory of a soldier who died from wounds received at the hands of Kickapoos I have taken the following inscription," says Chaplain Bateman:

> O pray for the soldier, you kind-hearted
> stranger;
> He has roamed the prairie for many a
> year;
> He has kept the Comanches away from
> your ranches —
> And followed them far over the Texas
> frontier.

"Fort Clark was regarrisoned by Federal troops Dec. 12, 1866. Company C, 4th Cavalry, commanded by Capt. John. E. Willcox, composing the force to which was committed the two-fold task of fighting Indians and restoring the place. In March, 1868, the 4th Cavalry was reinforced by troops of the 41st Infantry, joining in command of Brevet Brig. Gen. R. C. Mackenzie. This officer occupies a large page in the history of the post. All through the years we come upon autographs of distinguished men who served here To have 'served at Clark' was at one time nearly equivalent to honorable mention, for such an entry in one's record was a sure token that the fortunate or unfortunate individual had been really initiated into army life."

Chaplain Bateman says that in the old days if they did not have a compulsory church attendance they had something that was a good deal worse. The Chaplain of the Post was ordered to present himself on the parade ground at 2 P. M. Sundays before the garrison in line and read the Articles of War, after which he was authorized to conduct any service he might choose for the occasion.

Fort Prices Were High

"The high cost of living bore heavily upon the slender purses of those days," the Chaplain continues. "Old schedules framed by post councils of administration show that tomatoes were 50 cents a can, while a glass of jelly sold for $1.25. Whisky varied in price from $4 to $7 per gallon. All whiskey was supposed to be 'good' in those days, but some brands were 'better' than others. For close quarters and quick action the four-dollar grade was probably the 'best' the country afforded. It is a remarkable fact that, although Fort Clark was established so long ago, the Government did not secure a deed to the land of this military reservation until 1885, when the sum of $80,000 was paid for 3,693.2 acres. During the war with Spain (1898) Fort Clark was garrisoned by the 3rd Regiment of Texas Infantry and kept in good condition.

"Fort Clark today is one of the most desirable locations in the Southwest. Blessed with an abundance of pure spring water and the purest of air from the Gulf and great plains, the sick reports have always been low. All talk of abandonment has long since ceased. A period of enlargement and reconstruction began in 1917 and work is still in progress. One of the best Y. M. C. A.'s (now the Service Club) in the Department was dedicated by Maj. Gen. John W. Ruchman early in 1918. Since that time nearly $200,000 have been expended in modern improvements such as electric lighting, sewerage system, concrete walks and driveways. Parks have been laid out by which reason of the presence of ancient oaks and pecans lend themselves to every form of beautification. Bridle paths follow the shade of forest monarchs centuries old at Clark."

---

*The foregoing historical sketch of Fort Clark was written by Chaplain Cephas C. Bateman, U. S. Army.

CHAPTER XVII

Campaign of 1874-1876

Actions of Tule and Palo Duro Cañons

IN the late summer of 1874, while General Mackenzie's command with headquarters of the Fourth U. S. Cavalry was at Fort Clark, Texas, rumors became rife of more unrest among certain tribes of Indians on the reservations. These rumors were soon verified by a threatened outbreak.

Shortly after this news reached the post, Sergeant John B. Charlton, Troop "F," Fourth Cavalry, was sent by General Mackenzie with dispatches to Fort Sill, with orders to travel by night only, as the country at that time was infested by numerous small bands of Indians; this to avoid much delay and many dangers.

By changing horses at each army post on the route he was able to make the ride, a distance of about 580 miles, in six nights. It was an exceedingly hard, lonely and grueling ride.

On his return trip he found the General's command at Fort Concho and there learned that the threatened out break had occurred.

It became known that Lone Wolf's band of Kiowas, strengthened by warriors from other tribes, including the Southern Cheyennes, Qua-ha-da Comanches and Arapahoes, had left their reservations and with their families had established themselves in winter quarters somewhere well within the border of North Texas and the "Panhandle," or the many "breaks" or canyons of the "Staked Plains," and that General Mackenzie had been ordered out with his command to intercept them and break up their camps or villages of which it was believed there were at least five. It was to be a campaign of either driving these hostile Indians into their reservations or one of *subjugation* and *annihilation*.

473

On August 15th, Major General Augur, Commanding
the Department of Texas, having joined General Mackenzie at Fort Clark, arrived with the latter at Fort Mc-
Kavett with all of the troops from Clark, and Companies
C, I and K, Tenth U. S. Infantry. Being joined here by
Troops A and H, of the Fourth, on the morning of the
18th the entire command, consisting now of A, C (joining
from Kerrville), D, F, G, H, I and K Troops with the Infantry, started for Fort Concho. "Kickapoo Springs"
was reached that afternoon, where the command went into
camp. It was learned that some 20 miles from here a
citizen's wagon train had been run off by Indians the previous night. Troop "C" (Capt. John A. Wilcox) was
started out at once but returned at dark without having
struck the trail.

The command reached Fort Concho on the 21st and
went into camp near the post. The other troops having arrived, the organization of this column was as follows:

Troops A, C, D, F, H, I, K and L, 4th Cavalry; Companies A, C, I, 10th Infantry, and H, 11th Infantry.*

It moved out on August 23rd. About a mile from the
post the command was formed in column of companies
and was inspected by Generals Augur and Mackenzie,
after which we broke into column of fours and proceeded
for our base of supplies, which was to be on the Freshwater Fork of the Brazos, otherwise known on the maps
of those days as "Catfish Creek," from the fact, it is
presumed, that there were no catfish in it. It was also
called "White River." This was at or near the mouth of
Cañon Blanco, about where our camp had been both in
1871 and 1872. There were to be four columns, operating from the North, South, East and West.

About August 3rd, Troop "C" was at Kerrville; "E"
was at Fort Duncan, and "A" and "H" were at Fort

---

*Additional companies of Infantry joined before the end of the campaign, so that
there were at one time the following: Companies A, C, I and K of the Tenth Infantry,
commanded respectively by Captains Lacey and Lieut. Kelton, Capts. Parks and Hampson, and Company H of the Eleventh Infantry, commanded by Lieut. Kislingbury and
Capt. Schwan's company of the latter regiment, all under command of Major T. M.
Anderson, Tenth U. S. Infantry. His camp was known as "Anderson's Fort" from the
many boxes, barrels, bales and filled bags piled up for defense.

McKavett, while the balance of the regiment, with the band, was at Fort Clark, Texas.

Upon Sergeant Charlton's return from Fort Sill and reporting the result of his perilous trip, he was detached from his troop and was assigned to duty with the scouting party just being formed. This party consisted of six white men, thirteen Seminoles, a few Lipans, and twelve Tonkaway Indians, Lieutenant William A. Thompson, Fourth Cavalry, being made Chief of Scouts, and Charlton as Sergeant of Scouts.

Headquarters, Department of Texas,
Fort Griffin, Texas, August 28th, 1874.

Colonel R. S. Mackenzie, 4th Cavalry,
Commanding Troops in the Field,
Fort Griffin, Texas.
Colonel:

In addition to the troops already placed under your Command and now enroute from Fort Concho to your Old Supply Camp, Lieutenant Colonel Buell, 11th Infantry, has been instructed to report to you with six Companies of Cavalry and two of Infantry for field service, to act from this point.

As you are aware, the object of the proposed Campaign against the hostile Cheyennes, Comanches, Kiowas, and others from the Fort Sill Reservation, is to punish them for recent depredations along the Kansas and Texas frontiers, and you are expected to take such measures against them as will, in your judgment, the soonest accomplish the purpose.

The Country accessible to these hostile bands is very large, and affords innumerable hiding places for themselves and their families and herds, and it is not expected that the object of the Campaign is to be accomplished in a day, unless by great and unexpected good fortune; but it is not proposed, however, to release efforts in the least, until the Indians are eventually found and punished, and made to subject themselves to such terms as the Government may impose upon them.

In carrying out your plans, you need pay no regard to Department or Reservation lines. *You are at liberty to follow the Indians wherever they go, even to the Agencies.* In this latter event great care must be exercised not to involve such friendly bands as have already gone to the Agencies and have remained peaceful.

Should it happen in the course of the Campaign, that the Indians return to the Agency at Sill, you will follow them there and assuming Command of all troops at that point, you will take such measures as will insure entire Control of the Indians there, until such time as you can report the condition of affairs to Department Headquarters. While the Indian Agent is to be consulted and to be treated with great respect, he will not be permitted to interfere in any way with the hostile bands, until the Orders of the Government for the disposition of the Indians are received.

Lieutenant Colonel Davidson, 10th Cavalry, with eight Companies of his regiment and two of Infantry, will operate against the same Indians from a Camp established on Otter Creek. The distance of this Command from the theatre of your operations and the difficulties of your communicating with it, make it necessary that he operate independently. If, however, it should occur at any time that you can make his column more effective by acting in concert with you in carrying out a particular plan, he will be instructed to comply with your orders in this respect.

Your own familiarity with Indians and Indian warfare, renders it unnecessary to give you any instructions in detail. I hope, however, as I do not doubt you will impress upon your subordinates when acting away from you, that in a hostile Indian Country, there is never a moment when it is safe to relax in vigilance and precautions against surprise. A Commander against hostile Indians is never in such imminent danger as when fully satisfied that no Indians can possibly be near him.

It is desired that you have maps made of the Country passed over, and as accurately as your means and opportunities will permit. These should be accompanied with descriptions of the route and adjacent Country.

Supplies for your Command will be sent to Fort Griffin, until you suggest some other point. In making your requisitions be careful to designate amounts and the time you desire them to be at Fort Griffin to connect with your trains, and every means will be taken to carry out your wishes.

Make reports by every opportunity and give as much of detail as possible.

Very respectfully,
Your Obt. Servant,
(Signed) C. C. AUGUR,
Brigadier General,
Commanding.

Memorandum for the information of the Department Commander, Department of Texas.

The troops from the Dept. of Texas, designated for field operations are as follows: for depot on the Fresh Fork of the Brazos, five (5) companies of Infantry. 1st Cavalry Column. Eight (8) Companies of 4th Cavalry operating from Supply Camp on Fresh

Fork. One or two Companies of Infantry with train. 2d Column, operating from Fort Griffin and Fresh Fork of the Brazos, Lieut. Colonel Buell, commanding. Five (5) companies 9th Cavalry, one (1) company of the 10th Cavalry and two (2) companies of Infantry. 3d Column. Lieut. Colonel Davidson commanding. Eight (8) companies 10th Cavalry, two (2) Companies of Infantry, operating from Fort Sill and Elk Creek.

The first Column will move north from the Fresh Fork along the edge of the Staked Plains, passing either from the head of the Brazos to the head of the main Red River and thence to the head of the Salt Fork, or by Quita Que, crossing Red River and thence to the head of Salt Fork and perhaps eventually going into Camp Supply. This movement to commence September 15th to 18th.

2d Column from a point selected on Beaver Creek, crosses Pease River and marches up main Red River to trail of 1872 and then according to circumstances. Both columns will disregard any general directions if any probability offers of overtaking Indians; to disregard small parties and endeavor to strike Indian Camps. Greatest care to be exercised with reference to keeping horses in condition. Both columns to take with them as nearly as possible six weeks rations and thirty days half forage. Both columns to move 1st from Fresh Fork, 2d from the Beaver, September 18th.

In all columns it must be borne in mind that superiority of Cavalry soldiers over Indians with immense herds of horses can only be maintained by the constant use of sufficient short forage.

Additional Memoranda

Since the above was written it has been reported from Fort Sill that the Qua-ha-da Comanches had gone to the Staked Plains. The indications prior to the departure of the Comdg. General of the Department from Fort Concho, in numerous depredations south of that post, seemed to sustain this report.

Major Anderson was directed on leaving Concho that should the trails lead him to believe that a considerable body of Indians were camped West of his line of march, to detach a sufficient command to look them up.

Captain Boehm has since been directed on his march to the Fresh Fork to send two or three Seminole Negroes with fast led horses to go into the plains fifty miles west of the head of the Double Mountain Fork and endeavor to find such a Camp. Should they be successful in finding a column it might delay the movement of the column from the Fresh Fork a few days.

Respectfully submitted,
(Signed) R. S. MACKENZIE,
Colonel 4th Cavalry,
Commanding.

A true copy respectfully furnished for the information of the lieutenant General Commanding the Military Division of the Missouri, Chicago, Illinois.

(Signed) C. C. Augur,
Brigadier General,
Commanding.

H.Q. Dept. Texas.
Ft. Gfn., Texas,
28th August, 1874.

Our command was to be designated as "The Southern Column." That night (August 23d) our camp was at the "Stone Ranch" on the North Concho, some 16 miles from the Post of Concho. Proceeding up the North Concho for the next three days for about 50 miles, we diverged to the North, heading for a range of hills, which we crossed. We camped the same night (26th) at Rendlebrock Springs, named after the Captain of G Troop, 4th Cavalry. During this day's march we crossed two small Indian trails leading south, one of seven, the other of thirteen ponies. On the 27th the command remained in camp all day to rest the men and horses. About 10 o'clock P.M. a heavy wind carried a brand from one of the fires into a ravine close by, full of long dry grass, and set the camp afire. The men were turned out and with empty corn sacks and old blankets well soaked with water, after working hard for half an hour, put the fire out, after which we had a drill and inspection of the whole command. The tent of Captain T. J. Wint, commanding Co. L, was destroyed.

Moving at 5:30 A.M. the next morning (28th) we marched to Henry's Creek, or Salt Fork of the Colorado River, over a high, rolling country, with two deep ravines to cross for heavily loaded wagons. The crossing of the creek was also hard, with a heavy pull on the other side. The water, in holes, was bad; grass very poor, and no wood except limited amounts of mesquite brush. The Cavalry went into camp at 11 A.M.; the Infantry at 1:30 P.M. The next morning the Infantry and teams left camp at 2:30 A.M., the Cavalry at 5 o'clock. Crossed the Colorado River about 5 miles from camp. It was forded. The sand being heavy it took three quarters of an hour to march through it. The Infantry had arrived and were 3 miles beyond the river in camp, eating breakfast. The Cavlary pushed on to Culver's Creek, named for Acting Assistant Surgeon Ira Culver, who, in 1873, had been on a scout to this point. He was also with the writer on the Double Mountain Fork of the Brazos in November 1871. The creek was dry so we marched two miles beyond it, finding water in holes. The infantry came in two hours later and the teams did not get in until 4 P.M. after a hard pull through sand. There was a night alarm which proved to be a false one. At 4 A.M. August 30, the infantry and teams pulled out, the cavalry an hour later. Between 2 and 3 P.M. reached Hemphill's Creek, named after Lieut. Hemphill, Troop "G", but not finding water followed the creek up for a couple of miles and found some brackish water in holes on both sides of the stream, and went into camp. Glad enough to get anything to drink. This point was "just opposite Kelly's Creek where a private of that name had been killed by Indians in 1872, his horse having stumbled and thrown him when his company had fallen back before a large body of Indians".

On August 31st we marched to the Double Mountain Fork of the Brazos River and went into camp on the west bank. Many antelope seen and killed. The next day's march was the hardest as the command pushed on to the Freshwater Fork of the Brazos, on the banks of which we knew our permanent supply camp was to be located, and from which point we also knew that the real business of the expedition was to be undertaken. We were 12 hours in the saddle on this day. The march for the past two days had been through immense herds of buffalo, affording plenty of meat for the entire command. The wagons failed to arrive that night and our mess was without its usual meal.

On September 2nd Lieut. H. W. Lawton, Quartermaster of the expedition, as well as regimental quartermaster of the 4th Cavalry, one of the very best quartermasters the service ever had (later Major General of Volunteers and killed at San Mateo, P.I., Dec. 19, 1899), started with the now empty wagon train for Fort Griffin, Texas—a distance of about 140 miles—and designated as our future base of supplies. His route was by our old trail—"The Mackenzie Trail", via Double Mountain Fork of the Brazos, California and Paint Creeks and Clear Fork of the Brazos.

Our camp was moved the next day (Sept. 3) about one mile above the infantry camp to a high plateau, bleak and dreary, open on all sides to the full power of a "Norther" then blowing, having sprung up in the night. It continued all that day and night. It did not interfere, however, with our having a long and thorough skirmish drill on foot in the middle of the day, and late in the afternoon the entire command was turned out to attend the funeral of one of our men who, having become sick on the march, died the day previous (Sept. 2). It was a scene that made such strong impressions on the mind that one remembers them during a life time. His grave was far from home and friends, on the lonely, desolate plains of Texas. Not far from here we had buried nearly three years before Private Gregg of "G" Troop, who had been killed by Quan-ah Parker, the half breed chief of the Qua-ha-ha Comanches, at the mouth of Canon Blanco.

We remained in this camp some ten or twelve days, little better than a bivouac, drilling every day, collecting supplies, and getting ready for our pack mule scouting, etc., while we awaited the arrival of General Mackenzie.

Headquarters, Department of Texas.
Fort Sill, Sept. 17th, 1874.

Dear General Sheridan :—

I enclose copies of a number of letters received from Mackenzie. Although of different dates they were all received here the same day. You will see from these that he has had the same trouble as ourselves in getting forage to load his train. I have sent for Holabird to go to Dallas and other points and to see exactly what we can depend upon from our Contractors. Meanwhile I will ask you to send four thousand bushels more corn to Dennison or Dallas for Fort Griffin. Since the secretary broke up the Dallas arrangement I am entirely in the dark about matters there. The quartermaster who ships it should notify Holabird, that he may notify the Contractor. Buell's train, I am sorry to say is still detained south of Red River. There seems to have been a very great and a very unexpected rise in that stream. I sent the train there in order to hasten matters, as it did in the case of Davidson's command. But owing to this high water it will cause delay instead. It cannot be helped. Buell is very impatient as well as myself. I really do not think however that this delay will be in the least detrimental, as the Indians are effected by the other Columns they will fall back probably upon the main Red, and Buell will be in good time to meet them. Meanwhile the presence of his command has been beneficial.

Yours Respectfully,

(Signed) C. C. AUGUR,

Brig. General,

Commanding.

On September 17th the command moved up the valley some 9 miles and camped near "The Lake." Here we found a spring of pure water, a real blessing as all of the water we had drank had been impregnated with gypsum. Here three Lieutenants joined the 4th Cavalry, from detached duty. On the same day three wagons arrived with corn for the horses, they having had none for some days. Another troop ("E") joined here from Fort Duncan where it had been stationed.

On the morning of the 19th General Mackenzie, Lt. Col. John P. Hatch (Maj.-Gen. Volunteers 1862), 4th Cavalry, and Major T. M. Anderson (later Brig.-Gen. and Maj.-Gen. U.S.A.), 10th Infantry, came in escorted by two companies of infantry. The cavalry command was now divided into two battalions; the first, composed of Troops D, F, I and K, under Captain and Brevet Brigadier General of Volunteers (Brigadier General during the Civil War), N. B. McLaughlin, now senior captain; the second, composed of Troops A, E, H and L, under Captain E. B. Beaumont (brevet Lt. Colonel), both gallant officers of long service and much experience.

The entire cavalry command, consisting of 450 enlisted men, 21 commissioned officers and 3 Acting Assistant Surgeons, moved across the east side of the creek (Catfish) and final preparations were now made for a start on the 20th to hunt up the hostiles known to be away from their reservations at Forts Sill and Reno—Comanches, Kiowas, Arapahoes and Southern Cheyennes, and supposed to be in or about the "breaks" of the "Staked Plains."

On Sunday, September 20th, at 5 o'clock A.M. the long column marched out of camp East, up the valley, and on to the "Staked Plains"—("Llauo Estacado"). After marching some 15 miles we came to some water holes (rain water) and there found Lawton, who had started several hours ahead of the column with two companies of infantry escorting the train. We halted here for dinner. The scouts came in and reported that they had been attacked by some 20 Indians. The cavalry moved out at a trot in the direction the scouts pointed out. Held a course due north for 1½ hours, and then diverged northwest, marching that course for some 12 miles without seeing any signs.

Having found some running water nearby, we halted, unsaddled and bivouacked for the night. Every precaution was taken against surprise, as we now knew the Indians having discovered us would be on the alert day and night. This camp was at the head of the Big Wichita River, 30 miles from our starting place of the morning.

On the 21st we waited for the train, which had been left far to the rear, to come up. It arrived at 7:30 A.M. We then saddled up and the First Battalion moved out on a trail leading north, supposed to be made by the party our scouts had discovered the day before.

The Second Battalion moved northwest over some sand hills to the Salt Fork of the Wichita, and as soon as we arrived there, Troop E was sent to the west on a reconnoissance; the other three troops halted, unsaddled, the mules were unpacked, and the men got dinner. At 1 P.M. we repacked, saddled up, and marched to the head of

Pease River—a running stream of clear water in Quit-a-Que Valley, and camped.

A terrific thunderstorm, for which the "Staked Plains" are noted, came up that night. It rained in torrents and the lightning was incessant and so vivid as to illuminate the entire bivouac. "Sheets of flame" hardly does it justice. Officers stood under a high bluff, expecting to see the horses struck and to drop every moment. During this frightful storm a part of this bluff fell and compelled everybody to move away from there *"pronto."*

Lawton managed to get one wagon up with a supply of fresh beef, which was a welcome addition to our slim supply of grub. The balance of the train, owing to the mud, was back some 8 miles. It took 12 mules to haul that wagon.

We remained in camp all the next day waiting for the 1st Battalion to join headquarters, which had moved with the 2nd Battalion. A sergeant and 2 men, one of them being Private E. M. Beck of Co. H, Fourth Cavalry, were sent with dispatches to the First Battalion, which had advanced to Tule Canon, to recall them. On the afternoon of the 26th they, in "their company", rejoined the rest of the command at "Boehm's Canon". Early in the forenoon the train with its infantry escort came into our camp. It continued to rain and grow cold with a heavy gale. Shelter was sought in the small valleys and breaks. The command started to march west to some low hills and where we could get better grass for the horses, but were forced to go into camp again owing to the continuous heavy downpour of rain. Near sundown the 1st Battalion joined us. Some of the horses were now showing signs of giving out and had to be shot to prevent their falling into the hands of the Indians.

After 5 hours of hard pulling through the soft, slushy mud—making but 7 miles—Lawton succeeded in getting the supply wagons up late in the evening.

On September 24th a "wet Norther" set in and contin-

ued all night. One who has never passed through a
"Norther" can hardly appreciate the condition of a cavalry command at that period exposed to all its fury. No
move was made until 1 P.M. The train moved out towards the pass in the hills from Quit-a-Que Valley. Reaching the foot hills once more, the command was halted,
bridles taken off the horses and they were "staked out" to
graze—a herd guard being put on for safety. The balance
of the men manned the ropes which had been attached to
the wagons and hauled them up over the steep and slippery grade. The teams were "doubled up." Before dark
the last wagon was out of the valley and out on the
"Staked Plains" once more. We bivouacked. We had
made but 4 miles.

On September 25th the column had moved out early,
leaving the wagons—not a wheel could be turned. We
pushed on to Tule Spring, reaching it about sunset. While
waiting dismounted, to go into bivouac for the night, one
of our scouts galloped up and reported Indians to the east
of us and that Lieutenant Thompson, commanding scouts
and guides, had, with most of the scouts (Ton-ka-ways and
Seminoles), started for them.

Orders were given for the 2nd Battalion to mount and
move out. The moon was full. It was a weird sight—this
long, dark column of mounted men moving almost silently
over the thick, short buffalo grass, which deadened all
sounds, not a word being spoken, expecting every minute
to come upon the enemy. Failing to meet the Indians,
after being in the saddle about 16 hours, we went into
camp very late at night in a series of ravines which we
had struck on our march. Strong guards were posted
about the horses, pickets were thrown out and "sleeping
parties" were placed among the horse herds now lariated
out, to guard against any surprise or attempt to stampede
our animals. Everybody slept with their boots on, ready
on the instant of any alarm for immediate action. It
proved to be a quiet night. After remaining here all day,

at 5 P.M. we moved south some distance until we came to a depression in the plains—or "lagoon", full of good rain water—and went into bivouac, grazing our horses in the meantime. Shortly after this a corporal with 6 men arrived from the 1st Battalion, which we had left at Tule Spring the day before, and reported that Indians had been hovering around the 1st Battalion all day and had even exchanged shots with it. Some of our scouts also reported that Indians were beginning to gather in our own vicinity and we might expect a visit from them almost any time that very night.

On the march from Tule to Boehm's Canon three Indians approached Henry, one of the Ton-ka-way scouts, who was well out on the flank, and began circling about him. When within easy range they opened fire. Their rifles were muzzle loaders and when all had fired, Henry with his Winchester repeating rifle, put spur to his pony and charged them. As they disappeared over a slight rise in the prairie, a large party of the enemy, concealed in the grass, opened fire on Henry. Stopping his pony he waved his rifle in the air and cantered slowly back to the column. This was one of the usual pieces of bravado incident to Indian actions.

The horses were carefully "side lined" and "staked out", and all precaution in the way of pickets, sleeping parties, etc., taken as usual, so that we would not be caught "napping."

As was fully expected that night—Sunday, September 26-27, the Indians attacked our camp. Our horses proved safe from stampede as long as good leather and rope held together. The men were run out on a skirmish line with a 5 yard interval, outside the horse herds—the "sleeping parties" inside of the herds, ready with their boots on for quick fighting, consisted of from 12 to 20 men with selected non-commissioned officers. Upon an alarm they were to rush out to points designated during daylight, and from four to five hundred yards. These points were known to the Commanding Officer, Officer of the Day, and Officer of the Herd. They were posted so that they could not be observed by the Indians—in some ravine or hollow. A running guard was kept up all night in each party, so that nothing could approach the command or steal in upon it through these hollows. The party was strong enough to put up a stubborn fight, if necessary, until the entire command could be got under arms, and come to their support. They were really *inner outposts* within the *outer picket line.* This bivouac was in a slight basin-like depression, or "sink", with a skyline which gave a good view of anything passing while the command was practically invisible. Private Goodwin, Co. H, who was on guard at one end of the camp, hearing galloping ponies, challenged; receiving no answer, he opened fire, which aroused the command.

It was about 10:30 when the first attack came and a large body of mounted Indians charged along our lines, in fact, all around us, firing and yelling, to try and start our horses. The latter were securely *anchored.* The 1st Battalion was camped about three-quarters mile to the east, and as the Indians charged around it the night was so still that, without seeing them in the dim moonlight, the voices of the officers could be distinctly heard giving their commands. Now occurred a very unusual thing during an Indian fight. About midnight, with every one alert, keyed up and with nerves tightened, we could hear the rattling of the wheels of our wagons in the distance, moving up to us, we having cut loose from it the day previous. It was a *"cold day"* when Lawton could not move his train. Between 1 and 2 o'clock A.M. the Indians withdrew and the firing ceased. We then stretched ourselves on our blankets once again to snatch a little more of that much needed rest. About 5 o'clock A.M. the whole command was "turned out" under arms, the Indians having begun to fire into us from a ravine to the right quite a distance beyond our farthest picket post in that direction.

The firing was so desultory, however, that the men were directed to attend to their horses, but after a short time it began to grow more lively and Indians came faster and thicker, but without doing much damage, the range being very great. Orders were sent to each troop commander to "saddle up", which was done in quick time. "E" Troop being nearest to the General it was mounted and started off towards the position held by the Indians, who, when they saw the troop coming towards them, ran to their ponies, mounted and galloped off in a body on to the high and level ground, there being, at a rough guess, about 300 of them. "E" Troop, Captain P. M. Boehm, and "H" Troop, Captain S. Gunther, charged and the Indians fled. Some few shots were exchanged, and a couple of our Ton-Ka-way scouts, or "trailers," caught one Comanche who got separated from the rest, whom the "Tonks" killed and scalped.

The entire 2nd Battalion was out on the high ground by this time, but the Indians had disappeared as completely as if the ground had swallowed them. Several scouts and spies had been scouring the country in advance for long distances the past few days, and—from after events—had undoubtedly made discoveries which they had reported to headquarters and which accounted for our not taking up the trail of the Indians who had been firing into us. In this action "Woman Heart," a famous Ki-o-wa Chief, and 15 warriors were killed.

We returned to our camp of the previous night and let the men get breakfast, without unsaddling, after which our rations were overhauled, and deficiencies made good (to last ten days) from our wagon train, which, under the indefatigable Lawton, had once more worked up to us. Packs, carbines and equipments generally were closely inspected to see if everything was in good order, and at 3 o'clock P.M. the command moved from its camp, taking a course due North. Each troop had its pack mule train, in charge of a non-commissioned officer and a small detach-

ment of men as a guard, the whole marching in rear of
the column and under the immediate charge of "the Officer
of the Day."

We marched steadily for 12 hours before we halted,
which we finally did, and the order was quietly passed
along the column to unsaddle the horses and to unpack the
mules. All of the animals were "staked out" but the
ground was bare, there being no grass. We spread our
blankets on the wet ground and every man, excepting the
guard, sought rest and sleep, but the fortunes of war permitted neither, for in about half an hour we were quickly
routed out and ordered to "pack up" and "saddle up"
again, and at once.

The scouts, Sergeant John B. Charlton and Johnson and
Job, Ton-ka-way Indians, had come in and reported a
"fresh trail." We mounted and moved out quickly, every
man alert. It was yet dark about 4 o'clock A.M. when we
resumed our march, still going North, and just as the first
faint streaks of daylight came in the East we suddenly
came to a wide and yawning chasm or cañon, which proved
to be Palo Duro Cañon.

In the dim light of the dawn, away down hundreds of
feet we could see the Indian "tepees" or lodges, and as we
had to march along the edge of the cañon some distance
before we could find any path or trail to descend by, the
morning had become quite light and the Indians, who had
now discovered us, rushed out of their lodges and began
gathering in their herds of ponies and driving them off
towards the head of the Canon. How we got down into
the Canon was, and always will be, to the few surviving
members of the old 4th Cavalry, who participated in the
Palo Duro fight, a great mystery.

The whole command dismounted and each officer and
man, leading his horse in single file, took the narrow zig-
zag path, which was apparently used by nothing but Indian
ponies and buffalo. Men and horses slipping down the

steepest places, stumbling and sliding, one by one we reached the bottom.

By this time the Indians nearest us had fled with their stock up the Cañon. Each troop, as it reached the bottom, was formed and mounted and sent off at a gallop after the Indians, all of whom succeeded in getting away, abandoning lodges and everything in their flight, scrambling and climbing up both sides of the Canon and hiding behind immense boulders of rocks.

"A" Troop with its gallant Captain, Brevet Lt. Colonel Eugene B. Beaumont, was the first to reach the bottom and as soon as the last man and horse was down, mounted, and took the gallop up the Canon after the fleeing Indians and pony herds. "H" and "L" troops got down, somehow, on parallel lines and galloped off together and abreast —General Mackenzie in the lead. As we galloped along we passed village after village of Indian lodges both on the right and left, all empty and totally abandoned. The ground was strewn with buffalo robes, blankets, and every imaginable thing, in fact, that the Indians had in the way of property—all of which had been hastily collected and a vain attempt made by the squaws to gather up and save, but finding the troops coming up so rapidly they were forced to drop their goods and chattels and suddenly take to the almost inaccessible sides of the Cañon to save themselves from capture. Numbers of their pack animals were running around loose with their packs on, while others stood tied to trees—all having been abandoned by their owners, who were pressed so hard by our command that they had to hastily flee to the friendly shelter of the rocks that towered above us to the right and left.

One portion of the command continued up the Canon at a gallop for about 2 miles, with the object of overhauling the bucks who had run off the pony herds, when we met Colonel Beaumont with his troop returning and driving before them a large number of ponies which they had captured. In fact Beaumont had rounded up almost the entire herd. "H" and "L" troops were halted, formed line, and now waited for orders.

While waiting mounted and calmly taking in the surroundings, the Indians who had succeeded in safely placing themselves behind the immense breastwork of rocks, some 800 or 1000 feet above us, opened fire upon us and in a very few minutes made it so hot and galling that we were forced to fall back—the Indians being so thoroughly protected in their position that we could do nothing with so many captured horses on our hands.

As we made this move a trumpeter of "L" troop was shot through the body and fell from his horse. He was picked up and carried to the rear, everyone expecting to find him dead in twenty minutes, but, thanks to the care and skill of Acting Assistant Surgeon Rufus Choate (already referred to in the "Tragedies of Canon Blanco in 1871), the man lived to sound his trumpet-calls for many years after. This trumpeter's name was Hard. The surgeon said that his having fasted for about 30 hours had saved his life.

Troop "H" wheeled about in column of fours, struck the dry bed of a creek, moved back about 200 yards and halted there, as it was supposed under fairly good cover, but the Indians, soon getting the range, for a few minutes gave us a rattling fire, although not a man was hit.

Troop "H" being in line across the Canon at this time was exposed to an enfilading fire from both bluffs. Six or eight horses had been shot in as many minutes. The men were now dismounted, and leaving the horses in charge of the horse holders (No. 4) they were ordered by Captain Gunther to clear the bluffs of Indians. There was little or no cover. The movement had just begun when Gen. Mackenzie, who was near by, upon discovering it called out, "Sergeant, where are you going with those men"? "To clear the bluff sir"! "By whose orders"? "Captain Gunther's"! "Take those men back to their company. Not one of them would live to reach the top", and riding

over to the Captain he gave him to understand that he dis-
approved of such a move.

Private McGowan's horse was shot from under him and
fell in an exposed position where he was under a severe
fire. McGowan was down on his knees, tugging away at his
saddle, a fair target, the bullets whistling all about him
and kicking the sand over his body. Mackenzie happening
to see him, shouted, "McGowan, get away from there or
you will be hit"! "Yes, Sir", replied McGowan, and
made a motion as if to leave the spot; but the General's
back being turned, he dropped on his knees and resumed
his tugging. Twice Mackenzie ordered him away and
when he (Mackenzie) turned the third time and found him
still at his work, he spoke sharply, "I told you to go away
from there, are you going"? McGowan replied, "D—d if
I am until I get my tobacco and ammunition," which were
in the saddle pockets under his horse. The General then
gave it up.

A large number of Indians had disappeared around a
sharp elbow of the Canon, and Mackenzie wanted to know
what they might be up to. One of the scouts, Private
Comfort of Troop "A", volunteered to find out. In a few
minutes he came back, his horse on the run, with a large
bunch of Indians after him. In a shallow ravine crossing
the Cañon, a party of the command was posted, and when
Comfort had passed, they checked his pursuers and drove
them back. Near where the command halted a badly
wounded Indian lay on the slope of an embankment. One
of the Ton-ka-way squaws who had accompanied her scout
husband approached him. He spoke to her. She flew into
a rage, calling him vile names and dismounting from her
pony, finished him.

At a time when the fire was the hottest, one of the men
said on seeing that the command was nearly surrounded,
"How will we ever get out of here"? The General on
hearing him said, "I brought you in, I will take you out".
Most of the men did not question when he led, we knew we
could depend on his care and guidance.

About noon the General saw a movement among the Indians on top of the bluff, and surmised that they were going to try and block the way by which the command had entered. He ordered Captain Gunther to take his company ("H") to clear the way and hold it until the command came out. It was a race between that company and the Indians, but in favor of the former, as they (the Indians) would first have to cross a deep branch of the Cañon. The Company reached the top first without opposition, the Indians evidently not caring to attack the company in that position. On the way down the Cañon one company was held in reserve at a small cottonwood grove.

. . . The command, after destroying all the camps and contents and capturing all of the ponies, ceased fighting as the Indians offered no further resistance.

At this moment the Adjutant rode up with an order for us to take the command back at a gallop to the pass which the command had used to get down into the Canon, follow up the pass out of the Canon, and hold the head so that our retreat could not be cut off—as a demonstration had been made by a large party of Indians on the high tableland to make a detour towards that point.

The troop wheeled "fours to the left about," the command "Gallop" was given, and away we went on the same trail we had come over not many hours before. When we reached the foot of the "Jacob's ladder"—like arrangement—almost precipitous cliffs—we had to climb up to get out of the Canon. To do this we dismounted and began the toilsome, almost perilous ascent, which, after one-half to three-fourths of an hour's hard work, we accomplished, but did not find an Indian in sight.

Meantime, the Indians in the Canon, having recovered somewhat from their complete surprise of the early morning and having occupied the many strong strategic positions referred to, began to grow bold and come down the

Note:—This account of the Palo Duro fight is given more fully in "The Old Sergeant's Story."—R. G. C.

sides, hiding behind rocks and trees, and finally reaching a natural breastwork or barricade made by some huge boulders that had rolled down the sides of the Canon and were spread pretty thickly over its bottom in places. These Indians kept up a lively and continuous fire upon the command. Troops D, I and K were dismounted and deployed as skirmishers across the bottom of the Canon and commenced to shoot at long range with the Indians. While this rather desultory firing was going on another portion of the command was engaged in pulling down the lodges, chopping up the lodge poles and gathering up the various miscellaneous belongings of the Indians into immense piles, of which huge bonfires were made.

Still another detachment was employed in rounding up the pony herd and getting it out of the Canon by the same trail we had already used.

As our skirmish line advanced, the Indians retired, springing from one rock to the protection of another, until finally they took to the inaccessible sides of the Canon once more; then, in order to hold the large number of ponies captured the command commenced to withdraw from the Canon, which was finally vacated between 3 and 4 o'clock P.M. The whole command now assembled, with the immense herd of captured ponies, on the high prairie ("Staked Plains"). A "hollow square" or huge parallelogram was formed as follows: One troop in line of battle rode in advance; on either side marched two troops in column of twos; and one troop, in line, rode in rear. In the center of this huge hollow square the captured herd of about 2000 was driven along. One troop marched in rear of all as rear guard. It was a living corral and our march was nearly 20 miles.

We had adopted this formation when we lost Quanah Parker's band of Qua-ha-da Comanches in that bleak, sleeting Norther in October 1871—only in that case we had a line of advanced skirmishers and a flanking column out, ready for instant action, as the Comanches were constantly threatening to close in upon us for a fight.

We marched rapidly until nearly 1 A.M. on the 29th, when we came in sight of the welcome light of the camp-fires of our infantry guarding our wagon supply train. The noise made by the command on its approach alarmed the inmates of the Supply Camp at Tule Canon and the Infantry guard opened fire from their outposts, believing it to be in the darkness a large body of Indians. Lieut. Wentz C. Miller rode forward and informed the camp guard of its mistake. On the morning of the 29th the men had their first meal in over 48 hours.

The Indians afterwards admitted losing 15 at the Tule Canon action, and 50 or 60 at the Palo Duro Canon.

The captured ponies were at once driven into the corral formed by the wagons, and a strong guard placed over them. Our horses were unsaddled, staked out and fed a full ration of corn, which the poor animals sorely needed.

After getting a cup of coffee all rolled up in their blankets and "turned in," i.e., lay down on "Mother Earth" to secure some of "Nature's sweet restorer, balmy sleep."

In view of what we had gone through—thirty-four hours in the saddle, riding over seventy miles, and having two or three hours fighting and hard work generally, that same Mother Earth was as welcome as any soft feather bed.

On September 29th reveille was late. Immediately after breakfast a detail was made to shoot the captured ponies, which, owing to the great number, it was found impossible to take along and properly guard them, or to take them into the nearest military post—the nearest being nearly two hundred miles away. The Indians would follow us and be upon us every night in an effort to stampede and recapture them. Experience had been our lesson. The number, as has been stated, were variously estimated at from 1500 to 2200. The "Tonks" were permitted to select the best. Numbers of them were young and handsome, and it seemed a pity to be compelled to kill them, but there was no other alternative. It was the surest method of crippling the Indians and compelling them to go into and stay upon their reservations which they had fled from. Many were the best race ponies they had and many pesos had been waged upon them. Some were used to replace those which had died on the march or been wounded in the fight. It was a heavy blow. They were such valuable property that they were held in higher esteem than their squaws. It took Lawton the most of one day, with one troop, to pile these bodies up on the plains. They were still there—on the "Tex" Rogers ranch some years ago—an enigma to the average Texas boy who looked upon them with wondering eyes. About noontime there was a false alarm.

We moved camp about 4 P.M. on the 29th, some three or four miles away from the dead animals and went into camp in a good grass bottom, through which ran a clear creek of water called "Tule Creek." There was no wood for our cook fires except what the wagons had brought from our last camp. We had a quiet peaceable night, without alarm of any kind, and next day (30th) moved our camp a few miles farther west.

At dark some of the "Tonks" left camp with dispatches for our permanent supply camp on the Freshwater Fork of the Brazos River. The horses were tied into a picket line at night, a rope being stretched from wagon to wagon. The entire command was deployed on a skirmish line entirely around the camp, outside of everything, and lay down to sleep, with the necessary sentinels and picket outposts.

A few Indian spies were seen about sunset, to the North, sent out to observe our command. Every precaution was taken to guard against surprise.

The 1st Battalion was camped some distance from headquarters, which was now with the 2nd Battalion but was, after dark, sent to join the latter so as to have the entire command together.

The night passed quietly. Soon after breakfast we moved on our old trail back towards Palo Duro, where we had captured the ponies. When we had marched about half way, or about 5 o'clock P.M., having found some good water, it was decided to go into camp.

Shortly after camping one of our officers with some "Tonks" and a citizen guide (Strong ?) made a reconnoissance towards Palo Duro Canon. Upon their return they reported seeing no signs of Indians and that all was perfectly still and quiet.

At 9 A.M. on October 3rd the entire command—cavalry, infantry and wagons—left camp and marched to the wagon crossing of Canon Blanco, where we halted for dinner. After which we resumed the march till late in the evening, when camp was made in a large basin-like depression or "sink" in the prairie—where there was no wood, no grass, and but little water. Here each animal received one quart of corn.

About an hour or so after camping, the camp was alarmed by two shots. Every officer sprang up expecting that the Indians were upon us. It proved to be a false alarm, the shots having been fired in the killing of two beeves for the use of the men.

On Sunday, October 4th, we "packed up," "saddled up" and left camp without getting breakfast. After marching till 9::30 A.M. we reached the Palo Duro Canon, where we halted, took off the bridles, staked the horses out on good grass, and placing a strong guard on the herds, the command had its breakfast. This meal was generally fried bacon, coffee without milk, and "doby" biscuits baked in "Dutch ovens," or in an open fry pan.

At 3 o'clock, moving North—parallel with the Canon for about 6 or 7 miles—we went into camp, dense masses of clouds threatening a heavy storm for which the "Staked Plains" were famous.

CHAPTER XVIII

"Mopping Up" the "Texas Panhandle"

WHILE some had wall tent flies for shelter at night, there was nothing on the bare plains for tent poles. So a dismal rainy night was worn out with what shelter could be found, which was with a brother officer who had rank enough to have a "fly" that was not rotten and who had two small crotched stakes over which our lariats had been passed and the tent thrown over them and made fast to the ground. Shortly after starting on the march the next morning (Oct. 5) we struck a trail made by the 8th Cavalry under Col. J. I. Gregg in 1872. After following it for a few miles some excitement was noticed among the scouts at the front. The order was given to trot and soon the long column of fours was covering the ground at a lively gait. Soon the "Tonks" going still faster, the gallop was taken up. This continued for fully three miles, when all came down to a trot and walk. We had come to a place where a large Indian village had been, signs of which were all about, but now not a single Indian was to be seen. All the ravines and arroyas were searched on the north side of the Palo Duro Canon, but without avail, and we soon bore off to the North about three miles, and finding a great lagoon of fresh water from the recent rain we went into camp at sundown. There was plenty of grass and scrub oak. All the sick men and weak horses were left here with a supply train, which always kept on our trail wherever it was possible, and by detours Lawton managed to bring it up to us before our 15 days supply on our pack mules had been exhausted.

At 3 o'clock P.M., October 6th, the cavalry broke camp and marched steadily with scarcely a halt until 8 o'clock that night. The tremendous rains of the previous day had made the country miry, which exhausted the horses, compelling the command to halt and bivouac for the night.

The ground was wet and there was little or no grass. After a miserable night with no rest for man or beast, at daybreak a "wet norther" set in, making the going almost impossible; more than half of the time the men were on foot working their way through the mud now nearly a foot deep. During the forenoon we came up with six Mexican wagons drawn by oxen. The Mexicans said they were hunting buffalo. Shortly after we struck a trail and followed it till 1:30 P.M., when we halted for the men to get breakfast, having been without food for 24 hours. The march was resumed over the same kind of "dobe," wet country. About one hour before sundown we struck a large Indian trail running southeast. After following it about a mile we struck one of the ponds or lagoons (rain water), and were directed to halt and unpack. At dark orders were again given very quietly to "pack up" and "saddle up" and after everything was ready to move a second order was as quietly given for us to "unpack" and "unsaddle" again and to remain where we were for the night. We never knew why these orders were changed so soon.

The next morning (Oct. 7) we moved out on foot, leading our horses. We alternated riding and marching afoot for about ten miles, when we struck a very broken country and came across two Mexicans with a wagon ("Carreta") and 8 oxen. We made the Mexicans prisoners. They confessed that they had been trading with the hostiles, so we took the whole "outfit" along. Following down a small creek until 10 o'clock A.M. we halted, unsaddled, unpacked, staked out the animals and proceeded to get breakfast. The last few days had almost "played out" all of the animals. The Mexican wagon was broken up and their oxen were turned into the beef herd for food, while their owners were put under guard. At 2:30 we packed and saddled up and resumed our march. Some of the men whose horses had given out were now mounted on mules. It was ride the Mexican burros or small donkeys or walk. Our route continued down the valley of the creek, until sundown when camp was made. We continued to outpost our camp as usual, and place the command sleeping on a skirmish line all around the outside of where the animals were staked out and "side lined" for grazing.

During the night some of the scouts, who usually rode a long way in advance of the column, came in. Whatever they reported, the command did not always learn; but in the morning (Oct. 8) upon taking up the march we followed the back trail—evidently going to show that there was no fear of hostile trails ahead. It was surmised that we were looking for their villages where the squaws, papooses and the ponies saved from the Palo Duro fight might be found, and which if we now could only capture would prove to be the most decisive blow that could be given to the confederated bands, and which would surely result in their accepting defeat and retiring to the reservations.

> Headquarters Supply Camp Southern Columns,
> On Fresh Water Fork Brazos River, Texas.
> October 7th, 1874.

Adjutant General,
    Military Division of the Missouri,
        Chicago, Ill.

Sir :—

I have the honor to acknowledge the receipt of copies of the letters of Generals Pope and Miles sent from your Headquarters on the 22nd of September, and forwarded by courier from Fort Griffin October 3rd.

The Courier delivered them to me yesterday the 6th instant. I will forward the communications to Colonel Mackenzie as soon as I learn the direction of his next movement, which I expect to be advised of in a few days.

Colonel Mackenzie has, however, already met and defeated the Cheyennes, and moved directly North for McClellan's Creek on the 2d instant, taking twelve (12) days rations on pack-mules. He took his eight (8) Companies of Cavalry, and his Seminole and Tonk-a-way Scouts, leaving his wagon-train to follow under the guard of Companies "A" and "I", 10th Infantry.

Colonel Mackenzie, if he marched without detention, probably reached McClellan's Creek on the night of the third, or morning of the fourth instant, where he probably communicated with General Miles' command, and possibly with that of Lieut. Colonel

Buell, who was to have started with his command from his camp
on "Wanderers' Creek" on the 27th of September.

If the Kiowas move Southwest from McClellan's Creek, making
for the Paladuro Canon, Colonel Mackenzie must have crossed
their trail on his march North.

As we have had frequent rains in this vicinity, trailing is very
easy, and there must now be an abundance of water on the plains
to the Northwest.

Four days before the arrival of your Dispatches, I forwarded to
Colonel Mackenzie, letters from General Augur, containing substantially the same information.

As there are still twenty-three days rations for his whole command with the train, and a fair amount of Buffalo in the country,
I do not expect the Southern Column to return to this Camp for
more than a month from this date.

I remain, Sir,

Your obedient servant,

(Signed) THOMAS M. ANDERSON,

Major 10th U. S. Infantry,

Commanding Camp.

When we reached the place where we had breakfasted
the day before, we found a Lieutenant with three wagons
of corn sent ahead from our supply trains, which he reported as being some 25 miles to the rear, to which the
next day's march (Oct. 9) brought us. Here we learned
that the Mexican train which was after buffalo, and which
we had met a few days previous, had been joined by some
one hundred Indians with about 300 head of ponies. We
struck out in the direction of their trail, and reaching the
edge or "breaks" of the "Staked Plains" descended
through which ran a small creek. Here we met one of the
Lieutenants, who had been off with three Lipan Indians,
scouting the country for any fresh trails.

They reported a large trail of Comanches, Kiowas and
Cheyennes going towards the broken country about Red
River.

On October 12th the supply train with its infantry escort, a cavalry lieutenant with some 60 broken down
horses and all of our sick and disabled men, left us for the
supply camp on the Freshwater Fork of the Brazos River;
and the same day the column, with its pack mules loaded

with 15 days rations, took a southeast course through a terribly rough and broken country, leading in the direction of Red River, and camped that night on some rain water holes. The next day (Oct. 13) our march was along a high ridge and down a steep mountain side, making a winding course through ravines and over ridges, until finally we struck the bed of the river again. After about 2 miles the trail suddenly struck across the river to the north side, over more ridges and more ravines, coming out finally to a level country, sloping down to what proved to be "Mulberry Creek," where a halt was made for the night as it was too dark to follow the trail any longer. We had passed several worn out ponies left by the Indians, showing that they were being hard pressed. Some more of our own horses gave out, although much of the time the men had marched afoot.

The next day (Oct. 14) we found the trail much scattered out. We passed some ponds—in one place two together—the smaller of the two being clear and deep and free from alkali. It was called by the Indians "Medicine Lake," as bottom had never been reached by them in this lake. There was another large pond to the east. We were about to halt at this pond to give the men something to eat, when a detachment of our Seminole scouts galloped up and reported "Indians!"—at which the orders "forward," "trot," "gallop" followed each other in qiuck succession, the column taking a steady gallop over hill and through hollow for a good five miles, and finally pulling up without having seen an Indian. While at a halt, one of the Lipan scouts came up with 13 ponies, captured from the hostiles (a hunting party) which took to their heels, leaving the ponies behind. We retraced our steps and reached the nearest pond at sundown. There was but little grass and the animals suffered for food.

Left this camp at daylight (Oct. 15) and after marching a few miles we came to a fine large bottom, full of splendid grass, with Red River flowing to the south of us. Here we halted, turned out our half starved animals on the luxurious grass and then looked after our own stomachs—a long neglected function.

At 10 o'clock we moved south and forded the Salt Fork of the Red River near its mouth. The crossing proved to be a dangerous one, with much quicksand, making it difficult to get the animals out safely. We camped on the bluffs near some water full of gypsum. Several buffalo had been killed during the day, adding fresh meat to our rations. The horses were now growing thin and poor and weak very rapidly.

Moving at daylight (Oct. 16) we marched south till nearly 10 o'clock before halting for breakfast at a large rain water hole. While here a large herd of buffalo was sighted and some men with the Tonks were sent out and succeeded in killing nine. At 1 o'clock we were on the move again over a rolling country. We did not halt until 5 P.M. and then there was no grass for the horses. At 7 the orders came "pack up," "saddle up," and the column moved off in a dim, misty moonlight across a sandy plain. It was what is termed a "shin oak" country, and the horses were constantly stumbling over the hummocks or small sand dunes. As we descended from this plain to the bottom we found ourselves on the banks of "Pease River." We had to "stake out" our horses on the spot where we halted, like all of our halting places lately—no grass—a discovery only made by groping with our hands in the dark.

We unpacked, unsaddled, watered, and picketed out our animals, posted the sentinels and outposts, rolled ourselves in our blankets, and settled ourselves to rest on the bosom of Mother Earth, the black canopy of heaven for our roof.

In the morning (Oct. 17) the companies were spread out along the stream, in the best places for grass, and here we remained all day so as to allow the animals to fill up with grass, which they really needed.

On the 18th we resumed the march, going south, passing

Quit-a-que Mountain, halting to "noon" (lunch) at the very same place where we "nooned" September 21st—twenty-seven days before—in the Valley of the Salt Fork of the Wichita. We continued the march to the head of the Big Wichita, and went into camp just as the sun went down.

The next morning (Oct. 19) a wagon came into camp escorted by a Lieutenant and a small detail of men. He brought a mail which, in that vast solitude was always a most welcome event. We remained in camp all day and late in the afternoon the command marched a couple of hours to Cottonwood Springs, where we camped, having plenty of good grass, wood and water. As our supplies were running low and it was known that Lawton with his supply train was not far off, we laid over the 20th, 21st and 22nd, so as to rest men and horses and allow the latter to fill up on grass. In the meantime the train reached camp, having 20 days rations and 5 days forage. The rations were speedily issued to the men and transferred to the pack mules. The corn was unloaded and turned over to the companies and the train pulled out again over the same old route ("Mackenzie Trail"), which we had been over several times en route for Fort Griffin, our main depot, for a fresh load, to meet us at the supply camp on the Freshwater Fork of the Brazos, where it was pretty well understood that our next move would take us.

On the 23rd we broke camp early, and marched until 11 o'clock that night, making two halts to rest and graze, when we struck the Freshwater, near the "lake" from which we had started one month previous. The long and heavy marches frequently made at night with little rest, poor grass, and little or no forage for the animals, had told fearfully upon the latter and made it absolutely necessary to nurse them for a few days if anything further was to be accomplished.

The command was spread all along the valley, leaving considerable space between each troop for the purpose of grazing the animals—the infantry battalion being camped about 1 mile from the cavalry. Here we remained several days, performing the usual routine of duties, besides overhauling equipments of every kind, shoeing horses and mules.

COPY

TELEGRAM

Head Qrs Supply Camp Southern Column on Fresh Water Fork of Brazos River, Tex, Oct. 19, via Fort Worth, Tex. Oct. 28, 1874.

A.A. Genl Head Qrs D. T. San Antonio, Tex.

Sir:

I send today two dispatches from Col. MacKenzie; his train came in last night much broken down, also some captured mules and horses; eight mules will have to be put to each wagon and many wagons left without teams; the train coming in crossed a trail of a war party of about three hundred Indians moving towards the head of this valley. I believe they are in Camp there fifty miles above here. Col. MacKenzie, who is tonight about thirty-five miles distant at Cotton Wood Springs, has been informed of this; one team with rations and forage is sent out to him today and another will start to Griffin in two days. The Camp train is expected out in five or six days. No clothing has yet arrived and is much needed for the entire command. The train after parting from MacKenzie's command found Genl Miles trail and battle ground.

I am sir Very Respectfully Your Obdt Servt

(Signed) Thos. M. Anderson,
Col. 10th U. S. Infty., Comdg Post.

242 Collect
484 & 242 Govt.
Via Dallas Texas
A True Copy
J. H. Taylor,
A. D. C.

TELEGRAM

Headquarters Department of Texas
San Antonio, Texas, October 29, 1874.

Lt. Genl. Sheridan, U. S. A.,
Fort Dodge, Ks. via Ft. Leavenworth, Ks.

MacKenzie reports from camp on branch of Pease River Oct. 16, that he followed large trail Comanches, Kiowas, and Cheyennes to near mouth of Mulberry Creek on Red River where trail turned north. Horses could follow no farther—hopes to move again shortly. Has sent train in to Camp Supply. Thinks corn should be pushed from Camp Supply to McClellans Creek and from Bascom, N. Mexico to Junta des Cordose on upper Red River. Thinks Indians will hang about ravines on edge of plains between Head-

waters of North Fork and Red River or Canadian. Anderson
from Camp Supply Oct. 19, reports arrival of MacKenzie's train
much broken down. Supplies go out fast as possible. Train
crossed trail of large war party on way down moving towards
head of the valley Fresh Water Fork of Brazos, he supposed them
to be in camp fifty (50) miles from him and has notified Mac-
Kenzie, presumed to be then at Cotton Wood Springs thirty-five
(35) miles distant.

(Sgd) J. H. TAYLOR,
Asst. Adjt. Genl.

Official copy respectfully furnished by mail.

J. H. TAYLOR,
Asst. Adjt. Genl.

While in this camp a Captain with a few men went on a
buffalo hunt to get meat for his troop. Not returning by
dark, a Lieutenant and 20 men were sent out in search of
him. He came in, however, shortly after the moon rose,
which he waited for to enable him to see his way.

On October 31st the cavalry was concentrated on the
bank of the creek near Mackenzie's headquarters; 12 days
rations were issued to each troop; the mules were once
more packed, and at dusk the command—composed of all
the serviceable men and horses of eight troops—moved out
again, in the direction of the hostiles, who were now reported to be near the head waters of the Double Mountain
Fork of the Brazos River. The disabled men and horses
were left behind in camp under command of the senior
Captain with two Lieutenants to assist him.

The day after we started out, the Infantry major (Anderson), with one troop of cavalry (E), a captain and two
lieutenants left en route to Fort Concho. The weather had
been growing gradually cold, and this day culminated in a

---

*Gen. M. reports that Lieut. W. A. Thomson, commanding Indian Scouts, with nine
scouts, "several miles away from the command," killed two (2) Indians and captured
twenty-six (26) horses and mules. He further states—"Shall try one more trip on the
plains after which there will be no more use looking for Indians there this winter.
Intend going to the northwest between heads of Brazos and Red River."
  The women (squaws) said that "the bands of two (2) warriors, Patchaquiri and
Horseshoe, were with eight lodges of Cheyennes (Southern) on the Staked Plains.
Many of their people had gone into the reservation with Mow-wi, head Chief of the
Comanches; that the intention of the remainder was to leave for the reservation in a
few days; to try and slip around the troops, send in a party and get authority to go
into Fort Sill; that the Staked Plains Apaches left for the mountains about a month
before." Some of these women were those captured on North Fork of Red River in
1872 and released.
  Mackenzie commends Adam Payne, Seminole Indian Scout, for "habitual courage and
more cool daring than any scout I have ever seen."

regular "Norther," which is simply indescribable and had to be experienced to be fully appreciated.

On November 2nd, a courier arrived from Fort Griffin with a mail. Nothing had been heard from relatives and friends for some time.

Nov. 3. The marching column passed a deserted Indian camp, "signs" being quite fresh. This was near Las Lagunas Quatros and finding water prepared to go into camp. But discovering a herd of horses moved on at a gallop four miles East N.E. and here captured a small Indian village and encamped at this point.

On the 4th a supply train arrived from Fort Griffin, and on the 5th it started back—Captain Lacy and Lieutenant Duggan, with their company (?) of the 10th Infantry, accompanied the train as guard. Broke camp at 2 P.M. and marching east 10 miles, camped at Laguna Tahuca, without incident. Grass good.

Nov. 5. Broke camp at 12 M. Marched E.S.E. 16 miles. On this day a small Indian camp was struck and a short, hot fight ensued in which four Indians were killed and 12 squaws, seven papooses and 156 ponies were captured. Went into camp here for the night. Good grass but no wood or water. (Another report gives five Indians killed and 16 or 18 wounded.)

Nov. 6. Broke camp at daylight. Marched E.N.E. six miles, striking the edge of the plains and descending into the Arroyo (Canon) Riscata (Wild Cat Canon). Water in arroyo and continuing the course five miles, camped and grass bad; wood plenty. Moved again in the evening three miles N.E., and camped again, this time for the night.

Nov. 7. Broke camp at 10 A.M. and marched N.E. 10 miles and camped on an Arroyo. Containing running water, good grass and wood. On November 7th a Lieutenant of Cavalry with a citizen scout (Henry Strong(?)) arrived in camp about 7 P.M. They reported that on the 2nd instant some Indians had been seen by the command that left Camp on the 1st. The Indians were chased some miles but succeeded in getting away.

Nov. 8. Left camp at 10:30 A. M. Marched 15 miles and camped on a stream of running water (a tributary of the Brazos). Good water and grass. The scouting column returned to the permanent camp, everybody being glad to get back to its comforts.

The next day, Nov. 9th, the various detachments which had been left behind joined their respective commands.

On the 11th our never-to-be-forgotten quartermaster, Lawton, left camp with a large train for Fort Griffin for more supplies—and by way of variety, on the 12th we had another "Norther" that double discounted the previous ones. Everybody stuck close to what shelter they had. For a couple of days we had some active drilling on foot, and meantime orders were issued for each company to prepare to start on the 16th on a 30 days scout; but on that day we had another severe wet "Norther," making it impossible to move. For the next three days rain, hail, sleet and snow alternated. There was one consolation, however, the Indians could not move any better than ourselves. They were very susceptible to cold weather and sudden changes.

On the morning of the 19th reveille found us literally frozen as tight as though we had been in the Artic regions. It was one of the hardest freezes experienced during all of our service in Texas. The tents were like boards, one solid sheet of ice. The poor animals, standing out all night tied in to a picket line and exposed to such a cold blow, were nearly frozen stiff, although care had been taken to blanket them.

A change came on the 20th, which was soft and mild. Large numbers of wild geese and ducks with wild swans flew over our camp during the day—a sure "sign" that winter was approaching from the North as their flight was South.

Everything and everybody being thawed out on the 22nd, the command left camp on another scout after the hostiles, leaving, as before, the disabled men and horses behind. They were consolidated and moved to the Infantry camp about 2½ miles from the supply camp. A gale of wind blew all day. On this day another supply train left for Fort Griffin for more supplies. On this day and the day following (23rd) the command marched up Canon Blanco about 30 miles—"well up the valley"—where, on account of mud it remained in camp several days.

On the 26th a corporal and four men came in from the column and reported it in Canon Blanco, 32 miles from camp. Another hard "Norther" struck us the same day.

On November 27th Lieutenant Kislingbury, 11th Infantry, left the camp with another wagon train for Fort Griffin. These trains were kept in motion alternately— one going back empty while another was returning loaded. Poor Kislingbury little thought at that time that his bones would rest at Camp Clay, Grimmell Land, Arctic Regions, where he died June 1, 1884, while with the Greely Arctic Expedition. He was a fine man and soldier.

At noon sleet began to fall and at 5 P. M. a heavy fall of snow, with a piercing, cold wind. The poor horses tied in to the picket lines again suffered terribly while thus exposed. The sun came out bright and clear on the 29th and the next two days of sunshine made the snow disappear very rapidly.

During the next few days all of the cavalry and infantry detachments, with all camp supplies were moved from the Freshwater Fork across the country by our old trail ("Mackenzie Trail" of 1871) to Duck Creek where we had had our supply camp for a part of that period, but we had scarcely got settled in camp before orders were received to pack up again and proceed to the mouth of Duck Creek, joining the scouting column there. This was done preparatory to the breaking up of the expedition, and the return of the various troops to their respective posts.

The day after the entire command was concentrated at the mouth of Duck Creek, the expedition was broken up and the various companies were put in motion for those points, the cavalry with the exception of one troop (D) being ordered to Fort Richardson. The march to Fort Griffin was by the usual trail, Double Mountain Fork of the Brazos, California and Paint Creeks, Clear Fork of the Brazos and old Camp Cooper. On the march from Fort Griffin to Fort Richardson, especially across the 12 mile stretch of Salt Creek prairie, we experienced, as we had in November 1871, some of the most excessively cold weather ever felt in Texas. On the night of January 9, 1875, the Brazos River (at old Fort Belknap) froze over thick; the mercury stood at 10° below zero and two of our mules were frozen stiff and dead at the picket line—and *this* in "Texas."

Headquarters Southern Column,
Head of Fresh Fork Canon,
Nov. 27th, 1874.

General C. C. Augur,

General:

I have received your telegram of Nov. 18th addressed to myself, and, also, copy of one addressed to Commanding Officer of Fort Richardson. These telegrams have passed Major Davis and the dispatches by him are not yet received.

The mud on the Plains I found very bad and was compelled to lay up at the head of running water since the 24th—my teams being entirely unable to get through.

I send back Lieut. Lawton, tomorrow, to bring out a very fine train due tomorrow (at the Supply camp, a little more than thirty miles from here) with additional forage and rations.

Finding that there would be delay, three parties of spies were sent out on the 25th: one, consisting of two Mexicans and three Seminole negroes, to look about certain hiding places in the Staked Plains between here and the Salado Lake towards Sumner on the Mucha Que trail; another, consisting of a Lipan Indian in charge and four Tonkaways, to look up the cañon of Red River between the mouth of Canon-Cita Blanco and the mouth of Tule, and another consisting of Mr. Strong, Post Guide of Richardson, and Sergt. Charlton, Co. "F" 4th Cav., with three other enlisted men of the Regiment, to look up the head springs of Quita Que and the heads of the canons entering the Red River between the head of Pease's River and Tule.

These men, of course, take very great risks but I suppose where I send one, I could get a dozen anxious to go. I wish to stay here a few days longer to get their reports, which will cover a very great extent of country—and the parties will all go—the Indians being to my mind, the least likely to go far. The Mexicans in one case before, I feel sure, laid up and came back and reported nothing, but they have with them now a Seminole negro, who is a very determined man on a scout, and they will be afraid not to go. The soldiers and Mr. Strong are all bright and all determined men who have been used away from the column a good deal and were anxious to make the trip.

If any of them find a camp of any size. I suppose, judging from your dispatch, and not having received my orders, that it will be best for me to try and strike it first, but I expect that the orders will reach me tomorrow or the next day.

I have with me detachments of seven company's, that of "G" being taken to make up for men of "I" left back, in all with the various detachments of Cavalry, 13 officers and 265 enlisted men, and fourteen guides, Seminole negroes and Indians. There are two officers and 36 men present in the Infantry company. The cavalry officers, as a rule, regard their horses as much stronger than they were on the date of my report alluded to, and on the day following that report.

Finding a necessity of moving, a part of the command marched about thirty miles in the first twenty-four hours, a little over thirty the next, then laid over a day and moved about fifty in less than twenty-four hours. Of course, the weak horses were then left back and they are behind now. There are two men in the cavalry who complain of being sick who will be sent back tomorrow. There is one man sick in the Infantry. The cavalry have with them one hundred rounds of carbine ammunition per man and there are ten thousand rounds in the train.

The Infantry have two hundred rounds per man. The Officers and men are, I think, all in all, in better health and spirits than when you saw them at Concho.

The seven detachments have about the strength of five companies when the horses are in order.

We have had a great deal of compulsory laying up for the last two weeks, and today have had another sleet and snow with cold, northeast wind. I expect to be here till I get the orders spoken of, and then do not anticipate serious difficulty in going to McClellans Creek or, to any other point you desire: at any rate, taking the spirit of your telegram as showing your wishes, you can count on our leaving for McClellans Creek when the strong train arrives. That is, unless our scouts bring news of some very good opportunity of catching Indians elsewhere. Two of the parties are, however, looking up the country near the road. We can go to McClellans creek from here, with fair weather and roads in five days, and I believe, on a pressure, in four. I have not sent the companies to Richardson, because some of the dispatches indicated that the troubles were probably about over and the forage has come, recently, freely.

Another column can be made up to take the place of this one by taking the two companies from Clark and the three now at Concho and McKavett.

The seven companies now out will have to go in to Posts in January, and if this business is to last, had best be kept on this line, say five at Concho and two at McKavett, or elsewhere, as is thought best. The stations of the companies should be changed, and the effects of Officers and men sent to them, as they will need them very badly.

It appears to me that there will be but little trouble in keeping a strong column from this regiment out all the time. It is very important that this business be got through with satisfactorily before we let go of it.

I will write again when the command leaves. It is important for me to see the orders by Major Davis, as they will give me a clear understanding of your wishes.

Very respectfully,
Your obdt. servt.,
(sgd) R. S. MACKENZIE,
Colonel, 4th Cavalry,
Commanding.

Headquarters Southern Column,
Camp in Canon Blanco, Dec. 2nd, '74.

General C. C. Augur,
   Comd'g. Dept. of Texas.
General:

The several letters and copies of telegrams sent me by Major Davis were received last evening. When I wrote on the 27th, I had simply received the telegram of the 17th and did not understand the radical change that was desired.

In my opinion it will be best, unless there is some pressing necessity, which I do not gather from the spirit of the communication, to get together the five companies not in the field for this supply camp.

I have before written you that indications pointed to a considerable body of Indians as living somewhere southwest of Mucha Que. I had intended neglecting these people till a scout had been made to the north of the Red River, but the camp here ought not to be moved out of the country, leaving them there undisturbed.

My opinion is that, it will be best for the condition of the Regiment and, for its efficiency in a future campaign that it should change stations at once.

The Regimental Headquarters, band and dismounted men and all baggage at Clark and Duncan, under such officer as Col. Hatch may select, to move at once with transportation which would have to be hired, and ox tranportation can be hired reasonably at Eagle Pass or in the vicinity.

This party with heavy baggage, to go to Austin, then by rail to Caddo, and then by wagon transportation to Sill.

Companies "B" and "G" thoroughly fitted for a campaign of several months, and with no surplus property, to be, at the very earliest moment, put on the march, via Concho, for Griffin—Company "M" joining from McKavett and Companies "C" and "E" from Coenho.

This march should be made slowly, the greatest care being taken not to injure the horses.

There is sufficient post transportation which can be let go for a time, at Clark and Duncan, to move the two companies referred to, taking what they need for the field. Company "C" has with it, at Concho, property belonging to Company "D," and, perhaps, a little belonging to other companies—this property should be moved with the command as far as Fort Griffin, and then, sent, by first opportunity to Sill.

This should give, by late in February, five companies, with horses in good order at Grffin.

After looking up these people to the south, the companies here can go to Sill, or they will, I think, be able to make a trip to McClellans creek.

I do not think that it would be wise to attempt to keep them there the entire winter—this gives time for perfecting arrangements for supplies.

I send "K" and "F" Companies, as I had previously ordered, but order suspended, to Richardson.

Will start tomorrow, moving for the lower plains with the effective men of the other companies and shall probably be gone but ten or fifteen days.

Detachments from companies "F" and "K" can be used for bringing new horses to Richardson and the two Captains would make a good board for purchase.

If you think best to make the movement to McClellans creek at once, without waiting for new companies, everything will be in train, and all orders will be with that view till I get return courier from you.

There should be more forage here than I now have (12 days three quarters) to start for McClellans creek.

Very respectfully,

Your obdt. servt.,

(sgd) R. S. MACKENZIE,

Colonel 4th Cavalry,

Commanding.

Dec. 2nd, 1874.

My Dear General:

I cannot add much to what I have written. I am strongly of opinion that it will be best to wait for the change for a fresh command and strong horses.

At the same time I will arrange to move after this scout without waiting, if you think best.

My own opinion is that it is best to commence the change, bag and baggage, at once. I am very anxious, for the comfort of the men, to get them and their belongings together again, which are at Clark, Duncan, and, in part, at Concho.

The boxes belonging to the men should be opened by a reliable detail and their clothing and property put in a few large boxes, marked with the company letter and, so far as possible, with the names of the men.

If you agree with me, I had best start the Cavalry in to Griffin, and go on and see you, if you are at Sill.

It would be best, if practicable, to change the Infantry.

Please attend to new horses and recruits for me.

Should you determine to keep the same Infantry, Major Anderson should come out again, or, Captain Parke's company should go in,—Parke is a good man but has no head.

If he goes in, the other Captains are all competent.

The 10th Cavalry can be, in part, started for its new destination at once, using transportation at Sill, and the two companies "F" and "K" enroute for Richardson, turned by courier, to Sill.

If there is Infantry to spare to accumulate supplies at McClellans creek, it can be commenced at any time—The forks are a good point well up, and, change of camp could be made at any time.

Captain Lee's Company at Griffin is, I understand, a very good one, and I believe he is anxious to do service: and I suppose other people, as well as myself have horses not so fat as they were—I, therefore mention it, I am scouting now with about two hundred men after sending two more companies in. Lee's company, with such companies as may be strong, of the 10th should take up this section after we leave.

Another matter that will need looking after is the country about the lower Pecos, and the Guadalupe Mountains: Morrow would be a first rate man to attend to this: The Quahada Comanches and a large band of Mescaleros, with whom they associate, will go to one of those places after this scout, I think, if they have not already gone there.

There are two companies at Stockton and Davis that could be got hold of, and, perhaps, more could be got from Ringgold.

Certain districts will have to be taken, and the troops and posts got in convenient relations. If I take McClellans creek and the country north of Red River and south of Canadian, I want Sill and Richardson for stations.

Grierson taking the heads of the streams as far as the Concho, would want Concho, McKavett and Griffin, etc.

This is very general, of course, but it is very important to get the companies, their property and all, at the posts nearest which they are to be used, and relieving those on hard field service, from time to time, or the horses are bound to go, and the men to run down.

Please send a courier with your decision in this matter at the earliest moment.

If your decision is to get together the new command, it will be well to order me in to see you at Sill or elsewhere as soon as possible, as I much desire to talk with you on this subject.

My guides and scouts have been many miles from here, to the north and northeast and west, without finding any indications of Indians except to the west, near Casa Maria, which is between the Salado and Mucha Que, and there, a party, several weeks before, had gone south.

Morrow had best, if you can spare him, start at once for Stockton.

A good many parties are sure eventually, to turn up about the Guadalupe Mountains or lower Pecos.

Very respectfully,

Your obdt. servt.,

(sgd) R. S. MACKENZIE,

Colonel 4th Cavalry,

Commanding.

Dec. 3. From this point, 30 miles above "Supply Camp," wagon train was sent back and F and K Companies were ordered to proceed to Fort Richardson. This was in view of breaking up the expedition. Set out at 10 A.M. and marched 15 miles S.W. and camped at some small ponds or waterholes on the Staked Plains. Grass poor, no wood, water good.

Dec. 4. Broke camp at 6:45 A.M. without breakfast. Halted for breakfast at 11:15 A.M. in Canon Riscata. General course South, distance 14½ miles. Wood and grass sufficient. Water good. Set out after dinner in a heavy rain storm which soon became a strong "Norther" and continuing the march till night, about 9 P. M., in rain and sleet, the storm became so severe and in the darkness, the command was forced to halt, unsaddle and bivouac on the plains in column. The command passed one of its most wretched and uncomfortable nights. Several horses were frozen to death and some of the men barely escaped a like fate. Everything was frozen stiff.

Dec. 5. It was still storming heavily with a gale of wind. Saddled up at daylight; received orders to have all carbines, pistols, etc. in good condition and ready for action as word had come in from the scouts that the column was in the near vicinity of a large camp of Indians. On reaching that point, however, it was found that the Indians had disapeared. The men and horses were now in such a condition that a halt was made in a deep ravine or arroyo for shelter where it remained the balance of the day, big fires of mesquite roots being built to thaw the command out. The distance marched was only 3 miles, course generally S.E., and the bivouac was on Laguna Tahuca; but little wood or grass. Sleet turned into snow.

Dec. 6. Left camp at 6 A.M. Clear and frosty; soon struck a trail which was followed to Las Laguna Quatras—about 13 miles "a little Southwest"; here quitting the trail and turning Southeast and marching 8 miles went into camp near the head of Mucha Que on Aqua de Toro. No grass, water and wood good.

Dec. 7. Broke camp at 8:45 A.M. for Mucha Que and marched about 12 miles, halting near an alkali lagoon, where the horses were unsadded and where it was thought the command would remain for about two hours. After remaining here about an hour firing was heard in the direction the scouts had taken. The command saddled up and moved forward at a gallop but the fight was over before the command arrived. One Indian had been discovered and killed by the scouts. At 5 P.M. went into camp after marching generally a S.E. course for 24 miles. A Lipan Indian killed the enemy, although one Strong, a guide with the column, claimed that he did it, and appropriating the scalp boastfully displayed it as his trophy, giving the Lipan no credit.

Dec. 8. Changed camp 5 miles S.W. on running water. This was a tributary of the Double Mt. Fork of the Brazos. Indians were sighted by our lookouts or outposts from the rise above the camp "on which were located several Indian graves". Lieut. Warrington with a small party started in pursuit. He overtook them. Two Indians were killed and one, a boy, named Vidot, about 15 years old, was captured. He was taken to Fort Richardson and later returned to his band (Comanche) at Fort Sill. (See Lieut. Warrington's report annexed). Between 7 and 9 P.M. the command saddled up and marched all night, expecting to strike an Indian camp, but on reaching the spot found that they had disappeared. The march was continued until about 11 A.M. on the 9th, reached Lagunas Sabinas and went into camp. Distance 33 miles, general course South 20 West. Remained in camp until dark. Grass and wood poor. Water sulphur.

Dec. 9. Marching in dark, made 10 miles on the return. Camped on plains, a sand prairie to get grass for the animals. Grass good, no wood or water. General coures East.

Scouting Expedition, Southern Column,
West Fork, Brazos River, Texas,
December 19th, 1874.

Act'g Asst. Adj't General
    Scouting Expedition.
Sir:

Receiving orders from General R. S. MacKenzie, 4th Cavalry, Dec. 8th, while camped at Head of Mooch o Kaway to move out after a party of Indians which had been seen in vicinity of the camp, I started with ten men of Co. "I" 4th Cav'y; after riding three miles five Indians were seen. Taking advantage of a *ridge* for two miles, I managed to get within a mile of them before being discovered and immediately gave chase. After running two miles one of the Indians abandoned his horse and endeavored to catch one of a number driven by them, but, being unsuccessful ran on foot about a mile when he was overtaken by men. As he made no attempt to use his arms and thinking possible he would be of service to the command, I took him prisoner. By this time my men were strung along the trail. Ordering two men who were near me to push and turning the prisoner over to a man with a jaded horse, I started in pursuit of the others. After a run of two miles, the remaining four Indians dismounted to fight and by closing upon them by two men and wounding one of their number who was assisted upon a horse they mounted horses they were driving and for a time lengthened the distance. Within three miles one of the number dismounted and ran over a mile on foot when he was overtaken by myself and private Bengenchall, Co. "I" 4th Cavalry, who shot and mortally wounded him; Pvt. O'Sullivan of the same Company shooting him a second time. Encouraging the men to urge their jaded horses on, two more Indians were dismounted and ran for some distance when one was overtaken and turned to fight. Being within a few yards I shot him through the lungs and dismounted from my horse. His bow being broken by one of two men, he threw an arrow which missed its mark and then rushed upon and endeavored to stab me. Keeping him off with my carbine while endeavoring to get at the cartridges which had broken through the lining of my coat, he turned and attempted to mount my horse. Being weak from loss of blood, a well directed shot put an end to his existence. The wounded Indian made his escape on horseback and the remaining one on foot. My horse being completely broken down and the Indian the best man on the run, as the sun was setting and but two men within a mile, I returned to the Camp of the command which was distant nearly eighteen miles, having one warrior and satisfactory evidence of the death of two together with nine captured horses.

During the chase a party of about twenty Indians scampered off to the right. I did not pursue them owing to the tired condition of my horses and having but two men with me.

Hoping that the above may meet the approvation of the Commanding Officer, I have the honor to be,

Very respectfully,

Your obed't serv't,

(sgd) LEWIS WARRINGTON,

1st Lieut. 4th Cavalry.

The Asst. Adj't General,   San Antonio, Texas,
    Department of Texas,   January 7, 1875.
    San Antonio, Texas.

Sir:

I have the honor to enclose itinerary of Scout and Report of Lieut. Warrington.

It was much hoped that the Quahada Comanches with other hostile Indians could be caught at the Laguna de Sabinas, sixty miles West of the Mucha que Peak; the hostile Indians are packing buffalo meat from the Laguna Sabinas and the Laguna

---

Note—Warrington was awarded a M. H. for this action.

Cuarto far to the West in the Staked Plains. Their families are generally believed to have gone to the country near the Rio Grande above the mouth of the Pecos or to the Guadaloupe mountains.

On this scout Mr. Strong, Post Guide at Fort Richardson and Private McCabe, Co. "E" 4th Cavalry, deserve mention for good conduct on the 7th December in an affair with an Indian.

Lieut. Warrington deserves some reward for very gallant conduct on December 8th. Private Burgendall, Reg'l Band, on this expedition as a private with his former Company at his own request, and Private O'Sullivan, Co. "I" deserve consideration for gallantry on Dec. 8.

Very respectfully,
Your obed't serv't,
(sgd) R. S. Mackenzie,
Col., 4th Cav'y.

Dec. 10. Moved out at sunrise and after marching about 18 miles camped on the head of the Double Mt. Fork in the Mucha-Que Valley. Grass, wood and water good. General course North 20 East.

Dec. 11. Broke camp at 9 A.M. and marching 10 miles North 20 East. Camped on same stream. Wood and water good, but grass poor and horses growing very weak for lack of forage and good grass.

Dec. 12. Moved at 8 A.M. and after marching about 15 miles North 20 East camped at an arroya (water hole) on the prairie, near Mucha-que. Grass poor, water and wood good. Many horses dropped on the trail; rations gave out, and the men were on short rations of buffalo meat only. It was this camp that Sergeant Major Morfost was reduced to the ranks. One of the packers asked Morfost to hold his mule for him while he loosened the pack —"Oh, get one of the men to do it" M. said. It happened that the other packers were busy at some other work. General Mackenzie heard the answer, and calling Morfost said, "Take those chevrons from your arm, I will make a man of you"!

Dec. 13. Moved at 8:30 A.M. Marched 18 miles. Course North 50° East. Wood, water and grass good. Camped on Arroyo.

Dec. 14. Remained in camp all day. A severe "Norther" set in, rain and snow.

Dec. 16. Remained in camp, rain last night and snow this day. This storm lasted three days and the command suffered very greatly. Some of the horses were frozen to death, due to their weak condition. Many of the men were nearly barefooted and even the officers, among them Captain Gunther, were in the same plight. The wagons, after a terrible trip over the soaked prairie, reached the command this day (15th) at dark, with supplies and forage for the half-frozen and starving horses.

Dec. 16. Moved out at 9:45 A.M. Ground very heavy, marched about 20 miles North 45° East, crossed and camped on the Brazos on the old Concho trail. Wood, water and grass good. The ice was about 1½ inches on the river and was very severe on the first horses to cross. The night was very cold.

Dec. 17. Camp on the Brazos. Snow fell to the depth of 5 or 6 inches. Set out at 9 A.M. and after crossing the Double Mt. Fork of the Brazos camped on an Arroyo. good wood and water but grass poor. Marched 12 miles. General course N.E.

Dec. 18. Moved out at 8 A.M. and after marching 12 miles N.E. camped on main Brazos. Wood good, grass poor, water alkili.

Dec. 19. Heavy fall of snow last night. Moved N.E. 3 miles and camped on Duck Creek with wagon train. Here orders were received for General Mackenzie to proceed to go in and he left for Fort Griffin this date.

Dec. 20. Left Duck Creek for Fort Griffin. Arrived there on Dec. 28. Heavy rains last several days.

Headquarters, Department of Texas,
Fort Sill, Decr 3d, 1874.

Dear General Sheridan:

I have received your telegram of the 28th of November, and am glad to observe its tone regarding the transportation contractor. I enclose a copy of my letter to him by the last mail. My impression is, however, that at this season of the year, he will find it difficult to obtain transportation for this large amount of stores, except at as high, or higher rates than he receives himself. I am informed that he has few or no teams of his own, and that he depends upon hiring almost entirely. He is therefore at the mercy of individuals owning teams.

But after receiving my letter, and seeing it backed by your telegram—as he will—the telegraph office at Denison being leaky —I believe he will do the best he can without losing money. If the stores are not loaded in proportion, Robinson will proceed to hire transportation under the tenth article of the contract, and charge difference to him. But all this will require time—more, I am afraid, than we can spare if the camp on McClellan's Creek is to be established this winter.

I have heard nothing as yet from MacKenzie. Morrow gets off to-morrow and Davidson on Monday. I encloe copies of my instructions to them. I want to get the 9th towards Fort Clark as soon as possible, as there a few Indians on the lower Pecos that must be cleared out in Spring.

Two days since two of Mowwis's sons came in. They are youngsters and say they left their father on Staked Plains. Last night three Qua-ha-das, who had gone into the Wichita Agency and surrendered their arms, were brought here. They belonged to the party struck by MacKenzie early in November on Staked Plains. They have been since that time coming in. Their information is not important. They report a few bands of Kiowas and five lodges of Cheyennes on some point on head of Brazos, and that the Qua-ha-das under Otter Belt, and some Cheyennes are on Pecos towards Guadalupe mountains. They report Mowwi and his people as anxious to come in.

Kicking Bird has given me the names of four of his people now confined here in *ice house, who participated in the murders in this vicinity last Summer. Horse-back has given the names of three Comanches likewise engaged in those murders. I shall in consequence release from confinement ten of the Kiowas and a few of the Comanches. This is done however with the distinct understanding that the chiefs are responsible for them, and will return them when required, and has nothing to do with the final settlement by the Government with these tribes. It is merely done to relieve the crowd in the ice house, which is the best available place for their confinement. Those temporarily released are either quite old or very young. From those accused I think we can eventually obtain names of others, and may succeed in convicting the worst characters. I doubt if it is best to proceed to extremities until the Cheyennes and all the others have come in.   I am General very respc.,
              Your obdt sevt.,
                              C. C. Augar,
                                   Brig. Gl.

---

*The guard house had not yet been built at Fort Sill.—R. G. C.

Headquarters Department of Texas,
Fort Sill, I.T. Dec. 5, 1874.

Colonel R. S. Mackenzie 4th Cavalry,
  Comd'g Southern Column.

Colonel:

Since the date of instructions and dispatches sent you from San Antonio, and that of the telegraphic dispatches sent through the Comd'g Officer Fort Griffin, it has been determined to defer the establishment, of a camp on McClellan's Creek, until spring.

The General, Commanding has decided to bring your command in for the winter. He directs therefore that you break up your supply camp, sending Lee's Co. "D", Davis' Co. "F", and Wint's Co. "L", 4th Cavalry, to Fort Richardson, with sufficient trains and supplies. Beaumont's Co. "A", Gunther's Co. "H", 4th Cavalry. Parks' Co. "I", Kelton's Co. "C", and Hampson's Co. "K", 10th Infantry, to Fort McKavett, McLaughlin's Co. "I", 4th Cavalry, Lacey's Co. "A", 10th Infantry, and Kislingburg's Co. "H", 11th Infantry, to Fort Concho, and the balance of your transportation to be divided between Concho, and McKavett, wherever they can be made most comfortable. In this arrangement it is supposed that Boehm's Co. "E", and Heyl's Co. "K", 4th Cavy. are at Fort Concho.

If you have already ordered in any of the other companies, to any of these posts, let the arrangement you have made stand, unless you desire to change it.

The General desires that you report to him in person at San Antonio, where he will be by the 25th inst. You can come by whichever route you prefer, bringing maps, reports, &c.

Enclosed please find copies of letter to the Lieut. General, and his telegraphic reply.

You can send your Indian prisoners to Concho or Richardson, preferably Richardson.

I am, Colonel with respect,

Your obedt. servant,

(sgd)   G. B. RUSSELL,
Aide de Camp.

Official:
  G. B. Russell,
    Aide de Camp.

Headquarters Department of Texas,
Fort Sill, December 9th, 1874.

Dear General Sheridan:

Your telegram to me of Dec. 1st. reached me in such imperfect state, that I could not make much of it, except that you wanted the camp on McClellan's Creek established this winter. I immediately answered by my telegram of the fourth to which I sent by special messenger and which I suppose you have received, it being too late to stop it when I received your telegram of the 3d inst., which you stated was your final decision in the matter of winter operations. I immediately ordered Mackenzie in, with his command—this will bring him in about last of December and shall arrange at once with him in person for starting with his command for McClellan's Creek by first of March, promptly. By that time, too, I will have a column of the 9th Cavalry, from Clark operating on the Pecos, McCuskon is just down from the Cheyenne Agency and reports that Colonel Neill has sent a messenger to the Cheyenne Agency and reports that Colonel Neill has sent a messenger to the Cheyennes, to tell them to come in. If this be so, it would seem to be a departure from the policy toward these Indians that I had supposed to be authorized and prescribed. The Indians here say that every Kiowa and Comanche would come in at once, could they be assured the troops would not interfere with them, on the way.

I have thought it best to hold out no inducements for these people to come in, but to let them remain out until fatigue and hunger forced them in. They will be the better for it hereafter. But, if the Cheyennes have been invited in, I think the same course should be pursued toward the Kiowas and Comanches. The Indians here complain too, that, while their people here, who were captured or surrendered, are kept in confinement the Cheyennes are permitted to live in camp with their people. I do not know if this be true, or if it is very material if it is true.

Although Lieut. Colonel Davidson desired me to go on the scout which left here on Monday, last, and was originally ordered to command it, I thought it best, for some reasons, to send Major Schofield, in command, and keep Col. Davidson in immediate command of his post, which I found required attention.

I am, General with respect,

Your obedt. servant,

(sgd)   C. C. AUGAR,
Brig. General U. S. Army.
Commanding.

There is a rumor among the Indians here that the Cheyennes under Greybeard have gone North, and that they are now North of the Arkansas.   C. C. A.

A true copy:
(sgd)   J. H. TAYLOR,
A. A. General.

(1st End't)
                                    Hdqrs. Dep't. of Texas,
                                        San Antonio, Tex.,
                                           8th Jan'y 1875.
A true copy respectfully forwarded to the Asst. Adj't General
Military Division of the Missouri for the information of the
Lieut. General Commanding.
                            (sgd)   C. C. AUGAR,
                                       Brig. General,
                                         Commanding.

On January 13th we arrived at Fort Richardson.

During the four months the "Southern Column" was in
the field, the efforts to punish and subdue or exterminate
the four hostile tribes of Indians—which had left their
reservations early in the summer of 1874 and had taken
the warpath—were unceasing, as the reader will observe.
The Comanches, Kiowas, Southern Cheyennes and Arapahoes had banded together and foolishly imagined they
could whip out all the whites in that section of the country, but sad experience taught them that they were play-
ing with fire. They did not recover for many a year;
in fact, they never recovered from the blow which Mackenzie and the 4th Cavalry struck them in the Palo Duro
Canon on September 28, 1874, when their various camps
were destroyed and about 2200 ponies were captured and
killed, which was the greatest blow of all, as the Indians
without their ponies were comparatively helpless. They
began going in a few families at a time, until by the last
of April 1875 only one band, Comanches, were remaining
out of the Fort Sill and Fort Reno Reservations. Previous to this period, as has been shown, they had been the
terror to the settler, on that border for many years—especially the Qua-ha-da Comanches, under Quanah Parker and
the Kiowas, who, under Sa-tan-ta, Se-Tank, Lone Wolf and
other bold chiefs, had frequently crossed Red River into
Texas and raided the country for hundreds of miles, going even as far as San Antonio, Fredericksburg, San Marcos, New Braumfels and other towns, driving off horses
and cattle, and, as has also been shown, in more instances

than one, carrying off women and children into captivity which proved to be worse than death. Even General Sherman could scarcely believe at the time Sa-tan-ta raided Henry Warren's corn train on Salt Creek prairie and committed his wholesale massacre in May, 1871, that the Fort Sill reservation Indians were connected with that affair. The Indians in the southwest began to recognize the power of the army from that date, and while it took some time to get them shaken down so that they were willing to travel the "white man's road" it was ultimately accomplished, as will be shown in a succeeding chapter.

On January 30, 1875, the headquarters of the Fourth Cavalry with the regimental band, left Fort Clark, Texas, under Special Orders No. 7, Department of Texas, January 11, 1875, en route to Fort Sill, I. T. (now Oklahoma), then in the Department of the Missouri.

The companies of the regiment which had come in from the expedition and were now somewhat scattered at different posts—Forts Concho, Griffin and Richardson—soon followed under the same orders—"A" on April 1st, "B" on February 21st, "C" on April 17th, "D" on March 27th, "E" on April 17th, "F" on March 14th, "G" on March 19th, "H" on April 11th, "I" on April 18th, "K" on March 14th, "L" on March 14th, "M" on March 27th.

As soon as General Mackenzie assumed command of the regiment at Fort Sill, and most of the Indians had come in and surrendered their arms and what few ponies they had remaining after their various actions with the Fourth Cavalry, it was quite certain that they were permanently crippled and their power to make any further war upon the whites was gone forever. But it was deemed necessary to punish their leaders and orders were soon received to select from among them the principal ringleaders who had incited these outbreaks and had led their bands of hostiles in the many outrages which had occurred along that border for many years. They were to be sent to Fort Marion, Florida, there to be kept in close confinement. Among these chiefs was old Lone Wolf, then principal war chief of the Kiowas, who, next to Sa-tan-ta, had proved to be about the worst Indian along the southwest border.

Lieutenant C. L. Hudson had killed Lone Wolf's son on December 10, 1873, near Kickapoo Springs, Texas, and eight other Indians, besides wounding several and recapturing 81 stolen horses,—losing but one soldier wounded.

Several of these Indian prisoners were later transferred to Fort Sill but Lone Wolf died in captivity at Fort Marion, Florida.

In the report of the Secretary of War for 1875 (June 30) General Sheridan, on page 58, in referring to the campaign against the Cheyennes, Kiowas and Comanche Indians, 1874-5, by the Columns of Mackenzie, Miles, Price, Davidson and Buell, declares that—"This campaign was not only comprehensive, but was the most successful of any Indian Campaign in this country since its settlement by the whites; and much credit is due to the officers and men engaged in it." He further adds, "The high standard of honor and integrity attained by officers and men is deserving of commendation." * * * "The result of my observations makes me believe the moral standing of the officers and men in the service is higher at the present time than at any period within my knowledge."

Mr. LeGrange, clerk in charge of Records in Chief of Engineers Office, No. 2850, finds a letter written to Major Gillespie, C. E., Engineer for the Military Division of the Missouri, from the A. G. O., War Department, June 13, 1876, that Lieut. Wm. Hoffman's map of the expedition of 1874-5 will be unnecessary to print as Gen. Gillespie will publish the same as a compilation on a sheet (No. 2) with many other topographical, geological and military survey maps.

The Hoffman map (tracing) was, however, sent in with his (Major Gillespie's) annual report. (Bender, No. 1850, in charge of maps in Chief of Engineers office, says) 4 maps and a book on July 17 "will be forwarded in a few days. An endorsement on this letter states that they were received. Maps should be embodied in the book, "Outline Description of the Posts in the Military Division of the Missouri," which has been prepared in the A. G. O. (See Library of Army War College, Miss Barndollar, librarian.)

Further correspondence in the Chief of Engineer's Office, Munitions Bldg., War Department, discloses the fact that after Hoffman's map (tracing) was received at the War Department (Chief of Engineers Office) it was returned to the Military Division of the Missouri.

The Division of the Missouri, as first established, comprised four (4) Departments—Department of the Platte, Department of Dakota, Department of Missouri and Department of the Gulf. The Department of Texas was later added—about 1870. There were in these five (5) Departments eight (8) regiments of Cavalry, eighteen (18) regiments and four (4) companies of Infantry, and six (6) companies of Artillery—comprising 14,813 officers and men. There were ninety-one (91) posts and camps. There were ninety-nine (99) Indian bands, comprising 192,000 Indians and covering over one million (1,000,000) square miles of territory.

General Augur in his report to the Commanding General, Division of the Missouri, (embodied in Report of Secretary of War for 1875) on page 40, dated Fort Sill, I. T., Sept. 28, 1874, makes mention of Gen. Mackenzie's operations for that year. This, however, was before Mackenzie was directed by General Augur to report to him in person on or before December 25, 1874, bringing his *"maps and report."* General Augur makes his next report after being transferred to the Department of the Gulf, *March,* 1875, but makes no further mention of Mackenzie, nor does he include Mackenzie's report if he ever made one. Neither Mackenzie's report or map is given in his two reports, with an interval between, as Commanding these two Departments. Neither does Gen. E. O. C. Ord, who took over the Department of Texas in March 1875 in his report for that year, make any mention of Mackenzie's report or map of the Expedition of 1874-5. Gen. N. A. Miles, however, for that same period, Commanding the Northern Column, reports to Gen. John Pope, Commanding the Military Department of the Missouri, his detailed operations on *March* 4, 1875.

CHAPTER XIX

Surrender of Mow-Wi ("Hand Shaker"), the
Qua-ha-da Comanche Chief.

Charlton's Brave and Nervy Deed.

The daring act of the scout, Jack Stilwell, in his rescue of Gen. ("Sandy") Forsythe's command at Beecher Island in 1868, so many times recorded as an unparalleled feat, was nearly excelled in nerve and daring by this famous sergeant, John B. Charlton, Troop "F", Fourth U. S. Cavalry,—so often referred to in this story,—in April, 1875, when he was requested but not ordered by General R. S. MacKenzie, then Commanding that Regiment to bear a message to Mow-wi a hostile Qua-ha-da Comanche Chief, whose savage band was the last in the South West to come in and surrender at the Fort Sill reservation. The story as told by Charlton in his simple and most modest way to the writer is as follows:

"I did not know until I received your P.C. that my wife had written to you about my being sent by General Mac-Kenzie as messenger to the Qua-ha-das. The few times I've told the story, (two or three on request) I have been accused of telling romance, but to you who have declared yourself as willing ''to believe me before a regiment of Varilys" I will relate it with out fear of your not believing me. There is not much to the story but I have nothing at hand to offer in support of these statements unless by a far fetched chance some of the old officers of the old 4th may have told you at some time that General Mackenzie had induced Mow-wi and his band, by threat, to come in and surrender.

After we came in from the '74 scout Headquarters went to Fort Richardson, all excepting "H" Troop which was left at Fort Griffin. We reached Fort Richardson sometime in January, (1875). I think, and in March we were ordered to Fort Sill to relieve Colonel Davidson then commanding the Tenth Cavalry. After we got there my troop was sent to the Cheyenne Agency on the North Fork Canadian River (now Fort Reno). General MacKenzie kept me at Fort Sill on special duty as a scout until April 14th, 1875, when my time of service expired. Fully convinced that I was tired of the army, after my discharge, I went by stage to Caddo and on by train to Leavenworth, Kansas; bought a suit of citizen's clothes in which I felt as awkward as a "pig with a saddle"; wandered around for several days thoroughly miserable, and finally wound up my trip by chucking my new suit into the stove donning the old uniform and returning to Fort Sill. As I was crossing the parade grounds on my way to the Adjutants Office to reënlist I met General MacKenzie. He asked me where I was going and expressed himself as "much pleased" to find that I had decided to again enlist. He went with me to the Adjutant's office and had a set of papers made out. I took the papers and went to the doctor to receive my physical examination but he rejected me. Went back and gave the papers to General MacKenzie who, nothing ruffled by the doctor's rejection of me, had the Adjutant make out another set of papers and "swore me in" any how. He then told me that he wanted me to go on a very dangerous trip. He made clear that it was not an order, but he would like very much to have me go. The half breed interpreter's name was Storms or Sturm whom I was to accompany. His first name I've forgotten if I ever knew it. He was an old bear hunter who lived somewhere on the Washita. He claimed to be a friend of Mow-wis, which was the main reason for General MacKenzie's selecting him as messenger. General MacKenzie then called Storms or Sturm in and delivered to him the message he was to convey to Mow-wi, which was necessarily verbal and as follows:

"If Mow-wi and his band would come into Fort Sill and surrender, give up their Arms and Ammunition, he would be made comfortable and be taken care of by the

Government. Would be, in a manner, free so long as he gave no trouble; but if he did not come in that he (General MacKenzie) would follow him until his band was exterminated."

I do not know the names of the two Comanches. They had no American names like the Tonks, and Indian and Spanish names were always hard for me to remember.

This was the 23rd day of April, 1875. On the 24th, the following day, the four of us started. Storms and I with the two Comanches. We traveled in a general Westerly direction and on the third day out discovered two Indians hunting. The Comanches signaled to them and they came up and talked with Storms. They belonged to Mow-wi's band and when Storms explained our mission they led us to Mow-wi's Camp. On reaching there they took our arms, ammunition, horses, etc. away from us and placed the four of us together in a tepee with sufficient guards around us to keep us secure. Mow-wi then called his warriors and old men together for a "pow-wow". This continued until the third day. In the meantime we were treated well. Had plenty to eat and were not molested. I don't deny the strain was beginning to be felt by all of us. Our fate, should they refuse to go in with us, we tried hard to not think about it. On the third day when our nerves were most tense, suddenly we heard a yell followed by more shouts. I caught Storms by the arm and asked him what it all meant. He wasn't sure himself, but told me he thought it was alright. In a few minutes, sure enough, Mow-wi followed by bucks, squaws and papooses (such as could walk), came over and told us he would accept General Mackenzie's terms and go in with us. Then followed a tiresome time of handshaking and over done manifestation of friendship.

The return to Fort Sill was made in four days. General MacKenzie shook hands with me and said that he

---

Note:—Sergeant Charlton and "Jack" Stilwell were Post Scouts at Fort Sill for several years. See "The Old Sergeant's Story."

was glad the trip was a success. Mow-wi's band at this time was the only band off the reservation. All the others were quiet enough. Storms was really the messenger though we each took chances alike.

My letter of recommendation and my "complete record", which you have so kindly furnished me, I am very proud of and if this very ordinary, commonplace ex-Sergeant of the Old 4th Cavalry would dare pass judgment on you and speak his private opinion of his (one time) superior officer (the barrier still exists to a certain extent) he would say this: That you are one man who never cheapened his first estimate of your character by bigotry, intolerance, or an undue desire for self advancement. And he is very glad that you are selected by Providence to be the remaining officer of the Old 4th.

With the best of good wishes, I am very sincerely,

Your Friend,

P.S.   (signed) JOHN B. CHARLTON.''

The Indian pictures and scenes are affording the people of Uvalde much entertainment. Young and old.''

Some readers might look lightly upon such a daring deed as has been described all too briefly in the foregoing sketch and be likely to characterize it as merely a romantic adventure, but when the real truth of the act dawns upon the mind, especially to one who has had to deal with the subtle treachery of the Indian heart, of all the hostile Chiefs with whom we had dealt during that long period of Indian outbreaks, of endless murders, pillaging, and all the outrages in the category of crimes, for this brave sergeant to voluntarily risk his life by entering the village of the most ferocious Comanche of the Plains, Mow-wi the "Hand Shaker", and place himself in his power; many miles from any military post; remote from any possible chance for rescue—an unarmed white soldier in a tepee under Indian surveillance for three long days and nights, while the savages outside were engaged

in a "pow-wow," the result of which meant life or death
to him in their prolonged deliberations;—All this was the
most risky and daring act possible. One can readily see
what chances he took; upon what a slender thread his
fate hung, and why this nervy soldier's anxiety and apprehension of danger must have meant more for him
than a mere "strain" or "tense" nerves—and why his
name should be placed in the list with those other daring
spirits—our scouts—Cody, ("Buffalo Bill)", "Wild Bill"
—"Texas Jack"—Amos Grover—"Jack" Stilwell—etc., together with the many heroes, enlisted men of our little
regular army, whose deeds of valor, still unsung—should
be recorded in the Halls of Fame and handed down as
shining examples to the present youth of our land.

Closely following the return of all the hostile bands of
Indians to their reservations at Fort Sill and Reno in
1875, after the destruction of their villages and killing
of their ponies and the gradually disappearing herds of
buffalo in Northwest Texas, especially in the Texas Panhandle, or about 1876-1877, there was a gradual but steady
inflow of brave, hardy settlers into that entire frontier
section never before inhabited by white men. The first
of these bold frontiersmen was Charles Goodnight. He
built a ranch near the present site of the town of Goodnight at or near "Yellow House Canyon". He brought his
cattle there and soon had taken up a vast section of
country bordering on and crossing the "Staked Plains"
towards New Mexico. He was probably one of the largest
cattle owners in that entire region. To the east of him
many other great cattle ranches were established, among
them the Spur Ranch in Dickens County. Along in the
80's settlers or "Nesters" began to flock in and fencing
began. There was no longer thousands of acres of "open
range" and as the railroads were built across to the west
and shipment of cattle became easier, the business waned,
cattle trailing almost entirely ceased. Wells were bored,
water was found in plenty, windmills were installed, irri-

gation followed and cotton, wheat, and other crops followed, and this once great buffalo range, and the home of the wild, nomadic Indian became transformed into a great agricultural region, almost marvelous to conceive of. Goodnight died in 1928 at the age of 93. His memory is fondly cherished by the old pioneers. The writer being one of the last surviving officers who traversed the "Mackenzie Trail" in the '70's, having written some monographs and books relating to our service in that vast unknown country during its wild and woolly stage, was surprised one day a few years ago to receive a letter from a gentleman (C. B. Jones) who had been for some years connected with the great Spur Ranch, with much valuable descriptive literature connected with the same. The letter follows:

No. 61 Broadway, N. Y.
S. M. SWENSON & SONS
New York, October 7, 1926.

Captain Robert G. Carter,
    United States Army, Retired,
        Washington, D. C.
Dear Captain Carter:
    I recently read and was very much interested in the "OLD SERGEANT'S STORY". I was a resident of the west in the Indian days and have latterly been associated with the management of the Spur Ranche in northwest Texas. The history of that immediate section, such as events at Palo Duro and Blanco and Tule Canons, in which you took part, have been a matter of interest at all times. The old Mackenzie trail passed through the Spur Ranch and it may be of a little interest to you to know that the trail passed over land on which the Spur Inn has since been built. I enclose a picture of it. It is our thought to put up a tablet or marker of some kind at the hotel in commemoration of the trail with possibly some recitation of what Mackenzie's operations meant in freeing that country of the Indians. On the Spur Ranch and about ten miles from this hotel is "Soldier Mound." The local story is that Mackenzie made a winter camp at that mound which is just east of Duck Creek, one of the tributaries of the Salt Fork of the Brazos as shown on the accompanying map of Section 316. If you can by any chance assist me with information as to this encampment, it would be very helpful. There are one or two soldiers buried on top of this mound. If there is anything published intimately descriptive of the old Mackenzie trail, I would be ever so glad to have you say where

it can be procured. I judge, in reading the book above described, that you are probably one of the few living men who were intimately familiar with the old trail and the happenings in that particular part of the country. Possibly there is somewhere available a reliable map showing the Mackenzie trail in that region. If there is, and it is purchasable, I will like to have it. If you ever come to New York, I would very much appreciate a call from you as during the years when I was in the west, I became very appreciative of what the outlying posts had to contend with and in fact had some personal connections with Indian events from a civilian standpoint.

Not knowing your address, I am requesting a personal friend, Hon. John H. Small, of Washington, to locate you and present this letter.

Very truly yours,

(sgd)   C. A. JONES.

It occurs to me that you may possibly be interested in the Spur Ranch booklet from which you will see how completely that section of the country, wholly wild at the time you knew it, has become civilized and the home of many prosperous farmers and ranchmen.

———

This gentleman represented, as will be noted, Swenson Sons, who operate the great sulphur plant at Freeport, Texas, one of the largest plants in the world.

Illness in Mr. Jones' family, and various other causes, delayed him in carrying out his plans, but on Aug. 16, 1928, a bronze plate 32″x32″ with a suitable inscription was unveiled with appropriate ceremonies in the town of Spur, which includes Mackenzie's permanent supply camp, Canon Blanco and 763 square miles of ranch land, the plate being placed over the fireplace in the lobby of "Spur Inn," a very attractive hotel which was built directly on the "Mackenzie Trail." Thus after more than 50 years the hardships and sacrifices of a portion of our gallant little regular army has been recognized by these hardy and enterprising pioneers who, following closely in upon our trail have made that vast region "blossom like a rose." Houses, churches, school houses, beautiful residences, stores, motor plants for furnishing other towns with power, heat and light, have sprung up in towns nearby; automobiles, garages, filling stations, historical societies and all the culture and improvements of the modern civilization of the older Eastern cities have taken the place of what was once one of the most desolate spots in the entire United States. The old trail is still distinctly visible made by our wagon trains and pack mules, although the tons of bones which for so many years remained on the "Tex" Rogers ranch at the head of Tule Canyon after the Comanche ponies were shot there Sept. 29, 1874, have disappeared, having been hauled away to Colorado City to be made into fertilizer and to furnish the settlers with money for their necessary supplies.

The following is copy from a photo of the plate:

"THE MACKENZIE TRAIL"

"This famous, historic trail crossed the site of this inn and was made and used by the Fourth U. S. Cavalry, Tenth and Eleventh U.S. Infantries under command of General Ranald Slidell Mackenzie in their Indian campaigns of 1871 to 1875. Soldier's Mound, four miles north of this spot, was one of the important bases of operations. To him and his gallant officers and soldiers who freed West Texas of the predatory and murderous bands of Comanches, Cheyennes, Kiowas, Arapahoes and Lipans, this tablet is dedicated. Captain Robert G. Carter, formerly fourth U.S. Cavalry, is especially worthy of honor because of serious and permanent injuries received in action against the Indians on what is now Spur Ranch, compelling his early retirement from active service."

The following actions took place between General Mackenzie's command and Indians on or near the Spur Ranch:

Catfish Crek, mouth of Cañon Blanco, Oct. 10, 1871.

Near Lagoons, staked plains, Oct. 12, 1871.

Cañon Blanco (General Mackenzie and one soldier wounded, two Indians killed) Oct. 14, 1871.

Lynn Creek, May 23, 1872.

North Fork of Red River (near McClellan's Creek)
Sept. 29, 1872.

Near Sulphur Springs (18 miles east), Oct. 6, 1872.

Sulphur Springs, Oct. 8, 1872.—Boehm's Cañon, Sept.
24, 1874.

Tule Cañon, Sept. 26-27, 1874.—Palo Duro Cañon, Sept.
28, 1874.

Salt Lake, staked plains, Nov. 2, 1874.

Tahoka Lagoon (LaQuatra Rica) Nov. 5, 1874.

NEWSPAPER COMMENT

A bronze tablet (shown above), marking the famous
MacKenzie trail, commemorating the activities in West
Texas of the Fourth United States Cavalry under the leadership of Gen. Ranald Slidell MacKenzie, and with especial
mention of Capt. Robert G. Carter, U. S. A., retired, was
unveiled Thursday, Aug. 16, 1928 at the Spur Inn, Spur,
by Clifford B. Jones on behalf of the donors, S. M. Swenson & Sons of New York, owners of the Spur ranch.

The tablet was placed over the fireplace in the lobby of
the inn with fitting ceremony, in which the Spur Rotary
Club and guests participated.

It was with deepest regret to him and to the people of
Spur, that the condition of health of Captain Carter, now
in his eighty-fourth year, did not permit his attendance, as
had been planned. His home is at the Army and Navy
Club in Washington, and his doctors forbade the long trip.
A telegram was received and read expressing deepest regret at his enforced absence and heartfelt appreciation of
this tribute to himself and his comrades-in-arms.

Captain Carter is the only surviving officer of the old
Fourth United States Cavalry, which received the official
thanks of the Texas Legislature for its successful operations against the predatory bands of Indians in its campaigns in West Texas from 1871 to 1875.

With a prismatic compass Captain Carter laid out the
MacKenzie trail, which was used in their operations to

and from the Plains. He was desperately wounded in an engagement against the Comanches on what is now the Spur ranch, compelling his early retirement from service.

From surveys and data recently furnished by Captain Carter, a valuable map has been prepared for Texas Technological College and other educational institutions of the State, showing trails made and routes used by the Fourth United States Cavalry; old forts, posts and camps; actions with the Indians, 1871 to 1875; Fourth Cavalry detachments, and identifying by the names of those early years the creeks, springs, lakes and peaks of West Texas.

The MacKenzie trail crossed what is now the town of Spur at the northeast corner of the Spur Inn property. The broad trail was definitely in evidence when the town of Spur was begun in 1909. "Soldier's Mound" (known as "Anderson's Fort"), in Dickens County, just north of Spur, takes its name by reason of its use by General MacKenzie as a camp to which he withdrew for recuperation of men and horses after the battle of Palo Duro in September, 1874."

CONCLUSION

MacKenzie was not a military genius any more than Grant, Sherman, Thomas and Sheridan, or Lee, Longstreet, Johnston, Jackson and Stuart. He had to learn, as a perfectly new game—just as all of us had to learn in this difficult problem of Indian warfare—that side of his military profession. It differed so greatly from what we old Civil War veterans had seen, and so little was known of it that it proved to be an absolutely new kind of warfare, and the experience we had to gain, and that quickly—as we had no time in which to study or any books from which to gain it—was to everybody in that command of a kind we had never seen or encountered. Amidst all of this solitude of the vast plains, with its impressive—almost painful silence, and so remote then from all civilization and ordinary routes of travel, it required more patience and

really more human endurance than civilized warfare calls
for. The exposure to the elements, the extremes of heat
and cold seemed to be greater. The savage enemy seemed
to be more elusive, full of trickery, treachery and all kinds
of wily stratagems peculiar to the nature of the Indian—
all of which, with their strange methods, they did not consider as cowardice. They were such a very mobile force
and had such vast herds of sleek, well-fed and fleet ponies
as relays, that they could always outmarch—but not out-
speed in a race—our cavalry. Like all nomadic races they
could emigrate with the greatest ease and rapidity, because they carried their homes and all that was necessary
to furnish their bases of supply with them. With immense
herds of buffalo always all about them or nearby, they
were foot loose and independent. In taking with them
their wives, gun, lodge and horse, they transported their
entire fortune. They had little to lose and everything to
gain. They were the best light cavalry the world has ever
seen. As skirmishers, with their peculiar, elastic tactics,
they had few if any equals.

The big problem with our brave troopers was always
the one great one—that of supply—to feed our men and
animals to enable them to keep the field long enough to
run down, tire out and cripple our red foes. Once his
lodges were discovered in some far away, hidden and almost inaccessible canon and these and his pony herds
destroyed, the Indian was a helpless as a child. He could
no longer keep the field.

The fighting was a mere bagateele as compared to even
any skirmish the writer ever saw in front of our battle
lines during the Civil War.

The writer rode, ate and slept with MacKenzie; was
more than once his Adjutant and confidential advisor and
was a close observer of all his characteristics. He believed
in *force*—that force which, without being a mere brutal
exhibition of one's power, stands for moral restraint,
respect for the laws, enforcement of discipline, and all that

tended to make the good, self-respecting citizen and obedient soldier. He abhorred personal servility or self-seeking; could not tolerate "boot-licking", "molly-coodling" or "pussyfooting", and never tried mere moral suasion or special pleading with those men who manifested evil tendencies and whom he felt had entered the service to escape the restraints of the law in their own communities. To the murderer, thug, thief, shirker, skulker, coward, malingerer and deserter he never showed any mercy. In all this he was *"hard boiled"*. He considered it a waste of time and effort to play the role of reformer to that class. As grown men and soldiers in his command they must all perform their duty or take their punishment as a consequence of non-performance of the same. While he was strict and exacting, sometimes irritable or irascible, he was never tyrannical or unjust. Firmness and justice were his ruling characteristics. He wanted results—things accomplished. Sometimes in his intensity of purpose, he committed the error of imposing certain duties upon his more energetic and efficient officers and men—especially those who had served in the Civil War——when he had found by experience that the weaker ones were unable to perform those duties to his satisfaction. That was a fault, however, not alone confined to him in those strenuous days of Civil and Indian warfare when it was necessary to accomplish the seemingly impossible by every means possible.

He would never permit any hard drinking officer or men whom he had reason to believe were, in a way, outcasts of society, or toughs, gunmen, gamblers, thieves, deserters, mutineers, or men of that type to secure control, dominate or lower the morale of his regiment. He would never allow the organization of any cabals, cliques or societies to slumber, gather head and break out at intervals, or to show any hostile feeling—open or otherwise, towards the policies and plans or to embarrass his movements and methods of operation, certainly not to the extent of jeopardizing the safety of himself and sacrificing the lives of his men. He

did not drink or gamble or become unduly familiar or intimate with his officers, and while some may not have liked
or loved him, he had the respect and always their loyal
cooperation. Such a thing as a mutiny or the menace of a
strike in the Fourth Cavalry was never dreamed or
thought of even as a possibility. To this extent, and in all
this MacKenzie might be called "hard boiled". While it
was true that he was rather hard to serve with owing to
his ceaseless energy and temperamental irritability owing
to his many wounds, he could never be classed as an intolerable martinet.

*Official Record of Brigadier General Ranald Slidell Mac-
Kenzie U. S. A.*

He graduated in the Class of 1862, U. S. Military Acad-
empy—(*Star Graduate *No.* 1).

Second Lieut. C. E. June 17, 1862.

Battles——Kelly Ford August 20, 1862.

Second Battle Bull Run, August 29, 1862 *(*Wounded*)

Fredericksburg—Dec. 13, 1862.

Chancellorsville — May 2-4, 1863 — Building Ponton
bridges—guarding etc. U. S. Ford Rappannock River.

Commanding Engineer Company, June-July 1863—June
21, 1863—Ponton at Berlin, Md.

Aide General G. K. Warren, Chief of Engineer, A. of P.
Battle of Gettysburg, July 1-3, 1863.

Wilderness, May 5-6—1864.

Todd's Tavern, May 7, 1864.

Commanding Engineer, Regiment Richmond Campaign
—Laying Pontons at Germania Ford, Rapidan River.

Siege at Petersburg *(*Wounded*)

Colonel 2nd Conn. H. A. July 10, 1864.

Commanding Brigade 6th A. C. Shenandoah Campaign.

Battle of Opequan, September 19, 1864.

Battle Cedar Creek, October 19, 1864 *(*Wounded*)

*The negative from which this picture frontispiece was made by Brady, must have been taken shortly after he had been wounded at Cedar Creek. Oct. 19, 1864, and when he had been appointed Brigadier General of Volunteers. This proof was made from a Brady negative (date not given) in Photo. Division, Signal Corps (Captain Betts in charge) January 1921.

Battle Fisher's Hill, September 22, 1864.

Commanding Brig. 6th A. C. December 1864 to March 1865.

Brigadier General of Volunteers October 19, 1864.

Commanding Cavalry Division, Army of the James — March-April 1865. Attached to Sheridan's Cavalry Corps.

Battle of Five Forks, April 1, 1865. Wounded—Reported.

Surrender at Appomattox C. H. April 9, 1865.

Brevetted through every grade from First Lieutenant to Major General of Volunteers and Brigadier General U. S. Army—for "Gallant and Meritorious Services in the field during the Rebellion."

Colonel 41st U. S. Infantry March 6, 1867.

Commanding Baton Rouge, La. Brownsville, Ringgold Barracks.

Fort Clark, Fort McKavett, Tex. to April 19, 1870.

Transferred to 24th U. S. Infantry, March 15, 1869. (Consolidation.)

Transferred to Fourth U. S. Cavalry, December 15, 1869.

Commanding Fort Concho, Tex. February 1871, Fort Richardson, Tex., Fort Clark, Tex., Fort Sill, I. T.

Indian Campaigns August-November 1871.

Wounded October 15th, 1871 in Cañon Blanco by Comanche Indians (Was within a few feet of him when a spiked arrow buried itself in fleshy part of thigh. R. G. C.) Action of McClellans Creek, I. T. September 29, 1872. Remolina, Mexico, May 19, 1873. Never reported.

Tule Cañon September 27, 1874. Palo Duro Cañon.

September 28, 1874, Willow Creek, Wyoming November 25, 1876. (Tributary of Little Big Horn)—This is recorded as—"*MacKenzies Last Fight.*"

Commanding Camp Robinson, Neb. and Dis. of Black Hills, Neb.

Commanding District of Nueces, Texas. January to October 1878.

Commanding District of New Mexico. Fort Garland, N. Mexico.

Commanding Dept. of Arizona, Etc., Etc.

Brigadier General U. S. Army, October 26, 1882.

Commanding Dept. of Texas, Nov. 1 to Dec. 18, 1883.

Retired March 24, 1884—for "Disability incurred in line of Duty."

Died January 19, 1889 at New Brighton—Staten Island, N. Y. Age 49.

He was wounded five (5) times.

In memoirs of General U. S. Grant, he (General G.) declares: "He was the most promising Young Officer of the Army."

He was the youngest colonel in our army. He exhausted his vitality early and died from the overstrain upon his mental faculties and physical strength. With little or no sleep for weeks, and neglect of his food and rest, his restless energy soon wore out his brave spirit. He burned the candle at both ends and passed on—almost forgotten to an early grave—"The silver chord was loosed, the golden bowl was broken."

His record was an exceptionally brilliant one, in which he and his officers and men always felt a just pride. By reason of his four wounds and a none too robust constitution, he was constantly burdened with an almost ceaseless pain and physical suffering. He was impatient, impulsive, but always the brave, gallant and just soldier. In social life and garrison he was modest and retiring but dignified, affable and courteous. He was a true friend and comrade and all Texans may well declare with the writer —"May peace be with him, and rest, that rest which he earned by his sacrifices, to his—a soldier's reward, and when the last trumpet call shall sound his requiem may it not be the 'rude alarms of War' but the *sweet notes of* 'Taps!'"

MacKenzie did not secure the life, liberty and independence of the Texans. They secured that when they fought the Mexicans on many a sanguinary field, including that Thermopyle of their struggle as a Republic at the Alamo, with Davy Crockett, Travis Bowie and other brave spirits as a bloody sacrifice.

But MacKenzie with his gallant regiment of rough riding troopers did secure them their safety from constant harassing Indian incursions, their economic resources, their material prosperity, and their almost inexhaustible supply of mineral wealth, when he finally drove into their reservations for good their implacable enemies, the Kiowas, Comanches, Arapahoes and Cheyennes, and opened up all the western counties of Texas with their rich fertile valleys to settlement and to the almost unparalleled advance of civilization—now almost the marvel of the world —and those Texans will always owe him and his gallant command a debt of gratitude which the advance of time and the rapid history-making period of the country can alone adequately measure and record

To the Memory of Gen. R. S. MacKenzie.

By WILLIAM LAWRENCE CHITTENDEN
Anson, Texas.

(Published in *Ranch Verses* by G. P. Putnams Sons, 1893
Sixth edition, 1900.*)

MacKenzie, thy warfare is o'er —
  Thy bold, loyal heart is at rest,
Thy noble soul suffers earth's sorrows no more,
For the bark sailing seaward has reached the lone shore
  Of that far-away land of the blest.

Brave hero, we mourn not for thee,
  Thou hast gone from life's troubles and care;
Thy stern, soldier spirit forever is free;
It has joined the Grand Army encamped by the Sea
  In the bivouacked realms over there!

And yet since by love thou wert slain,
  In pity we bow o'er thy bier,
And we sigh when we think of thy story of pain,

Of that proud, loyal love that thou lavished in vain,
  And in secret we shed the sad tear.

But we feel that affection like thine
  Is not lost 'neath the gloom of the sod,
That beyond the dark valley where love is divine,
It will glow evermore and eternally shine
  In the balm-breathing Edens of God.

MacKenzie, true soldier, good-by;
  The wind wails the long reveille,
And tonight on the plains where the weird coyotes cry,
Far away o'er thy trail 'neath the tents of the sky,
  I breathe this slight tribute to thee.

—END—

Index

Index

Index

Index

Monterey, N. Mex., 431

Montezumas, 100

Montgomery, Ala., 25

monument of massacre of Salt Creek Prairie, 103–104

Moochas Indians (Crooked Mountain) band council, 152

Mooers (no given name), surgeon, 61

"mopping up" New Mexico, 504

Morgan, Sgt. (no given name), Troop "G," 169

Morgan Lines steamer, 4

Mt. Margaret, 59, 409

Mount Pleasant, Mass., district, 45

Mt. Scott, 139, 255, 258

Mt. Sylvan, 302

Mt. Webster, 125, 139

Mountain Creek, 271

Mountain Pass, 49, 62

Mow-wi ("Handshaker"), sub-chief: action against band, 529; camp, 336; capture of Comanche village, 376 ff.; handshake, 176; McClellan's creek, 388; Qua-ha-das, 176; Quanah, 157; raids, 157; sons, 520; women and children, 409; surrender, 527–542; Tatum letter, 144, 158

Mucha-Que, 501, 507, 508, 579; mountain peak, 509

Mulbery Creek, 501, 504

Mule Creek, 156

mule train, 85; Indians killed, 88

mules, 77; Charlton wagon, 91; Concord mail wagons, 50; Indian thefts, 95; "saw-buck" pack saddle, 119; Sherman letter, 88; tongue: Wright, 140; see also horses and mules

Mullen, John: memorial inscription, 104

murders, arrest for, 85; indictment of Indians, 99

Murphy's ranch, 158

Murray, Sgt. (no given name), 336

Nacoma, Pete, Comanche chief, 154; Quanah, 155, 157; Texas town, 216

Nacoma, Texas, 216

Nashville, battle of, 25 ff.

National Cemetery, Arlington, Va., xi, 185

National Museum, Washington, D.C., 200

National Soldiers' Home, Washington, D.C., 253

National Park, Fort Sill, 257

National Tribune, 92, 419

National Zoological Park, Washington, D.C., 63

Navasota Creek, 154

Nebraska "Bad Lands," 125

New Boggy Depot, 368

New Braunfels, Texas, 523

New England, 112

New Jersey, 95, 333

New Mexico, 504; border posts, 1; cave dwellers, 161; Mount Sumner, 196; McLean, 388

New Orleans, La., 301, 307, 310, 312, 315, 316, 326, 350

New York City: deserters, 223, 224

New York Tribune, 353, 357

Newcomb, James P., 464

Nichols, Mrs. (no given name), 351

Ninth U.S. Cavalry, 40, 62, 163, 334

No Man's Land, 448

No-ko-nees ("Wanderers"), Comanche band, 152

Nokong Comanche, 273

Norfolk, Va., 310, 333

North America, 126

North Angelo, 52

North Carolina, 366

North Concho River, 34, 51, 52, 409

North Fork of Red River, 123, 132, 376, 383, 384, 387, 505, 527

North Star, 130

"norther" (a Texas storm), 32, 44, 112, 115, 189–196, 206, 222, 226–228, 344, 480, 505–506, 508; deserters, 249, 251, 253; "dry," 340; Fourth Cavalry, 195; sleeting, 493; temperature, 252; "wet," 483–484, 498, 514, 519

Northern Cheyennes, 109, 142, 177, 299, 372

Nueces Cañon, 400, 445

O, Lt. and Mrs. (no given or surname), 8

Oak Creek, 59, 60

Oakes, Col. James, 69

O'Brian, Sgt. (no given name), 445

O'Connell, Capt. (no given name), 35, 435, 444, 445, 452

Oklahoma: Indian Nation, 245; Stilwell, 362; see also Indian Territory

Okmulgee Indian council, 89

Old Camp Cooper, 376

Old Fort Belknap: Fifth Infantry, 69; Sixth Cavalry, 69

"Old Henry," Ton-ka-way Indian, 191

Osages (Indians), 1, 275

O'Sullivan (no given name), 517, 518

Otis, Gen. Elwell, 110

Otter Creek, 12, 123, 124, 127, 137, 140, 141, 143, 325, 474

Oxford (no other name), trumpeter, 93

Oyner (no other name), packer, 153

pack mule, 130; see also mules

556

Index

CPSIA information can be obtained at www.ICGtesting.com
Printed in the USA
BVOW03s0919121113

336090BV00001B/1/P

9 780876 112465